THE JEWS OF MEDIEVAL ISLAM

ÉTUDES SUR LE JUDAÏSME MÉDIÉVAL

FONDÉES PAR

GEORGES VAJDA

DIRIGÉES PAR

PAUL B. FENTON
ELLIOT R. WOLFSON

TOME XVI

THE JEWS OF MEDIEVAL ISLAM

THE JEWS OF MEDIEVAL ISLAM

Community, Society, and Identity

Proceedings of an International Conference held by
the Institute of Jewish Studies, University College London
1992

EDITED BY

DANIEL FRANK

E.J. BRILL
LEIDEN · NEW YORK · KÖLN
1995

The paper in this book meets the guidelines for permanence and durability of the Committee on Production Guidelines for Book Longevity of the Council on Library Resources.

Library of Congress Cataloging-in-Publication Data

The Jews of medieval Islam : community, society, and identity : proceedings of an international conference held by the Institute of Jewish Studies, University College London / edited by Daniel Frank.
p. cm. — (Etudes sur le judaïsme médiéval, ISSN 0169-815X ; t. 16)
Includes bibliographical references.
ISBN 9004104046 (cloth : alk. paper)
1. Jews—Islamic Empire—History—Congresses. 2. Judaism—Islamic Empire—History—Congresses. I. Frank, Daniel. II. Institute of Jewish Studies (London, England) III. Series.
DS135.L4J48 1995
956'.004924—dc20 95–30702
CIP

Die Deutsche Bibliothek – CIP-Einheitsaufnahme

The Jews of medieval Islam : community, society, and identity : proceedings of an international conference held by the Institute of Jewish Studies, University College London / ed. by Daniel Frank. – Leiden ; New York ; Köln : Brill, 1995
(Études sur le judaïsme médiéval ; T. 16)
ISBN 90–04–10404-6
NE: [Hrsg.]; GT

ISSN 0169-815X
ISBN 90 04 10404 6

PRINTED IN THE NETHERLANDS

CONTENTS

CONTRIBUTORS

Yom Tov Assis, The Hebrew University
Menahem Ben-Sasson, The Hebrew University
Mark R. Cohen, Princeton University
Paul B. Fenton, University of Strasbourg
Daniel Frank, Oxford Centre for Hebrew and Jewish Studies
Moshe Gil, Tel Aviv University
Alfred L. Ivry, New York University
Y. Tzvi Langermann, Institute of Microfilmed Hebrew Manuscripts, Jerusalem
Daniel J. Lasker, Ben-Gurion University of the Negev
Gideon Libson, The Hebrew University
David E. Sklare, Ben-Zvi Institute, Jerusalem
Norman A. Stillman, University of Oklahoma
Yedida K. Stillman, University of Oklahoma
Sarah Stroumsa, The Hebrew University
David J. Wasserstein, Tel Aviv University

ABBREVIATIONS

A.M.	anno mundi
A.S.	anno seleucidae
b	Babylonian Talmud
m	Mishnah
AJSR	*Association for Jewish Studies Review*
BEK	*Bulletin d'Études Karaïtes*
BSOAS	*Bulletin of the School of Oriental and African Studies*
EI	*Encyclopaedia of Islam*
EIS	*Shorter Encyclopaedia of Islam* (Leiden, 1953)
EJ	*Encyclopaedia Judaica* (Jerusalem, 1972)
EJB	*Encyclopaedia Judaica* (Berlin, 1928–34)
HAR	*Hebrew Annual Review*
HTR	*Harvard Theological Review*
HUCA	*Hebrew Union College Annual*
IMHM	Institute of Microfilmed Hebrew Manuscripts
IOS	*Israel Oriental Studies*
JAOS	*Journal of the American Oriental Society*
JJS	*Journal of Jewish Studies*
JNES	*Journal of Near Eastern Studies*
JQR	*Jewish Quarterly Review*
JSAI	*Jerusalem Studies in Arabic and Islam*
JSS	*Journal of Semitic Studies*
KS	*Kiryat Sefer*
MEAH	*Miscelánea de Estudios Arabes y Hebraicos*
MGWJ	*Monatsschrift für Geschichte und Wissenschaft des Judenthums*
PAAJR	*Proceedings of the American Academy for Jewish Research*
REI	*Revue des Études Islamiques*
REJ	*Revue des Études Juives*
RSO	*Rivista degli studi orientali*
SBB	*Studies in Bibliography and Booklore*
SI	*Studia Islamica*
SMC	*Studies in Medieval Culture*
ZA	*Zeitschrift für Assyriologie*

INTRODUCTION

Scattered geographically throughout the Middle East and the Mediterranean basin, Jewish communities in medieval Islamic lands shared common languages, legal status, and, to a large degree, a world view. If knowledge of Hebrew (and to a lesser extent, Aramaic) enabled these Jews to preserve their religious and cultural identities, their Arabic enabled them to participate in the surrounding society. As "people of the book," they were universally accorded State protection, so long as they obeyed the special laws regulating minority life. Familial, cultural, and commercial ties all led to the formation of a general "Mediterranean Society," to use a phrase popularized by S.D. Goitein. At the same time, individual communities developed their own identities and mores, shaped by the local environment. The fifteen studies assembled in the present volume explore the variety and continuity of Jewish life under medieval Islam, emphasizing its unifying and differentiating features.

Jewish society in Arab lands was essentially urban in character. In the Prologue, Norman A. Stillman describes the growth of Middle Eastern cities during the early Islamic period and the concomitant development of urban Jewish populations. For a small religious minority it was far easier to conduct communal affairs and address common concerns within the city walls. The city afforded numerous economic opportunities, ranging from crafts to medicine and commerce. The close proximity of Jews, Muslims and Christians within urban settings, moreover, fostered a wide range of social and intellectual contacts.

As centers of Jewish settlement grew, they developed their own distinctive characters and institutions. And with the rise of regional Islamic powers, the fortunes of local Jewish communities waxed. In the East during the eighth-tenth centuries, the Exilarch and the Geonim succeeded in extending their authority under the Abbasid regime. In the West, the Andalusian community achieved pre-eminence in the days of the independent Umayyad Caliphate. The five studies in the first section, "Communities and Their Leaders: Iraq and Spain," examine key institutions and the elite groups which led them. Menahem Ben-Sasson reveals how relationships between the eastern centers of scholarship and "provincial" Jewish communities nominally under their jurisdiction shifted constantly, despite attempts by the Exilarchs and Geonim to regulate their individual spheres of influence (*reshuyot*). Moshe Gil assembles and evaluates the various historical sources relating to the Exilarchate whose principle claim to authority derived from Davidic descent. The Babylonian Geonim, by contrast, extended their influence by means of their legal expertise and creativity. As Gideon Libson shows, it was through the enactment of *taqqanot* on the one hand and recourse to *minhag* (local custom) on the other that they succeeded in adjusting halakhah to changing contemporary realities. Meanwhile, in the West, a small number of talented Jewish courtiers and scholars shaped a community whose intellectual and literary achievements have long been celebrated. In investigating this Sefardic élite, David Wasserstein points out that the sources available do not yield precise information concerning the actual constitution and workings of Jewish society in Islamic Spain. That the Sefardic identity was forged in al-Andalus, however, can be readily demonstrated: Yom Tov Assis identifies manifestations of the Judeo-Arabic tradition in Christian Spain and explores how it was tempered through contact with Ashkenazic culture.

As *ahl al-dhimma*, the Jews of Islam developed dual identities. While they belonged to the dominant, Arabic-speaking culture, they were members of a protected religious minority. Though they enjoyed communal autonomy, they were ever aware of their second-class citizenship: their status was determined as much by the attitudes of their Muslim neighbors as by Islamic law. The second section, "Self-Perceptions and Attitudes Towards Others," contains five papers that focus upon aspects of Jewish identity. In the *dār al-islām*, clothing conveyed a cultural message; Yedida K. Stillman examines the way costume communicates political ideology, socio-economic status, and religious affiliation. To a degree, Jewish dress in Muslim lands was color-coded by convention and determined by law; medieval societies took pains to prevent members of different faiths from mixing. Discrimination, however, does not necessarily imply active oppression. Mark R. Cohen claims that the Jews of Islam neither confronted the kind of persecution inflicted upon their brethren in Latin Christendom, nor commemorated the suffering they did experience in Ashkenazic-style martyrologies. That Islamic Jewry encountered Christians at close quarters, however, is beyond doubt: Daniel J. Lasker argues that several passages in Saadya Gaon's famous *Book of Beliefs and Opinions* reflect an ongoing polemic between rival *dhimmī* groups. At times, Jews in the East were tempted to abandon their faith, either for the dominant religion or, less commonly, for Christianity. Sarah Stroumsa shows how such intellectuals as the twelfth-century Abū ʾl-Barakāt al-Baghdādī and Samauʾal al-Maghribī could render the choice easier by a kind of rationalization.

But if some scholars found ways of philosophizing their Judaism away, others emphasized their particularism. Elitist, ascetic, and apocalyptic in orientation, the Karaite Mourners for Zion—or *Shoshanim*—of tenth-century Jerusalem constituted themselves as a self-defined community. DANIEL FRANK investigates the way they integrated their peculiar ideology into a strict regime of biblical exegesis and prayer.

If Arabic literacy afforded Jews access to Islamic society, Judeo-Arabic scholarly writings offer the clearest evidence of Jewish acculturation. By assimilating, adapting, and reacting to Islamic speculative, religious, and mystical works, Jewish thinkers East and West infused their own compositions with new energy and direction. The final part of this collection, "Religious Philosophy, Mysticism, and Spirituality in Islam and Judaism," opens with another study devoted to Karaism in Jerusalem. DAVID E. SKLARE surveys the legal writings of Yūsuf al-Baṣīr, one of the sect's leading teachers, and shows how they are imbued with Muʿtazilite theology. While Kalam attracted the Geonim and the Karaites in the East during the tenth and eleventh centuries, Aristotelianism gained ascendancy among Jewish intellectuals in twelfth-century Andalusia. Maimonides' dismissal of Kalam arguments is well known from the *Guide of the Perplexed*. ALFRED L. IVRY focuses upon an element of Maimonidean thought that has gone unnoticed: his dialectical relationship with Ismāʿīlī teachings. It is quite likely that Maimonides' lengthy sojourn in Egypt exposed him to works he had not previously studied. Certainly, the mystical tendencies of his descendants and their circles of adepts were strengthened through exposure to Ṣūfī teachings in the East. PAUL B. FENTON describes a lengthy treatise composed by one of these Jewish Ṣūfīs which integrates theosophical speculation with biblical exegesis. Bible commentaries naturally afford prime indices of acculturation: vernacular glosses, references to realia, and citations of gentile authorities are all ways of making Scripture meaningful to a contemporary audience. Y. TZVI LANGERMANN presents an exegetical genre, philosophical midrash, that reflects the particular intellectual world of Yemenite Jewry in the Middle Ages. Like the other studies collected here, his paper demonstrates the degree to which local communities developed distinctive, individual identities and cultures.

I would like to thank all of the institutions and individuals who made this volume possible.

The articles in this collection were, with two exceptions, originally presented at a conference in June, 1992 held by the Institute of Jewish Studies, University College London. Founded in 1954 by the late Alexander

Altmann, the Institute is an autonomous body affiliated with the Department of Hebrew and Jewish Studies at University College London. Through an ambitious program of public lectures, seminars, and international conferences, the Institute has promoted the academic study of Jewish culture for over forty years. Manfred Altman, Chairman of the IJS, played a major role in the realization of the conference and this volume. Mark Geller, Director of the IJS, extended invaluable assistance at every stage of this project. Without the Institute's generous financial support production of this volume would not have been possible.

The conference was co-sponsored by the Cohn-Haddow Center for Judaic Studies, Wayne State University. Jacob Lassner, formerly its Director and now Professor at Northwestern University, made necessary arrangements. Haggai Ben-Shammai of the Hebrew University offered helpful suggestions at the planning stages.

Paul B. Fenton (University of Strasbourg) and Elliot Wolfson (New York University), editors of ÉTUDES SUR LE JUDAÏSME MÉDIÉVAL, graciously accepted the volume for their series. Elisabeth Erdman-Visser, Senior Editor, E.J. Brill, Leiden, gave sound advice and was unstinting in her patience. Alun Ward and Emma Jane Muir of the Oxford Centre for Hebrew and Jewish Studies assisted with typing.

Adena Tanenbaum provided expert copy-editing and meticulous proofreading.

Princeton University Press kindly permitted us to include Mark Cohen's article in this volume; a slightly different version appeared in 1994 as the final chapter of his book *Under Crescent and Cross: The Jews in the Middle Ages*.

The following institutions graciously permitted the reproduction of the plates accompanying Yedida K. Stillman's article: The British Library; the Metropolitan Museum of Art, New York; the Museum of International Folk Art, Santa Fe, New Mexico; and the Museum of Islamic Art, Cairo.

Daniel Frank
Oxford Centre for Hebrew and Jewish Studies
and Wolfson College, Oxford

PROLOGUE

THE JEW IN THE MEDIEVAL ISLAMIC CITY

NORMAN A. STILLMAN

Islam is—and from its earliest days on the scene of world history has been—first and foremost an urban civilization, although as the late Samuel M. Stern has pointed out, "this statement . . . is somewhat devoid of meaning; for all civilizations—or let us be cautious and put it thus—most civilizations are urban civilizations."[1] (If Stern was exaggerating a bit here, it was to bring home a valid point.) Be that as it may, the Muslim Arab conquests of the seventh and early eighth centuries were followed almost immediately by a veritable wave of urbanization, the like of which the world west of India had not seen since Greco-Roman times.[2] Western Europe would experience no such burgeoning of cities and towns for another four or five centuries.

As a result of the Islamic conquests, the majority of Jews living in the world at that time came under Arab rule. During this period of urbanization, the Jews—particularly in their great demographic center of *Bavel*, which now became Arab Iraq—completed the transition that had already begun in talmudic times from an agrarian to a cosmopolitan way of life. Within the cities of the Muslim empire, Jews not only took part in creating the new and vibrant civilization that we call "medieval Islam," but also developed a flourishing Jewish culture along parallel lines.[3] For it was during the Islamic High Middle Ages (ca. 850–1250) that the Babylonian

---

[1] S.M. Stern, "The Constitution of the Islamic City," in *The Islamic City: A Colloquium*, ed. A.H. Hourani and S.M. Stern (Philadelphia, 1970), 25.

[2] The remark made by Ira Lapidus that "the Arabs, as other conquerors before and since, generated a wave of city building notable in intensity but too limited in scale to be equated with Muslim-era Near Eastern urbanization," simply does not square with the impressive body of historical evidence, nor does Lapidus offer any convincing evidence to support his assertion. See Ira M. Lapidus, "Traditional Muslim Cities: Structure and Change," *From Madina to Metropolis: Heritage and Change in the Near Eastern City*, ed. L. Carl Brown (Princeton, 1973), 52–53. It is not only the growth of towns and cities after a period of steady demographic decline that is so impressive in early Islam, but it is the conscious, programmatic nature of the expansion. As William Marçais has observed so succinctly: "Il n'y a guère de civilisation où se rencontre autant que dans la leur, la création urbaine, voulue, nommé, datée, revêtant en un mot tous les caractères de l'acte arbitraire." See William Marçais, *Articles et conférences* (Paris, 1961), 59.

[3] The best survey of this parallel evolution is still S.D. Goitein, *Jews and Arabs: Their Contacts Through the Ages*, 3rd ed. (New York, 1974). For the general history of the Jews in the Islamic world at this time, see Norman A. Stillman, *The Jews of Arab Lands: A History and Source Book* (Philadelphia, 1979), Chapters 1–3 and the parallel readings in Part Two.

Talmud gradually became the constitutional foundation of Diaspora Judaism, the synagogue service and the prayerbook text took on their familiar form, Jewish theology was systematized, Jewish law codified, and Hebrew language and literature enjoyed their greatest revival prior to their rebirth in modern times.

The founding of cities during the early Islamic period—or in some cases, the revitalizing of towns already in place—is amply documented in the Arabic historical and geographical literature, although the details of their development are not as clear as we would like them to be. The evolutionary process by which Middle Eastern Jewry came to play its part in so many medieval Islamic towns and cities is even hazier. The Arabic sources have relatively little to say about the internal history of the non-Muslim population at this time, while the Jews themselves wrote hardly anything on any subject—much less their own history—during the two crucial centuries of transition. As a result of their rapid military victories, the Arabs found themselves a tiny minority in a vast empire inhabited by Christians, Jews, and Zoroastrians. Two fundamental problems that faced the conquerors were how to deal with this non-Muslim, non-Arab majority, and how to keep themselves from being absorbed into this mass of humanity.

The basic administrative rule seems to have been that those who surrendered, paid tribute, and conducted themselves with the demeanor and comportment befitting a subject population were left more or less alone to carry on their lives and practice their faith without fear of molestation, which in medieval times was no small concession. Eventually, the diverse rules and regulations imposed upon the conquered peoples were regularized under the so-called Pact of ʿUmar which symbolized the social hierarchy of believer and non-believer in the traditional Muslim polity.[4]

So much for the problem of dealing with the subject population. As to the problem of preserving their own identity, the Arabs solved this by not settling at first in large numbers in the native population centers. Rather, they established military garrisons (the *amṣār*), located along their lines of communication safely inland from the Byzantine Sea (*baḥr al-rūm*), as they called the Mediterranean. (This represented a major change from the situation in classical antiquity when the Mediterranean was *Mare Nostrum* and important towns were built either along the coast or within easy

[4] Much ink has been spilled over this subject. See Norman A. Stillman, "Subordinance and Dominance: Non-Muslim Minorities and the Traditional Islamic State as Perceived from Above and Below," in *A Way Prepared: Essays on Islamic Culture in Honor of Richard Bayly Winder*, ed. Farhad Kazemi and R.D. McChesney (New York and London, 1988), 132–141, and the literature cited there.

access to it by navigable river or road.) The *amṣār* were laid out in a grid pattern. The Arab fighting men and their families settled in quadrangles reserved for their respective tribes or battle groups. These blocs eventually became urban quarters or neighborhoods, sometimes retaining the name of the original group that had settled there long after others had replaced them. Thus, for example, the al-Rāya Quarter of Fusṭāṭ (Old Cairo) was named for the troops that had borne the army's standard; half a millennium later, it had become a predominantly Christian neighborhood that was in the process of being bought up by Jews.[5]

The early Caliphate was a great welfare state for the benefit of the Arab ruling caste who were paid out of the treasury from booty and tribute. Like all armies of occupation with considerable sums of money to spend, the Arabs needed goods and services and individuals to provide them. While respecting commerce—the Prophet himself was, after all, a merchant, as were many of the leading figures in the early Muslim community—they despised physical labor.[6] As always in such situations, there was no lack of people among the conquered population willing to provide whatever the new overlords required. Newly converted natives (*mawālī*), flocked to the garrison towns to serve the conquerors. In short order, the *amṣār* began to grow into great urban centers, and the very word *miṣr* (sing. of *amṣār*) came to denote "metropolis" in the Arabic of the High Middle Ages.[7] Not only did the *amṣār* become the nuclei for Islamic urbanization in the Middle East and North Africa, but at the same time, they became the crucible for Arabization, since here the Arabs were the majority. Those coming to serve them and to attach themselves to their *umma* (religious community) had to meet them on their own terms and to learn their language.[8]

Many of the *mawālī* were—to say the least—bitterly disaffected with

---

[5] S.D. Goitein, "Cairo: An Islamic City in the Light of the Geniza Documents," in *Middle Eastern Cities: A Symposium on Ancient, Islamic and Contemporary Middle Eastern Urbanism*, ed. Ira M. Lapidus (Berkeley and Los Angeles, 1969), 85–86.

[6] This contempt is expressed, for example, in the *ḥadīth*: "The greatest liars among men are the dyers and the goldsmiths"; see Ibn Māja, *Sunan*, *Kitab al-tijārāt*, *bāb* 5 ("al-ṣināʿāt"). On the generally respected place of commerce in Islam, see the numerous sources cited in S.D. Goitein, "The Rise of the Middle-Eastern Bourgeoisie in Early Islamic Times," in his *Studies in Islamic History and Institutions* (Leiden, 1966), 217–41. See also the interesting Marxist analysis in Maxime Rodinson, *Islam and Capitalism*, trans. Brian Pearce (Austin, 1978), passim.

[7] See, for example, the classification of city types in the tenth-century geographer al-Muqaddasī, *Aḥsan al-tawāsīm fī maʿrifat al-aqālīm*, ed. M.J. De Goeje (Leiden, 1906), 7.

[8] For a summary of this process, see William Marçais, "Comment l'Afrique du Nord a été arabisé, 1. l'arabisation des villes," in his *Articles et Conférences*, 171–84; and A.N. Poliak, "L'arabisation de l'Orient sémitique," *REI* 12 (1938): 35–63.

the Umayyad regime (661–750) when they discovered that the Arab military caste not only was unwilling to allow them to pass from being tribute bearers to pension receivers, but treated them with thinly veiled contempt. In the end, however, the numbers of the newly converted swelled to such proportions that they would undermine the old tax base and with it Arab superiority, creating a new, more cosmopolitan social and economic order with expanded opportunities for all—including non-Muslims.

The Jews and Christians who did not convert could not at first go to the *amṣār* except as slaves, which in Islamic as in Jewish society was an intermediate step to conversion and assimilation. For the first two generations of Arab rule, all movement in the Caliphate was severely restricted for a variety of reasons—not least among them, military security. Added to this was the government's desire to ensure that taxes were not evaded. (Even in later, more liberal times, the *barāʾa*, or receipt for taxes paid, was the traveler's basic passport.) And finally, there was the need to maintain the agricultural labor force that produced not only food, but such essential raw materials as fibers for cloth and oil for lamp fuel.

The Arabs did, however, shift groups of native non-Muslims to repopulate strategic coastal towns abandoned by their Greek inhabitants when the Byzantine troops pulled out. The Muslim historian of the Islamic conquests, al-Balādhurī, informs us that Muʿāwiya, the governor of Syria and later caliph, moved a large body of Jews—from where, alas, we are not told but I would guess from the Syrian countryside—into the harbor fortification of Tripoli.[9] The same writer mentions that people from different regions were settled together with some Arabs in reconstructed towns up and down the Levantine coast, including Acre and Tyre.[10] Although he does not specify who these others were, we can assume that there were Jews among them, since these towns did indeed have visible Jewish communities in the years that followed.

As travel restrictions eased, Arabs began filtering into pre-existing towns, while Jews, Christians, and Zoroastrians began moving into the *amṣār*. Furthermore, despite the attempts by the Muslim authorities to staunch the flow, there was a wholesale flight of peasants from the villages to the anonymity of the cities in order to escape the crushing tax burden which weighed even more heavily upon them than upon any other element in the population.[11]

---

[9] Al-Balādhurī, *Futūḥ al-buldān*, ed. R.M. Riḍwān (Cairo, 1959), 133; English trans. by Philip Hitti, *The Origins of the Islamic State* (repr. Beirut, 1966), 195.

[10] Ibid., 124; Eng. trans., 180.

[11] The mistreatment of the hapless peasants, their flight to the cities, and the attempts to send

Since early rabbinic times, there has been an invidious distinction in Jewish society between the urban scholar, or *talmid ḥakham*, and the unlettered Israelite peasant, or *ʿam ha-areṣ*. In fact, in the words of one rather unkind mishnaic dictum: *ein bur yere ḥet ve-lo ʿam ha-areṣ ḥasid* ("An uncultured person does not fear sin, and a peasant cannot be a pious man").[12] The Jewish scholar had preferred living in town long before the advent of Islam because it was there that he could find the ten necessities and conveniences of the pious life ennumerated in the Talmud; namely: (1) a court with full authority; (2) a charitable welfare fund; (3) a synagogue; (4) a bath house; (5) toilet facilities; (6) a physician; (7) artisans; (8) a scribe; (9) a ritual slaughterer; and (10) a teacher for children.[13] In another talmudic passage, scholars are advised not to live in a town in which vegetables are unavailable. The great medieval French commentator Rashi explains this curious recommendation as meaning that the scholar should be able to buy this excellent foodstuff cheaply (and not have to spend time raising it), so that he can devote himself to study.[14]

Despite the urban proclivities of the Jewish scholarly elite, landownership and agriculture were still the norm in talmudic days, although the transformation to city and commercial life had begun even then. The social and economic upheavals that took place during the century following the Islamic conquests gave this process a new impetus.

Jewish law, as it developed in the medieval Muslim urban setting came to reflect these fundamental changes in the realities of Jewish socioeconomic life. Even though some of the Babylonian amoraim, such as Rav Assi (third century C.E.), had stated that "money is like real estate" (*kesafim harei hen ke-qarqaʿ*), a great many aspects of Jewish law are based upon the presumption of land ownership.[15] During the medieval Islamic period, movable goods (*miṭṭalṭelin*, in halakhic usage)—the mark of an urban commercial society—came to be recognized as the equivalent of land.[16]

them back to their villages are well-documented in the Arabic sources. See, for example, al-Mubarrad, *Kitāb al-kāmil*, ed. W. Wright, vol. 1 (Leipzig, 1864), 286; al-Ṭabarī, *Taʾrīkh al-rusul waʾl-mulūk* [Annales], ed. M.J. De Goeje, vol. 2, Secunda Series (Leiden, 1879), 1122; and Abū Yūsuf, *Kitāb al-kharāj* (Cairo, 1382 A.H.), 105–106.

[12] Avot 2:5.

[13] bSan. 17b.

[14] Commentary to bEruv. 55b.

[15] The quotation is from bB.Q. 9a. With respect to the presumption of land ownership, it should be noted, for example, that a woman's marriage contract (*ketubbah*) is not pledged to movables in talmudic law; see bKet. 81b and also Moses Maimonides, *The Code of Maimonides, Book XII: The Book of Acquisitions*, trans. Isaac Klein. [Yale Judaica Series, 5] (New Haven, 1951), 4–20.

[16] Maimonides, *Code: Acquisitions*, 21. As Goitein has observed, paragraph 5 of the fifth chapter

Moses b. Jacob, who was the Gaon of Sura in the first half of the ninth century, writes in a responsum that movables may be collected by a woman or a creditor instead of land because "nowadays, most people do not own real estate," and therefore the rabbis issued an ordinance (*taqqanah*) reforming the legal usage.[17]

It is true that the records of certain transactions before Jewish courts that have been preserved in the Cairo Genizah include ancient legal formulas mentioning land. But as S.D. Goitein has pointed out, these formulas were merely symbolic—as for example, those mentioning the sale of one's hypothetical share in the soil of the Holy Land—and did not involve the transfer of land at all.[18] The only real estate deals in the Genizah records have to do with urban properties: apartments, shops, and building complexes.[19] This is not to say that no Jews remained in agriculture, or that all of them had moved to the city. Until at least the twelfth century, there were Jews in Egypt with agricultural interests. Most of these, however, were absentee landlords who lived in the cities, while others worked their land. In medieval Spain, there were Jewish farmers and orchard owners, and they could also be found in North Africa up until modern times. But these were clearly the exception that proves the rule.[20]

By the time our historical sources begin to give us a detailed picture of Jewish life in the medieval Islamic world—that is, sometime around the tenth century—we find the Jews already transformed into an overwhelmingly urban group with a high degree of communal organization both on the local and international level. Within the medieval Islamic city, in fact, the Jews—like the Christians—constituted a semi-autonomous polity. The

---

here renders obsolete all of the preceding paragraphs which reflect the earlier agrarian society. See S.D. Goitein, *A Mediterranean Society* (Berkeley, Los Angeles, London, 1967–93), 2:329.

[17] H. Tykocinski, *Taqqanot ha-geʾonim*, ed. and trans. M. Havazelet (New York and Jerusalem, 1959), 30–50.

[18] Goitein, *Mediterranean Society*, 2:239.

[19] Concerning urban properties, see Goitein, *Mediterranean Society*, vol. 4 (Berkeley and Los Angeles, 1983), index, s.v., "Houses(s)" and "Store(s)"; also idem, "A Mansion in Fusṭāṭ: A Twelfth-Century Description of a Domestic Compound in the Ancient Capital of Egypt," in *The Medieval City*, eds. H.A. Miskimin, D. Herlihy, and A.L. Udovitch (New Haven and London, 1977), 163–78. A great deal of information on Jewish urban real estate may be found in Moshe Gil, *Documents of the Jewish Pious Foundations from the Cairo Geniza* (Leiden, 1976).

[20] See Goitein, *Jews and Arabs*, 99; Eliyahu Ashtor, *The Jews of Moslem Spain*, (Philadelphia, 1973), 1:267–71 and the sources cited in the notes, pp. 434–35. In 1979, I found a lone Jewish farmer still living in the village of Kerrando in the Tafilalet region of southeastern Morocco, who continued to work his family's fields. That same year, I came across a group of brothers who had settled their respective families in the town of Inezgane, near Agadir in southwestern Morocco, while they worked five days a week at their Saharan palmeries, 900 kms to the south in the oasis from which they hailed.

Islamic city was a place where people lived, not a corporation to which they belonged. This is a real, and not a sophistic distinction, and one that ought to be emphasized.

The medieval Islamic city was not a city in the Weberian sense. It may be recalled that for Weber the five distinguishing marks of a city were: (1) fortifications; (2) markets; (3) a court administering a partially autonomous law; (4) distinguishing urban forms of association; and (5) at least partial autonomy.[21] Weber based his model principally upon European cities as they developed in the Middle Ages. That Middle Eastern cities did not fit this categorization, is, of course, not to due to Islam, although the Islamic legal and social system helped to further the difference. As Gustave Von Grunebaum has pointed out, the principal difference between Muslim *adab* and Greek educational ideals was the absence in Islam of the political or civic element—the *bürgerliche Tüchtigkeit*.[22] Even the Hellenistic cities of the Near East had lost their corporate characters centuries earlier. They were population centers, conglomerations ruled by administrative representatives of centralized imperial bureaucracies whose seat of power was far away. Frequently, the officials were foreign military officers. Muslim urban administration was, on the whole, compatible with this tradition.

Even before Islam, corporate identity in the Middle East lay in religious communities. Civic life was congregational life. It so happened that the Jews and the Christians had preserved many of the Greco-Roman civic norms within their congregations. By contrast, the Zoroastrians, who had no such civic tradition at the communal level, quickly dwindled into insignificance.

The designation of the Jewish community as "holy congregation" (Heb. *qahal qadosh*) was—as Goitein has observed—the diaspora equivalent of the biblical "kingdom of priests and holy people" (Ex. 19:6).[23] Most often, the Jewish sources referred to the community at large simply as "Israel," that is, the nation itself. The synagogue was the assembly of the *polis*, hence the name *beit kenesset*, which to this day remains its most common Hebrew designation. (Naturally it was also a house of prayer and study, as well as a social club.) Where there was only one congregation, it was entirely coextensive with the Jewish community. Where there was

---

[21] Max Weber, *The City*, trans. D. Martindale and G. Neuwirth (Glencoe, 1958).

[22] Gustave E. von Grunebaum, *Medieval Islam: A Study in Cultural Orientation*, 2nd ed. (Chicago and London, 1971), p. 257, n. 90.

[23] Goitein, *Mediterranean Society*, 2:40.

more than one, as in those towns having both a Palestinian and a Babylonian synagogue, civic life was two-tiered.[24]

Public services were primarily the functions of the individual confessional communities, not those of the government. The Jewish community's civic organization and spirit were, therefore, all the more necessary for the administration of its own institutions of health, education, and welfare, which as we know from the Genizah records were highly organized and greatly sophisticated.[25]

Most of the large-scale pious endowments and charitable institutions established by rulers or government officials in Islamic states were done by them as individual Muslims for the benefit of their coreligionists and, of course, for their own salvation.[26] The directive issued by the Vizier ʿAlī ibn ʿIsā (d. 946) to his chief medical officer Sinān ibn Thābit to admit *dhimmīs* as well as Muslims to the great Bīmāristān (hospital) of Baghdad was exceptional. However, he made it clear that in the dispensaries outside the capital, where facilities were more limited, the rule was to be "humans before animals and Muslims before *dhimmīs*."[27]

Although Jews formed a tightly knit polity, they did not live in ghettos as such. In some cities, they did live within their own quarters. In Baghdad, which was built upon a site that had included Jewish villages, there was a section known as Qaṭīʿat al-Yahūd (the Jews' fief) or Dār al-Yahūd (the Domain of the Jews). Likewise, the bridge connecting the quarter with the next neighborhood across a canal was called Qanṭarat al-Yahūd (the Jews' Bridge).[28] In Jerusalem, too, the Jews seem to have inhabited their own quarters.[29] And for Islamic Spain Eliyahu Ashtor has reconstructed a number of Andalusian Jewish quarters, providing some interesting demographic estimates.[30] Goitein has concluded that in Fusṭāṭ (Old Cairo), on the other hand, there were no Jewish quarters as such, only neighborhoods

---

[24] Ibid., 51–55.

[25] Ibid., 91–143 and also Gil, *Documents of the Jewish Pious Foundations*, passim.

[26] See Norman A. Stillman, "Charity and Social Service in Medieval Islam," *Societas* 5 (1975): 105–15.

[27] Ibn Abī Uṣaybiʿa, *ʿUyūn al-anbāʾ fī ṭabaqāt al-aṭibbāʾ*, ed. Nizār Riḍā (Beirut, 1965), 301.

[28] See Jacob Lassner, *The Topography of Baghdad in the Early Middle Ages: Text and Studies* (Detroit, 1970), 101; also H.J. Cohen, "Baghdad," *EJ* 4:86.

[29] See Moshe Gil, "The Jewish Quarters of Jerusalem during Early Muslim Rule (634–1099)" (Hebrew), *Shalem* 2 (1976): 19–36; and idem, *A History of Palestine, 634-1099* (Cambridge, 1992), 635–53.

[30] For the Jewish quarters of major Spanish cities during the Umayyad period (756–1099), see Ashtor, *Jews of Moslem Spain*, 1:291–354; for the eleventh century, ibid. 2:190–300. For demographic estimates, see idem, "The Number of the Jews in Moslem Spain" (Hebrew), *Zion* 28 (1963): 34–56.

with highly concentrated Jewish populations. Menahem Ben-Sasson has observed a similar situation in medieval Kairouan.[31]

The existence of Jewish neighborhoods in some cities and Jewish quarters in others is in no way surprising. Jews had—as anyone familiar with the requirements of traditional Jewish life is fully aware—to live within easy walking distance of such facilities as the synagogue and *mikveh* (ritual bath). Because of the stipulations of the Pact of ʿUmar, it was advisable not to have the synagogue near a large concentration of Muslims. It was also preferable to have a route of access to the Jewish cemetery that did not go through a predominantly Muslim neighborhood. Indeed, *dhimmī* funeral processions were the object of occasional harassment—sometimes minor, sometimes serious—from medieval to modern times.[32] In light of this potential for interconfessional friction, it is noteworthy that the Jewish neighborhoods of Old Cairo, Kairouan, and (we may assume) other important cities as well, were mixed neighborhoods with some non-Jewish residents.

It was only in later medieval times, when the Muslim world began to close in upon itself as a result of a variety of pressures from without and within, as the non-Muslims became a more marginal element in the population, were the Jews restricted to enclosed quarters such as the *mellāḥ* in Morocco, the *ḥāra* in Tunisia, or the *qāʿat al-yahūd* in Yemen. It must be borne in mind that this was a rather late development, that it was by no means universal in the Islamic world, and that it took place primarily in those areas where the Jews were the only remaining non-Muslims. The transfer of the Jews of the *mellāḥ* of Fez, for example, took place in 1438, when the Merinid Sultan ʿAbd al-Ḥaqq b. Abī Saʿīd required them to move into special quarters next to the *dār al-makhzan*, the government administrative center in New Fez. This was the first of the enforced settlements. As it happens, this was done to protect the Jews from the increasing hostility of the population. It never fulfilled its protective function very well, however, and later came to denote the Jews' outcaste status.[33]

The Jews' transformation from an agrarian to a cosmopolitan people in the medieval Islamic city was followed by a socioeconomic evolution within the city itself. At first, it would seem, they formed—along with

---

[31] Goitein, *Mediterranean Society*, 2:289–293; Menahem Ben-Sasson, "The Jewish Community of Medieval North Africa—Society and Leadership: Qayrawan 800–1057" (Hebrew) (Ph.D. diss., The Hebrew University, 1983), 279.

[32] For examples, see Stillman, *Jews of Arab Lands*, 26, 158, 201, 304, and 313; also Goitein, *Mediterranean Society* 2:285.

[33] See Stillman, *Jews of Arab Lands*, 78–81.

other ex-country folk—part of the new urban proletarian mass. The ninth-century writer al-Jāḥiẓ in one of his well-known essays explains that one of reasons the Muslim masses have greater respect for the Christians than the Jews is that:

> among them [i.e., the Christians] are to be found government secretaries, attendants of kings, physicians of nobles, perfumers, and bankers; whereas you will find a Jew only as a dyer, a tanner, a cupper, a butcher, or a tinker.[34]

In other words, in the first century or so of their urbanization, the Jews were essentially working class and petit bourgeois, while the Christians were the professionals and upper middle class. In the tenth and eleventh centuries, however, this situation was to change as far as the Jews were concerned. Although there were still (and would always be) poor, working class Jews, many had entered the mercantile and professional ranks. Some of them even functioned at the very highest level, such as the Benei Neṭīra, who were court bankers (*jahābidha*) in tenth-century Baghdad. Neṭīra, the founder of this great merchant and banking house (d. 916), was a veritable *novus homo*, a man with no apparent pedigree or origins. His name appears in both the Jewish and the Muslim sources without the usual patronymic, as if he had no father or forefathers worth mentioning.[35]

Jews never came to dominate the financial scene in Baghdad or other medieval Islamic cities, despite the arguments to the contrary of the late Louis Massignon in a famous article, based, unfortunately, upon very scanty evidence.[36] Most of the great bankers of the eighth through tenth centuries in the Abbasid Caliphate seem to have been Christians, and it is Christians—not Jews—who remained the stereotypical men of money in Arabic literature and lore.[37] Even during the period of decline in the later Middle Ages, however, there were still a small number of Jews who played a significant role in the commercial and financial life of several major Islamic cities.

---

[34] Al-Jāḥiẓ, *Al-radd ʿala ʾl-naṣāra*, ed. J. Finkel (Cairo, 1926), 17–18; translated in Stillman, *Jews of Arab Lands*, 170.

[35] Almost all of the information on Neṭira and his house is collected in Walter J. Fischel, *Jews in the Economic and Political Life of Mediaeval Islam* (New York, 1969), 1–44. See also Stillman, *Jews of Arab Lands*, 35–37.

[36] Louis Massignon, "L'influence de l'Islam au moyen âge sur la fondation et l'essor des banques juives," *Bulletin des Études Orientales de l'Institut Français de Damas* 1 (1931): 3–12.

[37] See the observation of Goitein, *Jews and Arabs*, 116. For the stereotype of Christians and money, cf. the Arabic proverb quoted by the thirteenth-century writer Ibn al-Mujāwir, *Taʾrīkh al-mustabṣir*, ed. O. Löfgren (Leiden, 1951), 1:36: *inna lil-muslim farjahu lil-naṣrānī mālahu lil-majūsī riʾāsatahu lil-yahūdī baṭnahu* ("The Muslim enjoys his sex, the Christian his money, the Magian his status, and the Jew his food"). See also the passage from al-Jāḥiẓ cited in the text above, and n. 34.

At the close of the Middle Ages, the Jews in many Islamic urban centers began to enjoy a brief cultural and economic revival with the influx of Sephardi refugees expelled from Spain, Portugal, and Sicily. It was only in the last hundred years, however, that the Jews in the cities of the Muslim world once again underwent a tremendous social upheaval and transformation.[38]

---

[38] This transformation is surveyed in detail in Norman A. Stillman, *The Jews of Arab Lands in Modern Times* (Philadelphia, 1991).

PART ONE

COMMUNITIES AND THEIR LEADERS: IRAQ AND SPAIN

VARIETIES OF INTER-COMMUNAL RELATIONS IN THE GEONIC PERIOD

MENAHEM BEN-SASSON

The Islamic conquests of the seventh century signalled the beginning of a new era in Jewish history.* Between the time of Muhammad and the late eleventh century, over ninety percent of the world Jewish population lived under the domination of one religion (Islam), speaking the same language (Arabic) and possessing a similar legal status (as *ahl al-dhimma*). Throughout the Islamic world, Jewish communities maintained constant and extensive contacts with each other. Not surprisingly, developments which occurred within this Jewish society influenced Jewish centers both outside the realm of Islam and during later periods as well. The shaping of the whole Diaspora according to a single, unified code—the Babylonian Talmud—is one of several phenomena which mark this epoch as a formative period in Jewish history. This latter development can be credited both to the spread of Islam and the leadership of the Geonim. Indeed, if we wish to understand the special character of this formative period and its aftermath, we must attempt to make sense of the bonds between the Geonim and the Jewish Diaspora at large.

The organization of Jewish public life during the early Islamic period has been sketched many times; the traditional portrait looks like this: several centralized, super-communal institutions located in Babylonia and the Land of Israel stood at the top of a hierarchy. Claiming sacred authority, they prevented the rise of independent, local Jewish communities. Only with the decline of these central institutions did new, super-communal networks develop among Jews in Egypt, Yemen, North-Africa and Spain. By usurping the powers and responsibilities of the old sacred centers, however, the new regional centers in turn blocked the development of local Jewish communities in Islamic lands.[1]

---

* This lecture represents an attempt to summarize the results of recent research on the world of the Geonim. I have not deemed it necessary, therefore, to provide full documentation from primary sources but have referred, where possible, to more comprehensive scholarly treatments.

[1] See: H. Graetz, *History of the Jews* (Philadelphia, 1894), 3:93–101; S. Assaf, *The Geonic Period and its Literature* (Hebrew) (Jerusalem, 1955), 102–10; S.W. Baron, *A Social and Religious History of the Jews*, 2nd ed. (New York, 1957), 5:5–24; H.H. Ben-Sasson ed., *A History of the Jewish People* [= H.H. Ben-Sasson, *History*] (Cambridge, Mass., 1976), 423–28;

Such a highly organized picture of the central institutions governing the Jews of Islamic lands distorts the image of their society, which has been depicted within either a Geonic or a Mediterranean framework. Moreover, the tendency has been to overlook specific societal features, such as local and family identities, in order to present a simplified and unified historical picture.[2]

This study offers an alternative description of Jewish inter-communal relations during the Geonic and the Classical Genizah periods (eighth-thirteenth centuries C.E.). Dealing with Rabbanite communities throughout the Islamic world, it focuses on the variegated nature and sophistication of inter-communal relations during the Geonic and the Genizah periods.[3] It also seeks to describe the stages in the rise of local Jewish communities in Islamic lands. Finally, it may serve as a prolegomenon to a future investigation of changing identities within Islamic Jewish society. What should emerge is an alternative institutional history of Islamic Jewish society.

I

The basic structure of Jewish leadership—its institutions and organization—was rooted in the pre-Islamic period.[4] Following the Islamic con-

---

N. Stillman, *The Jews of Arab Lands* (Philadelphia, 1979), 41–42. This conception also functions as a working premise in other works; see, e.g., A. Grossman, "The Relationship Between the Social Structure and the Spiritual Activity of Jewish Communities in the Geonic Period" (Hebrew), *Zion* 53 (1988): 259–72.

[2] For this trend see: G.D. Cohen, "The Reconstruction of Gaonic History," Introduction to reprint edition of J. Mann, *Texts and Studies*, vol. 1 (New York, 1972) xiii–xcvi, reprinted in G.D. Cohen, *Studies in the Variety of Rabbinic Cultures* (Philadelphia and New York, 1991); H.H. Ben-Sasson, "A New Way to the World of the Geniza" (Hebrew), *Zion* 41 (1976): 1–46.

[3] Our time-frame has been determined by two considerations: for the period prior to the eighth century there is insufficient evidence; with the Mongol invasions and the rise of the Mamluks during the thirteenth century, Oriental Jewry experienced a sharp decline and the Geonim more or less ceased to function. With respect to scope, the present study is devoted exclusively to relationships between *Rabbanite* communities. On the wider authority existing over *all* Jewish minorities, i.e. Rabbanites, Karaites, and Samaritans, see now: S. Sela, "The Head of the Rabbanite, Karaite and Samaritan Jews: On the History of a Title," *BSOAS* 57 (1994): 255–67; idem, "The Headship of the Jews in the Fatimid Caliphate in Karaite Hands (Towards the History of David b. Isaac Ha-Levi)" (Hebrew), in the *Moshe Gil Festschrift*, ed. Y. Erder et al. [in press].

[4] See: S. Safrai, "The Era of the Mishna and Talmud (70–640)," in H.H. Ben-Sasson, *History*, 345–47, 355–56, 373–80; S.W. Baron, *Social and Religious History*, 5:3–9; G. Alon, *The Jews in Their Land in the Talmudic Age (70–640 CE)* (Jerusalem, 1984), 2:461–514; Y. Gafni, *The Jews of Babylonia in the Talmudic Era: A Social and Cultural History* (Hebrew) (Jerusalem, 1990), 177–203; M. Gil, *A History of Palestine 634–1099* (Cambridge, 1992), 495–501.

quest, we find that the leadership of the two sacred centers in Babylonia and the Land of Israel was regarded as authoritative for Jews both by the Jews themselves and by the non-Jewish rulers of these regions. Jewish leadership in these centers was concentrated in *yeshivot*. There were four such institutions: the three respective Babylonian Yeshivot of Sura, Pumbedita, and the Exilarch (*Rosh ha-golah*), and the Yeshivah of the Land of Israel.[5] (The term *yeshivah*, incidentally, was exclusively reserved at that time for these leading institutions; it never designated a local academy.) Claiming to be the sole legitimate successor to the Sanhedrin—not only in name but also in function—each Yeshivah demanded recognition as the absolute authority for directing Jewish life. The centers in the Land of Israel and in Babylonia both developed religious justifications for their supremacy. While the former pointed to its geographic location in the Holy Land as proof that it occupied the seat of the ancient Sanhedrin,[6] the latter derived its absolute authority from a tradition concerning Jehoiachin, one of the last kings of Judah who was exiled by the Assyrians to Babylonia. According to the legend, Jehoiachin established a *yeshivah* (i.e. a *sanhedrin*), accomplishing thereby the divine plan to transfer the teaching of the Oral Law to a more secure place than the Land of Israel, which would face mounting pressures and persecutions for more than five hundred years to come. In this way Babylonia became, according to its champions, the divinely-chosen place for Jews until the Last Redemption. And the word Zion came to designate a particular Babylonian virtue, excellence in study (*meṣuyanim be-limmudam*), rather than a geographic location.[7] Each center's claim to authority was translated as well into the system of leadership which prevailed at its Yeshivot. For generations, only members of certain sacred dynasties were permitted to hold the leading positions at these institutions—positions which invested national leadership in them as well.[8]

---

[5] See: S.D. Goitein, *A Mediterranean Society* (Berkeley, 1971), 2:5–23; Gil, *History of Palestine*, 490–95, 505–508. On the Yeshivah of the Exilarch see: Y. Brody, "Were the Geonim Legislators?" (Hebrew), *Shenaton Ha-Mishpat Ha-Ivri* 11–12 (1984–1986): 306–307.

[6] Claims for the supremacy of the Holy Land were stressed both in letters seeking financial support and during disputations over authority; see: Gil, *History of Palestine*, 495–97, 562–64, 610–14, 771–74.

[7] See: B.M. Lewin, "Geniza Fragments: Chapters of Ben Baboi" (Hebrew), *Tarbiz* 2 (1931): 383–410 ("excellence": p. 396 lines 13–15); S. Spiegel, "On the Polemics of Pirqoy ben Baboy," in *Harry Austryn Wolfson Jubilee Volume*, ed. S. Lieberman et al. (Hebrew section) (Jerusalem, 1965), 266–71. See also: Gil, *History of Palestine*, 793–94; M. Ben-Sasson, "The Jews of the Maghreb and Their Relations with Eretz Israel in the Ninth through Eleventh Centuries" (Hebrew), *Shalem* 5 (1987): 33–36.

[8] See: H.H. Ben-Sasson, *History*, 426–27; S. Assaf, *The Geonic Period and its Literature*,

With each institution claiming absolute authority, the communities they sought to control could, in fact, play one off against the other. In order to avoid such manoeuvering and to prevent the outbreak of controversies, the eastern regions were divided into four geographical areas or *reshuyot* (sg. *rashut*): Egypt, Syria and the Holy Land were under the Yeshivah of the Land of Israel; Persia and the region east of Iraq belonged to the Rashut of the Exilarch; northern and western Iraq were attached to the Gaon of Sura; and the South, including the Yemen, was under the Gaon of Pumbedita.[9]

With the support of non-Jewish rulers, through long established precedent and their claim to sacred supremacy, the Yeshivot succeeded in exerting their power. The local Jewish communities of the Rashut areas were compelled to accept the authority both of the Yeshivah's Head and of his local appointees; any official Jewish business done in these communities was performed, in effect, with the permission of the Head of the Yeshivah. Even lower officials in the local communities were nominated by the local judge, who was a member (*ḥaver*) of the Yeshivah and received his authority from its Head. By supplying the authority for a community's activities, the Yeshivah made that community its dependent. We will not be mistaken, therefore, in defining the Yeshivah as a super-communal institution.

The relations between these centers and the local communities are reflected in hundreds of documents discovered in the Cairo Genizah. Another important source is the detailed report of a certain Nathan ben Isaac the Babylonian (ca. 950 C.E.), which was based upon his personal experience at the Yeshivah of Sura.[10] Impressed with his objective tone, histo-

---

42–59; L. Ginzberg, *Geonica* (New York, 1909), 1:6–22; A. Grossman, "From Father to Son: The Inheritance of the Spiritual Leadership of the Jewish Communities in the Early Middle Ages" (Hebrew), *Zion* 50 (1985): 189–204, 216–20.

[9] See: L. Ginzberg, ibid.; Goitein, *Mediterranean Society*, 2:5–6; Gil, *History of Palestine*, 491–95. On Yemen see below, nn. 15–17.

[10] For Nathan the Babylonian's detailed description of these procedures see: A. Neubauer, *Mediaeval Jewish Chronicles* (Oxford, 1895), 2:78–88; A. Marx, "Studies in Gaonic History and Literature," *JQR* n.s. 1 (1910–11): 61–104. For Judeo-Arabic fragments of the source for Nathan's composition, see: I. Friedlaender, "The Arabic Original of the Report of R. Nathan Hababli," *JQR* o.s. 17 (1905): 747–61; M. Ben-Sasson, "The Structure, Goals, and Content of the Story of Nathan Ha-Babli" (Hebrew), in *Culture and Society in Medieval Jewry, Studies Dedicated to the Memory of Haim-Hillel Ben-Sasson*, ed. M. Ben-Sasson et al. (Jerusalem, 1989), 137–96. For documents testifying to this Babylonian framework see: J. Mann, *Texts and Studies*, 1:63–201; idem, "The Responsa of the Babylonian Geonim as a Source of Jewish History," *JQR* n.s. 7 (1917): 457–90; 9 (1919): 139–179; 10 (1920): 121–52, 309–365; 11 (1921): 433–71; S. Abramson, *Ba-merkazim u-va-tefuṣot* (Jerusalem, 1965); M. Ben-Sasson, "Fragmentary Letters from the Genizah: Concerning the Ties of the Babylonian Academies with the West" (Hebrew), *Tarbiz* 56

rians have tended to give the account special weight and have, for example, accepted uncritically his periodization of Geonic leadership.[11] At the same time, however, much has been incautiously projected from Nathan's description of the Babylonian center and scholars have assumed that its official authority extended over all Jewish settlements in the Islamic world. Support for such an assumption has been derived from the hundreds of surviving questions which were directed to Baghdad from the Maghreb. The evidence that thousands of dinars were sent as donations to the Yeshivot of Babylonia and the Land of Israel has suggested, moreover, that the two centers maintained similar types of relations with the Diaspora. Indeed, it seemed natural to conclude that throughout the lands of the Caliphate, Jewish communities remained subordinate to the centers in Babylonia and the Land of Israel and were thereby prevented from developing as independent entities.[12] Although the Genizah discoveries have led scholars to modify Nathan's harmonious picture, there is still a tendency to project it upon Jewish communities throughout the lands of Islam. Even if Nathan's account were wholly reliable, two main points would require emphasis:

1. Nathan never claimed that his report applied to communities outside the Reshuyot. The official authority claimed by the centers in Babylonia and the Land of Israel extended only over the areas mentioned above.[13] While these centers remained the sources of authority for their Reshuyot, the communities west of Egypt appointed their own officials and did not claim the authority of the centers for their daily communal activities. Sources relating to the history of North African and Andalusian Jewry reveal that the western communities took full responsibility for their members in both sacred and secular walks of life. We shall return to this point shortly.
2. With more than one institution claiming absolute authority, the Heads of the different Yeshivot struggled constantly with each other in order

---

(1987): 171–209; B.M. Lewin, *Ginzei Qedem*, vols. 1–6 (Haifa and Jerusalem, 1922–1944). For the material relating to the Land of Israel see: M. Gil, *Palestine During the First Muslim Period, 634–1099* (Hebrew), vols. 1–3 (Tel Aviv 1983).

[11] See, e.g., J. Mann, "Varia on the Gaonic Period" (Hebrew), *Tarbiz* 5 (1934): 148–79. Mann's reservations concerning Nathan's chronology have gone virtually unremarked in the subsequent literature.

[12] See works cited above in note 1. See also: Y.F. Baer, "The Origins of the Jewish Community of the Middle Ages" (Hebrew), *Zion* 15 (1950): 1–41. Even Gil, *History of Palestine*, 494–95, follows the same pattern.

[13] See above n. 9.

to establish their supremacy. The existence of distinct Reshuyot did not fully alleviate this tense situation which some communities succeeded in exploiting. Outside the Reshuyot, for example, certain communities systematically approached the Heads of two Yeshivot with the same question in order to compare their respective responsa. While this practice infuriated the Heads of the Yeshivot, they were powerless to stop it.[14] Within the Reshuyot on the other hand, communities might seek to switch allegiance from one Yeshivah to another. This was especially true when a community was distant from the center and the Yeshivah under whose authority it lay was experiencing troubles. A collection of epistles sent by Nehemiah Gaon to the Yemen in the mid-tenth century sheds light on just such a situation.[15] Nehemiah's Gaonate (960–967/68) was fraught with difficulties, since he was opposed by a faction within his own Yeshivah.[16] From his epistles we learn that Yemenite communities which had sent their dues to his Yeshivah in the past had severed their relationship with him and established contact with his opponents. The super-communal network that had been loyal to his Rashut was thus completely transferred to another party. But this was not the last time that the Yemenite communities shifted their loyalties. During the mid-eleventh century they came under the authority of the Exilarch, and by the beginning of the twelfth, they had switched allegiance once again—this time to the Yeshivah of the Land of Israel whose Head dwelt in Egypt![17]

Two episodes described by Nathan reflect this pattern of changing loyalties and the general tendency of one Rashut to encroach upon another.

[14] See: S. Abramson, "One Question and Two Answers" (Hebrew), *Shenaton Ha-Mishpat Ha-Ivri* 11–12 (1984–1986): 1–40. The Karaites exploited this phenomenon in order to reveal the inconsistency of the Rabbanite oral tradition. See the characteristic responsum by Naḥshon, Gaon of Sura, to the community of Kairouan in Mann, *Texts and Studies*, 1:558–567.

[15] The manuscript presumably originated at the Yeshivah and was then brought to Egypt where it was split up, one part eventually going to a Parisian library and the other to the Cambridge collection. The fragments are: Paris AIU E 26, ed. B. Lewin, *Ginzei Qedem* 3 (1925): 14–23 and Cambridge T-S 16.95, ed. S.D. Goitein, *The Yemenites: History, Communal Organization, Spiritual Life* (Hebrew) (Jerusalem, 1983), 20–25, 28–31. Their ascription to Nehemiah Gaon can be proven on the basis of style and content; this will be dealt with in a separate study.

[16] For the civil population in Babylonia this was a difficult period both because of the Buwayhids' activities and the general decline of the Iraqi economy; see: G. Le Strange, *Baghdad during the ʿAbbasid Caliphate* (London, 1900), 317–23; M. Canard, "Baghdad au IVe siècle de l'Hegire," *Arabica* 9 (1962): 267–87. On the revolutionary actions initiated against Nehemiah and his party see B.M. Lewin, *The Epistle of Rav Sherira Gaon* (Hebrew) (Haifa, 1921), 121.

[17] See Goitein, *The Yemenites*, 53–74.

The deposition of the Exilarch Uqba II in 917 C.E. followed upon charges that he had appropriated funds belonging to the Yeshivah of Pumbedita:

> For the Rashut of Khorasan had in olden times belonged to Pumbedita, whence the *dayyanim* used to be sent thither and all the tax on her revenues used to go to Pumbedita. Uqba, however, wished the *dayyanim* to be sent to her [Khorasan] by himself, in order to take possession of her and get hold of her revenues for himself alone, to the exclusion of Pumbedita.[18]

And the controversy between Saadya Gaon and David ben Zakkai moved rapidly into its final phase when the latter's officials took measures against a person outside the Exilarch's Rashut.[19] These events in Babylonia indicate that even with clearly defined areas of responsibility—i.e. the Reshuyot—there was great potential for instability within the super-communal network.[20] We may sum up by saying, therefore, that the traditional model of super-communal, sacred leadership does not adequately describe the situation of all Jewish communities under Islam. Indeed, as we have seen above, it does not even adequately describe the situation in the classic Geonic period.

II

While the sacred centers in Babylonia and the Land of Israel retained super-communal responsibility for those areas under their jurisdiction and tried to demonstrate their perfect superiority, the real battles for sacred authority took place in the West, outside the Reshuyot. Because they represented a new potential sphere of influence, these unaffiliated western regions greatly interested the old centers in the East. The western communities attracted them, moreover, for three specific reasons. First, their intensive involvement in international commerce had made them very affluent. Second, as a result of general population shifts, they were growing rapidly in size.[21] And finally, certain individual Jews in the West had found

[18] See I. Friedlaender, "Arabic Original," 753, 756; M. Ben-Sasson, "Structure, Goals, and Content," 181–82; A. Neubauer, *Mediaeval Jewish Chronicles*, 2:78–79.

[19] For this part of the report we do not yet possess the Arabic original; see A. Neubauer, *Mediaeval Jewish Chronicles*, 2:82.

[20] The same may be said with regard to the Rashut of the Land of Israel. In the Tiberias community, for example, there was more than a hint of rebellion; see Gil, *History of Palestine*, 542–43. (The Yeshivah's move from Tiberias to the south may be connected with this; cf. Gil, *History of Palestine*, p. 569, no. 790.) The case of the Babylonians in Fusṭāṭ and Ramla affords another instance of such instability; see Gil, *History of Palestine*, 527–39.

[21] For the rapid growth of their economic activities see: S.D. Goitein, "The Origin and

their way to the courts of Muslim rulers; the influence which they consequently acquired enabled them to play key roles both in the activities of their own communities and in international politics.[22]

While the leadership of super-communal networks in the East was largely determined by pedigree, the western communities were often headed by skilled individuals lacking any sacred lineage. This should come as no surprise when we remember that the Maghreb was very much an immigrant society. To these westerners economic and political talent counted for more than noble ancestry. For their part, the western communities succeeded in assuming total control of their own affairs by fully exploiting the physical distance which separated them from the centers. Taking advantage of the fact that there was no local tradition of sacred authority, they were able to define their own developing, basic needs. Beginning in the ninth century, therefore, we find the Maghrebi Jews involved in multi-faceted public activities. These included:

1. The establishment of academies where local scholars could sharpen their dialectical skills. When halakhic difficulties of a practical or theoretical nature arose, these academies frequently contacted the centers.
2. The creation of libraries for the use of local scholars. These collections were developed through overseas book-orders, the topical organization of rabbinic responsa, and the composition of new works on a variety of subjects, including, e.g., daily rulings.
3. The nomination of local judges and other officials both in accordance with the communities' specific needs and the nominees' own education and skills.
4. The exploitation of contacts at the courts of Muslim rulers for the communal good.

Historical Significance of North African Jewry," *Proceedings of the Seminar on Muslim Jewish Relations in North Africa* (New York, 1975), 2–13; Goitein, *Studies in Islamic History and Institutions* (Leiden, 1968), 559–79; and Stillman, *The Jews of Arab Lands*, 42–53. The demographic changes resulting from massive movements to the west began already in the early eighth century; see: Lewin "Geniza Fragments: Chapters of Ben Baboi" (on students who immigrated from the east and founded local academies in the west); H.Z.W. Hirschberg, *A History of the Jews in North Africa* (Leiden, 1974), 1:143–45; E. Ashtor, *The Jews of Moslem Spain* (Philadelphia, 1973), 1:29–42.

22 There are numerous examples of such individuals; see: H.Z.W. Hirschberg, *A History of the Jews in North Africa*, 1:271, 304–306 [Isaac Israeli], 109, 112, 210 [Judah Rosh ha-Seder], and 211–213 [Abraham Ibn ʿAṭā]; Goitein, *Mediterranean Society*, 2:243; B. Lewis, "Paltiel. A Note," *BSOAS* 30 (1967): 177–81 [Moses b. Eleazar]; E. Ashtor, *The Jews of Moslem Spain*, 1:376–79

Naturally, the smaller communities in these areas came under the influence of several major centers, e.g. Tahert and Kairouan, which were important commercial stations, or Cordova and al-Mahdiyya, which were Islamic capitals.[23]

Before discussing the day-to-day relationships of neighboring communities, we should note the existence of certain special links among the mercantile class. We are not referring here to the intensive and enduring business partnerships characteristic of the period, but to a wider network based mainly on regional contacts between merchants of different communities. While these relationships were, in fact, originally grounded in common economic interests, shared public interests could be translated into regional activities as well. There were, for example, cases where merchants from a particular place adopted a common line and became recognized as the "group" of that area. The merchants of the Maghreb, the Sicilians, and the Indian Karim,[24] for example, all knew how and when to organize themselves into pressure groups either to obtain tax-breaks or to proclaim a ban against other groups.[25] They might even express their collective dissatisfaction with the leaders of other communities and support an alternative leader, who would serve their interests better.[26]

[Joshua Ibn Jau], 155–227, [Ḥasdai Ibn Shaprut], and vol. 2, 41–189 [Samuel ha-Nagid and his son Joseph].

[23] See: M. Ben-Sasson, "Qayrawan," *Proceedings of the First Conference of the Society for Judaeo-Arabic Studies* [in press]; idem, *The Rise of the Local Jewish Community in Islamic Lands* (Hebrew) (Jerusalem, 1995), 189–345; idem, "The Jewish Community of Gabes in the 11th Century," in *Communautés juives des marges sahariennes du Maghreb*, ed. M. Abitbol (Jerusalem, 1982), 264–84. For Cordova and Lucena only the latter two activities are documented and this for a period when the level of scholarship in Andalusia was not at its height; see: I. Ta-Shma, "Shipput 'ivri u-mishpaṭ 'ivri ba-me'ot ha–11-ha–12 bi-sefarad," *Shenaton Ha-Mishpat Ha-Ivri* 1 (1974): 353–72; D. Rosenthal, "Rav Paltoi Gaon and his Place in the Halakhic Tradition" (Hebrew), *Shenaton Ha-Mishpat Ha-Ivri* 11–12 (1984–1986): 603–609.

[24] On the Maghrebis see: S.D. Goitein, "The Origin and Historical Significance of North African Jewry"; idem, *Mediterranean Society*, 1:540 (index, s.v. Maghrebi[s]). On the Sicilians see: M. Ben-Sasson, *The Jews of Sicily 825–1068* (Hebrew) (Jerusalem, 1991), vi; idem, "Mediterranean Sicily," in *Proceedings of the Fifth Conference of the Society for Judaeo-Arabic Studies* [in preparation]. On the Karim see: Goitein, *The Yemenites*, 35–36; *EI*, 2d ed., s.v. "Karim."

[25] On The Maghrebis' interests see: Goitein, *Mediterranean Society*, 2:67; M. Ben-Sasson, "The Jews of the Maghreb and Their Relations with Eretz Israel," p. 64, n. 112, no. III (and see the next example for their involvement in the community's activities). The Sicilians attempted to have the special taxes which had been imposed upon them repealed; see M. Ben-Sasson, *The Jews of Sicily*, p. 723, s.v. 'Ushr. For the Karim merchants see Goitein, *Studies in Islamic History and Institutions*, 351–60.

[26] On several occasions during the late tenth and early eleventh centuries, the Maghrebis living in the Land of Israel, Egypt, and North Africa actively sought high positions in the Yeshivah of the Land of Israel for their own candidates. One of the main objectives was to secure influence in the economic sphere; see M. Ben-Sasson, "The Jews of the Maghreb and Their Relations with Eretz Israel," 64–76.

Another expression of inter-communal development in the West was the promotion of certain local academies into the authoritative institutions of the region. This was the case with Kairouan, whose scholars were not at first officially acknowledged by the Jews of the Maghreb. Consequently, the city did not enjoy the advantages of the sacred centers in the East. Because of their location and availability, however, the sages of Kairouan did in the end come to be accepted. And once they were recognized by the Maghrebi communities as halakhic authorities, these scholars were consulted on other public issues of a non-halakhic nature as well.[27]

For the eastern centers, who badly needed the local communities in the West, the problem was clear: how to ensure that the Maghrebis remained tightly bound to them. Knowing the needs of western communities for responsa, books, and commercial contacts, the Geonim employed existing inter-communal ties to develop their influence in the Maghreb. As leaders, they were not unique in combining economic ties with politico-religious aims. The Muslim Caliphs also used the Maghreb-Mashreq caravan merchants, as well as the merchants who went to India, in order to deliver their messages and propaganda.[28] In Jewish society economic ties facilitated the delivery of mail, halakhic questions and responsa, new books, and money.[29] In order to develop contacts with the western communities which lay outside the Reshuyot, the eastern centers took several initiatives:

1. They bestowed honorary titles upon the regional leaders. Traditionally, such honorifics as Rosh Kallah, Rosh Seder, Aluf, Ḥaver be-Sanhedra Rabba, and Nagid belonged exclusively to the world of the sacred centers.[30]

---

[27] The scholars of Kairouan were even consulted by Egyptian communities who were officially under the Rashut of Land of Israel; see: S. Abramson, *R. Nissim Gaon: Libelli Quinque* (Hebrew) (Jerusalem, 1965), 25–26, 43–46; M. Ben-Sasson, *The Rise of the Local Jewish Community*, section 3, end of chapter 3.

[28] See: S.M. Stern, "Cairo as the Centre of the Ismāʿīlī Movement," *Le Millénaire du Caire: mélanges* (Cairo, 1972), 437–50, repr. in *Studies in Early Ismāʿīlism* (Jerusalem and Leiden, 1983), 234–53; J. Lassner, "Propaganda in Early Islam: The ʿAbbasid in the Post Revolutionary Age," *IOS* 10 (1980): 74–85; idem, *Islamic Revolution and Historical Memory: An Inquiry into the ʿAbbasid Apologetics* (New Haven, 1986); B. Lewis, "The Fatimids and the Route to India," *Revue de la Faculté des Sciences Économiques de l'Université d'Istanbul* 11 (1953): 50–54.

[29] See: N.A. Stillman, "East and West Relations in the Islamic Mediterranean in the Early Eleventh Century: A Study in the Geniza Correspondence of the House of Ibn Awkal" (Ph.D. diss., University of Pennsylvania, 1970); idem, "A Communal Leader in the Eleventh Century," in *The Eleventh Century* (Binghamton, New York, 1974); idem, "Quelques renseignements biographiques sur Yosef Ibn Awkal médiateur entre les communautés juives du Maghreb et les académies d'Irak," *REJ* 132 (1973): 529–42.

[30] See: Goitein, *Mediterranean Society*, 2:22–40, 196–99; Gil, *History of Palestine*, 575–601.

2. They composed books and dedicated them to the regional leaders.[31]
3. They encouraged regional leaders to build a local network—upon the existing commercial network—for the collection of funds and the delivery of responsa.[32]

Throughout this period from the ninth to the eleventh centuries the eastern centers greatly encouraged the development of regional networks which were also intended to serve their own interests. The relations between West and East, however, remained at all times voluntary. And while the western communities were not subordinated to the centers, they were loyal to them. If they participated in activities sponsored by the latter, it was because they accepted their special authority. Paradoxically, the selfsame initiatives taken by the eastern centers in order to strengthen their influence in the West, ultimately served to undermine their interests by supplying the means for complete independence. The establishment of a legitimate alternative network, the replacement of direct contact with the Geonim by recourse to their books, and the appropriation of the centers' exclusive honorary titles all paved the way for spiritual, halakhic, and political autonomy.[33] The question then remains: what exactly was the nature of the relations established between the eastern centers and the western regions?

Since the latter were not part of any Rashut, their relationship with the former was clearly unofficial. During the ninth and tenth centuries, the western communities' need for practical guidance in halakhic matters led the Heads of their academies to initiate contact with the Babylonian Yeshivot. Having developed links with the Babylonian center, the communities adopted a deferential attitude towards the Yeshivot by the beginning of the eleventh century.[34] At the same time, however, the Maghrebis

[31] For commentaries and monographs on a variety of topics (law, prayer, philosophy) and their dedication to regional leaders see M. Ben-Sasson, "Fragmentary Letters from the Genizah," 183–84, 188, 195–98.

[32] See, e.g., the epistles in Mann, *Texts and Studies*, 1:63–201.

[33] Towards the seventh decade of the eleventh century, after the local communities of the West had become partially disengaged from the East, the letters of the Geonim take on a certain pointed tone. These epistles reflect an awareness that the western communities no longer felt the need for Babylonian instruction, since they had developed their own local institutions; see M. Ben-Sasson, "Fragmentary Letters from the Genizah," 180–84.

[34] For the local communities' dependence upon the Yeshivot—in varying degrees and manifestations—see: M. Ben-Sasson, "Maghrib-Mashriq Ties from the Ninth to the Eleventh Centuries" (Hebrew), *Pe'amim* 38 (1989): 35–57; Z. Groner, "The Maghrib and the Geonic Academies in Iraq as Reflected in Responsa Literature (Ninth to Eleventh Centuries)" (Hebrew), *Pe'amim* 38 (1989): 49–57.

remained respectful towards the Yeshivah of the Land of Israel, even though they did not seek its advice. Recognizing the geographical superiority of the Holy Land, they also required the Yeshivah's support for those of their brethren who lived within its Rashut. Consequently, the Maghrebis sent the Yeshivah a steady stream of donations; and whenever necessary, they intervened on behalf of its members before the non-Jewish authorities in the Maghreb and in Egypt. From the Yeshivah's point of view such actions expressed deferential subordination to the center and were, therefore, of considerable political and economic value.[35] To sum up at this point: during the Geonic period, the western communities maintained relationships with both a super-communal, sacred center in the East and an inter-communal, regional authority. By the late tenth century, this balance of power would tip in favor of the latter. The process of vesting the regional institutions with authority heralds a new era in Jewish history—an era in which the relationships between the centers and the local communities were irrevocably altered. This trend marks the beginning of real regional independence from the centers and the emergence of local replacements, viz. the *qehillot*.[36]

As previously mentioned, there were two main types of inter-communal relationship. The "super-communal" relations between a sacred center and its subordinate area entailed mutual obligations and responsibilities. The communities of a particular Rashut were obliged to participate within this system and were expected to accept their center's authority. In the West, however, we may properly speak of "inter-communal" relationships which did not involve subordination to any center but operated rather on a voluntary basis. Up to the eleventh century, relationships of both type existed simultaneously: there were super-communal organizations within the Reshuyot and practical, inter-communal contacts in the West. The two were by no means incompatible; indeed, the inter-communal network served the sacred centers for a long time, without being part of the super-communal system. Even when the centers weakened during the second half of the eleventh century, the leaders of the regional, inter-communal networks made no attempt to claim sacred authority—which remained,

---

[35] Their political interest was expressed via disputes over the highest positions of the Yeshivah; see n. 26 above. The sizable donation made by the Maghrebis to the Yeshivah of the Land of Israel—which was found to be larger than their contribution to the Babylonian Yeshivot—is evidence of this financial commitment; see M. Ben-Sasson, "The Jews of the Maghreb and Their Relations with Eretz Israel," 60–63.

[36] *Contra* Baer's ideas concerning the tenth-century beginnings of the local Jewish community in medieval western Europe and Ben-Sasson's view that the regional connections constituted an organized replacement for the central sacred institutions of the East; see Y.F. Baer, "The Origins of the Jewish Community of the Middle Ages" and H.H. Ben-Sasson, *History*.

after all, the prerogative of the Geonim and the Exilarchs.[37]

Of all Jewish regional centers under Islam, only Spain asserted total sacred authority. During the twelfth century, Moses Ibn Ezra, Abraham Ibn Daud, and Judah Ibn Tibbon each alluded to the claim that Sefarad in their time—and even before—was the "divinely-chosen, temporary center."[38] For Jewish refugees from Islamic Spain to the Christian North there were obvious reasons for developing such a claim, especially when they began to encounter Jewish intellectuals of different cultural backgrounds.[39] Even in this extraordinary case, however, there was no attempt to build a super-communal network; the Sefardim continued to work within an inter-communal framework.

III

While the inter-communal networks continued to function during the eleventh and twelfth centuries, providing services which the local communities had come to expect of them, the old sacred centers collapsed. The advent of the Seljuks in 1071 forced the Yeshivah of the Land of Israel into exile for some fifty years—first in Tyre, then in Damascus. Based outside the borders of the Holy Land, the Yeshivah's members now found it difficult to claim sacred authority. It was only in 1127 that the Geonic families of the Land of Israel rectified a serious tactical blunder by relocating to Cairo.[40] Egypt, after all, was now the seat of power in the area

[37] Cf. the recent article of Zvi Groner, "The Geonim," in *Leaders and Leadership in Jewish and World History: Collected Essays* (Hebrew), ed. I. Malkin and Z. Tzahor (Jerusalem, 1992), 143–163 which argues that the Geonim were not leaders within the Jewish world at large. In evaluating the Geonim as leaders, he tends to confuse two different criteria: (1) the nature of their leadership as *official* authorities responsible for dealing with the official activities, organization, and regulation (e.g. nominating judges, collecting taxes) of the communities under their jurisdiction; and (2) the extent of their influence within the communities which voluntarily accepted geonic authority. Because of the basic institutional framework, the Geonim did not figure as *official* authorities within the communities outside the Reshuyot. As we have endeavored to show, however, they did succeed in exerting considerable influence in areas which were geographically remote from them for almost two hundred years.

[38] Spiritual justification for this assertion derived most famously from Obadiah 20. For the claims see: Moses Ibn Ezra, *Liber discussionis et commemorationis (Poetica Hebraica)* (Judeo-Arabic and Hebrew), ed. A.S. Halkin (Jerusalem, 1975), 54–87; Abraham Ibn Daud, *The Book of Tradition*, ed. G.D. Cohen (Philadelphia, 1969), 263–304; and Ibn Tibbon's ethical will in *Hebrew Ethical Wills*, ed. and trans. I. Abrahams (Philadelphia, 1926), 1:54–92.

[39] Living at period of decline in Muslim Spain, all strove to perpetuate the cultural achievements of Andalusian Jewry in the havens which they found on Christian soil, in the less-developed north; see R. Drory, "The Hidden Context: On Literary Products of Tri-Cultural Contact in the Middle-Ages" (Hebrew), *Pe'amim* 46–47 (1991): 9–28.

[40] See: Gil, *History of Palestine*, 739–50, 774–76; M.R. Cohen, "Administrative Relations

and would remain so until the sixteenth century. The Egyptian center had meanwhile assumed control over those areas which had previously been under the jurisdiction of the Yeshivah of the Land of Israel. Although it functioned as a super-communal authority, the powerful Egyptian community did not at first develop claims for total religious superiority. The situation changed briefly around the end of the eleventh century with the coming of outsiders possessing sacred lineage, such as David ben Daniel ben Azariah, who claimed both Davidic and Geonic descent.[41] A further boost to the authority of the Egyptian center was expected when the Yeshivah of the Land of Israel arrived a quarter of a century later.

In Babylonia toward the end of the twelfth century, a similar situation existed when the Gaon Samuel ben Eli sought to gain power in order to rebuild the super-communal network and reissue the age-old claims for sacred authority. His epistles to eastern Jewish communities carried with them the old message of Babylonian superiority and strongly emphasized the holiness of the Geonic dynasties. At the same time, descendants of the Exilarchs issued claims for their sacred lineage and demanded recognition and support.[42] In both centers, then, descendants of the Geonim headed a super-communal network. They continued to employ traditional formulae evocative of their divine authority to rule the Jewish people.

These authorities soon had to confront a new phase of leadership in the East—the intellectual supremacy of Egypt beginning with Moses Maimonides (1138–1204). With the ascent of Maimonides to political power, there is a marked change of attitude towards the idea of sacred authority. Maimonides was more than an intellectual leader who participated in Jewish political life. Not only did he wage successful campaigns against the Gaon in Babylonia and the Geonim of the Land of Israel who were based in Egypt, but he was also the first to develop a complete ideology in opposition to the power and respect vested in the so-called "sacred Geonic families." The harsh remarks which he directed against the Geonic dynas-

---

Between Palestinian and Egyptian Jewry During the Fatimid Period," in *Egypt and Palestine: A Millennium of Association*, ed. A. Cohen and G. Baer (Jerusalem, 1984), 130–35; and M. Ben-Sasson, "Egyptian Jewry in the 10th–12th Centuries: From Periphery to Center," *Bulletin of the Israeli Academic Center in Cairo* 8 (1987): 14–16.

[41] Gil, *History of Palestine*, 750–74.

[42] See: S. Poznanski, *Babylonische Geonim im nachgaonäischen Zeitalter* (Berlin, 1914), 15–36; Mann, *Texts and Studies*, 1:214–21, 251–53, 401–403; S. Assaf, "Letters of R. Samuel ben Eli and His Contemporaries" (Hebrew), *Tarbiz* 1 (1930): 43–84; D.S. Sassoon, *A History of the Jews in Baghdad* (Letchworth, 1949), 6–99. On the Exilarchs see: Mann, ibid., 228–254; Goitein, *The Yemenites*, ibid.; A. Grossman, *The Babylonian Exilarchate in the Gaonic Period* (Hebrew) (Jerusalem, 1984).

ties in his epistles and other literary works might have pointed the way to a new type of super-communal leadership, one which would have derived its authority from the power of pure scholarship.[43] Unfortunately, his call for reform came too late: the thirteenth century was a period of decline for eastern Jewish communities. There is more than a grain of irony in the fact that the Maimonidean dynasty adopted the super-communal system as a framework for its activities, claiming Maimonidean descent as a sacred justification.[44] Irony aside, the framework during this period for inter-communal relations in the East—including the Yemen—remained decidedly super-communal.

In analyzing the two main types of contacts between the Jewish communities of Islam, we have seen how leading communities within the inter-communal network did not assume responsibility for the local activities of smaller ones. In actual fact, the local community was the basic cell of Jewish public life. Unjustifiably dismissed as a later development in Islamic lands, the local community existed already in the ninth century. Outside the Reshuyot it took full responsibility for its members in most aspects of their life, giving them their secondary, communal identity.[45] During the late Middle Ages, Jewish populations in Islamic lands developed predominantly regional, local, and communal identities. The super-communal relationships which had so long played such a central role were, however, consigned to oblivion.[46]

---

[43] See M. Ben-Sasson, "Maimonides in Egypt: The First Stage," *Maimonidean Studies* 2 (1991): 10–11, 15–17.

[44] See: E. Strauss (Ashtor), *Toledot ha-yehudim be-miṣrayim ve-suriyah taḥat shilṭon ha-mamlukim* (History of the Jews in Egypt and Syria under the Rule of the Mameluks) (Jerusalem, 1944), 1:117–43, 228–33, 298–302. That their power derived ultimately from their lineage is evident from their role as custodians of Maimonides' literary legacy. Not only did they preserve the best versions of his writings but they also claimed to be the authoritative interpreters of his oeuvre; see: P.B. Fenton, "The Literary Legacy of David b. Joshua, last of the Maimonidean Negidim," *JQR* 75 (1984): 1–56. They were expected to take a leading part as well in defending Maimonides against his opponents; see: J. Sarachek, *Faith and Reason: The Conflict Over the Rationalism of Maimonides* (Williamsport, 1935), 120–27, 142–48; D.J. Silver, *Maimonidean Criticism and the Maimonidean Controversy, 1180–1240* (Leiden, 1965), 65–67, 126–27, 153–54, 160–61. And they were also expected to transmit the oral teachings of their illustrious ancestor; see: Ashtor, ibid., 227–28. Not surprisingly, they were addressed by such sacred titles as "his greatness" or "his holiness"; see, e.g., *Abraham Maimuni: Responsa*, ed. A.H. Freimann and S.D. Goitein (Jerusalem, 1937), 1, 4, 17, 27, 143, 149, 153, 161, 173, 175, 203, 207.

[45] See: M. Ben-Sasson, *The Rise of the Local Jewish Community*, section three.

[46] Nowadays, it is, ironically, only Ashkenazic Jews who preserve a memory of these super-communal networks. Every Sabbath, when they recite the prayer *yequm purqan* for the Geonim of Babylonia and the Land of Israel, they send their blessings to all officials of the Yeshivot and the Exilarchs—a sign of stubborn discontinuity! Although this prayer reflects an oriental reality, it has not yet been documented in eastern sources; the earliest known attestation is in *Maḥzor Vitri*, ed. S. Hurwitz (Nürnberg, 1923), 172.

THE EXILARCHATE*

Moshe Gil

The Exilarchate was undoubtedly the oldest of the central institutions to emerge in the Diaspora. A tradition connecting it with the House of David goes back as far as Jehoiachin, the exiled King of Judah. While the validity of this tradition is questionable, I believe it to be fundamentally genuine, for one simple reason: a Jewish community as sizable as that of Babylonia and Persia would not readily have acknowledged unfounded claims of kinship to the House of David for any length of time. All the same, the family of the Exilarchs has not left us a complete and convincing genealogy. In the *Seder Olam Zuta*, for example, there is a list of names beginning with Zerubabel that has been imaginatively adapted from I Chronicles 3—interspersed among the biblical names are Nathan and Huna, contemporaries of Rabbi Judah the Prince (d. ca. 225 C.E.). The utterly fanciful notion that Zerubabel returned to Babylonia from Palestine in order to become Exilarch is also to be found here.[1]

Nevertheless, it is reasonable to assume that the Babylonian exiles acknowledged the legitimacy of the descendants of the royal house, who maintained their leadership throughout the Persian period. According to Talmudic tradition, the Exilarch enjoyed a secure status at the Persian court, wearing special vestments, such as the *qamra* and the *himyān*, that he received from the Persian monarch as marks of his high rank.[2] He was granted complete authority over the Jewish community. Collectively, the ancient Exilarchs projected a strict and dominating personality. In keeping with Persian custom, they maintained courts of their own, possessed

---

* The English version of this article was prepared by Mrs. Ethel Broido. I would like to thank the Institute of Jewish Studies, University College London for funding the translation. A number of texts cited below are included in a corpus of 846 Genizah documents which I have edited (in press); these are referred to as *Corpus*, no. __, with the shelfmark given in parentheses. I am grateful to Dr. Yoram Erder who helped me elucidate certain chronological problems relating to the early Exilarchs.

[1] See M. Gil, *A History of Palestine, 634–1099* (Cambridge, 1992), 490ff. (= Gil, *History*). For the skeptical attitude towards the Exilarch's claim of Davidic descent, see bSan. 31a. See also J. Liver, *Toledot bet david* (Jerusalem, 1958/59), 42–45. On the genealogical list's lack of credibility, see S. Assaf, *Tequfat ha-ge'onim ve-sifrutah* (Jerusalem, 1955), 25.

[2] Al-Tanūkhī still uses the word *himyān* in the sense of a girdle or waistband for holding money; see *Nishwār al-muḥāḍara* (Beirut, 1971), 2:45.

considerable property and income, indulged in pomp and ceremony, and surrounded themselves with courtiers, servants, and slaves. They appointed their own judges and availed themselves of the best minds of their times. While the Talmud mentions several Exilarchs who were outstanding scholars and legislators, it is evident that even in those days, the spiritual leadership of the Diaspora was for the most part not in their care. The occupations and aspirations of the Exilarch were mainly secular and political, although in ancient times these would have been inseparable from the general religious system. The comparatively low spiritual profile they maintained evidently derived from the hereditary character of their position, which was limited to a single family.

Under Islam, the Exilarchs' status and responsibilities were reduced despite the respect that virtually all Muslims had for their Davidic ancestry.[3] At the same time, tensions between the Exilarchs and the Yeshivot that had originated during the Persian period seem to have increased under Islamic rule, becoming almost unbearable at times.

From the story of Bustanai—which I have discussed elsewhere—we learn that the Muslims regarded the Exilarch as the central figure within the Jewish community. Islamic sources which describe his personality, status, and struggles confirm this impression.[4] Half a millennium later, Benjamin of Tudela (latter half of the twelfth century) states that in his day, the Exilarch still received the Caliph's "seal for all the Jewish communities." The Exilarch was, in fact, appointed in much the same way as the Nestorian Katholikos. Muḥammad b. al-Ḥasan Ibn Ḥamdūn (mid-twelfth century) records the Caliph's appointment of such a Katholikos in 1138 after he had been elected by the fathers of the Church; this act symbolically expressed the rulers' authority to confirm or reject the leadership which the "protected peoples" had designated for themselves. The document cited by Ibn Ḥamdūn enumerates the leader's powers—e.g. the authority to make local appointments, the management of communal property, and the administration of pious foundations—and warns against disobedience to the rulers.[5] This text is not unique: there are at least two

[3] See Benjamin of Tudela, *Sefer massaʿot*, ed. E.N. Adler (London 1907), 40. In 1211 Samuel b. Samson wrote: "And from there we went to Hebron; and the Exilarch brought a seal (i.e. a written order) with him from the king and (in the name of) Muhammat (!) who is *al-khalīfa*." The Exilarch, then, still went about with the writ of appointment—"the seal" given him by the Caliph; see A. Berliner, "Mikhtav mi-rabbi shemu'el ben shimshon," *Ozar Tob* (Berlin, 1876), 36ff. and A. Yaari, *Iggerot ereṣ-yisraʾel* (Ramat Gan, 1971), 79.

[4] On the Bustanai affair see M. Gil, "The Babylonian Encounter" (Hebrew), *Tarbiz* 48 (1978/9): 35; F. Lazarus, "Neue Beiträge zur Geschichte des Exilarchats," *MGWJ* 78 (1934): 285, 295.

[5] On Ibn Ḥamdūn and his book (the *Tadhkira*), see C. Brockelmann, *Geschichte der arabischen*

similar, earlier documents from the latter half of the eleventh century that deal with the appointment of Patriarchs. And from the beginning of the thirteenth century, there is a parallel letter of appointment that was granted to Daniel b. Eleazar, Head of the Yeshivah of Baghdad. We may assume, therefore, that similar letters of appointment were originally sent to the Exilarchs; ultimately, however, it was the Heads of the Yeshivot in Baghdad who received such official recognition.[6]

In the mid-tenth century, however, the Exilarch still enjoyed special status. According to Nathan the Babylonian, the appointment of the Exilarch represented a sort of pact with the people, "public opinion" counting as the decisive voice: "Then the two Heads of the Yeshivot come together with members of their Yeshivot, with all the heads of the community and the elders." The meeting would take place in the home of a leading Baghdadī financier, "such as Neṭira," thereby conferring upon the host lasting prestige. Once the election of the Exilarch had been completed, the ceremonies would be planned. These were set for the end of the week. On the Thursday, the Exilarch would be blessed in synagogue and the shofar would be blown; the entire community would send him gifts—money, clothing, jewelry, and precious vessels. Huge feasts with "all sorts of foodstuffs, beverages, desserts and sweetmeats" were served on both

Literatur, 2d ed. (Leipzig, 1937–49), 1:281, Supp. 1:493. This document has already been published four times, most recently by L.I. Conrad, "A Nestorian Decree," in *Iḥsān ʿAbbās Jubilee Volume* (Beirut, 1981), 83; for the Arabic version, see 91–94. (On p. 97 he translates *wuqūfihim*, "their concerns"; this should, in fact, be "their *waqf*s." Here the document deals with a central issue: the maintenance and administration of the pious foundations, which formed the main economic basis of communal life and activities.) A. Grossman's assertion that the writ of appointment was discovered is incorrect; see his *Rashut ha-golah be-vavel bi-tequfat ha-geʾonim* (Jerusalem, 1984), 45.

[6] For similar writs of appointment see Mārī ibn Sulaymān, *Kitāb al-majdal, akhbār faṭārika kursī al-mashriq*, ed. H. Gismondi (Roma, 1899): 1:133, 147 (The appointment of ʿAbdīshūʿ Patriarch by Caliph al-Qāʾim either in 464 [1071/2] or at the end of Muḥarram 480 [May 1087]; the appointment of Makīkhā by Caliph al-Muqtadī in Ṣafar 480 [April–May 1092]). Note the expression *amwāl wuqūfihim*, "the assets of their pious foundations" in a writ of appointment issued by al-Qāʾim, ibid., 135, line 8. The Muslim authorities undoubtedly employed an ancient, fixed formulation for these documents, as is confirmed by the writs of appointment found in the Genizah. For a Genizah document appointing a *raʾīs al-yahūd* in Damascus (1193) see G. Khan, *Arabic Legal and Administrative Documents in the Cambridge Genizah Collections* (Cambridge, 1993), 460–66, no. 121 (T-S Arabic Box 38, f. 93). There is also a writ from the Egyptian vizier al-Afḍal (end of the 11th c.) appointing a Christian dignitary; see T-S Arabic Box 39, fs. 452 + 453. Cf. S.D. Goitein, *A Mediterranean Society* (Berkeley, Los Angeles, London, 1967–93), 2:527, n. 14; Gil, *History*, 508ff. Confirmation that it was a long-standing custom for the ruler to appoint the heads of the communities comes from the draft (or copy) of a writ of appointment issued by the Fāṭimid Caliph to the head of the Palestinian Yeshivah, Solomon b. Judah; see M. Gil, *Palestine During the First Muslim Period* (Hebrew), vol. 2 (Tel Aviv, 1983), doc. 311 (= Gil, *Palestine*) and the discussion in idem, *History*, 508–10.

the Thursday and Friday. Thus far, the Hebrew version of Nathan's account; the Arabic original—which is, alas, partially lost—contains many more details including a report of the great ceremony on the Sabbath. On the Friday, a wooden podium (*migdal*) would be constructed in the synagogue. Behind this platform, which was covered with rugs and hung with a sort of curtain, the Exilarch together with the Heads of the Yeshivot would await the opening of the ceremony which was accompanied by the singing of psalms and hymns. With the appearance of the Exilarch on the podium, the entire congregation would rise in his honor and remain standing until he took his seat. The Heads of the Yeshivot would appear and kneel before him; they would then take their seats by his side. After the cantor had blessed him quietly, the Exilarch would give a sermon on that day's reading from the Torah which the *meturgeman* ("translator" or "transmitter") would loudly declaim to the assembled throng. Next would come a homily on some *halakhic* issue to which one of the scholars would respond. The cantor would then bless the Exilarch again together with the Heads of the Yeshivot; afterwards he would call out the names of the various communities, announcing their donations in the order of their largesse. This would be followed by the Torah reading: after a priest (*kohen*) and a levite were called up, the Exilarch would receive the scroll from the cantor and would read a portion from it. Standing beside him, the Head of the Sura Yeshivah would read the *targum*. Following the service, the Exilarch would invite the gathering to his home and would offer hospitality to all of his followers during the ensuing week. Henceforth, he would cease to go out, remaining at home in state to receive his numerous callers; even religious services would be conducted within his walls. The sole exceptions to this rule, of course, were his own visits to the Caliph in the royal palace: ensconced in a carriage similar to those used by royal ministers, the Exilarch would be escorted by an entourage which was soon swelled by Jewish onlookers who would accompany him along the way.[7]

While the Exilarch seems to have enjoyed greater power than the Heads of the Yeshivot, the extent of his authority became geographically restricted

[7] For Nathan the Babylonian see A. Neubauer, *Mediaeval Jewish Chronicles* (Oxford, 1888–93), 2:83ff. I plan to discuss Neṭira and the other wealthy personalities in Baghdad elsewhere. In certain respects, the "coronation" ceremony resembles the appointment ceremony of ʿAḍud al-Dawla as described by Ibn al-Jawzī; note, e.g. how the Caliph sits behind the *sitāra* in order that none of the Daylamīs should see him before he is seen by ʿAḍud al-Dawla. See Ibn al-Jawzī, *Al-muntaẓam* (Hyderabad, 1358/9 A.H.), 7:98–100. Some scholars have tried to identify the specific Exilarchs whose coronations Nathan describes; see, e.g., S.W. Baron, "Saadia's Communal Activities," in *Saadia Anniversary Volume* (New York, 1943), 28 who tries to prove that the coronation ceremony in 940/1 of Judah, the son of David b. Zakkai, is being described. It seems

during the early Islamic period to the eastern sector of the Caliphate—i.e. the area east of the Tigris. According to Jewish sources, the Exilarch administered his own court (*bava de-maruta*) and issued legal decisions.[8] Thus, we encounter a certain Rav Ṣemaḥ, "chief judge of Maruta Ḥisdai the Exilarch, son of Maruta Naṭronai the Exilarch," who is referred to elsewhere as Ṣemaḥ b. Solomon "judge at *bava de-maruta* Ḥisdai" or "Mar Ṣemaḥ bar Solomon, Head of the Yeshivah" (although we are not aware of a Head of a Babylonian Yeshivah named Solomon).[9]

Originally, the Exilarch appointed—or at least confirmed—the Heads of the Yeshivot; thus, for example, Solomon b. Ḥisdai appointed Mar Rav Samuel and later Rav Yehudai b. Naḥman, as Heads of the Sura Yeshivah. Subsequently, according to Nathan the Babylonian, a three-fold confirmation process developed involving the Exilarch and Heads of the Sura and Pumbedita Yeshivot, each requiring the approval of the other two to confirm any appointment.[10] By then, however, the Exilarchate had entered a lengthy period of decline.[11]

According to Nathan the Babylonian, the Exilarch had residences in both Baghdad and Qaṣr. The latter was evidently his main abode, where he maintained an estate. While several places in Iraq bore this name, Qaṣr Ibn Hubayra, a thriving city midway between Baghdad and Kūfa, was undoubtedly intended.[12] The Exilarch's residence in Baghdad was located

to me, however, that Nathan is offering nothing more than a general description of what he had seen in Baghdad without referring to any specific Exilarch or occasion. On the ceremonial procedures shared by the Exilarch and the Heads of the Yeshivot, see also *Ḥemdah genuzah* (Jerusalem, 1863), par. 4.

[8] On the Exilarch's court, see bB.B. 65a: "Since you have a close relationship with the gate of the Exilarch." On the Exilarch's decisions see: Nathan the Babylonian in Neubauer, *Mediaeval Jewish Chronicles*, 2:80f.; A. Harkavy, *Teshuvot ha-ge'onim* (Berlin, 1887), 276f., par. 555; and cf. J. Mann, "The Responsa of the Babylonian Geonim as a Source of Jewish History," *JQR* n.s. 7 (1916–17): p. 483, n. 29, and 10 (1919–20): 338f.

[9] For Ṣemaḥ b. Solomon, see L. Dukes, "Literar-historische Beiträge: Rosch ha-Seder," *Ben Chananja* 4 (1861): 141: *ṣemaḥ rosh dayyanei de-vava de-marwata* ("Ṣemaḥ head of the judges of the Gate of the Exilarchs").

[10] A. Harkavy, *Teshuvot*, 389; *Halakhot gedolot*, ed. A. Hildesheimer (Jerusalem, 1972), 1:173, 296, 387. For the appointment of the Head of the Sura Yeshivah see: B.M. Lewin ed., *Iggeret rav sherira gaon* (Haifa, 1921), 106; cf. H. Graetz, *Divrei yemei yisra'el* (Warsaw, 1890 et sqq.), 3:427 and S. Eppenstein, *Beiträge zur Geschichte und Literatur im gaonäischen Zeitalter* (Berlin, 1913), 9f.

[11] At the very least, it seems that the Exilarch required the approval of the Yeshivot. Thus, Elijah ha-Kohen b. Abraham, who was apparently a judge in Raqqa (Syria), writes ca. 1100 that he requires letters of appointment from both the Exilarch and the Heads of the Yeshivot; see *Corpus*, no. 73 (New York, JTSA ms. Schechter 4).

[12] The Arabic word *qaṣr* ("fortress" or "palace") apparently derives from Latin *castrum*. Qaṣr Ibn Hubayra was simply called "Qaṣr" by the Muslims; see al-Muqaddasī, *Aḥsan al-taqāsīm fī maʿrifat al-āqālīm* (Leiden, 1906), 121. According to Ibn al-Jawzī, the *qāḍī* Muḥassin b. Alī began

in the *sūq al-ʿatīqa*, which was apparently the center of Jewish public life in Baghdad.[13] This was situated in the *sharqiyya* ("eastern") quarter of western Baghdad, i.e. to the east of the original city built by al-Manṣūr; it stretched from the *ṭāq al-ḥarrānī* ("The Harranian Arch") to the *bāb al-shaʿīr* ("The Barley Gate").[14]

The Exilarch in Arabic Sources

As I have noted elsewhere, Arabic sources mention the son of the Exilarch (*ibn raʾs al-jālūt*) with relative frequency; significantly, perhaps, they rarely mention the Heads of the Yeshivot. From the Islamic texts it is possible to glean genuine information concerning the Exilarch's status and authority in the eyes of contemporary educated Muslims. At the same time, however, we encounter some curious remarks which, though lacking in real historical value, reflect contemporary attitudes.

Al-Ṭabarī, for example, seeks the origins of the institution in the days of Pontius Pilate.[15] Al-Khawārizmī, on the other hand, explains that the Exilarch (*raʾs al-jālūt*) is the "Head of the Jews": *jālūt* means exiles, i.e.

---

his career in Qaṣr and Sura in 349 A.H./ 960/1 C.E. This statement implies that Qaṣr was not far from Sura; see Ibn al-Jawzī, *Muntaẓam*, 7:178 and Suhrāb, *ʿAjāʾib al-āqālīm*, ed. H. von Mzik (Vienna, 1929), 124. There is also an account of a man who conveyed people by boat along the canal between Qaṣr and Sura; see al-Tanūkhī, *Nishwār*, 2:99; V. Minorsky trans., *Qazwīnī's Ḥudūd al-ʿÂlam*, 2d ed. (London, 1970), 139. According to Yāqūt, the place received its name from the palace of the governor of Iraq which was unfinished at the time of the Abbasid revolution and completed by the Abbasid Caliph, al-Saffāḥ; see *Muʿjam al-buldān*, ed. F. Wüstenfeld (Leipzig, 1866), 4:123. Cf. also I. Friedländer, "The Arabic Original of the Report of R. Nathan Hababli," *JQR* o.s. 17 (1904–1905): 760; L. Ginzberg, *Geonica* (New York, 1909), 1:40, n. 3; H. Busse, *Chalif und Grosskönig* (Wiesbaden 1969), 482; and Mann, "The Responsa of the Babylonian Geonim," *JQR* n.s. 7 (1916–17): 466, who errs by saying that Qaṣr was a suburb of Baghdad.

[13] Nathan the Babylonian refers to a place called *ereṣ ʿattiqah*; see Neubauer, *Mediaeval Jewish Chronicles*, 2:78, 80. A legal decision emanating from the court of Sherira Gaon and dated 997 was written "in the *shuqa ʿattiqa* ('ancient market') of Baghdad"; see *Corpus*, no. 29, lines 8–9 (Oxford, Bod. ms. Heb. c. 28, fol. 49).

[14] See: Yāqūt, *Buldān*, 3:613; Ibn al-Athīr, *Al-lubāb fī tahdhīb al-ansāb* (Cairo, 1357 A.H.), 2:17; al-Baghdādī, *Marāṣid al-ittilāʿ ʿalā asmāʾ al-amākin waʾl-buqāʾ* (Cairo 1954), 2:757, 919. Cf. G. Le Strange, *Baghdad during the Abbasid Caliphate* (Oxford, 1924), 90. It has been suggested that there had been an early Jewish town on that spot in ancient times; see J. Obermeyer, *Die Landschaft Babylonien* (Frankfurt a.M., 1929), 150. Canard thought that the neighborhood was part of the *karkh* and explained the name "Sharqiyya" as being derived from a location east of the *Ṣarāh* canal, i.e. between the canal and the Tigris; see M. Canard trans., *Al-Ṣūlī: Akhbār al-rāḍī waʾl-muttaqī* (Alger, 1946), 221, 6. Cf. J. Lassner, *The Topography of Baghdad in the Early Middle Ages* (Detroit, 1970), p. 258, n. 56 and Busse, *Chalif*, 482.

[15] Al-Ṭabarī, *Taʾrīkh al-rusul waʾl-mulūk* (Leiden, 1964), 1:741.

those who were exiled from their homeland in Palestine (*bayt al-maqdis*).[16] Al-Bīrūnī notes the Exilarch's Davidic ancestry, quoting Genesis 49:10 ("The sceptre shall not depart from Judah"): "The kingdom will not depart from Judah until the arrival of the Messiah whom they await; the Jews claim that this had already happened, for the *raʾs al-jālūt* is master of all the Jews in the world, who obey him in all their cities."[17] Abūʾl-Fidāʾ (fourteenth century, drawing upon ancient sources) believes the *raʾs al-jālūt* to be the ruler of the Jews since the destruction of the Second Temple. According to him, Bukht Naṣr (Nebuchadnezzar), banished their king and appointed Herod to rule over them; Herod's authority was confirmed successively by the Persians, the Greeks, and the Roman Emperors. Subsequently, Titus waged war against the Jews and annihilated them, destroying their Temple once again. Abūʾl- Fidāʾ's account implies an awareness that Exilarchs no longer existed in his time.[18]

Al-Qāsim b. Ibrāhīm, a Shīʿite of the Zaydī sect (first half of the ninth century) wrote a comparatively detailed survey of the Exilarchate. Speaking of the *waṣiyya* (the heritage of the divine vision), a term of considerable significance in Shīʿite theology, he asserts that it was bestowed upon the Jews and became the legacy of the House of David, which claimed that it was passed on from generation to generation. Al-Qāsim extols the Jews for not compromising their *waṣiyya*: they are, he says, prepared to kill anyone who claims to be a prophet but does not stem from the House of David. The Exilarch is an expression of their wisdom. When questioned about the Jews' educational system, for example, the Exilarch replied that the Jews had no special program: children acquire their values, one by one, in the course of their games. Whoever asks: "Who will join me?" possesses a desirable quality and is likely to become a good man. But whoever asks: "With whom is it worthwhile being?" shows evidence of a bad character.[19]

---

[16] Al-Khawārizmī, *Mafātīḥ al-ʿulūm*, ed. G. van Vloten (Leiden, 1895), 34–35.

[17] Al-Bīrūnī, *Al-āthār al-bāqiya ʿan al-qurūn al-khāliya*, ed. E. Sachau (Leipzig, 1927), 14.

[18] Abūʾl-Fidāʾ, *Kitāb al-mukhtaṣar fī akhbār al-bashar*, 1:88.

[19] See the passage from al-Qāsim b. Ibrāhīm, from his book: *al-radd ʿalā al-rawāfiḍ* (according to Berlin ms. Glaser 101, fol. 110a) cited by S. Pines, "Une notice sur les Rech Galuta chez un écrivain arabe du ixe siècle," *REJ* 100 (1935): 71. On al-Qāsim, see W. Madelung, *Der Imam al-Qāsim ibn Ibrāhīm* (Berlin, 1965), 86ff., esp. 90 on his positive and tolerant attitude toward non-Muslims. On education see Ibn Abīʾl-Ḥadīd, *Sharḥ nahj al-balāgha* (Beirut, 1963), 5:811. It is possible that the Muslim writers copied some of this general information from eastern Christian Arabic literature. There are some Arabic Jacobite manuscripts which contain chapters on "the history of the Bible" where "the order of the generations" according to the Jews is recorded. In one of these works, it states that the Bible was rescued when Hadrian conquered Jerusalem, and that personalities from the House of David brought it to Baghdad, where they live "until

Several Muslim authors deny that the Exilarch had any real authority. Al-Jāḥiẓ (d. 868) notes that when the Exilarch wishes to punish someone, he forbids any communication with that person, the shofar being sounded as the punishment is pronounced. After describing the announcement of the ban, al-Jāḥiẓ adds:

> This ban on communication is not a punishment laid down in their books. Neither the Katholikos nor the Exilarch possesses the authority in the Muslim world to impose imprisonment or flogging; they can only impose fines or excommunication (literally: "forbid speaking"). The Katholikos would frequently overlook matters involving members of the wealthier class or those with connections at court. Timotheos, for example, wanted to impose a ban on ʿAwn al-ʿIbādī, the Nestorian, because he took two concubines into his household; Shashkīl (?), Michael, and Theophilus refrained from having Manuel blinded, for in their law whoever sides with the Muslims against the Byzantines is to be killed, but if he is a man of standing, then blinding may be imposed instead of execution. In this case, (i.e. that of Manuel), however, they did not observe their own law but spared him.

From al-Jāḥiẓ's account, it can be seen that while both the Exilarch and the Katholikos lacked the authority to judge criminal cases, there were, in fact, exceptions. As far as the Katholikos was concerned, he is here accused of favoritism. We do not have a similar precedent specifically attributed to the Exilarch. A much earlier incident, however, provides evidence for court-ordered arrests and flogging: "Bar Ḥama killed a person. Then the Exilarch said to Abba b. Jacob: 'Go look into the matter; if he did indeed commit murder, let his eyes be blinded.'" While one version reads *le-kaḥlinhu*, i.e. "with white-hot iron," Hananel interpreted it to mean that the man should be made to pay a (large) fine.[20]

Similarly, the Andalusian writer Ibn Ḥazm (994–1064) denied Samuel ha-Nagid's claim that the Exilarchs enjoyed status and authority:

> Actually, the *ra'y al-jālūt* possesses no authority whatsoever, neither over the Jews nor over others; his title is purely nominal. He has neither rights nor prerogatives

today." It is they who copied it and sent copies to all the Jewish tribes, see G. Graf, *Geschichte der christlichen arabischen Literatur* (Vatican, 1940 et sqq.), 2:290ff.

[20] See al-Jāḥiẓ, *Al-maḥāsin wa'l-aḍdād*, ed. G. van Vloten (Leiden, 1898), 4:27f.; cf. Mann, "The Responsa of the Babylonian Geonim," *JQR* n.s. 10 (1919–20): 360. On ʿAwn al-ʿIbādī, see: J.M. Fiey, *Chrétiens syriaques sous les abbasides* (Louvain, 1980), 51f. According to Fiey, Christians were called *ʿibādī* in Ḥīra; but it seems to me that the term specifically signified a Nestorian. Fiey assumes that *darb ʿawn*, one of the famous streets of Baghdad in the Middle Ages, was named after him. According to al-Masʿūdī, *Murūj al-dhahab*, ed. C. Barbier de Meynard (Paris 1861–77), 6:305ff., ʿAwn was Head (*ṣāḥib*) of Ḥīra and he tells of his meeting with the Caliph al-Ma'mūn; according to al-Ṭabarī, *Ta'rīkh*, 3:752, the Caliph Harūn al-Rashīd stayed with him. For the tradition on Bar Ḥama, see bSan. 27a.

> and owes his position to the Muslim rulers, who respect the descendants of the House of David. Herod, his son and grandson[21] were not even Jews, as some historians claim, but were apparently Romans.[22]

Several sources, beginning with al-Khawārizmī's *Mafātīḥ al-ʿulūm*, record a curious detail: only someone possessing a wide arm-span (*ṭawīl al-bāʿ*) may be appointed Exilarch, i.e. "his finger tips must reach his knees when they are outstretched." The origin of this notion apparently derives from the Hebrew expression *orekh yad* (lit., "length of hand"), encountered in connection with Bustanai; while the phrase simply means "mighty," it was understood literally by Muslim writers. Not surprisingly, certain Shīʿites detected similarities between the Exilarchs and the descendants of ʿAlī b. Abī Ṭālib, to whom they also attributed particular physical characteristics.[23] Analogies between the Exilarchs and the House of ʿAlī could be drawn in other ways too; al-Ṭabarī quotes a tradition attributed to an anonymous Exilarch, who heard it from his father:

> Whenever I passed near Karbala (where Ḥusayn b. ʿAlī was killed), I would spur on my beast, in order to distance myself from the place. I asked him: "Why?" He replied: "We have a tradition that a descendant of a prophet would be murdered on this spot and I feared that I was that person. But when Ḥusayn was killed, I said: 'He is the man of whom our tradition speaks.' From that time onwards, when I passed that place I would ride as usual, without hurrying past.[24]

---

[21] As we have seen, several Islamic sources consider Herod to have been an Exilarch.

[22] See Ibn Ḥazm, Leiden ms. Warner no. 480, fol. 60b, cited by Goldziher, "Proben muhammedanischer Polemik gegen den Talmud," *Jeschurun* 8 (1871): 76f. See also: idem, "Notes et mélanges," *REJ* 8 (1884): 125; W.J. Fischel, "Resh-galuta ba-sifrut ha-ʿaravit," in *Judah L. Magnes Volume* (Jerusalem, 1938), 181–87; and see Ibn Ḥazm, *Al-faṣl fīʾl-milal waʾl-ahwāʾ waʾl-niḥal* (Cairo, 1317/21 A.H.), 1:118. In *Jamharat ansāb al-ʿarab* (Cairo, 1962), 506 Ibn Ḥazm states the contrary: "The rulers and authority over the Jews are in the hands of the descendants of David, until this very day." See M. Zucker, "Beirurim be-toledot ha-viqquḥim she-bein ha-yahadut we-ha-islam," in *A. Kaminka Jubilee Volume* (Vienna, 1937), 31–48, with its discussion of Ibn Ḥazm's comments on the Jews; he refers especially to an anonymous medieval Jewish polemical compendium against Islam, from a Breslau ms. published by J. Perles in the supplement to his *R. Salomo b. Abraham b. Adereth* (Breslau, 1863). I am grateful to Prof. Paul B. Fenton for drawing my attention to Zucker's article.

[23] For the expression *ṭawīl al-bāʿ*, see al-Khawārizmī, *Mafātīḥ al-ʿulūm*, 34 and al-Bīrūnī, *Āthār*, 58, who refers to the descendants of ʿAlī immediately following the tradition concerning the Exilarch. On the "arm-span" in the Bustanai story, see J. Heilprin, *Seder ha-dorot* (Warsaw, 1876–77), 177; cf. Gil, "The Babylonian Encounter," p. 42, n. 18. Al-Qāsim b. Ibrāhīm cites the tradition concerning the arm-span but denies it absolutely; see Pines, "Une notice," 72f. From the Ismāʿīlī traditions collected by W. Ivanow, *Ismāʿīlī Traditions Concerning the Rise of the Fatimids* (Oxford, 1942), 63 one can conclude that the Arabs viewed the Jews as having superior physical constitutions. For comparisons of the Jews' faithfulness to the House of David and the Shīʿites' faithfulness to the House of ʿAlī, see, e.g., Ibn ʿAbd Rabbihi, *Al-ʿiqd al-farīd* (Cairo, 1331/1913), 1:353 and cf. J.W. Hirschberg, in *Sefer ha-zikkaron le-veit ha-midrash la-rabbanim be-vin* (Jerusalem, 1946), 123.

[24] See al-Ṭabarī, *Taʾrīkh*, 2:287.

Similarly, we may note the remark of the Exilarch to the Shīʿite Abū'l-Aswad, one of the first grammarians:

> Although King David and I are separated by seventy generations, I still command enormous respect among the Jews. They recognize my rights as a descendant of the royal house and feel obliged to protect me. You and your Prophet, on the other hand, are but one generation apart and yet you have already killed his offspring, Ḥusayn.[25]

Another tradition mentions the visit by the Exilarch's son to the Umayyad Caliph, Hishām b. ʿAbd al-Malik on an occasion when Muḥammad b. ʿAlī, the son of al-Ḥanīfiyya, was also present. Comparing the two men, the Exilarch's son noticed that there was something special about the latter: he seemed more like a prophet than did Hishām and therefore more entitled to the role of Caliph. By way of example, the son of the Exilarch pointed to himself: his status was assured, despite the forty generations that separated him from his ancestor.[26] At about the same time, on the eve of the Abbasid revolution, a group of ten great scholars was known to have met in Basra: a Sunnī, a Shīʿite, a Manichean, a Christian, several sectarians, and the son of the Exilarch, who was also a poet.[27]

The vizier Abū'l-Qāsim Ismāʿīl b. ʿAbbād (938–995) reportedly held a colloquium in Rayy (ca. 985) with the Exilarch, concerning the inimitability of the Qur'ān (*iʿjāz al-qur'ān*).[28] While the Muslims offered their standard argument, viz. that the Qur'ān's divine origin is manifest in its literary perfection and inimitability, the Exilarch argued that the vizier's own writings, which were models of literary perfection, furnished ample proof that the Qur'ān could be imitated.[29]

Finally, there is the strange legend of a miraculous mirror in which it was possible to see the future: handed down generation after generation, from Adam to King Solomon, it ultimately passed into the possession of the Exilarch who gave it to the last Umayyad Caliph, Marwān, during his

---

[25] The tradition is quoted in the name of Ibn Lahīʿa (late 8th c.); see al-Jāḥiẓ, *Al-maḥāsin*, 14, 362, cited by Goldziher, "Proben" and "Notes et mélanges." Goldziher, however, was not aware that al-Jāḥiẓ was the source of these comments. See also Ibn ʿAbd Rabbihi, *Al-ʿiqd al-farīd* (Cairo, 1940), 2:309. Abū'l-Aswad al-Du'alī (or al-Dīlī, d. 688), one of the settlers in Basra, was a poet and ardent follower of ʿAlī. He is considered (on insufficient grounds) one of the foremost grammarians and vocalizers of the Qur'ān; see *EI*, 2d ed., s.v. "Abū'l-Aswad al-Du'alī."

[26] See *Akhbār al-dawla al-ʿabbāsiyya* (Beirut 1971), 171f.

[27] See Ibn Taghrī Bardī, *Al-nujūm al-zāhira fī mulūk miṣr wa'l-qāhira* (Cairo, 1929/56), 2:29, under the year 156.

[28] Abū'l-Qāsim was vizier to the Buyid, Fakhr al-Dawla ʿAlī (977–997).

[29] This Exilarch may have been Azariah b. Solomon, father of Daniel, who later became the Palestinian Gaon.

struggles with the Abbasids. Upon seeing distressing things in the mirror, Marwān had the Exilarch killed. The mirror remained with Marwān's maidservant and was taken from her by the Abbasid Abū Jaʿfar al-Manṣūr.[30]

The Rashut

The term *rashut* refers to one of four regions under the respective jurisdiction of the Exilarch and the Yeshivot of Sura, Pumbedita, and Palestine. To a large degree, the administration of these four domains was stable for long periods but there were also "unaffiliated" territories where authority depended largely upon the predilections of the local community. At times, therefore, considerable friction and even real conflicts developed over matters of *rashut*.

As we have mentioned, it seems that during both the Persian and the early Islamic periods, the Exilarch enjoyed precedence even in regions outside his own *rashut*.[31] This precedence undoubtedly afforded him many advantages which increased his prestige, privileges, and—to no small degree—his finances and property. It is no accident that in his *Epistle*, Sherira Gaon refers to "the days of the Persians and the early Islamic period as well when one used to buy the Exilarchate for large sums."[32]

He who wished to be appointed Exilarch, therefore, was compelled to bribe the rulers excessively, despite his own hereditary rights. According to Nathan the Babylonian, the Exilarch's domain comprised the eastern regions, i.e. the Persian territories, which were entirely separate from the *reshuyot* of the Yeshivot. "The Heads of the Yeshivot," reports Nathan, "have no jurisdiction over anyone from the Exilarch's *rashut*." Officially,

---

[30] See Ibn al-Zubayr, *Al-dhakhāʾir waʾl-tuḥaf*, ed. M. Ḥamidullah (Kuwait, 1959), 166ff. Al-Qazwīnī, *Āthār al-bilād wa-akhbār al-ʿibād*, ed. F. Wüstenfeld (Göttingen, 1849), 203 (under Babil, in the description of Daniel's cave), relates a tradition according to which Mujāhid met the Exilarch in the days of al-Ḥajjāj b. Yūsuf (with al-Ḥajjāj's approval), and requested that he show them the two devils, Hārūt and Mārūt. The Exilarch sent for one of the Jews to go with him and the Jew warned him lest he use the name of the Almighty in the presence of those devils; Mujāhid was so disturbed by the sight that he forgot the warning and with difficulty managed to extricate himself. Cf. Goldziher, "Notes et mélanges," 124.

[31] Assaf, *Tequfat ha-geʾonim*, 22 also stresses the Exilarch's precedence at the beginning of the period. See the account of Nathan the Babylonian in Neubauer, *Mediaeval Jewish Chronicles*, 2:85–87.

[32] Lewin, *Iggeret rav sherira gaon*, 92. Eppenstein, *Beiträge*, 7 has his own explanation for Sherira Gaon's version: it was the Persian kings who bought the Exilarchs "with large sums of money"; this is exactly the opposite of what Sherira meant.

there was no appealing the decision administered in one *rashut* to the authority of the other. Nevertheless, Nathan himself describes just such an appeal which was the source of the dispute between Saadya Gaon and the Exilarch David b. Zakkai.[33]

According to Nathan, the Exilarch ʿUqba made a blatant attempt at extending the boundaries of his jurisdiction to distant Khurāsān, which had previously been attached to the Yeshivah of Pumbedita.[34] The Exilarch's precedence in earlier times is reflected in a responsum of Natronai b. Hilai (around 855), that quotes his predecessor's definition of a "letter of the *rashut*": "A document written by the Exilarch to the judge, giving him permission to go and teach the Jews what is forbidden and what is permitted and instruct them in the words of the Torah; in Aramaic it is called, *Pitqa de-dayyanuta*."[35] In contrast, Judah of Barcelona's *Book of Deeds* offers the following definition: "a document written by the Exilarch for a judge, giving him permission to go and judge . . . similarly, when the people of the Yeshivah grant authorization (e.g. to judge) (the document employed) is called a 'writ of authorization' (*pitqa de-rashwata*)."[36] In truth, in these matters, there was evidently no consensus of opinion and it seems that there was a constant struggle over who had the right of appointment. We may assume that in quieter times, appointments were made on behalf of the Yeshivah (or Yeshivot) and also on behalf of the Exilarch.[37] At a later

---

[33] For Nathan's account, see Neubauer, *Mediaeval Jewish Chronicles*, 2:81ff. Similarly, we read in one of the responsa published by Harkavy: "(This is) the text of a legal decision taken in the court of the Exilarch (*bava de-maruta*) David *rosh galuta* . . .; viz. that this document, sewn and folded, was issued (and brought) before us with the purpose of ordering (our court) to read it carefully and validate it, and decide what legal measures are to be taken after its validation"; see Harkavy, *Teshuvot*, 276, par. 555. It is, however, possible that there were special arrangements in Baghdad, which was a new city; the rights acquired earlier may not, therefore, have been applicable. See also *Corpus*, no. 12, a, line 7 (T-S Loan 48, together with T-S Ar 48.121).

[34] Neubauer, *Mediaeval Jewish Chronicles*, 2:78.

[35] Natronai b. Hilai citing Zadok Gaon (i.e. Isaac Zadok b. Jesse, ca. 810), *Shaʿarei teshuvah* (Leipzig, 1857–58), par. 217.

[36] Judah b. Barzilai of Barcelona, *Sefer ha-sheṭarot* (Berlin, 1898), 134.

[37] See Harkavy, *Teshuvot*, 355–56. Cf. V. Aptowitzer, "Formularies of Decrees and Documents from a Gaonic Court," *JQR* n.s. 4 (1913): 31 who disputes Harkavy's assertion that the Exilarch's prerogative to appoint judges only began after the crisis in the Exilarchate (first half of the 9th c.). (Harkavy, in fact, was referring to the period of Hai Gaon, without specifying when the Geonim started to issue writs of appointment.) Aptowitzer's argument is based upon Nathan's account which expressly mentions judges appointed by the head of the Yeshivah, and this also becomes clear from the dispute between David b. Zakkai and Saadya Gaon; see Neubauer, *Mediaeval Jewish Chronicles*, 2:81–82, 86. Harkavy bases himself upon *Halakhot pesuqot*, ed. J. Müller (Krakow, 1893), 80, par. 156 (the sayings of the Gaon Isaac Zadok, which I quote). See also Abraham b. Isaac of Narbonne, *Sefer ha-eshkol*, ed. B. Auerbach (Halberstadt, 1868), 2:158: "Both the *halakhot gedolot* and the Gaon Rav Zadok explained that a letter of the *rashut* means one which was issued by the Great Court."

date, we even find local judges asking to receive their writs of appointment from the Heads of the Yeshivot as well as from the Exilarch.[38]

Concerning the Exilarch's funds, al-Qāsim b. Ibrāhīm states that the Jews pay a fifth part of their income to the Exilarch. In addition, he is given the first-born of every cow, a dirham and a third for every cow which is slaughtered and an eighth of the liver, four dirhams for a marriage or a divorce, and a similar amount for the building of a house. Divorce requires the permission of the Exilarch's appointee. Children born of adulterous relationships or of uncertain parentage are given over to the Exilarch until they reach maturity; when they are adults, they have the status of his slaves and he is entitled to do with them as he pleases, i.e. to manumit or sell them. These young men are his bearers, carrying him on high through the thoroughfares and never allowing him to go on foot. The Exilarchs treat the Jews as their own property.[39] Obviously, this description is quite fanciful, though it may contain a grain of truth. Underlying the statements concerning marriage and divorce taxes, for example, is undoubtedly the obligation to draw up the requisite documents properly through the local court. The information concerning payments (for slaughtering and building) also seems credible. The term *akhmās* ("fifths") is found as well in a letter from the Exilarch Hezekiah to the Fuṣṭāṭ community (ca. 1036). He requests them not to send him funds from a Jewish pious foundation (*heqdesh*), but rather from the *akhmās*.[40] Nathan the Babylonian supplies us with additional details. There is a place in Babylonia (Baghdad?), he says, where twice a year, on Passover and Sukkot, the Exilarch receives the large sum of two dinars from every Jewish household. He receives tribute as well from Nahrwān and "all its surroundings," from Ḥulwān (some one hundred and fifty dinars annually), and from his main place of residence, Qaṣr (thirty dinars per year). From each of the *ṭabbaḥim* ("ritual slaughterers") he receives a quarter of a dinar per year. During hard years, he imposes quotas upon the communities and collects the money with the assistance of the Muslim authorities. Nathan estimates the Exilarch's annual income at seven hundred dinars. This estimate is, of course, suspect: since it seems unlikely that Nathan had access to the Exilarch's accounts, his information was probably based upon hearsay.[41]

---

38 N.N. Coronel, *Teshuvot ha-ge'onim* (Vienna, 1870/71), 17a, par. 110 mentions the principle that a judge had to receive his appointment from the head of the Yeshivah; in what follows Hai Gaon's dictum is cited, viz. that he must receive his appointment from the Exilarch.

39 For al-Qāsim b. Ibrāhīm's account see Pines, "Une notice," 71.

40 *Corpus*, no. 68, II, lines 2ff. (T-S Loan 40 [I]). And see below, n. 102.

41 Neubauer, *Mediaeval Jewish Chronicles*, 2:85–86. Baron compares the Exilarch's income

Did the Exilarch really collect the poll tax on behalf of the Muslim authorities? Drawing an analogy from the Katholikos's letter of appointment, Graetz concluded that the tax was paid centrally through the head of the community—in this case, the Exilarch. But in fact, the letter of appointment lays down no more than a general moral obligation to fulfil this duty for which the *dhimmī* is personally responsible.[42] Today we know for certain that a qāḍī was directly in charge of collecting the poll tax in every locality and that the payment was made on an individual basis, except in those towns which had arranged to pay a lump sum at the time of the conquest, such as Jerusalem and Tiberias.[43]

The Exilarchs in the Early Period

As we have seen, the Exilarchs enjoyed great prestige within the Jewish community during the Islamic period. For their part, the Muslim rulers certainly regarded them as the community's leaders. This reality is reflected in Sherira's complaint that he did not know the proper sequence of the Geonim in Sura because of the frequent turnover that took place before 689 C.E.: "Since the Nesi'im (i.e. the Exilarchs) would dismiss the Heads of the Yeshivot and appoint them."[44]

Reconstructing the list of Exilarchs who succeeded Bustanai is no easy task. While there are some details in Sherira's *Epistle*, the Gaon did not attribute much importance to genealogical trees and the order of succession to the office. He does, however, mention some of the ancient Exilarchs in passing. In addition, there are ten lists, recording the sequence of Exilarchs:

---

with the much larger incomes of the Muslim dignitaries; see "Saadia's Communal Activities," 92. The analogy with the qāḍīs is certainly not apt, since the income of a qāḍī was not uniform but depended on his rank, geographic location, and various other factors. Ibn Hujayra, the qāḍī of Egypt (699–702), received eight hundred dinars annually, two hundred of which were his regular income, the remainder being payments for additional functions. Other qāḍīs received thousands of dinars a year; see E. Tyan, *Histoire de l'organisation judiciaire en pays d'Islam*, 2d ed. (Leiden, 1960), 338f.

[42] Graetz, *Divrei yemei yisra'el*, 3:125.

[43] Gil, *History*, 143–57. From the famous responsum ascribed to Sheshna Gaon of Sura (ca. 670) one can understand that taxes were indeed collected on an individual basis: "whenever the authority or the tax collector demands that a community pronounce a ban" (on a debtor); see, *Sha'arei teshuvah*, par. 195. The use of such phraseology would be impossible if the taxes were collected by a central Jewish body, such as the Exilarch. Assaf's opinion that the collection of taxes was done through the local community (except in certain instances, as mentioned above) is without foundation; see *Tequfat ha-ge'onim*, 19.

[44] Lewin, *Iggeret rav sherira gaon*, 105; cf. Eppenstein, *Beiträge*, 7.

(1) T-S 12.138;[45] (2) Mosseri I.107;[46] (3) Dropsie 462;[47] (4) T-S AS 150.148; (5) al-Bīrūnī, *Al-āthār al-bāqiya ʿan al-qurūn al-khāliya*, 58f.; (6) A Damascus ms.;[48] Harkavy, *Teshuvot ha-geʾonim*, 378 (7) S. Pinsker, *Lickute Kadmoniot* (Vienna, 1860), 2:53; (8) N.N. Coronel, *Ḥamishah quntresim*, 110a; (9) The Tripoli Bible;[49] (10) Oxford ms. Heb. f. 40.[50]

These lists differ from each other to a considerable degree. Most include additional names at the beginning; while some of these are based upon talmudic sources or Sherira Gaon's *Epistle*, others are imaginary. Different versions of the same name also occur: ʿUqba, ʿUqbah, and ʿAqiva; Nehemiah and Naḥmeimar; Abhamar, Abamar, Aba Mari, and Aba; Ḥunah, Ḥuna, Huna, Ḥanina, Ḥaninai, Huna Mar, and Hunamar. Hunamar son of the Exilarch Mar Zuṭra was imprisoned in Tevet 781 A.S. (December–January, 469–70 C.E.), and executed in the same month (January 470).[51] In one list the Exilarch Huna is said to have died in 819 A.S. (508 C.E.), but elsewhere it is stated that he died in 822, i.e. 511 C.E. These lists were clearly intended to demonstrate the legitimacy of a particular lineage, rather than to fulfill some abstract need for historical information. List 1 records the lineage of Ṣemaḥ, the Gaon of Palestine. His sons, however, were banished—evidently when they had linked up with the members of the other branch of the family, the heirs of Daniel and Anan II. List 2 presents the lineage of Hezekiah, the fourth generation after Jehosaphat and the brother of Ṣemaḥ, who was also Gaon in Palestine, while his offspring joined the Karaite Nesiʾim.[52] List 3 gives the lineage of Zakkai, the grandson of Zakkai b. Azariah; that Zakkai was the brother of Daniel, the Palestinian Gaon.[53] List 4 records the descendants of Nehemiah, who is not known from any other source and seems to have been descended from David b. Zakkai, Exilarch during the first half of the tenth century. List 5 provides the lineage of Anan II, who lived during the latter half of the ninth century, about a century before al-Bīrūnī, who possibly obtained the list from Anan's descendants or the descendants of

[45] J. Mann, *Texts and Studies in Jewish History and Literature* (Cincinnati, 1931), 2:131.

[46] *Corpus*, no. 70 (Mosseri I.107), and see the introduction to this document.

[47] J. Mann, "Misrat rosh ha-golah be-vavel ve-histaʿafutah," in *Livre d'hommage à la mémoire du Dr. Samuel Poznanski* (Hebrew Section) (Warsaw, 1927), 20.

[48] Neubauer, *Mediaeval Jewish Chronicles*, 1:196.

[49] Ibid., 2:248.

[50] Ibid., 2:110.

[51] On Hunamar and Huna see Lewin, *Iggeret rav sherira gaon*, 96–98.

[52] On Josiah, Jehosaphat, and their descendants, see Gil, *History*, 657–69.

[53] On Zakkai b. Azariah, see ibid., 583f. and idem, "A Supplement to 'Palestine During the First Muslim Period'" (Hebrew), *Teʿuda* 7 (1991): 302.

Comparative table of lists of
the Exilarchs and Nesi'im (ca. 450–1050)

(1) T-S 12.138	(2) Mosseri	(3) Dropsie	(4) T-S AS 150.148	(5) Bīrūnī	(6) Damas-cus. Ms.	(7) Pinsker	(8) Coronel	(9) Tripoli	(10) Oxford
Hanina				Rav Huna			Huna	Huna	Huna Būs
Mar Zutra				Zutra			Mar Zutra	Mar Zutra	Zutra
Huna-mar							Bar Huna	Huna	Huna-mad
Kafnai		Kafnai		Qafnai	Kafnai	Kafna		Kafnai	Kafnai
Haninai	Huna	Huna				Hanina			
Bustanai	Bustani	Bustanai	Bustanai (Hanina)	Bustanai	Bustanai	Bustani	Bustanai	Bustānī	Bustānī
Hisdai	Hisdai	Baradai	....	Hisdai	Hisdai	Hisda	Hisdai		Solomon
David	David	Hisdai	Hisdai	David	David	David	Solomon		Isqawai
Anan	Anan	Solomon	Solomon	Anan	Isaac (Isqawai)	Anan	Judah		Judah
Saul	Saul	Isaac	....	Saul	Judah (Zakkai Baboi Moses)	Saul	Judah		David
Josiah	Josiah	Judah	Baradai	Daniel	Isaac	Josiah	David		Zakkai
Semah	Jeho-saphat	David	Boaz	Anan	David (b. Judah)		Jeho-saphat	Judah	David
	Boaz	Judah	....		Hisdai	Boaz et al.	Zakkai		
	David	Zakkai	Zakkai				Josiah		
	Solomon	Josiah	David				Solomon		
	Hezekiah	Solomon	....				Azariah		
		Azariah	David				Solomon et al.		
		Zakkai	Nehe-miah						
		Joseph	....						
		Zakkai							

his followers who joined the Karaites.[54] List 6 contains the lineage of the descendants of Isaac (Isqawai) b. David, the David who likely was the brother of Solomon and father of Anan. Isaac the Exilarch, about whom some information exists, seems to have been the cousin of this Isaac.[55] List 7 records the first part of the lineage of Solomon b. David, one of the later Karaite Nesi'im, whose ancestor was the aforementioned Jehosaphat, Gaon in Palestine. List 8 gives the first part of Jedediah b. Jesse's lineage; he was descended from Solomon b. Azariah, the same Azariah who was the father of Daniel, the Palestinian Gaon. We possess no additional information concerning a brother of Daniel named Solomon. In List 9 we are given the first part of Sar Shalom's lineage; the "Nasi of Judah," he was a descendant of Solomon b. Zakkai, evidently the father of the famous David who was Exilarch during the first half of the tenth century.[56] List 10 gives David b. Zakkai's lineage.[57]

It is obvious that in seven of the lists—including two of Rabbanite Exilarchs and Nesi'im—Ḥisdai, the son of Bustanai, is listed as the head of the dynasty. Ḥisdai, it will be recalled, was one of Bustanai's two sons by his Jewish wife; Anan b. David was also one of his descendants. In List 3 Ḥisdai's brother Baradai (Baradoi) heads the lineage and Ḥisdai is given as the name of Baradai's son; presumably, this was the real lineage of Daniel b. Azariah and his family, for it emphasizes that they were of different extraction than Anan's family. List 2 provides an additional column (after Bustanai): Solomon—Isqawai—Judah—Zakkai—David; it thus resembles Lists 9 and 10. In this column in List 2 and in List 10, Ḥisdai's name is omitted entirely; Bustanai is followed by Solomon, who was actually his grandson. This Solomon is mentioned only in the lists of Zakkai and his sons David and Josiah; the lists of Anan's descendants naturally include David, brother of Solomon and father of Anan. Most of the early Exilarchs about whom we have information from other sources have clearly been omitted from these lists: Hananiah b David (Anan's brother), Naṭronai b. Ḥaninai, Zakkai b. Ahunai, Ḥisdai b. Naṭronai, and ʿUqba. From the outset, we can discredit the possibility that all those mentioned in the lists

---

[54] In List 5, the name of Zuṭra is blurred, and because of the illegibility of the Arabic writing, it was read (and copied) as Nushra.

[55] List 6 is from a ms. by Elisha Crescas, copied in 1383.

[56] The Tripoli Bible (Tripoli, Libya), was copied and completed in 1312. The sons of Sar Shalom who are mentioned there are: Melchizedek, the *khawāja khalīfa* (i.e. the Nasi); Phineas, the *khawāja badīʿ al-zamān* (approximately, "the wonder of his time"); Hezekiah, the *khawāja jumhūr* (perhaps, "the excellent," or "head of the community"); and Josiah.

[57] List 10 was written in 1470 A.S., 4919 A.M., i.e. 1159 C.E.

actually were Exilarchs, unless this is confirmed by some other source.

Previously, both Lazarus and Goode attempted to reconstruct the sequence of Exilarchs during the Geonic period. The following discussion departs from their conclusions which also differ from each other.[58]

During the first few generations, the Exilarchate was apparently held by Ḥisdai b. Bustanai and his descendants. All of the lineage lists mention him and note that Anan, who was considered to be the founder of the Karaite sect, was descended from him.[59] In his *Epistle*, Sherira Gaon recalls that the Gaon of Pumbedita, Naṭronai b. Nehemiah (719), was related by marriage to the Exilarch's family and ruled so high-handedly that the scholars of his Yeshivah fled to Sura and remained there until he died.[60] Sherira also informs us that in 730 the Exilarch Solomon b. Ḥisdai, grandson of Bustanai, appointed Samuel, the grandson of Rabba, as Gaon of Pumbedita.[61]

The Exilarch Isaac or Isqawai, son of the aforementioned Solomon, is mentioned in connection with the release of slaves in a responsum (ca. 760) by "one of the children of the Nasi (that is, of an Exilarchic family) called Nathan b. Shahriar." This Nathan evidently had no sons for it says there that his heir was "Shemaiah son of Isaac, the Exilarch."[62] It should be noted that it was not Nathan who was Exilarch. The Exilarch referred to here is Isaac himself, presumably Isaac b. Solomon b. Ḥisdai, who is named Isqawai in a geonic responsum from ca. 810.[63]

In the lists preserved by the Karaites, which refer mainly to the house

---

[58] See A.D. Goode, "The Exilarchate in the Eastern Caliphate, 637–1258," *JQR* n.s. 31 (1940–41): 154–165 and F. Lazarus, "Die Häupter der Vertriebenen," *Jahrbücher für jüdische Geschichte und Literatur* 10 (1890): 174–179.

[59] On Bustanai's descendants, see *Corpus*, no. 1 (T-S 13 G 1) and the parallel version in T-S 8 G 1. See also Gil, "The Babylonian Encounter," 35 and idem, *Palestine*, vol. 2, no. 29, lines 28–29.

[60] Lewin, *Iggeret rav sherira gaon*, 102f. Cf. H. Malter, *Saadia Gaon: His Life and Works* (Philadelphia, 1921), 103.

[61] Lewin, ibid., 106–107. And see S. Rapoport, *Toledot rabbenu natan ish romi* (Warsaw, 1902–1903), 50 and Harkavy's corrected reading in *Teshuvot*, 357. See also Harkavy, ibid., 82: ". . . One says that (this halakhah) was also declared in the days of the Exilarch Solomon b. Ḥisdai and of Mar Rav Samuel Gaon, on a *shubta de-rigla* ('a Saturday of reunion') before the Exilarch." This is the same Solomon the Exilarch mentioned in *Sefer ha-pardes* (Warsaw 1869/70), par. 280 = (Budapest, 1923/24), p. 15; cf. V. Aptowitzer, "Deux consultations des gueonim," *REJ* 57 (1909): 245. Solomon b. Ḥisdai is missing from the genealogical lists of the Karaite Nesi'im; Graetz has explained this according to the Karaite view that Anan was the legitimate Exilarch. Since Anan was the son of David (Solomon's brother), they included David in their lists and omitted Solomon; see Graetz, *Divrei yemei yisra'el*, 3:416.

[62] See Oxford ms. Heb. c. 18, fol. 38; cf. Goitein, *A Mediterranean Society*, 1:144.

[63] The fifty year time-span (760–810) defined by the two responsa does seem incredible and

of Anan, David is mentioned as if he were the Exilarch. It seems, in fact, that he was actually the brother of the Exilarch, Solomon b. Ḥisdai. As the father of both Anan and Hananiah—who was chosen over Anan to be Exilarch in the early 760's—David was, nevertheless, included in the lists.[64]

From the geonic responsum which speaks of the Bustanai affair, it is evident that Bustanai had five sons—two (Baradai and Ḥisdai) by his Jewish wife, the other three (Shahriar, Gūrdānshāh, and Mardānshāh) by his Persian spouse. At the beginning of the eleventh century, the Palestinian Gaon Josiah b. Aaron, writes that *five* of Bustanai's children were born of the "daughter of kings" and were "the sons of foreskin and shame; while two of them were heirs to holiness." The responsum of the Babylonian Gaon, however, which was written somewhat earlier, says that some of the descendants of the Persian wife "reigned over" the Yeshivot and the Exilarchate. One version of the responsum even records that they were the descendants of Rūzbīhān, the son of Shahriar (one of the Persian wife's sons), i.e. the great-grandsons of Bustanai.[65] The same responsum states that one of these unnamed grandsons married "the daughter of Rav Ḥaninai." Now, the version of this responsum found in *Shaʿarei ṣedeq* mentions that "Ḥaninai, Judge of the Gate" wrote "the document of release for that slave-girl"; this implies that he was the first to legitimize the Persian wife's descendants, even going so far as to give his daughter in marriage to one of her great-grandsons.[66] There is a further hint in the Gaon's responsum that even Naṭronai b. Hilai Gaon was related to the

---

remains unexplained in the the sources. On Isaac-Isqawai b. Solomon, see Harkavy, *Teshuvot*, par. 389, p. 205 and see his comments ad loc.; see also idem, "Über die handschriftliche Responsensammlung in der kaiserlichen öffentlichen Bibliothek in Petersburg," *MGWJ* 32 (1883): 376. Lazarus, "Die Häupter der Vertriebenen," p. 175, n. 1 refers to the killing of the Exilarch ordered by the last Umayyad Caliph, Marwān b. Muḥammad (744–750), mentioned by al-Ṭabarī, *Ta'rīkh*, 3:166; this story, however, which is related in connection with the legend of the Exilarch's magic mirror (mentioned above) seems entirely fanciful. B.M. Lewin assumed that the Isaac mentioned in an ancient *qaddish* (JTSA ms. ENA 4053, b) was Isaac (Isqawai) the Exilarch; see his "Qaddish ʿattiq," *Ginzē Qedem* 2 (1922–23): 46. David b. Ḥisdai is also mentioned by the 17th c. Karaite Mordechai b. Nissan in *Dod Mordekhai*, ed. J.C. Wolf in *Notitia Karaeorum* (Hamburg, 1714), 42 = (Vienna, 1830), 4b–5a. Cf. Lazarus, "Die Häupter der Vertriebenen," 174ff. who connected a seal inscription with the name Isaac b. Moses to another (presumed) Exilarch by that name; there may be a trace of this individual in List 6 (= Harkavy, *Teshuvot*, 378).

[64] On David's sons Anan and Hananiah, see Pinsker, *Lickute Kadmoniot*, 2:53, n. 103 (in Elijah b. Abraham's "Ḥilluq ha-qara'im we-ha-rabbanim").

[65] G. Widengren interprets the name Shahriar as the satrap of a *shahr*, which means a district; see "Iran, der grosse Gegner Roms," in *Aufstieg und Niedergang der römischen Welt*, II (9.1) (Berlin, 1976), 276. It seems to me that in Jewish sources "Shahriar" corresponds to "Sherira."

[66] We still do not know precisely who this Ḥaninai was and whether he was a "judge of the gate" of the Exilarch or of the Yeshivot.

family of the Persian wife's descendants and therefore issued decisions in their favor. On the basis of this kinship, we may perhaps assume that this same Ḥaninai, "Judge of the Gate," afterward became Gaon in Sura, that Naṭronai b. Hilai was one of his daughter's descendants, and that it was Haninai's daughter who married the great-grandson of Bustanai by his Persian wife.[67] Now since the son of Rūzbīhān (i.e. Yomtov) who became Exilarch can probably be identified with Zakkai b. Ahunai, we may offer the following conjectural lineage:

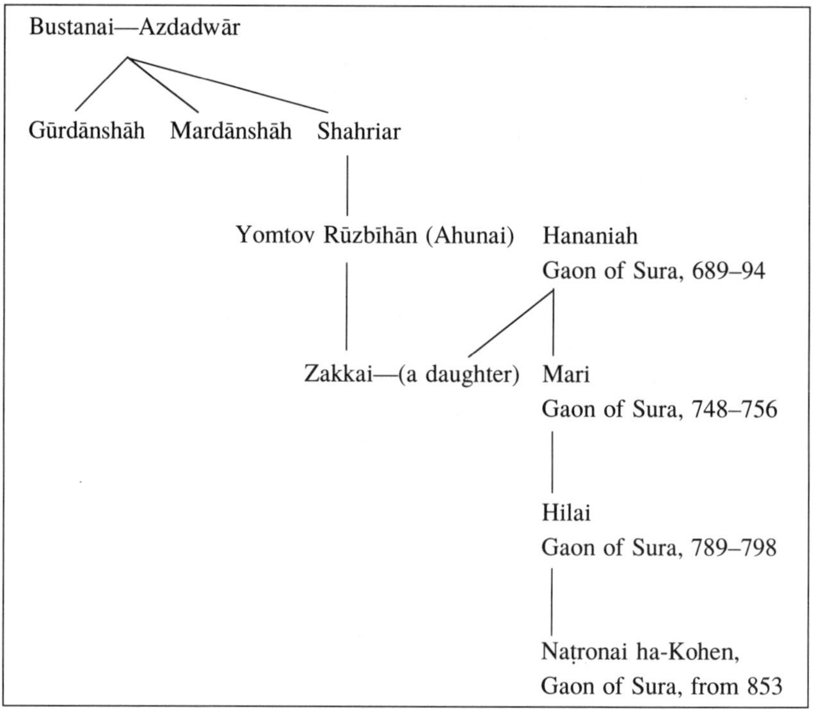

[67] Cf. J. Mann, "On the History of the Gaonate in the X Century" (Hebrew), *Tarbiz* 5 (1933–34): 289f.; Neubauer, *Mediaeval Jewish Chronicles*, 1:196; Lewin, *Iggeret rav sherira gaon*, 104. See the version of the responsum edited by Ginzberg, *Geonica*, 2:83. Assaf, *Tequfat ha-geʾonim*, 31f., attempted to solve the problems of the Exilarch's lineage and order of descent by making them all the descendants of the Persian wife; only the slanderous Genizah account makes this claim, however, which should not be credited.

Zakkai, the son of Yomtov-Rūzbīhān-Ahunai—i.e. the great-grandson of Bustanai's Persian wife—became involved in a serious controversy over the office of Exilarch with Naṭronai b. Ḥaninai. If we identify Haninai with Hananiah, we find that Naṭronai the Exilarch was the son of Hananiah b. David. Having held the Exilarchate for a few years, Naṭronai was ousted by Mar Rav Malka b. Mar Rav Aḥa, Head of the Yeshivah of Pumbedita (771–773): "... (Rav Malka) dismissed Naṭronai b. Ḥaninai the Nasi during the conflict over Zakkai b. Ahunai, who had been Nasi previously for several years. The two Yeshivot then convened with Zakkai the Nasi and dismissed him. Subsequently, Rav Malka went to Paradise, and Naṭronai the Nasi went to the West."[68]

From the wording of the letter, it is difficult to discern who was the one in office "previously for several years"—Malka b. Aḥa or Naṭronai. The dismissal made a great impression, for it was decided at a joint meeting of the two Yeshivot, with the participation of the designated Exilarch, Zakkai b. Ahunai. If the lineage above is correct, the Sura Gaon who collaborated in the dismissal was none other than Zakkai b. Ahunai's brother-in-law, Mari (b. Hananiah). There is almost no doubt that while Naṭronai b. Ḥaninai stemmed from the "legitimate" dynasty—the branch of Ḥisdai and Anan—Zakkai b. Ahunai was descended from the Persian wife, who married the daughter of Hananiah.[69] It was said that after his dismissal, Naṭronai left Babylonia and "went to the West," i.e. the Maghrib (North Africa or Spain). In his *Sefer ha-ʿittim*, Judah b. Barzilai mentions that Naṭronai bar Ḥakinai (!) was the man who "wrote the Talmud out from memory for the Andalusians, without a written text." In the commentary to the *Sefer Yeṣirah* he quotes "the obviously well-known fact ... that Mar Naṭronai Gaon(!), of blessed memory, came to them (to Spain) from Babylonia by means of a miraculous journey (*qefiṣat ha-derekh*), disseminated knowledge, and returned."[70] A responsum ascribed to Ṣemaḥ b. Solomon, the head of the Exilarch's court, mentions both Naṭronai

[68] Lewin, ibid.

[69] It appears that the phrase "previously for several years" refers to Naṭronai, not to Rav Malka. I.H. Weiss interpreted the episode as a plot hatched by the Heads of the Yeshivot, who did not want a scholarly Exilarch. They succeeded in forcing Naṭronai to emigrate; see *Dor dor ve-doreshav* 6th ed. (Vilna, 1910–11), 4:29. I. Halevy understood Sherira's statement differently: according to him, Zakkai b. Ahunai was the Nasi whom Natronai opposed. The two Geonim thus acted properly in expelling the man who provoked the controversy; cf. *Dorot ha-rishonim* (Berlin, 1923), 3:231.

[70] See Judah b. Barzilai of Barcelona, *Sefer ha-ʿittim* (Krakow, 1903), 267 and idem, *Peirush sefer yeṣirah* (Berlin, 1885), 103f. And see Harkavy's correction in Graetz, *Divrei yemei yisraʾel*, 4:8.

b. Ḥaninai and his son Ḥisdai. It seems that Ḥisdai assumed the office of Exilarch, from which his father had been ousted, some time after 800 C.E.[71]

With regard to those changes and reversals that occurred in the last quarter of the eighth century, there is ample justification for linking developments within the Jewish world with the events in the surrounding world. This was the first generation after the Abbasid revolution, in which surviving representatives of the Persian aristocracy enjoyed great prestige within the ruling circles. The influence and power of the Barmacides, members of the Persian elite who ruled in Khurāsān, was singularly impressive. Khālid b. Barmak took an active part in the Abbasid revolution and was the right-hand man of the first Abbasid Caliphs; his son Yaḥyā was the vizier of Hārūn al-Rashīd. Barmacide supremacy continued until their sudden and brutal elimination in 803. It is not unlikely, therefore, that when Zakkai b. Ahunai sought the Exilarchate in the latter part of the eighth century, his illustrious "Persian" descent afforded him a decided advantage. With the annihilation of the House of Barmak, however, the "legitimate" descendants of Bustanai were restored to office, as we have seen with the return of Ḥisdai b. Naṭronai b. Ḥaninai. Against this background, there is also some significance in what was said in the various versions of Sherira's responsum, regarding a sort of collusion among the sages to keep the affair of the illegitimate lineage quiet, because the descendants of the Persian "had royal backing since they were related to royalty, their mother's brother being a Marzūbān."[72]

The affair of Aḥa of Shabḥa, author of the *She'iltot*, also occurred at about this time. According to Abraham Ibn Daud, Aḥa was hated by the Exilarch and was therefore passed over for the office of Gaon in favor of his secretary Naṭronai; angered at this treatment, Aḥa emigrated to Palestine. Ibn Daud's account of these matters is, however, based wholly upon Sherira's *Epistle* and may involve certain misinterpretations. According

[71] For Ṣemaḥ b. Solomon's responsum, see Dukes, "Literar-historische Beiträge," 141f. Cf. Harkavy, *Teshuvot*, 389; *Halakhot gedolot*, 86, 188, 190 (mentioning Ṣemaḥ b. Solomon). There has been extensive discussion of the episode and its aftermath. See: N. Brüll, "Recensionen," *Jahrbücher für jüdische Geschichte und Litteratur* 9 (1887): 116ff.; L. Ginzberg, *Geonica*, 1:17ff.; A. Marx, "Notes," *JQR* o.s. 18 (1905–1906): 770. For evidence that a copy of the Talmud with commentaries was sent to Spain a century after Naṭronai's time by the Gaon Palṭoi b. Abayye (842–858), see *Corpus*, no. 13, c, lines 8ff. (Oxford ms. Heb. f. 34, fols. 39–44). Naṭronai b. Ḥaninai is also mentioned in *Sefer ha-pardes*, 127; cf. Graetz, *Divrei yemei yisra'el*, 3:417f. For another possible reference to him, see Hai Gaon's responsum concerning magic and superstitions in E. Ashkenazi, *Ṭa'am zeqenim* (Frankfurt a.M. 1854), 56a: "As to the tradition of the people of France that you mentioned regarding Mar Rav Naṭronai, perhaps a swindler happened to come among them, saying: 'I am Naṭronai.'"

[72] Regarding the political background to these events, see *EI*, 2d ed., s.v. "al-Barāmika."

to Sherira, Aḥa was passed over for the office of Nasi in favor of his disciple Mar Rav Naṭroi ha-Kohen b. Mar Rav Emuna. At that time, the title Nasi referred exclusively to the Exilarch or a member of his family. The man in question, then, is evidently Naṭronai b. Ḥaninai, the demoted Exilarch, and not Naṭroi ha-Kohen—Naṭronai, according to the *Book of Tradition*—Head of the Pumbedita Yeshivah. Obviously something has been omitted from Sherira's *Epistle*; possibly, he meant that Naṭronai b. Ḥaninai was Aḥa's pupil. When Naṭronai was dismissed and went to the west, Aḥa also left Babylonia and went to Palestine.[73] One should also note that Aḥa's name is found twice more in the same short passage of Sherira's *Epistle*: as Head of the Sura Yeshivah for half a year in 756 and as the father of Malka Gaon of Pumbedita (771–773). Whether or not these are all references to the same individual remains an open question.

From this point onward, we have no actual information relating to the Exilarchs, apart from a few names in the genealogical lists which are not worth investigating in this context. We do not know which Exilarch dismissed the Gaon of Pumbedita, Ḥaninai ha-Kohen b. Abraham, in 786, as reported by Sherira Gaon in his *Epistle*. Possibly this was still Zakkai b. Ahunai or one of his offspring.[74] At any rate, when we again have some real information about the Exilarchs from approximately 820, there is no further mention of the descendants of Bustanai from his Persian wife. The conflict between David and Daniel which I shall describe below, was a controversy between descendants of Ḥisdai and Baradai, the two sons of his Jewish wife. It is possible that in 803, the year in which the Barmacides were annihilated, the descendants of the Persian wife were ousted as well, and that at the same time, Ḥisdai b. Naṭronai b. Ḥaninai-Hananiah may have returned from the west and been granted the office of Exilarch, but I must stress that this is merely conjecture.

The Crisis at the Beginning of the Ninth Century

During the Muslim period, the Exilarchate undoubtedly suffered decline. Sherira states this explicitly:

> During the middle of the Islamic period, in the days of David b. Judah the Nasi, they (i.e. the Exilarchs) were humiliated by the royal authorities, so that the Heads

[73] See Lewin, *Iggeret rav sherira gaon*, 103 and G.D. Cohen ed. and trans., *The Book of Tradition (Sefer ha-Qabbalah) by Abraham Ibn Daud* (Philadelphia, 1967), 37 (Heb.), 47–48 (Eng.).

[74] Lewin, *Iggeret rav sherira gaon*, 104.

> of (the) Pumbedita (Yeshivah) would no longer go to them. On the contrary, when the Nesi'im wished to hold a convocation at Pumbedita, it was they (i.e. the Exilarchs) who went thither.[75]

Similarly, Samuel b. Eli, Head of the Baghdad Yeshivah at the end of the twelfth century, writes:

> And in the days of David b. Judah they (the Exilarchs) were dismissed from the service of the Sultan and returned to join the sages and the Yeshivot. They were received, however, only if they accepted the conditions of the Yeshivah; for it was the Yeshivah which authorized them (and gave them) certificates (of appointment) to serve as Exilarchs. And some of the evidence for this (i.e. the lists) is in our keeping.[76]

Five months after these lines were written, in October 1191, Maimonides came to the defense of the Exilarch whom Samuel b. Eli had attacked.[77] In a letter addressed to Raḥba, Raqqa, and other communities in Iraq and Syria, Samuel b. Eli extolled the Yeshivah, comparing its role to that of Moses and noting that even King David sought the counsel of such sages as Mephibosheth. By contrast, he censured the Exilarch who lacked scholarly credentials, owed his appointment solely to political connections, and received his exalted position without Samuel's approval. Samuel's criticisms tally with our information concerning the Exilarch's declining status. Apparently, he had recourse to Sherira's *Epistle* which he adapted for his own purposes, employing his own characteristic style and wording.

Syriac sources provide parallel evidence. A passage from the (lost) chronicle of the Jacobite Patriarch of Baghdad, Dionysius of Tel Maḥre, describes the circumstances surrounding the conflict between David and Daniel. The account has been transmitted by Michael the Syrian (ca. 1170):

> At that time, an order was issued by Ma'mūn that if ten people of any religion were to come together and desire to appoint a leader over themselves, no man should interfere, arguing, "if there are too many leaders, we will become weaker and will be overcome; we have gone down to him, therefore, in order to annul this law." Now (this practice) had spread among all the religions on account of

---

[75] Lewin, *Iggeret rav sherira gaon*, 93. Cf. ibid., 111 concerning the "dispute between Daniel and David, the Nesi'im" that occurred during 816–828, when Abraham b. Sherira was Gaon of Pumbedita.

[76] See the letter of Samuel b. Eli, published by S. Assaf, "Letters of R. Samuel ben Eli and His Contemporaries" (Hebrew), *Tarbiz* 1 (1929–30), printed separately as *Qoveṣ shel iggerot rabbi shemu'el b. ʿeli* (Jerusalem 1930), 49–55 and see Assaf's comments, ibid., 25–27. Samuel b. Eli reiterates the fact that there was no longer any need for an Exilarch; what was needed in exile was someone to teach the Law and administer it.

[77] This was apparently David, Exilarch in Mosul after the death of Samuel; both of them were descendants of Zakkai.

> the Jews' conflict over the Exilarchate, for those in Tiberias had appointed a man called David, while those in Babylonia had appointed a man named Daniel from the Ananite sect that profanes the Sabbath and observes Wednesday (as a holy day). When their affair came before Ma'mūn, he decreed that each side should choose as its head whomever it pleased.[78]

Michael also relates a passage in which Dionysius, then head of the Jacobites in the Abbasid Caliphate, tells of having gone to a meeting with the Caliph on this issue.[79]

These events relate to the same period described by Sherira in his *Epistle*, approximately 825. The dispute between David and Daniel obviously concerned the succession to the Exilarchate. While it is commonly held that David b. Judah was the victor in this quarrel, we shall soon see that the dispute likely continued at least until 834 and that possibly both contenders viewed themselves as Exilarchs.[80]

It is quite likely that the Daniel involved in this dispute was the grandson of Anan—the same Anan who has been considered the founder of Karaism. The sources indicate, however, that the Ananite branch of the Exilarch family only joined the Karaites in the ninth century when Daniel b. Saul b. Anan and his son Anan (II) went over to the sectarian camp. At

[78] See J.-B. Chabot ed. and trans., *Chronique de Michel le syrien* (Paris 1899–1910), 517 (French translation: 3:65). Cf. the almost identical version of Bar Hebraeus (ca. 1270) where, however, the sequence of events is reversed, i.e. al-Ma'mūn issues his decree in the *wake* of the Jews' dispute; see Gregorius Bar Hebraeus, *Chronicon ecclesiasticum*, ed. J.B. Abbeloos (Louvain 1872), 1:366. It is impossible to tell whether Bar Hebraeus relied directly upon the chronicle of Dionysius or whether he merely summarized Michael the Syrian's version. I am most grateful to Prof. Gideon Goldenberg for his suggestions concerning these Syriac texts and their translation.

The assertion that the Ananites profane the Sabbath and keep Wednesday sacred is, of course without foundation and must be based upon a garbled understanding of earlier sources and ancient accusations. According to al-Qirqisānī, the sectarian leader Yudghān abolished the Sabbath and some Karaites agreed with him in this matter. From al-Qirqisānī's account it appears that Yudghān was a contemporary of Anan b. David; see Yaʿqūb al-Qirqisānī, *Kitāb al-anwār wa'l-marāqib*, ed. L. Nemoy (New York, 1939–43), 1:52–53 and 4:876, lines 12ff. Al-Bīrūnī asserts that the sect of the "Maghāriyya" sanctified Wednesday, when "the lights in the firmament" were created; see al-Bīrūnī, *Āthār*, 284. Cf. S. Poznanski, "Philon dans l'ancienne littérature judéoarabe," *REJ* 50 (1905): 16ff. Cf. also al-Shahrastānī, *Kitāb al-milal wa'l-niḥal* (London, 1846), 127.

[79] These details are recorded in connection with the rebellion of Bishop Lazarus of Baghdad, who was dismissed and excommunicated, but nevertheless claimed that he had the right to retain his status according to the Caliph's decree. The Patriarch visited the Caliph, who argued that his decision resulted from problems among the Jews. While the Caliph stressed that he did not wish to impose leaders, the Patriarch claimed that such an approach would contradict the agreements between the Muslims and the Christians, according to which the Christians need not change anything in the laws of their forefathers. The meeting took place in Adar (March) 829; it is clear that the dispute among the Jews had taken place a number of years earlier.

[80] According to Sherira's *Epistle*, David b. Judah appointed Isaac b. Huna (Hananiah) as Gaon of Pumbedita in 832/3; see Lewin, *Iggeret rav sherira gaon*, 112.

that time, his brother Josiah b. Saul served as Head of the Palestinian Yeshivah; Josiah's sons Jehosaphat and Ṣemaḥ, the cousins of Anan (II), undoubtedly also held the office of Palestinian Gaon in later years.[81]

A Genizah letter, apparently written by the Gaon of Pumbedita and addressed to the people of Kairouan, offers striking confirmation of the sources concerning this dispute.[82] While neither the letter's date nor the name of its author has been preserved, we may assume that it was written by Hai b. David Gaon of Pumbedita (ca. 850). The writer boasts of the many sages who sit in the "first row" of his Yeshivah; Sura can claim only a quarter of this number. But this is not all: half the Sura Yeshivah supports Daniel of the house of Anan, from the lineage of Ḥisdai (!) the Nasi! Naṭronai's charge leads us to conclude that the Babylonians, i.e. the people of Pumbedita, together with many Surans, supported David b. Judah, who—it is implied—stemmed from the lineage of Baradai, son of Bustanai's Jewish wife. This letter must date from the period after David's victory, when Sar Shalom b. Boaz was Gaon of Sura. Several years later, as we have seen, Naṭronai b. Hilai actively opposed Daniel and accused him and his followers of heresy.

From another Genizah letter, written in Baghdad in 1095, we learn that David's victory was no small matter, for Daniel was in fact deposed from the office of Exilarch. The writer, a refugee who had fled Ramla some twenty years earlier, recalls visiting the graves of the sages and the Heads of the Yeshivot buried in al-Anbār (evidently Pumbedita) "on the mountain," including the grave of Daniel, who—he says—was the Exilarch in

[81] On the Nesi'im of Anan's family, see Gil, *History*, 790–94; on Jehosaphat and Ṣemaḥ, ibid., 657–60. Mann believed it unlikely that this Daniel stemmed from the family of Anan, for the sages of Pumbedita would not have supported a Karaite. He maintained, in other words, that Daniel, the grandson of Anan, and Daniel, the contestant for the Exilarchate, were two different people; see *Texts and Studies*, 2:129f. I. Markon even denied that Anan had a grandson named Daniel; in his opinion, the contestant for the Exilarchate was the Daniel mentioned in a responsum of Naṭronai Gaon; see "Wer ist der in einem Responsum des Natronai Gaon II erwähnte Karäer Daniel," in *Moritz Schaefer Jubilee Volume* (Berlin, 1927), 130ff. In light of what we now know, however, about the Anan family's circumstances, Mann's conclusion cannot stand. It is true that the family was already reputed to have sectarian tendencies in Anan's time. Naṭronai b. Hilai Gaon of Sura (c. 860) attacks those "*minim* (heretics) who deride and despise the words of our sages, of blessed memory," calling them "the disciples of Anan"; see his responsum, cited in *Seder rav amram gaon*, ed. L. Frumkin (Jerusalem, 1912), 1:207. This statement, however, mainly reflects the animosity directed towards the house of Anan and should be viewed with a degree of skepticism. What *is* apparent is that this branch of the Exilarchic house was attacked and slandered in Babylonia while it still held a leading position in Palestine. Some of the aspersions cast upon this family also seem to have made their way into the Syriac source (Dionysius—Michael the Syrian—Bar Hebraeus), for it states there that the Ananites profaned the Sabbath and made Wednesday sacred.

[82] See *Corpus*, no. 4 (T-S NS 308.122).

the days of al-Ma'mūn.[83] We may conclude, therefore, that either each faction proclaimed its own candidate Exilarch or that one of the two men was ousted from office.[84]

In light of what we have shown above, it is necessary to reconsider the Exilarch's letter identified and published by Mann.[85] In the letter, which deals with the calendar for the year 1147 A.S. (835/56 C.E.), the Exilarch declares that on matters of intercalation he and the Heads of the Yeshivot rely upon the sages of Palestine. While Mann attributed the letter to David b. Judah, who was, he believed, allied with the community in Palestine, the writer's identity remains uncertain. In fact, the letter may have been written during the controversy by none other than Daniel b. Saul (b. Anan) at the time that his brother Josiah and his nephews Jehosaphath and Ṣemaḥ were Heads of the Yeshivah in Palestine. If this is the case, the Exilarch's stern adherence to the principles of the Jewish calendar (i.e. that Passover should not fall on Monday, Wednesday or Friday) obviously contradicts the Syriac source which states that the Ananite Daniel sanctified Wednesday rather than Saturday.[86]

As long as the family of Anan controlled both the Palestinian Yeshivah and the Babylonian Exilarchate, the Holy Land continued to enjoy its traditional supremacy in all calendrical matters. When the family was deposed from the Palestinian Gaonate, however, friction developed between the two centers. Matters reached a head during the early tenth century with the great calendar controversy between the family of Meir Gaon of Palestine and Saadya b. Joseph Gaon of Sura.

At this point, I should stress that the events described above—i.e. the decline of the Exilarch's status and the dispute between David and Daniel—are interrelated. The decline of the Exilarchate had both internal and external aspects: while the Heads of the Yeshivot exerted greater authority internally, al-Ma'mūn's decree afforded legitimacy to the external

[83] For the letter see *Corpus*, no. 86, a, line 11 (ENA NS 9, fol. 15).

[84] For further discussions of the dispute—not all of which, however, take into account the latest Genizah findings—see: Graetz, *Divrei yemei yisra'el*, 3:419f., n. 1; S. Abramson, *Ba-merkazim u-va-tefuṣot* (Jerusalem, 1965), p. 13 and n. 4; Grossman, *Rashut ha-golah*, 64; F. Lazarus, "Neue Beiträge zur Geschichte des Exilarchats," *MGWJ* 78 (1934): 281f.; D. Rosenthal, "Rav Paltoi Gaon and His Place in the Halakhic Tradition" (Hebrew), *Shenaton ha-Mishpat ha-Ivri* 11–12 (1984–86): 590.

[85] J. Mann, *The Jews in Egypt and in Palestine Under the Fatimid Caliphs*, 2d ed. (New York, 1970), 1:52ff. and 2:41, where *Corpus*, no. 3 (T-S 8 G 7, fol. 1) is edited.

[86] See Gil, *History*, 566f. and cf. Mann, "The Responsa of the Babylonian Geonim," *JQR* n.s. 10 (1919–20): 360. See also *Corpus*, no. 4 (T-S NS 308.122) edited by Abramson, *Ba-merkazim*, 16ff. Abramson assumes that this letter, which lacks the full name of its author, was written by

organization and re-grouping of religious dissidents. We may assume, in fact, that the decree encouraged the spread of religious dissent among Jews, a phenomenon familiar to us from our knowledge of early Karaism. What is confirmed by all our sources—both Jewish and Christian—is the development of a profound public crisis that engulfed the Diaspora during the first half of the ninth century.

The Exilarchs in the Tenth and Eleventh Centuries

Somewhere towards the end of the ninth century, we encounter the Exilarch ʿUqba. Both he and his successor, David b. Zakkai, undoubtedly belonged to the dynasty of David b. Judah which, as we have seen, remained Rabbanite, while the competing "Ananite" dynasty of Daniel b. Saul went over to the Karaite camp.[87] Following the death of David b. Zakkai in 940 C.E., his son Judah assumed the Exilarchate but he remained in office for only seven months.[88] Since Judah's son Hezekiah died at the age of twelve, it seemed that the Exilarchate would come under the control of distant relatives from Nisibis, the family of a certain Heman.[89] The family's candidate for the Exilarchate was accused, however, of cursing the Prophet Muḥammad and was executed. For the descendants of Zakkai the latter half of the tenth century was an especially critical period; as Sherira Gaon writes in 987: "Of the family of the Nesiʾim there now remains but one little child."[90]

In the mid-tenth century, Solomon, b. Josiah (the brother of David) b. Zakkai assumed the Exilarchate. Solomon b. Josiah is mentioned in a letter from the Pumbedita Yeshivah written in 953 C.E. which states that he entered office two years earlier, i.e. in 951. He also is mentioned in a

---

the son of David b. Judah. In his view, Judah was the Exilarch—an opinion which finds corroboration in one of the lists (MS Dropsie 462); see no. 3 in the table above. Abramson dates the letter before 857. While this supposition is possible, it is more likely that the letter was written by Hai b. David.

[87] The subject of ʿUqba and David b. Zakkai should be discussed in the context of the various tenth-century disputes; I shall not touch upon it here.

[88] See Neubauer, *Mediaeval Jewish Chronicles*, 2:82f. and Mann, "Misrat rosh ha-golah," 18ff.

[89] He is perhaps Heman b. Hanamel the Nasi whose name is found on a seal inscription; see S. Shaked, "Jewish and Christian Seals of the Sasanian Period," in *Gaston Wiet Memorial Volume* (Jerusalem, 1977), 125.

[90] According to another version, it is in Sura (Mata Maḥsiya) that but one child of the entire family remained. A third version states that not even a single child of the family remained; but this is rather illogical. See Lewin, *Iggeret rav sherira gaon*, 93 and the many versions cited there.

genealogical list from the Genizah.[91] He was succeeded by his son Azariah.[92]

For some unknown reason, the Exilarchate was transferred from the descendants of Josiah to the descendants of David. As is known, Azariah's son Daniel became Head of the Palestinian Yeshivah in 1052 and was granted the titles of Nasi and Gaon.[93] After the office had passed out of the hands of David b. Zakkai's descendants—apparently in the days of Hezekiah I b. Judah—it reverted to this branch of the family when Hezekiah II became the Exilarch.[94]

According to Abraham Ibn Daud, "the members of Rav Hai's Yeshivah" appointed Hezekiah to Hai's seat after his death (March, 1038). Two years later, Hezekiah was betrayed by "informers" and then the "King"[95]

> imprisoned him, put him in chains, tortured him grievously and left him no survivors. His two sons fled to R. Joseph ha-Levi the Nagid b. R. Samuel the Nagid, who had great affection for Hezekiah the Exilarch and head of the academy. They remained there with him until the time of the massacre in Granada, when the Nagid was killed [December 30, 1066]. One of the sons of Hezekiah then fled to the land of Saragossa where he married and had children. Afterwards, his descendants migrated to Christian Spain. One of them was R. Ḥiyya b. al-Daudi, who passed away in Castile in 4914 [i.e. 1154]. After him there did not remain in Spain a single person known to be of the house of David. After Hezekiah the Exilarch and head of the academy, there were no more academies or geonim.[96]

Apart from this tantalizing account in *The Book of Tradition*, some information on the Exilarch Hezekiah can be found in the Genizah documents.[97] In a letter to Elhanan b. Shemariah (early February 1018), Hai Gaon mentions his having written to the Exilarch, evidently referring to

---

91 For the letter, see *Corpus*, no. 13, f, line 8 (Oxford ms. Heb. f. 34, fols. 39–44); for the genealogical list, see *Corpus*, no. 70, line 14 (Mosseri I.107).

92 The opening of a letter from Azariah has been preserved in the Genizah; it may be reconstructed as follows: ". . . [Azariahu Exi]larch of all Israel b. Solomon b. Josiah Exilarch of all Israel." See Philadelphia, ms. Dropsie 462, ed. B.Z. Halper, *Descriptive Catalogue of Genizah Fragments in Philadelphia* (Philadelphia, 1924). See also ms. Mosseri I a 19 (L 289) for the name "Azariahu"; on the verso can be found the name of the addressee's father, "Rabbana Ḥusayn, of blessed memory." See also Mann, "Misrat rosh ha-golah," 20.

93 On Daniel b. Azariah and his son David, see Gil, *History*, 719–39, 750–74.

94 On the sons of Azariah see Mann, "Misrat rosh ha-golah," 21 and my criticisms in "A Supplement to 'Palestine During the First Muslim Period,'" pp. 302–303 and n. 53. See also the lineage on the verso of ms. Heidelberg no. 10; for the recto see Gil, *Palestine*, 2:44–45, no. 27 and additional references there.

95 It is not clear whether this occurred under Buyid or Seljuk rule, i.e. before or after 1055. We can assume, in any event, that the "two years" in this version is inaccurate.

96 See Cohen, *The Book of Tradition*, 61–62 (Hebrew, 44–45).

97 See Gil, *History*, pp. 540–42, 578–79 and the references there.

Hezekiah.[98] In a letter dated Nisan, 1332 A.S. (1021 C.E.), Hezekiah provides his family tree: Zakkai—David—Judah—Hezekiah—David—Hezekiah I—and Hezekiah II; all are styled Exilarchs.[99] And writing to an unknown addressee in July 1036, Hezekiah requests that queries on matters of biblical exegesis and halakhah be submitted to him; he would like to see the ties between them strengthened.[100]

From a letter of Daniel b. Azariah of September 12, 1038, we learn of Hezekiah's close relationship with the people of Fuṣṭāṭ.[101] This is confirmed by another letter, written in July or August 1040, in which he requests the Babylonian community of Fuṣṭāṭ to obey their leader Sahlān b. Abraham in every possible way.[102] The letter also contains praise for Abū Naṣr, i.e. Ḥesed al-Tustarī; we may infer that this wealthy Karaite, who enjoyed close ties to the authorities, was involved in the release of some prisoners. Although there are no specific references to the dispute between Solomon b. Judah Gaon and his rival Nathan b. Abraham, this conflict probably motivated Hezekiah's remarks. The "Babylonians" in Fuṣṭāṭ are known to have sided with Nathan b. Abraham, who was supported both by their leader, the above-mentioned Sahlān, and the Karaite Tustarī brothers. There is also a fragmentary letter written by Hezekiah in 1040 to Jacob b. Amram, Nagid of Kairouan praising the latter for supporting scholars.[103]

Another Genizah letter also refers to Hezekiah; it was written by one Elijah ha-Kohen b. Abraham to Jacob *he-ḥaver* of the Great Sanhedrin b. Joseph, the leader of the Jews of Aleppo, who, as his title would indicate, was loyal to the Palestinian *rashut*. The letter is replete with greetings to all manner of dignitaries, e.g. various Aleppan notables as well as "the teachers, cantors, *parnasim* and *gabba'im* of the synagogue." Its author was a local *dayyan*, or judge who lived five days' journey from Baghdad—perhaps in Raqqa, Syria on the banks of the Euphrates. Elijah had received writs of appointment from the Heads of the Yeshivot in Baghdad; subsequently, similar documents "were brought to him by Rav Ezekiel the Babylonian . . . renewed by our master Hezekiah Exilarch of all Israel . . . and Rabbenu Rav Hai, Head of the Yeshivah." From this passage, we may infer that when Hai succeeded his father Sherira as Gaon in 998, it was

[98] *Corpus*, no. 39, lines 3–4 (T-S 10 J 27, fol. 10).
[99] Ms. Heidelberg no. 10, mentioned above n. 94. This is the draft of a letter in Hezekiah's own hand (or that of his scribe), expressing opposition to Elhanan b. Shemariah.
[100] *Corpus*, no. 67 (T-S 13 J 9, fol. 1).
[101] See Gil, *Palestine*, 2:627–30, no. 344, a, lines 14ff.
[102] *Corpus*, no. 68 (T-S Loan 40 [I]). See above n. 40.
[103] *Corpus*, no. 69 (T-S Loan 40 [II]).

necessary to have such appointments renewed. Indirectly, we may also conclude that Hezekiah rose to the office of Exilarch at approximately the same time. Significantly, our *dayyan* affixes to his signature the phrase, "by appointment of the gate of the *nesi'ut* (i.e. the Exilarchate) and the Yeshivot of the Diaspora."[104]

The Exilarch Hezekiah is also mentioned in the Arabic passages interspersed in Samuel ha-Nagid's *dīwān*. Following the description of a military victory in 1055 in which the Nagid took part, we find the phrase: *fa-kataba ilā mar rav yiṣḥaq yeḥezqiyahu rosh galut*, i.e. the Exilarch Hezekiah wrote words of praise and flattery to Rav Isaac. Samuel calls Hezekiah "my king" and "prince of a pure tribe" comparing his teachings to those of Moses which "burn and destroy the depraved." Alluding to Hezekiah's adversaries, he writes: "Ascending on high, he founded a kingdom for his sons with a covenant of salt; so long as there is light, it will not be overturned." In other words, he believes that this particular Exilarchic dynasty will rule in perpetuity.[105]

A manuscript of *Seder ʿolam zuṭa* and *Seder tanna'im va-amora'im* contains the following scribal addition: "After Rav Hai, no Head of the Yeshivah was appointed in Babylonia; (they did) however, (appoint) an Exilarch by the name of Rav Hezekiah who is now Head and who stems from the House of David."[106] In the continuation, Hezekiah's son David is mentioned as is Solomon b. Judah, Gaon of Palestine. Since the date is recorded, we learn that Hezekiah still occupied the office of Exilarch in summer of 1045; this accords with the information in the *Book of Tradition* cited above.[107] Ibn Daud, who seems to have used this source,

---

[104] See *Corpus*, no. 73 (New York, JTSA ms. Schechter 4). And see: S. Schechter, "Genizah Ms.," in *A. Berliner Festschrift*, (Hebrew section) (Frankfurt a.M., 1903), 108ff.; S. Poznanski, *Babylonische Geonim im nachgaonäischen Zeitalter* (Berlin, 1914), 1ff.; Mann, "Misrat rosh ha-golah," 22; and idem, *Texts and Studies*, 1:179. On Jacob b. Joseph of Aleppo, see: Gil, *History*, 187f. See A.S. Kamenetzki, "Deux lettres de l'époque du dernier exilarque," *REJ* 55–56 (1908): 51ff.

[105] For Samuel's *dīwān*, see New York, JTSA ms. ENA 1731, fol. 9, first quoted by A. Marmorstein, "Les gueonim en Palestine aux XIe et XIIe siècles," *REJ* 68 (1914): 41f. The passage mentioning Hezekiah has also been published by J. Marcus, "Mi-shirei rav shemu'el hanagid," *Mizraḥ u-maʿarav* 4 (1929–30): 313 (with errors and without translation). See also D.S. Sassoon ed., *Diwan of Shemuel Hannaghid* (Oxford, 1934), 101ff., no. 143 and D. Jarden, *Diwan Shemuel ha-Nagid* (Jerusalem, 1966), 134.

[106] The ms. was copied by a certain Jerahmeel who evidently hailed from southern Italy. On "Ms. Jerahmeel," see Neubauer, *Mediaeval Jewish Chronicles*, 1:178 and the editor's comments on p. xxi.

[107] The date is given as 15 Elul 4807 A.M.; this is undoubtedly a mistake and should read 4805. The date is also given both according to the Seleucid calendar and from the time of the Temple's destruction.

apparently understood it to imply that Hezekiah served simultaneously as Exilarch and Head of the Yeshivah. This reading, however, is not confirmed by the letters of Hezekiah and his contemporaries. Judah b. Barzilai's statement that following the death of Hai Gaon, Hezekiah, the Nasi, was consulted would also suggest that the latter did not become Head of the Yeshivah.[108]

Hezekiah's son David stayed in Palestine during the third and fourth decades of the eleventh century, returning to Baghdad sometime after 1050—possibly after having stayed in both Egypt and Spain.[109] In our sources, he is called both Nasi and *nesi galuyot kol yisra'el* but no contemporary source has yet been found that refers to him as Exilarch.[110] In his diary, Abū ʿAlī al-Ḥasan b. Aḥmad al-Bannā records that a controversy over the Exilarchate took place within the Baghdad community around 1068. Ibn Faḍlān, the most important Jewish financier of that period, supported a pretender from the House of David, while the majority favored another candidate. Apparently, he was referring to David b. Hezekiah, who may have been the central figure in this controversy and who was subsequently discharged from the Exilarchate.[111] His victorious rival was possibly Azariah b. Solomon. In any case, David's son Hezekiah was subsequently appointed Exilarch, as is confirmed by a letter from Abiathar ha-Kohen b. Elijah, Gaon of Palestine, dated July 4, 1091.[112] With his tenure, we come to the end of our survey. Below is a tentative list of

---

[108] On the problem of Hezekiah's "Gaonate," see Gil, *History*, pp. 541–42 and n. 46. On Ibn Daud's account, see also: W. Bacher, "Ein neuerschlossenes Capitel der jüdischen Geschichte," *JQR* o.s. 15 (1902–1903): 80; Mann, "Misrat rosh ha-golah," 22f.; Goitein, *A Mediterranean Society*, 2:17; Grossman, *Rashut ha-golah*, 11.

According to the aforementioned letter by the refugee from Ramla, Hezekiah was buried in al-Anbār (Pumbedita?); see *Corpus*, no. 86 (ENA NS 9, fol. 15) and n. 83 above. For further information on Hezekiah, see A. Ben Jacob, *Yehudei bavel mi-sof tequfat ha-ge'onim ʿad yamenu* (Jerusalem 1965), 10 and the memorial list (post 1100) in Mann, *The Jews in Egypt and in Palestine*, 2:100 which mentions "Hezekiah, Exilarch of all Israel . . . and his son, our Lord and Master David the Nasi of all diasporas of Israel." See also the letters in Gil, *Palestine*, 2:113, no. 65 and 3:8–9, no. 416. And cf. also Mann, *The Jews in Egypt and in Palestine*, 1:112f.

[109] On David b. Hezekiah, see Gil, *History*, 543–44.

[110] I retract my statement in *History*, 554 that David b. Hezekiah was Exilarch (as assumed also by Mann, "Misrat rosh ha-golah," 23). There is, at any rate, no evidence that he was; for evidence suggesting that he was not, see *Corpus*, no. 255 (T-S 8 J 22, fol. 10).

[111] For the diary of Ibn al-Bannā, see G. Makdisi, "Autograph Diary of an Eleventh-Century Historian of Baghdad," *BSOAS* 19 (1957): 25.

[112] For Abiathar's letter, see Gil, *Palestine*, 3:370f., no. 553. Hezekiah may have had another son named Joseph, who evidently lived in Fuṣṭāṭ. This Joseph b. Hezekiah is said to have written a treatise on ritual slaughter; see Mann, *The Jews in Egypt and in Palestine*, 2:145, n. 7 and idem, *Texts and Studies*, 2:47f. and n. 94, where he notes the need to distinguish between Hezekiah b. David and Hezekiah b. Solomon, a Karaite Nasi.

the Exilarchs until approximately the end of the eleventh century. (Their dates of office are only approximate.)

1. Bustanai b. Kafnai, in the first half of the 7th century
2. Ḥisdai b. Bustanai, in the latter half of the 7th century
3. Solomon b. Ḥisdai, mentioned in 730 and 758
4. Isaac b. Solomon, ca. 760
5. Hananiah (ʿAnan's brother) b. David, ca. 762
6. Naṭronai b. Hananiah, until ca. 770
7. Zakkai b. Ahunai, from 770 until ca. 803
8. Ḥisdai b. Naṭronai, after ca. 803
9. Daniel b. Saul b. Anan, ca. 820
10. David b. Judah, probably in the 30's of the 9th century
11. Judah (Zakkai) b. David b. Judah, ca. 840
12. ʿUqba, until ca. 908
13. David b. Zakkai, ca. 915 until 940
14. Judah b. David b. Zakkai, 940
15. Hezekiah I b. Judah b. David b. Zakkai, from ca. 941
16. Solomon b. Josiah b. Zakkai, mentioned in 951
17. Azariah b. Solomon b. Josiah, ca. 975
18. Hezekiah II b. David b. Hezekiah, ca. 1000 until ca. 1060
19. Hezekiah III b. David b. Hezekiah, ca. 1060 until ca. 1100

HALAKHAH AND REALITY IN THE GAONIC PERIOD: TAQQANAH, MINHAG, TRADITION AND CONSENSUS: SOME OBSERVATIONS

Gideon Libson

Introduction

It is a fact of life that legal systems, if they are to survive, must respond to the challenges posed by the dynamic, changing circumstances of human society, constantly creating new norms and rules in order to govern and regulate social organization and interpersonal behavior. This is true not only of legal systems in general but even of religious law, although at first sight one might think that, being by definition of divine origin, it would be entirely intolerant of human intervention.

Judaism, too, no less than other religions, relies on a variety of legal tools and sources to bridge the gap between a changing reality and the principles of religious law—halakhah. Over the generations, therefore, there emerged a limited number of legal sources—the tools through which Jewish law was able to evolve and adapt to new circumstances, while still maintaining the formal halakhic framework.

Halakhah recognizes several such sources: *qabbalah* (tradition), *taqqanah* (enactment), *minhag* (custom, usage), *midrash* (exegesis or interpretation), *sevarah* (legal logic) and precedent.[1] These sources were particularly important during the Gaonic period, when the legal authorities of the time, the Geonim of the great academies in Babylonia-Iraq, faced new challenges, due to the great historical changes then in progress. In this article I will be concerned mainly with three of these sources: *taqqanah*, *minhag*[2] and *midrash*—though I shall also touch on some aspects of tradition and precedent, which to my mind are closely related, both directly

[1] On the sources of Jewish law, see M. Elon, *Jewish Law* (Hebrew) (Jerusalem, 1973), 2:221.

[2] On *minhag* during the Gaonic period see J.L. Fishman, "Minhag in Gaonic Literature" (Hebrew), in *B.M. Lewin Jubilee Volume* (Jerusalem, 1940), 132–59, reprinted in idem, *Portraits of Great Men* (Hebrew) (Jerusalem, 1946), 97–122; M. Havazelet, "On Minhag in Gaonic Literature" (Hebrew), *P'raqim* 3 (1963): 97–108; idem, "On Some Minhagim in the Works of Maimonides and the Geonim" (Hebrew), *P'raqim* 4 (1964): 57–70, reprinted in idem, *Maimonides and the Geonim* (Hebrew) (Jerusalem, 1967), 144–99. For *minhag* in the works of Hai Gaon, see Z. Groner, "R. Hai Gaon and His Approach to Halakhah" (Hebrew) (Ph.D. diss., The Hebrew

and indirectly, to *minhag*. Some attention will also be devoted to the question of consensus, a legal source that gained some acceptance at this time in the Jewish legal literature, possibly as a result of Muslim influence; it, too, is not entirely unrelated to *qabbalah* and *minhag*.

It is my aim here to look at the way the Geonim used these legal sources and to try to characterize the specific role played by each source in the broader gamut of legal innovation: were certain sources appealed to more than others? Was any specific source considered preferable? The answers to these and similar questions should undoubtedly reflect the changing circumstances of the Gaonic period, which forced the Geonim to grapple with a variety of legal problems. For it is a commonplace, as accepted in the scholarly literature, that the nature of legal creativity, both in theory and in practice, is intimately bound up with political and social conditions.

Influences on the Development of Halakhah

Before clarifying the relationship between such considerations and the new reality of the Gaonic period, I would like briefly to survey the factors that forged that reality. These may be grouped into four categories: (1) center versus Diaspora; (2) social structure and economic change; (3) political developments and the advent of Islam with its various sects and legal schools; and (4) modes of study, legislation and literary creativity.

The first category, center versus Diaspora, concerns the political and social structure of the Jewish communities in the Gaonic period. The dispersal of Jewish communities over all parts of the Muslim world, far distant from the center in Iraq (Babylonia), naturally weakened their ties with the central religious authorities. Conditions were thus ripe for the emergence of numerous local customs, on the one hand, and for the enactment

University, 1974) (= Groner, "R. Hai Gaon"), 115–91. The *taqqanot* of the Geonim have been discussed at much greater length; see: H. Tykocinski, *The Taqqanot of the Geonim* (Hebrew) (Jerusalem, 1960); I. Schepanski, "The Taqqanot of the Geonim" (Hebrew), *Ha-Darom* 24–25 (1967): 135–97; E. Shochetman, "The Methodology of Ascertaining Geonic Enactments with Specific Reference to 'kim lei be-gavei' " (Hebrew), *Shenaton ha-Mishpat ha-Ivri* 11–12 (1984–86): 655–86; Y. Brody, "Were the Geonim Legislators?" (Hebrew), *Shenaton ha-Mishpat ha-Ivri* 11–12 (1984–86): 279–315; A. Beeri, "Takkanoth and Quasi-Takkanoth in Gaonic Halacha" (Hebrew), *Mizraḥ u-Maʿarav* 1 (1974): 285–93. Some Gaonic *minhagim* have nevertheless been included in studies of Gaonic *taqqanot*, as rabbis and later also scholars dealing with the subject have not infrequently treated various practices, originally considered *minhagim*, as *taqqanot*; see below. Only recently have Brody and Shochetman, contrary to the dominant tendency hitherto, suggested that the number of genuine *taqqanot* was in fact much smaller.

of special *taqqanot*, on the other. No less important than geographical distance was the political fragmentation of the Muslim world, which at times created political borders that cut off individual communities from the center, thus encouraging a degree of legal autonomy vis-à-vis the prevailing Muslim influence of Iraq.[3] The geographical divisions naturally promoted legal pluralism (or, to use a phrase coined by Haym Soloveitchik, "halakhic federalism").[4] As Isadore Twersky has written concerning *minhag*, in reference to Maimonides: "This dispersal bears the historical responsibility for the emergence of the *minhag*, with its limited scope, in contrast to the universal halakhah, which is binding on Jews wherever they may be."[5]

At the core of the tension between the center and the Diaspora was the long-standing rivalry between the centers in Iraq-Babylonia and Palestine, which reached new heights during the Gaonic period. It was not merely a question of each center wishing to impose its will on the other; the rivals were at pains to assert their respective hegemonies over Jewish communities throughout the Orient and, in particular, North Africa and Egypt. The main controversy stemmed from different legal traditions, which produced correspondingly different customs in many areas, from the laws of prayer and mourning to those of personal status, legal procedure and deeds.[6]

In addition to these two external aspects—geographical divisions and political fragmentation—there were two "internal" factors that may also be subsumed under the political and social category. One was the weakness of the Babylonian academies at different times. Their waning influence was due to inner tensions among the different academies or, some-

---

[3] On the effects of such political divisions see S. Spiegel, "On the Polemic of Pirkoi b. Baboi," *H.A. Wolfson Jubilee Volume* (Hebrew Section) (Jerusalem, 1965), 262; M. Ben-Sasson, "Inter-Communal Relations and Regional Organization in the Maghreb in the Ninth to the Eleventh Centuries" (Hebrew), *Pe'amim* 18 (1984): 15, 18.

[4] H. Soloveitchik, *Pawnbroking* (Hebrew) (Jerusalem, 1985), 80.

[5] I. Twersky, "Land and Exile in Maimonides," in *The Land of Israel in Medieval Jewish History* (Hebrew), ed. M. Hallamish and A. Ravitzky (Jerusalem, 1991), 104. Twersky is relying on Maimonides' own statement in the Introduction to the *Mishneh Torah*, in which he stresses the relationship between the physical effect of life in the Diaspora and the development of *taqqanah* and *minhag*: "Every *beit-din* that was established later than the Gemara in any country, and that decreed or enacted or instituted a custom for the people of its country or of several countries—its actions did not spread throughout Israel, because of the distances between their settlements and the poor state of the roads."

[6] The question of Palestine vs. North Africa has received much attention. See, e.g., S. Büchler, "The Ketubbah among the Jews of North Africa during the Gaonic Period and the Relationship between the African Communities and Babylonian and Palestinian Jewry" (Hebrew), *Shenaton ha-Mishpat ha-Ivri* 11–12 (1984–86): 55; M. Ben-Sasson, "The Jewish Community of Medieval North Africa—Society and Leadership: Qayrawan 800–1057" (Hebrew) (Ph.D. diss., The Hebrew University, 1983), 1:36; idem, "The Jews of the Maghreb and their Relation with Israel in the Ninth through Eleventh Centuries" (Hebrew), *Shalem* 5 (1987): 36ff.

times, between the Geonim and the Exilarchs.[7] These weaknesses created a vacuum that frequently facilitated the action of various influences; these, in turn, forced the Geonim to commit themselves to particular positions.

The other internal factor was the dependence of the academies on financial aid from the Diaspora communities, which sometimes made the Geonim more tolerant of local tradition and custom. In fact, although the Geonim considered the Babylonian academies legislative bodies, whose decisions were binding for all Jews—"For this body is in place of the Sanhedrin and its head is in place of Moses our Master, and the customs (*minhagot*) of the Sanhedrin are issued by it"[8]—this was in the nature of wishful thinking, which rarely stood the test of reality. Hai Gaon, as just quoted, was referring not only to the position of the academies, but also to the importance of *minhag* for the Babylonian Geonim. He was not alone in equating the academy with the Sanhedrin and the Great Court; this was the view of many other Geonim, as we may conclude from the introductory remarks to their letters and responsa.[9]

The second category of factors influencing the use of legal sources was economic in nature: the transition from an agricultural society to an urban, commercial society engaged in local and international trade. This transformation created patterns of commerce and techniques of credit, methods of authorization and agency, legal procedures and methods of collection—all or some of which frequently did not fit exactly into the frame of accepted halakhah and was therefore a source of tension between the halakhah and the economic facts of life. The Geonim were thus obliged to accommodate halakhic theory to economic reality. Even the surviving islands of agricultural society challenged the accepted halakhic norms and demanded legal solutions to various new problems.[10]

[7] On these tensions and the relations between the center and the Diaspora, see A. Grossman, "From Father to Son: The Inheritance of the Spiritual Leadership of the Jewish Communities in the Early Middle Ages" (Hebrew), *Zion* 50 (1985): 203; Ben-Sasson, "Inter-Communal Relations," 15, 18.

[8] *Iggeret rav sherira ga'on*, ed. B.M. Lewin (Jerusalem, 1972), 28. For the use of the word *minhagot*, see below.

[9] For the sources, see A. Grossman, "The Relationship Between the Social Structure and Spiritual Activity of Jewish Communities in the Geonic Period" (Hebrew), *Zion* 53 (1988): 266; M. Ben-Sasson, "The Story of Nathan Ha-Babli: Structure, Goals and Content" in *Culture and Society in Medieval Jewry: Studies Dedicated to the Memory of Haim Hillel Ben-Sasson* (Hebrew), ed. M. Ben-Sasson et al. (Jerusalem, 1989), p. 179 n. 102; Schepanski, "The Taqqanot of the Geonim," 136; and cf. the reservations expressed by R. Brody, "Toward a Correct Evaluation of Maimonides' *Mishneh Torah*" (Hebrew), *Tarbiz* 53 (1984): p. 319, n. 10 and the sources cited there.

[10] On this factor and its influence, see my article, "Custom as a Mediating Factor Between Law and Economic Contingency in Jewish and Islamic Society," in *Religion and Economy:*

The third category—though not necessarily third in order of importance—was political in nature: the Persian Sassanids gave way to the Muslims, whose culture and law spread throughout the Middle East and directly affected almost every sphere of Jewish life—society, philosophy and law. Besides the receptive attitude of some Geonim—particularly since the days of Saadya Gaon—to Arabic culture, the social tensions and political-economic factors outlined above also made it easier for Islamic influence to penetrate the Jewish legal system. In actual fact, the political and economic transformations took place concurrently, so it is not always easy to determine which sphere was more decisive in relation to a given halakhic development.

The fourth category of influences on the formation of legal sources—modes of study, legislation and literary creativity, which were among other things a response to halakhic and social needs—is in a sense the inverse of the first, political-social category, although the two categories stand in a two-way relationship of causality. There is of course a strong link between this factor, on the one hand, and social and political conditions, on the other. Indeed, the scholarly world is well aware of the connection between political distress and cultural decline, which encourages the composition of codificatory works.[11] It is not impossible that the prevalence of halakhic monographs in the Gaonic period, from the time of Saadya Gaon on (aside from the codificatory literature of the previous generations), as against the paucity of exegetical works on the Talmud, is indicative of some such tendency.

Halakhic monographs, in fact, played a more significant role than might be supposed; they represented a balanced response to the needs of the time as we have described them, filling a vacuum for those unable to study the Talmud, preserving the talmudic tradition, and leading their readers safely, purposefully, and systematically down the paths of talmudic law. As such, they provided a counterweight to deviant traditions, thus in some measure moderating the influence of the latter. The monograph literature also

Connections and Interactions, Collected Essays (Hebrew), ed. M. Ben-Sasson (Jerusalem, 1995), 265–307.

[11] See I. Twersky, "Maimonides' *Mishneh Torah*, its Object and Function" (Hebrew), *Proceedings of the Israel Academy of Sciences and Humanities* 5 (1972): 11. Cf. A. Grossman, *The Early Sages of Ashkenaz* (Hebrew) (Jerusalem, 1981), 413. I. Ta-Shma links the phenomenon in question to the culture of the host societies; see "Law, Custom and Tradition in Early Jewish Germany—Tentative Reflections" (Hebrew), *Sidra* 3 (1987): 96. Cf. also G. Blidstein, "The Idea of Oral Law and its History in the Epistle of R. Sherira Gaon" (Hebrew), *Da^cat* 7 (1980): 9–10; N. Danzig, "Halakhot Pesukot ('Hilkhot R. Yehudai Gaon')," (Ph.D. diss., Yeshivah University, 1984), p. 11 n. 9.

stressed the above-mentioned Gaonic view of the academy as a surrogate Sanhedrin and judicial institution of universal authority, thus reinforcing the position and authority of the academies in their ties with the communities.[12]

Some support for this conjecture may be derived from a comparison of the situation in the East to what was then happening in Central Europe. Indeed, the activity of the Ashkenazi rabbis as a whole indicates that halakhic and codificatory literature, the attitude to the Talmud and the development of custom stand in a three-way relationship. No large-scale codificatory works were composed in Central Europe, so that the Talmud itself—sometimes in non-standard interpretations—was freely used to substantiate prevalent practices.[13]

How did this complex of factors and circumstances affect the Gaonic use of legal sources? The legal writings of the Geonim contain virtually no theoretical discussion of such questions; the scant references that can be identified do not permit any conclusive answer. For an evaluation to be possible, we must also consider the responsa literature—in fact, the Gaonic responsa furnish our principal source for any attempt to trace the development of Jewish law in the Gaonic period.[14]

Taqqanah

The most important legal source that the Geonim used as a tool to adapt halakhah to changing conditions was the *taqqanah* (enactment). The *taqqanah* in general, and in the Gaonic period in particular, may be defined in terms of three characteristics. First, it was a unique measure, a deliberate response to a major shift in reality, which created, so to speak, a halakhic emergency and an urgent need for a legal solution. Failure to provide a solution might engender a major violation of talmudic law and, consequently, might undermine halakhic authority.[15] As it was intended to bridge a particularly acute gap between the needs of reality and talmudic law, the change created by a *taqqanah* might be quite significant. Second,

[12] See Grossman, "Relationship." For the role of monographs in reinforcing the academies' position see Ben-Sasson, "The Story of Nathan Ha-Babli," 161.

[13] See, e.g., Ta-Shma, "Law, Custom and Tradition," 110. Other differences between the Orient and Ashkenaz in this context will be discussed at length elsewhere.

[14] For the legal status of the responsa literature, see Elon, *Jewish Law*, 3:1213ff. and B. Lifshitz, "The Legal Status of the Responsa Literature" (Hebrew), *Shenaton ha-Mishpat ha-Ivri* 9–10 (1982–85): 266f. For its status in Gaonic literature, see G. Libson, *Halakhah and Legal Procedure in the Gaonic Period* (forthcoming).

[15] See Ta-Shma, "Law, Custom and Tradition," 131 and Groner, "R. Hai Gaon," 139.

any *taqqanah*, once enacted, was applicable equally to all parts of the community at large. Third, the enactment of a *taqqanah* was subject to certain procedural prescriptions. Once enacted, a *taqqanah* enjoyed priority over other legal sources and was considered absolutely binding; it was to be enforced under any circumstances.

Nevertheless, although the actual word *taqqanah* occurs quite frequently in Gaonic writings—as has been cited by scholars as evidence for the promulgation of numerous *taqqanot*—there are only two well-documented *taqqanot* that may be attributed with confidence to the Geonim; namely, those dealing with the rebellious wife (*moredet*) and with chattels or movable property (*miṭṭalṭelin*), each of which is related (in its own sphere) to a fundamental revolution then taking place.[16] The *taqqanah* of the rebellious wife related to the social sphere—the changing status of women. It addressed itself particularly to the danger that women might sue for immediate divorce by way of the Muslim authorities and courts, rather than wait the statutory period of one year as required by the Talmud. The second *taqqanah* permitted loans to be collected from movable as well as landed property—a reaction to new economic conditions in which real estate was no longer the principal object of commerce. This change influenced many laws and regulations relating to property transactions. Common to both *taqqanot* is their allowance for a radical transformation in one specific area—their adoption of a new halakhic position, more lenient than allowed by the original talmudic law; in both cases the innovation was supposed to apply to all Jewish communities.

Although the two *taqqanot* ostensibly pertain to different areas of everyday life, one cannot ignore a significant common element: both affect the status of women, as they were designed, among other things, to safeguard the wife's personal and financial rights should she be divorced or widowed. In both *taqqanot* the Geonim modified accepted halakhah in the direction of increased leniency—once again, as a bridge between reality and the letter of the law—and both were diametrically opposed to the talmudic ruling. It is perhaps not insignificant that both measures date from the early stages of the Gaonic period: one was enacted in the middle of the seventh century, the other in the last quarter of the eighth century. We have no concrete, documentary evidence of any *taqqanot* enacted at a later date.

[16] Concerning these *taqqanot* see Brody, "Were the Geonim Legislators?" The *taqqanah* of the rebellious wife, in particular, has received copious attention in the literature; see, esp., M.A. Friedman, *Jewish Marriage in Palestine: A Cairo Geniza Study* (Tel Aviv and New York, 1980), 1:312ff. and the bibliography cited there in n. 42.

To my mind, this dearth of *taqqanot* is no accident: it reflects, on the one hand, a decline of the *taqqanah* as a legal source in the Gaonic period, and, on the other, the increasing significance of custom. The decline of the *taqqanah* is corroborated by several phenomena. First, the mere fact that the two documented instances were more than one century apart and that both involved the participation of a large number of scholars is in itself evidence that their promulgation was no easy matter. The *taqqanah* of the rebellious wife was apparently issued with the agreement of the Geonim of all the academies of Sura and Pumbedita; that of the chattels, however, was enacted by the Geonim of Sura only, those of Pumbedita having objected—at least, at an early stage.

An important cause of the eclipse of the *taqqanah* should be sought in the many practical and exegetical problems occasioned by the enactment of these two specific *taqqanot* by the Geonim, both at the time of enactment and later. We have evidence of a series of confrontations, both among the Geonim themselves and between them and the communities or community representatives, in connection with the application of the new *taqqanot*. Thus, for example, we know that several Geonim had to rebuke local judges who objected to the collection of debts from chattels. In addition, the different possible interpretations of the enactments seem to have hindered their widespread acceptance, both during and after the Gaonic period. The *taqqanah* of the rebellious wife raised several questions: under what circumstances was it effective? did it apply only to a woman claiming to find her husband repulsive, or even to one refusing conjugal rights without apparent legal justification? did it apply in a levirate marriage as well? what financial loss did it involve for the woman? was she to be recompensed for property under her husband's control and now lost? The *taqqanah* of chattels also raised difficult questions: did it apply to the main, statutory part of the *ketubbah* (*ʿiqqar ketubbah*) only or to the increment (*tosefet*) as well? did the *taqqanah* apply as well to the husband's obligation to maintain his wife, included in the terms of the *ketubbah*? once the *taqqanah* had been enacted, did collection from chattels enjoy the same priority as collection from real estate in talmudic law? Such questions in time necessitated modification of the *taqqanah* itself, but no such measures were ever taken.

Thus, the weaker status of the *taqqanah* was, at least in part, due to intrinsic factors, rooted in the very nature of the institution.[17] The chief

---

[17] On the interpretations and controversies aroused by these *taqqanot*, see Brody, ibid., and S. Assaf, *The Period of the Geonim and its Literature* (Hebrew) (Jerusalem, 1955), 62–63.

reason for its decline as a legal source, however, was the expanding role of *minhag*, custom.

Custom as Opposed to Taqqanah

The Gaonic period witnessed a veritable proliferation of practices specifically referred to, then and later, as "customs," *minhagim*. Gaonic writings feature a broad spectrum of different types of custom: the custom of the academy (*yeshivah*) or of the two academies; ancestral custom (*minhag avot*); the ancients' custom (*minhag qadmonim* or *rishonim*); local customs, merchants' customs; customs of the country; and so on.[18]

Nowhere in Gaonic literature, however, do we find an explicit, as opposed to implicit, definition of a custom. In the literature of jurisprudence in general, a custom is defined as a practice or act, adhered to repeatedly out of an individual's or society's conviction that such is the proper course of action; it is binding in consequence of its very existence.[19] The characteristics of custom are the opposite of those of *taqqanah* listed above. First, "custom" denotes a course of action that existed generally prior to being so named; it reflects a solution adopted after the fact. Second, a custom is persistent, pertaining generally to limited, specific and, in particular, unpredictable problems. Third, "custom" is not necessarily opposed to talmudic law; sometimes it only reinforces and confirms the strict law when the latter is not firmly enforced, or when the aim is to decide between conflicting authorities. One manifestation of this tendency is the expression, "that is the law and that is the custom," quite common in Gaonic responsa (see below). Fourth, a custom is generally based on some prevalent popular practice or on a legal precedent issuing from the Gaonic courts. The nature of a custom precludes the formulation of procedural norms for its creation, though we do, very occasionally, read of criteria for the status and authority of a specific custom. Fifth, any custom is *ipso facto* assumed to be temporary in nature, hence its lower position on the scale of legal sources vis-à-vis *taqqanah*.[20]

---

[18] These types of *minhag* will be treated at length elsewhere.

[19] For a definition of *minhag* see R. Gavison, "Abolition of the *Mejelle* as a Source of Law" (Hebrew), *Mishpatim* 14 (1984): 333; for the problematic nature of the definition in the Gaonic literature see my "Custom as a Mediating Factor."

[20] On the difference between custom and enactment in the general literature of jurisprudence, see L. Fuller, "Human Interaction and the Law," in *The Rule of Law*, ed. R.P. Wolff (New York, 1971), 114; L. Hamstead, *Introduction to Jurisprudence*, 3d ed. (London, 1972), 572–85, 619–21; L.K. Allen, *Law in the Making*, 7th ed. (Oxford, 1964), 82. On the difference between these

We intend to show that the Geonim, when confronted with the exigencies of a changing reality, were inclined to prefer custom to other available legal tools. The legal system could absorb custom in a variety of ways and, as we have mentioned, there were also different categories of custom, which go beyond the limited scope of this article.

Custom and Precedent

As we have pointed out, a specific custom might be related to precedents issuing from the Gaonic courts, such precedents being the origins of various customs. There are several illustrations of this phenomenon in Gaonic literature. One particularly interesting example will be considered below—the practice of excommunicating an assailant until he appeases his victim. Another example is the injunction against the annulment of oaths: "It is not the custom in Israel to release any person from an oath." This derives from a ruling of Yehudai Gaon, touching on both vows and oaths. It is first mentioned, as a judicial ruling, by Pirqoi ben Baboi in the name of Yehudai Gaon: "And that is the law in practice, for litigants came before Rav Yehudai of blessed memory . . . and he told them, I am not competent to annul oaths and vows." Another, similarly phrased, reference appears in a responsum of Natronai Gaon: "For thus said Rav Yehudai Gaon of blessed memory, that we do not possess the power . . . to annul [lit., "to make an opening for"] an oath."[21] In later sources, however, the injunction is referred to as a custom. Thus, in the words of Sar Shalom Gaon: "For thus it was said in the name of Rav Yehudai . . . it is not the custom in Israel to release any person from an oath." Similarly, Hai Gaon writes, "Now Master Yehudai imposed a custom (*hinhig*) upon all the scholars . . . Neither we nor our ancestors will rule in connection with a person who has sworn an oath in the name of the God of Israel." Or, in another res-

---

sources in Gaonic law, see Brody, "Were the Geonim Legislators?" 280. Brody's conception of deliberately created *minhagim* is rather dubious, since occasional, random emergence is, in fact, a major characteristic of *minhagim* and their development does not depend upon the guiding hand of authority. Even a practice whose origin lies in legal precedent was not *a priori* intended to be a *minhag*. Brody includes the custom of administering the oath "I have no means" in this particular category; for my part, I am convinced that this oath was a practice that first gained popular acceptance and was only later confirmed by the Gaonic courts, which perhaps only accelerated its popularity; cf. my "Custom as a Mediating Factor."

[21] See S. Abramson, "On the Benediction over Annulment of Vows and Oaths" (Hebrew), *Sinai* 50 (1964): 185. For R. Natronai's responsum, see *Teshuvot ha-ge'onim: ḥemdah genuzah* (Jerusalem, 1863, repr. Jerusalem, 1968) (= *Ḥemdah genuzah*), no. 6, and parallels, *Oṣar ha-ge'onim*, ed. B.M. Lewin et al. (Jerusalem and Haifa, 1928–63), "Nedarim," nos. 48–51.

ponsum: "And it is not the custom in either academy or anywhere in Babylonia . . . so do not depart from the custom of the academies."[22]

Conversely, legal precedents not infrequently put the stamp of judicial approval on a course of action that had become accepted practice, thus representing an advanced stage in the formation of the custom in question.[23]

Custom and Interpretation of the Talmud

Although custom already acts as a determining factor in the establishment of law in the Talmud, it became more widely applied in the Gaonic period, especially in areas where talmudic law proper left a vacuum or did not render an explicit ruling. Thus, custom will interpret a passage of the Talmud or settle an amoraic dispute. For example, the Geonim of Sura ruled, in contrast to the Geonim of Pumbedita, on the talmudic controversy (bBava Meṣiʿa 67a) as to whether a creditor may benefit ("eat") from a pledge in return for diminishing the amount of the loan. Thus, we read in *Sefer ha-metivot*, in the name of Kohen-Ṣedek Gaon: "It is our custom to permit 'eating against deduction' as ruled by Ravina, and that was the custom in the time of Rav Simeon Qayyara."[24] Similarly, we read in *Sefer halakhot gedolot* that such was the accepted practice of the early authorities (*rishonim*; the term used there, however, is *maʿasim*, practice, rather than *minhag* as in the Gaonic literature). There were also Geonim, however, who opposed the practice.[25]

No less interesting is the occasional role of custom as a decisive factor

---

[22] For Sar Shalom Gaon's responsum see *Ḥemdah genuzah* no. 75; Hai Gaon: *Oṣar ha-geʾonim*, "Nedarim," nos. 51, 56; cf. ibid. nos. 60, 61, 63, 66. The source of the custom, originally a legal precedent, was the practice of the host society; see ibid., no. 67, and M.D. Herr, "Matters of Palestinian Halakha during the Sixth and Seventh Centuries C.E." (Hebrew), *Tarbiz* 49 (1980): 62. To my mind, the popularity and prevalence of oaths in Islam, in a slightly later period, provided an additional stimulus. There are numerous other examples of customs that originated in legal precedents.

[23] The difficult question of the relationship between custom and juridical decision has been discussed in the general literature as well; see Allen, *Law in the Making*, 120; A. Schiller, "Custom in Classical Roman Law," *Virginia Law Review* 24 (1938): 269, 274; H.F. Jolowicz, *Roman Foundations of Modern Law* (Oxford, 1957), 36.

[24] Isaac b. Abba Mari, *Sefer ha-ʿiṭṭur, apotiki*, ed. Meir Jonah (Warsaw, 1883; New York, 1956), 65a.

[25] *Halakhot gedolot*, ed. S.A. Traub (Tel Aviv, 1963), "Laws of Interest," 191 = ed. Hildesheimer (Berlin, 1870), 387: "And today it is common practice (*maʿasim she-ve-khol yom*) that such deduction is permitted. Early authorities (*rishonim*) would deduct four hundred *zuzim*." And see *Shaʿarei ṣedeq*, 36a, no. 12 and H. Soloveitchik, "An Analysis of the Provençal Mortgage Contract" (Hebrew), *Tarbiz* 41 (1972): pp. 318–19 and n. 15 ad loc.

in the formation of halakhah, sometimes dictating the "correct" interpretation of a talmudic text. In a responsum on whether the collection of a wife's marriage money takes precedence over that of an ordinary debt, we read, for example: "Thus we learn from our ancestors and our masters the Geonim, of blessed memory, and thus we are accustomed to do in connection with a wife's marriage money and a debtor: whosoever presents a deed with an earlier date than another person, his debt is collected first."[26] Here the "custom of the academy" not only decided the issue, but also rejected an opposing interpretation of Sar Shalom Gaon, according to which the woman should collect her due first, as the husband's property was considered collateral for her *ketubbah*.

The Geonim were similarly divided on the correct interpretation of the talmudic discussion of whether collection of a debt contrary to the above rule ("late debtor") should be allowed when proper procedure has been violated; Sherira Gaon interpreted the passage as meaning that such a measure was illegal ("what he has collected is as if not collected"), pointing out that such was the prevailing custom: "That is the law and thus do we conduct ourselves."[27] The power of custom to shape both the law and the correct interpretation of the Talmud, seen in both examples cited above in relation to the collection of debts, may well reflect certain problems that arose at the time in the economic sphere.

Although custom, as we have stated, already acted as a deciding factor in the Talmud itself, its similar role in the Gaonic period seems at times to reflect a heightened sensitivity to everyday life. We have already mentioned, for example, the legal precedent created by Yehudai Gaon in connection with absolution from vows and oaths, when he ruled according to the view of Rav Assi, who would not allow such absolution—despite the fact that Rav Assi's view was not considered legally binding.[28] Yehudai's usage in this respect fits into a general picture. In reaction to the prevalent disregard for oaths and vows during the Gaonic period—possibly under the influence of the non-Jewish environment in general, probably including Muslim practice—Jewish legal authorities made efforts to impose stricter rules in this sphere. Another example is Nahshon Gaon's ruling on the subject of wills written by healthy persons, where he upholds the

[26] *Sha'arei ṣedeq*, 89b, no. 80 (= *Oṣar ha-ge'onim*, "Ketubbot," no. 646). Sar Shalom (ibid.), however, held that the wife has precedence.

[27] *Oṣar ha-ge'onim*, "Ketubbot," no. 735. Other Geonim, however, such as Amram, Ṣemah and Nahshon, permitted a person who had thus illegally collected his debt to keep his money; see *Oṣar ha-ge'onim*, loc. cit., and also ibid., no. 739.

[28] See *Oṣar ha-ge'onim*, "Nedarim," no. 51, in a responsum of Hai.

view of Judah that the legator must bequeath his property with the words "from today and after death."[29] The Talmud, however (bBava Batra 136a; bGiṭṭin 72a), rules in favor of Yose, who invalidates this formula—in accordance with the general rule that, in any dispute between Judah and Yose, the latter's view is considered binding (bTa'anit 26b). Nahshon's usage found its way into the halakhic literature, reflecting the custom that actually prevailed.

When the Geonim based their interpretation of the talmudic text on custom, they were putting into practice Hai Gaon's view of custom as an exegetical instrument to be considered, together with tradition and consensus, even when it dictated a forced interpretation of talmudic law proper, as he explicitly writes in a responsum concerning the blowing of the shofar:

> And the greatest proof is: go out, see how the people conduct themselves; and that is the chief support. Only then do we examine everything that has been said in the Mishnah or the Gemara on that matter and what can be derived therefrom. If it can be explained as we wish, that is good. But if it contains a dissenting view, which can be neither explained nor supported by proof, this does not alter the chief ruling.[30]

Although in theory Hai Gaon does try to uphold the supremacy of the Talmud, in practice he allows custom such power that it essentially supplants talmudic law proper.

There emerges, therefore, a style of expansive, extremely free interpretation—of the kind capable of producing legal fictions—and it is sometimes difficult to decide just where custom ends and the art of interpretation begins.[31] It thus becomes possible to mitigate the clash between custom

---

[29] See Isaac Alfasi on bB.B. 136a; Isaac b. Abba Mari, *Sefer ha-'iṭṭur* 30d, rules in accordance with Nahshon's view, though the latter seems to be relying on a ruling cited in the Talmud (bGiṭṭ. 85b) counter to the view of Yose.

[30] *Oṣar ha-ge'onim*, "Rosh ha-Shanah," Responsa, p. 61; on this responsum see D. Rosenthal, "Rav Paltoi Gaon and his Place in the Halakhic Tradition" (Hebrew), *Shenaton ha-Mishpat ha-Ivri* 11–12 (1984–86): 624; Z. Groner, *The Legal Methodology of Rav Hai Gaon* (Chico, Calif., 1985), 16–17, 19; Ta-Shma, "Law, Custom and Tradition," 133. Hai's concern to stress the threefold sources of halakhah supporting his view may have been motivated by the Rabbanite-Karaite controversy; the appeal to popular consensus was a powerful weapon in the anti-Karaite struggle. I am indebted to M. Ben-Sasson for this last comment; in that connection see Ben-Sasson, "The Jewish Community of Medieval North Africa," 1:34.

[31] See Allen, *Law in the Making*, 126, 149–50; D. Even, "Desuetude" (Hebrew) (Ph.D. diss., The Hebrew University, 1977), 234 and the references cited ad loc. to Erlich and Main. In this connection one might well cite the comment of Israel Isserlein in *Terumat ha-deshen*, no. 242: "At any rate, it is preferable to find support in the words of the Sages and interpret them in accordance with logic and reason."

and the strict ruling of the Talmud, by reinterpreting the text and thus promoting the final acceptance of the practice in question as law.

The Geonim did not usually offer bold interpretations, involving far-reaching constructions and tacit assumptions, as one finds in the writings of other halakhic authorities throughout the generations. Nevertheless, such methods are not entirely absent in Gaonic responsa. Though they are indeed very rare, we do find attempts at what Haym Soloveitchik has called "harmonious assimilation"[32] or reinterpretation of various textual difficulties. To my mind, such expedients became necessary in order to overcome a clash with what had become accepted practice—custom, though rarely does the written material provide any indication to that effect. Hai himself had recourse to the above device, which enabled him to further the legitimation of various customs without explicitly naming them as the motive for his free interpretation.[33]

To conclude this section I refer to an example, which I have discussed elsewhere in a different context, where Hai uses an interpretative device to narrow the gap between a certain usage and the talmudic literature. The amoraim addressed themselves on various occasions to the question of whether a court concerned with the case of an impoverished debtor should institute "arrangement of assets" (*siddur nekhasim*); that is, make provisions to leave the debtor minimal means for his sustenance.[34] Most authorities, including the Geonim, ruled in favor of this measure;[35] but the question then arose whether the needs of the debtor's wife and children should also be considered. Almost all authorities ruled that "arrangement of assets" should not include the debtor's family; the sole exception in the halakhic literature is Hai Gaon, who ruled, both in a responsum and in his work *Mishpeṭei shevuʿot*, that the needs of the wife and children should

[32] H. Soloveitchik, *Pawnbroking*, 74.

[33] Elsewhere, however (*Oṣar ha-geʾonim*, "Pesaḥim," p. 125), we find Hai explicitly rejecting a reinterpretation of text in favor of prevailing custom: "One does not infer from generalizations to reject their practice." He states similarly with respect to the practice of administering an oath to women: "And though our Sages said that one infers from the verse, 'Hear out your fellow men,' an admonition to the judge not to listen to one litigant before the other's arrival, the fact is that we act thus because it is a highly beneficial practice"; see S. Assaf, *Teshuvot ha-geʾonim*, in *Maddaʿei ha-Yahadut* 2 (Jerusalem, 1927, repr. Jerusalem, 1970); no. 3. In connection with Hai's attitude to custom, see J. Katz, "The Evening Service at the Proper Time and at the Wrong Time," in *Halakhah and Kabbalah* (Hebrew) (Jerusalem, 1984), 190. For Sherira's method of settling conflicts between halakhah and practice, see ibid., 186, where Katz also considers the Tosafists' method of settling contradictions between the source and prevailing custom.

[34] See mArakh. 6:3–4 and mB.M. 9:13.

[35] See, e.g., *Nimmuqei yosef* on Alfasi, bB.M. 114a, ad *ashkeḥeih*: "And the Geonim ruled that arrangements are made. . . ." Cf. Alfasi, ibid., 113a and Maimonides, *Mishneh Torah*, "Hilkhot malveh ve-loveh," 1:7.

also be taken into account.[36] This ruling flies in the face of the tannaitic and talmudic sources; the Mishnah in tractate Arakhin and the *baraita* in bBava Meṣiʿa are quite explicit: "One allows him [= the debtor] food . . ., clothing . . ., *for himself; but not for his wife and children.*" Not surprisingly, Hai's ruling aroused considerable debate and was in fact finally rejected.[37]

To my mind, there is no doubt that Hai's exceptional opinion was inspired by the accepted practice in the Muslim law courts, as upheld by all the Sunnī legal schools; the wording of his ruling actually echoes that of the Muslim sources. In order to remain faithful to the relevant talmudic passages, while still making allowance for the needs of the debtor's dependents, Hai cites a passage from the Babylonian Talmud (bKetubbot 65b), which is not really relevant to our situation:

> And [the court] should allow him from his earnings his own needs and those of his household [= wife] and his small children, not yet six years old, for whose sustenance he is responsible; but not those of his older children, for we have learned: "Rav ʿUla taught. . . . Although they said that a man need not sustain his sons and daughters when they are small, he should sustain the smallest of the small. Till what age? Till they are six." The balance of his earnings is then given to the creditor.

Though we do not wish here to go into a thorough discussion of the talmudic material, it is clearly concerned with a case in which the talmudic law is quite explicit: the "arrangement of assets" for the debtor in question should not include his wife and children. In fact, though the Talmud clearly lays down the debtor's continuing responsibility for the payment of his wife's *ketubbah* (marriage money), it rules, just as explicitly, that the wife's needs are disregarded in connection with "arrangement of assets." To my mind, Hai appeals to ʿUla's homily, which draws a distinction between "small" children and the "smallest of the small," in order to justify the accepted practice of his time, which dictated consideration for the needs of the family, including the debtor's children; only thus can he smooth over the clash between custom and the text of the Talmud. I believe this to be an illustration of Hai's use of custom on an exegetical plane, though he himself does not mention custom but seeks to incorporate his innovation smoothly into the talmudic discussion.

---

[36] For Hai's responsum see A.A. Harkavy, *Teshuvot ha-ge'onim: zikhron la-rishonim ve-gam la-aḥaronim*, vol. 1 (Berlin, 1887), no. 182; *Mishpeṭei shevuʿot* (Venice, 1602), 20.

[37] See G. Libson, "Legal Status of the Jewish Woman in the Gaonic Period: Overt and Covert Muslim Influence," in *The Jews of Islamic Lands (an International Conference)*, ed. J. Lassner (Detroit: Wayne State University) [in press].

Interchanged Usage of "Custom" and Taqqanah

Despite the differences we have indicated between *taqqanah* and custom, the distinction between the two concepts as understood in the Gaonic period and the relationship between them present twofold difficulties: linguistic-semantic and juristic; we shall discuss each of these in turn.

In the linguistic-semantic arena, we find that the Geonim frequently use the term *taqqanah* rather imprecisely, meaning a judicial remedy or solution to a problem, rather than a *taqqanah* ("enactment") in the strict sense of the word. Thus, we have such phrases as "If there is a *taqqanah* (= remedy, repair) for this matter," or "to explain to you what the *taqqanah* is" (i.e., what can be done to remedy the situation).[38] Moreover, the terms *taqqanah* and *minhag* are sometimes used interchangeably in Gaonic responsa; this usage may well have more than linguistic-semantic significance, perhaps implying a tendency to equate treatment of the two sources.[39]

Some support for this conjecture may be derived from the use of the term *minhagot* (rather than *taqqanot*) in Gaonic writings, particularly by Sherira and Hai, as a general expression for rulings issued by Gaonic circles. We have already cited Hai's letter concerning the position of the academy, in which he refers to the *minhagot* of the Sanhedrin;[40] in a responsum on the subject of testimony he writes, "And thus we have heard in all courts in all generations of whose *minhagot* we have heard."[41] A similar locution may be found in Sherira's responsum concerning the

---

[38] *Ḥemdah genuzah*, no. 37; *Sha'arei ṣedeq*, 9b, no. 3. Cf. Assaf, *Teshuvot ha-ge'onim*, nos. 3, 116; J. Mueller ed., *Ge'onei mizraḥ u-ma'arav* (Berlin, 1888), no. 24 and passim.

[39] See, e.g., Hai's responsum (Harkavy, *Teshuvot ha-ge'onim*, no. 335) concerning the revocation of a declaration of protest (*moda'ah*) and Sherira's responsum (*Sha'arei ṣedeq*, 15b, no. 30) on the question of whether an agent may appoint a second agent. Cf. Maimonides, *Mishneh Torah*, "Hilkhot mamrim," 2:2, 6:2. Elon also discusses the interchangeability of these terms; see *Jewish Law*, 2:404, p. 714 n. 6. Groner, however, asserts that Hai clearly distinguishes the two concepts; see "R. Hai Gaon," 139. One sometimes finds the reverse situation, with a well-documented Gaonic *taqqanah* being referred to as a *minhag*. See, e.g., Isaac b. Reuben's comment (*Sha'arei shevu'ot*, chap. 13), on the *taqqanah* of chattels: "The Geonim and all the Heads of the academies agreed to institute this *minhag* as a permanent measure." And see the comment by Z.M. Rabinowitz, "Sefer ha-ma'asim li-venei ereṣ yisra'el," *Tarbiz* 41 (1972): 301 and cf. ibid., 281, where a woman is awarded cash rather than land, in order to prevent landed property leaving the family—it follows that chattels were considered legitimate payment for a woman's *ketubbah* long before the Gaonic period, albeit for a different reason. Maimonides, however, understands the Gaonic *taqqanah* as contrary to custom; see *Mishneh Torah*, "Hilkhot ishut," 14:14. Cf. Menaḥem Meiri, *Commentary on Ketubbot*, ed. A. Sofer (Jerusalem, 1968), 270.

[40] See above, n. 8.

[41] Assaf, *Teshuvot ha-ge'onim*, no. 110.

wording of the *ketubbah*: "... concerning your actions in accordance with our *minhagot* and our Talmud."[42]

There is a passage in Sherira's account of the period of persecution that would also seem to corroborate the tendency to equate the two sources; the term *minhag* in this text, however, possesses a different sense and the passage proves to be irrelevant to our point.[43] In another responsum, however, touching on the distinction between what appear to be two different types of prophetic enactment, *yesod* and *minhag*, he is evidently making a distinction between *taqqanah* and *minhag*: "A *yesod* of the prophets is something that they enacted for all Israel to act accordingly and established it for them; while a *minhag* of the prophets is something that they were accustomed to do without proper enactment and establishment."[44]

The confusion that reigns in the juristic area is related in part to the linguistic-semantic aspect already discussed, primarily in a broader context; namely, the tendency of later authorities to refer to Gaonic rulings and legal decisions by such terms as *taqqanah*, *gezerah* or *haskamah*, although the rulings in question may be unquestionably rooted in custom.[45] Such instances may well testify to a gradual transition from custom to *taqqanah*, not attributable to a formal act but to a transformation which ultimately conferred *taqqanah* status on a custom when the latter had gained universal acceptance. The first signs of such transitions were already obvious in the Gaonic period; but they were to become most prevalent in later times.[46]

A prominent example of such a transformation in the status of a Gaonic legal norm occurs in connection with the excommunication of an assailant until he appeases the injured party. The practice makes its first

---

[42] *Oṣar ha-ge'onim*, "Ketubbot," no. 121. Maimonides also frequently uses the word *minhagot*; see: Introduction to the *Mishneh Torah*, *Sefer ha-Madda'*, ed. S. Lieberman (Jerusalem, 1964), 9; *Mishneh Torah* (standard editions), "Hilkhot mamrim," 1:1; "Hilkhot ishut," 14:14; "Hilkhot sanhedrin," 21:5. That is, possibly, why Maimonides treats *taqqanot*, *gezerot* and *minhagot* in the same context; see, e.g., "Hilkhot mamrim," 2:2, 6:5. Abraham b. David of Posquières also writes (*Temim De'im*, no. 51): "They adjudicate according to the *minhagot*," but he is referring there to gentile law courts. Sometimes, however, it is clear that the word did actually denote customs; see, e.g., *Oṣar ha-ge'onim*, "Pesaḥim," p. 161 and passim.

[43] See *Iggeret rav sherira ga'on* (French version), 99: "And they were unable to hold study sessions and establish academies and institute *minhagei* on behalf of the Gaonate."

[44] J. Mueller, *Halakhot pesuqot min ha-ge'onim* (Cracow, 1883, repr. Jerusalem, 1963), no. 180, and, somewhat differently worded, *Sha'arei teshuvah*, no. 307; cf. Groner, "R. Hai Gaon," 136 and Elon, *Jewish Law*, 2:721.

[45] See Shochetman, "The Methodology of Ascertaining Geonic Enactments," p. 659 and n. 19.

[46] See, e.g., a Gaonic responsum in *Sha'arei ṣedeq*, 52b, no. 48 and cf. the responsum ibid., 51a, no. 37. See Shochetman, ibid., 660.

appearance in a precedent issuing from the circles of Zadok, as reported by Ṣemaḥ Gaon. It is subsequently referred to as "*minhag*,"[47] and finally, in the writings of the last Geonim, as a "*taqqanah*." This is explicitly attributed to Sherira and Hai: "Thenceforth, the last scholars and heads of the academies, whenever they feared a substantial loss [to the injured party]—since fines cannot be collected—instituted a *taqqanah*, that the assailant be excommunicated until he appeases the injured party."[48] Similarly: "For the Geonim enacted (*takinu*) that the assailant must compensate the injured party according to the limits set by our Sages."[49]

As we have stated, this tendency to regard Gaonic customs as *taqqanot* occurs frequently in the later sources.[50] Indeed, several Gaonic norms generally referred to as *taqqanot* actually began life as customs; and it is not improbable that the two reliably documented *taqqanot* mentioned above were originally customs. I would suggest that this terminological shift was not merely semantic or due to misunderstanding; it may well represent a major development, whereby certain legal norms, originally of a temporary and occasional nature, were considered in later generations to assume proper halakhic authority, as if they were *bona fide taqqanot*.[51] If this is true, the transition from custom to *taqqanah* is due not only to the wide dissemination and acceptance of a practice—which are of course necessary conditions for its very recognition as a custom—but also to the chronological dimension, that is, the time elapsed from its beginnings as a custom. In historical perspective, the practice in question assumes the validity

---

[47] See *Oṣar ha-ge'onim*, "Bava Qama," no. 192 (= ibid., "Ketubbot," no. 260), and another responsum ibid., "Ketubbot," no. 264. A responsum of Natronai, however, reporting the case, makes no mention of *minhag*; see ibid., "Bava Qama," no. 192.

[48] *Oṣar ha-ge'onim*, "Ketubbot," no. 267 = ibid., "Bava Qama," no. 188.

[49] Ibid., "Ketubbot," 267 = ibid., "Bava Qama," no. 188. Maimonides, however, continues to refer to the practice as a custom; see *Mishneh Torah*, "Hilkhot sanhedrin," 5:17: "The custom of the academies abroad . . . is that they excommunicate him until he pacifies the plaintiff." This *taqqanah*/*minhag* was subjected to modifications both in content and in scope; we shall discuss them elsewhere.

[50] See Maimonides, *Mishneh Torah*, "Hilkhot sheluḥin ve-shuttafin," 3:11—*ḥerem setam*; "Hilkhot malveh ve-loveh," 2:2, 4; 14:12; 22:10—the oath "I have no means"; and cf. Isaac Alfasi's responsum in Assaf, *Teshuvot ha-ge'onim*, no. 131. Joseph Ibn Migash, *Sefer ha-Terumot*, chap. 43, pt. 1, no. 13—power of attorney; *Teshuvot rashbash*, no. 511—excommunication of an assailant until he pacifies the injured party; Ibn Migash, ibid., and Maimonides, "Hilkhot sheluḥin ve-shuttafin," 7:11—power of attorney by acquisition of four cubits of land.

[51] See Fuller, "Human Interaction and the Law," who discusses the difference between law and custom and states that, once a custom has become universal, it has in fact taken on one of the characteristics of a law. W.S. Salmond, *On Jurisprudence*, 11th ed. (London, 1957), 223, also writes that the fact that a given norm has received the sanction of custom implies that it is worthy of receiving legal sanction, so that custom is, in fact a hallmark of national recognition. See also Allen, *Law in the Making*; Hamstead, *Introduction to Jurisprudence*.

of a *taqqanah*, and the authorities in whose lifetime it emerged are considered to have instituted it accordingly.

From the point of view of jurisprudence, perhaps the transition from "custom" to *taqqanah* indicates a preference on the part of jurists to base legal norms on formally established, written laws, albeit artificially conceived, rather than continue to appeal to the independent status of custom, which was deemed to be a weaker source. In any case, of course, the very consideration of dissemination and prevalence as the definitive criterion for acceptance of a custom, sometimes even for its definition as a *taqqanah* in later sources, implies a certain tendency to equate its status with that of *taqqanah*, since the ultimate test for the authority of the latter is similar—mere enactment of a *taqqanah* does not guarantee its future acceptance and validity.[52]

The Gaonic Attitude to Custom

Although, as we have seen, it is often difficult to decide whether the words "custom" and *taqqanah* are being used in their precise technical senses, we must nevertheless assume a general marked distinction in the Gaonic use of these terms. It is therefore pertinent to ask why the Geonim appealed to custom in some situations and to *taqqanah* in others, despite the fact that both sources served the same purpose in dealing with a given reality, generally aiming at the achievement of greater lenience rather than severity. If we work on the virtually undeniable assumption that Geonim did distinguish between the two sources, it is a fact that they enacted only a very small number of *taqqanot*—only two, if we limit ourselves to the most reliably documented instances. By contrast, they made broad use of custom in their legal activities. We have already indicated the interpretational difficulties encountered by the Geonim in their enactment of *taqqanot*. It would appear that these difficulties and the obstacles involved in the application of the Gaonic *taqqanot* weakened the position of this legal source and forced it into decline.

The prevalence and force of custom during the Gaonic period does not represent a deliberate preference for one legal source over another, but the outcome of immanent processes, not always controllable by halakhic

[52] See, e.g., Maimonides, *Mishneh Torah*, "Hilkhot malveh ve-loveh," end of chap. 11; "Hilkhot nizqei mammon," 8:12; "Hilkhot ishut," 16:7, 4:14. Cf. Shochetman, "The Methodology of Ascertaining Geonic Enactments," 684; Schepanski, "The Taqqanot of the Geonim," 139.

scholars. Indeed, by definition, custom is created at the grass roots level, a reflection of human needs combined with elements of imitation, beyond any considerations of logic or utility. The dissemination of any specific custom is accelerated by informal processes, such as the individual's feeling of obligation to adapt his or her behavior to accepted social norms.

Elsewhere I coined the terms "borrowed custom" and "responsive custom."[53] By "borrowed custom" I mean the many Gaonic customs that were borrowed from the legal environment, their main characteristic being that they emerged from current practice and were not imposed from above by the Geonim. "Responsive custom," in contrast, has its origins in the Gaonic courts and is far more similar to a *taqqanah*. It was such processes that allowed many Muslim laws, representing the prevailing practice of the environment, to enter the Gaonic world of halakhah. Many customs sanctioned by the Geonim, therefore—both "borrowed" and "responsive"—largely reflect the society in which they lived and acted.

Although, as we have intimated, the Geonim did not initiate the adoption or absorption of a specific *minhag*, they undoubtedly deemed it their task to regulate and control the process, supervising the development and consolidation of such originally informal practices by virtue of their authority as the recognized interpreters of Jewish law. We do not wish to dwell here on the various considerations that guided Gaonic decisions in such matters. Suffice it to say that the Geonim sometimes fully recognized the growing encroachment of reality on halakhic territory and often actually allowed everyday needs to supersede the dictates of formal law. They might do so, in particular, when they felt themselves powerless to invalidate or eradicate a specific custom, or that any attempt to do so might adversely affect their authority, engendering tension and controversy.

Such motives could be subsumed under the heading of the public good. Thus, for example, Sherira and Hai permit a judge to consult with a litigant concerning the latter's plea against his wife, contrary to the Rabbinic interpretation of the verse, "Hear out your fellow men . . ." (Deuteronomy 1:16): "We infer from the words of the Torah an injunction upon the judge not to hear the words of one litigant before he hears the other."[54] The reason for disregarding talmudic law and adopting the deviant practice as a custom was the fear that the wife's honor might be compromised by appearing in a public place: "But in accordance with this principle, which is highly beneficial, one acts thus." Elsewhere Hai cites the consideration,

---

[53] Libson, "Custom as a Mediating Factor."

[54] See Assaf, *Teshuvot ha-ge'onim*, no. 3 and my comments in this connection above.

"lest they come to quarrel among themselves" as justification for the acceptance of a custom, despite his disapproval of it.[55] He gives a similar explanation for the Gaonic dispensation allowing litigants and witnesses to remain seated during legal proceedings: "Perhaps it was considered beneficial not to discriminate between a scholar and his fellow man, that the matter should not be put to the test."[56] Incidentally, Maimonides expresses a similar sentiment with respect to this Gaonic innovation: "For it is not within our power to uphold the authentic religious law."[57] This admission strikingly illustrates the tug-of-war between reality and halakhah; moreover, it complements Maimonides' statement in the Introduction to the *Mishneh Torah* concerning the relationship between the geographical dispersal of Jewish communities and the emergence of different customs.[58]

In connection with the attitude of the Geonim to custom in general, there are three questions to be considered: their willingness to use custom as a legal source in general; their attitude to specific local customs that deviated from those of the academies; and their readiness to impose the custom of the academies (essentially another aspect of the second question). We cannot go into a comprehensive discussion of all these questions, but limit ourselves here to the first—the willingness of the Geonim to use custom as a legal source. As a rule, the Geonim do not take a uniform stand on this question; their views were largely shaped by the times in which they lived and by their consideration of other sources of law, such as the Talmud itself and oral traditions.

It is not surprising that the earlier Geonim, as far as we know, almost never appeal to custom. Later representatives of the period, however, refer to it repeatedly, perhaps because different customs had already crystallized by then. In some cases we can even trace the stages in the evolution from a mere practice or legal precedent to an accepted custom, one example being the excommunication of assailants mentioned previously. Nevertheless, it is clear that, for some of the Geonim, the theoretical, legal element was decisive in governing Gaonic attitudes to custom.

In this connection it is striking that Saadya Gaon makes almost no reference to custom among his legal sources, despite the fact that the concept was certainly current among the earlier Sura Geonim, such as Zadok, Shalom and Natronai, particularly—but not exclusively—in the phrase "the

---

55 See, e.g., Harkavy, *Teshuvot ha-ge'onim*, no. 208; Groner, "R. Hai Gaon," 157.

56 Assaf, *Teshuvot ha-ge'onim*, no. 110.

57 Maimonides, *Mishneh Torah*, "Hilkhot sanhedrin," 21:5.

58 Cf. my discussion of this point in my "Custom as a Mediating Factor."

custom of the two academies."[59] Though other Sura Geonim, such as Samuel ben Hophni, made scant use of custom, they do occasionally mention it,[60] while Saadya almost completely avoids the term in his responsa, preferring such locutions as "this is the law," "as dictated by the proper law," "this is the proper situation according to the law and no changes should be made," and so on.[61] These expressions are by no means stylistic peculiarities, but indicate rather Saadya's individual, specific preference for halakhah over *minhag*.[62]

Saadya's rejection of the use of *minhag* is also evident from his attempt to renew the line of oral tradition. As he writes in *Sefer ha-galuy*:

> . . . And I have set down . . . when the Talmud was finalized. Now these (texts) in their entirety were transmitted orally without break until the time that they were fixed (in writing). I was motivated (to elaborate a chronology) because I found that

---

[59] For Sar Shalom's use of *minhag* see S. Weinberg, *Responsa of Rab Sar Shalom Gaon* (Jerusalem, 1976), nos. 24, 25, 26, 45, 59, 103, 118, 123. On the extent of Natronai's use of *minhag* see R. Brody, "The Halakhic Responsa of Rav Natronai bar Hilai Gaon" (Hebrew) (Ph.D. diss., The Hebrew University, 1981), pt. 5, p. 46; he discusses the types of *minhagim* used by Natronai, the different reasons in each case and Natronai's flexibility in relation to local customs.

[60] Samuel b. Hophni is mentioned as appealing to *minhag* in a responsum in *Oṣar ha-ge'onim*, "Giṭṭin," no. 291. Only rarely does he refer to the "custom of the academies"; see, e.g., ibid., "Ta'anit," no. 71. This attitude may be due to his reliance on legal tradition, on the one hand, and to legal logic and reason, on the other. It is quite possible that Saadya Gaon's position on the subject also influenced Samuel b. Hophni.

[61] I have counted some twenty such turns of phrase; see J. Mueller, *Sifrei rav saadya gaon*, vol. 9 (Paris, 1897, repr. Jerusalem, 1968), 88–89, 93, 97, 100, 104, 109, 112, 117–19, 123, 126, 129–30, 138–39.

[62] The exceptional cases in which Saadya does refer to *minhag* are readily explained. Thus, in one responsum (Mueller, p. 99), he writes: "No departure should be made from the custom. . . . For the law in [matters of] *ketubbot* is like the custom of the land, as she marries him in keeping with that custom." Here Saadya is adhering to custom because the Mishnah (Ketub. 6:4) appeals directly to custom. He presumably did so whenever the talmudic sages similarly rely directly upon custom. Thus, Saadya relies upon custom twice in *Sefer ha-sheṭarot*—again in connection with *ketubbot*—following the talmudic argument in bB.M. 104b; see M. Ben-Sasson, "Fragments from Saadya's *Sefer ha-Edut ve-ha-Sheṭarot*" (Hebrew), *Shenaton ha-Mishpat ha-Ivri* 11–12 (1984–86): 221–22. On another occasion, Saadya prescribes adherence to ancestral custom (*minhag avot*); see M. Zucker, *A Critique Against the Writings of R. Saadya Gaon by R. Mubashshir Halevi* (Hebrew) (New York, 1955), 102. Cf. also idem, "From R. Saadiah Gaon's Commentary on the Torah" (Hebrew), *Sura* 2 (1955–1956): 314; but ancestral customs constitute a separate category in the context of Saadya's treatment of legal sources, as we shall see later. Another relevant passage may be found in A. Karlin, "Halakhah and Law in the Teaching of R. Saadiah Gaon" (Hebrew), in *Saadiah Anniversary Volume* (Jerusalem, 1943), 435, citing from *Sha'arei ṣedeq*, 63a, no. 35: "And one should not change these customs in any way." The text, however, is corrupt and the original printed text reads: "And one should not change these *matters*" (not *minhagim* but *'inyanim*). In *Mishpeṭei shevu'ot* Isaac b. Reuben attributes to Saadya a reference to *minhag* in connection with the "shifted" oath: "The ban shall be finalized in keeping with the custom." But here again, the source does not refer to custom; see S. Abramson, *'Inyanot be-sifrut ha-ge'onim* (Jerusalem, 1974), 63. Finally, there is indeed a responsum attributed to Saadya in which he justifies *suftaja* (signature with a particular sign) by stating that the device is in general use. The attribu-

> those known today as "rabbis" are ignorant of these matters and do not (actually) follow the ways of their ancestors, whom they cite and upon whom they rely.[63]

What was the reason for Saadya's stand on custom? A natural suggestion might be that, having emigrated to Iraq from Egypt, he was unfamiliar with the tradition of the academies and therefore does not refer to their customs. I believe, however, that his attitude was more a matter of principle: it should be traced to his unrelenting war against the Karaites and his view that the law derives "from the Torah and the Prophets and the Mishnah and the Talmud," as he points out in one responsum.[64] That is why Saadya lays special emphasis on oral tradition (and ancestral custom), trying whenever possible to link talmudic law to the Bible, even when there is no source to that effect.[65]

Though the laws of preemption (abutters' rights; *mazranut*), for example, are a late development, mentioned only in the Babylonian Talmud, Saadya traces them to the Bible; he does the same for *ḥerem setam* ("anonymous ban")—also an exclusively Gaonic practice.[66] And perhaps his literary innovation, the composition of halakhic monographs, is also related to his objective of reinforcing talmudic law proper, preserving halakhic tradition and, seemingly, rejecting custom.

In contrast to the late Sura Geonim, the last Geonim to officiate at Pumbedita, Sherira and Hai, assign to custom a prominent and far-reaching role. Hai is particularly at pains to broaden the application of *minhag*,

---

tion, however, is by no means certain and even if the author was Saadya, it touches on the limited area of commerce and, in fact, does not explicitly use the word "custom"; see Libson, "Custom as a Mediating Factor." Saadya's rejection of custom as a legal source is so thorough that he does not even mention it in response to an explicit question on the subject; see *Shaʿarei ṣedeq*, 74b, no. 13.

[63] A. Harkavy, *Ha-sarid ve-ha-paliṭ me-sefer ha-egron ve-sefer ha-galuy le-rav seʿadyah gaʾon* (St. Petersburg, 1882), 152. See also M. Zucker, "Fragments of the Kitāb Taḥsīl al-Sharāʾiʿ al-Samāʿīyah" (Hebrew), *Tarbiz* 41 (1972): 446. On the juxtaposition of custom and authentic tradition see D. Sklare, "The Religious and Legal Thought of Samuel ben Ḥofni Gaon: Texts and Studies in Cultural History" (Ph.D. diss., Harvard University, 1992), 1:68.

[64] Mueller, *Geʾonei mizraḥ u-maʿarav*, no. 22 (= Mueller, *Sifrei rav seʿadyah gaon*, 129).

[65] Cf. M. Zucker, *Saadya's Commentary on Genesis* (Hebrew) (New York, 1984), 14: "Inspired by his objective of strengthening the ties between prophetic lore and the teachings of our Sages, the Gaon endeavored to create a halakhic-talmudic foundation for the stories of the Torah, even when there was no suitable source in the talmudic-midrashic literature." Saadya's reluctance to appeal to legal analogy may have been similarly motivated; see Zucker, "Fragments," 375, who cites Japheth b. Eli: "There are few who reject analogy in matters of law, and one of them is al-Fayyūmī."

[66] Concerning pre-emption see Zucker, "Fragments"; on *ḥerem setam* see G. Libson, "*Gezerta* and *Ḥerem Setam* in the Gaonic and Early Medieval Periods" (Hebrew) (Ph.D. diss., The Hebrew University, 1979), 96, 205. And cf. the comment by B. Lifshitz, "Evolution of the Court-Oath with Imprecation" (Hebrew), *Shenaton ha-Mishpat ha-Ivri* 11–12 (1984–86): 394ff.

though he does strive to avoid any contradiction of or deviation from strict talmudic law.[67] Hai is generally faithful to these restrictive principles, though he does show his preference upon occasion for custom over other legal sources. Moreover, as we have seen,[68] he will also sometimes employ interpretative means in order to adapt a "custom" to talmudic sources, thus justifying it without actually terming it a "custom."

Whatever the situation in practice, in legal theory custom is generally placed on a relatively low level on the scale of legal sources; indeed, a reference to custom is generally an indication that a certain practice has gained acceptance via a nonstandard process, not in accordance with the natural evolution of talmudic law, that is, normative exegesis and theoretical study of the sources. Custom, as it were, signifies that the needs of reality dictated some temporary measure, or a radical new departure in the evolution of halakhah. The acceptance of a practice by force of custom is therefore doubly significant. On the one hand, the new practice is indeed absorbed into the world of halakhah; on the other, the halakhic innovation involved is identified by its very designation as custom, thus permitting the Geonim and later authorities to single it out, keeping it apart from the "pure" theoretical foundations of Jewish law. Thus, custom is generally considered somewhat extraneous to halakhah. The development is, therefore, somewhat paradoxical: the ostensibly weak legal status or temporariness of a custom makes it easier for halakhah to absorb and accept it, even at the cost of yielding on certain points of principle. One might say that the apparent ease with which a custom can be abolished provides a safety valve that can be opened wide whenever the need arises.

Halakhah ("Law") and Custom

At this point, I believe it is worthwhile to amplify our previous cursory mention of the relationship between law and custom. We have already pointed out the relationship between halakhah proper and custom, where custom frequently confirms an existing law or decides between conflicting views.[69] This situation is frequently indicated by the common Gaonic expression "that is the law and that is the custom" or vice versa. We find this phrase, for example, used by Paltoi in connection with the duty of a

[67] On *minhag* in Hai's legal system see Groner, "R. Hai Gaon," 115ff.
[68] See above, n. 33 and text ad loc.
[69] See above, n. 19 and text ad loc.

husband in conflict with his wife to divorce her and pay her *ketubbah*,[70] and by Natronai in relation to testimony of relatives in a deed ("that is the law and that is the custom, that any deed containing testimony of relatives, if two competent witnesses can be added, is valid").[71] We find similar wording in a responsum of Mattityah[72] and in a ruling of Sherira regarding the mandate of an agent to appoint another agent in matters of divorce: "And thus it was customary (*nahagin*) . . . and that is the law."[73] Hai, discussing the wording of the benediction of betrothal, writes: "[It would befit] you to restore the law and our custom in accordance with general consensus."[74] Elsewhere Hai appeals to custom in connection with the familiar rule, accepted by all Geonim, that the law should be decided in accordance with the last version cited in the Talmud; this despite the fact that the rule itself would have been quite sufficient without appealing to custom: "In the matter of two versions, . . . [the law is according to the last version] and our custom too is according to the last version."[75] Similarly, in an anonymous Gaonic responsum, concerning the rule that a woman collecting her *ketubbah* should be treated as a debtor, we read: "That is the custom . . . and that is the law."[76] Only rarely do we find the term "law" (*halakhah*) used in opposition to "custom" (*minhag*), as in "that is the law, but the custom of the two academies. . . ."[77] In all these examples, there is an appeal to custom so as to reinforce the law where the latter reflects tradition or, sometimes, consensus; it may occasionally represent a wish that the practice indeed be followed.

---

70 See *Oṣar ha-ge'onim*, "Ketubbot," no. 474.

71 *Ḥemdah genuzah*, no. 79 (= *Oṣar ha-ge'onim*, "Sanhedrin," no. 170). This actually seems to have been accepted practice; see Harkavy, *Teshuvot ha-ge'onim*, no. 42; Assaf, *Teshuvot ha-ge'onim*, no. 8; L. Ginzberg, *Geonica*, 2:139.

72 *Oṣar ha-ge'onim*, "Mashkin," no. 102.

73 *Sha'arei ṣedeq*, 15b, no. 30 (= *Oṣar ha-ge'onim*, "Giṭṭin," no. 112).

74 *Oṣar ha-ge'onim*, "Ketubbot," no. 71. Cf. also Natronai Gaon's responsum concerning the bridegroom's benediction where he uses a similar phrase: "That is the custom and thus is the practice in both academies"; see *Ginzei qedem* 4:101; L. Ginzberg, *Genizah Studies in Memory of Doctor Solomon Schechter* (New York, 1929), 2:106 = *Oṣar ha-ge'onim*, "Ketubbot," no. 62. And cf. the wording in Isaac b. Abba Mari, *Sefer ha-'iṭṭur*, III, 63c. In a parallel, however, cited in Nahshon's name, we read only, "and that is the custom"; see *Sha'arei ṣedeq*, 19b, no. 14.

75 S. Assaf, *Gaonic Responsa from the Genizah* (Hebrew) (Jerusalem, 1942), 45, as completed by Assaf. Custom is also added as a justification in another responsum, relating to the proper decision of halakhah; see Groner, "R. Hai Gaon," 43, 146.

76 *Oṣar ha-ge'onim*, "Ketubbot," no. 806; cf. ibid., "Pesaḥim," no. 335.

77 See *Oṣar ha-ge'onim*, "Ketubbot," no. 134. A similar tendency to combine tradition and practice may be found in Muslim jurisprudence; see, e.g., J. Schacht, *The Origins of Muhammadan Jurisprudence* (Oxford, 1950), 63, 68. Cf. also the comment by J. Wansbrough, *Quranic Studies* (Oxford, 1977), 57, 200.

Custom, Tradition and Consensus

The ostensible weakness of custom as a legal source is balanced by frequent efforts to trace a specific custom, on the one hand, to halakhic tradition, and, on the other, to the consensus of public opinion, that is, its degree of general acceptance. In the first case custom assumes a historical dimension, in the second, a geographical one.

Evidence of this "triangle"—custom, tradition, consensus—is quite frequent in Gaonic writings. Hai, for example, in his responsum concerning the blowing of the shofar,[78] refers to all three elements: "an inheritance handed down" (= tradition); "the words of the many are the proof for every Mishnah and every Gemara" (= consensus); "and the greatest proof is: go out, see how the people conduct themselves" (= custom). A similar definition is offered in Nissim Gaon's *Megillat setarim*:[79] *naql muttaṣil mutasalsil ʿalā ʿaṣr al-nabī ʿalay(hi) al-salām* ("a tradition, continuous and handed down [literally: descending by a chain] since the time of the prophet [= Moses] of blessed memory"). Incidentally, this passage indicates that the Hebrew word *mishtalshelet* used by Hai in the above-mentioned responsum derives from the Arabic *mutasalsil*, confirming our understanding of its meaning as "handed down."[80]

1. *Custom and Tradition*

The element of tradition[81] is frequently stressed, as early as Pirqoi ben Baboi, and later by Ṣemah in his responsum to Eldad Ha-Dani;[82] similar references are made by Saadya and Samuel ben Hophni.[83] Even Hai, whose attitude to the various legal sources is far more balanced, rejects the prin-

[78] See above, n. 30 and the text ad loc.

[79] S. Abramson, *Rav Nissim Gaon* (Hebrew) (Jerusalem, 1965), 354.

[80] This interpretation was originally suggested by A.D. Rosenthal, as reported by D. Rosenthal, "Rav Paltoi Gaon," p. 624 n. 214. Cf. the expression "chain of wisdom and prophecy," as used by Ṣemah in a responsum addressed to a group representing Eldad Ha-Dani; see A. Epstein, *Kitvei rav avraham epstein* (Jerusalem, 1950), 1:37, 40.

[81] On tradition as a legal source see Maimonides, *Mishneh Torah*, "Hilkhot mamrim," 1:2; cf. Elon, *Jewish Law*, 1:221. Non-Jewish legal systems, too, stipulate that a custom be practiced "from time immemorial" as a prerequisite for its acceptance; see H.F. Jolowicz, *Lectures on Jurisprudence* (London, 1963), 208. On the special status of an ancient custom in Jewish law see J. Roth, *The Halakhic Process* (New York, 1986), 212.

[82] For Pirqoi see Spiegel, "On the Polemic of Pirkoi b. Baboi." For Eldad ha-Dani, see A. Epstein, *Kitvei rav avraham epstein*, 1:37.

[83] As we have indicated, Saadya's propensity for this emphasis is probably a result of his reluctance to appeal to custom. As to Samuel b. Hophni, see Sklare, "Samuel ben Ḥofni," 1:241; 2:16, 61, and esp., 64.

ciple of exegesis in favor of tradition, as in connection with the exemption of a master who has injured his slave.[84] While it is true that, as a rule, custom is cited as a proof of tradition, I believe that the desire to justify and legitimize prevailing custom led the Geonim to stress, on the one hand, its antiquity, and, on the other, its derivation from a reliable tradition. These two aspects are essentially two sides of the same coin; so much so that on occasion the difference between custom and tradition is obscured and the two are interchanged or even combined. In such cases, one might even say that the distinction between the two types of source is merely semantic rather than one of substance, making it difficult to determine which derives from the other.

Another instructive instance of a link between custom and tradition concerns the rights of a creditor in the case of an absentee debtor. The discussion is based on a passage in the Babylonian Talmud, Ketubbot 88a. According to Gaonic tradition, first reported by Amram Gaon, the rule that, in such a situation, the creditor may take the oath and collect his debt is not applicable to any absentee debtor, but only to a debtor who fled after the case had been decided or who defied the court. Hai touches on this question in several responsa, in one of which he bases his ruling on tradition: "The ruling laid down by Rav Amram, though not mentioned explicitly in the Gemara, is considered accepted tradition."[85] In another responsum, however, he refers to the same practice as a custom: "Such is the practice of our courts as a custom."[86] In the matter of absentee debtors, therefore, we again find Hai conjoining tradition and custom in order to justify the law; here, however, in contrast to his shofar responsum, he does so in two different responsa, seemingly using the two terms interchangeably and blurring the difference between them. The element of "practicality" in the custom/tradition of collecting a debt from an absent person is quite prominent in Hai's responsa.[87] Although it seems reasonable to assume here that the tradition does not derive from the custom but is being cited as a source for the latter, this responsum does not provide

---

[84] *Oṣar ha-ge'onim*, "Bava Qama," 28. Cf. also his important comments on the subject of a promiscuous unmarried woman, Harkavy, *Teshuvot ha-ge'onim*, no. 228. On Gaonic responsa appealing to ancient (or ancestral) tradition, see Rosenthal, "Rav Paltoi Gaon," 626, 634–35.

[85] Abramson, *'Inyanot be-sifrut ha-ge'onim*, 188. Cf. also Assaf, *Gaonic Responsa from the Genizah*, 102 and the abbreviated version in Harkavy, *Teshuvot ha-ge'onim*, no. 434 (= *Oṣar ha-ge'onim*, "Ketubbot," no. 190).

[86] Harkavy, *Teshuvot ha-ge'onim*, no. 234.

[87] Abramson, *'Inyanot be-sifrut ha-ge'onim* and *Sefer ha-terumot*, chap. 15, pt. 1. *Contra* Abramson (n. 1), Assaf, *Gaonic Responsa from the Genizah*, believes it to be an abbreviated version of the responsum in Harkavy, *Teshuvot ha-ge'onim*, no. 434.

conclusive proof to that effect and the opposite may be true. At any rate, it surely provides further evidence of the close relationship between tradition and custom.[88]

Sherira also combines custom and tradition when he affirms: "Thus we have heard from the ancients, it was their tradition and that is the custom of all the sages."[89] Many other examples could be adduced; in some cases we find the two concepts (or the related verbs) being used in a single context, as in the phrase, "we are accustomed (*nahagin*) to do so as a tradition from our ancestors."[90]

2. *Custom and Consensus*

The appeal to consensus as a legal source is in effect a Gaonic innovation. The Talmud never explicitly recognizes consensus, in the sense of general agreement, as a formal legal source, whereas the Geonim accord it, in practice, quasi-formal status as a legal source and a major element in deciding the law.[91]

Consensus is clearly distinguished from *taqqanah* and represents a differ-

---

[88] Cf. Hai in *Oṣar ha-ge'onim*, "Rosh ha-Shanah," no. 85: "Thus are we accustomed to act, in the tradition of our ancestors." Similarly ibid., "Pesaḥim," p. 6, in connection with the benediction on the burning of leaven: "It is an inheritance from our ancestors and thus do the people conduct themselves (*ʿamma dabbar*)." The geonim frequently use the expression *ʿamma dabbar* to mean a custom; this indicates their conception of the significance of custom/*minhag* in general. See, e.g., *Oṣar ha-ge'onim*, "Eruvin," no. 86; ibid., "Pesaḥim," p. 125: ". . . since all conduct themselves so and thus Israel has inherited from their ancestors"; ibid., "Rosh ha-Shanah," p. 62; Assaf, *Teshuvot ha-ge'onim*, nos. 61, 2 (cf. Assaf's comment ibid.); D. Rosenthal, "Rabbanan desiyyuma and Bene siyyume" (Hebrew) *Tarbiz* 49 (1980): p. 54 n. 15; M.A. Friedman, *Jewish Polygyny in the Middle Ages* (Hebrew) (Jerusalem, 1986), p. 14 n. 42. Cf. Sherira's comment in *Shaʿarei teshuvah*, no. 15, concerning the parallel use of these terms: "Thus we have heard from the ancients, it was their tradition and that is the custom of all the sages." A comment of Isaac Ibn Ghiyāth, in *Shaʿarei simḥah*, 2:93, implies that tradition and *minhag* are actually two distinct legal sources: "And therefore Rav Sherira made the prohibition conditional on tradition and accepted it as a custom." One could cite dozens of additional examples of such combinations. A recently published example occurs in a Gaonic responsum cited by Sklare, "Samuel ben Ḥofni," 2:116, in connection with the appointment of judges; in that case custom is considered to reinforce tradition and is not apparently considered as an independent legal source.

[89] *Shaʿarei teshuvah*, no. 15; cf. *Iggeret rav sherira ga'on*, 21; *Oṣar ha- ge'onim*, "Pesaḥim," no. 221: "And that is still the custom of all the sages." Cf. Hai on the wording of the marriage benediction, in *Oṣar ha-ge'onim*, "Ketubbot," no. 71, as cited above, n. 74 and text ad loc. Cf. *Oṣar ha-ge'onim*, "Pesaḥim," p. 125 (cited above, n. 88).

[90] *Oṣar ha-ge'onim*, "Rosh ha-Shanah," p. 51. One could cite many more expressions attributing customs to tradition; see, e.g., ibid., "Moʿed Qatan," p. 39; ibid., "Megillah," p. 60; Mueller, *Ge'onei mizraḥ u-maʿarav*, no. 3.

[91] See Ben-Sasson, "The Jewish Community of Medieval North Africa," 2:20, n. 118. Although the references cited there do not refer to our specific question, they certainly seem to treat *taqqanah* and consensus as distinct concepts.

ent legal process, despite a certain degree of similarity. The essence of consensus is *a posteriori* approval, generally extending over a period of one or two generations, not necessarily deriving from a legitimate authority, for it is sometimes determined by *vox populi*. In either case, it is considered proof of divine will and *ipso facto* infallible, generally in harmony with legal tradition. *Taqqanah*, by contrast, as we have already pointed out, is an *a priori* act, associated with a set point in time and involving an authoritative human agency; moreover, it generally runs counter to legal tradition.

Consensus is invoked as a legal source mainly by the later Geonim, such as Samuel ben Hophni and Hai. The former treats it specifically in his work *ʿAshr masāʾil*, recently discussed by David Sklare.[92] He does not, however, consider it to be an independent legal source but conjoins it with generally accepted tradition, considering the two as essentially a single source. The tendency to identify consensus with tradition was apparently influenced by early Muslim legal practice, which combined the two elements. Eventually, however, Muslim jurists considered their version of consensus (*ijmāʿ*) to be an independent legal source. A similar tendency to consider consensus as an independent source, not necessarily bound up with tradition, may be detected—albeit in a rather rudimentary form—in Hai's discussion of the criteria for the accuracy of the biblical text: "[It is not possible] that this is a corruption of the text, for all Israel unanimously read it thus and [that] is the version of all the Rabbis."[93]

It is an interesting point that the Karaites adopted the conception of consensus as a legal source, identifying it more or less with tradition (perhaps also under the influence of the Muslim environment). Samuel ben Hophni's definition of consensus differs, however, from that of the Karaites, in that he demands approval of only a majority of the people, whereas they stipulate general agreement in the strict sense of the word (though al-Qirqisānī was also inclined to accept a partial consensus in cases of conflicting traditions). One might add here that, though the Karaites and

---

92 Sklare, "Samuel ben Ḥofni," 1:83, 241.

93 *Oṣar ha-geʾonim*, "Berakhot," p. 6; cf. his commentary to bBer. 32b, ibid., *Commentaries*, 45, where consensus is not mentioned as a source. Cf. *Iggeret rav sherira gaʾon* (French version, 30): "But we in Israel rely on this law and all Israel have agreed to it. . . ." See S.Z. Havlin, "On Literary Finalization" (Hebrew) in *Researches in Talmudic Literature* (Jerusalem, 1983), 181. Cf. Sklare, "Samuel ben Ḥofni," 1:68. As to Sklare's comment (ibid., p. 142 n. 91) that the use of the phrase *hassagat gevul*, "overstepping the boundary," to mean violation of a custom is new, one should note that the expression appears in a responsum of Sherira concerning the justification of a custom (*Shaʿarei ṣedeq*, 32a, no. 20), perhaps indicating that the author of this responsum was also Sherira.

Rabbanites debated these questions in relation to the biblical text (see Hai above), their attitudes to the question in the context of legal science were largely similar.[94]

The Geonim essentially envisaged two variants of consensus—popular and scholarly. As we have already pointed out, the most frequent definition of custom in Gaonic writings—the familiar quote from the Talmud, "go out, see how the people conduct themselves"—essentially sees custom as dependent on popular consensus. Put differently: there is an organic relationship between popular consensus and custom; the prevalence of a custom is evidence of consensus regarding the practice in question, and the reverse is generally also true. In contrast to popular consensus, scholarly consensus often appears as confirmation of the law as practiced by the Geonim, though it may sometimes mean nothing more than scholarly agreement with talmudic law.[95]

The Gaonic attitude toward the importance of a custom based on consensus, popular or scholarly, is determined by the degree to which the custom in question is accepted. This criterion is also frequently cited in post-Gaonic sources in references to the development of various customs, when consensus often appears as a parallel to custom or tradition. Thus, on the one hand, we read in a responsum, concerning the custom of administering an oath to a widow upon collection of her *ketubbah*: "Her vow is not sufficient; she must swear a solemn oath. That is the *custom* since the earliest days."[96] On the other hand, another responsum on the same subject stresses the degree of consensus on that point: "And all the Geonim of the academies *have agreed* that one does not rely on that Mishnah or on that law . . ."[97] Sherira similarly combines tradition, *minhag* and scholarly consensus in a passage already quoted above.[98] Many further instances could be given.

The prevalence of a custom, reflecting, as we have pointed out, the extent of consensus toward it, is not only a criterion for acceptance of the prac-

---

[94] On the attitude of the Karaites and the sources to *ijmāʿ* see G. Khan, "Al-Qirqisānī's Opinions Concerning the Text of the Bible and Parallel Muslim Attitudes towards the Text of the Qurʾan," *JQR* 81 (1990): 69–73. On the possibility of Muslim influence on Karaite legal sources see D.J. Lasker, "Islamic Influences on Karaite Origins," in *Studies in Islamic and Judaic Traditions*, ed. W.M. Brinner and S.D. Ricks, vol. 2 (Atlanta, 1989), 23.

[95] See, e.g., Mueller, *Halakhot pesuqot*, no. 40, and parallels, concerning uncooked spelt. See also Sherira's responsum, *Shaʿarei ṣedeq*, 94a, no. 5, concerning a person who contracted a partnership with another and died. And cf. Sherira's wording in connection with the same question in *Ḥemdah genuzah*, no. 132; cf. Danzig, "Halakhot Pesukot," p. 15 n. 27.

[96] *Oṣar ha-geʾonim*, "Giṭṭin," no. 162.

[97] Ibid., no. 161.

[98] See above, n. 90.

tice in question but also a kind of filter, determining its status and the degree to which it should be enforced. Such is the situation with regard to all types of custom, including what are known as *minhagei beit-din* ("customs of the court"). This conclusion follows, e.g., from the already cited responsum concerning the dispensation permitting litigants to sit during legal proceedings,[99] which implies a connection between the prevalence of a practice and the discretion allowed the judges in respect of its enforcement. Similarly, discussing the custom of not using the Divine Name in oaths, Hai writes: "The accepted custom of not administering the oath undoubtedly refers to such oaths specifically, and it is in accordance with the law and is accepted throughout Israel."[100] Again, in connection with music performed during wedding festivities, he states: "It is the custom of all Israel in places of feasting . . . that they rejoice with sounds of rejoicing. . . . But the songs that Mar ʿUqba prohibited were not of this kind." Clearly, then, it was the fact that the custom had taken root throughout Jewry that made it binding; hence songs performed at wedding festivities, which were the rule in all Jewish communities, were not considered in the category of those forbidden by Mar ʿUqba.[101]

This principle governed customs accepted by all Jews. Practices current only in specific localities, however, were not considered binding elsewhere. Thus, for example, in connection with the administration of oaths, there was a custom that a sacred object was to be held by the official administering the oath but not by the litigant himself; on this matter we read: "Places where the object is held not by the person who takes the oath but by the person who administers it . . . this is not the proper procedure, and this custom has not gained acceptance in our place in scholarly circles."[102] Similarly, Sar Shalom, writing of the sum of money to be collected on account of the *ketubbah*, states: "Your custom, that you collect four hundred *zuzim*, if that is the custom of all of you, you are entitled to do so."[103] The sum of four hundred *zuzim*, therefore, was considered a specifically local custom, contrary to the custom of the academies; hence the wording, "you are *entitled* to do so"—but not "obliged."

---

[99] Assaf, *Teshuvot ha-geʾonim*, no. 110.

[100] Ibid., no. 106.

[101] See Groner, "R. Hai Gaon," 174. Hai applies a similar criterion in a responsum (ibid., "Sukkah," no. 151) relating to two other popular customs, avoidance of drinking water at the *tequfah* and the procession in the synagogue during the Sukkot holiday: "The custom has spread (*pashaṭ*) throughout Israel and we have not heard of any place that does otherwise; therefore, do not depart from the custom of your ancestors."

[102] *Oṣar ha-geʾonim*, "Giṭṭin," no. 167; and cf. Groner, "R. Hai Gaon," 155.

[103] *Oṣar ha-geʾonim*, "Ketubbot," no. 88.

It would appear from many Gaonic responsa that the geographical prevalence of a custom not only implied its validity but was also considered evidence of its justness and logic.[104] The reasoning is similar to one of the arguments through which Muslim tradition justifies *ijmāʿ*: "My community would never agree to an error."[105] The Geonim appealed to a similar criterion of geographical distribution, as representing the degree of acceptance of a practice, in connection with the enactment of *taqqanot*. This criterion was applied in the case of the two clearly documented Gaonic *taqqanot*—the *taqqanot* of chattels and of the rebellious wife—and it surely helps to explain why *taqqanah* and custom were sometimes confused, as we have already shown.

Conclusion

We have touched briefly on only one aspect of the use of legal sources in the Gaonic period—custom versus other legal sources. In the final analysis, however, I believe that any evaluation of this aspect of Gaonic legislation will find that, eventually, the actual sources used—*taqqanah*, custom, exegesis or tradition—were not the decisive factor in determining

---

[104] In this sense one should understand Hai's comments on music at wedding festivities (see above) and on drinking water at the time of the *tequfah*: "Although we are ignorant of the reason, we must obey, for not in vain has the custom spread throughout Israel"; see *Oṣar ha-geʾonim*, "Pesaḥim," no. 320. See also Hai's ruling on the question of whether the Scroll of Esther should be considered Scripture: "Moreover, all Israel include it in Scripture" (ibid., "Megillah," no. 36). And cf. Groner, "R. Hai Gaon," 126–27; for further examples see ibid., 161, 174.

[105] In this article I have touched only very briefly and incidentally on the question of the relationship between the legal sources of Jewish law and those of Muslim law. Though this topic has received some attention in the literature, it still awaits a thorough treatment. Here we will only note that the relationship between the legal sources of the two systems may involve a feedback model, according to which the Jewish system first influenced the Muslim, which at a later stage exerted influence on Jewish law—at least, as far as consensus and the emphasis on continuous tradition are concerned. We have not given proper attention to the development of parallels in Islamic law in the context of legal sources either, particularly as regards the relationship between custom and consensus. Concerning the relationship between the sources see, for the time being, J.R. Wegner, "Islamic and Talmudic Jurisprudence: The Four Roots of Islamic Law and their Talmudic Counterparts," *American Journal of Legal History* 26 (1982): 26–29. Wegner, however, stresses the Jewish influences on Muslim law, disregarding the "feedback." Cf. also P. Crone and M. Cook, *Hagarism* (Cambridge, 1977), 30–32, 37, 151, 180; see also my "Custom as a Mediating Factor." Of the Jewish legal sources, only *taqqanah* is entirely foreign to the Muslim system; see S.D. Goitein, *A Mediterranean Society* (Berkeley, Los Angeles, London, 1971), 2:65–66. On the possible influence of Islamic law on Karaite halakhah see Lasker, "Islamic Influences on Karaite Origins," 23–47; cf. also M. Cook, "ʿAnan and Islam: The Origins of Karaite Scripturalism," *JSAI* 9 (1987): 161–82 and the sources cited there. On the subject of legal analogy (*qiyās*), see Zucker, "From R. Saadiah Gaon's Commentary on the Torah," 320ff.

whether a specific innovation or new practice would be accepted as binding by later generations. Over the centuries, halakhic authorities reexamined Gaonic rulings on a theoretical basis, applying purely halakhic criteria; as a result, enactments, customs and interpretations which did not meet such theoretical criteria, though originally created to answer real needs, were rejected. The various legal sources provided a tool for emergency measures, in ways that were recognized by halakhah itself; but once the reality that had necessitated such measures changed, the old law was often reestablished, in accordance with the principle, "once the reason has been canceled, the innovation should be canceled."[106] The Gaonic period was a time of many changes, which gave birth to many innovations. With the close of the period and the disappearance of some of the changes, many regulations and temporary measures instituted by the Geonim were rejected, irrespective of the legal sources on which they had been based.

---

[106] Elon, *Jewish Law*, 2:445 and cf. the discussion in n. 201. Concerning the attitude of later halakhic authorities to the Geonim and their rulings see my "Halakhah and Judicial Procedures in the Gaonic Period," in *Introduction to the History of Jewish Law*, ed. B.S. Jackson et al. (Atlanta: Scholars Press) [forthcoming].

JEWISH ÉLITES IN AL-ANDALUS

DAVID J. WASSERSTEIN
(Tel Aviv University)

At the end of the fifteenth century, shortly before the fall of Granada, there were roughly one thousand Jews in the whole of Islamic Spain. Four hundred and fifty were enslaved upon the fall of Malaga in 1487; a further fifty-five (fifty men and five women) were in the town of Velez Malaga, which also fell in that year; and in Granada itself at the capitulation there were something like five hundred and fifty Jews. There may have been a few dozen others scattered over the rest of the kingdom.[1]

These are precious data. They are precious in two ways. First, they provide us with fairly reliable information about numbers of Jews in a medieval context. Such information is all too rare, and when it does occur we have to weigh the possibility of its being actually far less reliable than it may appear to be. The absolute (or nearly absolute) figures that we have in these cases show every sign of being reliable.[2] Second, the numbers involved are very small. Rachel Arié, the doyenne of modern students of the Nasrid kingdom of Granada, wisely and carefully avoids attempting to reach an estimate for the size of the total population of Granada in this period, but she does suggest that the proportion that was Jewish was no more than "faible."

The value of this information is considerable. It shows us that, even

---

[1] See Rachel Arié, *L'Espagne musulmane au temps des Nasrides (1232–1492)* (Paris, 1973), 332–33. On p. 340, Arié cites Torres Balbás' estimate of fifty thousand for the population of the city of Granada. It should be noted, in connection with Arié's figure for the number of Jews in Malaga, that she also reports, in a separate context, an estimate of only fifteen hundred inhabitants for the total population of Malaga (p. 338). While this need not conflict with the suggestion that the Jews formed only a "faible" proportion of the total population of the kingdom, it certainly raises questions (unless it is merely a misprint). See now also R. Arié, "Une métropole hispano-musulmane au bas-moyen âge: Grenade nasride," *Cahiers de Tunisie* 34, 137–38 (1986): 47–67, reprinted in her *L'Occident musulman au bas moyen âge* (Paris, 1992). On pp. 65–67 (reprint, 123–25), more recent research is cited which seems to put the figures for the numbers of Muslims in the Islamic state of Granada somewhat higher than had been thought. Such changes do nothing, however, to improve the absolute or the relative size of the Jewish element in the population.

[2] In using the word "reliable" here I do not mean to suggest anything more than that the figures in question offer us reliable indicators of the sorts of numbers involved; I do not, of course, intend to suggest that the numbers are completely accurate.

taking account of the afflux of Jewish immigrants and refugees from Christian Spain in preceding years, especially since the establishment of the Inquisition there a decade earlier, the Jewish community in the Granadan kingdom was tiny. This *may* point to difficulties, geographical and other, encountered by Jews from Christian Spain in moving to the relative safety of Islamic Granada; it certainly indicates that the Jewry of Granada was itself not particularly flourishing.

This conclusion is confirmed indirectly by the other information available to us on the overall position of the Granadan community on the eve of the capitulation. We know of the last rabbi of the kingdom, Saadya Ibn Danan, and a small number of his writings are still extant.[3] We also know of a Jewish physician at the Granadan court near the end, Isaac Hamon; and we hear of interpreters and people engaged in commerce and even in international trade with Genoa. In addition, we hear of a small number of people involved in literary activities, both religious and secular.[4]

This does not add up to very much: perhaps as many as half a dozen or so people of intellectual pretensions, and another small group—probably overlapping slightly with the first—of people involved in vaguely middle class economic activity. It is more or less what we might expect of a small community in a state which was itself on the verge of total collapse in the face of the completion of the Christian reconquest. It also suggests that the Jews were a very small minority in the Muslim state. What we know of the overall size of the population of the Granadan kingdom is not very certain, but if Torres Balbás is anywhere near right in his estimate of some fifty thousand for the population of the capital city alone towards the end, then our overall figure of around one thousand for the Jewish population of the entire kingdom is unlikely to represent more than something like one per cent. This is small indeed. I shall return to this below.

I stress these two aspects of the conclusions offered by these figures—

---

[3] See, e.g., *EJ* 8:1158–59; Arié, *L'Espagne musulmane au temps des Nasrides*, p. 336, and n. 2, where his death is recorded as occurring on December 11, 1492, within a few months of the Expulsion. For the surviving writings of this last rabbi in al-Andalus see the studies of Judit Targarona Borrás: "Poemas de Seʿadyah Ibn Danan. Edición, traducción y notas," *Sefarad* 46 (1986): 449–61; "La transmisión de la Ley Oral según «El tratado sobre la sucesión de las generaciones» de Seʿadyah ibn Danan," *Estudios Mirandeses* 8 (1988): 141–67; "Ma'amar ʿal seder ha-dorot de Seʿadyah ibn Danan. Edición, traducción y notas," *MEAH* 34 (1986): 81–149; and (with A. Sáenz-Badillos), "Los capitulos sobre métrica del granadino Seʿadyah ibn Danan," *Homenaje al Prof. D. Cabanelas* (Granada, 1987), 2:471–89.

[4] Arié's statement (ibid., p. 335) that these included Abraham Gavison, the author of *ʿOmer ha-shikheḥah*, seems to be an error: according to the *EJ* entry for the family (7:338), this author died in 1578, which makes it unlikely that he was active in Granada itself, although his family moved there from Seville after the persecutions of 1391.

on one hand their absolute smallness and on the other the relative insignificance of the community both within the larger population of Muslims and as a culturally active group in the Jewish world—for another reason. The natural comparison for us to make with the Jewish community of Granada, the Islamic Spain of the late fifteenth century, is the Jewish community of al-Andalus, Islamic Spain, in earlier periods. That comparison inevitably brings to mind the great achievements of the Jewish communities of al-Andalus, especially during the central period in its history, from the tenth to the twelfth centuries, as it also brings to mind the Jewish community of Granada in its greatest phase, under the leadership of Samuel ha-Nagid and his son Joseph, in the middle of the eleventh century.

My concern here is those small, even tiny, groups of intellectuals and merchants, rabbis and doctors and court officials, who formed the Jewish élites of al-Andalus. Who were they? How did these groups come into being, where did they recruit their membership, how did they change and pass away? What roles did they fulfill? How, in particular, did they interact with the surrounding, Muslim-dominated society, or societies, of al-Andalus and with their élites? How did they compare with the élite groups of the other minority in al-Andalus, the Christians? How, for that matter, did the élite groups of both *dhimmi* communities compare with those of the Muslims? Did the Jewish élites in this as in so much else resemble those of the Muslims? Or did they operate very differently? It seems clear that the answer is probably a mixture of these possibilities, for at least one good reason.

However else they behaved, as individuals and as a community, the Jews of al-Andalus, as also of other Islamic territories, functioned as members of a *dhimmi* category: this affected élites and élite activity perhaps more than other spheres of life. In economic life there were scarcely any real restrictions on Jews, or *dhimmis*, qua Jews or *dhimmis*. In religious life real constraints on Jewish practice were minimal and relatively unimportant—I am of course not referring here to the rare outbursts of persecution. Even the punishments that awaited Jews who attacked Islam or who uttered what were considered to be blasphemies against Allah or criticisms of the Prophet did not single Jews out for special treatment: Christians and *Muslims* too were subject to the same laws in this area. In literary activity, there was scarcely any discrimination against Jews, and indeed it may be argued, with great force, that, at least in literary terms, the Jewish encounter with Arab Islam was highly productive, and especially so in al-Andalus.

But élites, and élite activity, are slightly different. They are *different* because the élites of a minority group in an Islamic society are differently structured from those of the majority; they must interact with that majority at a variety of levels; and they are to a great extent dependent on that society and on its continuing goodwill. In all this there is, at base, a reflection of the *dhimmi* status of mandated inferiority, and also of dependency: a minority élite is different because in the majority's eyes it may actually not constitute an élite at all. A good example of this is provided by a Jew who served as a vizier in the petty kingdom of Almería, in south-eastern Andalusia, in the middle of the eleventh century. In the (public) baths one day, a learned Muslim spotted him in the company of a young Muslim; not liking what he saw, the older Muslim picked up a stone lying conveniently to hand, and dashed out the Jew's brains—the point is not this alone, but also, and rather, that nothing happened to the murderer, and this in a territory where law and order were generally maintained at a relatively high level.[5]

But I said above that élites, and élite activity, are *slightly* different. That word "slightly" is worth a moment's consideration. The Jewish élites are only slightly different, I think, because certain important limitations affected members of Muslim élites themselves too. Chief among these was the element of lawlessness which is so prominent a feature of life at the top in a medieval Islamic society. This will appear a little odd to anyone who has read much of the substantial scholarly writing on these societies produced in the last twenty years or so, for one of the main impressions left by this literature is of overall social stability: whatever the thin crust of rulers and armies might get up to, decent respectable people in the equivalent of our middle class—"our sort of people"—were busy getting on with the job, and keeping Islam, and themselves, going. Nonetheless, the very structure of such a formulation, together with the interest in precisely that middle level in societies that it reflects, is only half the story. Rulers and their armies, in varying degrees, do get up to things too, and a lot of what they do is lawless and unpredictable and outside the control of others; it is also in some ways damaging to the élites of their own societies, élites of which, it may be noted, rulers and their armies also formed a part. In Toledo, for example, shortly after the middle of the eleventh century, the local ruler dealt with widespread hostility to his own incompetence by executing a large number of members of the local élite. In one sense this reflects the vagaries and risks of small-scale local factionalism,

[5] Cf. D. Wasserstein, *The Rise and Fall of the Party-Kings: Politics and Society in Islamic Spain, 1002–1086* (Princeton, 1985), 210–11.

but it also reflects that lawlessness and lack of stability which feature strongly in the Islamic Middle Ages.[6]

These questions about Jewish élites matter in a further way. Some of the best known names in Jewish history, like Ḥasdai Ibn Shaprut and Samuel ha-Nagid, belong to members of Jewish élites in al-Andalus (and I deliberately refrain from any attempt to define these élites): an examination of the élites of *dhimmi* communities, unless it descends into mere antiquarianism, is likely to throw light on the nature and significance of their activities both within their own communities and outside them. Despite all the promise that this implies, the results of such an investigation are disappointing. There are two main reasons for this. First, the sources available for such inquiries tend to impose their own character and limitations on our ability to formulate answers to these problems. The nature of the problems means that one is, perhaps a trifle paradoxically, less interested in the great figures, like Samuel ha-Nagid—or even the anonymous Almerian vizier whose goings-on in the bath so enraged the Muslim scholar—and we are more interested in the greater mass of lesser lights. For the Muslims, this presents no real difficulty, especially in al-Andalus. We are well provided with numerous and excellent biographical dictionaries from the Middle Ages. Between them these contain many thousands of entries on individual Muslims covering virtually the whole period of the Islamic political presence in the Iberian peninsula, from the eighth to the end of the fifteenth centuries.[7] If the range of their coverage is limited in certain areas, which means that there are questions which cannot be fully dealt with, a lacuna can generally be noticed and to some extent allowed for, thanks to the sheer mass of the other information available in the biographical dictionaries and thanks to other types of source altogether.

For the Jews, the situation is very different. We have no biographical dictionaries at all. We do have two works—Ibn Daud's *Sefer ha-Qabbalah*, and Moses Ibn Ezra's *Kitāb al-Muḥāḍara wa'l-Mudhākara*[8]—which contain a certain amount of biographical information and in this respect resemble the biographical dictionaries of the Muslims. Although all of these works suffer from important limitations which make them less than ideal sources in this field, each does nonetheless furnish us with a little serviceable material.

---

[6] Ibid., 255.

[7] Cf. Ch. Pellat, "The Origin and Development of Historiography in Muslim Spain," in *Historians of the Middle East*, ed. B. Lewis and P.M. Holt (London, 1962), 118–25.

[8] Abraham Ibn Daud, *The Book of Tradition (Sefer ha-Qabbalah)*, ed. and trans. G.D. Cohen

However, that material is difficult to use. One question which we should very much like to be able to answer, regarding élite members, and especially those who are at least in part élite members through links with the outside society, concerns their origins. One such character is Ibn Jau, who was in charge of the collection of the poll-tax levied on the Jews of al-Andalus in the latter part of the tenth century. Who was he? Where did he come from? To what sort of background can we assign him? There are no answers to these questions. Even his name, strikingly, raises problems: what kind of linguistic or other source does it reflect? Again, there are no good answers.[9]

This may seem like an excessive eagerness for detail. But Ibn Jau is not the only person about whom these problems exist; others can be cited. The list includes almost every Andalusian Jew whose name is known to us; even Samuel ha-Nagid. This is particularly odd, given that we know a good deal about the Andalusian community. It is odd in the specific case of the Nagid because we *seem* to know a good deal about him and about his family. But what do we in fact know about him and his family before the collapse of the Umayyad state and his own flight from Cordoba in about 1013? It is also odd for another reason, and this is the second reason for disappointment which I mentioned earlier.

One of the features of Muslim élites which seems to emerge from recent work is a kind of social and professional differentiation. Families, and sometimes ethnic groups, tended to stick to certain types of profession: the law did not overlap very much with civil service jobs, narrowly considered; army careers were separate again, and so on. The great families of civil servants in Umayyad Andalusia, like the Banū Abī ʿAbda or the Banū Hudayr, of course offer a couple of eccentrics who went off and became ascetics or even studied *fiqh*, but by and large they stuck to what they were born to, senior posts in the central administration of a strong state. What we see is fairly clear differentiation of employment: separate or virtually separate élites.[10] For such long-term differentiation to be possible, relatively large numbers of people are indispensable.

How big were these Jewish élites? Or, for it is really the same question, how many Jews were there in al-Andalus? Of course, we do not know, and we cannot know, the answer. But we do have some indicators. S.D.

(Philadelphia and London, 1967); Moses ibn Ezra, *Kitāb al-Muḥāḍara wa'l-Mudhākara*, ed. and trans. A.S. Halkin (Jerusalem, 1975).

[9] For Ibn Jau see Wasserstein, *Rise and Fall*, 196–97, with references.

[10] This has of course implications of great importance for those societies, but these are not relevant here.

Goitein once suggested that the Jews may have constituted something like one per cent of the population of the Islamic lands in the Middle Ages, with a higher concentration in the cities, reflecting their lesser interest and participation in rural activities like agriculture.[11] It is not my intention here to argue with Goitein; but it is worth pointing out that in offering this figure of one per cent overall he cannot have meant one per cent as against half a per cent, or one per cent as against one and a half per cent. There is no information at all which would make it possible to offer such an exact estimate.[12] Clearly, one per cent is a very rough approximation. But the differences between half a per cent and one per cent, or between half a per cent and one and a half per cent, are very large: in the first case one per cent is twice as large as half a per cent; and in the second the difference is one to three. We also have estimates by Ashtor.[13] He made use of the overall estimates for urban population sizes in medieval Islamic Spain worked out by the Spanish scholar Leopoldo Torres Balbás on the basis of the actual sizes and shapes of medieval urban landscapes. The overall estimates of the population sizes of these cities worked out by Torres Balbás carry a certain amount of persuasive force; but there are too many uncertainties and variables and excessively large margins of error in Ashtor's methods to make his results either acceptable or usable.

Another datum that we have concerns Granada, a city where the Jews were said to be very important in the eleventh century. Here, in the famous massacre of the Jews in 1066–67, some four thousand of his coreligionists, many of them tax-collecting civil servants, are reported to have been killed along with Joseph Ibn Naghrila, the son of the Nagid.[14] If this

---

[11] S.D. Goitein, "Jewish Society and Institutions Under Islam," in *Jewish Society Through the Ages*, ed. H.H. Ben-Sasson and S. Ettinger (New York, 1971), 173.

[12] On the general problem of counting Jews in pre-modern periods, see Abraham Wasserstein, "The Number and Provenance of Jews in Graeco-Roman Antiquity: A Note on Population Statistics" (forthcoming). See also, more generally, S.W. Baron, "Reflections on Ancient and Medieval Jewish Historical Demography," in *Ancient and Medieval Jewish History* (New Brunswick, N.J., 1972), 10–22. More recently, P. Chalmeta, "An Approximate Picture of the Economy of al-Andalus," in *The Legacy of Muslim Spain*, ed. S.Kh. Jayyusi (Leiden, 1992), 755 (741–59), attempts to calculate the size of the population of al-Andalus: his calculations, however, precisely because they purport to be exact and specific, rather than approximate and general, carry little conviction. It is in the nature of such an investigation that it cannot provide exact figures, especially for a pre-modern period, and the figures which result from such an investigation can be relied on only to the extent to which they are tentative, cautious, and not too ambitious.

[13] See E. Ashtor, "The Number of Jews in Islamic Spain" (Hebrew), *Zion* 28 (1963): 34–56; and his greatly expanded study of the same question in *The Jews of Moslem Spain*, (Philadelphia, 1973; repr., with new introduction and bibliography by D.J. Wasserstein, 1992), 2:190–300; Wasserstein, *Rise and Fall*, 191–92.

[14] Cf. Wasserstein, *Rise and Fall*, 206–209, with references.

were true, it would be a most useful datum in the present context. But, like most figures in medieval narrative sources, it is not. Torres Balbás' estimates of population sizes for medieval Islamic cities in al-Andalus are less subject to uncertainties and large margins of error than Ashtor's derivations from them: Torres Balbás showed that, with the single significant exception of tenth-century Cordoba, the capital of the peninsular state of the Umayyads, large cities in al-Andalus had populations ranging in size between twenty and thirty thousand—cities like Valencia and Malaga, Denia and Almeria, Saragossa and Badajoz and Granada. He may of course have been mistaken, but by how great a margin?[15] Granada's population may perhaps have been as large as double his average: say fifty thousand—or it may not, and may have been only some twenty thousand. The majority Muslim population was, as is well known, split, between the ruling Berbers and the Andalusians—and there were probably a good number of Christians there too. Four thousand Jews, the number given in our narrative sources for the victims of the massacre, is nearly ten per cent of fifty thousand; in a population of only twenty thousand it is exactly twenty per cent. The only context in which we hear anything of how many Jews there were in Zirid Granada is the context of the massacre. We should have more evidence. We do not have it. We can be pretty sure that even in Granada, to which they were probably attracted by the success of the Nagid, the Jews formed a very small proportion of the population.

This must also be true in other cities. A city (in modern terms, little more than a village) of twenty thousand inhabitants of whom even three per cent or four per cent are Jews will have had only six or eight hundred Jews; and probably few cities will have had so heavy a concentration.[16]

This has serious implications for many questions, including élites.[17] One of these questions relates to élite differentiation: we know of really rather a lot of individual Jews in al-Andalus between the tenth and the twelfth centuries; many, or most, of them belonged in some ways to an élite—

[15] See L. Torres Balbás, "Extensión y demografía de las ciudades hispanomusulmanas," *SI* 3 (1955): 37–59; *Ciudades hispanomusulmanas*, 2 vols. (n.p., n.d.).

[16] It is worth noting here the phenomenon of drift in Jewish communities in the British Isles (and elsewhere): this operates to increase the numbers of Jews in the larger cities and reduce those in the smaller and less important provincial centers. There is every reason to suppose that a similar process was at work in al-Andalus (though it is also true that the existence of some very small communities in medieval Egypt may argue against this). If this was the case, it raises other questions, both about the sizes of the Jewish populations in larger and in smaller centers, and about the possible existence of different types of Jewish élites, in larger and in smaller centers.

[17] Another question is that of critical mass: how many Jews does a community need to count before it can produce poets, scholars, etc.? Although this question of critical mass is not touched on here explicitly, it is implicit in everything contained in this paper.

and again I want to stress my unwillingness to attempt any definition of the élite; among the Jews there seems to have operated some degree of occupational differentiation too. But occupational differentiation calls for a solid demographic base. Indeed, even if we disregard this matter of distribution and differentiation of Jewish élite occupations, we are faced with a problem regarding our demographic base: our élite seems to have been quite large. No Andalusian city of thirty thousand is likely to have had Jews forming as much as ten per cent of its population. The largest Jewish community in al-Andalus is unlikely to have counted more than eight or nine hundred individuals. And this figure includes roughly fifty per cent who were females, who effectively do not count for élite studies in this period, as well as many children, not to mention the masses, who, by definition, however we define the élites, did not form, or at least did not belong to, the élites.

There is another, related, problem here. On the basis of the great biographical dictionaries we can, as I indicated above, reconstruct, among other things, the shape and membership of whole families whose members belonged to the élites of the Muslims. It stands to reason, even without such material to help us, that there must have been such families among the Jews too; in a community, or a series of communities, of very small size, this likelihood is all the greater; and in small communities with relatively large élites it is larger still. Where are these families? Where are the dynasties of the Jewish communities of al-Andalus?

Of course there are one or two. The family of Ibn Ḥasdai in Saragossa (although they ended up as converts to Islam) formed one such dynasty among the Jews; and, but for the (most unusual and atypical) event of the massacre, it is likely that Samuel ha-Nagid's family would have been another.[18] But what happened to the family of Ḥasdai Ibn Shaprut? And to all the others? We simply do not know.

Almost everything contained in this paper seems very negative. I set out to try and ask about Jews and their élites in al-Andalus questions similar to those which we can ask about Muslims in that country. Can we draw any useful conclusions at all from the material that we have? The full response seems to be two-fold. On the one hand, we can track a fair number of individuals who served as members of the broader élite of the country and also of internal Jewish élites—in such cases we have to ask, of course, whether élite membership in the one society served as cause, or effect, of

[18] For the possibility that it might not, and that its members might also have ended up as converts to Islam, see my "Samuel Ibn Nagrīla Ha-Nagid and Islamic Historiography in al-Andalus," *Al-Qanṭara* 14 (1993): 109–25.

élite membership in the other. In some cases, as that of Ṣamuel ha-Nagid, and even that of his son Joseph, may indicate, membership of the external élite may have been born of the internal status and then have proceeded to feed that source in its turn. On the other hand, our information is such, in quantity and in quality alike, that it may be dangerous to attempt deeper analysis: we simply cannot answer for Jews the sorts of questions that we can answer for Muslims. This is particularly true for questions about élite *processes*: how membership was attained, how it could be passed on, and so on. Granada at the end of the fifteenth century, to return to my starting point, is a good example here: all our information about what may be termed its Jewish élite amounts to some half a dozen or so scattered individuals. Affected, it is true, by the long-term decline—social, economic, political, and cultural—that affected Granada as a whole, this tiny group of élite-type Granadan Jews illustrates well the difficulties of research in this area, and the practical limitations on the results which may be realistically expected.

We appear to be left with slightly gloomy conclusions, some of them reflections on methodological difficulty rather than historical problems as such. First, how far can we go in studying the real extent of Jewish integration in this, or in any, Islamic society?[19] We know, in relative terms, quite a lot about this particular Jewish society, so it is especially important, and instructive, to ask this about al-Andalus. Second, how well can we expect to be able to analyze the inner functioning of the Jewish societies or elements within these broader societies? For Egypt, possibly, thanks to the Cairo Genizah, and for one or two other areas, we may now have more and better material, but this only serves to point up our difficulties here. Finally, and to my mind most usefully, all this shows the great importance of keeping numbers in mind: not counting how many Jews there were per square metre in tenth- or eleventh-century Saragossa or Almeria, but estimating very roughly what sorts of numbers are involved. The first sort of number cannot be arrived at, but the second sort can, and numbers of this sort matter critically for any consideration of social patterning and occupational differentiation. They also, incidentally, show how very much the Jewish people today owes to a very small absolute number of medieval inhabitants of the Iberian Peninsula.

---

[19] See now the suggestive article of Mercedes García-Arenal, "Rapports entre groupes dans la péninsule ibérique: la conversion de juifs à l'Islam (XIIe–XIIIe siècles)," *Revue du Monde Musulman et de la Méditerranée* (= *Minorités religieuses dans l'Espagne médiévale*) 63–64 (1992): 91–101.

THE JUDEO-ARABIC TRADITION IN CHRISTIAN SPAIN

Yom Tov Assis
(The Hebrew University of Jerusalem)

The rise of Islam marks a turning point in the history of the Mediterranean world. In less than a century the Islamic Empire dominated the territories stretching from Asia Minor in the north to the Sahara in the south, and from India in the east to the Iberian Peninsula in the west. The forces of Islam now controlled large areas inhabited by members of various ethnic, religious, linguistic and cultural groups, including Christians and Jews, who unlike the rest, were considered *ahl al-dhimma* or *ahl al-kitāb*, i.e. tolerated People of the Book, members of the revealed religions.[1]

The conquests of Islam ushered in a new epoch in the history of the Jews. Following the establishment of the Islamic Empire the vast majority of the Jews were now living in the same political, cultural and linguistic framework. The major Jewish center in Babylonia, for more than a millennium under Persian rule, was now united with the Jewish communities in the Mediterranean basin which had been under Christian rule. Muslim domination and the encounter with Arabic culture had a tremendous influence on Jewish life. Jewish history changed its course.

Politically, the change was radical. While the Christians and Zoroastrians rapidly declined under Islam, disappearing altogether in many places, Jews flourished.[2] This was not due to any difference in the attitude of Islam to the non-Muslim subjects but rather to the fundamentally different reaction of Christians and Jews to the political changes of the eighth century. For the Christians, political supremacy and theological truth went hand in hand; the Arabs' victories, therefore, shattered their theological doctrines and religious beliefs. The Jews, on the other hand, never considered their sad lot in Exile to be a reflection of the truth and validity of their faith, so the change from Christian or Sassanian rule to Muslim government did not affect their religious fundamentals. Furthermore, there was

---

[1] On the attitude of Islam to Christians and Jews, see: A.S. Tritton, *The Caliphs and Their Non-Muslim Subjects: A Critical Study of the Covenant of 'Umar* (London, 1970); C.E. Bosworth, "The Concept of Dhimma in Early Islam," in *Christians and Jews in the Ottoman Empire*, ed. B. Braude and B. Lewis (New York, 1983), 1:37–51.

[2] S.W. Baron, *A Social and Religious History of the Jews*, 2nd ed. (New York, 1957), 3:99–114.

great comfort to be had in the sight of their Christian adversaries' downfall and the punishment of their oppressors. The victory of Islam over its Byzantine and Sassanian adversaries was seen by many Jews as the precursor of their own messianic age.[3]

The conquests of Islam brought unity and uniformity to Jewish religious life. As communication within the ever expanding Jewish Diaspora improved, the influence of the Babylonian center, which coincided with the center of the Abbasid Caliphate, extended to the most distant communities. The Babylonian Talmud and the teachings of the Geonim could now be disseminated far more easily than before.[4]

The encounter with Islamic culture, on the other hand, produced nothing less than a revolution. The Jewish world became essentially Arabic-speaking. There had not been such a process of acculturation since the Jews' engagement with the Hellenistic and Aramaic cultures. Islamic culture, which encompassed the philosophical and scientific works of antiquity as well as original, Arabic compositions, was now accessible. On the whole, the Jews proved to be most receptive and open to external influences, while retaining their Jewish identity and Hebrew culture. Their success in combining their culture with that of their environment by far surpassed that of their ancestors living in the Greco-Roman world. The greatest achievement of Judeo-Arabic culture was its ability to remain an integral part of mainstream Judaism. It is in this context that its survival in a Christian milieu and its efforts to meet the challenge from the northern Jewish centers should be evaluated.[5]

The beginnings of Sephardic culture go back to the conquest of the Iberian Peninsula by the Arabs in 711 C.E. The Jews of the Iberian Peninsula now became part of the Umayyad Empire and the Arabic-speaking Jewish world. The impact of the Arab conquest and of Arabic culture in Spain was paramount for all its inhabitants.[6] For the Jews, contact with the Babylonian center was now easier than ever before. The Jews, who had been persecuted for more than a century under Visigothic rule, prospered and flourished. It was, however, in the middle of the tenth century that the

[3] A.Z. Aescoly, *Jewish Messianic Movements* (Hebrew), (Jerusalem, 1956), 98–102.

[4] A.S. Rosenthal, "The History of the Text and Problems of Redaction in the Study of the Babylonian Talmud" (Hebrew), *Tarbiz* 57 (1988): 1–36.

[5] A.S. Halkin, "The Judeo-Islamic Age," in *Great Ages and Ideas of the Jewish People*, ed. L. Schwarz (New York, 1956), 215–263; idem, "Judeo-Arabic Literature," in *The Jews, Their Religion and Culture*, ed. L. Finkelstein (New York, 1949), 2:121–154.

[6] R. Dozy, *Recherches sur l'histoire et la littérature de l'Espagne pendant le moyen-âge*, 3rd ed. (Leiden, 1881), 1:1–83; idem, *Histoire des musulmans d'Espagne*, 2d ed. revised E. Lévi-Provençal (Leiden, 1932), 1:270ff. (= *Spanish Islam*, trans. F.G. Stokes [London, 1913], 230ff.).

Iberian Peninsula became the center of Jewish culture, which subsequently developed into Sephardic culture.[7]

The Judeo-Arabic tradition that transformed the cultural life of Iberian Jewry originated and developed in the East. Its most illustrious representative was Saadya al-Fayyūmī Gaon, an Egyptian and the only non-Babylonian to reach the Headship of a Yeshivah. A proper understanding of his scholarly endeavor and his disciples' achievements is important for an appreciation of Andalusian Judeo-Arabic culture. In practically every field Saadya Gaon was a pioneer. His translation of the Bible into Arabic, his commentary, his prayer book, his philosophical work *Kitāb al-amānāt wa'l-i'tiqādāt* (*The Book of Beliefs and Opinions*), his work on Hebrew lexicography and grammar, his poetry—all were innovative works of outstanding quality.

Saadya Gaon's works were all designed to respond to the challenge posed by Islamic culture. If we analyze his works and those of his disciples, we reach the inescapable conclusion that their activities were the result of an inferiority complex vis-à-vis Arabic culture. For the first time, since the earlier contact with Hellenism, Jewish intellectuals began to doubt the superiority of their religion and culture. Naturally, nothing in their writings explicitly indicated such uncertainty, but it was implicit in their very attempt, which was largely apologetic, to show the supremacy of Judaism over any other culture, faith or religion. And it was through such attempts that Saadya Gaon and his eastern successors produced masterly pieces of Jewish scholarship.[8] But only in Spain did political circumstances permit this fascinating cultural program to attain maturity.

Following the establishment of the Abbasid regime in Baghdad, a survivor of the Umayyad dynasty, based in Damascus, found refuge in Spain. The emergence of an Umayyad Caliphate in Spain independent of, and hostile to, Baghdad provided the opportunity for Spanish Jewry to appropriate and pursue the literary, linguistic, philosophical and theological work begun in the East. In the days of 'Abd al-Raḥmān III, when the Caliphate of Cordova became totally independent of Baghdad, the political conditions became ripe for the emergence of a Jewish center independent of Sura and Pumbedita. Understandably, 'Abd al-Raḥmān favored the end of Spanish Jewry's dependence on the Babylonian academies. Ḥasdai Ibn

---

[7] For earlier contacts between Spanish Jews and the eastern centers, see B.M. Lewin, *Oṣar ha-ge'onim*, vol. 3, pt. 1 (Jerusalem, 1930), pp. 24f., no. 64 (Natronai's famous responsum to the community of Lucena on the order of prayer).

[8] E. Fleischer, "Reflections on the Character of Hebrew Poetry in Spain" (Hebrew), *Pe'amim* 2 (1979): 15–20.

Shaprut, ʿAbd al-Raḥmān's famous Jewish courtier, therefore enjoyed his Caliph's full support in establishing an Andalusian center of Jewish learning independent of Babylonia. As is well-known, he spared no efforts to attract the finest Jewish scholars of the day, including some of Saadya Gaon's own disciples.[9] The contributions of Menahem ben Saruq, Dunash ben Labraṭ and Judah Ḥayyūj constitute a key stage in the development of Hebrew linguistic studies, and the foundations laid by their generation remain to this day basically unchanged and unchallenged.[10] In all branches of Jewish learning, except poetry, the scholars of Sepharad followed the lead of Saadya Gaon and his disciples but reached a level of unsurpassed maturity and excellence.

Medieval Jewish philosophy in all its ramifications was intimately linked to general philosophy expounded in Arabic; north of the Pyrenees, by contrast, there was no medieval Jewish philosophy.[11] In their attempts to show the superiority of Judaism over other religions, Jewish philosophers did not hesitate to use Judeo-Arabic, that is Arabic written in Hebrew characters. They did so despite their complete mastery of the Hebrew language. Neither in details nor in substance can the achievements in Hebrew grammar be grasped without reference to Arabic. And in Hebrew verse Arabic meters predominated: they were the innovation of Dunash ben Labraṭ, who was otherwise very critical of Spanish Jews for adopting the fashions of the Arabs. Poetry in Andalusia took its very special course as the total fusion of sacred and profane.[12]

The culture of Sephardic Jewry reflects contact between the Judeo-Arabic tradition of Andalusia and the Jewish culture that developed in Christian Spain. Contacts between Jews from the Muslim south and the Christian north were frequent, with movement in both directions. It is a fascinating, but often forgotten fact, that some of the masterpieces of the Sephardic "Golden Age" were produced in Christian Spain, in a different cultural and linguistic environment. Authors such as Moses Ibn Ezra felt the necessity of formulating the essence of their Andalusian tradition as a

---

[9] On Ḥasdai Ibn Shaprut's role in the emergence of the Jewish center of learning in Muslim Spain, see E. Ashtor, *The Jews of Moslem Spain* (Philadelphia, 1973), 1:155–227.

[10] S. Morag, "The Jewish Communities of Spain and the Living Traditions of the Hebrew Language," in *Moreshet Sepharad: The Sephardi Legacy*, ed. H. Beinart (Jerusalem, 1992), 1:103–114; A. Sáenz-Badillos and J. Targarona Borrás, *Gramáticos hebreos de Al-Andalus (siglos X–XII)* (Cordoba, 1988).

[11] For a brief overview of Jewish philosophy in Muslim Spain, see M. Idel, "Jewish Thought in Medieval Spain," in *Moreshet Sepharad: The Sephardi Legacy*, 1:263–267.

[12] A. Mirsky, "Hebrew Literary Creation," in *Moreshet Sepharad: The Sephardi Legacy*, 1:147–187.

result of their contact with the Jews of Christian Spain. In many respects, Moses Ibn Ezra tried to justify the deep debt of Andalusian Jewish culture to Arabic and show that the result was not at all harmful. In doing so, he was, in fact, laying the foundations of the unique Sephardic culture that developed in Spain, through contact with both the world of Islam and Christian Europe. What occurred in the cultural sphere had its analogue in other areas. The history of the Jewish communities in Christian Spain cannot be understood without reference to these dual influences.[13]

Even after the decline and total disappearance of Judeo-Arabic culture from Andalusia, the process did not come to an end. For while we often refer to the transfer of the Andalusian Judeo-Arabic tradition to the Islamic East and the south of France after the Almohade invasion, we tend to overlook the emigration of Andalusian Jews to the neighboring Hispanic kingdoms of Christian Spain—Castile, Aragon, Navarre—and Portugal. While much attention has been devoted to the activities of Maimonides in Egypt and the Ibn Tibbon and Qimḥi families in Provence, not much research has been conducted on the cultural impact of the Andalusian Jewish migration to the Hispanic kingdoms.[14]

Judah Alḥarizi, Israel ben Joseph Israeli, Todros ha-Levi Abulafia and many others were not born under Muslim rule. Their absorption of the Judeo-Arabic culture of Andalusia in a Christian Romance milieu is a fascinating phenomenon that is the key to the proper appreciation of Sephardic culture. This culture was not lacking in contradictions, pressures and competing rival elements, but it was typical of the life of Jews who, with the advance of the Reconquista, had gradually passed from an Arabic milieu to a Latin and Romance environment. Sephardic culture, as it developed in Christian Spain from the twelfth century onwards, differed from Jewish culture in both the Islamic East and in Ashkenaz. Arabic remained an essential ingredient and the wide-ranging interests characteristic of Andalusian Jewry also typified the Sephardim of Christian Spain.[15]

---

[13] R. Drory, "The Hidden Context: On Literary Products of Tri-Cultural Contacts in the Middle Ages" (Hebrew), *Pe'amim* 46–47 (1991): 9–28.

[14] For one such study of Meir ha-Levi Abulafia (ca. 1165–1244), see B. Septimus, *Hispano-Jewish Culture in Transition: The Career and Controversies of Ramah* (Cambridge, Mass., 1982).

[15] On Alḥarizi, see: Y. Ratzaby, "On the Sources of the *Taḥkemoni*" (Hebrew), *Tarbiz* 30 (1956): 424–439; J. Dana, "On the Source of the *Taḥkemoni*" (Hebrew), *Tarbiz* 44 (1975): 172–81; R. Brann, "Power in the Portrayal: Representations of Muslims and Jews in Judah al-Harizi's Taḥkemoni," *Princeton Papers in Near Eastern Studies* 1 (1992): 1–22. On Todros Halevi, see: Y. Baer, "Todros ben Yehudah Halevi and His Times" (Hebrew), *Zion* 2 (1937): 19–55; R. Brann, *The Compunctious Poet: Cultural Ambiguity and Hebrew Poetry in Muslim Spain* (Baltimore and London, 1991), 143–157. On Israel Israeli, see *The Commentaries of R. Yiṣhaq ben R. Shelomo*

From the end of the eleventh century to the end of the thirteenth, the Jews of Christian Spain participated in the translation of numerous works of science, philosophy and medicine. Arabic remained the language of the intellectual and religious elite in Jewish society within the Hispanic kingdoms. Knowledge of Arabic, Hebrew and a Romance language enabled Jews to perform a vital task in the process of transmitting works from Arabic into Latin or the Romance languages of the Iberian Peninsula, mostly Castilian and to a lesser extent Catalan. The titles *trujaman* and *alphaquim* given to Jews in the Crowns of Castile and Aragon indicate the extent of their involvement in the process.[16] There is, however, no evidence that a school of translators operated in Toledo as suggested by some scholars.[17] The most important Jewish translators in Castile were Judah ben Moses ha-Kohen, Isaac ben Sid, Abraham Alphaquim, Samuel ha-Levi, and Moses Alphaquim.[18] Jaime I and Pedro III of Aragon and Fernando III and Alfonso X of Castile employed many Jews as administrators, diplomats and interpreters; they were chosen primarily for their expertise in Arabic.[19]

Arabic remained the language of the ordinances of Toledo, long after its conquest by the Christians in 1085. Even in the fourteenth century, knowledge of Arabic was widespread among the intellectual elite. Abraham ben Nathan ha-Yarḥi, the author of *Sefer ha-manhig*, who came to Toledo at the end of the twelfth century and again at the beginning of the thirteenth, apparently felt it necessary to study Arabic in the Castilian capital that had already been ruled by Christians for more than a century.[20]

Arabic, however, was not the main characteristic of Sephardic culture. Like the Jewish culture of the so-called "Golden Age," Sephardic culture was characterized above all by its diversity, exceptional receptivity, and

---

from Toledo on Ethics of the Fathers, ed. M.S. Kasher and Y.Y. Blechrowitz (Jerusalem, 1972), Introduction.

[16] D. Romano, "Judios escribanos y trujamanes de árabe en la Corona de Aragon (reinados de Jaime I a Jaime II)," *Sefarad* 38 (1978): 71–105; idem, "Li opere scientifiche di Alfonso X e l'intervento degli ebrei," *Oriente e Occidente nel Medioevo: Filosofia e Scienze. Convegno Internazionale 9–15 aprile 1969* (Roma, 1971), 677–711.

[17] See, for instance, J.L. Teicher, "The Latin-Hebrew School of Translators in Spain in the Twelfth Century," in *Homenaje a Millás Vallicrosa* (Barcelona, 1956), 2:403–444.

[18] D. Romano, "El papel judío en la transmisión de la cultura," *Hispania Sacra* 40 (1988): 955–978.

[19] Studies on Jews at the service of the Catalano-Aragonese rulers show the extent of the phenomenon; see: D. Romano, *Judios al servicio de Pedro el Grande de Aragon (1276–1285)* (Barcelona, 1983); J.L. Schneidman, "Jews in the Administration of 13th-Century Aragon," *Historia Judaica* 21 (1959): 37–52; and Y. Assis, "Jewish Diplomats from Aragon in Muslim Lands" (Hebrew), *Sefunot* 3 (18) (1985): 11–34.

[20] *Sefer ha-manhig*, ed. Y. Raphael (Jerusalem, 1978), 2:555, lines 53–54.

sympathetic attitude to philosophy and the sciences. The contact of Spanish Jewry with Christian-Iberian culture modified Andalusian Jewish culture, resulting in, for example, the limited use of Romance languages in Jewish literature. Apart from Renaissance Italy, Christian Spain was the only region in medieval Christian Europe where the Jews wrote in the local language. Noteworthy in this respect are the Castilian poetry of Shem Tov Ardutiel (Santob de Carrión) and the Catalan proverbs of Jafuda Bonsenyor.[21]

The advance of the Christian conquests opened new channels of cultural interchange for Spanish Jewry. Until the middle of the twelfth century, the contacts between Spanish and Franco-German Jewry were limited. In the second half of the twelfth century the relations and mutual influence between the Jews of the two regions increased considerably. Rashi's commentaries and the Tosafists' glosses penetrated into Sepharad. Jonah Gerondi, who studied in the Tosafist *yeshivah* of Evreux at the beginning of the thirteenth century, and his cousin Moses Naḥmanides were the representatives of the Tosafists in Spain. Naḥmanides' two teachers, Judah ben Yaqar and Nathan ben Meir of Trinquetaille, also studied in northern France; upon their return to Spain, they propagated their newly-acquired learning. Judah ben Yaqar, who taught in Barcelona and died in 1220, was the first Catalan rabbi to have studied in France. He deeply influenced Naḥmanides. He was followed by Jonah Gerondi who studied in Evreux. The *yeshivah* of Evreux attained academic excellence, combining the talmudic erudition of the French Tosafists with German pietism. The young Catalonian student, Jonah Gerondi, was totally captivated by the system of learning developed in Evreux which was designed to reduce the intellectual import of the individual scholar to a minimum. Rather than adding *ḥiddushim* (novellae) to the Talmud, the system advocated the study of the old halakhic works on the Talmudic text.[22] Solomon Ibn Adret, Aaron de Na Clara, and Yom Tov Alishbili were deeply influenced by Naḥmanides' teachings and absorbed much of the Ashkenazic scholarship through him and other channels. Ibn Adret's great respect for Ashkenazic

[21] Santob de Carrión, *Proverbios morales*, ed. I. González Llubera (Cambridge, 1947); C. Colahan, "Santob's Debate: Parody and Political Allegory," *Sefarad* 39 (1979): 87–107, 265–308; S. Shepard, *Shem Tov: His World and His Words* (Miami, 1978); A. Cardoner Planas, "Nuevos datos acerca de Jafuda Bonsenyor," *Sefarad* 4 (1944): 287–293.

[22] A. Grossman, "Relations between Spanish and Ashkenazi Jewry in the Middle Ages," in *Moreshet Sepharad: The Sephardi Legacy*, 1:227–234; I. Ta-Shma, "Ashkenazi Ḥasidism in Spain: R. Jonah Gerondi—the Man and His Work" (Hebrew), in *Exile and Diaspora: Studies in the History of the Jewish People Presented to Professor Haim Beinart*, ed. A. Mirsky et al. (Jerusalem, 1988), 165–194.

customs is best illustrated by his tolerance of those that even contradicted his convictions.[23]

Furthermore, there were some rabbis from Franco-Germany who visited Spain or settled there. The first well-known rabbi from north of the Pyrenees who came to Spain was Abraham ben Nathan ha-Yarḥi of Lunel, in Provence, who arrived in Toledo in 1207, joining the *beit din* of Meir ha-Levi Abulafia in the Castilian capital where he wrote his book *Sefer ha-manhig*. Before settling in Spain, Abraham ben Nathan had studied in the north; through him Ashkenazic and French influences began to penetrate Sepharad. It is not insignificant that the first opposition to Maimonides was raised by Meir ha-Levi Abulafia who had welcomed his Provençal colleague most enthusiastically. Another northerner, Moses of Coucy, visited Spain in 1236. He preached in Castile and in the Introduction to his *Sefer miṣvot gadol*, he boasts that he convinced many Sephardic Jews to send away their foreign women, i.e. their Muslim concubines.[24] His visit followed the great Maimonidean controversy of 1232 that had divided Sephardic Jewry and had culminated with the pronouncement in Toledo of a ban against Maimonides' works.

The greatest impact, however, was made by those Ashkenazic scholars who settled in Spain. Undoubtedly the key figures in the consolidation of Ashkenazic influence in Sepharad were Dan Ashkenazi, Asher ben Jehiel, and the latter's children. With the appointment of Asher as the rabbi of Toledo, this northern influence reached a new stage.[25] In the fourteenth century, the community of Majorca engaged Solomon Ṣarfati as a rabbi, a man whose French talmudic training had a great impact on the island Jews. He was opposed by Vidal Ephraim Gerondi whose education combined broad Jewish studies and sciences.[26] Another French rabbi who was offered a post in Spain was Perez ha-Kohen who was highly recommended by Nissim Gerondi.[27]

---

[23] A good example is the custom of the *kapparot*, that is the slaughtering of fowls for atonement on the eve of Kippur, to which he was opposed. Upon hearing from Ashkenazi students in his *yeshivah* that the custom was prevalent in Germany, he voiced no criticism; see R. Solomon Ibn Adret, *Responsa*, vol. 1 (Bologna, 1539), No. 395.

[24] Y. Assis, "Sexual Behaviour in Hispano-Jewish Society," in *Jewish History: Essays in Honour of Chimen Abramsky*, ed. A. Rapoport-Albert and S.J. Zipperstein (London, 1988), 37; Moses of Coucy, *Sefer miṣvot gadol*, Prohibition 112, no. 3.

[25] Y.M. Ta-Shma, "Rabbenu Asher and His Son R. Ya'akov Ba'al ha-Ṭurim—Between Ashkenaz and Sepharad" (Hebrew), *Pe'amim* 46–47 (1991): 75–91; idem, "Rabbeinu Dan from Ashkenaz who was in Sepharad" (Hebrew), in *Studies in Kabbalah, Philosophy and Ethical Literature: Anniversary Volume dedicated to Y. Tishby* (Jerusalem, 1985), 385–394.

[26] Y. Baer, *A History of the Jews in Christian Spain*, vol. 2 (Philadelphia, 1961), p. 463, n. 13.

[27] Nissim Gerondi, *Responsa*, ed. L.A. Feldman (Jerusalem, 1984), nos. 88–89, pp. 417–20;

There was also an important kabbalistic influence from the north. Indeed, the Gerona school of Kabbalah owed much to Provençal mystics.[28] Those kabbalists and talmudists who had absorbed much from Ashkenaz found themselves allied against such champions of Sephardic culture as Judah ben Samuel Ibn ʿAbbas (mid-thirteenth century) who wrote: "One should not occupy himself with the study of the *novellae*, *tosafot*, and other works written by many people, for they all waste man's time with worthless matters. All this is unnecessary and futile to achieve the aim of the Talmud—that is the interpretation of the commandments and halakhic decisions and rulings." He suggested an alternative syllabus in keeping with Sephardic culture, a broad curriculum of Bible, Hebrew, Talmud, philosophy, and the sciences.[29] The nature of talmudic studies in Spain prior to the thirteenth century has not been thoroughly investigated. In the opinion of some scholars these studies did not reach the level of talmudic scholarship of Franco-Germany and concentrated mainly on searching for the halakhic decisions to guide Jews in their daily conduct. This explains the enthusiastic welcome accorded Maimonides' *Mishneh Torah* in thirteenth-century Spain.[30]

In its two stages, the so-called Maimonidean controversy provides the best illustration of the conflict between Sephardic and Ashkenazic culture on Spanish soil. Social and religious polarization in Hispano-Jewish society reached its peak during the thirteenth century. Various complex factors led to the growing division among Spanish Jewry during this period. One of the major causes for these internal conflicts was undoubtedly the clash between two interpretations of Judaism and two Jewish lifestyles that differed in details and substance. The Maimonidean controversies were the most obvious but by no means the only manifestations of a clash between two camps that differed on crucial religious, theological, cultural and philosophical issues. While it would be an oversimplification to represent this conflict solely along Sephardic/Ashkenazic lines, it is certainly

J. Shatzmiller, "Rabbi Isaac Ha-Cohen of Manosque and His Son Rabbi Peretz: The Rabbinate and its Professionalization in the Fourteenth Century," in *Jewish History: Essays in Honour of Chimen Abramsky*, 61–83.

[28] M. Idel, "Jewish Thought in Medieval Spain," 272–75.

[29] Judah ben Samuel Ibn ʿAbbas, *Yair nativ*, cited in S. Assaf, *Sources for the History of Education in Israel* (Hebrew), (Tel-Aviv, 1931), 2:29–30; A. Grossman, "Relations Between Spanish and Ashkenazi Jewry in the Middle Ages," 229.

[30] On the level of talmudic studies in Muslim Spain, see: I. Ta-Shma, "Jewish Judiciary and Law in the Eleventh and Twelfth Centuries in Spain (as Reflected in the Reponsa of Alfasi)" (Hebrew), *Shenaton Ha-Mishpat Ha-Ivri* 1 (1974): 353–72; I. Twersky, "Maimonides' Mishneh Torah—Its Aim and Function" (Hebrew) *Proceedings of the Israel Academy of Sciences and Humanities* 5 (1976): pp. 3–4, n. 12.

true that Spain and Franco-Germany had developed by this time into the two major centers of Jewish life, providing leadership to the Jewish world after the decline of the Babylonian center.[31]

In Spain both concepts were well represented. Franco-German traditions and methods of learning had penetrated deeply into Hispano-Jewish society. One camp was much influenced by the talmudic erudition and kabbalistic beliefs emanating from the Franco-German and Provençal centers, while the other was the product of centuries-old Spanish experience, both under Muslim and Christian rule, which attached great importance to all branches of Jewish learning, philosophy and science. Yitzhak Baer, the great historian of Spanish Jewry, described one camp as traditionalist, pietistic and mystical and the other as rationalistic and philosophically-inclined. It is not difficult to understand where his sympathy lay. Scholars and students saw in the conflict a clash between tradition and modernity when in reality the crisis was the result of a confrontation between two radically different traditions, neither possessing greater legitimacy. Sephardic culture—at least in Spain—represented *the* tradition while Ashkenazic culture was a northern import.[32]

It has been suggested that religious laxity and moral permissiveness were found primarily in one camp while the other was totally committed to Jewish tradition and values. Adherence to one led to assimilation, while membership in the other ensured the preservation of traditional Jewish life. In one camp, it is claimed, we find allegorization of the biblical texts and precepts, while the other stood for the practice of the halakhah in its minutest details. From the fact that courtiers were mainly found in one camp, it has automatically been assumed that Sephardic culture necessarily meant the partial or total abandonment of Jewish identity. We search in vain for the names of all those who advocated an allegorical interpretation of the biblical precepts so that they might lead their fellow Jews away from traditional practices to an estrangement from Jewish values, and in extreme

---

[31] J. Saracheck, *Faith and Reason: The Conflict over the Rationalism of Maimonides* (Williamsport, 1935); D.J. Silver, *Maimonidean Criticism and the Maimonidean Controversy, 1180–1240* (Leiden, 1965); E.E. Urbach, "The Participation of German and French Scholars in the Controversy about Maimonides and his Works" (Hebrew), *Zion* 12 (1947/8): 149–159; J. Shatzmiller, "Towards a Picture of the First Maimonidean Controversy" (Hebrew), *Zion* 34 (1969): 126–144. Some of the doubts cast by Urbach on the role played by French rabbis in the controversy have been eliminated by Shatzmiller. See also Septimus, *Hispano-Jewish Culture in Transition*, 61–74.

[32] For Baer's evaluation of the controversy, see Baer, *History*, 1:96–110, 289–305; for a different view, see Ch. Touati, "Les deux conflits autour de Maimonide et des études philosophiques," *Juifs et Judaïsme de Languedoc* (Toulouse, 1977), 173–184.

cases, even to apostasy. We search in vain for the heretical movement that supposedly devastated Sephardic Jewry. Instead we find individual Jews of different backgrounds, rationalists as well as mystics, who developed antinominian attitudes—and some of whom finally broke away from Judaism.[33] There is absolutely no evidence that there was any mass movement of Jews of one particular cultural background away from their community and identity as Jews. It is true that during the 1391 massacres and the subsequent persecutions there was a proportionately higher number of converts from the higher social classes. Their reasons for converting, however, were no less social and economic than religious and cultural. Were Solomon Halevi (*alias* Paulus de Santa María) or Joshua ha-Lorqi (*alias* Jerónimo de Santa Fé) rationalist philosophers? Were there no kabbalists who were attracted to the mysteries of Christianity? Was Abner of Burgos a rationalist Jew before his apostasy?[34]

The cultural background of the two sides in the Maimonidean controversies is clear. In the dispute around 1200, Meir ha-Levi Abulafia appealed to the scholars of Provence and northern France for support in combating the views concerning resurrection set forth in Maimonides' *Sefer ha-madda*ʿ. In the 1232 controversy, the involvement of French scholars was deeper. They criticized the Spanish Jews who read Maimonides' *Guide of the Perplexed* and later pronounced a ban against them. The kabbalists and talmudists, followers of the Tosafists, were in full agreement with their northern colleagues. The chief instigator in 1232, in fact, was Solomon of Montpellier (originally from Barcelona), the teacher of Jonah Gerondi. At the beginning of the controversy he sent Jonah to France to lead the campaign. Interestingly, Jonah was in Paris in 1240 when the Talmud was burned in the city streets. So far as we can tell, the Maimonidean side was not a camp of heretics and transgressors. David Qimḥi, who journeyed all the way from Provence to Toledo in order to defend Maimonides only to be expelled by the anti-Maimonideans, was no heretic. Nor was Menahem ha-Meiri of Perpignan who belonged to the rationalist camp. While the Maimunists were accused of terrible crimes by their opponents, their writings, in fact, contain nothing anti-halakhic; in the Judeo-Arabic fashion, they interweave Sephardic traditions with philosophy and science. The loyalty of a David Qimḥi, a Menahem ha-Meiri, a Levi ben Gershon, or a

---

[33] D. Schwartz, "The Spiritual-Intellectual Decline of the Jewish Community in Spain at the End of the Fourteenth Century" (Hebrew), *Pe*ʿ*amim* 46–47 (1991): 92–114.

[34] For polemics between Jews and apostates and criticism of rationalists who were held responsible for the calamities of 1391 and for the disastrous consequences of the Tortosa Disputation, see Baer, *History*, 2:139–158, 232–243.

Jedaiah Bedersi to the halakhah cannot be questioned. The syllabus proposed by the so-called rationalists was in the best Judeo-Arabic tradition; Joseph Ibn Kaspi's curriculum for his son included Bible, Talmud, and general sciences. The struggle, then, was not between tradition and heresy, but between the Sephardic or Judeo-Arabic and Ashkenazic traditions.[35]

The arrival in Toledo of Asher ben Jehiel, the disciple of Meir of Rothenburg, illustrates the affinity of certain Spanish circles for the Franco-German brand of Judaism. That an Ashkenazic Jew and his children who never gave up their traditions, should have led the Jewish community of Toledo was no small matter and shows that the ground was well prepared. His son Judah was particularly strict in his adherence to Ashkenazic traditions. On more than one occasion Asher came into conflict with champions of the Judeo-Arabic-Hispanic tradition. It was around this period that the next round of controversy broke out. Although the initiative against Sephardic traditions seemed once again to originate in Provence, the campaign's leadership was based right in Barcelona. Solomon Ibn Adret was the greatest halakhic authority at the end of the thirteenth century. His writings are imbued with Kabbalah and the teachings of the Tosafists. His meeting with Asher in Barcelona had a crucial influence on the events that followed. The ban pronounced in Barcelona in 1305 by Ibn Adret and his group prohibited the study of philosophy and all science, except for medicine, to anyone under the age of twenty-five; a second ban was pronounced against the allegorists. The significance of the first ban was nothing more or less than the destruction of the Judeo-Arabic-Hispanic tradition.[36]

Meanwhile, that special type of casuistry and dialectics introduced from France and known as *pilpul* was developed in Toledo by Asher. His glosses to the Talmud, the *Tosafot ha-rosh*, were disseminated in Castile and his approach overtook the traditional Sephardic method of *ʿiyyun*, i.e. the study of the Talmudic text in order to reach a halakhic decision.[37] Newcomers in Spain, Asher ben Jehiel and his children propagated the Ashkenazic heritage which they considered a superior—or, indeed, the *authentic*—form of Judaism. To them various Sephardic customs seemed erroneous; nevertheless, they had enthusiastic supporters in Toledo and elsewhere in Spain.[38]

---

[35] For Joseph Ibn Kaspi's proposal, see B.Z. Dinur, *A Documentary History of the Jewish People* (Hebrew), Pt. 2 (Jerusalem, 1972), 6:62.

[36] On the ban of 1305, see Ch. Touati, "La controverse de 1303–1306 autour des études philosophiques et scientifiques," *REJ* 127 (1968): 21–37.

[37] On the method of study of the Talmud in Spain on the eve of the Expulsion, see D. Boyarin, *Sephardi Speculation: A Study in Methods of Talmudic Interpretation* (Hebrew) (Jerusalem, 1989).

[38] There is ample evidence that Asher ben Jehiel and his children—particularly Judah—continued to adhere to their Ashkenazic traditions. See, for instance, Asher ben Jehiel, *Responsa*, XX, no. 20; I.M. Ta-Shma, "Rabbenu Asher and His Son R. Yaʿakov Baʾal ha-Ṭurim."

After the disaster of 1391 and the Disputation of Tortosa (1413–14) many blamed the so-called philosophers and rationalists for all the calamities. The northern trend grew in strength, the champions of the Sephardic approach weakened. In 1422, Moses Arragel writes: "Thus, our science has vanished." Even such an opponent of philosophy and science as Solomon Alʿami describes talmudic studies in very pessimistic terms: "Some of our later sages lost their way in the desert . . . Their study is in the Talmud and the composition of different works, which can neither help nor redeem. . . ." In his Introduction to *Or ha-ḥayyim*, Joseph Yaʿaveṣ, an exile of 1492, disparages talmudic scholarship in Spain, attributing the generally poor level to the methods of study employed. "Never before," he claims, "did Sepharad have as many *yeshivot* and students as at the time of the Expulsion. The students, however, were divided into several groups. . . ." Of the most important group of scholars he says: ". . . their only interest was in *pilpul* (casuistry) so as to display their ingenuity—they could demonstrate with their *pilpul* the purity of a reptile."[39]

For nineteenth-century scholars, Jewish culture in Islamic Spain represented the ideal of enlightenment. In nineteenth-century Jewish historiography the "Golden Age" of the Jews corresponded to the two centuries under Muslim rule. For Jewish apologists in Christian Europe this "Golden Age" was the most eloquent testimony to the Jews' capabilities under a tolerant régime. The impression they created was that during the Middle Ages, Jewish life under Islam invariably flourished. In the eyes of these enlightened Jewish scholars, the terrible lot of Ashkenazic Jewry was, on the other hand, the direct result of persecution and intolerance in Christian Europe. Conveniently, they ignored similar persecutions under Islam. "The Golden Age," as they defined it, came to an abrupt and tragic end with the Almohade invasion. In their enthusiasm for this construct, many scholars did not bother to follow the subsequent history of those twelfth-century refugees and their descendants in the Hispanic kingdoms of Christian Spain. Baer was quite right to observe that historians tended to ignore the "Golden Age" of the Jews in Christian Spain. He himself, however, considered the "Golden Age" of the Islamic period as an assimilationist trend in comparison to the authentic and pure faith and piety that characterized Franco-German Jewry. Though his head was fully immersed in the research of Iberian Jewry, Baer's heart remained with the Jews of Ashkenaz.[40]

[39] For all these references, see J. Faur, *In the Shadow of History* (New York, 1992), 19–20.

[40] See D. Myers, "'From Zion will go forth Torah': Jewish Scholarship and the Return to History" (Ph.D. diss., Columbia University, 1991), 227, 244–51.

The deep penetration of Ashkenazic influence in Jewish Spain did not totally eradicate the spirit of Sepharad. Even with the Expulsion, this spirit was not extinguished. The exiles from Spain formed a new Diaspora within the old Exile. Outside Spain their Sephardic culture contained elements of the two trends that had clashed in Spain but were now merged in the Sephardic Diaspora. The *Shulḥan Arukh* of Joseph Karo combined both, for his halakhic decisions took into consideration Maimonides' rulings and—via his son Jacob—Asher's traditions, those of Sepharad and Ashkenaz.[41] The decline of Sephardic culture would be resumed in many parts of the new Diaspora, as the inevitable result of the general cultural decline of the Islamic world. On Spanish soil two illustrious versions of Judaism had clashed, each legitimate in its own way, neither more authentic than the other. For all the differences between them were the products of their long sojourns in the lands of their Exile. That which united them was their Torah, their common past, and their future aspirations—hopes which they interpreted through their different experiences under Ishmael and Edom.

[41] I.M. Ta-Shma, "Rabbi Joseph Caro and His Beit Yosef: Between Spain and Germany," in *Moreshet Sepharad: The Sephardi Legacy*, 2:192–206.

PART TWO

SELF-PERCEPTIONS AND ATTITUDES TOWARDS OTHERS

COSTUME AS CULTURAL STATEMENT: THE ESTHETICS, ECONOMICS, AND POLITICS OF ISLAMIC DRESS*

YEDIDA K. STILLMAN

In France, in the autumn of 1989, the appearance of North African Muslim girls with their heads covered at school caused a national scandal and stirred an enormous debate throughout the country. Practically all the newspapers, journals, magazines, and television stations followed the story which was also covered by the international media.[1] Due to the rules prohibiting any display of religious identity in public places, these girls broke the so-called laws of "*Laïcité*" (separation of Church and State), and thus were thrown out of school, at which time a nationwide debate ensued involving the Ministry of Education. Eventually a compromise was worked out, and the girls were allowed to return to school with their heads covered upon arrival, but with their scarfs down once in class.

This incident reveals several points: first that the French did not understand that costume makes a cultural, ideological, religious, and political statement. Or perhaps they did understand this, but did not condone the values attached to the act. In fact, the terminology used in the various French newspapers ranged from *foulard*, i.e. scarf, to *hijāb* which indicates veiling, and *chador*, the huge black body wrap worn by Iranian women. Could it be that the escalation of terminology was a deliberate manipulation exercised by the media in order to convey that which the individual journalist desired? After all, it would seem that journalists should know what a *chador* is when night after night, during the hostage crisis in Teheran, American and European television viewers saw women totally shrouded in the traditional black *chador* demonstrating in the streets. Similarly, we can ask whether the journalists wished to suggest that such veiling represented a throwback to the ninth century or an alignment with the forces of Middle East terrorism and fundamentalism, either of which would

* I would like to thank the Lynde and Harry Bradley Foundation, Inc. for the generous grant that enabled me to conduct the research for this article.

[1] See, e.g., Jaques Julliard, "Les maisons d'intolérance," *Le Nouvel Observateur* (26 octobre); Elisabeth Schemla, "Un principal intransigeant sur la laïcité. . . ." ibid. (1 novembre); idem, "Les foulards de madame le Principal," ibid. (8 novembre); J.D., "nne!: Le foulard et la loi," ibid. (30 novembre)

seriously undermine the ideals of the French revolution. Possibly they were displaying a measure of ignorance, even racism. In any event, this debate split even the Muslim community in France. One French journalist, Françoise Giroud, writing a retrospective piece in *Le Nouvel Observateur* noted insightfully, "On dit 'foulard' quand on veut minimiser les choses, on dit 'tchador' quand on veut les enfler." In other words, when one wants to minimize this issue, it's just a scarf; but when one wants to inflate it, it becomes a *chador*.

The recent cause célèbre concerning headcoverings in French schools bears eloquent testimony to the fact that dress communicates a great deal of information about society and the individual. Clothing provides insight into the structure and values of a particular period or social group. Particular fashions may have significant symbolism. For example, the Phrygian sock cap was worn to indicate patriotism after the French revolution, while the Mao jacket in China conveyed conformity and discipline, as well as reverence for the leader. Nazi uniforms and skinhead styles today represent a rejection of democratic values. And finally, closer to our field of interest, the return to the *chador* by many university-educated or otherwise modern women in Iran during the uprising against the late Shah reflected rebellion against his autocratic, westernizing policies.

In the open display of returning to fundamental Islam, there was relative freedom, rarely accorded to women, to demonstrate in the public domain usually reserved for men. However, these women were able to do so only because they adhered to a strict code of behavior; thus, when in public they were totally covered, or, at least, dressed modestly. Nevertheless, their act displayed radical changes in social structure. We see this again and again whenever pressure from within is exerted for change—be it in Tehran, Baghdad, Amman, the West Bank, or Algiers. Women seize this opportunity to step out and not only take part in the demonstrations, but be at the forefront.

Dress actually becomes a barometer of change and a mirror of a changing society. That Iranian women were allowed to mix with men during demonstrations is remarkable, considering the usual segregation of their society along gender lines. The return of Iranian women to traditional garb after the Shah had attempted to bring about social, cultural and religious reforms (perhaps too quickly) is clearly an indication of a rejection, not only of what he had tried to impose on them, but of the West and its values. The same process can be seen throughout the Islamic World, not just in Libya, Saudi Arabia and Pakistan, but also in Morocco, Algeria, Tunisia, and Egypt. The case of Egypt is a setback for what was once the strongest feminist movement in the Arab world, which began early in this century, under the leadership of Bāḥithat al-Bādiya, Hudā Shaʿāwī, and Qāsim Amīn, author of *Taḥrīr al-marʾa*.[2] And now, even educated women have voluntarily returned to the veil to demonstrate a variety of factors, from femininity to religiosity. Hence, a new style of veiling has emerged in such places as Morocco and Egypt.

There exists, then, a definite correlation between changes in dress and political changes. During a cultural renaissance and/or period of heightened nationalism, there is an increase in the wearing of indigenous dress. This is true with immigrant societies as well: in Israel, for example, with the emergence of ethnic pride, people from Islamic countries are no longer shy about wearing their traditional dress, or at least a headpiece, from the old country—although only for festive occasions. The wide array of Afro hairdos and dashikis that became popular among Blacks in the United States with the "Black is Beautiful" movement is a manifestation of the same phenomenon.

In traditional Middle Eastern societies dress conveys cultural messages regarding tribal and regional identification or clan affiliation. The women of the towns of Jericho and Salt and the Taʿamreh Bedouin tribe in Jordan/Israel had a special long dress.[3] The fibula (Ar. *khellāla*; Berb. *tizerzay*) holding the outer wrap (*izār*) worn by women in North Africa identifies the village or area of the wearer's origin (Pl. 1).[4] Another sign of affiliation can be tatoos on the face, hands, or feet, and hairdos or headdresses (Pl. 2).[5]

In Islamic society, dress also constitutes a visual statement of one's (1) political ideology, (2) socio-economic status and (3) religious affiliation:

1. Political ideology: The wearing of the checkered *kafiyyeh* by Arabs in the Middle East (and even by some students on our campuses) often denotes sympathy with the PLO and Yasser Arafat. A person in the Middle East might even wear Western-style clothes, with a *kafiyyeh* on

---

[2] Cairo, 1899. He also wrote another feminist tract *Al-marʾa al-jadīda* (Cairo, 1901).

[3] See Yedida K. Stillman, *Palestinian Costume and Jewelry* (Albuquerque, 1979), 80, 84. It is known as a *berameh* or *khalaga*.

[4] For numerous examples, see Jean Besancenot, *Bijoux arabes et berbères du Maroc* (Casablanca, 1953) and Paul Eudel, *Dictionnaire des bijoux de l'Afrique du Nord (Maroc, Algérie, Tunisie, Tripolitaine)* (Paris, 1906).

[5] For examples of ethnic and regional headdresses, see Stillman, *Palestinian Costume and Jewelry*, 37–40, 52–54, 61–66, and 73–75; and idem, "The Costume of the Jewish Woman in Morocco," in *Studies in Jewish Folklore*, ed. Frank Talmage (Cambridge, Mass., 1980), 345–48 and 351.

his head. In the political world of medieval Islam, black robes were the mark of loyalty to the Abbasid Caliphate (750–1250) and white was the mark of loyalty to the Umayyad (661–750). Red hats (the so-called *tāj Ṣafavī*, or "Safavid crown") were the mark of the Safavids (1502–1736)—hence their epithet *kulāh-i surkh*, or "red caps" used by their Sunnī opponents. Green over many centuries was associated with the ʿAlids.[6]

2. Socio-economic status: Every garment in the Islamic and Jewish wardrobe can be made luxuriously or very simply, depending on the fabric, the weave, the embellishments, etc. It is amazing to observe that of all the fabrics used in the medieval period, silk and linen were the most popular textiles. This, according to S.D. Goitein, "is one of the most distinctive expressions of a refined and extravagant urban civilization."[7] The twelve different kinds of silk are among the more than sixty fabrics mentioned in the Genizah documents for this period. Forty-six of these fabrics appear in trousseau lists, the remainder in mercantile accounts. No fewer than one hundred and sixty-six names of medieval fabrics from Arabic and Persian literary sources were collected by R.B. Serjeant in his monograph *Islamic Textiles*, which covers the length and breadth of the Muslim world from the seventh to the mid-thirteenth century. Seventeen of the Genizah textiles were not known to Serjeant.[8]

3. Religious affiliation: One of the most obvious signs of religious affiliation is the covering of the head (by both sexes) and veiling (by women, upon reaching puberty or upon marriage)—hence, the enormous variety of headgear and veils in Middle Eastern Islamic and Jewish societies. The ubiquity of veils of all sorts in the Genizah marriage contracts proves conclusively that Jewish women, like their Muslim counterparts, went veiled, despite Baron's view to the contrary.[9] Indeed, more than half of the names of garments in the Genizah trousseau lists are for headgear and veils: *mindīl*, *bukhnuq*, *ʿiṣāba māʾila*, *khimār*, *khirqa*, *miʿjar minshafa*, *miqnaʿa*, *niqāb*, *ṭarḥa*, to mention only a few. Some

[6] See Yedida K. Stillman, "Libās," *EI*, 2d ed., 5:736, 749.

[7] S.D. Goitein, *A Mediterranean Society* (Berkeley, Los Angeles, and London, 1983), 4:165.

[8] R.B. Serjeant, *Islamic Textiles, Material for a History up to the Mongol Conquest* (Beirut, 1972); Yedida K. Stillman, "New Data on Islamic Textiles from the Geniza," *Textile History* 10 (1979): 184–95.

[9] Salo W. Baron, *A Social and Religious History of the Jews*. 2d rev. ed. (New York and Philadelphia, 1957), 3:142. For the evidence *contra* Baron, see Yedida K. Stillman, "Female Attire of Medieval Egypt: According to the Trousseau Lists and Cognate Material from the Cairo Geniza" (Ph.D. diss., University of Pennsylvania, 1972), 116–202.

of the terms, such as *ʿaqbiyya* or *ʿaqabiyya*, *mukallaf*, *radda*, and *rumiyya* are not commonly found in any dictionary. This plethora of veils, headgear, and enveloping wraps in the Genizah clearly shows that Jews shared notions of feminine modesty with Muslim society; indeed, they continued to do so up until modern times. The headgear and veils worn by men of religion and scholarship are mentioned in al-Maqrīzī and al-Suyūṭī. The latter wrote an entire book on head covering, entitled *Al-aḥadīth al-ḥisān fī faḍl al-ṭaylasān* (Fine Hadiths on the Excellence of the Ṭaylasān).[10] Al-Suyūṭī uses the term, *ṭaylasān*, somewhat loosely for a variety of head veils worn by men in Egypt, especially by qadis and members of the *fuqahāʾ* (Pl. 3). These head veils and shawls, such as the *ṭaylasān* and the *ṭarḥa*, were also the mark of Jewish scholars in the Middle Ages in places as far apart as the geonic academies of Baghdad and synagogues in Islamic Spain.[11]

The Ottoman Empire exploited this phenomenon in an opulent and extravagant way. The size and shape of one's turban, for example, indicated not only the religious position of the *ʿulamāʾ* and qadis, but also one's rank and station in life as well as death; this is clearly indicated upon tombstones in old Turkish cemeteries.[12] The turban was considered *tijān al-ʿarab* or the "crown of the Arabs" and was technically the prerogative of Muslims only, being a "badge of Islam" (*sīmā al-Islām*) and a "divider between believers and non-believers" (*ḥājiza bayna ʾl-īmān waʾl kufr*). However, during periods when the laws of differentiation were less strictly or less consistently applied—e.g. in Fāṭimid times—Jews did wear turbans that were not, as far as we know, markedly different from those worn by Muslims.

One practical display of religious affiliation can be seen in the renowned Bethlehem embroidery into whose floral and geometric designs the Arab Christian women sometimes work the sign of the cross (possibly under the influence of missionaries, who opened girl's schools at the turn of the century where embroidery was taught).[13]

---

[10] Jalāl al-Dīn al-Suyūṭī, *Al-aḥadīth al-ḥisān fī faḍl al-ṭaylasān*, ed. Albert Arazi (Jerusalem, 1983).

[11] Ibn al-Fuwaṭī, *Al-ḥawādith al-jāmiʿa*, ed. M. Jawād (Baghdad, 1932), 218 and 248, mentions Daniel b. Samuel and Eli b. Zechariah putting on the *ṭarḥa* after their investiture as Geonim by the Islamic state in 1247/48 and 1250/51, respectively. The passages are translated in Norman A. Stillman, *The Jews of Arab Lands: A History and Source Book* (Philadelphia, 1979), 181–82.

[12] See for example the representations of turbans at Rūmī's tomb in Konya in *Islam and the Arab World*, ed B. Lewis (New York, 1976), p. 139, Pl. 22.

[13] Stillman, *Palestinian Costume and Jewelry*, p. 34 and Pl. 5 (between pp. 16 and 17).

In the Islamic system, dress was used to set Muslims apart from non-Muslims, i.e, Christians, Jews, and other minorities. Elsewhere, I have discussed the function of clothing in the early Islamic period as a mark of differentiation between the tolerated religious minorities (*ahl al-dhimma*) and the community of the Believers (*al-umma*). I have also shown how legislation governing the dress of the non-Muslim subject population represents one of the earliest and most significant phenomena of Islamic costume history.[14] It should be mentioned here, however, that during some periods the minorities became color-coded: in Mameluke Egypt, for example, Jews were required to wear outer garments of yellow, Christians of blue, and Samaritans of red. In Sharifan Morocco, too, color—black for Jewish men in the urban communities as opposed to the Believers' white—was a primary mark of religious differentiation (Pl. 4).[15]

With colonialism, the replacement of a well-established traditional form of dress with European clothing was inevitable. From the non-Muslim minorities' point of view, the Europeans were liberators. Adopting their mode of dress symbolized freedom from the social hierarchy that Islam had imposed upon them. Eventually, albeit more gradually, even members of the Muslim majority began modifying their own attire as Western attire came to be perceived as modern and international. The issue of costume change as a result of prolonged interaction between the natives and the intrusive Europeans is an important subject that has not yet received sufficient scholarly attention.[16]

In addition to the garments themselves, other related topics are of interest to the historian of dress: fabric and its production; weaving and looms; dyeing and substances used as dyes, such as pomegranate, onion skin, and prickly pear. Ornamentation is another important ancillary topic. Embroidery patterns and motifs can reflect an urban/rural dichotomy. Sometimes they may display elements of a belief system. The most feared symbol in North Africa, for example, is the evil eye (*al-ʿayn*); its representation—or that of prophylactic signs to ward it off—are sometimes worked into the

[14] Yedida K. Stillman, "Sumptuary Laws, Islamic," *Dictionary of the Middle Ages* XI (New York, 1988), 507–509; idem, "Libās," *EI*, 2d ed., 5:736.

[15] Al-Suyūṭī cited in Sylvestre de Sacy, *Chrestomathie arabe* (Paris, 1826), 1:145–46.

[16] Among the few studies that treat the phenomenon are R. Tresse, "L'évolution du costume des citadins syrolibanais depuis un siècle," *La Géographie* 70 (1938): 1–16 and 76–82; idem, "L'évolution du costume des citadines en Syrie depuis le XIXe siècle," *La Géographie* 71–72 (1939): 257–71 and 29–40; Nancy Micklewright, "Women's Dress in Nineteenth-Century Istanbul: Mirror of a Changing Society" (Ph.D. diss., University of Pennsylvania, 1986). See also Michèle Kasriel, "Le Vêtement comme langage," in *Femmes du Maghreb au présent*, ed. M. Gadaut and M. Kasriel (Paris, 1990), 175–89.

ornamentation of clothing worn by both Jews and Muslims (Pl. 5). Among the most popular anti-evil eye motifs are the ubiquitous hand, or *khamsa*, and its geometrical or numerical representations (Pl. 6). Another decorative element with talismanic properties is the bird motif, which was popular in Near Eastern art long before the advent of Islam and is found on textiles and clothing from medieval Andalusia to nineteenth-century Palestine and modern North Africa (Pls. 7–8).[17]

Colors can convey messages regarding one's age (darker for older women) or rites of passage (for example, white for certain rituals such as the *ḥajj*). Color terminology is probably the richest in Arabic. There is a verb form in Arabic, *ifʿalla* (form IX), which is specifically used for color (and, curiously enough, for physical defects). The verb in this form designates the process by which an item is, turns to, or becomes yellow (*iṣfarra*), red (*iḥmarra*), green (*ikhḍarra)*, etc. Names to denote shades are drawn from spices (turmeric, saffron, pepper), fruits (quince, pomegranate, apricot), nuts (pistachio), vegetables (chick peas), birds (peacock, sand grouse), as well as flowers and gemstones. Colors worn by Jews and Muslims during the medieval Islamic period were phenomenally exquisite. To paraphrase Goitein, the Genizah people were "color intoxicated."[18]

Jews in the medieval Islamic *oikoumene* adopted not only the fashions of the society in which they lived, but also its psychology and culture of dress. Fine clothing was highly prized in the medieval Muslim world. The ruling elite hoarded fine clothes and precious textiles. The Genizah documents confirm that clothes formed part—and at times a considerable part—of a family's investment. The Jewish bourgeoisie, like its Muslim counterpart, passed valuable garments from parents to children as heirlooms, to be converted into cash (far more easily than real estate, for example) in case of an emergency. Valuable clothes were stored in chests and were lovingly cared for. Clothing constituted anywhere from two-fifths to more than half of a Genizah bride's trousseau, which formed the actual wealth that she brought into her marriage.[19]

Another aspect of Islamic vestimentary culture adopted by Jews was the ritual bestowal of garments. The giving of clothing in the Islamic world

---

[17] See Yedida K. Stillman, "The Evil Eye in Morocco," in *Folklore Research Center Studies*, ed. D. Noy and I. Ben-Ami (Jerusalem, 1970), 81–94; idem, "Hashpaʿot sefardiyot ʿal ha-tarbut ha-ḥomrit shel yehudei maroqo," in *Moreshet yehudei sefarad veha-mizraḥ: meḥqarim*, ed. I. Ben-Ami (Jerusalem, 1982), 359–72.

[18] S.D. Goitein, *A Mediterranean Society* (Berkeley and Los Angeles, 1967), 1:106.

[19] Goitein, *A Mediterranean Society*, 1:101; ibid., 4:184–90. The inventory of Hārūn al-Rashīd's storehouses show that garments were a significant part of his treasures. See Ibn al-Zubayr, *Kitāb al-dhakhāʾir waʾl-tuḥaf*, ed. M. Ḥamīd Allāh (Kuwait, 1959), 214–15.

has always been a highly ritualized activity. Muhammad gave his *burda* to his favorite poet, Kaʿb b. Zuhayr. The Prophet also received garments from others (for example, a *burda* from a woman who wove it herself). Up until modern times rulers received—or more often presented—cloaks of honor, *khilaʿ* (sing. *khilʿa*), to whomsoever they wished to favor, irrespective of religious confession or gender, and these were inscribed with *ṭirāz*, or embroidered bands produced in royal factories (Pl. 9). We know of instances where Jews and other *dhimmīs* received robes of honor. The custom of bestowing embroidered garments of honor was imitated by the bourgeoisie. We find, for example, a twelfth-century Jewish merchant in India ordering a gift for his son: a fine linen (*dabīqī*) *ṭirāz* turban, complete with the boy's name embroidered on it. In a *sheṭar eirusin* (document of betrothal) from around 1100, a groom promises to give his bride a *khilʿa* (*wa-an yadfaʿ lahā ʿinda ʾl-dukhūl khilʿa*).[20]

It is probably not fortuitous that evidence for the Jewish practice of bestowing garments of honor in imitation of Muslim usage dates from the Fāṭimid period. This was a time of great and ecumenical prosperity. It also was a period when the discriminatory laws of *ghiyār* were least enforced. Furthermore, perhaps no medieval dynasty combined clothing and ritual more publicly and to better effect than did the Fāṭimids. Indeed, clothing played a major part in their pomp and ceremony.[21] The first Fāṭimid Caliph in Egypt, al-Muʿizz (d. 365/975), founded a special government costume supply house known as the *dār al-kiswa* or *khizānat al-kiswa* with an outlay of 600,000 dinars. An official bureau (*dīwān*) oversaw the production, storage, and distribution of the costumes. Every official and functionary from the Caliph down to government clerks was supplied with a ceremonial outfit (*badla mawkibiyya*) for public occasions. According to al-Maqrīzī, (who is the almost exclusive source of information for Fāṭimid ceremonial costume), each person was provided with an entire wardrobe "from the turban to the underdrawers."[22]

---

[20] For two recent surveys of the *khilʿa* phenomenon, see Norman A. Stillman, "Khilʿa," *EI*, 2d ed., 5:6–7 and Patricia L. Baker, "Islamic Honorific Garments," *Costume* 25 (1991): 25–35. For a Jewish merchant in India ordering a *dabīqī ṭirāz* turban for his son, see Westminster College Cambridge Cair. Misc. f. 9, lines 19f. (*India Book* 50). For a groom contracting to present his bride with a robe of honor, see TS 8 J 9, f. 9.

[21] There are numerous studies dealing with Fāṭimid ceremonies. The most up-to-date and analytical is Paula A. Sanders, "The Court Ceremonial of the Fatimid Caliphate in Egypt" (Ph.D. diss., Princeton University, 1984). For an assessment of the specific role of *ṭirāz* in Fāṭimid ceremony and politics and its wider impact on the medieval Mediterranean world, see Irene A. Bierman, "Art and Politics: The Impact of Fāṭimid Uses of Ṭirāz Fabrics" (Ph.D. diss., University of Chicago, 1980).

[22] Al-Maqrīzī, *Al-mawāʿiẓ wa ʾl-iʿtibār bi-dhikr al-khiṭaṭ wa ʾl-athār* (Bulaq, 1853), 409–13 is devoted entirely to a description of the Storehouse of Costume. The quote is from p. 409.

The most outstanding item of the Caliph's attire was his enormous turban which was ornamented with jewels. An enormous solitaire (*yatīma*) mounted on a silk band was centered on the Caliph's forehead. The entire headgear was called "the noble crown" (*al-tāj al-sharīf*). The rest of the imperial retinue wore a variety of less splendid headdresses. Each rank and office was distinguished by its costume, as al-Maqrīzī states: "It was customary for the Caliph to honor his close subjects and servants during this feast day and other similar feast days with dresses befitting their rank, dresses that combined honor and beauty." Furthermore, "each dress would have the name of the one to whom it was offered in Ibn Sayrafī's handwriting." One glance at the items given and to whom reveals that gold garments were given to men in general as well as to higher-ups, while silk dresses were reserved for women and lesser functionaries such as the carpet spreaders and shield holders.[23]

The feudal military elites that ruled the Middle East in the later Middle Ages also made considerable use of costume in their pomp and ceremony, but they were less willing than the Fāṭimids to let anyone outside their own caste, much less non-Muslims, emulate their fashions. Yet occasionally, some elements of their uniforms were popularized and were even worn by *dhimmīs*. One such example, known from the Genizah, is the *bughluṭāq*, a short-sleeved military coat that was modified into a woman's garment and is listed in several trousseaux.[24] But on the whole, the later Middle Ages witnessed a decline in the freedom of *dhimmī* attire. Thus the abandonment of traditional *dhimmī* dress in favor of Western clothes over the past century and a half was a political and cultural statement no less than the example of the young schoolgirls in contemporary France cited at the beginning of this essay.

---

[23] Ibid., 448–49.

[24] TS 16.206, TS 24.8, TS 24.28, and TS Arabic Box 30, f. 1. For the Mameluke version of this garment, see L.A. Mayer, *Mamluk Costume: A Survey* (Geneva, 1952), 24.

1. Maghrebi fibulae for securing women's outer wraps. Jean Besancenot, *Bijoux arabes et berbères du Maroc* (Casablanca, 1953), Pl. X.

2. Coiffures of Married Moroccan Jewish Women: *1*. Fez, Meknes, Sefrou; *2*. Taroudant (Sūs); *3*. Tiznit (Sūs); *4*. Rabat. Jeanne Jouin, "Le costume de la femme israélite au Maroc," *Journal de la Société des Africanistes* 6 (1936), Fig. 20.

3. Scene from the *Maqāmāt* of al-Ḥarīrī, showing a qadi (on the right) wearing a white *ṭaylasān* or *ṭarḥa* (probably Syria, ca. 1300). British Library ms. Add. 22.114, f. 15.

4. The *amīn* of the goldsmith's guild in traditional urban Jewish black attire, Mogador, Morocco, 1935.

5. *Akhnīf* (hooded cloak) worn by Berber Muslims and Jews in the High Atlas Mountains. Gabriel Rousseau, *Le costume au Maroc* (Paris, 1938), Pl. 3.

6. Various Moroccan *khamsas*. Besancenot, *Bijoux arabes et berbères du Maroc*, Pl. XXIII.

7. Bethlehem woman's jacket (*taqṣīra*) from the late 19th or early 20th century with various embroidered motifs, including the bird. Museum of International Folk Art, Santa Fe, New Mexico, No. 3907

8. Twelfth-century Hispano-Islamic silk textile with bird.
The Metropolitan Museum of Art, New York, No. 58-85-2.

9. A piece of *ṭirāz* textile. Museum of Islamic Art, Cairo, no. 14174.

PERSECUTION, RESPONSE, AND COLLECTIVE MEMORY: THE JEWS OF ISLAM IN THE CLASSICAL PERIOD*

MARK R. COHEN

At the outset of this paper it is important to state some premises. First: a definition of "persecution." As employed in the following discussion, the word means unwarranted violence against persons or property, including individual and mass murder. It means unlawful compulsion in matters of religion, such as forced conversion, and it includes physical expulsion. Other forms of mistreatment—what we would call discrimination, be it bias, sumptuary laws, restrictions upon public display of religion, negative attitudes, or false statements—may lead to persecution. In and of itself, however, such intolerance was considered "normal" in the medieval societies in which Jews lived. Hierarchy and inequality were accepted as part of the natural order of things.

Equally important: I wish to emphasize that I subscribe to the premise that monotheistic religions are, historically and structurally, intolerant and that they often persecute. This has been well put by the historian G.R. Elton, writing in 1983 about persecution and toleration with reference to Christianity:

> Religions organized in powerful churches and in command of their scene persecute as a matter of course and tend to regard toleration as a sign of weakness or even wickedness towards whatever deity they worship.[1]

Further, in the Middle Ages, the persecutor rarely considered violent assault on members of another faith to be "persecution." He believed that

---

* The paper read at the conference in June, 1992, was drawn from the final chapter of a book in progress. That book appeared in 1994 under the title, *Under Crescent and Cross: The Jews in the Middle Ages*, © Princeton University Press. I have made some changes in the paper in the light of revisions I made before the book went to press. The first two sections are treated at much greater length there, and the third and main part of the paper is also somewhat longer in the book. I am grateful to Princeton University's Committee on Research in the Humanities and Social Sciences and to my own Department of Near Eastern Studies Publication Fund, which provided support for various stages of the research and writing, and also to The Institute for Advanced Studies at the Hebrew University of Jerusalem, where, as a Fellow in 1992–1993, I made the final revisions to this paper and to the book.

[1] *Persecution and Toleration: Papers Read at the Twenty-Second Summer Meeting and the Twenty-Third Winter Meeting of the Ecclesiastical History Society*, ed. W.J. Sheils (Oxford, 1984), xiii.

he was implementing the law—or that he was fulfilling the unspoken wish of God. His victim, by contrast, felt persecuted, and typically wondered why God let him suffer so. Over time, persecution could and often did generate a collective memory of persecution at the hands of members of another religion. Applied to the Jews of Islam in the Middle Ages, that is the principal question addressed by the present paper.

Third: the time-frame. I deal here with the formative and classical centuries of Islam, up until the thirteenth century, when the situation of the Jews began to deteriorate largely as a result of the general economic, social, and political decline in the Islamic world, and the level of intolerance and persecution intensified accordingly.

Persecution

It is largely accepted (though vociferously challenged in recent years by what I have called the "neo-lachrymose conception of Jewish-Arab history") that in the Middle Ages, the Jews of Islam did not experience persecution on a scale remotely approaching Jewish suffering in Western Christendom, especially among the Ashkenazic Jews of northern Europe, but also among the Sephardic Jews of Christian Spain beginning with the fierce pogroms of 1391.[2] Oriental persecutions of the Western variety are few and far between.[3] The major ones are the following: (1) Muḥammad's expulsion of two Jewish tribes from Medina and his massacre of the male members of a third; (2) the oppression of Christians and Jews under the Abbasid Caliph al-Mutawakkil in 850 C.E., during which the humiliating restrictions of the so-called Pact of ʿUmar were rigorously enforced; (3) the persecution of Christians and Jews in Egypt and Palestine during the reign of the "mad" Fatimid Caliph al-Ḥākim (996–1021), during which many non-Muslims converted to Islam under duress; (4) the pogrom that struck the Jews of the Spanish-Muslim Berber kingdom of Granada in 1066, after Joseph Ibn Nagrela, the Jewish vizier who succeeded his illustrious father, Samuel ha-Nagid, was assassinated on December 31, 1066; (5) the

[2] M.R. Cohen, "The Neo-Lachrymose Conception of Jewish-Arab History," *Tikkun* (May/June, 1991): 55–60. Cf. also my earlier article, "Islam and the Jews: Myth, Counter-Myth, History," *The Jerusalem Quarterly* 38 (1986): 125–37.

[3] In his classic three-volume history of Jewish persecutions, *Sefer ha-demaʿot* (Berlin, 1924–26), Simon Bernfeld was only able to fill 25 pages on the topic, "Muḥammad and Islam" (vol. 1, 114–34). Bernfeld's proclivity for finding persecution mainly under Christendom was consistent with the "lachrymose conception of Jewish history," as Salo Baron coined the term, but was also in part a result of the availability of sources. Today we have more information on the subject.

reign of terror of the puritanical Berber Almohades during and after their conquests in North Africa and Spain beginning in the 1140s, when, with their militant preaching of the absolute unity of God and of a morality based on the scriptural sources of Islamic law, they turned all resistors, Muslim and non-Muslim alike, into enemies and offered Jews and Christians the choice of death or conversion; (6) and finally, the persecution of Jews in Yemen some years later.[4] This last event was made famous by Maimonides' "Epistle to Yemen," in which he stated what—taken out of context—has become the watchword or "prooftext" of the "neo-lachrymose conception of Jewish-Arab history":

> You know, my brethren, that on account of our sins God has cast us into the midst of this people, the nation of Ishmael, who persecute us severely, and who devise ways to harm us and to debase us. This is as the Exalted had warned us: "Even our enemies themselves being judges" (Deuteronomy 32:31). No nation has ever done more harm to Israel. None has matched it in debasing, humiliating, and hating us.[5]

These persecutions differed, qualitatively, from those in Christendom in a number of ways.[6] Generally, they were directed, not at the Jews per se,

[4] This apparently took place in 1172; see S.D. Goitein, *Letters of Medieval Jewish Traders* (Princeton, 1973), 212.

[5] Moses ben Maimon, "The Epistle to Yemen," trans. Norman A. Stillman, *The Jews of Arab Lands: A History and Source Book* (Philadelphia, 1979), 241 (slightly altered here). The translation in A. Halkin and D. Hartman, *Crisis and Leadership: Epistles of Maimonides* (Philadelphia, 1985), 126, varies a bit. For instance, the Arabic, *al-tafaqquh fī sharrinā*, is rendered "passed baneful and discriminatory legislation against us." Stillman's rendition is somewhat closer to the Arabic text, as is also the Hebrew translation of J. Qafiḥ, "Iggeret teiman" in his edition with Hebrew translations, *Iggerot le-rabbenu moshe ben maimon* (Jerusalem, 1972), 53.

[6] Some less well known instances of persecution include the following: in 1032 the Jewish quarter of Fez came under attack along with the rest of the city when the town was taken over by a Berber chief. Over 6000 Jews are said to have been slain and other barbarisms also to have taken place; see: H.Z. Hirschberg, *A History of the Jews in North Africa*, 2d rev. ed. (Leiden, 1974–81), 1:108 and Bat Ye'or, *The Dhimmi: Jews and Christians under Islam* (Rutherford, New Jersey, 1985), 61. In 1177/78, in Mada'in (near Baghdad), local Muslims complained after Jews had attempted to have the intrusive call of the muezzin in a nearby mosque toned down. Thwarted by the authorities, they joined up with the local mob and went on a rampage, destroying Jewish shops and a synagogue and burning a Torah scroll in the process; see: A.S. Tritton, *The Caliphs and their Non-Muslim Subjects: A Critical Study of the Covenant of 'Umar* (1930; reprint London, 1970), 56; Salo W. Baron, *A Social and Religious History of the Jews*, 2d ed. (Philadelphia, 1957), 3:136 (with some inaccuracies, including the date, which is given by Tritton as 573 A.H.). An anti-Jewish riot that I have not seen mentioned in the secondary literature occurred in the year 1135 in Cordova, during the Almoravide period in Spain, when warfare between Islam and militant, crusading Christendom raised fears and passions in the beleaguered Muslim population. The sentence, in Ibn al-Qaṭṭān's (mid thirteenth-century) historical account of the Almoravide-Almohade period, in an entry for the year 529 (1134–35), reads: "A Jew killed a Muslim, whereupon the Muslims overcame the Jews, plundering their possessions and destroying their residences." See: Ibn al-Qaṭṭān, *Juz' min kitāb naẓm al-jumān*, ed. Mahmud 'Ali Makkī

but at the non-Muslims (*dhimmīs*, "protected people") as a group or at the Jews in their capacity as members of the *dhimmī* class. Persecutions did not accompany "irrational" accusations against the Jews, such as the infamous ritual murder, or blood libel. And we do not hear of expulsions during the formative and classical centuries of Islamic history.[7] By and large, even when *dhimmīs* as a group experienced growing oppression and persecution in the postclassical period, the grim conditions found in Europe were not matched. The Black Death, which raged through Europe between 1348 and 1350, witnessed massive pogroms against the Jews, who were believed to have poisoned wells in an attempt to destroy Christian civilization.[8] The Black Death also ravaged the Islamic world, but nowhere did people there blame the Jews, let alone try to eliminate them.[9]

Responses to Persecution

Like persecution itself, Jewish *response* to persecution differed markedly in Christian and in Islamic lands. In northern Europe, Jews faced with the alternative of death or forced conversion, a choice commonly encountered during anti-Jewish eruptions, frequently chose a noble death—martyrdom

(Rabat, n.d.), 217. A parallel in *Al-bayān al-mughrib fī akhbār al-andalus wa'l-maghrib* of Ibn ʿIdhārī (d. after 1312/13) elaborates somewhat: "In that year, during Rajab [April 17–May 16, 1135], also in Cordova, a mob (*al-ʿāmma*) attacked the Jews—God curse them—when a dead body was found in their midst. They stormed their houses, plundered their possessions, and killed a number (*nafar*) of them." See A. Huici-Miranda, "Un fragmento inédito de Ibn ʿIdari sobre los almorávides," *Hespéris Tamuda* 2 (1961): 101.

[7] It is sometimes stated in secondary literature that forced exile was one of the choices the Almohades offered the Jews. But this is unfounded. Abraham Ibn Daud's statement that Jews "were compelled to wander from their homes" does not refer to expulsion; see *Sefer ha-Qabbalah* (*The Book of Tradition*), ed. and trans. Gerson D. Cohen (Philadelphia, 1967), 87–88 (English). The Hebrew, *ve-yaṣe'u be-galut mi-meqomotam* (ibid., p. 65), lit., "they went into exile from their homes [or localities]" is misrepresented in the English edition of Hirschberg's *History of the Jews in North Africa*, 1:125, "they were exiled from their localities." It clearly means voluntary departure to escape death or forced conversion. This is precisely what Maimonides urges as the desirable strategy for the besieged Jews in his "Epistle on Apostasy" (see below), a recommendation that is incomprehensible if the Jews had been ordered expelled. For a more complete discussion of expulsion see my *Under Crescent and Cross*, 167–69.

[8] Philip Ziegler, *The Black Death* (New York, 1969), 96–109; Norman Cohn, *The Pursuit of the Millenium*, rev. and expanded ed. (New York, 1970), 138–39.

[9] In his study of the Black Death in the Middle East, Michael Dols discusses the contrasting responses of Christian and Muslim societies to their respective infidels during the pandemic. The Christian concepts of "millennialism, militancy toward alien communities, [and] punishment and guilt" that contributed to persecution of the Jews during the plague were not operative in Muslim society. See Michael Dols, *The Black Death in the Middle East* (Princeton, 1977), 293–301 (quotation from pp. 300–1).

(*qiddush ha-shem*, "sanctification of the divine name," in their language)—either at the hands of the Christian enemy or by suicide (including taking the lives of other family members). These martyrs were "canonized" by later generations as Jewish saints who, like Father Abraham, had passed the test of absolute faith in God. The medieval martyrs even surpassed the trial of Abraham, for they died, and even killed their children, in order to avoid baptism and prove their faith. Many explanations for this characteristically Ashkenazic response to persecution have been suggested.[10]

In Islamic lands, by contrast, Jews threatened with extinction unless they converted typically accepted the religion of Islam rather than a martyr's death. Many factors determined this characteristically "Sephardic" response to violent persecution, which, of course, would become the norm for the Jews of Christian Spain beginning in 1391.[11]

Jewish history and Jewish collective memory

I believe that the divergent responses to persecution in Christian and in Muslim lands correlate with their fundamentally different collective historical memories of suffering. Collective memory—the memory preserved by a group of people—mirrors the perception of what was meaningful from that people's past, and, in turn, what is salient in their present.[12] It also

[10] (1) The Ashkenazic conviction that Christianity was theologically idolatrous, obliging Jews to heed the mishnaic ruling that a Jew must die rather than succumb to idolatry; (2) the Jews' revulsion at the sight of certain Christian symbols, notably the cross; (3) the challenge of the age-old Christian readiness to suffer martyrdom to avoid apostasy and bear witness with one's life to the truth of Christianity; (4) the "messianic posture" of Ashkenazim, including an unquestioned belief in the dogma of resurrection, which added to their willingness to undergo martyrdom. For more on these matters, with references, see my *Under Crescent and Cross*, 174–75.

[11] (1) The exclusion of Islam from the category of idolatry by scholars such as Maimonides; (2) rationalism, that undermined faith in miracles such as the resurrection; (3) the relative absence of repulsion by symbols of the dominant religion, which correlates with the dearth of anti-gentile invective and hatred so characteristic of the Ashkenazic depiction of Christians and Christianity (this is true both of literary works and of the private letters of the Cairo Genizah, in which derogatory remarks about gentiles as a group might occasionally be expected, but are not to be found); (4) the absence of martyrdom as a salient, central response to persecution in orthodox (Sunni) Islam, and its replacement by outward accommodation or dissimulation (*taqiyya* in Arabic), while inwardly maintaining belief in Islam; (5) Jewish awareness that forced conversion was contrary to Islamic holy law and that, notwithstanding the law forbidding apostasy from Islam, converts to Islam through duress were often allowed to revert to their former religion. For more detail and documentation, see ibid., 175–76.

[12] In his classic work on collective memory, Maurice Halbwachs states, regarding the opposition between history and collective memory: "Collective memory . . . retains from the past only what still lives or is capable of living in the consciousness of the groups keeping the memory

reflects, even if on an unconscious level, the actual historical experience of their ancestors. The study of *Jewish* collective memory is still in its infancy. Yosef Hayim Yerushalmi's eloquent *Zakhor: Jewish History and Jewish Memory*[13] is the best known work on this subject, though Bernard Lewis' *History: Remembered, Recovered, Invented,*[14] which examines Jewish evidence as part of a broader, comparative inquiry using Middle Eastern examples, preceded it and anticipated many of its conclusions.[15]

Yerushalmi traces the Jewish tradition of writing history back to the Bible. Side by side with written history, biblical Israel preserved memory—with its inherent selectivity—in the form of ritual observance and recitation of past events, as in the Song of Deborah. The rabbis of the Talmud focused all their attention on the biblical account of the Jewish past, evincing little interest in the history of postbiblical times. Yerushalmi and Lewis concur that the store of Jewish historiographical works from the Middle Ages is also paltry.[16] The most important vehicles for transmitting historical memory, they argue, were commemorative acts of ritual and liturgy: elegies, fasts, and penitential prayers (*seliḥot*).[17] In addition, Jews of the Middle Ages took inspiration from the biblical Book of Esther, the first and archetypical Jewish literary response to antisemitism, which relates the triumph of the Jews of Persia over their enemy Haman, who had sought

alive." Unlike history, which deals with change, which is unitary, and which means to be "objective and impartial," collective memory is not universal, but selective, and the selection is determined by the self-perception of the group in the present. "History is a record of changes. . . . The collective memory is a record of resemblances and, naturally, is convinced that the group remains the same because it focuses attention on the group, whereas what has changed are the group's relations or contacts with other groups." See *The Collective Memory*, trans. from the French by Francis J. Ditter and Vida Yazdi Ditter (New York, 1980; French original: Paris, 1950), 78–87 (quotations from 78, 80, 86). I have found this formulation helpful in organizing my own approach to the subject. But, I feel that the dichotomy between history (written) and memory, as far as medieval Jewry is concerned, may not be so absolute. For instance, as I argue below, I believe there exists a bit more "history" from the Ashkenazic Middle Ages than is usually recognized and that these texts convey the same kinds of thematics of Jewish collective memory that Yosef Hayim Yerushalmi's *Zakhor* finds in the premodern period only in non-historiographical formats. Historical texts themselves are inexorably intertwined with the commemorative acts of ritual and liturgy that mark the principal vehicles of Jewish collective memory in the premodern Jewish world.

[13] Seattle and London, 1983.

[14] Princeton, 1975.

[15] Other studies of Jewish memory include Lucette Valensi and Nathan Wachtel, *Jewish Memories*, trans. from the French by Barbara Harshav (Berkeley, 1991) and Ivan G. Marcus, "History, Story, and Collective Memory: Narrativity in Early Ashkenazic Culture," *Prooftexts* 10 (1990): 365–88.

[16] The most recent book on this subject, Reuven Michael, *Jewish Historiography: From the Renaissance to the Modern Time* (Hebrew) (Jerusalem, 1993), echoes the conviction that no significant Jewish historical writing existed in the Middle Ages (see the Introduction to the book).

[17] Yerushalmi, *Zakhor*, 40–52; Lewis, *History*, 23, 45–48.

to destroy them. The book served as a model for medieval *megillot*, "scrolls" of deliverance—even "Second Purims," commemorating narrow escapes from catastrophic persecutions of local Jewish communities.[18] Only in the sixteenth century, Yerushalmi asserts, following the traumatic expulsion of the Jews from Christian Spain in 1492, did the Jewish people begin to take historiography seriously. There appeared at that time a cluster of chronicles recounting in novel fashion the litany of persecutions during the preceding centuries.[19]

What little there is that resembles genuine history-writing in the Middle Ages comes mainly, though not exclusively, from the Ashkenazic world.[20] It is a body of so-called "chronicles," describing acts of persecution by Christians—especially during the First and Second Crusades—and Jewish martyrological responses. Yerushalmi dismisses such writings as transmitters of Jewish memory because, in his words, "they describe something in the most recent past, be it the latest persecution or the latest deliverance" and, more importantly, because "historiography never served as a primary vehicle for Jewish memory in the Middle Ages."[21]

Yerushalmi is overly categorical in his statement of the case. In addition, he makes the distinction between collective memory and historiography too sharp. First, we can point to other medieval examples of "chronicles" that go beyond the short term in their description of past instances of persecution. The best example is Ephraim of Bonn's *Book of Remembrance* (*Sefer zekhirah*), which contains the last of the four Hebrew Crusade chronicles. The *Book of Remembrance* is often, but imprecisely, characterized simply as a chronicle of the Second Crusade (1147). True, the writer *begins* with the suffering of the Jews during that Crusade. But he goes on to recount in sequence *seven other* persecutions that occurred in France, Germany, and England during the second half of the twelfth

[18] Yerushalmi, *Zakhor*, 46–48. Zvi Malachi discusses, and also republishes some of the medieval "megillah" literature in *Studies in Medieval Hebrew Literature* (Hebrew), vol. 1 (Tel Aviv, 1971).

[19] Yerushalmi, *Zakhor*, 53–75; cf. Lewis, *History*, 26–28. On the issue of how "new" the historical outlook of the sixteenth-century chroniclers was, see Robert Bonfil, "How Golden was the Age of the Renaissance in Jewish Historiography?" *History and Theory* 27 (1988): 78–102. For a critique of Yerushalmi's assumption that the expulsion of 1492 represented a watershed in Jewish history, thus giving rise to the works of history in the sixteenth century, see Ivan G. Marcus, "Beyond the Sephardic Mystique," *Orim: A Jewish Journal at Yale* 1 (1985): 35–53.

[20] See Marcus, "History, Story, and Collective Memory: Narrativity in Early Ashkenazic Culture."

[21] Yerushalmi, *Zakhor*, 34, 37–39 (the second quotation is at the bottom of p. 39). Further on (p. 45), he observes that "[t]he single most important religious and literary response to historical catastrophe in the Middle Ages was not a chronicle of the event but the composition of *seliḥot*, penitential prayers, and their insertion into the liturgy of the synagogue."

century, starting with the first occurrence of the ritual murder accusation on the European continent—the case of Blois, France, in 1171, for which Ephraim drew upon letters contemporary with the incident.[22] The Blois narrative, with its martyrdoms, catches Yerushalmi's attention as an artifact of Jewish collective memory because the event produced *seliḥot* and, significantly, an annual fast day in memory of the victims that took hold in the Jewish calendar. In the seventeenth century, moreover, that fast assimilated a new element—the memory of the pogroms against the Jews of Poland and the Ukraine during the Cossack rebellion of 1648–49.[23]

In its *literary form*, however, Ephraim of Bonn's *Book of Remembrance* anticipates by several centuries the "chain of persecutions" chronicles that proliferated among the Sephardim in the sixteenth century. And there are others. An annalistic Hebrew narrative of Jewish travails in southern France (mostly from persecution), compiled near the end of the thirteenth century by a Provençal Jew named Shemtov Shanzolo, was borrowed in the sixteenth century by the Iberian refugee Joseph Ibn Verga to serve as an appendix to his father Solomon's chronicle of persecution, *Sheveṭ yehudah*, which Joseph published in 1554, in Turkey.[24] Another short chronicle, compiled between the middle of the fourteenth and the end of the fifteenth century, recounts a series of tribulations experienced by Jewish communities and individuals from the days of the Merovingian king, Dagobert, to the Black Death.[25] There is also the lost *Remembrance of Persecutions*

---

[22] See Ephraim of Bonn's chronicle, *Sefer zekhirah*, in *Sefer gezerot ashkenaz ve-ṣarfat*, ed. A.M. Habermann (1945; reprint Jerusalem, 1971), 115–32. The first part of Ephraim's chronicle, dealing with the persecutions during the Second Crusade, is translated in Shlomo Eidelberg, *The Jews and the Crusaders: The Hebrew Chronicles of the First and Second Crusades* (Madison, Wisc., 1977), 121–33. The part about Blois is translated in Jacob R. Marcus, *The Jew in the Medieval World* (Cincinnati, 1938, and reprints), 127–30. On the Blois persecution, see Robert Chazan, "The Blois Incident of 1171: A Study in Jewish Communal Organization," *PAAJR* 36 (1968): 13–31. On the "chronicle" as a work of historiography see idem, "R. Ephraim of Bonn's *Sefer Zechirah*," *REJ* 132 (1973): 119–26. The text of the letters used by Ephraim has been published in Habermann, *Sefer gezerot ashkenaz ve-ṣarfat*, 142–46. There is a partial translation in Robert Chazan, *Church, State, and Jew in the Middle Ages* (New York, 1980), 300–304; cf. idem, "The Blois Incident of 1171," 17–21. At some time (probably not long after the event), the text of the letters was tacked onto the end of the longest of the three Hebrew chronicles of the First Crusade. The copyist may have wished to show that the main narrative was but a link in a "chain-of-persecutions," a function the Blois libel assumed when it was absorbed into Ephraim of Bonn's *Book of Remembrance*.

[23] Yerushalmi, *Zakhor*, 48–52.

[24] Solomon Ibn Verga, *Shevet yehudah*, ed. A. Shohat and Y. Baer (Jerusalem, 1947), 146–49. Joseph Shatzmiller, "Provençal Chronography in the Lost Pamphlet by Shemtov Schanzolo" (Hebrew), *PAAJR* 52 (1985): 43–59.

[25] A. David, "Stories Concerning Persecutions in Germany in the Middle Ages" (Hebrew), in *Papers on Medieval Hebrew Literature Presented to A.M. Habermann*, ed. Zvi Malachi (Jerusalem, 1977), 69–83. The account was copied in 1485, at the end of a manuscript containing astronomical and astrological texts.

(*Zikhron ha-shemadot*) of the fourteenth-century Catalonian Jew Profiat Duran ("Efodi"), known only from citation in a messianic work of the sixteenth century by a prominent exile from Christian Spain, Don Isaac Abravanel.[26]

This type of literature, anticipating by generations the post-Spanish expulsion chronicles singled out by Yerushalmi and serving to recount (and often sacralize) the suffering of European Jewry, is consistent with the collective memory of the Jews of Western lands under Christian rule. Viewed alongside a much larger corpus of liturgical poetry—elegies and dirges—they form the basis for a collective memory of suffering inflicted by Christians.[27] This, in turn, is linked with the older, biblical-rabbinic historical conception of persecution in exile (*galut*), usually viewed as punishment for past sins, eventually to be relieved by the Redemption. The "lachrymose conception" of Jewish history in Christendom had its origins in this medieval collective memory of tragic fate in the Christian world.

Collective Memory of Persecution Among the Jews of Islam

Compared to the sorrowful memorialization of past oppression at the hands of Christians, Jewish literary remembrance of persecution by Muslims in the classical centuries of Islam is surprisingly sparse and even casual. This is not because episodes of persecution were not widely known to contemporaries. Letters from the Cairo Genizah describing such crises as the al-Ḥākim persecutions and the Almohade terror prove the opposite.[28] Yet, unlike the situation in the Ashkenazic lands, epistolary reports did not feed

[26] Mentioned in Fritz (Yitzhak) Baer, *Untersuchungen über Quellen und Komposition des Schebet Jehuda* (Berlin, 1936), 2. In a monograph entitled *The "1007 Anonymous" and Papal Sovereignty: Jewish Perceptions of the Papacy and Papal Policy in the High Middle Ages* (Cincinnati, 1984), Kenneth Stow argues that the Hebrew account of an episode of persecution at Rouen in 1007 during the reign of King Robert of France assumes background that makes it necessary to date its composition to the thirteenth century, rather than the eleventh. It fits with what Stow calls a realistic Jewish awareness that the papacy was their most dependable protector—a conviction, he says, that first emerged in the post-Gregorian reform period, grew during the period of the Crusades, and became firm during the thirteenth century. If this revisionist interpretation gains acceptance, it will mean that the "chronicle" constitutes yet another exception to Yerushalmi's rule that medieval Hebrew chronicles "dwell either on the distant, ancient past, up to the destruction of the Second Temple (i.e., *Yosippon*), or else they describe something in the most recent past, be it the latest persecution or the latest deliverance."

[27] On the liturgical poetry, see, for instance, Alan Mintz, *Ḥurban: Responses to Catastrophe in Hebrew Literature* (New York, 1984), 89–105; and, for numerous examples in the original Hebrew, Bernfeld, *Sefer ha-dema'ot*, vols. 1–2.

[28] For details, see my *Under Crescent and Cross*, 180–82.

a literature of suffering in the Muslim world—not in the aftermath of the Almohade persecution nor following the earlier persecution of al-Ḥākim.

A Hebrew poem mourning Jewish suffering and originally thought to have been composed at the time of the al-Ḥākim persecutions was mistakenly connected with that episode.[29] The massacre of 1066 in Granada, unequivocally anti-Jewish, had its "memorialization" in Arabic historiography, but left hardly any literary trace among the Jews themselves.[30] It is mentioned briefly in Moses Ibn Ezra's (b. 1055/60; d. after 1138) Arabic book on Hebrew prosody, where he speaks of Joseph Ibn Nagrela in his biographical survey of poetic personalities,[31] and it crops up in a passing notice in Abraham Ibn Daud's *Book of Tradition*, composed ca. 1160, a source devoted to rabbinic history, not to Muslim-Jewish relations. In the passage, Ibn Daud "blames" the pogrom on Joseph Ibn Nagrela's lack of humility and haughty behavior, which corresponds to the reason given by the Muslim chronicler of the events for the outbreak of anti-Jewish violence.[32]

---

[29] This is the dirge by the Spanish-Hebrew poet, Joseph b. Isaac Ibn Abitur, which begins "Weep, my brothers, and lament/ over Zion with great commotion." See Hayyim Schirmann, "Elegies on Persecutions in Palestine, Africa, Spain, Germany, and France" (Hebrew), *Kobez al Jad* 3 (13) (1939): 27–29, and idem, *Ha-shirah ha-ʿivrit bi-sefarad uve-provans* (Jerusalem and Tel-Aviv, 1954), 1:64–65. Goitein argued in an article first published in 1964 that Ibn Abitur mourns Jews who died as a result of the atrocities committed against the populace in general when rebellious Bedouin tribes overran Fatimid Palestine in 1024 and 1025; Genizah letters, similarly, depict Jewish suffering during this time of troubles in Palestine. See Goitein, *A Mediterranean Society* (Berkeley, Los Angeles, London, 1967–94), 5:58–59 (with references there). On the events, see Moshe Gil, *A History of Palestine 634–1099* (Cambridge, 1992), 385–97. Goitein's theory has been confirmed by Ezra Fleischer's discovery of a Hebrew quasi-liturgical poem from about the same time by an otherwise unknown poet, which, however, dwells only on the general depredations, not on Jewish suffering. See "A Historical Poem Describing Some Military Events in Syria and Erez Israel in the Early 11th Century" (Hebrew), *Zion* 52 (1987): 417–26.

In contrast to the Jews, Egyptian Christians had a literary framework into which to fit a memorialization of the persecutions under al-Ḥākim. Pages of the official chronicle of the patriarchs of the Coptic church brim over with stories of the bizarre and evil acts that the Caliph wrought against the Christians. The account features acts of martyrdom and ends with joy over the deliverance after the apparently deranged Caliph rescinded all oppressive decrees and restored forced converts to their Christian faith. Sāwīrūs ibn al-Muqaffaʿ, *Taʾrīkh baṭārikāt al-kanīsa al-miṣriyya* (History of the Patriarchs of the Egyptian Church), vol. 2, pt. 2, ed. and trans. Aziz Suryal Atiya et al. (Cairo, 1948), 183–209 (English translation).

[30] The "memoirs" of Abdallah, the grandson of Joseph's patron, Sultan Bādīs, who later became Sultan himself, contain a graphic eyewitness description of the background to the events and of the massacre itself. English translation of the long passage in Bernard Lewis, *Islam from the Prophet Muhammad to the Capture of Constantinople* (New York, 1974), 1:123–34.

[31] Moses Ibn Ezra, *Kitāb al-muḥāḍara waʾl-mudhākara*, ed. and trans. A.S. Halkin (Jerusalem, 1975), 66–67.

[32] See Ibn Daud, *Sefer ha-Qabbalah*, 75–76 (English):

> R. Joseph ha-Levi the Nagid, succeeded to his [father's] post. Of all the fine qualities which his father possessed he lacked but one. Having been reared in wealth and never having had

We possess only three Jewish literary responses to Islamic persecution during the classical centuries, though none of them forms a "chronicle" of suffering of the Ashkenazic or later Sephardic variety. Two of them are the famous treatises written in response to the Almohade terror, Maimon the Dayyan's "Epistle of Consolation"[33] and his son Maimonides' "Epistle on Apostasy,"[34] both of which have the consolatory purpose of rationalizing the mass Jewish apostasy to Islam. The third is Maimonides' "Epistle to Yemen," already mentioned. The author counsels the beleaguered and despondent Yemenite Jews to resist both the missionizing message of a Jewish convert to Islam who argued that the advent of Muḥammad was foretold in the Torah, and the preaching of a local Jewish messianic pretender who proclaimed that the persecution heralded the imminent, long-awaited Redemption.[35]

Maimonides' younger contemporary, the Barcelona-born philosopher Joseph b. Judah Ibn ʿAqnīn, devotes considerable attention to the Almohade persecution and forced conversions in one chapter of his still unpublished Judeo-Arabic ethical treatise, *Ṭibb al-nufūs* (Therapy of the Soul).[36] Ibn ʿAqnīn had succumbed to Islam during the terror that accompanied the Almohade conquest of Spain and North Africa in the 1140s, and lived as a crypto-Jew in Fez. The passage in question responds to the second "wave" of Almohade intolerance under the third Almohade ruler, Abū Yūsuf Yaʿqūb al-Manṣūr (1184–99). The Almohades directed their renewed persecution at the descendants of the first generation of forced Jewish converts, whom they suspected—rightly, it turns out—of secret allegiance to Judaism.

to bear a burden [of responsibility] in his youth, he lacked his father's humility. Indeed, he grew haughty—to his destruction. The Berber princes became so jealous of him that he was killed on the Sabbath day, the ninth of Tebet [4]827 [December 31, 1066], along with the community of Granada and all those who had come from distant lands to see his learning and power. He was mourned in every center and in every town. (Indeed, a fast had been decreed for the ninth of Tebet as far back as the days of our ancient rabbis, who composed *Megillat Taʿanit*; but the reason had not been known. From this [incident] we see that they had pointed prophetically to this very day.).

[33] L.M. Simmons, "The Letter of Consolation of Maimun ben Joseph," *JQR*, o.s., 2 (1890): 62–101; Arabic text, 335–69. See also Eliezer Schlossberg, "The Attitude of R. Maimon, the Father of Maimonides, to Islam and Muslim Persecutions" (Hebrew), *Sefunot*, n.s. 5 (20): 95–107.

[34] Moses ben Maimon, "Iggeret ha-shemad" in *Iggerot le-rabbenu mosheh ben maimon*, ed. Qafiḥ, 107–20; English trans. Halkin, *Crisis and Leadership: Epistles of Maimonides*, 13–45.

[35] Moses ben Maimon, "Iggeret teiman," in *Iggerot le-rabbenu moshe ben maimon*, ed. Qafiḥ, 15–60; English trans. Halkin, *Crisis and Leadership: Epistles of Maimonides*, 91–149.

[36] Oxford ms. Huntington 517 (Neubauer, *Catalogue*, 1273), beginning at fol. 138v, lines 27–28. The section, from Part 6 of *Ṭibb al-nufūs*, was first made available in Paul Fenton's partial translation in Bat Yeʾor's *The Dhimmi*, 346–51. I consulted the manuscript on microfilm at the

Ibn ʿAqnīn's prose recalls the doleful tone of many Ashkenazic elegies, beginning with his chapter title: "On the Explication of the Trials and Tribulations [*al-imtiḥānāt wa'l-ḍayqāt*] That Have Befallen Us." He even praises martyrdom as being preferable to forced abandonment of Judaism.[37] But, the passage in question is not part of a persecution "chronicle" like those Ashkenazic narratives memorializing Jewish suffering and martyrdom in Europe. Rather, Ibn ʿAqnīn uses the episode to illustrate his broader ethical message about punishment for sins—here, the sin of apostasy—for which, he confesses at the end, his generation had received its rightful due from God.

The Almohade devastation is reported in Ibn Daud's *Sefer ha-Qabbalah*, but in a brief and low-keyed manner:

> After the demise of R. Joseph [ha-Levi Ibn Megash] there were years of war, evil decrees and persecutions that overtook the Jews, who were compelled to wander from their homes, "such as were for death, to death; and such as were for the sword, to the sword; and such as were for famine, to the famine; and such as were for captivity, to captivity" (Jeremiah 15:2). To Jeremiah's prophecy, there was now added "such as were [destined] to leave the faith." This happened in the wake of the sword of Ibn Tumart, which came into the world in [4]873, when he decreed apostasy on the Jews, saying: "Come, and let us cut them off from being a nation; that the name of Israel may be no more in remembrance."[38]

The casual treatment of the persecution in this passage, written a scant fifteen years after the event, when its consequences were still keenly felt, and by an author who apparently thought the persecution was a prelude to the imminent messianic event, is surprising.[39] Even though Ibn Daud's purpose was to trace the unbroken chain of rabbinic learning and authority—not a chain of persecutions—we are nonethless left wondering why

Jewish Theological Seminary and at the Bodleian Library. Abraham S. Halkin described and discussed the passage in "On the History of the Almohade Persecution" (Hebrew), in *The Joshua Starr Memorial Volume* (New York, 1953), 101–10. I am grateful to Saul Zucker for sharing his knowledge of the book with me.

[37] In Part 3 of *Ṭibb al-nufūs* (fol. 29r, lines 2–3, in the manuscript), Ibn ʿAqnīn mentions the Jews of "the community of Fez, of Sijilmasa, of Darʿa, and of other places, all of which, together, have singular standing in that they martyred themselves (Hebrew: *qiddeshu et ha-shem*)." Cf. also Joseph ben Judah Ibn ʿAqnīn's commentary on the Song of Songs, *Inkishāf al-asrār wa-ẓuhūr al-anwār*, ed. and trans. A.S. Halkin (Jerusalem, 1964), 308, referring to forced conversion and *qiddush ha-shem* (martyrdom).

[38] Ibn Daud, *Sefer ha-Qabbalah*, 87–88 (English). On the possibly symbolic meaning of the incorrect date of 4873 (1112–13), see Cohen's supplementary note, ibid., 141ff. A few pages later in the book, Ibn Daud returns to the Almohade persecutions in order to describe how God, "who prepares the remedy before afflictions," had previously arranged for the installation of the Jewish notable, Judah Ibn Ezra, in the good graces of King Alfonso, so that the Jews fleeing Almohade terror could find refuge in the Christian North (ibid., 96–97).

[39] Ibid., 219–20.

neither he nor any other Andalusian Jew of his time left an account memorializing the terrible calamity.

In poetry, there is the famous eulogy of Abraham Ibn Ezra (1089–1164) for the Jewish communities in Spain and North Africa, which were annihilated by the Almohade oppressor in the mid-1140s, "Aha yarad ʿal sefarad" —"O woe! Misfortune from heaven has fallen upon Sefarad (Spain)."[40] But in sharp contrast to the large output of Ashkenazic elegies (*qinot*) on persecution, among the *thousands* of Hebrew poems written during the classical Arab centuries, this is the only clear-cut example of a poetical Jewish reaction to an outbreak of Islamic persecution to which one can point.[41]

It is true that poems about historical acts of persecution were not part of the literary tradition of the Jews of the East.[42] By the time of the Almohade invasion of Spain, Abraham Ibn Ezra had spent several years living among the Jewish communities of Christian lands; quite possibly, he was influenced in writing "Aha yarad ʿal sefarad" by the Ashkenazic model. On the other hand, simliar poems may turn up as the vast corpus of medieval Hebrew poetry, much of it still unstudied, becomes better known (or when the questions raised by the present analysis are asked of the material in a systematic fashion).[43] Nonetheless, I believe that the apparent near-absence of Jewish poetical memorialization of persecution under

---

[40] For discussions see, e.g., Hirschberg, *A History of the Jews in North Africa*, 1:123–25 (cf. also the Hebrew edition, *Toledot ha-yehudim be-afriqah ha-ṣefonit* [Jerusalem, 1965], 1:90–91) and I. Levin, *Abraham Ibn Ezra: His Life and Poetry* (Hebrew) (Tel Aviv, 1969), 18–20 and p. 344, n. 58. Levin discusses evidence for the single authorship of both "Aha yarad ʿal sefarad" and another, imitative eulogy beginning "Eikh neḥerav ha-maʿarav," "O how the Maghreb has been destroyed," found in the Genizah among some leaves containing lamentations on the destruction of the Temple (Dropsie College, now Annenberg Institute, ms. 316), and excerpted by Schirmann for his article, "Elegies on Persecutions in Palestine, Africa, Spain, Germany, and France," 31–35. See also Dan Pagis, "Dirges on the Persecutions of 1391 in Spain" (Hebrew), *Tarbiz* 37 (1968), p. 357 and n. 19, where Pagis expresses his opinion that the Genizah version is from Ibn Ezra's pen. For a fresh treatment of the poem, in a comparative context, see Ross Brann, "Power and Poetry: Constructions of Exile in Hispano-Hebrew and Hispano-Arabic Elegies," in the *Israel Levin Jubilee Volume* (Hebrew), ed. R. Tsur and T. Rosen (Tel Aviv, 1994), 45–61.

[41] In thinking through this next section, I consulted several scholars of medieval Hebrew poetry: I would like to thank Professors Ross Brann, Ezra Fleischer, Ephraim Hazzan, Raymond Scheindlin, Yosef Yahalom, and Masha Yitzhaki for their bibliographical assistance and comments. I am also grateful to Professor Sasson Somekh for his criticism of the argument.

[42] As Professor Fleischer commented, the tradition developed in Italy and passed to the Ashkenazic lands.

[43] Professor Fleischer kindly showed me several *piyyuṭim* from the Cairo Genizah by Solomon Sulaymān Ibn ʿAmr—whose floruit he has convincingly dated to the second half of the ninth century—which he is planning to publish in an article in *Zion*. Extremely hostile toward Muslims (who are called *meshuggaʿim*, a common Jewish pejorative for the Prophet Muḥammad), these poems contain allusions to specific acts of oppression: the imposition of "colored" garb (apparently alluding to the distinctive clothing for non-Muslims prescribed by the Pact of ʿUmar); the plundering of "tents and dwellings"; and the exaction of taxes. Possibly the verses allude to

Islam in the classical centuries says something important about the difference between Jewish collective memory of suffering in the East and the West.[44] To my mind, the hypothesis is enhanced by the fact that, when we do find examples of Hebrew elegies about persecution from Andalusian poets, they refer to acts perpetrated by *Christians*.[45] Moreover, "Aha yarad ʿal sefarad" was not, as far as we know, incorporated into the liturgy of Andalusian or North African Jewry, at least during the immediately succeeding period.[46] To the contrary, and consistent with the hypothesis that

---

the oppressive decree of Caliph al-Mutawakkil in 850 and/or to some other general violence during the ninth century from which Jews suffered. On the poet Solomon Sulaymān al-Sinjārī, see Ezra Fleischer, *The Yoẓer: Its Emergence and Development* (Hebrew) (Jerusalem, 1984), 191–93; and, idem, "Piyyuṭ and Prayer in *Maḥzor Eretz Israel*" (Hebrew), *KS* 63 (1990–91): 257. For some Jewish reactions to the early Islamic conquests in poetry and prose, see Yosef Yahalom, "The Transition of Kingdom in Eretz Israel (Palestine) as Conceived by Poets and Homilists" (Hebrew), *Shalem* 6 (1992): 1–22.

[44] Regarding the dirge of Joseph Ibn Abitur, once thought to have been dedicated to the al-Ḥākim persecution, see above. Two elegies on the death of Joseph Ibn Nagrela by the contemporary Hebrew poet Isaac Ibn Ghiyāth (1038–89) lack even the faintest allusion to the gruesome circumstances surrounding his demise, let alone to the fact that it was followed by a pogrom against the Jewish community. See: Yonah David ed., *The Poems of Rabbi Isaac Ibn Ghiyyat* (Hebrew) (Jerusalem, 1987), 165 (no. 84), and 219–20 (no. 120). A dirge by Judah Halevi included in Sephardic and Yemenite collections of lamentations for the Ninth of Av (also published in Schirmann, *Ha-shirah ha-ʿivrit bi-sefarad uve-provans*, 2:325–26) and formerly ascribed incorrectly to Isaac Ibn Ghiyāth and believed to refer to the destruction of the Jerusalem Temple, actually relates atrocities suffered by the Jewish community of Majorca when it was ruled by or in the name of the Muslim Almoravides. See David Wasserstein, *The Rise and Fall of the Party Kings: Politics and Society in Islamic Spain 1002–1086* (Princeton, 1985), 89. The historical background of this elegy has not yet been investigated. See also, Ezra Fleischer, "Materials and Considerations for a Future Edition of the Poems of R. Judah Halevi" (Hebrew), *Asufot* 5 (1991): 111.

[45] The eleventh-century Hebrew poet of Muslim Spain, Solomon Ibn Gabirol, penned two elegies, each about the brutal murder by *Christians* ("Edomites") of possibly one and the same friend (the method of death, by stabbing, and other details occur in both poems); see: H. Brody and J. Schirmann eds., *Solomon Ibn Gabirol: Secular Poems* (Hebrew) (Jerusalem, 1974), 122–24 (no. 198), 164–66 (no. 248). Two lamentations by an unidentified poet, found in the Genizah, bemoan the murder of a Jew that took place in Guadalajara, in Christian Spain; see: J. Schirmann, *New Hebrew Poems from the Genizah* (Hebrew) (Jerusalem, 1965), 446–50. A *seliḥah* (penitential poem) for the Day of Atonement by the Saragossan Hebrew poet Levi Ibn al-Tabbān describes anti-Jewish persecutions thought to have occurred at the time of the sacking of the city by King Alfonso VI of Castile and Leon (ca. 1090) or on the Christian reconquest of the city from the Muslims by King Alfonso I of Aragon (1118); see: Dan Pagis ed., *Shirei Levi Ibn al-Tabban* (Jerusalem, 1968), 68–72 and p. 6 in the editor's introduction. Two elegies on a local persecution written by Judah Halevi pertain, it seems, to an outbreak of popular violence in *Christian* Toledo (one of the poems mentions Toledo in the rubric, and E. Fleischer assumes that the other refers to the same event); see: Fleischer, "Materials and Considerations for a Future Edition of the Poems of R. Judah Halevi," 121–30. See also Yisrael Levin, "Suffering in the Poetry of Judah Halevi from the Time of the Crisis of the Reconquista" (Hebrew), *Oṣar yehudei sefarad* (*Tesoro de los Judíos Sefardíes*) 7 (1964): 49–64.

[46] Dr. Masha Yitzhaki kindly informed me that "Aha yarad ʿal sefarad" is contained in a

a vivid historical memory of persecution is more characteristic of the Jews of Christendom than of the Jews of Islam, Abraham Ibn Ezra's lament over the Almohade destruction of Jewish communities in Andalusia was assimilated a century and a half later into the famous Lisbon manuscript of Hebrew dirges written in the wake of the antisemitic pogroms in Christian Spain in 1391.[47]

That we find virtually no memorialization of a major persecution in the classical centuries of Islam analogous to the chronicle and elegiac literature of the Jews of Ashkenaz and of Reconquista and post-expulsion Spain should not be taken to mean that the Jews of Islam were incapable of recollecting, mourning, and commemorating. Quite the contrary. The Genizah, for example, contains manuscript fragments of a Hebrew "scroll" (*megillah*) of deliverance from persecution, reminiscent of the genre discussed by Yerushalmi and others.[48] Composed by the Palestinian-born scholar and celebrated poet, Samuel b. Hosha'na, this "Egyptian Scroll"

Yemenite collection of lamentations (*qinot*) for the Ninth of Av, dating from the beginning of the seventeenth century (Paris ms. héb. 1332, fol. 60a) as well as in a manuscript of diverse Hebrew poems copied at the end of the eighteenth century by a certain Rabbi Abraham Ḥalfon, who lived in Tripoli, Libya (D. Cazés, "Antiquités judaïques en Tripolitaine," *REJ* 20 [1890]: 83–87). The version "Eikh neḥerav ha-ma'arav" found in the Genizah is contained among poems of lamentation by Ibn Ezra on the destruction of the Jerusalem Temple. Possibly some Jews used these pages during the recitation of *qinot* (lamentations) on the Ninth of Av. Many other liturgical poems (*piyyuṭim*) by Ibn Ezra can be found in the good company of those by other famous Andalusian poets in Sephardic prayerbooks; see, e.g., the *Sefardi Maḥzor for Yom Kippur from the Year 1481*, Parma De Rossi ms. 1377, facsimile edition by Makor (Jerusalem, 1973), fols. 24a, 77b, 96b, 102a. Hirschberg writes regarding the main phase of Almohade oppression in North Africa during the reign of 'Abd al-Mu'mīn, that "Moroccan-Jewish popular tradition preserves no memory of these events"; see *A History of the Jews in North Africa*, 1:138.

[47] See: Simon Bernstein ed., *'Al naharot sefarad* (Tel Aviv, 1956), 243–44 (as truncated in the manuscript), 114–19 (reproduced according to the full version in *Diwān des Abraham ibn Ezra*, ed. Jacob Egers [Berlin, 1886]). Egers's Yemenite manuscript places the poem in a section on dirges "for the Ninth of Av, the Exile, the Destruction [namely, of the Jerusalem Temple], and for the persecution [lit., forced apostasy, Hebrew *shemad*] in North Africa and Andalusia" (66–69 in the Egers edition). Bernstein also reprints (112–13, 241–43), from the Sephardic Maḥzor printed in Venice in 1524, another dirge ascribed to "Abraham [Ibn Ezra]," beginning *Yom nilḥamu vi yaḥad shekhenai*, "On the day my [gentile] neighbors did battle against me." This poem does not, however, appear in the Lisbon Manuscript nor in any of the printed editions of Abraham Ibn Ezra's works. Professor Ezra Fleischer kindly gave me his opinion (private communication, February 11, 1992) that, despite its inclusion in Y. Levin's critical edition, *The Religious Poems of Abraham Ibn Ezra* (Jerusalem, 1980), 2:297–99, the poem remains of doubtful authorship.

[48] Jacob Mann, *The Jews in Egypt and in Palestine under the Fāṭimid Caliphs* (2 vols., 1920–22; repr. as 2 vols. in 1, New York, 1970), 1:30–32, 2:31–37; idem, "A Second Supplement to 'The Jews in Egypt and in Palestine under the Fāṭimid Caliphs,'" *HUCA* 3 (1926): 258–63; Goitein, *A Mediterranean Society*, 2:28–29; Gil, *Palestine*, 376–77. Yerushalmi says imprecisely (*Zakhor*, p. 119, n. 37) that the Scroll "refers to deliverance from the persecution of the Caliph Al-Ḥākim in 1012." The text is also discussed briefly in Malachi, *Studies*, 1:25–26 and reprinted there, 1:34–39.

reports how, on December 31, 1011, a Muslim mob attacked a Jewish funeral procession on its way from Old Cairo to the cemetery outside the town.[49] The outbreak in question, which occurred at the very height of the general anti-*dhimmī* persecution by Caliph al-Ḥākim, resulted in the arrest of twenty-three Jews. The victims were imprisoned and the community panicked. People hid in their homes, mourning, fasting, and weeping. On the third day, a group of Jews gathered outside the palace and beseeched the Caliph to spare their captive brethren. Al-Ḥākim found wrongdoing on the part of the Muslims—false testimony, which Islam, particularly, condemns—and released the Jews. So great was the joy of the community that an annual fast was instituted to commemorate the deliverance. Samuel b. Hoshaʿna, who himself had been incarcerated, composed celebratory *piyyuṭim* and *seliḥot* to be recited during the fast.[50] These acts recall characteristic Ashkenazic responses to disaster. So does the rhetoric of "memory" in the *megillah*. Samuel urges his readers: "Remember this and place it before your eyes. Tell it to your children, your children to their children, and their children to another generation." The scroll, fulfilling the commandment to memorialize the miraculous deliverance, is also our only source about the terrifying incident itself.[51]

In light of this document, it is all the more mystifying that we have no comparable response to the decade-long, even more terrifying persecution of non-Muslims by the same Caliph. Jacob Mann, who discovered the Hebrew celebratory scroll of 1012, surmises that the persecution, which began as early as 1004, must have affected only the Christians at first and must not have struck the Jews before 1012. Otherwise, there is no easy explanation for the warm words for the Caliph.[52] This makes sense. But we are still left wondering why the Jews apparently did not leave behind

[49] Non-Muslim funeral corteges vexed Muslims because they violated the prohibition in the Pact of ʿUmar against public display of religious ceremonies. The Genizah documents, as well as Arabic historical sources, attest that this type of anti-*dhimmī* flare-up was not uncommon; Goitein, *A Mediterranean Society*, 2:285; Tritton, *The Caliphs and Their Non-Muslim Subjects*, 109.

[50] M. Zulay, "Liturgical Poems on Various Historical Events" (Hebrew), *Studies of the Research Institute for the Study of Hebrew Poetry* 3 (1936): 163–75.

[51] Some years earlier, Samuel b. Hoshaʿna composed a similar prose/poetic account of deliverance from a different "persecution." Two individuals, one in Palestine and the other in Egypt, had attempted to harm the Jews by leveling accusations against them before Christian clerks in the Fāṭimid government, but were seized and punished by the authorities before they could effectuate their evil designs. This was under the rule of the same Caliph al-Ḥākim of the infamous persecutions. See Benjamin Z. Kedar, "Notes on the History of the Jews of Palestine in the Middle Ages" (Hebrew), *Tarbiz* 42 (1972–73): 401–5. Kedar gives this text the nickname "Megillat Shenei Ha-Soṭenim," or "The Scroll of the Two Fiends."

[52] Mann, *The Jews in Egypt and in Palestine under the Fāṭimid Caliphs*, 1:34.

some apposite literary response to the dreadful wave of persecution.

The *megillah* itself shows that the Jews of Islam were capable of reacting to distress in similar fashion to Jews in Ashkenazic lands, with typological acts of collective commemoration, although they do not seem to have instituted a formal "Second Purim" to "remember" the deliverance of 1012 in some future ritual.[53] It seems, moreover, that Jews in Islamic lands were aware of the Ashkenazic-style chronicle of persecution. Many must have read or at least heard about the engrossing narrative of the Norman-Christian proselyte from southern Italy, Johannes-Obadiah, numerous fragments of which were discovered in the Cairo Genizah. Arriving in the Near East at the turn of the twelfth century, this fascinating individual composed an "autobiography" in Hebrew that highlighted the saga of his life and conversion to Judaism in 1102. It included news of the persecution of the Jews in Europe in 1096 during the First Crusade, which Obadiah seems to have taken from an Ashkenazic source, as well as episodes of oppression of Jews in the Muslim lands that he had observed during his roamings in the Near East.[54] The absence of a similar literary commemoration of the major persecutions experienced by the Jews of Islam suggests the nature of their collective memory: neither the murders of 1066, nor those in twelfth-century Spain and North Africa, constituted holy or noble acts worthy of memorialization for posterity. Nor, certainly, was this true of the apostasies in Egypt and Palestine under al-Ḥākim, in North Africa under the Almohades, or in the Yemen. Moreover, neither the pogrom of 1066, nor the al-Ḥākim depredations, nor the Almohade terror, nor the oppression of the Jews of Yemen fit the Book of Esther's typology of gentile persecution miraculously thwarted.

When, on the other hand, an anti-Jewish episode fit the paradigm, the Jews reacted accordingly—as, for example, in the *megillah*, fast, and *piyyuṭ*

[53] Samuel ha-Nagid Ibn Nagrela's call for a "Second Purim" at the end of his triumphal poem, "Eloha ʿoz" ("Mighty God"), celebrating the victory of his Granadan troops over the army of the "party kingdom" of Almeria in 1038, memorializes a deliverance from harm that Samuel feared would have come to himself and his Jewish community had he lost the battle. Fascinating in the poem are: (1) the application of the typology of the Book of Esther to what was essentially a "cover" for a human victory; (2) the poet's prideful command that his (and God's) local victory be commemorated throughout the Arabic-speaking Jewish communities of Ifriqiya (Tunisia), Egypt, Palestine, and Babylonia (Iraq) with a special Purim; and (3) his call that it be recorded "in their books" so that the event would be "remembered forever after and by generation after generation." Unlike the instance of the "Egyptian Purim" of 1524 discussed below, however, there is to my knowledge no evidence that the anticipated deliverance from danger in 1038 entered the collective historical memory of the Jews, even in Spain itself. See: *Divan Shmuel Hanagid*, ed. Dov Jarden (Jerusalem, 1966), 1:4–14 and the discussion by Yerushalmi, *Zakhor*, 46–47.

[54] See Malachi, *Studies*, 1:61–97.

celebrating the redemption from persecution at the turn of the year 1012. Letters and poems in the Genizah use the typology of Haman, enemy of the Jews, to describe local Jew-baiters and apply the title "Mordecai of Our Time" (*mordekhai ha-zeman*) to Jewish victors over the evildoer's oppression.[55]

More remarkable, the Jews of Arab lands used the *megillah* genre to record and commemorate deliverance from *intra*-Jewish persecution—further suggesting that they lacked a collective historical memory of persecution at the hands of Muslims. Again, the texts are found in the Genizah. Abiathar b. Solomon, dynastic successor to the Gaonate (headship) of the Palestinian Yeshivah, composed a *megillah* at the end of the eleventh century in order to relate how the authority of the Gaonate had been usurped between 1082 and 1094. The *megillah* culminates with the defeat of his evil rival in Egypt, with God's miraculous intervention.[56] In the next century, an Egyptian Jewish "historian" recounted a triumphal struggle between the legitimate holders of the office of head of Fatimid Jewry, among them Maimonides, and an evildoing usurping "Haman" pejoratively nicknamed Zuta (the Small) in a scroll consciously modeled on the *megillah* of Purim and expressly intended to memorialize the episode for future generations.[57]

The application to internal Jewish disputes of the model of the Scroll of Esther, the paradigmatic depiction of Jewish triumph over gentile victimization, would seem to reveal a Jewish perception of persecution as a general phenomenon, and not the monopoly of Muslims. While the Jews believed that salvation always came from God, they learned from their own communal, interpersonal disputes that self-righteous oppression of rivals and of the community-at-large was political in a worldly sense, even if it had religious underpinnings.[58]

Going further, I believe that the dearth of literary sources devoted to persecution of Jews in the Islamic world during the classical centuries reflects a milieu in which there was simply much less of the kind of violent persecution of Jews *as Jews* than that which gave rise to the doleful lit-

---

[55] Mann, *The Jews in Egypt and in Palestine under the Fāṭimid Caliphs*, 1:212–14, 2:257–63; Mark R. Cohen, *Jewish Self-Government in Medieval Egypt* (Princeton, 1980), 279–80.

[56] Best edition in Moshe Gil, *Palestine During the First Muslim Period (634–1099)* (Hebrew) (Tel Aviv, 1983), 3:391–413 (no. 559). See also Gil, *Palestine*, 750–74. The *megillah* and the episode are also treated in my *Jewish Self-Government in Medieval Egypt*, 178–226.

[57] See the edition by A. Kahana, "The Scroll of Zuta the Evil-doer" (Hebrew), *Haschiloach* 15 (1905): 175–84; repr. in Malachi, *Studies*, 1:41–51.

[58] My *Jewish Self-Government in Medieval Egypt* is devoted to the subject of administration, politics, and political conflict within a Jewish community of the Islamic High Middle Ages.

erature and other memorializing traditions of Christian lands. Missing, too, was the entire cluster of theological factors rooted in ancient religious conflict that underlay Jewish responses to persecution in Europe.

Only later, beginning in the sixteenth century, at the same time that Sephardim expelled from Christian Spain began to compose their chronicles of persecution, do we encounter Jewish literary texts from the Muslim world memorializing suffering and persecution at the hands of gentiles. From Egypt comes a *megillah*, in Hebrew and Judeo-Arabic versions, echoing the Book of Esther. Composed in 1524, the scroll describes the deliverance of the Jews of Cairo from a local persecutor, Aḥmad Pasha, the newly-appointed governor of Egypt who rebelled against Ottoman overlordship.[59] The episode, which occurred two weeks after the holiday of Purim, was recorded in some of the Hebrew chronicles of the sixteenth and seventeenth centuries, including Ibn Verga's *Sheveṭ yehudah*. Memorialized in the holiday cycle and liturgy of the Jews of Cairo as an "Egyptian Purim," it was observed as recently as the early 1950's.[60]

One example of the "chronicle of suffering" genre from the late Islamic Middle Ages is a work partly in Hebrew and partly in Judeo-Arabic.[61] The work consists of episodes recorded by members of a family of rabbis named Ibn Danan, descendants of Sephardic exiles who had lived in Morocco since their expulsion from Spain in 1492. The text was first redacted in 1724, but did not take final form until after 1879. It relates in disorderly annalistic fashion the afflictions of the Jews of Fez and other North African Jewish communities from the sixteenth to the nineteenth century.[62] In contrast to the Ashkenazic chronicles, it does not focus exclusively on persecution but, rather, interweaves accounts of mistreatment by Muslims with episodes of misfortune caused by natural catastrophes, especially drought and famine. The anecdotes themselves are replete with depictions of classic, Ashkenazic-like responses to suffering: fasting, prayer, and chronicling of events for posterity. The emergence of such a

---

[59] He is called "the well-known Satan" in several Hebrew versions of the story; Muslim sources refer to him as *al-khā'in* or "the traitor."

[60] See the study, with edited texts, linguistic analysis, and English translation, by Benjamin Hary, *Multiglossia in Judeo-Arabic* (Leiden, 1992), with discussion of all earlier bibliography on this source. For a literary discussion, see Malachi, *Studies*, 1:53–60. Cf. also Yerushalmi, *Zakhor*, 48.

[61] The work was described and translated into French by Georges Vajda and later published in the original by David Ovadia. See: Georges Vajda, *Un recueil de textes historiques judéo-marocains* (Paris, 1951); David Ovadia ed., *Fas ve-ḥakhameha* (Fez and its Scholars) (Jerusalem, 1979), 1:1–63, and Vajda's translation included as an appendix.

[62] Vajda reorders the episodes chronologically.

literary specimen in the late Islamic Middle Ages is suggestive, since it derives from a time when the position of the Jews had come more to resemble the plight of their brethren living in Christendom. This was especially true in Morocco, where, since the mid-twelfth century, the Jews had been the only infidels. (Jews had returned to their original faith at the end of the Almohade persecution, whereas Christians had not.) It casts into sharp relief my argument about the earlier, relatively secure period, when the level of persecution was low and there was no significant Jewish collective memory of suffering at the hands of gentiles.[63]

[63] Two other "chronicles," from late medieval Iran, written in Judeo-Persian, recount the disastrous persecution and forced conversions of Jews by the intolerant Shiʿite regime of the Safavids. One of them, composed by Bābāī Ibn Luṭf, covers periodic persecutions between 1617 and 1662. The other, by Bābāī Ibn Farhād, the grandson of Bābāī Ibn Luṭf, relates the oppression that led to the mass conversion of the Jewish community of Kashan around 1729. Vera B. Moreen's publications on these two sources make it feasible for students of Jewish collective memory in Europe to compare the well-known Ashkenazic and Sephardic chronicles with Oriental counterparts from a period of great oppression; see: V. Moreen, *Iranian Jewry's Hour of Peril and Heroism: A Study of Bābāī Ibn Lutf's Chronicle (1617–1662)* (New York and Jerusalem, 1987); and *Iranian Jewry during the Afghan Invasion: The Kitāb-i Sar Guzasht-i Kāshan of Bābāī b. Farhād* (Stuttgart, 1990).

SAADYA GAON ON CHRISTIANITY AND ISLAM*

DANIEL J. LASKER

Anyone with even a cursory knowledge of Saadya Gaon (882–942) and his oeuvre knows that he was an argumentative individual. From Ben Meir and the calendar, to Ben Zakkai and the role of the Exilarch, to Anan and the Karaites, to Ḥiwi al-Balkhi and his heresy, Saadya was rarely reluctant to take on an adversary (which is why the Karaite claims that he refused to debate them directly seem unlikely).[1] Saadya's writings are full of polemics against groups with whom he disagreed, such polemics affording him, among other things, the opportunity to make his famous copious lists of wrong opinions.[2]

Among the many non-Jewish groups with whom Saadya disagreed, two stand out. The first are the Muslims, about whom Saadya had surprisingly little to say, given the fact that Islam was the dominant religion of the world in which he lived. The second are the Christians, against whom Saadya polemicized quite often, despite their own official minority status in Islamic society. In fact, judging by the amount of attention Saadya paid to the two religions, one might conclude that he lived in a Christian

* Over half a century ago, my uncle Herman Hailperin dealt with some of the issues raised here in an article entitled, "Saadia's Relation to Islamic and Christian Thought," *Historia Judaica* 4 (1942): 2–16. This article was published to commemorate the thousandth anniversary of Saadya's death. Fifty years on, I would like to return to the same subject, this time from a different perspective. I would also like to thank the Institute of Jewish Studies, University College London, for inviting me to the conference of which this volume forms the proceedings. The Institute was founded by my professor and teacher, the late Professor Alexander Altmann, and it provided a framework which allowed him to continue the research that had been so cruelly interrupted in Germany by the rise of Nazism.

[1] The standard biography of Saadya is still Henry Malter, *Saadia Gaon: His Life and Works* (Philadelphia, 1921). On Saadya's polemics with various groups, see: Samuel A. Poznanski, "The Anti-Karaite Writings of Saʿadiah Gaon," *JQR*, o.s. 10 (1898): 238–76, repr. in *Karaite Studies*, ed. P. Birnbaum (New York, 1971), 89–127; Israel Davidson, *Saadia's Polemic Against Ḥiwi al-Balkhi* (New York, 1915); and Arnold A. Lasker and Daniel J. Lasker, "642 Parts—More Concerning the Saadia-Ben Meir Controversy" (Hebrew), *Tarbiz* 60 (1990): 119–28.

[2] See, e.g., *Kitāb al-amānāt waʾl-iʿtiqādāt* (*Sefer ha-emunot ve-ha-deʿot*), 1:3 (twelve wrong opinions about creation of the world); 6:1–2 (seven opinions concerning the nature of the soul). In this paper I cite the Arabic edition and Hebrew translation of Joseph Qafiḥ, *Sefer ha-nivḥar ba-emunot u-va-deʿot* (Jerusalem and New York, 1970) [= *Amānāt*]. I also refer to Samuel Rosenblatt trans., *Saadia Gaon: The Book of Beliefs and Opinions* (New Haven, 1948). It should be noted that the relevant passages dealing with anti-Christian polemic have been censored in standard editions of the medieval Hebrew translation by Judah Ibn Tibbon.

society in which Islam was but a peripheral factor. Even though that, of course, was not the case, it would appear that the sizable Christian populations of Saadya's native Egypt and his adopted city of Baghdad left an impression upon him.[3]

Before trying to answer the question as to why Saadya polemicized more against Christianity than Islam, it would be useful to review what exactly he said about these two religions. Although he offered very few arguments against Islam, Saadya referred to this religion both explicitly and implicitly on many occasions. Thus, as Eliezer Schlossberg has recently shown, Saadya understood the Book of Daniel to be replete with references to Islam (such as "the little horn" of Daniel 7:8) and, therefore, in his *Commentary on Daniel*, often mentions Islam specifically.[4] In his other writings, however, Saadya was much more circumspect. In his exegetical works, he refers to Muslims as descendants of Ishmael, but in his halakhic writings, he generally discusses various issues concerning relations with non-Jews without mentioning Muslims by name. Given the paucity of actual arguments against the majority religion,[5] Schlossberg's contention that Saadya was more ill at ease with Islamic society than with Islam itself seems reasonable. We should also remember that Saadya's world-view was greatly affected by Islamic *kalām* from which he borrowed freely in his theological works.[6]

The situation is different when we look at Saadya and Christianity. The Jewish-Christian polemics of the late medieval period have led us to view the Jewish critique of Christianity as a function of the Christian threat to Judaism that was expressed in missionary efforts. Nevertheless, the substantial number of Jewish anti-Christian polemics emanating from Islamic countries indicate that certain Jewish thinkers considered Christianity to be an important target even in the absence of a conversionary threat.[7] Saadya was such a thinker.

---

[3] On the Christian population of Baghdad in the tenth century, see Joel L. Kraemer, *Humanism in the Renaissance of Islam* (Leiden, 1986), 75–77; Guy Le Strange, *Baghdad During the Abbasid Caliphate* (Oxford, 1924), 207–14; Michel Allard, "Les Chrétiens à Baghdad," *Arabica* 9, 3 (1962): 375–88.

[4] See Eliezer Schlossberg, "Concepts and Methods in the Commentary of R. Saadia Gaon on the Book of Daniel" (Hebrew), (Ph.D. diss., Bar-Ilan University, 1988), esp. 216–89; idem, "R. Saadia Gaon's Attitude Towards Islam" (Hebrew), *Daat* 25 (1990): 21–51.

[5] Moses Ibn Ezra refers to anti-Islamic arguments which can be found in a number of Saadya's works, but it is unclear to which precise works he is referring; see his *Kitāb al-muḥāḍara wa'l-mudhākara*, ed. and trans. A.S. Halkin (Jerusalem, 1975), 38.

[6] Saadya was a (not uncritical) follower of the Mu'tazilite school of *kalām*, and in his *Book of Beliefs and Opinions* he borrowed many *kalām*-type arguments.

[7] See my "The Jewish Critique of Christianity Under Islam in the Middle Ages," *PAAJR* 57 (1991): 121–153.

Saadya's critique of Christianity is concerned with three major topics, all of which he discusses employing both exegetical and rational arguments. These three topics are the nature of God (trinity versus unity and the possibility of incarnation); the status of the messianic redemption (whether or not it has already occurred); and the status of the Law at the present time (whether the laws of the Torah are still applicable).

Book II of Saadya's *Beliefs and Opinions* is devoted to the subject of divine unity. In Saadya's day, there were two groups that denied God's absolute unity: the Dualists, who believed in two gods; and the Christians, who believed in one God with three separate Persons. After dismissing the claims of the Dualists,[8] Saadya turns to the Christians.[9]

According to Saadya, the Christians misunderstand God's attributes of wisdom and life as separate hypostases, arriving, thereby, at a belief in a divine trinity. Saadya responds that God's attributes should not be understood as separate Persons, since God's incorporeality assures that His unity is absolute. And if one wants to understand attributes as Persons, why are there but three? For God possesses more attributes than just life and wisdom. Saadya adds that the Christians arrive at their trinitarian belief by extrapolating from the human condition in which attributes are distinct from essence. God's life and wisdom, however, are not to be distinguished from His essence in the manner in which an individual's life and wisdom can be distinguished from his or her essence. Turning to exegetical arguments, he claims that biblical verses used by the Christians to show divine multiplicity do not have a trinitarian meaning.[10]

A corollary of the doctrine of the trinity is the Christian belief in incarnation, namely that the Person of the Son took on flesh in Jesus. Saadya does not offer new arguments against this Christian belief, relying instead on a reference to his arguments against creation of the world by divine emanation.[11] This last issue also affords him the opportunity of demonstrating his close knowledge of the various Christian denominations, each

---

[8] *Beliefs and Opinions* 2:1–3 (*Amānāt*, 82–88).

[9] Ibid., 2:4–7 (*Amānāt*, 88–95).

[10] Saadya's concern with the Christian doctrine of the trinity finds expression as well in his *Commentary on Genesis*. A discussion of God's attributes in the Preface to this commentary stresses the fact that the three divine attributes of life, power, and wisdom should not be understood as separate, distinct attributes as they are in the case of humans. Christianity is not mentioned by name, but comparison with *Beliefs and Opinions* demonstrates the intended target of the discussion. Furthermore, Saadya named the Christian trinity explicitly in his commentary to Gen. 1:26 ("Let *us* make man"), as well as responding to Christian exegesis to Gen. 18:1–2 (and cf. *Beliefs and Opinions*, 2:6). See Moshe Zucker ed. and trans., *Saadya's Commentary on Genesis* (New York, 1984), 22, 51, 122–123 (Arabic); 200, 252, 373 (Hebrew).

[11] *Beliefs and Opinions*, 1:3 (third opinion; *Amānāt*, 49–51).

of which have a different understanding of the relationship between Jesus' divine and human natures.[12]

The subject of the Christian view of the messianic redemption arises in both *Beliefs and Opinions* and in Saadya's *Commentary on Daniel.*[13] The difference between Judaism and Christianity can be summarized as follows: Christians believe that the biblical promises concerning the messiah have already been fulfilled whereas Jews hold that these promises have yet to be realized. In both *Beliefs and Opinions* and the *Commentary on Daniel*, Saadya argues that the Jewish interpretation of messianic verses is correct. By comparing the biblical promises with contemporary reality, he hopes to demonstrate the impossibility of maintaining that the messiah has already arrived.[14]

The third subject which occupies Saadya in his anti-Christian polemic is the abrogation of the Law (*naskh*). Even though Jews and Christians both believed that the Hebrew Scriptures were divinely revealed and had continued validity, the Christians argued that, with the coming of Jesus, there was no longer a reason to observe the ritual law of the Bible. The latter part of *Beliefs and Opinions*, Book Three is devoted to arguing that the Torah is to be observed eternally. There is no warrant for the Christian abandonment of Jewish law.

By claiming that Saadya's discussion of the annulment of the Torah in *Beliefs and Opinions* 3:7–9 is specifically anti-Christian, I am disagreeing with the assessment made by Eliezer Schlossberg and a number of other scholars. Understanding this section to be anti-Islamic, Schlossberg asserts that Saadya engaged in anti-Muslim polemic.[15] If this were true, my con-

---

[12] Saadya's critique of the Christian doctrines of trinity and incarnation is discussed in my *Jewish Philosophical Polemics Against Christianity in the Middle Ages* (New York, 1977), 55–57; 109. See also Harry A. Wolfson, "Saadia on the Semantic Aspect of the Problem of Attributes," in *Salo W. Baron Jubilee Volume* (New York and London, 1975), 2:1009–1021; idem, "Saadia on the Trinity and Incarnation," in *Studies and Essays in Honor of Abraham A. Neumann*, ed. M. Ben-Horin et al. (Leiden, 1962), 547–568, reprinted in Wolfson, *Studies in the History of Philosophy and Religion* (Cambridge, Mass. and London, 1973–77), 2:393–414.

[13] *Beliefs and Opinions* 8:7–9 (*Amānāt*, 252–60); for the *Commentary on Daniel*, see Schlossberg, "Concepts," 323–50. Note that Schlossberg maintains (p. 350) that the Christological interpretations of Daniel were an important factor in Saadia's decision to write a commentary on that book.

[14] Christians were not the only group to claim that the messianic passages in the Bible had already been fulfilled. Referring to a group which ostensibly claimed to be Jewish (*qauman mimman yatasammawna bi'l-yahūdiyya*), Saadya claims that they also have no future messianic hope. This group has not been identified with any certainty; see *Beliefs and Opinions*, 8:7; Schlossberg, "Concepts," 325–27.

[15] See his "R. Saadia Gaon's Attitude," 39–49. Schlossberg also raises the possibility that this section is directed against Karaites as well as against Muslims but rejects that possibility in favor

tention that Saadya polemicized against Christianity while almost ignoring Islam would be called into question. It is important, then, that we clarify the object of Saadya's polemic against the annulment of the Torah.

It is true that the dominant religion in Saadya's day was Islam and that Muslims also believed that the laws of the Hebrew Bible were no longer applicable. Nevertheless, the fact that Saadya polemicized against Christianity concerning trinity, incarnation, and messianism demonstrates his concern with that religion's doctrines, one of which is the nullification of Mosaic Law. In addition, it would seem *prima facie* that a Jewish discussion of abrogation of the Law which relies to a great extent on arguments from the Hebrew Scriptures would be directed at Christians, who accepted those Scriptures, but who disagreed with Jews as to their correct interpretation, rather than at Muslims, who did not accept the validity of the Hebrew Scriptures.[16]

In his discussion of Saadya's polemic concerning abrogation, Schlossberg admits that certain references in Saadya's work, such as his citations of Jeremiah 31 and Obadiah, should be understood as anti-Christian. He believes, nevertheless, that Saadya's discussion of abrogation is predominantly anti-Islamic. To substantiate this claim, Schlossberg adduces parallels from Islamic sources concerning abrogation. Most of these authors, however, such as al-Baqillānī (d. 1013) and ʿAbd al-Jabbār (d. 1024/25)

---

of his original anti-Islamic thesis. While he admits that specific arguments are directed at Christianity (see, e.g., p. 44, n. 146), he does not consider a possible Christian background to the discussion of *naskh* in general.

Among other scholars who have understood Saadya's discussion of abrogation in an Islamic context are Hava Lazarus-Yafeh and John Wansbrough (references in next note), Moshe Zucker, *Saadya's Commentary on Genesis*, pp. 368–69, n. 132; idem, *Rav Saadya Gaon's Translation of the Torah* (New York, 1959), p. 29, n. 60*; and Andrew Rippin (see n. 34). See now also Mark R. Cohen, *Under Crescent and Cross: The Jews in the Middle Ages* (Princeton, 1994), 156, where the author refers to the oral presentation upon which this article is based and argues that Saadya's discussion is directed at Islam.

[16] Islamic attitudes toward the Hebrew Bible are discussed in Hava Lazarus-Yafeh, *Intertwined Worlds: Medieval Islam and Bible Criticism* (Princeton, 1992). In her discussion of abrogation (35–41), Lazarus-Yafeh assumes that Saadya was responding to Muslim arguments in *Beliefs and Opinions* 3:7–9.

We have at least two pre-Saadyanic instances of Islamic anti-Jewish argumentation in favor of abrogation that rely on discussion of the Hebrew Bible; neither of them is totally devoid of a Christian connection. The first, the mid-ninth century *Kitāb al-dīn wa'l-dawla*, was written by Alī ibn Rabbān al-Ṭabarī, a Christian convert to Islam; see the edition of A. Mingana (Manchester, 1923) and his English translation, *The Book of Religion and Empire by Alī Tabarī* (Manchester, 1922). Alī Ṭabarī defends *naskh* on the grounds that Jesus and Paul had abrogated the Law first and that therefore, it is permitted for Muslims to do so; see 134–36 (Arabic) and 158–60 (English). The second, an account of a discussion between the Muʿtazilite author Ibrāhīm al-Naẓẓām (d. ca. 840) and a Jew, was preserved by Christian scholars. For the text, see L. Cheikho,

postdate Saadya and should be used with caution when determining Saadya's target.[17] Furthermore, while the Muslim texts adduced by Schlossberg do talk about abrogation (*naskh*), the parallels are not particularly striking, and almost no parallels are adduced for arguments based on specific scriptural verses or contradictions. My position is that there are much closer parallels to Saadya's arguments in Christian writings which predate Saadya; it makes much more sense, therefore, to interpret his discussion in *Beliefs and Opinions* of the law's annulment as being directed primarily at Christianity, although Islam may have been a secondary target.

Saadya begins his discussion of the Torah's eternity by citing three prophetic statements to that effect: Deuteronomy 33:4, Jeremiah 31:34–35, and Malachi 3:22–23 (4:4–5). The last two passages are particularly significant, since already in the New Testament, Christians referred to Jeremiah 31 ("the new covenant") and the end of Malachi ("Behold, I will send you Elijah the Prophet") as predicting the new Christian religion.[18] He adds an additional argument for the Law's eternity, which others had already made: had the Torah been intended for a limited time only, to be superseded in due course by another, this would have been stated explicitly.[19]

Saadya then turns to arguments for the possibility of annulment. The

Vingt traités théologiques d'auteurs Arabes chrétiens (Beirut, 1920), 68–70; an English translation is provided by John Wansbrough, *The Sectarian Milieu: Content and Composition of Islamic Salvation History* (Oxford, 1978), 110–12. A slightly different version (and English translation) of this encounter has been published by A.S. Tritton, "'Debate' Between a Muslim and a Jew," *Islamic Studies* 1:2 (1962): 60–64. Tritton states that the mention of Jeremiah (see below, n. 32) is "suspicious." For the decisive influence of Christian converts to Islam upon Muslim anti-Jewish polemics, see Moshe Perlmann, "The Medieval Polemics Between Judaism and Islam," in *Religion in a Religious Age*, ed. S.D. Goitein (Cambridge, Mass., 1974), 106.

[17] Not only do al-Baqillāni and ʿAbd al-Jabbār postdate Saadya, but their knowledge of the Bible was also not very extensive. It certainly was not sufficient for the type of arguments for abrogation adduced by Saadya; see Schlossberg, "R. Saadia Gaon's Attitude," pp. 40–41, n. 125.

Hava Lazarus-Yafeh uses Saadya's discussion of *naskh* as evidence that this topos was already well developed in Islamic anti-Jewish polemics by the tenth century. If, however, the thrust of Saadya's argument is against Christianity, such a conclusion would not be warranted; see *Intertwined Worlds*, 37. On the generally poor knowledge that Muslims had of the biblical text see ibid., 111–29.

Saadya's Karaite contemporary, Yaʿqūb al-Qirqisānī also refuted the concept of *naskh* held by certain Ananites and Karaites, as well as by Muslims; see his *Kitāb al-anwār wa'l-marāqib*, ed. Leon Nemoy (New York, 1939–1943), 2:440–468 (Fourth Discourse, Chs. 52–57), trans. G. Vajda, "Études sur Qirqisānī IV," *REJ* 120 (1961): 234–56.

[18] For Jeremiah, see Heb. 8:8–12; 10:16–17; for Malachi, see Matt. 17:11; Mk. 9:12; cf. also Tertullian, "An Answer to the Jews," in *The Ante-Nicene Fathers*, ed. Alexander Roberts and James Donaldson (Grand Rapids, Mich., 1973), 3:154; Hippolytus, "Treatise on Christ and Antichrist," in ibid., (Grand Rapids, Mich., 1971), 5:213. See also A. Altmann, *Saadya Gaon, Book of Doctrines and Beliefs* (Oxford, 1946), p. 113, n. 1, reprinted in *Three Jewish Philosophers*, ed. H. Lewy et al. (New York, 1972).

[19] *Amānāt*, 132–33.

first group of arguments are presented as follows: "Now I have seen someone who presents seven arguments in favor of the possibility of the abrogation of the Law which, he maintains, are advanced by reason, and all of which would corroborate such a view."[20] No indication is given as to the identity of this person. Since the arguments are claimed by their exponent to be rational (*naẓariyya*), not exegetical, there is no reason to assume that they were necessarily advanced by a Christian rather than by a Muslim. The advocate of abrogation argues, for instance, that just as dates turn from green to red, so the Torah can be annulled; just as people are rich and then poor, or alive and then dead, seeing and then blind, the Torah can change; just as the living are commanded to observe commandments but at their death they are released from them, so, too, the Torah can be annulled; just as one is commanded to work one day and to rest on another, or to fast one day and eat on another, the Torah can order certain actions for a circumscribed period and then abrogate those actions.[21]

Not all seven arguments, though, are of this "rational" variety. The sixth proof is that just as work on the Sabbath is permitted by reason and forbidden by a revelational commandment, so too, a new revelational commandment can be given to allow work on the Sabbath.[22] The seventh argument is that just as the Law of Abraham was replaced by the Law of Moses, in like manner the Law of Moses can be replaced by another Law. This last argument can be found, for instance, in a second-century polemic, Tertullian's *Against the Jews*, in which it is argued that the various divine laws, namely those of Adam, Noah, Abraham, and Moses, all have the same core, and one replaces the other without there being any real change.[23] Interestingly enough, Saadya also argues in this context that the Law of Moses is based upon the Law of Abraham. This position appears to be identical with Tertullian's stance—yet Tertullian employs this claim in order to argue that the Law of Moses may be abrogated, while Saadya understands it as a refutation of the idea that God changes His mind.

Other Christians also argued that pre-Mosaic figures did not observe the Law of Moses, and, therefore, that the Law of Moses abrogated previous divine laws.[24] It would seem, then, that although there is no

[20] Rosenblatt, *The Book of Beliefs and Opinions*, 159–60.

[21] *Amānāt*, 133–35. Saadya responds to these arguments by claiming that the analogies are not relevant to the claim of abrogation.

[22] The distinction between rational and revelational commandments is drawn in *Beliefs and Opinions* 3:1–2.

[23] Tertullian, "An Answer to the Jews," 3:152.

[24] See, e.g.: Jacob Neusner, *Aphrahat and Judaism: The Christian-Jewish Argument in Fourth-Century Iran* (Leiden, 1971), 22 (concerning circumcision), 43–46 (concerning the Sabbath);

evidence that the seven arguments for abrogation were advanced by a Christian rather than by a Muslim, at least part of the argumentation accords well with Christian theology.

Saadya then turns to what he considers to be a major argument for abrogation, namely, the possibility of a prophet's arising who could abrogate the Torah by performing miracles greater than those of Moses.[25] Saadya may very well have Muḥammad in mind here, since Christians claim that Jesus was messiah and God, not a prophet. Nevertheless, the Christians did argue that Jesus' miracles were greater than Moses' and that, therefore, he possessed greater authority than did Moses. This claim was made, for instance, by Origen in his treatise *Against Celsus* as well as by the Christian Arab author Theodore Abū Qurra (c. 750–825).[26] Furthermore, the Nestorian Patriarch Timothy I (late eighth century) contrasted the abrogation of the Law of Moses, which was brought about by the miracles of Jesus, with the ongoing validity of Christianity, because Muḥammad had not performed any miracles.[27] Jesus was identified in the New Testament (Acts 3:22–23; 7:37) as the new prophet about whom Moses spoke in Deuteronomy 18:15–19, and this remained the standard Christian exegesis.[28] In addition, a Jewish anti-Christian polemic, *Qiṣṣat Mujādalat*

Eutychius of Alexandria (attributed), *The Book of Demonstration (Kitāb al-burhān)*, Pt. 2, trans. W. Montgomery Watt (Louvain, 1961), 116–19 (just as the Law of Moses replaced the Law of Adam, so, too, can the Law of Jesus replace the Law of Moses).

[25] Saadya responds to this argument by contending that one does not accept a prophet on the basis of his miracles but rather on the basis of the prophetic message which is then corroborated by the miracles. This statement seems to contradict Saadya's epistemology as found in the Introduction to *Beliefs and Opinions*, as well as the methodology of most of the book. Since, however, this passage is polemical, there is no reason to expect consistency on the author's part.

[26] See: Origen, "Against Celsus," in *The Ante-Nicene Fathers*, ed. A. Roberts and J. Donaldson (Grand Rapids, Mich., 1972), 4:452; Constantine Bacha ed. and trans., *Un traité des œuvres arabes de Théodore Abou-Kurra* (Tripoli, Syria and Rome, 1905), 8–10 (Arabic), 17, 19 (French). On Abū Qurra, see Sidney H. Griffith, "Theodore Abū Qurra: The Intellectual Profile of an Arab Christian Writer of the First Abbasid Century," *Annual Lecture of The Irene Halmost Chair in Arabic Literature* (Tel Aviv University, 1992).

[27] See *The Apology of Timothy the Patriarch before the Caliph Mahdi*, in A. Mingana, *Woodbrooke Studies* (Cambridge, 1928), 2:36–37. In the introduction to this work (6–8), Rendel Harris concludes that Christian arguments from the Islamic period exhibit great affinity to patristic Christian traditions. This would reinforce the contention here that one should read Saadya's polemic in the context of earlier Christian writings, even ones from the pre-Islamic period.

[28] See the sources listed by David Berger, *The Jewish-Christian Debate in the High Middle Ages* (Philadelphia, 1979), 262.

Alī Ṭabarī understood Deut. 18:15–19 as referring to Muḥammad, specifically denying this passage's applicability to Jesus (demonstrating thereby that this was the standard Christian understanding of his day); see *Al-dīn wa'l-dawla*, 73–74, 134 (Arabic); 85–86, 158 (English). The Caliph Mahdī is represented by Timothy as saying that these verses refer to Muhammad; see *Apology*, 50. Cf. also Maimonides, "Iggeret teiman" ("Epistle to Yemen"), in *Iggerot le-rabbenu moshe ben maimon*, ed. J. Qafiḥ (Jerusalem, 1972), 35–36.

al-Usquf (*The Account of the Disputation of the Priest*), roughly contemporary with Saadya, presents the Christians as arguing for Jesus' divinity on the basis of the miracles which he had performed.[29]

Saadya next turns to biblical proofs employed by those who argue for abrogation and it is here that the Christian context is most clearly observed. These verses include Deuteronomy 33:2 (as understood in light of Habakuk 3:3), Obadiah 1:1, and Jeremiah 31:30 (31). While the verse from Deuteronomy is understood by the Muslims as referring to Muḥammad,[30] the follow-up verse from Habakkuk is often cited by Christians as predictive of Jesus.[31] The other two verses also should be seen in terms of Christian exegesis. Obadiah refers to Edom, whom Saadya identifies with Christianity, and the verse from Jeremiah was a particularly favorite Christological passage.[32]

The aforementioned verses are then reinforced with ten so-called scriptural doubts which are claimed to prove the possibility of abrogation. Such doubts include: the permission for Adam's sons to marry their sisters;[33] the fact that Cain was not sentenced to death in opposition to biblical law; the prohibition of non-priests' offering sacrifices after they were allowed to be offered by anyone; the permission to offer sacrifices on the Sabbath; God's changing His mind concerning the sacrifice of Isaac;[34] the

---

[29] This text, along with its Hebrew version, *Sefer nesṭor ha-komer* (The Book of Nestor the Priest), will be available in Daniel J. Lasker and Sarah Stroumsa, *The Polemic of Nestor the Priest* (forthcoming). In the meantime, see Leon Schlosberg, *Qiṣṣat mujādalat al-usquf* (*Controverse d'un évêque*) (Vienna, 1880); and my "*Qiṣṣat Mujādalat al-Usquf* and *Nesṭor Ha-Komer*: The Earliest Arabic and Hebrew Jewish Anti-Christian Polemics," in *Geniza Research After Ninety Years: The Case of Judaeo-Arabic*, ed. Joshua Blau and Stefan C. Reif (Cambridge, 1992), 112–18.

[30] Alī Ṭabarī, *Al-din wa'l-dawla*, 74–75 (Arabic); 86–87 (English); cf. also Maimonides, "Epistle to Yemen," 34–35.

[31] Cyprian, "Treatise XII, Three Books of Testimonies Against the Jews," in *The Ante-Nicene Fathers*, 5:524; see also the sources listed in Berger, *The Jewish-Christian Debate*, 286. In the Arabic-speaking world, see Eutychius (attributed), *The Book of Demonstration*, 69, 71.

[32] Schlossberg agrees that the verses from Obadiah and Jeremiah are directed at Christians; see "R. Saadia Gaon's Attitude," p. 44, n. 146. For the Christian exegesis of Jeremiah, see, in addition to the references in n. 18: Tertullian, "An Answer to the Jews," 154; Cyprian, "Against the Jews," 511; Bacha, *Abou-Kurra*, 11 (Arabic), 20 (French); *The Disputation of Sergius the Stylite Against a Jew*, trans. A.P. Hayman, (Louvain, 1973), 4 (and cf. n. 34 there for further references).

The verse from Jeremiah is also cited in the description of the dispute of al-Naẓẓām; see: Cheikho, *Vingt traités*, 69; Wansbrough, *Sectarian Milieu*, 111; Tritton, "Debate," 61–62, 64.

[33] Schlossberg interprets this passage as referring to Adam's marrying his own daughters (perhaps on the basis of an unclear note by Qafiḥ, *Amānāt*, p. 139, n. 82); the text (as well as the biblical story as mediated by the Midrash) would seem to argue against this understanding of Saadya's words.

[34] The accusation that God changed his mind in regard to the binding of Isaac is found in the

permission to Balaam to go with the Moabite messengers after having been forbidden to do so; the annulment of the death sentence passed against Hezekiah; the replacement of the obligation of the first-born Israelites by the Levites; Joshua's putative non-observance of the Sabbath during the siege of Jericho; and the change in the direction of prayer from the sanctuary to Jerusalem.[35]

Parallels to a number of these arguments can be found in either the New Testament, the Church Fathers, or Christian Arabic works. The question of laying siege to Jericho on the Sabbath, for example, may go back to Hebrews 4:8–9 and is developed by both Tertullian and the Syriac Aphrahat.[36] The permission to offer sacrifices on the Sabbath is already noted in Matthew 12:5 and discussed further by John Chrysostom and John of Damascus.[37] Concerning the monopoly of the priests over the sacrificial system, Jesus is described in Hebrews 9:11–12 as having taken the place of the High Priest in the offering of sacrifices.[38]

Saadya's concluding arguments against abrogation of the Law concern

---

account of the discussion between al-Naẓẓām and a Jew (see above, n. 16), and, therefore, may have an Islamic flavor to it (an account of the binding of Abraham's son is found in Qur'ān 37:99–110). For discussions that assume an Islamic background to this point, see: Wansbrough, *Sectarian Milieu*, 109–14; Andrew Rippin, "Sa'adya Gaon and Genesis 22: Aspects of Jewish-Muslim Interaction and Polemic," in *Studies in Islamic and Jewish Traditions*, ed. William M. Brinner and Stephen D. Ricks (Atlanta, 1986), 33–46; Tritton, "Debate." Cf., however, Heb. 11:17–19.

Abraham Ibn Ezra's Commentary on Gen. 22:1 shows evidence that he was aware of the geonic discussions of God's changing His mind (*ḥazarah*) in the case of the binding of Isaac.

For Christians, the binding of Isaac is a prefiguration of the crucifixion; see, e.g., Theodoret, "Dialogues," in *A Select Library of Nicene and Post-Nicene Fathers*, ed. Philip Schaff and Henry Wace (Grand Rapids, Mich., 1969), 3:225.

[35] Some of these objections go back at least to Marcion and were refuted by Tertullian; see "Against Marcion," in *Ante-Nicene Fathers*, 3:317 (sentence of Cain), 313–314 (Joshua in Jericho); and 310, 452 (the reprieve for Hezekiah). It is also possible that, in Saadya's day, these objections circulated in heretical circles, such as that of Ḥiwi al-Balkhi.

[36] See: Tertullian, "Answer to the Jews," 155; Neusner, *Aphrahat*, 48–49; John of Damascus, "Exposition of the Orthodox Faith," in *A Select Library of the Nicene and Post-Nicene Fathers*, 2d Series, 9:95.

[37] John Chrysostom, "Homilies on the Gospel According to St. Matthew," in *A Select Library of the Nicene and Post-Nicene Fathers*, 1st Series, 10:256; John of Damascus, "Exposition," 95.

Saadya's answer to this argument also shows a possible anti-Christian context. Saadya writes that pre-Sinaitic commandments, such as sacrifices and circumcision, were not annulled by the Sabbath. Mention of circumcision would seem to indicate that Saadya has Christians, rather than Muslims, in mind, since both Jews and Muslims accept circumcision, and Christians do not. Another possibility is that there is a veiled reference here to Anan's prohibition of performing circumcisions on the Sabbath day. See also Zucker, *Commentary on Genesis*, 368 (and cf. n. 132).

[38] The example of Cain's not receiving the death sentence is raised by the thirteenth-century Christian Paul Rahib; see Cheikho, *Vingt traités*, p. 64. Such late evidence, however, should not be introduced.

the meaning of "eternal" (*'olam*), and the possible objection of the Brahmans against certain Pentateuchal laws.[39] There is nothing particularly Islamic about these arguments.

There is one more indication that the section on abrogation in *Beliefs and Opinions* is directed at Christians. At the end of both explicitly anti-Christian passages in *Beliefs and Opinions*—Book Two, Chapter Seven (against trinity and incarnation) and Book Eight, Chapter Nine (against the Christian doctrine that the messiah has already come)—Saadya refers to his discussion of abrogation as further proof that Christianity is a false religion. Thus, after enumerating the various Christian views on incarnation, Saadya writes that his discussions of abrogation and redemption refute the Christian doctrines.[40] And at the end of Book Eight, after demonstrating that the messiah has not yet come, Saadya concludes: "These are, then, the arguments that may be offered in refutation of the doctrine of the Christians aside from the objections to be raised against their theory of the abrogation of the laws of the Torah and those that might be urged against them on the subject of the unity of God."[41] In other words, Saadya himself saw his arguments against abrogation as directed at the Christians. Not one word is said about the Muslims.[42]

When all the evidence is analyzed, it appears that many of Saadya's specific arguments against abrogation of the Torah were in response to Christian and not Muslim claims. While Saadya's exact sources may elude us in a number of cases, there is no reason in their absence to assume necessarily that the contentions were derived from Islamic polemics. When

---

[39] The enigma of the Brahmans has been discussed by quite a number of scholars; see the recent article and summary of previous opinions by Binyamin Abrahamov, "The Barāhima's Enigma: A Search for a New Solution," *Die Welt des Orients* 18 (1987): 72–91.

[40] *Amānāt*, 95.

[41] Rosenblatt, *The Book of Beliefs and Opinions*, 322 (translation slightly modified); *Amānāt*, 260.

[42] Bernard Septimus has seen a hint of an anti-Islamic polemic in a passage explicitly directed at Christians, *Book of Beliefs and Opinions*, 2:7. Septimus argues that the group of "Christians" which had recently arisen was really a reference to Muslims. See Septimus, "A Prudent Ambiguity in Saadya Gaon's Book of Doctrines and Beliefs," *HTR* 76 (1983): 249–54. Harry A. Wolfson, with whom Septimus takes issue, had identified the object of Saadya's reference with "a splinter group of Nestorians"; see the articles mentioned in n. 12; and idem, "More About the Unknown Splinter Group of Nestorians," *Revue des Études Augustiniennes* 11 (1965): 217–22. There is, however, another possibility. A ninth-century *summa theologiae arabica*, now being edited by Sidney Griffith, describes a group of Christians which tried to please the Muslim majority by denying the divinity of Jesus. Saadya may very well have this group in mind when he discusses the different Christian views of incarnation; see Griffith, "The First *Summa Theologiae* in Arabic: Christian Kalam in Ninth-Century Palestine," in *Conversion and Continuity* (Papers in Medieval Studies 9), ed. Michael Gervers and Ramzi Jibran Bikhazi (Toronto, 1990), 15–31.

one considers Saadya's obvious reluctance to polemicize against other Islamic tenets while exercising no such restraint vis-à-vis Christianity, it would seem that the discussion of *naskh* should be seen in the context of Saadya's anti-Christian polemic. This does not preclude Saadya's having the Muslims in mind as a secondary target.[43]

Why did Saadya polemicize against Christianity, while almost ignoring Islam? There are three possible explanations, none of which excludes any of the others. First, Saadya was being circumspect. Whereas Muslims apparently did not exercise censorship of Jewish writings, and few of them in any case could read Arabic in Hebrew script, there were Jewish apostates to Islam who might inform on their former co-religionists to curry favor with their new-found brethren. It was, therefore, much safer for Saadya to criticize Christianity than Islam.[44]

Second, there are greater theological differences between Judaism and Christianity than between Judaism and Islam. The strict monotheism of Islam was generally indistinguishable from the Jewish doctrine of God. Furthermore, while Muslims might have charged Jews with distorting the Hebrew Bible, they did not expropriate the biblical text and claim it as their own, as the Christians did. Whereas Islam was the majority religion and might have been a more realistic challenge to Judaism, in theory at least, Christianity presented the greater threat.

Finally, it may very well be the case that tenth-century Babylonian Jewry felt quite at home as a minority among a Muslim majority. There was no overwhelming conversionary pressure upon them, and, hence, no sufficient reason to pick a fight, as it were, with Islam. Notwithstanding Saadya's

[43] A shorter, Hebrew version of the present article was published in *Daʿat* 32–33 (1994): 13–17, under the title: "Against Whom Did Rav Saadia Gaon Polemicize in his Discussion Concerning Abrogation of the Torah?". The editors of that journal provided Dr. Schlossberg with the right of response to my article. Without going into detail, suffice it to say that Schlossberg's response did not convince me any more than his original article did. The argument which Schlossberg makes from a consensus of earlier scholarly opinion is irrelevant. While it may be true, as Schlossberg maintains, that Saadya did not know the works of Tertullian, Origen, or Aphrahat, it is still much more likely that he knew their works than that he knew those of al-Baqillānī or ʿAbd Al-Jabbār which were composed long after his death. To argue that Muslims contemporaneous with Saadya must have attacked the Jews concerning abrogation because Saadya responds to such attacks is circular and begs the question as to whether Saadya's discussion is directed at Christianity or at Islam.

[44] It may be the case that sometimes polemics explicitly directed at Christianity in Islamic countries were really meant against Islam. Even if that were true, later Jewish writers in Christian countries employed the anti-Christian polemics from Islamic countries as the basis of their own polemics; see my "Judeo-Christian Polemics and Their Origins in Muslim Countries" (Hebrew), *Peʿamim* 57 (1993): 4–16.

comments on the burden of the Islamic exile, the situation was not so terrible as to provoke him into attacking the majority religion openly. The challenge posed by a rival *dhimmî* religion—a religion which believed in the same holy scriptures as the Jews—did, however, call for a carefully-argued response. As we have seen, Saadya Gaon did not shrink from the task.[45]

[45] Dr. Sarah Stroumsa, who was kind enough to discuss some of the issues raised here with me, is of the opinion that Saadya's discussion of abrogation is not directed at any particular group, but rather is intended as a general refutation of the doctrine of abrogation.

ON JEWISH INTELLECTUALS WHO CONVERTED IN THE EARLY MIDDLE AGES*

Sarah Stroumsa

"Minorities living amidst a huge majority are prone to be partly absorbed by it," remarks S.D. Goitein in his discussion of converts and proselytes in light of the Genizah documents.[1] From this generalization it is apparent that, in the Islamic world, conversion of Jews to Islam is essentially both a natural and a foreseeable process. Nevertheless, when we scrutinize individual instances of conversion, we are likely to find immediate factors which bring about—or at least hasten—the decision in each case to adopt another faith. In his discussion of Jewish conversion to Islam, Goitein counts among these factors alienation from the Jewish community—both in a geographic and social sense—on the one hand, and attraction to Islam, on the other. In this context, he presents the conversion of Jewish dignitaries to Islam as an expedient measure adopted for the sake of advancement as well as a means of avoiding persecution. Indeed, Goitein's opening sentence cited above reflects his conviction that the conversion of Jews to Islam can be explained by the force of the dominant faith.

Obviously, Jewish intellectuals living under Islamic rule were affected by the same forces of attraction and repulsion which affected the larger Jewish community.[2] On occasion, intellectuals were forcibly converted;[3] we certainly can find instances of Jewish humanists who apostasized half-heartedly—as did Heine in his time solely in order to gain an entrée into society.[4] In devoting a separate study to conversion among intellectuals,

* An earlier version of this paper was published in Hebrew in *Pe'amim* 42 (1990): 61–75. I wish to express my gratitude to Daniel Frank, who translated the Hebrew and offered many judicious remarks for its revision.

[1] S.D. Goitein, *A Mediterranean Society* (Berkeley and Los Angeles, 1971), 2:299. See further his comments, 300–301.

[2] For lack of anything better and despite its slightly modern flavor, I have used the term "intellectuals" in this paper to designate those learned individuals whose writings and deeds testify to their particular interest in ideas.

[3] According to Muslim sources, this was the case with Maimonides—see: Ibn al-Qiftī, *Ta'arīkh al-ḥukamā'*, ed. J. Lippert (Leipzig, 1903), 317–19; B. Lewis, *The Jews of Islam* (Princeton, 1984), 100; D.S. Margoliouth, "The Legend of the Apostasy of Maimonides," *JQR* o.s. 13 (1901): 539–41. The same was true of Joseph Ibn 'Aqnīn, as he himself testifies; see Joseph ben Judah Ibn 'Aqnīn, *Commentary on the Song of Songs*, ed. A.S. Halkin (Jerusalem, 1964), 500.

[4] *See EJB*, s.v. "Heine, Heinrich." A note of skepticism as to the sincerity of Jews converting

however, we begin with the underlying assumption that it is possible to discern some sort of unifying element in their conversion processes—an element bound up with the fact of their being intellectuals. It is possible, moreover, that such a unifying element finds expression in motivations for conversion which do not exist—or at least not to the same degree—among other segments of the population.

Since intellectuals by definition engage in ideas, we might initially expect the influence of the majority upon them to express itself in spiritual and intellectual terms. Some scholars have suggested the attraction to a "wiser," "more spiritual" religion and to religio-mystical experience as a factor in the conversion of Jews.[5] In support of this theory, it may be noted that Jews who converted to Christianity indeed explicitly expressed their attraction to the more "spiritual" religion.[6] It seems to me, however, that among Jewish intellectuals living in Islamic lands—as among their Christian counterparts—this was not one of the stated factors for conversion to Islam. Even the role of Sufis in disseminating Islam probably expressed itself not so much in their presentation of a more "spiritual" religion, as in other aspects of their activity.[7] Nevertheless, it can be assumed that for the intellectually inclined, the desire to assimilate within the majority society also encompasses a longing to participate in a world of ideas regarded as superior, to be admitted to the cultured world.[8]

Also, because the intellectuals were literarily inclined, we may expect them to have recorded the circumstances of their decisions to convert, thereby affording us a glimpse of the apostates' inner world. In the writings of those intellectuals who apostasized out of inner conviction we can also hope to find some analysis of those spiritual factors which they found to be superior in their new faith. In instances of opportunistic or forced

---

to Islam may be discerned in *The Apology of al-Kindi*, which says: "A Jew remains true to his Judaism and preserves the laws of his Torah (even) when he shows himself to be Muslim" (*inna al-yahūdī innamā taṣiḥḥu yahūdiyyatuhu wa-yaḥfaẓu sharā'iʿ tawrātihi idha aẓhara al-islām*), see Georges Tartar, *Dialogue Islamo-chrétien sous le calife al-Ma'mun (813–834), les épîtres d'al-Hasimi et d'al-Kindi; thèse pour le doctorat de 3 cycle* (Strasbourg, 1977), 94.

[5] See Lewis, *Jews of Islam*, 95.

[6] This was the case, e.g., with Herman of Cologne—see J. Cohen, "The Mentality of the Medieval Jewish Apostate: Peter Alfonsi, Herman of Cologne, and Pablo Christiani," in *Jewish Apostasy in the Modern World*, ed. T.M. Endelman (New York and London, 1987), 33–35.

[7] See N. Levtzion, "Toward a Comparative Study of Islamization," in *Conversion to Islam* (New York and London, 1979), 16–21.

[8] An anonymous polemical treatise found in the Firkovich collection at St. Petersburg (II Firk. Heb.-Arab.I.3022) tells us of the intellectual attraction that Islam had for Jews in his time. The author, writing in tenth-century Iraq, says that Islam was presented to them in a beautiful, logical way, and many converted.

conversion, on the other hand, we may also expect our literary sources to reveal a certain tension between an author's past and his inner convictions and between the day-to-day existence which he chose to live.[9]

In fairness, it ought to be stated that the study of intellectuals and their religious conversions is necessarily marred by a certain measure of arbitrariness. The limitations of such a study may be illustrated by one defining aspect of these intellectuals, viz. their professions. Learned businessmen and craftsmen were certainly to be found in the medieval Jewish world; by virtue of their employment, however, these people were not considered intellectuals. Even when such individuals appear in texts and documents, what is recorded generally—though not always—reflects their financial problems rather than their intellectual pursuits.[10] By way of contrast, for the period under consideration, physicians were generally regarded as scholars whose intellectual interests were manifest in their profession. Biographical works were, therefore, devoted to them; these enable us to become acquainted with them and their life-stories. Physicians figure prominently, therefore, in our discussion of intellectuals, even though there is no certainty that they actually constituted such a high proportion of the intellectual elite. From the distance of several hundred years, however, we can identify as "Jewish intellectuals who converted" only those individuals who were raised and educated as Jews, who were sufficiently important to have made an impression upon their contemporaries, and whose conversion was, therefore, duly noted. We may well suppose that there were numerous instances of educated individuals and men of letters who converted. If, however, the Muslim chroniclers did not mention them by name or if they themselves left no written accounts, then we have no way of knowing about them or of following their conversion.

In the following pages I neither claim to describe a social stratum nor offer a comprehensive sociological analysis of Jewish intellectuals who converted within the Islamic world. The quantity of factual evidence available to us does not, in my opinion, warrant such an analysis. Historians and sociologists must necessarily make do with the "socio-biographical" description of isolated instances that have come down to us. What follows is an attempt to analyze some such isolated instances from the perspective of intellectual history.

---

[9] See, e.g., Heine's "Hebrew Melodies."

[10] An exception to this can be seen in the *Kitāb al-manāẓir*, which records the weekly scholarly meetings of learned merchants and artisans in tenth-century Mosul. See H. Ben-Shammai, "A Philosophical Study Group in Tenth Century Mosul—A Document for the Socio-Cultural History of a Jewish Community in a Muslim Country" (Hebrew), *Peʿamim* 41 (1990): 21–31.

Kaʿb al-Akhbār

For the period of Islamic origins we lack real documentation relating to the subject of this inquiry.[11] The Muslim tradition literature relates that Kaʿb al-Akhbār awaited the advent of the Prophet foretold by the Scriptures, even before he became the first Jew to convert to Islam. It is further related that his expectations were strengthened and fuelled by dream visions; ultimately he converted, having recognized in Muḥammad the likeness of the expected prophet. Numerous Jewish traditions (*isrāʾīliyāt*) have been transmitted in Kaʿb's name. The figure of Kaʿb thus personifies the processes of Jewish influence upon early Islam. Certain features of Kaʿb's story which recur frequently in the conversion accounts of intellectuals shed light upon the individual's personal process of conversion to Islam: the tendency to provide intellectual justification by citing and analyzing biblical prooftexts; the production of supernatural justification in the form of dream-experiences[12]; and the attempt to preserve a cultural and spiritual continuity between the old and new faiths even after the conversion had taken place. At the same time, however, it must be said that the figure of Kaʿb belongs more to the realm of myth than of history.[13]

More detailed documentation concerning conversion becomes available for the third Islamic century; even here, however, our information remains scarce indeed. There is a gap of some three centuries between the first and second documented instances of conversion by Jewish intellectuals. I shall deal below with these two examples from the classical period of Islam. It must be emphasized, however, that the chronological gap between these two cases makes it impossible to argue that they are in any way representative of the period as a whole: the most that can be said is that they contribute to our understanding of the conversion phenomenon among Jewish intellectuals.

---

[11] I refer here to the first and second centuries A.H., i.e. the seventh and eighth centuries C.E. This is the period commonly referred to as "The Early Islamic Middle Ages," a term which reflects the periodization of European historiography. It may be more appropriate to speak of "the period of high caliphate," as suggested by M. Hodgson, *The Venture of Islam: Conscience and History in a World Civilization*, Vol. I: *The Classical Age of Islam* (Chicago and London, 1979), 234–35. On the question of periodization, see also B. Lewis, *Jews of Islam*, 107–11; R. Brague, "Elargir le passé, approfondir le présent," *Débats* 72 (1992): 34.

[12] On dreams paving the way for conversion see, for instance, H.J. Fischer, "Dreams and Conversion in Black Africa," in *Conversion to Islam*, 218–19, 231–35.

[13] See *EI*, 2d ed., s.v. "Kaʿb al-Akhbār" and Lewis, *Jews of Islam*, 96–97.

Conversion to Christianity under Islamic Rule: Dāwūd al-Muqammaṣ

We begin with the conversion of Dāwūd ibn Marwān al-Muqammaṣ (ninth century C.E.). The Karaite al-Qirqisānī reports that al-Muqammaṣ converted to Christianity and lived for many years among the Christians of Nisibis.[14] Under Islamic rule, the Christians were designated a protected minority (*ahl al-dhimma*). The protection, however, depended on the good will of the ruler, and the Christians were sometimes persecuted. Thus, the Christian theologian, Nonnus of Nisibis, who was probably al-Muqammaṣ's teacher, languished for many years in prison where he had been cast by the Caliph al-Mutawakkil.[15] We certainly cannot maintain, therefore, that someone converting to Christianity under Islamic rule was attracted either to the power of the dominant religion or to the convenience of the majority faith. Moreover, since Islamic law does not permit any conversion within its realm save to Islam, such an act could even entail some danger.[16] We have, however, no evidence to suggest that al-Muqammaṣ in any way endangered himself by converting to Christianity. It is possible that the Muslim authorities refrained from interfering with the domain of the Christian academies; it is also possible that the conversion of a Jew to Christianity was sufficiently rare in this period to be conveniently ignored by the Muslim authorities.

Al-Qirqisānī does not attempt to describe the psychological changes experienced by al-Muqammaṣ at the time of his conversion to Christianity; al-Muqammaṣ, for his part, does not inform us of his innermost feelings. We may assume that we have before us a classic instance of *conversio*—the adoption of Christianity out of a real change in faith.[17] If this was indeed the case, it would seem that al-Muqammaṣ found the experience to his taste, for he indulged in it a second time: from his writings it appears that subsequent to becoming a Christian, he returned to Judaism, devoting his best literary efforts thereafter to refuting Christianity.

At first glance, then, it would seem that this example is in no way

---

[14] See Yaʿqūb al-Qirqisānī, *Kitāb al-anwār wa'l-marāqib*, ed. L. Nemoy (New York, 1939), 1:44. Concerning al-Muqammaṣ, see S. Stroumsa, *Dāwūd ibn Marwān al-Muqammiṣ's ʿIshrūn Maqāla* (Leiden, 1989). On the vocalization of his name, see S. Stroumsa, "La perception maïmonidienne du kalām juif; sa véracité et son influence" *Genos* (Lausanne, forthcoming), n. 12.

[15] On Nonnus see A. Van-Roey, *Nonnus de Nisibe, traité apologétique* (Louvain, 1948).

[16] See Goitein, *Mediterranean Society*, 2:305 and A. Fattal, *Le Statut légal des non musulmans en pays d'Islam* (Beirut, 1958).

[17] On the distinction between "conversion" and "adhesion" see A.D. Nock, *Conversion: The Old and New in Religion from Alexander the Great to Augustine of Hippo* (Oxford, 1933), 7ff.

representative of the conversion of Jews under Islamic rule and that it offers us nothing beyond the eccentric deeds of one individual. In fact, the eccentric elements which we observe in al-Muqammaṣ's behavior reflect the typical peculiarities of an intellectual: the search for education and learning wherever they can be found, the quest for religious truth, and the tendency to identify the place of religious truth with the place of education and learning.

Certain scholars have cast doubts upon the reliability of al-Qirqisānī's assertion that al-Muqammaṣ actually converted to Christianity; others emphasize that we lack explicit evidence for his reversion to Judaism.[18] It seems to me, however, that taken together, both conversions may be accepted as true facts. Both conversions may be explained not only on the basis of the information in our sources but also on the basis of al-Muqammaṣ's personality and the cultural world in which he lived. For while it is true that during the third Islamic century there existed a Muslim intellectual elite—whose influence upon al-Muqammaṣ was considerable—its prestige at the time was still outstripped by Christian superiority in the study of philosophy and the sciences. The prestige enjoyed by Christians manifested itself in their status as translators, as appointees to positions in the Royal Library (*bayt al-ḥikma*), and as court physicians; it also aroused the jealousy of their Muslim neighbors.[19] While al-Muqammaṣ's writings do not, in fact, reflect great intellectual depth, a true intellectual curiosity is discernible in them. It was natural for such a person, determined as he was to study philosophy, to be attracted to the centers of Christian learning. If this was the situation in his day, we may suppose that such an attraction existed—perhaps to an even greater degree—in the first and second Islamic centuries. The letters of Bishop Timotheos I (eighth century, Baghdad) mention a learned Jew who was preparing to convert to Christianity. Like al-Muqammaṣ, Timotheos's Jewish novice reveals an interest in the archaeological discoveries of the day and in their significance for the history of religions.[20] If we do not maintain that these two apostates were one and the same person—a claim rendered problematic by chronological considerations—it appears that in the early Islamic period, Chris-

[18] See, e.g., the relevant article in *EJB*.

[19] Through the special honors accorded them, Christians frequently incurred an additional measure of hatred; see, e.g., al-Jāḥiẓ, "Al-radd ʿalā ʾl-naṣārā" in *Thalāth rasāʾil*, ed. J. Finkel (Cairo, 1344/1926). And see also A.S. Tritton, *The Caliphs and Their Non-Muslim Subjects* (London, 1970), 92–95.

[20] See O. Braun, "Ein Brief des Katholikos Timotheos über biblische Studien des 9 Jahrhunderts," *Oriens Christianus* 1 (1901): 299–313.

tianity held a fascination for a certain type of Jewish intellectual.

On the other hand, as we have already said, al-Muqammaṣ lived in a period when Muslims had already begun to compete with Christians in the fields of theology and philosophy. Traces of Muslim arguments against Christianity are observable in al-Muqammaṣ's writings. That same curiosity which had brought him to Christianity in the first place, also spurred him to become acquainted with the Muslim polemics against Christianity. We may suppose that such confrontations between Christianity and Islam sharpened his doubts—doubts which in the end led him back to Judaism.

Jews who converted to Islam

If we accept the premise that al-Muqammaṣ's attraction to intellectual superiority played a decisive role in his conversion to Christianity, we may also presume that Christianity lost its attractiveness for Jews living in Islamic lands when the Muslims achieved supremacy in philosophy and the sciences during the following centuries.[21] Saʿd b. Manṣūr Ibn Kammūna, a thirteenth-century Jewish intellectual—who, it has been suggested, may also have apostasized—summarized the reasons for converting to Islam as follows:

> That is why, to this day we never see anyone converting to Islam unless in terror, or in quest of power, or to avoid heavy taxation, or to escape humiliation, or if taken prisoner, or because of infatuation with a Muslim woman, or for some similar reason. Nor do we see a respected, wealthy, and pious non-Muslim well-versed in both his faith and that of Islam, going over to the Islamic faith without some of the aforementioned or similar motives.[22]

Ibn Kammūna thus explicitly rejects the possibility of conversion to Islam for any but the most pragmatic of motivations—especially in cases involving individuals who are "well-versed in both their own faith and that of Islam," i.e., people possessing religious learning.

We will examine below Ibn Kammūna's categorical statement concerning those Jewish intellectuals whose conversion to Islam left traces in the literary sources. The number of these individuals is extremely limited and

---

[21] However, the tenth-century Karaite author Japheth b. Eli, in his commentary on Deut. 4:28 (B.L. ms. Or. 2478, fol. 42a, lines 4–6) still speaks of Jews whom "you can see today apostasizing and converting to Christianity." For this reference I am indebted to Daniel Frank.

[22] See M. Perlmann, *Ibn Kammūna's Examination of the Three Faiths* (Berkeley and Los Angeles, 1971), 149. For the Arabic text see idem. ed., *Tanqīḥ al-Abḥāth li'l-Milal al-Thalāth* (Berkeley and Los Angeles, 1967), 102.

the impression made by their conversion to Islam is not sufficiently detailed to permit us any certain conclusions; what follows, therefore, should not be taken as anything more than reasonable postulation.

Ibn Kammūna's words, which unequivocally reject any possibility of an intellectual attraction to Islam, reflect a polemical stance. It is certainly reasonable to suppose, however, that not only did such an attraction actually exist but that it may even have caused certain individuals to convert. All the same, can we speak of a more general phenomenon of conversion to Islam due to intellectual motives?

A. *Abū'l-Barakāt al-Baghdādī*

The next apostate whom we will discuss—and who represents, incidentally, the next instance of a Jewish intellectual's conversion to Islam which is documented in some detail—has led scholars to posit the existence of just such a wide-spread phenomenon. Three Jewish scholars in twelfth-century Baghdad converted to Islam. Of this group, the two younger men—the poet Isaac ben Abraham Ibn Ezra and the mathematician, physician and polemicist Samuel Ibn Abbās ha-Maʿaravi (Samauʾal al-Maghribī)—were the disciples of the third—the philosopher, "Netanel, the Unique One of His Generation," i.e. Ḥibat Allāh Abūʾl-Barakāt al-Baghdādī. Various scholars have been inclined to suppose that the two younger men converted to Islam under the influence of their master.[23] From this, apparently, they have inferred the existence of a learned Jewish "circle," whose studies and discussions prompted its members to recognize the truth of Islam. Such a circle would offer an ideal object for the study of conversion among intellectuals in general. Before adopting such a theory, however, we ought first to re-examine the accuracy of the description upon which it is grounded.

Our knowledge of Abūʾl-Barakāt al-Baghdādī's conversion to Islam derives solely from Muslim sources; the Jewish sources are utterly silent on the matter. In the literary debate between Maimonides and Samuel ben ʿEli, Abūʾl-Barakāt's name is mentioned without any derogatory epithet.[24]

---

[23] Moshe Perlmann mentions this as a coincidence deserving of note, without insisting upon any necessary connection between the three instances; see the introduction to his "Ifḥām al-Yahūd," *PAAJR* 32 (1964): 16. See also: Menahem H. Schmelzer ed., *Isaac Ben Abraham Ibn Ezra: Poems* (New York, 1980), xi; N. Ben-Menahem, *Isaac Ibn Ezra: Poems* (Jerusalem, 1950), 44; and J.L. Fleischer, "Le-qorot yiṣḥaq ibn ʿezra," *Sinai* 21 (1947): 263–76. See also *Encyclopedia Hebraica*, s.v. "Ibn Ezra, Yiṣḥaq ben Avraham."

[24] See J. Finkel ed., "Maimonides' Treatise on Resurrection," *PAAJR* 9 (1938–1939): 12–13 of the text; S. Stroumsa, "On the Maimonidean Controversy in the East: The Role of Abū al-Barakāt al-Baghdādī" (Hebrew), in *Hebrew and Arabic Studies in Honour of Joshua Blau*

This fact was noted with mild surprise by scholars.[25] There is, in fact, no cause for astonishment: the Genizah documents record no custom of cursing apostates,[26] and it seems that instances of conversion to Islam whose pragmatic benefits were obvious were received with a measure of understanding.[27] While it is true that Abū'l-Barakāt's philosophical writings were not widely disseminated in Jewish intellectual circles, it appears that there was no connection between this fact and his conversion to Islam; his lack of popularity ought not to be regarded as evidence of any ban against him. The fact that his writings belong to the realm of general philosophy and that they were originally set down in Arabic rather than Hebrew script led to their not being classified as works of a specifically Jewish character but rather as philosophy proper.[28] And in this category there were other writers whose works were preferred to those of Abū'l-Barakāt among both Jewish and gentile audiences.

There are four reports extant concerning Abū'l-Barakāt's conversion to Islam.[29] All four recount that he became a Muslim at a very advanced age, and that the recognition of Muḥammad's prophethood was not a factor in his decision. Two of the reports connect his conversion to a craving for honor and the realization that he would not receive the respect due a court physician so long as he remained Jewish. According to Ibn Abī Uṣaybiʿah, Abū'l-Barakāt was enraged when the Chief Justice (*qāḍī al-quḍāt*) remained seated before him and did not rise out of respect.[30] Ibn al-Qiftī recounts that Abū'l-Barakāt was insulted by a satiric ditty composed against him by Ibn al-Aflaḥ.[31] The other two reports indicate that the elderly philosopher converted to Islam out of fear for his life: in this connection, Ibn al-Qiftī mentions a royal patient who died in Abū'l-Barakāt's care,[32] while al-Bayhaqī records that the decision to convert came when Abū'l-Barakāt

---

Presented by Friends and Students on the Occasion of his Seventieth Birthday, ed. H. Ben-Shammai (Jerusalem, 1993), 415–22.

[25] See Pines, "Studies in Abū'l-Barakāt al-Baghdādī's Poetics and Metaphysics," *Scripta Hierosolymitana* 6 (1960): 121 [= idem., *Studies in Abū'l-Barakāt al-Baghdādī: Physics and Metaphysics* (Jerusalem, 1979), 260].

[26] See Goitein, *Mediterranean Society*, 2:301.

[27] As, for example, in the case of Ibn Killis—see Goitein, ibid.

[28] On a copy of his main composition in Hebrew characters see Tzvi Langermann, "A Fragment of Abū'l-Barakāt al-Baghdādī's *al-Kitāb al-Muʿtabar*" (Hebrew), *KS* 61 (1986–87), 361–62.

[29] For a summary of the four reports see Goitein, *Mediterranean Society*, 2:303 and Pines, "Studies in Abū'l-Barakāt," p. 121, n. 4.

[30] See Ibn Abī Uṣaybiʿa, *Kitāb ʿuyūn al-anbā' fī ṭabaqāt al-aṭibbā'*, ed. N. Riḍā (Beirut, 1965), 375.

[31] See Ibn al-Qiftī, *Ta'rīkh al-ḥukamā'*, 343.

[32] Ibid., 346.

was in captivity.[33] From all of these accounts a self-evident conclusion emerges, viz. that under an Islamic regime it was much more pleasant and secure to be a Muslim.

Against this background, another story becomes all the more striking: it is said that Abū'l-Barakāt demanded as a condition for his conversion—and in contravention of Islamic law—that his Jewish daughters be granted the right to inherit him.[34] Now, we know of instances in medieval Europe in which pressure was exerted upon Jews to become Christians, while at the same time some effort was made to take their backgrounds and former lives into consideration.[35] From the story in which Abū'l-Barakāt lays down his conditions for conversion, however, a different picture emerges. Whether or not the account is historically accurate, it most certainly does not depict a fanatical Muslim regime whose Jewish subjects are forced to convert, while being permitted to retain their social fabric. On the contrary, the story presents a respected man who sets forth his conditions from a position of power, knowing even in that very moment of weakness that his adoption of Islam will meet with admiration.

It should be added that from the geonic responsa we learn that the phenomenon of an apostate leaving his property to his Jewish heirs was well-known and quite common. In this connection Maimonides writes:

> Cases of this kind are brought before us every day . . . and we always handle them in the same manner: the estate of anyone who apostasizes is distributed among his (Jewish) sons. Should he have no Jewish sons, it is transferred to another suitable heir.[36]

If this is the case, it is indeed possible that the story of Abū'l-Barakāt's laying down prior conditions before converting to Islam reflects a historical reality. Against the background of Maimonides' statement it becomes necessary to examine the possibility that the conditions laid down by Abū'l-Barakāt testify not only to the apostate's strong personality but also to the strength of a Jewish community whose laws achieved, at times, a certain priority over the laws of Islam.

---

[33] See Ẓāhir al-Dīn Abū'l-Ḥasan ʿAlī b. Zayd al-Bayhaqī, *Tatimmat siwān al-ḥikma*, ed. Muḥammad Shāfiʿ (Lahore, 1935), 151–52.

[34] See Ibn al-Qifṭī, *Ta'rīkh al-ḥukamā'*, 343.

[35] They were not, for example, required to annul existing marriages which—for reasons of consanguinity—would have been forbidden under canon law; see Cohen, "The Mentality of the Medieval Jewish Apostate," 22.

[36] See Moses Maimonides, *Responsa*, ed. J. Blau (Jerusalem, 1960), 2:657. And see on this S.W. Baron, *A Social and Religious History of the Jews*, 2d ed. (New York, 1957), 3:143–44 and pp. 300–301, nn. 26–28.

This description of Abū'l-Barakāt's own conversion offers sufficient grounds to call into question the argument that his two disciples adopted Islam under his influence. When we come to examine his relationship with these students, our doubts are heightened. Samau'al recounts that he studied medicine and pharmacology with Abū'l-Barakāt. By his account, it is apparent that Samau'al was no more than a young man at the time and that he pursued these studies some time—perhaps even several years—before reaching his decision to convert. His remarks in no way suggest that there was any theological dimension to his meetings with Abū'l-Barakāt.[37]

B. *Isaac Ibn Ezra*

The story of Isaac Ibn Ezra's conversion to Islam is more complicated.[38] As J.L. Fleischer showed, Isaac most likely converted to Islam outwardly and without conviction—before reverting to Judaism once he was in a position to do so.[39] At one time, the prevailing scholarly view held that Isaac's entire conversion process took place in Baghdad but this theory is now difficult to accept. As we have mentioned above, the Seljuk regime in Baghdad was not particularly zealous in this period. Moreover, it is difficult to conceive of a zealous regime which would both compel Jews to become Muslims and permit them to revert to Judaism with impunity. According to Islamic law, Jews may not be forced to convert; once they have become Muslims, however, they are liable to capital punishment should they return to their original faith.[40] In attempting to resolve this difficulty, Goitein posited that Isaac was forced to travel abroad to Christian lands in order to return to Judaism.[41]

Our information about Isaac's conversion to Islam derives entirely from two sources: his own verse and certain statements made by Judah al-Ḥarizi concerning him. In one poem attributed to Isaac he acknowledges that "he kept neither the oath sworn by his mouth nor all the laws learned from his prophet's lips." In another poem ("Yerivuni alei ozvi berit el") he explains that his profession of Islam—i.e., the *shahāda*—is entirely external:

---

[37] "Islām al-Samau'al" in Perlmann, "Ifḥām al-Yahūd," 97.

[38] Concerning him see Goitein, *Mediterranean Society*, 2:302 and Lewis, *Jews of Islam*, 99.

[39] See: Fleischer, "Le-qorot yiṣḥaq ibn ʿezra," 263–76; N. Ben-Menahem, "Kelum hemir yiṣḥaq ibn ʿezra et dato?" *Sinai* 12 (1943): 443–50.

[40] See Fattal, *Le Statut légal des non musulmans*, 165–68 and Goitein, *Mediterranean Society*, 2:304.

[41] See Goitein, ibid., 303.

> But if I still begin each prayer
> by professing a madman to be God's prophet,
> I do this with my lips alone, my heart responding,
> "You're a liar and your testimony is invalid."

Asserting that he has never tasted ritually unfit food he adds:

> I have come back beneath the shadow of Your wing;
> I ask You, God, for Your forgiveness.[42]

While some doubt exists concerning the attribution of these poems, there is an additional poem, whose attribution to Isaac is beyond question, in which the author refers to himself with the following words: "Embracing the faith of strangers I estranged myself from the speech of my fathers."[43] The identity of our author with Isaac ben Abraham Ibn Ezra is consistent as well with the testimony of al-Ḥarizi who recounts concerning Isaac:

> When he came to the lands of the East, the glory of the Lord did not shine upon him and he discarded the precious garments of the faith. He stripped off his garments and put on other vestments.[44]

Menahem Schmelzer, who published the poems from which the above citations were taken has shown that they were composed while Isaac was still in Egypt.[45] In this connection Schmelzer mentions an episode in which Judah Halevi was also involved. As is well known, Isaac arrived in Egypt as Judah Halevi's travelling companion.[46] From the Genizah documents we learn that one of Halevi's fellow travelers had been asked to convey a sum of money to a certain apostate in Alexandria, that Halevi had attempted to bring this apostate back to the fold of Judaism, that the apostate denounced Halevi to the authorities, and that only by virtue of Halevi's eminence did the affair conclude satisfactorily for him—the Muslim mobs venting their wrath, in the end, upon the hapless apostate.[47] Schmelzer suggested that Halevi's companion, Isaac Ibn Ezra, was involved in this affair and as a consequence was forced to "abandon the covenant."[48]

We may object, however, that such an episode—whose ultimate victim proved to be the apostate, Halevi escaping unharmed—can hardly have

---

[42] Schmelzer, *Isaac Ibn Ezra*, 146–47 and Ben-Menahem, *Isaac Ibn Ezra: Poems*, 16.

[43] Ben-Menahem, ibid., 7.

[44] Judah al-Ḥarizi, *The Taḥkemoni*, "The Third Gate," trans. V.E. Reichert, vol. 1, (Jerusalem, 1965), 79. For the Hebrew text see Taḥkemoni, ed. Y. Toporowski (Tel Aviv, 1952), 45.

[45] *Isaac Ibn Ezra*, 11.

[46] Goitein even maintains that Isaac was Judah Halevi's son-in-law; see *Mediterranean Society*, 2:303. This view is rejected by Schmelzer, ibid., 11.

[47] Goitein, ibid., 304.

[48] Schmelzer, ibid., 11.

brought about Isaac's conversion. Moreover, it is scarcely possible that Isaac could have renounced Islam under the same Muslim regime that he had previously embraced it. It seems to me, therefore, that Goitein was probably right in assuming that Isaac's conversion to Islam was undertaken strictly for appearance's sake. It was not, however, performed out of compulsion but rather for convenience. This being the case, it should in no way be connected with the aforementioned episode.[49]

Furthermore, from the poems published by Schmelzer it appears that by the time Isaac departed from Egypt, his "Muslim phase" was already past. Schmelzer attempted to add a second act: according to him, when al-Ḥarizi mentions Isaac's apostasy "upon his arrival in eastern lands," we must assume that he converted a second time in Baghdad, under the influence of Abū'l-Barakāt.[50] Now while it is true that Isaac was apparently a complicated person,[51] it seems most unlikely that he apostasized twice. Such fickleness would be much more natural for a person like al-Muqammaṣ who related to theology on a far more profound level. There are no signs of any such profundity in Isaac Ibn Ezra; his relationship to religion bears the stamp of a suffering, unfortunate personality. It seems more reasonable to me that by "lands of the East," al-Ḥarizi intended those countries to which Isaac journeyed from the "lands of the West," i.e. Spain. From al-Ḥarizi's perspective, once Isaac had left Spain, it made little difference whether he apostasized in Egypt or in Baghdad.

We see, therefore, that there are no grounds for connecting the conversions of Samau'al and Isaac with that of Abū'l-Barakāt. Each had his own motivations for becoming a Muslim which were unconnected to those of his fellows; these motivations, moreover, were probably unconnected to their mutual acquaintance, either causally or temporally. We cannot, in any event, speak here of a phenomenon: these three instances of conversion neither indicate the presence of a small circle of intellectuals whose intellectualism led them to embrace Islam, nor suggest the existence of any such widespread pattern of behavior.

C. *Samau'al al-Maghribī*

At the same time, Samau'al's autobiographical account of his conversion offers us a way of comprehending the phenomenon of conversion to

[49] Goitein, ibid., 303.

[50] Schmelzer, ibid., 11.

[51] From two of Isaac's letters which have been preserved in the Genizah, Goitein concludes that he was "a rather strange person." (p. 303)

Islam—not as some prevailing fashion but as a phenomenon within the realm of the individual.

Of the three instances discussed, Samau'al's conversion is the only one presented as being theologically motivated. Ibn Kammūna, who was familiar with Samau'al's writings, cast aspersions both upon the purity of his motivations and the power of his intellect. He rejects one of Samau'al's arguments as being "too unsound to be discussed seriously"[52]; elsewhere, he suggests that Samau'al's conversion to Islam was motivated less by his inner convictions than by a desire to enrage the Jews (*ʿānada al-yahūd wa-aslama*).[53] As Samau'al mentions repeatedly, his relationship with his father was a factor in his own religious behavior. (As he puts it, his fear of his father and his reluctance to offend him prevented him from converting at a much earlier date.) Comments of this nature lead us to wonder how a psychologist of religion might analyze his case. In this respect, Samau'al matches the general picture sketched by Goitein,[54] for he converted only after he had become geographically separated from his father. Nevertheless, the fact itself remains before us: Samau'al did convert publicly and of his own volition. In doing so, moreover, he acted out of sufficient conviction to record the story of his conversion in writing. We cannot, therefore, subscribe to Ibn Kammūna's assessment and permit ourselves to judge Samau'al's truthfulness.

According to Samau'al, the turning point in his conversion came with his dreams, in which the prophets Samuel and Muḥammad were revealed to him. The dream as an incitement to conversion is a well-known topos, one we have already encountered in the case of Kaʿb al-Akhbār. Samau'al, however, seeks to play down the dream's value in this context. He recounts that over the course of several years he refused to publicize the matter, because he sensed that his dreams would be regarded with scorn. Repeatedly, he emphasizes that his dream did not cause him to realize the soundness of Islam; it represented, rather, the crucial event which forced him to take the final step of severing himself from his faith and his father's house.[55]

---

[52] See Ibn Kammūna, *Examination of the Three Faiths*, 143 (= *Tanqīḥ al-Abḥāth*, 97).

[53] *Tanqīḥ al-Abḥāth*, 95. Perlmann renders *ʿānada* "turned against"; see *Examination of the Three Faiths*, 139. From al-Ḥarizi's words it is clear that Samau'al truly enraged the Jews. The latter is treated much more harshly than Isaac Ibn Ezra. See al-Ḥarizi, *Taḥkemoni*, trans. V.E. Reichert, 1:79 (= Taḥkemoni, ed. Toporowski, 45): "He [i.e. Judah Ibn Abbas] too begat a renegade son who acted with amazing and impudent shamelessness." On this passage see also H. Schirmann, *Ha-shirah ha-ʿivrit bi-sefarad u-ve-provans*, 2d ed. (Jerusalem, 1960), 3:112, lines 173–79 and the notes ad loc.

[54] Goitein, *Mediterranean Society*, 2:299.

[55] "Islām al-Samau'al" in Perlmann, "Ifḥām al-Yahūd," 118–20.

According to Samauʾal's conception, religious experience does not constitute a legitimate argument for conversion; the only legitimate argument is a rational one.

Samauʾal describes his path to Islam as an intellectual process of study and systematic analysis. We have already seen how Kaʿb employed his learning to argue that the Bible attests to the prophethood of Muḥammad. In his book *Ifḥām al-Yahūd* (*Silencing the Jews*) Samauʾal discusses similar biblical verses at great length. In his account of his conversion, however, they appear only as part of his dream, i.e. at a secondary, experiential stage of his conversion. In the first stage, which he terms the intellectual-rational stage, there is no mention of the biblical verses. In his autobiography, Samauʾal describes the course of his education—his curriculum included medicine, logic, history, and literature—leading up to his study of different religions. He writes as follows:

> Then . . . I asked myself about the differences among men in religious faiths and tenets. I received the greatest impulse to inquire into the subject from reading the epistle of Bardhawayh the physician, in the book Kalīla wa-Dimna.[56]

The conclusion to which this book led him was that "reason is the final arbiter" and that rationally speaking, no one religious tradition is superior to any other; we therefore ought either to accept or reject all of them. Samauʾal elects to accept them all.

An examination of "The Book of Barzawayh (Burzoe) the Physician" confirms that it served Samauʾal as the source for these arguments. "Barzawayh the Physician" is presented as a spiritual autobiography. Like Samauʾal's, it opens with Barzawayh's genealogy (*nasab*), an account of his parents' lives, and the education which they gave him. Barzawayh begins his account as well with the assertion that reason is God's greatest gift to man. He too passes on to a discussion of religions, stating:

> I found that there are many religions and creeds and that the followers of these creeds differ one from another. Some inherited their religion from their ancestors, others adopted it on account of fear and coercion, yet others hoped by means of it to acquire worldly goods, pleasures, and prestige. But every one of them claims that his religion is the true and correct one and that whoever contradicts him lives in error and deception . . . I decided to frequent the scholars and leaders in every religious faction and to examine what they teach and stipulate in the hope that

---

[56] Trans. M. Perlmann in "The Medieval Polemics Between Islam and Judaism," in *Religion in a Religious Age*, ed. S.D. Goitein (Cambridge, Mass., 1974), 115; Arabic text in idem., "Ifḥām al-Yahūd," 103. The English translation of the autobiography in N. Stillman, *The Jews of Arab Lands* (Philadelphia, 1979), 118–20 omits the passage relating to "The Book of Barzawayh the Physician."

> perhaps I could learn to distinguish truth from falsehood and attach myself confidently to the truth without having to accept on the authority of others something that I could not know or understand by myself. I pursued this plan, investigated and studied. But I discovered that all of these people merely repeat what was handed down to them. Each one praises his own religion and curses the religion of those who disagree with him. It became clear to me that their conclusions are based on illusions and that their speech is not motivated by a sense of fairness. In not one of them did I find that degree of honesty and rightmindedness which would induce rational persons to accept their words and be satisfied with them.[57]

The equality of religions and the fact that they contradict each other leads Barzawayh to reject them all. He chooses instead an ethical, ascetic way of life as a certain truth upon which all religions agree. Now Samau'al's explicit statement, that his familiarity with the argument for the equality of religions derived from Barzawayh, implies that he had seen both Barzawayh's argument and his atheistic conclusion. Samau'al's own innovation, in this case, is to impose a conclusion upon the argument which is diametrically opposed to the one originally presented, viz. the affirmation of belief in all religions and—it goes without saying—in Islam, the final revelation which encompasses all others.

Further support may be offered for our claim that Samau'al was familiar with the argument for the equality of religions in its atheistic context. As far back as the tenth century, there were those who maintained that the autobiography of Barzawayh was actually composed by Ibn al-Muqaffa' who sought to introduce skepticism into the Muslim world.[58] Indeed, arguments similar to Barzawayh's and similar universalistic conclusions were used by some notorious Muslim free-thinkers. These arguments are present in somewhat veiled form in the writings of Ibn al-Rāwandī, who championed—in the name of the Indian Barāhima—the superiority of reason, deducing thereby the invalidity of revealed religions.[59] More explicitly, they are to be found in the works of the tenth-century philosopher Muḥammad b. Zakarīyā al-Rāzī, who states:

> We have seen that those who hold fast to tradition [. . .] believe in the truth of their religion, basing themselves upon their faith in the truth of their ancestors' words. . . . He said: If this (religion) is true for this reason, then all faiths—Juda-

[57] Trans. F. de Blois in *Burzoy's Voyage to India and the Origin of the Book of Kalilah wa Dimnah* (London, 1990), 26; see the discussion on 28–32. For the Arabic text see Ibn al-Muqaffaʿ, *Kalīla wa-Dimna*, ed. L. Cheikho (Beirut, 1905), 33–34; see also esp. 42–40.

[58] On the authenticity of Barzawayh's autobiography, see now M. Chokr, *Zandaqa et Zindīqs en Islam au second siècle de l'hégire* (Damascus, 1993), 179–208.

[59] See P. Kraus, "Beiträge zur islamische Ketzergeschichte, das *Kitāb al-Zumurrud* des Ibn ar-Rāwandī," *RSO* 14 (1934): 93–129; 15 (1934): 335–79.

> ism, Christianity, Zoroastrianism, and others—are valid as well, since they employ the same demonstrative method as does Islam.[60]

Like Barzawayh, al-Rāzī derives the refutation of all revealed religions from the fact that they employ equivalent arguments to demonstrate their validity. This indeed is the logical conclusion to the problem as it is presented by Barzawayh. It stands to reason that Samau'al was acquainted with al-Rāzī's medical works; there is reason to believe, moreover, that he was acquainted as well with al-Rāzī's other writings—including this particular argument. Now, even if it were possible for him to have ignored Barzawayh's conclusion rejecting all religions, it is difficult to suppose that he could have ignored the same argument in the writings of al-Rāzī, who was well-known to have been an unbeliever. I am inclined, therefore, to suppose that Samau'al was conscious of the fact that he was adapting atheistic argumentation to the exigencies of a religious argument. Were al-Rāzī his only source in arguing for the equivalence of religions, it is doubtful whether Samau'al would have drawn upon him: aside from medical matters, in which he was regarded as a great authority, al-Rāzī was denigrated as an unbeliever. We may assume that Samau'al would not readily have mentioned such a dubious source in his autobiography. *Kalīla wa-Dimna* on the other hand—including "The Book of Barzawayh the Physician"—was a much more acceptable source, which might well be cited in polite company.

The argument for the equivalence of religious traditions made its way as well into orthodox Islamic circles and is widespread in theological writings.[61] I am unaware, however, of any other place in which the equivalence of religious traditions in and of themselves—without any further development—is taken as a proof for the validity of Islam. For comparative purposes, I shall bring one example which occurs as well in the context of religious conversion. ʿAlī b. Rabbān al-Ṭabarī was a Christian intellectual who, like Abū'l-Barakāt, converted to Islam at an advanced age. Like Samau'al, al-Ṭabarī attacked his former faith, while seeking to justify his new one. According to al-Ṭabarī, he is writing so that slanderers may not assert that he converted to Islam out of a pursuit of temporal pleasures. Like Samau'al, al-Ṭabarī too hastens to assert the superiority of reason as a fundamental principle. Al-Ṭabarī does not, however, in any

---

[60] P. Kraus, "Raziana," *Orientalia* n.s. 5 (1936): 363, 367.

[61] See, e.g., the spiritual autobiography of Abū Ḥāmid Muḥammad al-Ghazzālī, *Al-Munqidh min al-dalāl wa'l-mūsil ilā dhī al-ʿizza wa'l-jalāl*, ed. J. Ṣalība and K. ʿAyyād (Beirut, 1981), 81–82; trans. W.M. Watt, *The Faith and Practice of al-Ghazālī* (London, 1953), 21–22.

way allow for the possibility that all religious traditions are of equal value. His entire aim is to show the absolute superiority of the Islamic tradition on the one hand and the logical and historical distortions of the Christian tradition on the other.[62] Reliance upon reason is part of the Arabic polemical tradition; this is evident from the discussion's framework, a theological engagement of intellectuals. Any inclination toward religious relativism such as we may encounter with Samauʾal, however, belongs to this tradition only in a polemical way, as a strawman to be destroyed.

Summary: Relativism as a Factor in Conversion

It is possible to dismiss Samauʾal's relativism as the weak argumentation of an eclectic theologian who sought to combine incompatible ideas. Such a view, at any rate, is expressed by Perlmann, who regards Samauʾal's spiritual autobiography as no more than a youthful essay.[63] It seems to me, however, that the very presence of the argument in Samauʾal's work has more to teach us than does the quality of his theology. In his day, the relativist argument was undoubtedly widespread and well-known in various versions, but always with the same atheistic conclusion. The fact, moreover, that Samauʾal employs this as the single decisive argument which logically demands acceptance of Islam confirms the view that this argument was particularly widespread. It is possible as well that the relativist atmosphere prevailing in certain intellectual circles helped facilitate the transition between different religions—especially, of course, conversion to the dominant faith from an intellectual perspective.[64] To put it differently: although we have not encountered any systematic conversion of intellectuals to Islam in organized groups and under the influence of spiritual teachers, it appears that the subjects discussed by intellectuals during this period enabled them to adopt a detached position vis-à-vis reli-

[62] See A. Khalife and W. Kutsch, "Al-Radd ʿalā-n-naṣārā de Alī at-Ṭabarī," *Mélanges de l'université Saint Joseph* 36 (1959): 115. Chokr, *Zandaqa et Zindiqs*, regards Barzawayh's introduction as a literary convention rather than an expression of true skepticism. On pp. 204–205 he cites examples where authors, like al-Ṭabarī, start their quest for the true religion with the assumption of the primacy of the intellect and with a detached, objective examination of all religions. In none of these examples, however, does the author *conclude* with the equivalence of religions. Whereas the primacy of the intellect is indeed a commonplace theme in theological literature, the skeptical conclusion is not.

[63] See M. Perlmann, "Ifḥām al-Yahūd," 23.

[64] See M. Perlmann ed., *Tanqīḥ al-Abḥāth*, X–XII. On relativistic expressions in relation to all religions see also Lewis, *Jews of Islam*, 88 and p. 206, n. 29.

gion in general, a position which in certain circumstances, could lead them to embrace a new faith.

This relativism leads us again to Ibn Kammūna, with whom we will conclude: the claim that he converted to Islam is, apparently, incorrect. While Ibn Kammūna definitely drew upon Samau'al's anti-Jewish polemic, *Ifḥām al-Yahūd*, we do not know whether he was familiar with the latter's autobiography. And although it is true that Ibn Kammūna too mentions the relativist argument, this argument was, as we have seen, sufficiently widespread and well-known for him to have received it from many other sources. To a certain degree, Ibn Kammūna confirms the impression that relativism typified the spirit of the age: his detached, objective attitude toward the three faiths is generally presented against the background of toleration which characterized the Mongol regime prior to its conversion to Islam. There is certainly a great deal of truth to this. It seems, nevertheless, that we must factor in as well the relativist tradition in Islamic philosophy—a tradition which paradoxically expressed itself in the polemical words of Samau'al the apostate.

THE *SHOSHANIM* OF TENTH-CENTURY JERUSALEM: KARAITE EXEGESIS, PRAYER, AND COMMUNAL IDENTITY*

DANIEL FRANK

The Karaites of tenth- and eleventh-century Jerusalem were unusual—if not unique—among pre-modern Jewish communities: they were a self-consciously defined group which had constituted itself in the Holy City for specifically religious purposes.[1] Jewish sectarians who denied the authority of the rabbinic tradition, they viewed themselves as fulfilling a particular role in history, a role central to the imminent eschaton. As one of their leading scholars, Sahl b. Maṣliaḥ, explained:

> In the days of the "Little Horn," [i.e. the reign of Islam] God opened the gates of His mercy to His people and brought them to His Holy City. There they settled, erecting buildings in which to recite (Scripture), interpret (it), pray at all times, and establish night vigils.[2]

---

* I would like to thank the Oxford Centre for Hebrew and Jewish Studies, the Institute of Jewish Studies, London and the Jewish Memorial Foundation, New York for generously supporting my research. I would also like to thank the British Library, the Jewish Theological Seminary of America, and the Bibliothèque Nationale for permitting me to consult and publish manuscripts in their collections, and the Institute of Microfilmed Hebrew Manuscripts [IMHM] of the Jewish National and University Library for all the assistance extended me. I am especially grateful to three scholars: Professor Haggai Ben-Shammai offered his invaluable comments on this paper and gave me a copy of his article on Karaite prayer prior to its publication (n. 16 below); Dr. David Sklare kindly shared a recent discovery with me (n. 34 below); and Dr. Adena Tanenbaum read the typescript with her usual care, suggesting substantive refinements and stylistic improvements.

[1] The most comprehensive historical study of medieval Karaism is still Z. Ankori, *Karaites in Byzantium* (New York, 1959). For surveys of recent scholarship see: D. Frank, "The Study of Medieval Karaism 1959–1989: A Bibliographical Essay," *Bulletin of Judaeo-Greek Studies* 6 (1990): 15–23 and D.J. Lasker, "Karaites: Developments 1970–1988," *Encyclopaedia Judaica Yearbook 1988–89*, 366–67. On the Karaite community of tenth- and eleventh-century Jerusalem see: S. Poznanski, "Reshit hityashevut ha-qara'im bi-yerushalayim," in *Jerusalem*, ed. A.M. Luncz, vol. 10 (1913), 83–116; J. Mann, *Texts and Studies in Jewish History and Literature*, vol. 2 (Philadelphia, 1935), 3–66; H.H. Ben-Sasson, "The Karaite Community of Jerusalem in the Tenth-Eleventh Centuries" (Hebrew), *Shalem* 2 (1976): 1–18; H. Ben-Shammai, "The Karaites," in *The History of Jerusalem: The Early Islamic Period (638–1099)* (Hebrew), ed. J. Prawer (Jerusalem, 1987), 163–178 (English edition in press); Moshe Gil, *A History of Palestine, 634–1099* (Cambridge, 1992), 777–820.

[2] See Sahl b. Maṣliaḥ, Hebrew Introduction to the *Book of Precepts*, ed. A. Harkavy in "Me'assef Niddaḥim, no. 13," *Hameliṣ* 15 (1879), repr. in *Me'assef niddaḥim* (Jerusalem, 1970), p. 199, lines 26–28. For a slightly different translation, see N. Wieder, *The Judean Scrolls and Karaism* (London, 1962), 103. The Karaites' derogatory nickname for Islam, "the little horn," possesses eschatological associations which derive from its biblical source in Daniel 7:8; see

Study and worship, then, represented the group's two main activities, and it was through biblical exegesis and prayer that they were able to define themselves as a community.

Probably the most striking feature of this community's biblical exegesis is its prognostic quality, a quality shared by the *pesharim* of the ancient Dead Sea sect.[3] According to this method of interpretation, scriptural prophecies are related not so much to their biblical context as to contemporary events. Conversely, the world of today is viewed through the prophetic prism of the Bible. What lends this principle its power and urgency is the apocalyptic conviction that the present lies at the threshold of the Messianic Era.[4] Prognostic exegesis operates emblematically: biblical words and phrases are understood to be special appellations for the actors in a great eschatological drama. To be sure, this approach to Scripture can be found in rabbinic midrash and Christian typology as well; we have only to recall the late Gerson Cohen's analysis of Esau as a symbol among Jews and Christians in the early Middle Ages in order to recognize the force and popularity of the technique.[5] The Karaites, however, were particularly adept at developing such equations and using them in order to interpret the Bible, explain the world in which they lived, and establish their own place within that world.

The name "Shoshanim" ("lilies"), which they adopted for themselves, ultimately derived, for example, from their interpretation of the Song of Songs, which they read as a prophetic allegory. For the Jerusalem Karaites,

---

H. Ben-Shammai, "The Attitude of Some Early Karaites Toward Islam," in *Studies in Medieval Jewish History and Literature*, vol. 2, ed. I. Twersky (Cambridge, Mass., 1984), 8 (3–40). An oft-quoted passage by an older contemporary of Sahl's describes the origins and development of the Karaite community in Jerusalem until the mid-10th century; see *The Arabic Commentary of Salmon ben Yeruham the Karaite, Chapters 42–72*, ed. L. Marwick (Philadelphia, 1956), 97–98 on Ps. 69:1. On this text see S. Pinsker, *Lickute Kadmoniot*, pt. 1 (Wien, 1860), 21–22; J. Mann, *Texts*, vol. 2, p. 4, n. 3; Ben-Sasson, "The Karaite Community of Jerusalem," 1–2; Ben-Shammai, "The Karaites," 163; and Gil, *History of Palestine*, 618–19, containing an English translation of the passage.

[3] On this type of exegesis and the special significance with which it invests certain key words and phrases see the important studies of Naphtali Wieder: "The Qumran Sectaries and the Karaites," *J.Q.R.* n.s. 47 (1956–57): 97–113, 269–92; "The Dead Sea Scrolls Type of Biblical Exegesis Among the Karaites," in *Between East and West: Essays Dedicated to the Memory of Bela Horovitz*, ed. A. Altmann (Oxford and London, 1958), 75–106; and *The Judean Scrolls and Karaism* (London, 1962).

[4] See Wieder, "The Dead Sea Scrolls Type of Biblical Exegesis Among the Karaites," 75–76.

[5] See G.D. Cohen, "Esau as Symbol in Early Medieval Thought," in *Studies in the Variety of Rabbinic Cultures* (Philadelphia, 1991), 243–69. The compositions of the Palestinian payyetanim of the early Middle Ages are especially notable for their use of such emblematic appellations or *kinnuyim*; see E. Fleischer, *Hebrew Liturgical Poetry in the Middle Ages* (Hebrew) (Jerusalem, 1975), 104–107.

the "lily among thorns" of Canticles 2:1–2 was more than a lovely metaphor; it was a clear reference to their own place in the world:

> The Remnant of Israel is compared to "the lily among thorns" for just as the lily appears in the spring when the summer season is just beginning, so "those whose way is blameless" (*temimei derekh*; cf. Ps. 119) appear at the end of the Exile which is compared to the winter.[6]

Once the identification was made, other biblical references to *shoshan* or *shoshanim* were understood as allusions to the Jerusalem community.[7] The name by which these sectarians were best known, however, was *avelei ṣion*, or Mourners for Zion. This term and the related phrase *eilei ṣedeq* ("Oaks of Righteousness") both derive from Isaiah 61:3; the former title, in particular, was assumed by members of the group who adopted an ascetic lifestyle, lamenting the destruction of the Temple and the lengthy duration of the Exile. They cited another verse, Isaiah 62:6, to describe their program of activities: "Upon your walls, O Jerusalem, I have set watchmen; all the day and all the night they shall never be silent. You who put the Lord in remembrance, take no rest."[8] As they understood it, the verse indicates that the prayers of an elite will ultimately bring about God's return to Zion. The members of this elite are the Maskilim, or preachers and teachers of Karaism who settled in the Holy City.[9] The "watchmen" of Jerusalem, they observe ceaseless vigils and pray to God, interceding

---

[6] Japheth b. Eli, Comment on Ps. 45:1; see: J.J.L. Bargès ed., *Rabbi Yapheth Abou Aly . . . in Canticum Canticorum Commentarium Arabicum* (Paris, 1884), 185–186; and N. Wieder, "Qumran Sectaries," p. 280 and n. 80. For the epithet *temimei derekh*, which Wieder renders "The Perfect of Way," see ibid., 97–113 and 289–91 where he reproduces Japheth's comment on Ps. 119:1. On the phrase "The Remnant of Israel" see ibid., 278–83. The payyetanim of Byzantine Palestine referred emblematically to the Jewish people as a *shoshanah*; see J. Yahalom, *Poetic Language in the Early Piyyut* (Hebrew) (Jerusalem, 1985), p. 13 and n. 11.

[7] See, e.g., the comments of Japheth b. Eli on the superscriptions to Psalms 60, 69, and 80; for the comment on Ps. 80:1, see "The Psalms Relating to the Community (44, 80, and 90)" below and Appendix, Text B.6.

[8] On this verse see Wieder, *Judean Scrolls*, 97–100, 102–103; Gil, *History of Palestine*, 612, 617.

[9] On the meaning of *maskil* see Wieder, *Judean Scrolls*, 104–117, esp. 106 where he notes Daniel al-Qūmisī's gloss on Ps. 74:1: "'*Maskil* is one who teaches and instructs Israel in the *Galuth* lest they go astray from the way of the Torah.'" The term derives from Dan. 11:33 and 12:3. In his comment on Cant. 2:1 Japheth b. Eli explains that the "rose of Sharon" and the "lilies of the valleys" likely refer to two separate groups of Maskilim—he calls them "Maskilim of the Exile" (*maskilei galut*)—those, such as Anan b. David, who lived in the midst of the Exile, and those living during the "generation of salvation" (*dor yeshuʿah*). The latter, of course, are the Shoshanim who "burst forth in the spring"; see Bargès ed., *Rabbi Yapheth . . . in Canticum Canticorum Commentarium*, p. 22 (Ar. text) and cf. the comment on Ps. 45:1 cited above. On *maskil* in the Psalms superscriptions see n. 70 below.

with Him on Israel's behalf in the time of trouble (*ʿet ṣarah*).[10] As one Karaite scholar explains:

> ... The Shoshanim are the Maskilim of the Exile who were gleaned from the Tribes of Israel and brought to Jerusalem so that they might intercede with God for the sake of His people. It is with their help that Israel's salvation and the kingdom of the Messiah will come. They are the ones who in the (period of the) Exile are styled the "Mourners for Zion" (*avelei ṣion*) and who will be called the "Oaks of Righteousness" (*eilei ṣedeq*) at the time of salvation.[11]

From these passages it is evident that prayer and lamentation featured as prominently in the group's activities as biblical interpretation: both were integral to the program of settlement, scholarship, and devotion that was intended to hasten the coming of the Messiah.[12] A study of the Mourners' exegesis and liturgy would seem, therefore, one of the most natural ways of learning about their hopes, fears, and self-perceptions. But here we encounter a problem: while a great part of their enormous exegetical production is extant, their rite remains something of a cipher. Verbose and repetitive, the commentaries of Salmon b. Jeroham and Japheth b. Eli, for example, furnish an abundance of information on the sect's ideology, halakhah, and theology—materials which still await proper analysis.[13] But how are we to make sense of a liturgy which consists almost entirely of biblical passages and verses? To be sure, the Shoshanim *did* recite piyyutim and lamentations of their own composition; so far as we can tell, however, it was the Bible—notably the Books of Psalms and Lamentations—which furnished them with their prayer book. In interpreting a liturgy of this kind we must first identify the most central texts and then seek to grasp the principles governing their selection. Finally, we must discover the way these texts were understood by the community. In other words, we must try to find out what the Mourners for Zion *intended* when they recited these biblical passages.[14] Essentially, we are seeking two types of

[10] See Japheth b. Eli, Comm. Is. 62:6, B.L. ms. Or. 2502 (Cat. 281). (The folio numbers are not legible on microfilm.)

[11] Japheth b. Eli, Comm. Psalm 46:1, New York, JTSA ms. Mic. 3350 [ENA 96], fol. 22b = Paris ms. héb. 287, fol. 26a.

[12] For a brief but perceptive characterization of the Jerusalem Karaites' messianism see G.D. Cohen, "Messianic Postures of Ashkenazim and Sephardim," in *Studies in the Variety of Rabbinic Cultures*, 273.

[13] For a sense of the tenth-century Karaite literary enterprise, its aims and scope see: R. Drory, *The Emergence of Hebrew-Arabic Literary Contacts at the Beginning of the Tenth Century* (Hebrew) (Tel Aviv, 1988) and idem., "The Role of Karaite Literature in the History of Tenth Century Jewish Literature" (Hebrew), *Dappim le-Meḥqar be-Sifrut* 9 (1994): 101–10.

[14] Cf. Wieder's succinct formulation:

texts: a liturgy proper, containing the designated passages ordered and arranged according to occasional demands; and a commentary on the passages in question, providing a key to the meaning which the community attached to them.

The second type of text is, as we have said, abundantly represented: the extant literary legacy of the Shoshanim includes extensive commentaries on Psalms by Salmon b. Jeroham and Japheth b. Eli.[15] There is also a commentary on Lamentations by Salmon which, as has recently been suggested, actually constituted the Mourners' main order of lamentation.[16] It is the first type of text, the liturgy, which poses problems. The Karaite *siddur* that has come down to us is a late text, of Byzantine origin.[17] While it undoubtedly preserves certain features of the old Palestinian liturgy, it contains numerous later accretions — including piyyutim by some of the great Andalusian poets![18] As a means of evaluating the liturgy of the Shoshanim, therefore, it is virtually without independent value.[19]

There is, however, one work which can answer our present need. Sometime during the first decades of the eleventh century, Japheth b. Eli's son Levi composed a short but important treatise on prayer which he included in his *Book of Precepts*. In this treatise he enumerates *inter alia* the biblical

---

The question as to the guiding principle, or principles, which determined the selection of the passages is still unexplored ground and cannot be fully discussed here. For the present purpose, however, it will suffice to state briefly that a number of biblical quotations that were accorded a place in the Karaite order of prayers owe their selection to a distinctive sectarian interpretation given to them—an interpretation which associated them with aspects of Karaite history, practice and doctrine. ("The Qumran Sectaries and the Karaites," 110; cf. 288.)

[15] For a penetrating study of these works see U. Simon, "The Karaite Approach," chap. 2 in *Four Approaches to the Book of Psalms: From Saadiah Gaon to Abraham Ibn Ezra* (Albany, N.Y., 1991) and the literature cited there.

[16] Ben-Shammai has argued this most persuasively; see his "Poetic Works and Lamentations of Qaraite 'Mourners of Zion'—Structure and Contents," in *Kenesset Ezra: Literature and Life in the Synagogue, Studies Presented to Ezra Fleischer* (Hebrew), ed. S. Elizur et al. (Jerusalem, 1994), 191–234. The first chapter of the text was edited by S. Feuerstein, *Der Commentar des Karaers Salmon ben Jerucham zu den Klageliedern* (Krakau, 1898).

[17] It was redacted by the thirteenth-century Crimean scholar Aaron b. Joseph, "The Elder"; see S.B. Bowman, *The Jews of Byzantium, 1204–1453* (University, Alabama, 1985), 140–42.

[18] For a study of the Karaite *siddur* see P.S. Goldberg, *Karaite Liturgy and Its Relation to Synagogue Worship* (Manchester, 1957). For Karaite paraphrases of rabbinic prayers see pp. 108–14. For Rabbanite piyyutim appropriated by the Karaites see L. Zunz, *Die Ritus des Synagogalen Gottesdienstes* (Berlin, 1859), 160–61. A generous selection of Karaite piyyutim from the later Byzantine and Turkish periods can be found in L.J. Weinberger, *Rabbanite and Karaite Liturgical Poetry in South-Eastern Europe* (Cincinnati, 1991).

[19] The liturgy of the Damascus Karaites, which contains numerous payyetanic additions as well, also does not afford reliable evidence for the practices of the tenth-century Jerusalem community; for a description, partial edition, and translation see G. Margoliouth, "An Introduction to the Liturgy of the Damascus Karaites," *JQR* o.s. 18 (1906): 505–27.

passages which he deems most important for daily recitation. This text, then, furnishes us with a liturgy employed by the Shoshanim. And by correlating Levi's pronouncements concerning the passages most appropriate for prayer with his father's comments on those passages, it is possible, I believe, to answer some of the questions that we have posed above concerning the Jerusalem Karaites and their worship. In the present study we will restrict ourselves to the Book of Psalms, its recitation and exegesis. For reasons which will become readily apparent, the Psalter affords a natural focus for our inquiry. Before turning to Levi b. Japheth's liturgy, therefore, we will briefly discuss his father's general approach to Psalms. This, in due course, will lead us to a discussion of specific, paradigmatic passages in his commentary.

Japheth b. Eli and His Commentary on Psalms

During the last decades of the tenth century, the foremost biblical exegete among the Karaites of Jerusalem was undoubtedly Japheth b. Eli (Abū ʿAlī Ḥasan b. ʿAlī al-Baṣrī).[20] Japheth translated and interpreted virtually every book of the Bible; while his Judeo-Arabic commentaries survive in manuscript, few have been edited and published.[21] As a source for the intellectual and cultural history of the Jerusalem Karaite community in the tenth century, they are of unparalleled worth, presenting the raw material for descriptions of the group's theology, education, and attitudes to other groups.[22] The first complete set of Bible commentaries composed by

[20] See: *EJB* 8:754–59, s.v. "Jafet ben Ali ha-Levi" (S.L. Skoss); *EJ* 9:1286, s.v. "Japheth ben Ali ha-Levi (Yafith ibn Ali; Abu Ali al-Hasan ibn Ali al-Lawi al-Basri)." Much useful information can be gleaned as well from S. Poznanski, "The Karaite Literary Opponents of Saadiah Gaon in the Tenth Century," *JQR* o.s. 18 (1906): 228–38, no. 12 (209–50).

[21] On the problems entailed in the edition of these texts see: H. Ben-Shammai, "Edition and Versions in Yephet b. Ali's Bible Commentary" (Hebrew), *Alei Sefer* 2 (1976): 17–32. The manuscript evidence for Japheth's commentaries has been surveyed by Ben-Shammai, "Doctrines" [see next note], vol. 2, Hebrew Introduction and G. Tamani, "La Tradizione delle opere di Yefet b. Ali," *BEK* 1 (1983): 27–76; both works also list published editions. To date, Japheth's commentary on Lamentations has not been discovered. The ten Firkovich mss. (II Firk. Hebr.-Arab. First Series) ascribed to him that I examined all proved to be copies of Salmon's work; see Ben-Shammai, "Poetic Works and Lamentations," 193. It is possible that the Karaites' veneration of this text precluded their interest in any other commentary on Lamentations.

[22] The single most important study of Japheth's thought is H. Ben-Shammai, "The Doctrines of Religious Thought of Abū Yūsuf Yaʿqūb al-Qirqisānī and Yefet ben ʿElī" (Hebrew), 2 vols. (Ph.D. diss., The Hebrew University, 1977) [= "Doctrines"]; the second volume contains a valuable survey of the manuscript evidence for Japheth's oeuvre, an anthology of critically edited texts, and a long English summary.

a Jewish author, Japheth's exegetical works resemble in many respects those of Saadya b. Joseph Gaon (d. 942).[23] They feature programmatic introductions which discuss the authorship, style, and purpose of the biblical book under consideration. Key themes are abstracted, enumerated, and classified. The tone is measured and rationalistic, the language clear and largely unadorned. As a genre, this type of introduction (Ar. *ṣadr*) was, of course, appropriated from Arabic literature and ultimately derived from classical models.[24] Subsequently, it became a hallmark of Andalusian, Rabbanite writing.

In the Introduction to his Commentary on Psalms, Japheth discusses the nature of prayer and its relationship to the biblical text.[25] As mentioned above, the Karaites regarded the Psalter as their *dīwān al-ṣalāt*, their *siddur*. In this, they were notably at odds with Saadya, who denied the Psalms the status of mandatory prayer.[26] While that entire debate relates back to

---

Other studies of his exegesis and thought include: P. Birnbaum, "Yefet ben Ali and his Influence on Biblical Exegesis," *JQR* 32 (1941–42): 51–70, 159–74, 257–71; L. Marwick, "The Order of the Books in Yefet's Bible Codex," *JQR* 33 (1942–43): 445–60; G. Vajda, *Deux Commentaires karaïtes sur l'Ecclésiaste* (Leiden, 1971); idem, "The Opinions of the Karaite R. Yafeth b. Ali on the Destruction of the World in the End of Days" (Hebrew), in *American Academy for Jewish Research Jubilee Volume* (Jerusalem, 1980), 85–95; A. Schenker, "Der Karäer Jafet ben Eli, die Buyiden und das Datum seines Danielkommentar," *BEK* 1 (1983): 19–26; idem, "Die Geburtswehen der messianischen Zeit nach Japhet ben Eli," *BEK* 2 (1989): 39–46. See also Ben-Shammai, "Attitude," esp. 14–23.

[23] For an overview of Saadya's exegetical enterprise see: H. Ben-Shammai, "The Exegetical and Philosophical Writing of Saadya Gaon: A Leader's Endeavor" (Hebrew), *Peʿamim* 54 (1993): 63–81 and the bibliography cited there. Japheth's younger contemporary, Samuel b. Hophni Gaon of Sūra (d. 1013), belonged to the same exegetical school as Saadya; on his life, works, and thought see D. Sklare, "The Religious and Legal Thought of Samuel Ben Hofni Gaon: Texts and Studies in Cultural History," 2 vols. (Ph.D. diss., Harvard University, 1992). On his Bible commentaries, see vol. 1, 23–30.

[24] The "Arabic model" for Karaite and Geonic Bible commentaries is discussed by R. Drory in *The Emergence of Hebrew-Arabic Literary Contacts*, 110–23. On the writing of programmatic introductions, see esp. pp. 117–18 and n. 21.

[25] For an edition of Japheth's Introduction and Commentary on Psalms 1 and 2, see (J.J.) L. Bargès ed. and trans., *Rabbi Yapheth Ben Heli Bassorensis Karaïtae in Librum Psalmorum Commentarii arabici* (Paris, 1846). Bargès also published a complete edition and Latin translation of Japheth's Arabic translation of the Psalter; see *Kitāb al-zubūr: Libri Psalmorum David regis et prophetae versio a R. Japheth ben Heli Bassorensi Karaïta* (Paris, 1861). See also Th. Hoffmann, *Der XXII. Psalm in das Arabische übersetzt und erklärt von R. Jephet b. Eli ha-Baçri* (Tübingen, 1880). Ben-Shammai includes excerpts from the Psalms commentary in "Doctrines," vol. 2, App. V, 234–63. Recently, A. Schenker has announced plans to produce a facsimile edition and French translation of Japheth's Commentary on the First Book of Psalms; see "Auf dem Weg zu einer kritischen Ausgabe von Jafet ben Elis Kommentar zu den Psalmen," *BEK* 2 (1989): 29–38.

[26] The most important study of Japheth's commentary on Psalms remains U. Simon, *Four Approaches*, chap. 2 where the matter is fully discussed. The original Hebrew edition of Simon's book was reviewed by Ben-Shammai in *KS* 58 (1983): 400–406. For the phrase *dīwān al-ṣalāt* see Bargès, *Yapheth Ben Heli in Librum Psalmorum Commentarii*, 9.

the question of rabbinic versus scriptural authority, there is another aspect to the Mourners' approach which lends their reading of Psalms special vitality. The apocalypticism of the Jerusalem community manifested itself, as we have seen, in their prognostic interpretation of biblical prophecies. Believing the Psalms to be prophetic prayers, the Shoshanim fashioned their own personal liturgy from the Psalter.[27]

In introducing the Psalter, Japheth asserts that its numerous "categories" or "themes" (*tafnīnāt wa-abwāb*) can be subsumed under twelve rubrics (*abwāb*). After first listing the rubrics, he proceeds to catalogue the Psalms and individual verses which address each theme. Japheth's purpose in providing such a detailed listing is practical: "It is obligatory," he says, "for us to include these twelve themes in our mandatory prayers, day and night."[28] Obligatory, because reason demands that we praise our Benefactor, enumerate His wondrous deeds and acts of munificence, and thank Him for them.[29] The twelve rubrics themselves provide further insight into Japheth's conception of prayer; they are as follows: (1) mentioning the creation and its arrangement; (2) mentioning God's excellences and His general and particular beneficence; (3) mentioning the wonders, miracles, and signs performed (by God) in the past and those He will perform in the future; (4) the disobedience of our ancestors; (5) the punishment which overtook them; (6) the return of the repentant (*shavei pesha*ʿ), i.e. the Shoshanim; (7) their request to God for knowledge of His Scripture; (8) their request for salvation from their enemies; (9) their request that God fulfill His promises (to redeem them); (10) the conversion of the gentile nations to the true faith and their eternal thanks to God; (11) recounting universal and perpetual peace and the banishment of enmity among the nations; (12) the obedience of the nations to God's people and His Messiah.

[27] Here the liturgy of al-Qirqisānī, the Iraqi Karaite, offers an interesting contrast: while it prominently features Psalm recitation, it does not reflect the prophetic approach characteristic of the Jerusalem community. For al-Qirqisānī's liturgy see: Yaʿqūb al-Qirqisānī, *Kitāb al-anwār wa'l-marāqib*, ed. L. Nemoy (New York, 1941), 3:603–36. See also L. Nemoy, "Studies in the History of the Early Karaite Liturgy: The Liturgy of al-Qirqisānī," *Studies in Jewish Bibliography, History, and Literature in Honor of I. Edward Kiev*, ed. C. Berlin (New York, 1971), 305–32 (contains a partial translation of chs. xv–xix and a complete translation of chs. xx–xxi). While he was certainly familiar with the practices of the Jerusalem community, al-Qirqisānī did not fully identify with them. As Gil has observed, he was the only contemporary sectarian who did not employ the phrase "Mourners of Zion"; see *History of Palestine*, 620.

[28] See Bargès, *Yapheth Ben Heli in Librum Psalmorum Commentarii*, p. 6, lines 9–10 (Ar. text). Cf. Simon, *Four Approaches*, 72–74.

[29] Ibid., lines 10–11. The appeal to reason derives from Japhet's Muʿtazilite orientation in theological matters; see H. Ben-Shammai, "Doctrines," 1:8ff. On the phrase *fī faṭr al-ʿaql* ("known intuitively according to the nature of human reason") see ibid., 73ff.

Taken together, these themes describe a salvation history in which divine beneficence is met with human disobedience, and divine punishment (Exile) is ultimately replaced with redemption (Return). Particularly noteworthy are the sixth through ninth themes which deal explicitly with the Mourners for Zion—here called "the Penitent" (*shavei peshaʿ*)—and their requests for divine assistance.[30] Even from Japheth's initial presentation it is clear that the Jerusalem community regarded its own part in this historical drama as pivotal. And when we turn to Japheth's exegesis of individual Psalms, we feel the full force of the Mourners' assertions and appreciate the depth of their convictions. Rather than attempting the ambitious task of analyzing Japheth's commentary on the entire Psalter, however, we have chosen to focus on a small corpus of Psalms which the sectarians singled out for daily worship. This liturgy, as circumstances would have it, was set down by none other than Japheth's successor within the community, his son Levi.

Levi b. Japheth's Treatise on Prayer (Al-qawl fīʾl-ṣalāt)

Like his father Japheth b. Eli, Levi b. Japheth—or Abū Saʿīd Lawī b. Ḥasan al-Baṣrī, as he was known in Arabic—was one of the leading scholars of the Jerusalem community.[31] He is remembered today chiefly for his *Book of Precepts* which was frequently cited by later Karaite authorities.[32] Composed during the first quarter of the eleventh century, this work represents the oldest extant code to have been produced by the Jerusalem Karaites.[33]

---

[30] On the term *shavei peshaʿ*, which derives from Is. 59:20, see Wieder, "Qumran Sectaries," 269–78 and idem., *The Judean Scrolls*, 101–102, 125–26.

[31] On Levi see S. Poznanski, "The Karaite Literary Opponents of Saadiah Gaon in the Eleventh Century," *JQR* o.s. 19 (1907): 59–63, no. 15; Ankori, *Karaites in Byzantium*, index, s.v. "Levi b. Yefeth"; and H. Ben-Shammai, "*Sefer Ha-Mitzvoth* of the Karaite Levi ben Yefet" (Hebrew), *Shenaton Ha-Mishpat Ha-Ivri* 11–12 (1984–86): 99–133.

[32] Composed in Arabic, Levi's code was later translated into Hebrew by Byzantine Karaites. For citations of the *Sefer miṣvot* by such scholars as Judah Hadassi (12th c.), Aaron b. Elijah (14th c.), and Elijah Bashyachi (15th c.) see Poznanski, ibid., p. 60 and Ankori, ibid.

[33] While the work has traditionally been dated to 1006/1007 C.E., the fragment identified by Ben-Shammai—quite possibly an autograph—dates from the year 415 A.H., i.e. 1024 C.E. See Ben-Shammai, "*Sefer Ha-Mitzvoth,*" p. 100, n. 2 and p. 103, referring to British Library ms. Or. 2577 (Cat. 592), fol. 159a. While Levi's code has not survived intact in the original Arabic, it has been largely preserved in medieval Hebrew translation; see Ben-Shammai, "*Sefer Ha-Mitzvoth,*" 100–101 and n. 3 for the mss. which have been identified to date. Sahl b. Maṣliaḥ ha-Kohen (Abūʾl Surrī), whose *Book of Precepts* has been cited above, belonged to the generation of Levi's father. To date, only small fragments of his code have been discovered and published; see A. Harkavy, "Meʾassef Niddaḥim, No. 13"; M. Sokolow, "Kidnapping in Karaite Law According to the Commentary of Sahl Ben Maṣlīʾaḥ," *JQR* 73 (1982): 176–88.

Like al-Qirqisānī before him, Levi devoted one section of his code to the subject of prayer. This treatise, which seems to have circulated independently, comprises ten short chapters that define the obligation to pray and discusses the times, orientation, location, language, and physical postures appropriate to prayer.[34] Each subject is introduced in turn, diverse opinions are surveyed, and the author's own view is expressed clearly and unequivocally.

Levi's treatise is important for two reasons. As Japheth b. Eli's son and intellectual heir, Levi occupied a prominent and influential position among the Shoshanim; his statements concerning prayer must therefore have carried real weight. Moreover, his code as a whole may be taken to reflect not only the views of his father but also the consensus of the community: to a great degree, it faithfully preserves the practices and beliefs of the Shoshanim.[35]

It is immediately apparent from the treatise, in fact, that the community shared certain basic opinions concerning prayer, even if there were differences in matters of detail. As self-professed scripturalists, they traced all religious obligations back to biblical sources; their actual liturgical practices were based, therefore, directly upon their interpretation of the Bible. On the basis of I Chronicles 23:30, for example, most of them held two daily services to be obligatory; according to a minority view, however, Daniel 6:11 and Psalm 55:18 indicated the existence of three mandatory daily prayers. Levi necessarily founds his own halakhic opinion, therefore, upon the exegesis of a scriptural passage—in this case, a biblical

---

[34] For an annotated translation see: G. Vajda, "La Lex orandi de la communauté karaïte d'après Lévi ben Yefet," *REJ* 134, 1–2 (1975): 3–45. For most of the text, Vajda was compelled to rely upon two medieval Hebrew versions, the Arabic fragment preserved in British Library ms. Or. 2564 (Cat. 308/II) supplying chaps. 7–10; see Vajda's comments on the text, pp. 3–4. For the contents of the treatise, see pp. 7–8. The B.L. fragment contains a colophon indicating that it was copied in A.H. 437 (C.E. 1045) and collated with the original, i.e. the authorized copy; see G. Margoliouth, *Catalogue of the Hebrew and Samaritan Manuscripts in the British Museum*, Pt. I. (London, 1899), p. 232, col. b. From a statement at the beginning of the ms. we learn that the treatise was known as *Al-qawl fī'l-ṣalāt* and that it was copied independently of the rest of the code; see Margoliouth, ibid., p. 232, col. a. Recently, Dr. David Sklare has discovered two more fragments of the Arabic original (in Hebrew characters) containing portions of the first eight sections: II Firk Heb.-Arab. I.930, fols. 19–26 and II Firk Heb.-Arab. I.928, 141–148. Taken together with the B.L. fragment, they constitute virtually the entire treatise in its original language. The longer of these fragments, II Firk Heb.-Arab. I.930, originally belonged to a ms. of Levi's code, i.e. it was not copied as a separate text. From this fragment we learn that the treatise on prayer followed the treatise on the Sabbath; the title of the former, incidentally, is given here as *al-kalām fī'l-ṣalāt*. For another copy of the Hebrew trans. (ascribed to Japheth b. Eli) see Ms. I. Firkovich Heb. 761; my thanks to Dr. Sklare for bringing these mss. to my attention.

[35] Cf. the remarks of H.H. Ben-Sasson, "Tenth and Eleventh-Century Karaite Attitudes to Gentiles," in *Salo Wittmayer Baron Jubilee Volume* (Hebrew section) (Jerusalem, 1975), 75 (71–90). A complicating factor, of course, remains the degree to which the (largely extant) Hebrew

narrative.[36] The liturgy itself, as we have said, derived mostly from Scripture, although some sectarians permitted the use of piyyutim as well.[37] The specific biblical passages employed seem to have remained a matter of choice. It was, moreover, accepted practice to string unconnected verses together to form new, meaningful texts.[38] Several fragments containing florilegia of biblical verses attest to this convention; the presence of interspersed instructions to worshipers confirms their liturgical function.[39] Although at least one Karaite, a certain Abū Sulaymān Dāwūd, compiled an order of prayer, the community as a whole resisted the canonization of its liturgy. While they might regard certain forms of worship as obligatory—e.g. the declaration of divine unity, expressions of thanks and praise, and confession—they tended to leave the choice of specific liturgical texts to individual discretion, there being no scriptural prescriptions to determine their prayers.[40]

Despite the community's special esteem for the Psalter, some sectarians sensed a tension between the original setting of a Psalm and its contemporary use as prayer. On exegetical grounds—often on the basis of a superscription—they might ascribe the composition of a given Psalm to specific individuals who were reacting to particular historical circumstances.

---

translation accurately reflects the (mostly lost) Arabic original. On the relationship between the Arabic and Hebrew texts of the code see Ben-Shammai, "*Sefer Ha-Mitzvoth*," 110–12, 130–33.

[36] See Vajda, "*Lex orandi*," 12–13. While the Rabbanites ultimately restricted themselves to pentateuchal proof-texts in their halakhic argumentation, the Karaites derived their laws from the entire biblical corpus; see D.J. Lasker, "The Influence of Karaism on Maimonides" (Hebrew), *Sefunot* 20 (1991), pp. 155–56 and n. 53 (145–161).

[37] See Vajda, ibid., 15–16. For piyyutim recited by the Mourners for Zion see: S. Assaf, "Prayer by Salman ben Yerūham [?] the Karaite" (Hebrew), *Zion* o.s. 3 (1928–29): 88–94; Mann, *Texts*, 2:31–32 (attrib. Japheth b. Eli, trans. Nemoy, *Anthology*, 107–108); M. Zulay, "Mi-piyyuṭei ha-qara'im ha-qadmonim," in *Qoveṣ hoṣa'at shoqen le-divrei sifrut* (Tel Aviv, 1941), 139–45, partial trans. T. Carmi, *The Penguin Book of Hebrew Verse* (Harmondsworth, 1981), 250–51; Ben-Shammai, "Poetic Works and Lamentations," pp. 192–93 and nn. 6–10, 222, 229–31.

[38] Vajda, ibid., 17. Certain Rabbanite prayers, such as the "qedusha de-sidra" ("u-va le-ṣion go'el"), are constructed similarly; see I. Elbogen, *Jewish Liturgy: A Comprehensive History* (Philadelphia-New York-Jerusalem, 1993), 70–71.

[39] See G. Khan, *Karaite Bible Manuscripts from the Cairo Genizah* (Cambridge, 1990), mss. nos. 13–17, pp. 152–69. Ms. no. 14 includes liturgical instructions, e.g.: "Save us, Oh Lord (*hoshiʿenu adonai*)! Prostrate then complete the verse and say . . ."; "The leader says . . . and you say . . . (*wa-yaqūl al-ra'īs . . . wa-qul anta*)"; see 163–64. These manuscripts, like the others published by Khan, were all written in Arabic characters. The practice of transcribing biblical texts into Arabic characters was typically Karaite. On possible motivations for this convention see: Khan, ibid., 20–21; idem., "The Medieval Karaite Transcriptions of Hebrew into Arabic Script," *IOS* 12 (1992): 157–76 and the literature cited there.

[40] Vajda, "Lex orandi," 8–12 (II Firk. H.-A. I.930, fols. 191–20b). For Abū Sulaymān Dāwūd b. Ḥusayn see ibid., 17 (II Firk. H.-A. I.930, fol. 21b). While the medieval Hebrew rendering which Vajda had before him refers to Abū Sulaymān's work as a *siddur*, the original Arabic simply has *ta'līf* (compilation, composition). Levi criticizes his fellow Karaite for incorporating so much extraneous material—homilies (*dirāshāt*), exegetical comments (*tafāsīr*), and polemics

Confronted by the problem of adapting scriptural texts to current liturgical needs, they developed two effective solutions. First, they might preface the recitation of a Psalm with the words, "this is the prayer which so-and-so recited."[41] As al-Qirqisānī had put it, the worshiper, in effect, acknowledged: "Even though these prayers are compositions of so-and-so, yet I admit what he had admitted, and seek what he had sought."[42] Any passages within the Psalm which did not conform, however, to the worshiper's own situation could safely be regarded as a record or quotation (*ḥikāya*) pertaining to the original historical context.[43] Second, those Karaites who compiled florilegia effectively disengaged verses from their ancient settings. Such anthologizing brought an additional benefit: since individual Psalms often seemed incomplete from a liturgical standpoint, it was tempting to assemble all the necessary components from different sources. The evocation of God's creation in Psalm 136:4–9, for example, could be admirably supplemented by Psalm 104.[44] As Levi states:

> (The worshiper) may choose verses in accordance with what he desires his prayers to express. And this is the practice of all worshipers, for they glean verses expressing divine unity (*fawāsīq al-tawḥīd*) (from all of Scripture) for their prayers. In the same manner, (they select) verses of confession (*fawāsīq widduyīm*), verses of consolation (*fawāsīq nāḥāmōth*), praise and prayer (*wa-hillūl wa-tafillā*) which it would take too long to detail.[45]

One of the florilegia preserved, in fact, represents just such a sequence of verses. Here the verb *hodah* ("give thanks") works as a kind of magnet, attracting diverse phrases drawn almost exclusively from Psalms. Skilfully arranged and adapted, they constitute a new prayer of thanksgiving (*hodāʾāh*):[46]

> In the name of God, the merciful the compassionate.
> It is good to give thanks to the Lord (92:2); sing praises to the Lord, O you His saints and give thanks (30:5)! Give thanks to Him, bless His name! For the Lord is good; His steadfast love endures forever (100:4–5). For as the heavens are high

(*dalāʾil ʿalā ʾl-madhāhib wa-radd ʿalā ʾl-mukhālifīn*)—that the Psalms, the *sine qua non* of prayer, are indistinguishable.

[41] B.L. ms. Or. 2564, fol. 13a, lines 7–8: *ṣallā fulān kadhā wa-kadhā*, trans. Vajda, ibid., 32–33.

[42] See *Kitāb al-anwār*, vol. 3, p. 636, lines 9–10, trans. Nemoy, "Studies in the History of the Early Karaite Liturgy," 328.

[43] B.L. ms. Or. 2564, fol. 13a, lines 2–3; see Vajda, "Lex orandi," 33.

[44] See Vajda, ibid., 18.

[45] See B.L. ms. Or. 2564, fol. 13a, lines 10–14, trans. Vajda, ibid., p. 33 and nn. 151–53.

[46] See Khan, *Karaite Bible Manuscripts*, ms. 15, pp. 165–66. For the place of thanksgiving in Karaite prayer see al-Qirqisānī, *Kitāb al-anwār*, vol. 3, pp. 624–25, trans. Nemoy, "Liturgy of al-Qirqisānī," 314.

above the earth, so great is His steadfast love toward us [!][47] (103:11); for great is His steadfast love toward us (117:2). I will praise the Lord as long as I live (146:2). My soul is feasted as with marrow and fat, and my mouth praises You with joyful lips (63:6). I will thank You forever because You have done it (52:11). I give thanks to You, O Lord my God, with my whole heart (86:12). O give thanks to the Lord, for He is good! O give thanks to the God of gods! O give thanks to the Lord of lords, He who gives food to all flesh! O give thanks to the God of heaven (136:1–3, 25–26)! O give thanks to [!][48] the Lord for His steadfast love, for He satisfies him (who is thirsty) (107:8–9). The afflicted shall eat and be satisfied (22:27). O taste and see that the Lord is good! O fear the Lord, you His saints (34:9–10)! . . .[49]

Florilegia of this kind enabled worshipers to formulate their devotions in pure biblical phraseology. Selective by nature, such prayers include only those verses which address the specific liturgical matter at hand, be it praise, petition, or thanksgiving. Whether they were carefully constructed or associatively pieced together, composite texts of this kind present isolated verses stripped of their original contexts and interpretative frameworks.[50] Nevertheless, certain Psalms retained their special liturgical value for the community precisely because of the way in which they were integrally interpreted. Levi classifies such biblical prayers (*ṣalawāt*) as either divine communications to the prophets (*awliyāʾ*) which contain information about the future (*ʿattidot*) or lessons for the people of the exile (*ahl al-jāliya*).[51] In both cases, the Psalms were to be understood at once liturgically and prophetically, i.e. as prayers whose full significance would be realized long after their revelation, during the days of the Shoshanim. As we will argue below, Karaite exegesis of these texts functioned, therefore, as liturgical commentary. First, however, we must identify the scriptural texts which the Shoshanim themselves regarded as possessing special liturgical value.

Levi b. Japheth's Liturgy

Towards the end of his treatise, Levi offers some specific liturgical guidelines, indicating which biblical passages best express the themes that a

---

47 Ps. 103:11: ". . . toward those who fear him." The verse has been adapted, consciously or unconsciously, to accord with 117:2 which follows.

48 Ps. 107:8: "Let them thank." Another adaptation.

49 The prayer continues with Deut. 6:11, Ex. 23:25, and Joel 2:26 before reverting to the Psalter for the last dozen or so verses.

50 For an important collection of such texts see B.L. ms. Or. 2539, fols. 1–55; my thanks to Professor Ben-Shammai for this reference.

51 Ps. 90 ("A Prayer of Moses, the man of God") is an instance of the first category, Ps. 79 of

worshiper must address on a daily basis.[52] It is laudable, he says, for a person to begin with those Psalms which relate to the community (*al-mazāmīr allatī lil-jamāʿati*) such as Psalm 44, "We have heard with our ears, O God," Psalm 80, "Hear us, O Shepherd of Israel," and Psalm 90, "A prayer of Moses." Even prior to these, however, one should recite Psalms relating to the Temple (*mazāmīr al-quds*) such as Psalm 74, "Why have you rejected us forever O God" and Psalm 79, "O God, the nations have invaded your inheritance."[53] Following the Psalms relating to the community, one should recite Psalms relating to the individuals (*mazāmīr al-āḥād*), such as Psalms 25, 28,[54] and 86. Furthermore, it is laudable to recite the Psalms relating to the Exile (*mazāmīr al-jālūth*) prior to the Psalms relating to the Salvation (*mazāmīr al-yeshūʿōth*) according to the chronological sequence of events. Of all the Psalms, none combines communal concerns and historical issues so well as Psalm 90, *tefillah le-mosheh*.[55] Should worldly concerns intervene, however, and the worshiper prefer a condensed service, there is an abridged liturgy containing all of the essential elements: the proclamation of divine unity (*fawāsīq al-tawḥīd*)[56] is to be followed by Psalm 136 (*hodu ladonay ki tov al-kabīr*) and the portion concerning the daily sacrifice. This is to be followed, in turn, by Psalm 145 (*tehillah le-david*), the verses of Lamentation (*fawāsīq al-qīnōth*),[57] Psalms 79, 90, and 86,[58] and finally, the portion *va-yevarekh david* (I Chronicles 29:10–13).

---

the second; see see B.L. ms. Or. 2564, fol. 12b, trans. Vajda, "Lex orandi," 32. See also the comments concerning Pss. 79, 44, 80, 90, and 102 on fol. 13a, lines 14–19, trans. Vajda, 33–34.

[52] B.L. ms. Or. 2564, fol. 18a, lines 13ff., trans. Vajda, ibid., 41–42. See Appendix, Text A.

[53] Vajda, ibid., p. 41 (last line): "LXIX" should be corrected accordingly.

[54] Vajda, ibid., p. 42 (first line): "XXX" should be corrected accordingly.

[55] Ar.: *wa-laysa fīʾl-mazāmīr mā yajmaʿ umūr al-jamāʿa waʾl-azimna mithl tefillah le-mosheh.*

[56] It is not clear which verses Levi intends. The proclamation of divine unity (*yiḥud* or *yiḥud ha-shem*) figures at least as prominently in the Karaite liturgy as it does in the Rabbanite service. The scriptural verses which constitute the sectarian proclamation (*fawāsīq al-tawḥīd*) are not identical, however, with the Rabbanite *shemaʿ* (Deut. 6:4–9; 11:13–21; Num. 15:37–41). While both groups recite Deut. 6:4, the Karaites have, at different periods, employed other biblical verses as well. For one such text see the Genizah fragment published by Louis Ginzberg, *Genizah Studies in Memory of Doctor Solomon Schechter* (Hebrew) (New York, 1929), 2:441–42 (435–442). Commenting upon Ps. 44:18 (New York, JTSA ms. Mic. 3350 [ENA 96], fol. 13a) Japheth b. Eli explains: "The words 'we have not forgotten You' refer to the proclamation of divine unity (*yiḥud ha-shem*) for daily, in this world they (i.e. the Karaites) recite: 'Hear O Israel, the Lord is our God, the Lord is One (Deut. 6:4).' " On the other hand, later Karaites also regarded Neh. 9:6ff. as an expression of *yiḥud ha-shem*; see, e.g. Aaron b. Elijah, *Gan Eden*, "ʿInyan tefillah," ch. 2 (Gozlow, 1864), fol. 72b, line 12. And see the discussion in Goldberg, *Karaite Liturgy*, 64–70.

[57] Again, Levi does not indicate specific verses. See further below under "The Psalms Relating to the (Destruction of the) Temple (74 and 79)."

[58] In the Arabic text (fol. 18b, lines 7–8) these three Psalms are labelled "elohim baʾu goyim" (79), "tefillah le-mosheh" (90), and "tefillah le-david" (86). Vajda, p. 42 and n. 202 seems to

Figure: Levi b. Japheth's Abridged Liturgy

Proclamation of divine unity	*fawāsīq al-tawḥīd*
Psalm 136	*hodu al-kabīr = hoda'ah*[59]
Numbers 28 (the daily sacrifice)	*faṣl al-qorbān*
Psalm 145	*shevaḥ, hillūl*[60]
Verses of Lamentation	*fawāsīq al-qīnōth*
Psalm 79	*mazāmīr al-quds*
Psalm 90	*al-mazāmīr allatī lil-jamā'ati*
Psalm 86	*mazāmīr al-āḥād*
I Chronicles 29:10ff.	*va-yevarekh david*

From this passage, several basic features of the Jerusalem Karaite liturgy become clear. First—as may be seen from the abridged liturgy—the *essential* "prayer book" of the community is defined by a small core of biblical passages, each of which fulfills a specific liturgical function. Second, the recitation of individual Psalms occupies a prominent place. Particular Psalms have been chosen, moreover, because they express key communal concerns. The rubrics under which the Psalms may accordingly be classified are: the Temple; the Community; and the Individuals. The importance of these three categories is apparent, moreover, from the abridged liturgy where each rubric is represented by one Psalm. Third, two additional considerations determine both the selection of individual Psalms and the order in which they are recited: (1) the chronological sequence of events to which the Psalm is understood to relate, and (2) the Psalm's comprehensiveness, i.e., the degree to which it is seen to express both historical and communal issues.

Having identified which scriptural passages furnished the core of the Jerusalem Karaite liturgy, we may investigate the way the sectarians understood these texts when they prayed. Here, the Bible commentaries of Levi's father, Japheth b. Eli, are most informative. As Uriel Simon has demonstrated, Japheth's Psalms commentary reflects the sectarians' conviction

have read "tefillah le-david" as a heading for the following words, "va-yevarekh david" (I Chronicles 29:10–13). But as noted below, each of these three Psalms corresponds to one of the groups enumerated above.

[59] According to al-Qirqisānī Ps. 136 constitutes "Thanksgiving" (*hoda'ah*); see Nemoy ed., *Kitāb al-anwār*, vol. 3, p. 625, lines 5–7. It should be noted that in rabbinic literature Ps. 136 is commonly styled *hallel ha-gadol*; see, e.g., bPes. 118a.

[60] Levi speaks generally of "Praise" (*shevaḥ*, fol. 12b, line 15; *hillūl*, fol. 13a, line 13); Ps. 145 would seem to fit this category of prayer.

that the Psalter was their prayer book (*dīwān al-ṣalāt*).[61] In his Introduction, Japheth clearly and unequivocally expresses his commitment to examining liturgical issues, a tendency which becomes manifest in his comments on virtually every Psalm. We may reasonably assume that Levi understood Scripture as his father had expounded it. We will focus below, therefore, on Japheth's exegesis of Psalms, particularly the three groups singled out for recitation by Levi.

The Psalms Relating to the (Destruction of the) Temple (74 and 79)

As *avelei ṣion*, the Jerusalem Karaites naturally devoted themselves to mourning the destruction of the Temple. They donned sackcloth and ashes, observed nighttime vigils, and recited dirges—all practices which are well attested in both sectarian and Rabbanite sources.[62] In his liturgy, Levi mentions "verses of lamentation" (*fawāsīq al-qīnōth*); these likely refer to selections from the Book of Lamentations accompanied by the so-called commentary of Salmon b. Jeroham.[63] There were also poetic laments which had been composed in biblical Hebrew.[64] Not surprisingly, Levi recommends the recitation of two Psalms which feature the destruction of the Temple as their main subject.

Psalms 74 and 79—the *mazāmīr al-quds*—share certain thematic and stylistic similarities. Both report the defilement of the Temple and its destruction (74:3–8; 79:1–3, 7). Both describe the way the nations revile God and Israel (74:10, 18, 22; 79:4, 10). And both recount Israel's complaint to God for having abandoned them and for raging against them continually (74:1, 11; 79:5) as well as their entreaty to Him for vengeance against their enemies (74:11, 22; 79:6–7, 9–11).

For Japheth b. Eli Psalm 74 expresses Israel's plaint at the Temple's

[61] Simon, *Four Approaches*, 75. For the term *dīwān al-ṣalāt* see above, n. 26. From several references in Levi's treatise it is clear that there were other Karaite liturgies circulating; see Vajda, "Lex orandi," p. 17 (the *siddur* of Abū Sulaymān David b. Ḥusayn) and p. 42 ("les rituels composés par les Docteurs"—where, however, the Ar. *ta'līf al-ʿulamā'* is vague).

[62] See, e.g., D.S. Margoliouth ed. and trans., *A Commentary on the Book of Daniel by Rabbi Jephet the Karaite* (Oxford, 1889), p. 146, lines 19–20 (Arabic), p. 81 (English) (comment on Daniel 12:9). And see M. Gil, *History of Palestine*, 618–21 and the literature cited there. For Rabbanite reactions to the Mourners' practices see M. Zucker, "Teguvot li-tenuʿat avelei ṣion ha-qara'iyim be-sifrut ha-rabanit," in *Chanoch Albeck Jubilee Volume* (Jerusalem, 1963), 378–401.

[63] See Ben-Shammai, "Poetic Works and Lamentations," passim.

[64] See above, n. 37.

destruction in ancient times and the continuing defilement of its site during the present. He recognizes a clear two-part structure: verses 3–10 describe the destruction wrought by the Babylonians; verses 11–23 relate the contemporary injuries inflicted by the Muslims. As usual, Japheth begins by noting a thematic link with the preceding Psalm. He then offers some general, programmatic observations:[65]

74:1 A Maskil (*rushd*) of Asaph. O God, why have You utterly abandoned (us), Your anger smoking against the sheep of Your flock?

In the preceding Psalm he (i.e. the Psalmist) complained about what will befall them at the hands of the Fourth Kingdom, as we explained in connection with the verse "I was envious of the wicked" (Ps. 73:3). In the present Psalm, he has assembled (*jamaʿa*) (descriptions of) all that befell[66] them at the hands of the kingdom of the Chaldeans as well as what will befall them at the hands of the Fourth Kingdom. The verses "Direct Your steps" until "How long, O God, is the foe to scoff?" (Ps. 74:3–10) constitute a complaint about what befell them at the hands of the Chaldeans. (In the second part of the Psalm), from the verse "How long" until the end of the Psalm (Ps. 74:10–23) they complain about what will befall them at the hands of the Fourth Kingdom. This Psalm (deals with) two matters (*maʿnayn*): The first (relates) to the subject of the Holy Temple (*al-quds*), for (just as) the Chaldeans had defiled and burned it, so Ishmael ever defiles it, fulfilling thereby (the prophecy) that "they will scoff at God and revile His name"[67] as it is written, "Is the enemy to revile your name forever?" (Ps. 74:10). Second, it mentions the first and last kings[68] so as to include thereby the two (other) kings who come between them.

This Psalm, says Japheth, takes the form of a two-fold complaint (*shakwa*) in which Israel first recounts the destruction of the Temple in ancient times, before describing the current desecration of the holy site. By juxtaposing these descriptions the Psalm accomplishes two ends: it emphasizes that the current situation under Islam is, alas, comparable to the desolation wrought by the Chaldeans; and it suggests a historical continuum of oppression, by alluding to the so-called Four Kingdoms.[69] The comprehensiveness of the text is noteworthy: in encompassing a great historical sweep, it

---

[65] The text has been edited and translated from New York, JTSA ms. Mic. 3349 [ENA 95] (= Ms. A), fols. 16b–30b = Paris, Bibliothèque Nationale ms. héb. 288 (= Ms. P), fols. 13a–24a. See Appendix, Text B.1.

[66] Reading *jara* with Ms. P.

[67] Cf. Ps. 74:18.

[68] Ar. *al-malikān al-ṭarafāniyān*, lit. "The two kings at either end."

[69] For a survey of tenth-century Karaite views on Islam see H. Ben-Shammai, "Attitude." From this passage and his commentary on Ps. 73, it seems that Japheth regarded Islam as the Fourth Kingdom. According to Japheth's Commentary on Daniel, however, the Four Kingdoms were, in order, (1) the Chaldeans; (2) Persia; (3) Greece; and (4) Rome. The Arabs, who arose last, after the Romans, "have not indeed acted like the others in exiling them and destroying them [i.e.

describes the persecution of Israel, past and present. The Psalm's special significance for the Shoshanim is immediately apparent from its heading:

> The superscription employs (the term) *maskil,* since (this Psalm) contains guidance (*rushd*) and instruction (*taʿlīm*) for the remnant of Israel (*she'erit yisra'el*)—how they voice their complaints to God, beseeching Him to change their condition and the condition of their Holy Temple (for the better)!

While *Maskil* was, of course, employed by the Jerusalem sectarians as an appellation for teachers or preachers of Karaism, within a Psalm superscription it was understood to indicate divine guidance (*rushd*, *hidāya*) for the group as a whole which was to use the following text as a prayer.[70] The latter often styled itself "the Remnant of Israel" which had clung fast to the Law and would in the end be saved.[71] The Psalm, then, was seen as a divinely-inspired petition by means of which the community could voice its plaints to God and its pleas for deliverance:

> The words "O God, why" take the form of a question or entreaty like the words of Moses, peace be upon him, "O Lord, why does Thy wrath burn hot . . .? Why should the Egyptians say . . .?" (Ex. 32:11–12). And the words "have You utterly abandoned (us)" embrace all that befell them at the hands of the Chaldeans and until the present day. "Abandoned" means the cessation of (divine) support so that (Israel's) enemies accomplish their designs against them. "Your anger smoking" refers to the times of severe tribulations. The first of these occurred at the

---

Israel], but they have injured the nation in the way of contempt and scorn and humiliation, etc." See Japheth, *Commentary on Daniel*, 28–30, esp. p. 30, lines 19–20 (Ar.), 12–14 (Eng.) (comm. on 2:37–43). This comment suggests that Japheth seems to have experienced some difficulty in accommodating both Christendom and Islam within his scheme. His use of the standard Karaite epithet for Islam, "the Little Horn" (*qeren zeʿira*; see Dan. 7:8) may indicate that he regarded the latter as an outgrowth of the former and thus a *part* of the Fourth Kingdom; on "the little horn" see Ben-Shammai, "Attitude," 8 and n. 2 above. Japheth's near-contemporary, Sahl b. Maṣliaḥ offers a different, more symmetrical scheme with each of the Kingdoms corresponding to two nations: Babylonia and the Chaldeans, Media and the Persians, Greece and Macedon, Edom and Ishmael; see A. Harkavy, "Me'assef Niddaḥim, No. 13," 202–203. Cf. the respective solutions of Saadya Gaon, who divided the Fourth Kingdom between the Christians and Muslims, and Abraham Ibn Ezra, who unequivocally excluded "Rome" from his interpretation of the Four Kingdoms. See: G.D. Cohen, "Esau as Symbol in Early Medieval Thought," 260–61; idem., *The Book of Tradition (Sefer Ha-Qabbalah) by Abraham Ibn Daud* (Philadelphia, 1967), 237–40; E. Schlossberg, "The Nature and Exegetical Purpose of the Commentary of R. Saadia Gaon on the Book of Daniel"(Hebrew), *PAAJR* 56 (1990): 13 (5–15); idem., "R. Saadia Gaon's Attitude Towards Islam" (Hebrew), *Daʿat* 25 (1990): 28–29 (21–51).

[70] On *maskil* see above n. 9. For Japheth's interpretation of the term in the Psalms superscriptions see Simon, *Four Approaches*, 89 (citing the comment on Ps. 88:1) and p. 107, n. 66. Japheth discusses the meaning of the terms *mizmor*, *shiggayon*, *mikhtam*, *shir*, *maskil*, *tefillah*, and *tehillah* at the beginning of his comment on Ps. 3; see Paris ms. héb. 286, fols. 20b–21b and Simon, ibid., 93.

[71] For the Karaites' self-designation as "the Remnant of Israel" see N. Wieder, "Qumran Sectaries," 278–83.

> destruction of the Lord's Temple by the King of Babylon; this resulted from the Lord's burning wrath as it states: "The Lord gave full vent to His wrath" (Lam. 4:11). In the present verse he summarizes all that will befall them in the Exile; and indeed, He has fulfilled every single (prediction).[72] This is the force of the phrase "have You utterly abandoned (us)" which is similar to "cursed shall you be in the city" (Deut. 28:16) and all the rest of the curses (Deut. 28:16–68). For every one of (these) things will befall them at some time, e.g. the destruction of the two Temples, those periods when they will be pressed[73] to abandon their faith, and the time of confiscation[74]—all these (disasters) are included in the words "Your anger smoking against the sheep of Your flock." The phrase "against the sheep of Your flock" is (intended) to soften (the tone of) the statement, indicating that this nation has been "the sheep of Your flock" as long as it has existed and they have no other leader beside You. They are like sheep which cannot find their own way;[75] the gentle shepherd, however, leads them and protects them.

The entire Psalm is a communal plea for succor to an absent deity: "Do not send us away confounded but accept, rather, our prayers and entreaties and answer our requests."[76] "Divine guidance" (*rushd*) might at the least take the form of a *maskil*, an inspired interpreter who could explain the words "shut up and sealed until the end of time" (Daniel 12:9). But alas, "there is none among us who knows how long!" (Ps. 74:9):

> . . . We are perplexed and are unable to find a prophet in our midst whom we can consult or a *maskil* among us who correctly understands what Your scripture contains concerning the End (*qeṣ*) so that he might inform us how much (time) remains. We would then be certain as to how much remains and would be patient. For we have now (been waiting) a long time and still do not know when the end of this Exile (*galut*) has been decreed for us and when we will be saved.[77]

Lending this prayer urgency is the way individual phrases are understood in light of the Jerusalem Karaites' own experiences. As we have seen, Japheth believes that the second half of the Psalm—beginning with verse 10—constitutes Israel's complaint at their mistreatment by the Muslims:

74:10 Until when, O God, will the foe offer insult? Will the enemy despise Your name forever?

> This is (their) complaint at the situation (which they endure) under the Fourth Kingdom. They exclaim "Until when?" at the prolongation of the Exile and

---

[72] Ar. *fa-kull shay' huwa muqīm.*

[73] Reading *yuṭālabūna* (Form III, passive), lit. "it will be demanded of them."

[74] Ar. *waqt al-muṣādara.* The allusion is obscure.

[75] Or "lead themselves."

[76] See Japheth's comment on v. 21, Ms. A, fol. 29a.

[77] Comment on 74:9, Ms. A, fol. 23b. Cf. Japheth's comment on Ps. 90:12, Ms. A, fols. 193b–194a.

> the remoteness of the End (*qeṣ*). They are exasperated by the two types of abuse mentioned that the enemy has heaped upon them; these are (reflected in the words) "offer insult" (*yeḥaref*) and "despise"[78] (*yena'eṣ*). "Offer insult" refers to the way that they (i.e. the Muslims) revile Israel on account of the degradation (*dhull*) and insult that have befallen them (i.e. the Jews), all the while saying: "Where is your God?"[79] as we have explained in our comment on "With a deadly wound in my body" (Ps. 42:11). "Will the enemy despise" relates to the subject of religion (*al-dīn*), for they have despised the Law (*torah*) of the Lord, uttering all manner of evil things about it. Thus, they always accuse Israel (saying): "You have altered (*ghayyartum*) the Torah and have falsified it (*wa-ḥarraftumūhā*)!" One of them might even assert on his own authority that he denies the One who commanded this Torah, while affirming this "(Book of) Shame" which is replete with expressions of scorn (*ni'aṣot*), lies, and follies. Therefore, it says "Will the enemy despise."[80]

Japheth characteristically interprets the two verbs *yeḥaref* and *yena'eṣ* not as simple synonyms, but as allusions to distinct acts. In seeking to actualize the biblical text as far as possible, Japheth reads the verse as a plaint at two common anti-Jewish slurs. The insult that he describes recalls the Qur'ānic charge that "shame (*al-dhilla*) is pitched over them (i.e. the Jews) wherever they are found" (2:112).[81] Indeed, both Muslims and Christians regarded the Jews' adherence to their faith—despite their subjugation and degradation—as an act of blind persistence. The Muslims' rejection of the Torah, on the other hand, is rooted not only in their belief that it has been abrogated, but also in their conviction that it has been "altered" or "falsified."[82] But not only do they deny the Torah; they also affirm their own "Book of Shame"—*al-qalon*, a punning, derogatory epithet for *al-qur'ān*—a work packed with lies and absurdities![83]

---

[78] Or "reject," "abandon." Japheth regularly renders Heb. *na'aṣ* with Ar. *rafaḍa*; cf. his comment on Dt. 32:19 in M. Sokolow, "The Commentary of Yefet Ben Ali on Deuteronomy XXXII," (Ph.D. diss., Yeshiva University, 1974), 85–86.

[79] Cf. Pss. 42:4, 11; 79:10.

[80] Comment on Ps. 74:10, Ms. A, fols. 23b–24a. See Appendix, Text B.2.

[81] A.Y. Ali trans., *The Holy Qur'ān* (London, 1975), p. 151.

[82] See, e.g., Qur'ān 2:59, 75. On the Muslim charge that the Jews falsified the text of their Scripture see *EI*, 1st ed., s.v. "Taḥrīf" and H. Lazarus-Yafeh, "Muslim Arguments against the Bible," chap. 2 in *Intertwined Worlds: Medieval Islam and Bible Criticism* (Princeton, 1992), esp. 19–35, and the literature cited there. Oddly, perhaps, Japheth does not connect Heb. *yeḥaref* with Ar. *ḥarrafa* ("falsify"), though he does include the phrase *wa-ḥarraftumūhā* ("and you have falsified it") in elaborating Heb. *yena'eṣ*. But cf. Salmon b. Jeroham's comment on Ps. 44:17 cited in the next section.

[83] On Japheth's use of Heb. *qalon* ("shame") and *sefer qalon* ("book of shame") as a derogatory epithet for the Qur'ān see: M. Steinschneider, *Polemische und apologetische Literatur in arabischer Sprache* (Leipzig, 1877; reprinted: Hildesheim, 1966), 316 and the comments on Hab. 2:18 and Is. 47:9–10 translated by Ben-Shammai, "Attitude," 16–17.

The Muslim presence on the Temple Mount—manifest in the monumental Dome of the Rock and al-Aqsā Mosque—also deeply affronted the Mourners:[84]

> The phrase "eliminate (him) from within Your bosom" (v. 11) is a request to God asking that He eliminate Ishmael from the midst of His holy place. By the word *tashiv* ("hold back")[85] he as much as indicated his wish for speedy vengeance against them in the other places where Jews (dwell) in their midst. The phrase "eliminate (him) from within Your bosom" refers to those of them who are within His sanctuary (*miqdasho*). Concerning the latter he says "eliminate," since their sin is greater than others'. For while they have "mocked" (*yeḥarefu*) and "despised" (*yena'aṣu*)[86] as others have done, they have exceeded others in reviling the Lord's name in His sanctuary (*yena'aṣu et shem adonay be-miqdasho*). They have, moreover, polluted His sanctuary with their impurity, adultery, fornication, and funeral biers (*yeṭamme'u miqdasho be-ṭum'atam ve-ni'uf u-zenut u-miṭṭot metim*). Therefore he says "eliminate (him) from within Your bosom."[87]

The Muslims' desecration of the holy site is a recurring theme in the writings of the Jerusalem Karaites. Daniel al-Qūmisī, (late ninth-early tenth century), Salmon b. Jeroham and Sahl b. Maṣliaḥ (both mid-tenth century) all decry the comings and goings of gentiles who are contaminated with every kind of ritual impurity.[88] They are also very disturbed by the Muslims' daily services which they declare to be both obtrusive and profane:

> (23) Forget neither the clamor of Your foes, nor the uproar of Your adversaries which goes up continually!
>
> Previously he said "do not forget the life of Your poor forever"(v. 19) for the reason which we explained. At the conclusion of the Psalm he again says "do not forget" what they did in Your holy place. He has subsumed (*wa-jamaʿa*) the actions of both the Chaldeans and the Muslims (lit. "Ishmael") within this verse. "The clamor of Your foes" refers (back) to the phrase "Your foes have roared in

[84] Ben-Shammai has shown that the Jerusalem Karaites inhabited the City of David, a neighborhood situated just outside the present Dung Gate, to the south of the Temple Mount; see: "The Karaites," 166–68 (163–78); idem., "Meidaʿ ḥadash ʿal meqomah shel shekhunat ha-qara'im bi-yerushalayim ba-tequfah ha-muslemit ha-qedumah," *Shalem* 6 (1992): 305–13; idem., "Letoledot ha-shekhunah ha-qara'it bi-yerushalayim," *Cathedra* 70 (1994): 59–74. He observes that the Mourners, in looking up towards the city from their quarter, would have beheld the Muslim edifices upon the Temple Mount and the Nea Church on Mount Zion; see "Poetic Works and Lamentations," 223–24 and notes ad loc.

[85] Ps. 74:11a: *lamah tashiv yadekha* ("Why do You *hold back* Your hand?").

[86] On the verbs *yeḥarefu* and *yena'aṣu* see Japheth's comment on vs. 10, discussed above.

[87] Comment on Ps. 74:11, Ms. A, fol. 24b.

[88] See, e.g., the text attributed to Salmon, published by S. Assaf, "Prayer by Salman ben Yerūham [?] the Karaite," and Salmon's Commentary on Lam. 1:7, cited by Ben-Shammai, "Attitude," p. 9. As has often been remarked, the Karaites held extremely strict views on matters of ritual purity; see, e.g., Ben-Shammai, "Meidaʿ ḥadash," p. 308 and n. 15. See also Japheth's comment on Ps. 79:8, translated below.

the midst of Your holy place" (v. 4) which includes the rest of what we mentioned concerning "the enemy has destroyed everything in the sanctuary!" (v. 3). "The uproar of Your adversaries" refers (back) to the phrase "the foe mocks, the enemy reviles" (v. 10). He mentions thus the magnitude of their mocking and reviling, i.e. (the way) they assemble on the Temple Mount[89] with a great tumult, especially at the hour of prayer and behave in a provocative manner (Heb. *yargizu*) five times a day.[90] For this reason he says, "which goes up continually." By the words "do not forget" he means "to annihilate them from before You and from Your holy place" as it says, "eliminate (him) from within Your bosom" (v. 11).[91] In saying "do not forget" in connection with the actions of the Chaldeans he means, "Hasten to fulfill what You promised them (when You said): 'I will requite Babylon and all the inhabitants of Chaldea before your very eyes for all the evil that they have done in Zion etc." (Jer. 51:24).[92]

For Japheth the Psalm's final verse describes not only the destruction of the Sanctuary by the ancient Babylonians, but also the site's continued occupation by Muslims. Having usurped the holy place, the latter conduct daily religious services which create a disturbing din. The sound of these prayers serves as a constant reminder to the Jerusalem Karaites of the Temple's destruction, the extended Exile, and their abasement at the hands of the nations. In Japheth's reading, the verse perfectly encapsulates the frustrations of his fellow sectarians. For what could be more disturbing to the worshiper than the perpetual clamor of rival religious services?

The other Psalm of Lamentation, Psalm 79, addresses similar themes; it is likely that Levi b. Japheth preferred it for his abridged liturgy because of its comparative brevity. In his commentary, Japheth identifies two main subjects: a description of the Temple's destruction in ancient times and Israel's plea that God punish her enemies:

79:1 A Psalm[93] of Asaph. O God, the nations have invaded Your inheritance; they have defiled Your holy Temple; they have made Jerusalem a wasteland.

There is a very close thematic link (*niẓām*)[94] between the present Psalm and the preceding one, for just as he (first) recalled the destruction of Shiloh (Ps. 78:60–67) and then (said) "He built His sanctuary like the high heavens" (ibid., v. 69), he informed (us) afterwards that this Temple would be destroyed as well, and that Israel would suffer at the present time as it had not suffered when Shiloh was destroyed. The phrase "O God, the nations have invaded" (marks) the be-

[89] Or, "in Jerusalem"; Ar. *fī ʾl-quds*.

[90] For parallel passages in the exegesis of Salmon b. Jeroham see Ben-Shammai, "Attitude," p. 9.

[91] This refers to the Muslims.

[92] Comment on Ps. 74:23, Ms. A, fol. 29b–30a. See Appendix, Text B.3.

[93] Heb. *mizmor* (psalm) rendered here by Ar. *majd*, a (song of) praise.

[94] On the meaning of this term in Japheth's Psalms exegesis see Simon, *Four Approaches*, 86.

ginning of a narrative. It (deals) with two subjects: the first is His fulfillment of His threat **[78b]** against them; the second is their request that God exact justice of these nations, as we will explain in connection with verse 10.

In accordance with his historico-prophetic approach, Japheth relates the Psalm to the destruction of Jerusalem in ancient times as well as to Israel's continued suffering at the hands of the nations down to his own time. In praying for relief, Israel acknowledges and enumerates the transgressions which have incurred divine punishment. These sins are of two kinds: imitation of gentile practices and halakhic innovation. Israel's assimilation of foreign mores and general lawlessness represents contamination from without; the institution of new laws lacking scriptural foundation represents erosion from within.[95] Japheth's comment on 79:8 suggests that he discerns a prayer of confession (*vidduy*) embedded within the Psalm. The "Penitents of Jacob" (*shavei pesha*ʿ) whom he pictures proclaiming the verse are, of course, none other than the Mourners for Zion for whom repenting and returning to Scripture were fundamental.[96]

79:8 Do not remember against us the iniquities of our ancestors; may Your compassion come speedily to meet us, for we are brought very low.

Having said, "How long, O Lord? Will You be angry forever?" (v. 5) they ask God again to disregard the great sins which they have committed. The words "iniquities of our ancestors" refer to **[82b]** the transgressions committed by our forefathers whom we have followed and whose path we have taken. Now, however, since it has become clear to us that these (ways) are not right, we have returned from them; we ask You, therefore, not to remember them against us. (Here) it should be said that the sins of the people of the Exile can be classified (as follows): There were transgressions (committed by) the ruling nation[97] such as forbidden sexual relations, the profanation of the Sabbath, divination, enchantment, sorcery, and the like, as well as robbery, oppression, and theft, etc. There were also transgressions committed specifically by the people of the Exile, such as intercalation, by which they changed the festivals from their (appointed) times.[98] They abandoned (the laws of) ritual purity and impurity and (the laws

[95] Cf. the notion of unacceptable legal or doctrinal innovation in Islam; see *EIS*, s.v. *bid*ʿ*a*.

[96] On this epithet see the literature cited in n. 30 above. The Hebrew verb *shuv* encompasses both repentance from sin and return (to Scripture); Arabic *tawba*, which Japheth employs in his comment, is the standard term for repentance. On the significance of "returning" to Scripture see H. Ben-Shammai, "Return to the Scriptures in Ancient and Medieval Jewish Sectarianism and in Early Islam," in *Les Retours aux écritures: fondamentalismes présents et passés*, ed. E. Patlagean and A. Le Boulluec (Louvain-Paris, 1993), 319–39.

[97] I.e. sins endemic to the surrounding society that the Jews consequently committed.

[98] Heb. *ʿibbur*, lit. "pregnancy," i.e. the leap year. Japheth here attacks the Rabbanite practice of intercalating an additional month during seven years of every nineteen-year cycle. The Rabbanites do this in order to keep the lunar and solar years more or less aligned, ensuring thereby

relating to the consumption of) food prepared by gentiles (*ma'akhalot goyim*); being brought up with these practices in the Exile, they became habituated to them. Then the Penitents of Jacob (*shavei pesha' be-ya'aqov*) say: "O Lord! We beseech You not to remember against us the iniquities of our predecessors which we used to commit (as well) but of which we have now repented." **[83a]** The words "may Your compassion come speedily to meet us" mean "hasten the salvation which has been slow in reaching us."

The phrase "for we are brought very low" refers to those who have strayed, a people that has reached the most diminished of circumstances and for whom the divine promise, "for the Lord will judge His people" (Deut. 32:36) had already been fulfilled. The phrase "for we are brought very low" is (similar to) "the power is gone" (ibid.).[99]

Elsewhere it has been explained that Israel will repent (*yatūbūn*)[100] at the present time (*fī dhālika al-zamān*) and that God will have mercy upon them as it is stated: "When you are in tribulation, and all these things come upon you (in the latter days, you will return (*ve-shavta*) to the Lord your God and obey His voice)" (Deut. 4:30). This indicates that Israel will repent at a time of tribulation (*'et ṣarah*) and that God will have mercy upon them when they do so,[101] as it is stated: "For the Lord your God is a merciful God" (Deut. 4:31). Those who repent at the time of tribulation have said: "O God, behold how 'we are brought very low'! You have promised those who repent (*al-tā'ibīn*) that You will have mercy upon them; have mercy, therefore, upon us as you have promised" for "their power is gone and there is none remaining, bond or free" (Deut. 32:36).[102]

That the Psalm is to be understood as a *contemporary* text is clear from Japheth's reference to "the present time" (*dhālika al-zamān*), when, as he notes with reference to verse 10, "the signs of salvation (*'alāmāt al-yeshu'ah*) have already (begun) to appear."[103] What makes the Psalm particularly suitable for regular liturgical use, however, is its comprehensiveness: it rehearses the past and present afflictions of the Jews; relates their sinfulness; conveys their contrition, desire for mercy and vengeance; and expresses their thanks. Japheth's comment on the final verse provides the student and worshiper with a digest of the major themes which he has isolated in the Psalm:

---

that the festivals fall during their proper seasons. According to the Karaites, the months are determined by direct observation rather than calendation; the problem of keeping the lunar and solar calendars aligned, therefore, did not arise. See Ankori, *Karaites in Byzantium*, pp. 350–51, n. 138.

[99] For Japheth's commentary on Deut. 32:36 see M. Sokolow, "The Commentary of Yefet ben Ali on Deuteronomy XXXII," 138–41.

[100] Or "return."

[101] Lit. "with their repentance," Ar. *'inda tawbatihim.*

[102] Comment on Ps. 79:8, Ms. A, fol. 82a–83a. See Appendix, Text B.4.

[103] Ar. *wa-hādhā maqūl 'alā dhālika al-zamān alladhī qad ẓaharat fīhi 'alāmāt al-yeshu'ah.* Comment on Ps. 79:10, Ms. A, fol. 84b.

79:13 Then we Your people, the sheep of Your flock, will give thanks to You forever; from generation to generation we will recount Your praise.

Know that this Psalm comprises five themes: (1) the three ways in which the nations acted against Israel—by entering **[86b]** their domain, polluting their sanctuary, and destroying it (v. 1); by killing them there (vv. 2–3, 10); and by reviling them for the destruction which befell them (vv. 4, 10); (2) (Israel's) entreaty that God forgive their sins which were the cause of all this destruction (vv. 5, 8–9); (3) their entreaty for mercy and salvation (vv. 9, 11); (4) their exacting justice of their enemies (vv. 6–7, 9–10, 11); and (5) their conviction that they will thank and praise God (v. 13). For they said: "We are the nation (*qawm*) that is Your people (*shaʿbuka*) who belong to You, the sheep of Your flock whom You lead as You see fit. You save us from the enemy[104] and from the kings of the nations, tending us as You have said: 'I will be the shepherd of my sheep, and will make them lie down.' And we will thank You always, never ceasing to praise You; indeed, we will recount Your praise in each and every generation, as it is stated: 'But I **[87a]** will hope continually (and will praise You yet more and more')" (Ps. 71:14).[105]

The Psalms Relating to the Community (44, 80, and 90)

The second group of Psalms in Levi's liturgy relate, he says, to the community as a whole (*al-mazāmīr allatī lil-jamāʿati*). The interpretation of these Psalms by the Shoshanim should reveal much about their self-perception and corporate identity; more precisely, it should show us how they defined themselves as a group through prayer. In surveying the three Psalms which Levi singles out, we must first inquire why he felt them to be special, before noting certain key themes which they share.

First, the Psalm superscriptions not only guided exegesis but also influenced the process of liturgical selection. As we have seen, the terms *shoshanim* and *maskilim* were understood by the Jerusalem Karaites as prophetic references to their community and its leaders.[106] It was natural, therefore, that Psalms which include these words in their headings find their way into the liturgy. Thus, Japheth comments on the superscription to Psalm 80 (*la-menaṣeaḥ el shoshanim ʿedut le-asaf mizmor*):

80:1 In (our commentary on) the preceding Book (of Psalms) we have already mentioned to whom these "Shoshanim" refer. Similarly, we have explained the meaning of the term "testimony" (*ʿedut*). We have stated that these Shoshanim are the people who sprout up amidst the thorns.[107] They are the same (people)

[104] Lit. "the evil ones"; Heb. *raʿim*.
[105] Comment on Ps. 79:13, Ms. A, fol. 86a–87a. See Appendix, Text B.5.
[106] On the former appellation see above nn. 6–7; for the latter, nn. 9 and 70.
[107] The Arabic here accords with Japheth's translation of Cant. 2:2.

> who are described in "Blessed are those whose way is blameless" (*ashrei temimei derekh*) (Psalm 119) and "A prayer of one afflicted" (*tefillah le-ʿani*) (Psalm 102).[108] We have stated that "testimony" (*ʿedut*) denotes "lineage" (*nisba*), as we have explained concerning "To the leader about the Shoshan, a testimony" (Psalm 60), which concerns the Messiah. This (Psalm), however, was spoken concerning the Shoshanim who are the "worm of Jacob" (*tolaʿat yaʿaqov*).[109] They are mentioned in the superscriptions of three Psalms, "My heart overflows," "Save me, O God!" (Psalms 45 and 69), and here in order to inform us that this Psalm is their prayer.[110]

Whatever the word *shoshanim* ("lilies") might signify to other exegetes, to the Mourners for Zion it was a clear reference to their own community. This passage, in fact, offers a fine example of the serial identifications they favored: *shoshanim* = *temimei derekh* = *ʿaniyim* = *tolaʿat yaʿaqov*. The power of such equations will be obvious: they enable an inspired exegete—or community of interpreters—to read the Bible prognostically. For the Shoshanim, the term *maskil* seems to have denoted both the community as a whole vis-à-vis the rest of Israel (and the nations), as well as the leading teachers *within* the community who instructed the other Shoshanim. Commenting on the superscription to Psalm 44, Japheth explains:

> **44:1** The word *maskil* is used in the superscription because (this Psalm) contains guidance and instruction for Israel as to how they should present their case before God. Know that this Psalm refers to the Jewish people (*umma yisraʾel*) and it has (therefore) been expressed in the plural. Among all the Psalms none other compares to it in terms of comprehensiveness (*fī jawāmiʿ maʿānīhi*), for it commences with (the Exodus from) Egypt and concludes with the end of the Exile. There are three verses in this Psalm which are expressed in the singular, viz. vv. 5, 7, and 16—each for a reason which we will mention in due course.[111]

Second, the abstraction of certain key liturgical themes undoubtedly governed the choice of liturgical texts from Scripture. Psalms were, most likely, designated for liturgical use when both their superscriptions and content corresponded to these key themes. We have already seen how Japheth identifies twelve major liturgical themes according to which he classifies

[108] On the importance of these two Psalms for the Mourners of Zion see Wieder, *Judean Scrolls*, 203–204 (Ps. 102), 206–13 (Ps. 119) and the literature cited there.

[109] For the significance of this name, see Japheth's comment on Is. 41:14 ("Do not fear, O worm of Jacob . . .") which he explains as God's reply to the community's complaints. "They compared themselves to a worm," he says, "which is the lowliest of things and trodden upon by all"; see London, B.L. ms. Or. 2501 (= Cat. 280), fol. 203b, lines 6–13.

[110] Comment on Ps. 80:1, Ms. A, fol. 87a. See Appendix, Text B.6. Cf. Japheth's comment on Cant. 2:1 cited by Wieder, *Judean Scrolls*, p. 202, n. 4.

[111] Comment on Ps. 40:1, Ms. A, fol. 8b. See Appendix, Text B.7. On Ps. 44:5,7, and 16 see the next section, "Psalms Relating to the Individuals (25, 28, and 86)."

the Psalms.[112] Psalms 44 and 80 are, in fact, listed in his thematic catalogue under rubric 2b, "Psalms which express God's special acts of beneficence (*niʿamuhu al-khāṣṣa*) towards Israel."[113]

Third, and finally, the Shoshanim had a marked predilection for Psalms which they felt to be of a comprehensive nature, encapsulating the various doctrines emphasized by the community. In Japheth's view—as we have just seen—Psalm 44 is the most comprehensive of all, encompassing the entire history of Israel from the Exodus until the end of the Exile. His opening comment on Psalm 90, "A Prayer of Moses," contains a similar observation:

Ps. 90:1 This prayer (i.e. Ps. 90) comprises six themes: (1) the eternal and enduring nature of the Creator; (2) His creation of His creatures; (3) the varying life-spans of human beings and the fact that they are (in any case) short; (4) what befell Israel on account of God's wrath and the other things that happened to them in Exile,[114] all this being the cause of their sins; (5) their entreaty to God to inform them of the End (*qeṣ*) so that they might verify (the time); and (6) the anticipated fulfillment of the (divine) promises.[115] Now this (Psalm) comprises all that is necessary to mention on the subject of the two Exiles.[116]

From this observation, we learn that Japheth approaches Psalm 90 in much the same way as he interprets Psalm 74: the text is presented as a condensed, self-contained *Heilsgeschichte* which has been cast in liturgical form.

In terms of comprehensiveness, however, it is Psalm 44, he believes, which most completely surveys the course of Jewish history. In verses 3–4, he finds references to the expulsion of the seven nations from the Land and its inheritance by Israel's ancestors in the time of the judges and kings. "Within these two verses," Japheth explains, "(the Psalmist) has included all that God accomplished for them in the Land; it is possible that the words 'what deeds You did perform in their days' (v. 2) encompass what He did for them in Egypt and in the wilderness. He enlarged, however, upon what He did for them in the Land because (further on) He will mention the opposite, as we will explain."[117] In verses 5–6, Japheth sees allusions to the defeat of the Philistines, Moabites, Amonites,

[112] See above, "Japheth b. Eli's Commentary on Psalms."
[113] See Bargès, *Yapheth in Librum Psalmorum Commentarii*, 3.
[114] Ms. P. adds *bi-ikhtiṣār*, "in summary form."
[115] Lit. "the fulfillment of the anticipated promises," Ar. *injāz al-mawāʿīd al-muntaẓira*."
[116] Comment on Ps. 90:1, Ms. A, fol. 189b. See Appendix, Text B.8.
[117] Comment on Ps. 44:4, Ms. A, fol. 9b–10a.

and Edomites in ancient times; indeed he views the first nine verses as a description of the praiseworthy deeds which God performed for Israel of old.[118] With verse 10 there begins an enumeration of the punishments which God inflicted upon His people; significantly, the word *af* is also used in Leviticus 26:16 to introduce the curses which God will bring down upon Israel, should they violate the covenant. While Japheth relates the next five verses to the people's suffering in Exile, he connects verses 16 and 17 with the anti-Jewish polemics characteristic of the Islamic milieu in which he lived:[119]

44:16 My disgrace is before me all the time, and the shame of my face has enveloped me

44:17 at the voice of him that reviles and slanders, by reason of the enemy and avenger.

The expression "all the day" (*kol ha-yom*) has two connotations: "all day long" from morning to evening; and throughout the period of the Exile. He says "my disgrace is before me" and explains in the following verse "at the voice of him that reviles," informing (us) that he is perpetually ashamed when he hears "the voice of him that reviles and slanders." This refers to the one who reviles my religion and slanders my law and my God (*sharīʿatī wa-maʿabūdī*) as it is stated, "(with which) the servants of the king of Assyria have reviled me" (II Kgs. 19:6, Is. 37:6).

Next he says "by reason of the enemy," by which he means, "and the shame of my face has covered me . . . by reason of the enemy and avenger." By the words "and the shame of my face has covered me" he wishes to convey the fact that the shame which manifests itself on a person's face (can) envelop his body as well—an indication of deep humiliation. This is because "the enemy and avenger" has stated: "The Torah has been abrogated (*nusikhat*) by another (scripture) and there is no (possibility) of your returning (to your former prosperity)![120] For how are you faring now, after fifteen hundred years of degradation (*dhull*) ?" It is to these and similar (statements) that he refers, when he says "my disgrace is before me all the time . . . at the voice of him that reviles and slanders."

"The shame of my face" refers to the way they revile Israel for their disobedience as, for example, when they say: "You worshiped the Golden Calf and

[118] Comment on Ps. 44:10, Ms. A, fol. 11a.

[119] Comment on 44:16–17, Ms. A., fol. 12ab. See Appendix, Text B.9.

[120] "And there is no (possibility) of your returning (to your former prosperity)!" (Ar.: *wa-laysa lakum rajʿa*). I follow Professor Ben-Shammai's suggestion in translating this obscure phrase. For *rajʿa* meaning "return" in the sense of "profit" see E. Lane, *Dictionary*, p. 1041; the phrase might then mean, "And there is no (longer) any profit in it for you!" The technical, legal sense of the word may also be apposite, denoting remarriage with a wife who was previously divorced; see H. Wehr, *Dictionary*, 328. If the latter meaning is intended, then Israel is being taunted as a divorced wife to whom her husband will never return.

slew the prophets[121]!" These and the like are expressed by the phrase "and the shame of my face has enveloped me."

The phrase "the enemy and avenger" refers to Ishmael and Edom[122] and to the others as well who revile Israel.[123]

For the Mourners the word *meḥaref* represented a whole range of Muslim, anti-Jewish slanders: the charge that the Jews had falsified their Scripture (*taḥrīf*); the claim that the Bible had, in any case, been abrogated (*naskh*); and the libel that they declared Ezra to be the son of God. Thus Salmon b. Jeroham comments:

> A *meḥaref* is one who reviles (us) for (sins) which we have committed and (others) which we have not. The former includes (our) worshiping the calves, killing the prophets, and the like. The latter, our assertion that ʿUzayr was the son (of God) and our tampering with the text of Scripture (lit. 'changing the letters of the Torah,' i.e. *taḥrīf*) and other matters which it would take too long to expound.[124]

From such remarks, it is easy to see that the community recited these verses as a plea for relief from the insults that they endured. Despite the unbearable situation in which they found themselves, however, they remained firm in their faith and observance. Verses 18–19 encapsulated for them their own steadfastness, furnishing a suitable reply to their tormentors:[125]

44:18 All this has befallen us, although we have not forgotten You and not betrayed Your covenant.

44:19 Our heart has not turned back and our steps have not departed from Your ways.

They mentioned the four things observed by the entire nation. First, "we have not forgotten You"—this refers to the proclamation of divine unity (*yiḥud hashem*), for every day in this world they say: "Hear O Israel, the Lord is our God, the Lord is one" (Deut. 6:4). Second, "we have not betrayed Your covenant"—the meaning of this is that we have not abolished Your Law but rather, we continually assert "the Law of Moses is true."[126] For they proclaim as well

---

[121] For the charge that the Jews worshiped the (Golden) Calf see Qurʾān 2:51, 2:92; 4:153. According to Qurʾān 2:61, the Jews were subjugated and brought low (*wa-ḍuriba ʿalayhim al-dhilla wa'l-maskana*) because they used to deny God's signs and would kill (His) prophets unjustly; cf. 2:91, 3:21, 3:112, 3:181, and 4:155.

[122] I.e. to Islam and Christendom.

[123] Ms. P refers only to Ishmael and Edom and omits the last clause.

[124] Marwick, *The Arabic Commentary of Salmon ben Yeruham*, 9 on Ps. 44:17. For the charge that the Jews call ʿUzayr (i.e. Ezra) a son of God, see Qurʾān 9:30 and the discussion in Lazarus-Yafeh, *Intertwined Worlds*, 50–74. See also Salmon's comment on Lam. 1:8, ed. Feuerstein, p. XXXI, trans. Ben-Shammai, "Attitude," 15. On *taḥrīf* and *naskh* see ibid., 19–41. And see n. 82 above.

[125] Comment on 44:18–19, Ms. A., fol. 12b–13a. See Appendix, Text B.10.

[126] Heb. "*torat moshe emet*." On the liturgical function of *emet* among Rabbanites and Karaites,

> that God made a covenant with them beneath Mount Sinai and that that covenant will remain binding upon the generations of Israel until the end of time,[127] as it is stated: "Nor is it with you only that I make this covenant and this oath, but with him who stands here with us this day (before the Lord our God, and also with him who is not here with us this day)" (Deut. 29:13–14). (Third) it then stated, "Our heart has not turned back"—by this they meant, "Our hearts have not inclined toward any religion other than Yours." Now in the first verse (i.e. v. 18), they conveyed the plain meaning of their statement; subsequently, they imparted its hidden (sense). (Fourth,) by the words "Our heart has not turned back" and "and our steps have not departed from Your ways" they are referring to the commandments (*farāʾiḍ*) which both the righteous and wicked among them[128] perform such as facing in the proper direction for prayer,[129] circumcision, eating unleavened bread (on Passover)[130] and the like.

Yiḥud ha-shem, the daily affirmation of God's unity, figures as prominently in the Karaite liturgy as in the Rabbanite prayer book. Here its importance is underscored by a sort of cross-reference within the Psalm: our loyalty to the Covenant, proclaims the worshiper, is manifest in our recitation of the Shemaʿ.[131] We have, moreover, remained firmly committed to the Law of Moses, resisting all arguments that it has been superseded and its commandments abrogated. For even the least devout Jew observes such basic religious laws as circumcision and the eating of unleavened bread on Passover.[132] And this, in the face of unremitting persecution (vv. 20–23)! The conclusion of the Psalm (vv. 24–27) represents a request—the Mourners' request—that God no longer conceal Himself from them and reveal at last His salvation.

---

see now N. Wieder, "An Unknown Ancient Version of the Haftarah Benedictions—The Use of 'emet' to affirm Important Religious Principles," in *Knesset Ezra . . . Studies Presented to Ezra Fleischer* (Hebrew) (Jerusalem, 1994), 35–46, esp. pp. 44–46 and n. 34. Noting that *emet* figures in the four *hodayot* ("affirmations") of the Karaites, Wieder cites a passage from Japheth's commentary on Cant. 5:8: "They say: 'Hear O Israel etc.' and say: 'The Law of Moses is true, His prophets are true, and His Temple is true"; see Bargès, *Rabbi Yapheth . . . in Canticum Canticorum Commentarium*, p. 74 (Ar. text).

[127] Lit., "until the end of all the generations."

[128] Ar. "*ṣāliḥuhum wa-ṭāliḥuhum.*"

[129] Ar. *istiqbāl al-qibla.*

[130] Ar. *akl al-faṭīr.*

[131] As we have seen Levi b. Japheth's liturgy begins with *yiḥud ha-shem*. On this component of the Karaite liturgy see above n. 56.

[132] It is true that Japheth complains elsewhere of apostasy. Apparently, some Jews in his day were susceptible to the religious propaganda of the Ismāʿīlīs; see S.M. Stern, "Fāṭimid Propaganda Among Jews According to the Testimony of Yefet b. ʿAlī the Karaite," in *Studies in Early Ismāʿīlism* (Jerusalem, 1983), 84–95 for an allusion in Japheth's comment on Dan. 11:30–32. See also the article of Dr. Sarah Stroumsa in this volume and her n. 21. In commenting on Ps. 44:23, however, he recalls the willingness of Jews to suffer martyrdom at the hands of Christians and Muslims rather than abandon their faith.

In sum, the Psalm provided the Shoshanim with a compelling prayer for their community whose message can be recapitulated as follows:

> . . . Now this Psalm comprises four themes: (1) God's beneficence towards (our) ancestors throughout the various ages; (2) (Israel's) complaint at what has befallen them; (3) mention of their adherence to the religion and law of God; (4) (their) entreaty to God that He pay attention to their (present) situation and restore them to their former (condition).[133]

While Levi b. Japheth includes both Psalms 44 and 80 in his liturgy, it is Psalm 90 which he claims best combines communal and historical issues.[134] Most likely, his choice was affected by the Psalm's ascription to Moses. Like his father, he probably believed that Moses composed the Psalm through the same "holy spirit" (Heb. *ruaḥ ha-qodesh*) which inspired his songs at the sea (Ex. 15) and in the plains of Moab (Deut. 32)—texts which the Jerusalem Karaites read prophetically.[135] The Psalm's designation as a prayer moreover, made it a natural choice for the liturgy. According to Japheth, the heading *tefillah* signifies "a complaint at (one's) situation, and an entreaty to God for salvation and the fulfillment of the (divine) promise"—a definition which tallies with his exegesis of Psalm 90.[136] But Levi may also have been influenced by messianic considerations: the Psalm's popularity among the Karaites was stimulated by certain clues to the Messiah's coming which some detected in verses 4, 12, 14, and 15. Evidence for such calculations can be found both in Japheth's commentary and in a Hebrew fragment apparently copied in Byzantium.

In Japheth's reading, the Psalm does indeed become a comprehensive

---

[133] Comment on 44:27, Ms. A., fol. 15a.

[134] See above, n. 55.

[135] According to Japheth's theory of revelation, there were six or seven "degrees" (*marātib*) of prophecy. The highest of these, labelled "mouth-to-mouth" (*peh el peh*, see Num. 12:7) was uniquely attained by Moses when he received the commandments; his non-legislative prophecies, however, such as the Psalms of David, were revealed via prophetic inspiration (Ar. *ilhām*; Heb. *ruaḥ ha-qodesh*). See: C. Sirat, *Les Théories des visions surnaturelles dans la pensée juive du moyen-âge* (Leiden, 1969), 47–57; H. Ben-Shammai, "Doctrines," 1:259–78; idem., "On a Polemical Element in Saadya's Theory of Prophecy" (Hebrew), *Shlomo Pines Jubilee Volume* (= *Jerusalem Studies in Jewish Thought*, vol. 7), ed. M. Idel et al., Pt. 1 (Jerusalem, 1988): 127–46, esp. 137–43 and 143 where a portion of Japheth's comment on Ps. 90:1 is reproduced; D.J. Lasker, "The Influence of Karaism on Maimonides," 152–57; Simon, *Four Approaches*, 80–81.

[136] For Japheth's definition of *tefillah* see his comment on Ps. 3:1, Ms. P, fol. 21a, lines 10–11. Similarly, Ps. 86 ("A Prayer of David"), was chosen to represent the "Individuals"; see above "Levi b. Japheth's Liturgy" and further below. Al-Qirqisānī advances three reasons for the daily recitation of Ps. 90 in the morning: (1) its Mosaic authorship invests it with special value; (2) its subject matter—the Exile, the return following repentance, and reward—is apposite; and (3) the word "morning" (*boqer*) is mentioned several times. See: al-Qirqisānī, *Kitāb al-anwār*, vol. 3, p. 630, lines 1–9; Nemoy, "Studies in the History of the Early Karaite Liturgy," 320–21.

prayer which would certainly make a fitting liturgical climax: "You have been our refuge (Heb. *maʿon*; Ar. *maʾwan*) in every generation" (v. 1) alludes to God's all-encompassing nature and self-sufficiency on the one hand, and the way He has continually aided Israel, on the other. This divine assistance was granted in the days of Moses, the time of the Judges and the Kings, and during the Exile; at the End of Days, "in the future, it will be even greater than in the past."[137] Having succinctly described God's creation of the world and His relation to all of His creatures (v. 2),[138] the Psalmist (here: Moses) describes the nature of the human predicament (vv. 3–6), specifically the decreasing life spans of human beings.[139] These general statements introduce a description of what has befallen Israel: as a result of their sinfulness, the Jews have decreased dramatically and unnaturally in number and have suffered divine punishment at the hands of the nations (vv. 7, 9–11). The nature of their transgressions is familiar (v. 8): changing the times of the Sabbaths and festivals, eating forbidden foods, contracting illicit unions, and perverting justice. Whether willful or unintentional, these sins result primarily from ignorance of Scripture and adherence to man-made commandments (*miṣvat anashim melummadah*).[140] Beset by great troubles (*ṣarot gedolot*) in the last days of the Fourth Kingdom, the Teachers of the Exile (*maskilei ʿam*) realize that the words of the Prophet Jeremiah have been realized: "It is a time of distress for Jacob; yet he shall be saved out of it" (Jer. 30:7). When these troubles subside, however, and their hopes for redemption go unfulfilled, they beseech God to tell them the number of days remaining before the advent of the Prophet Elijah; for to date, none of the Sages of the Exile (*ḥakhmei galut*) has successfully computed the End (v. 12).[141] They ask God to repent of His anger and bestow upon them His favor so that they might rejoice all their days (vv. 13–14). In his comment on the following verse, Japheth exhibits his well-known antipathy to Messianic computations.[142] On the basis of

---

[137] Comment on 90:1, Ms. A, fol. 190a.

[138] Ms. A, fol. 190b.

[139] Ms. A, fol. 191ab.

[140] Ms. A, fol. 192ab. Cf. Japheth's comment on Ps. 79:8, Ms. A, fol. 82b (Appendix, Text B.4). On the significance of the phrase *miṣvat anashim melummadah* (Is. 29:13) for the Jerusalem Karaites see Wieder, *Judean Scrolls*, 259–63.

[141] Cf. Japheth's comment on Ps. 74:9, Ms. A, fol. 23b, cited above.

[142] In his Commentary on Daniel, Japheth makes it quite clear that precise calculation of the End is impossible. While the Bible does contain certain hints as to the timing of the final days, it has deliberately prevented any precise reckoning; see *Commentary on Daniel* 12:6, p. 143, lines 18ff. (Ar.), p. 79 (Eng.) where Japheth collects eight such biblical references and his comment at the end of Daniel on the mistaken computations of his predecessors, ibid., pp. 151–53 (Ar.), pp. 86–87 (Eng.). And see Ben-Shammai's comments, "Fragments of Daniel al-Qūmisī's

v. 15, some Karaite exegetes, such as Benjamin al-Nahāwandī, maintained that the days of salvation (*ayām al-yeshuʿah*) would number as many as the days of Exile (*ayām al-galut*).[143] Rejecting this reading, Japheth finds in the verse an expression of hope that the period of salvation will be as joyful and full of rejuvenation as the preceding period was miserable and full of oppression. The final two verses (16–17), he says, mention five deeds which God will perform in the "morning" (cf. v. 14), i.e. the advent of the salvation and the passing of the darkness of Exile (*zawāl ḥoshekh galut*): (1) the wreaking of divine vengeance upon Israel's enemies, Israel's salvation from them and return to their Land—all this is signified by the word "Your work"; (2) the bestowing of glorious dominion upon the new generation; (3) the favoring of Israel—after years of want—with the bounties of the Land; (4) the reestablishment of Jewish settlement in the Land; (5) and the reestablishment of the Temple for all eternity.

In his exegesis of verses 12, 14, and 15 Japheth unequivocally rejects the suggestion that the Psalm may contain intimations of some actual eschatological date. His explicit dismissal of Benjamin al-Nahāwandī's interpretation implies that some Karaites may have persisted in searching Psalm 90 for clues of this kind. The Hebrew fragment mentioned above, on the other hand, gives direct evidence of the Psalm's importance to the Jerusalem Karaites in Levi's time, both as a source for messianic calculations and as a liturgical text.[144] On the basis of verse 4, some had reckoned that the Salvation would begin in the year 1015—a hope which had been frustrated for some nine years! Quite possibly, these calculations were stimulated by the harsh conditions endured by the Jews of Jerusalem during this period: the severe persecution of non-Muslims by the Fāṭimid Caliph al-Ḥākim, beginning in 1012, extended to the Holy Land which was also ravaged by the revolt of Bedouin tribes.[145] Writing in 1024, the anonymous author emphasizes the importance of *this* prayer, i.e. Psalm 90, whose recitation by the *maskilim shavei peshaʿ* is essential preparation for the beginning of the Salvation.[146] The incorporation of Psalm 90 within Levi's liturgy, therefore, may well reflect not only his community's

---

Commentary on the Book of Daniel as a Historical Source," *Henoch* 13 (1991), p. 270 and n. 30 (259–81).

[143] Ms. A, fols. 194b–195a. Benjamin (fl. mid-9th c.), who was regarded as one of the founders of Karaism, lived in the Islamic East before the Jerusalem community was founded; see Nemoy, *Karaite Anthology*, 21–29.

[144] The fragment was published by Mann, *Texts*, 2:100–102; see also Gil, *History of Palestine*, 805 for a brief discussion.

[145] On the events of this period see M. Gil, *History of Palestine*, 376–85.

[146] Mann, *Texts*, 2:102, last eight lines of Hebrew text.

longing for salvation, but also a concession of sorts to their predilection for messianic computations.

Psalms Relating to the Individuals (25, 28, and 86)

"Following the Psalms relating to the community," declares Levi, "one should recite Psalms relating to the individuals (*mazāmīr al-āḥād*), such as Psalms 25, 28, and 86." The significance of this phrase is obscure. Most likely, Levi is contrasting prayer recited for the sake of the entire community with prayer recited for personal needs; the same terminology can be found at the beginning of his treatise.[147] On the other hand, for the Jerusalem Karaites, who were preoccupied with the notion of spiritual elitism, the term *āḥād* may have held greater significance: are they the Mourners for Zion, a special group within the entire nation of Israel? Or are they an elite group within the Jerusalem community, i.e. the Maskilim? Now, it is tempting to connect the "Individuals" (*āḥād*) with the "elite" (*al-khāṣṣ*) mentioned by Japheth on several occasions. Thus, at the very end of his comment on Psalm 44, he remarks:

> As for the three verses (5, 7, 16) which, we have noted, are expressed in the singular—they allude to the elite of the nation (*khawāṣṣ al-umma*). For He has also slain their elite.[148]

The elite in this case seem to be the nation's leaders through the ages: the judges, kings, priests, and—in Japheth's time—Shoshanim. This notion is borne out by his comment on Psalm 149:2 ("Let Israel be glad in his Maker, let the sons of Zion rejoice in their King!"):

> He mentions both "Israel" and "the sons of Zion." (First,) he mentions the community, i.e. the nation which rejoices in the Lord (i.e. in) His worship and His salvation. Then he mentions the elite (*al-khāṣṣ*), i.e. the sons of Zion, the sons of Kings, the sons of Priests and Levites, the singers (*meshorerim*), the servants of the city, and the "terebinths of righteousness" (i.e. the Mourners for Zion)[149] who are the most joyful just as during the Exile they were more aggrieved and distressed than the rest of Israel. Therefore, he says: "rejoice in their King."[150]

---

[147] See ms. II Firk Heb.-Arab. I.930, fol. 20a, lines 11–13: "The legal authorities differ concerning the obligation of prayer devolving today upon the communities and individuals (*ʿalā al-jamāʿāt wa'l-āḥād*).

[148] Comment on 44:27, Ms. A., fol. 15a. Cf. above, "The Psalms Relating to the Community," for Japheth's comment on Ps. 44:1.

[149] For the origin of this epithet see Is. 61:3 and see N. Wieder, "Qumran sectaries," 100–101.

[150] New York, JTSA ms. Mic. 3351 [ENA 97], fol. 207a.

Japheth's contemporary David al-Fāsī makes the identification explicit: he contrasts the elite (*al-khuṣūṣ*), "by which I mean the individuals" (*aʿnī al-āḥād*), with the general public (*al-ʿumūm al-jumhūr*) in his commentary on Psalms.[151] From all this, it would seem that the terms *khawāṣṣ* and *āḥād* refer to the Shoshanim. On the other hand, we have already seen how the term *jamāʿa* must designate the Jerusalem community as well, for Japheth relates Psalms 44, 80, and 90 directly to the Mourners.[152]

According to Levi, the three texts which most aptly represent the concerns of the Individuals are Psalms 25, 28, and 86. In his commentary, however, Japheth connects them with the Shoshanim generally. "This Psalm," he writes in connection with Psalm 28, "also refers to the Remnant of Israel (*sheʾerit yisraʾel*) and in it he related their prayer to the Lord for deliverance from their enemies among the nations and Israel."[153] A prophetic prayer vouchsafed unto David, it was "spoken concerning the 'Time of Trouble for Jacob' (*ʿet ṣarah le-yaʿaqov*) when they would be overtaken by dangers threatening their life and religion."[154] Similarly, Psalm 86—which at first blush seems to be David's prayer for his own deliverance—really relates to "those whose way is blameless" (*temimei derekh*, cf. Psalm 119), living at the Time of Trouble, i.e. the Mourners for Zion. This, then, is another prophetic prayer spoken by David but intended for recitation by the pious (*ḥasidim*) at the End of Days.[155] What sets these three Psalms apart, of course, is their voice: cast in the first-person singular, they furnish suitable texts for individual prayer. What Japheth and Levi may intend, then, is that each "pious servant" (*ʿabd ṣāliḥ*) recite these Psalms as a personal supplication for salvation from the afflictions he or she has endured as an individual member of an elite group.[156]

Conclusion: The Nature of Karaite Prayer in Tenth-Century Jerusalem

Since the best prayers, according to the Karaites, are in fact biblical prophecies, the most perfect worshipers ought to be ancient prophets. Indeed,

[151] See E.L. Marwick, "A First Fragment of David b. Abraham al-Fasi's Commentary on Psalms," *SBB* 6 (1962–63), p. 60, lines 21ff. (53–72).

[152] See above, especially the comment on Ps. 80:1.

[153] Comment on Ps. 28:1, Ms. P, fol. 159b.

[154] Ibid.

[155] Comment on Ps. 86:2, Ms. P, fol. 100a. Cf. Japheth's comment on Ps. 25:1, Ms. P, fols. 142ab.

[156] For *ʿabd ṣāliḥ* see Japheth's comment on Ps. 86:2, ibid.

as Simon has noted, the seeming opposition between prayer and prophecy—between human speech addressed to God and divine speech addressed to human beings — "disappears, because of the holy spirit, which descends from heaven and inspires the prophet's address to the Lord."[157] Scripture records the inspired prayers of many individuals, such as Moses, Hannah, David, Solomon, and Habakkuk all of whom serve as exemplars of piety. In the prophet Daniel, however, the Mourners for Zion likely saw a prototype for their own devotional practices. A prophet in Exile, Daniel lived in Babylonia, whence many of the Shoshanim themselves probably hailed.[158] As we have seen, his visions furnished the Shoshanim—as they did Rabbanite Jews—with the raw material for messianic speculation. His personal piety, moreover, served as a model which they strove to emulate. Defying a royal ban on prayer addressed to anyone but King Darius, Daniel retired to his chamber, faced Jerusalem, and prayed to God three times a day (Dan. 6:11). For the Karaites, this verse provided a halakhic source: it indicated that the worshiper was regularly to face Jerusalem in prayer evening, morning, and midday.[159] Far more important to the Shoshanim, though, was the prayer of Daniel (Dan. 9:3–20) in which he prays, offers confession, and beseeches God to relieve Israel's oppression.

Japheth's analysis of this passage tallies perfectly with his approach to the Psalter.[160] The following observation concerning the prayer's form and content accords with numerous statements in his *Commentary on Psalms*:

> The prayer contains four subjects (*maʿānī*): (1) praise of God (v. 4); (2) the enumeration of (Israel's) sins and transgressions (vv. 5–11a); (3) the enumeration of what has befallen Israel in consequence of their sins (vv. 11b–14); (4) a petition that God return from His wrath against the city and the nation and that He forgive their sins. . . . He prefaces the prayer with an account of God's deeds, as is the custom with all those who ask God for anything they desire.[161]

---

[157] Simon, *Four Approaches*, 81.

[158] Japheth b. Eli's *nisba*, al-Baṣrī, indicates his Iraqi origin; Salmon b. Jeroham was apparently also from Iraq.

[159] See Japheth, *Commentary on Daniel* 6:11, p. 24 (Ar.), p. 30 (Eng.). See also al-Qirqisānī, *Kitāb al-anwār* VI.16.3 and VI.18.1, trans. Nemoy, "Studies in the History of the Early Karaite Liturgy," 310–12. Levi b. Japheth, on the other hand, believed that only the morning and evening prayers were strictly obligatory; see Vajda, "Lex Orandi," 12–13 where he argues that Daniel's three daily prayers reflected his own personal practice. Levi did, of course, insist that Jerusalem was the proper *qibla*; ibid., 23–25.

[160] *Commentary on Daniel* 9:3–20, 91–98 (Ar.), 44–48 (Eng.).

[161] *Commentary on Daniel* 9:4, p. 91, lines 6–17 (Ar.), 44 (Eng.); I have modified Margoliouth's translation slightly. Cf. especially the twelve liturgical themes in Japheth's Introduction to Psalms; cf. also his comments on, e.g., Ps. 79:13 (Appendix, B.5) and Ps. 90:1 (Appendix, B.8).

Japheth's gloss on Daniel's closing words, "O Lord, hear; O Lord, forgive; O Lord, give heed and act," is strongly reminiscent of his definition of prayer as "a complaint at (one's) situation, and an entreaty to God for salvation and the fulfillment of the (divine) promise":

> *Hear*, i.e. hear our complaint concerning our condition (*shakwa ḥālinā*) and what has befallen us, and *forgive* our sins. *Give heed*, i.e. listen to our supplication and *do* something for Your people, Your city, and Your Temple.[162]

Daniel's behavior, moreover—his fasting, donning of sackcloth and ashes (v. 3) and lamenting the Temple's destruction (vv. 16–18)—established a program for the Mourners in tenth-century Zion.[163] And in calling themselves Maskilim, they clearly believed that their own activities were described in visions vouchsafed to the prophet.[164] For as Japheth observes elsewhere:

> After they have performed the commandment(s) and religious obligations, the Remnant of Jacob—i.e. the Penitent, the Maskilim—will take upon themselves the performance of such supererogatory acts (*nawāfil*) as fasting, (donning) coarse clothing, and refraining from permissible delights and celebrations, while praying continually at night.[165]

Certainly, the Shoshanim sought to imitate the actions of the prophets. Even more important to them, however, was the use of prophetic language in prayer. As we have tried to show throughout this paper, their exegetical and devotional activities were intimately related. Having interpreted a biblical passage, they incorporated its exegesis directly into their worship. For the most part, of course, this phenomenon was implicit and must have been invisible. But there can be no doubt that the teachings of their leading scholars were internalized. The commentary of Japheth b. Eli on the Psalter was intended as liturgical exegesis. His abstraction of key liturgical themes, his frequent references to prayer, complaint (*shakwa*), and entreaty (*mas'ala*), and his regular detection of references to the Jerusalem community within the Psalter can all be seen as an attempt to inculcate a

---

[162] *Commentary on Daniel* 9:19, p. 97, lines 6–17 (Ar.), 48 (Eng., modified); cf. 9:20, p. 98, lines 1–2 (Ar.), 48 (Eng.). The definition of *tefillah* can be found in the comment on Ps. 3:1 (*shakwa al-ḥāl wa-mas'ala allāh fī 'l-khalāṣ wa-injāz al-wa'ad*); see above n. 136. Cf. also the comments on Pss. 74:1 (Appendix, B.1), 74:10 (Appendix, B.2), and 44:27.

[163] Cf. *Commentary on Daniel* 10:2–3, 104–105 (Ar.), 52–53 (Eng.) where Japheth characterizes Daniel's actions as "after the ordinary fashion of mourners" (*min mabsūṭāt al-avelut*).

[164] See the comments on Daniel 11:32–35, 128–30 (Ar.), 68–69 (Eng.) and 12:9–10, 146–49 (Ar.), 81–84 (Eng.).

[165] *The Arabic Commentary of Yefet ben 'Ali the Karaite on the Book of Hosea*, ed. P. Birnbaum (Philadelphia, 1942), p. 220, lines 10–14 (comm. on 14:5).

certain way of reading the Psalms. Ultimately, the focused worshiper could not help but understand these texts according to their accepted interpretation as he recited them.

The Mourners for Zion developed a grand salvation history, giving themselves a leading role at the End of Days. The liturgy which they constructed for themselves plainly reflects this vision. Where possible, they tended to interpret individual Psalms as comprehensive, self-contained units which included praise of God, mention of Israel's past—notably their sins and sufferings—and a petition for divine help. Japheth sets forth twelve main liturgical themes in the Introduction to his Psalms commentary; the texts most suitable for prayer are those which encompass the greatest number of these rubrics. Comprehensiveness in a Psalm became, therefore, a prime liturgical desideratum.[166] But this was not all. The liturgy in its entirety was organized around the same principle; as Levi affirms: "It is laudable to recite the Psalms relating to the Exile prior to the Psalms relating to the Salvation according to the chronological sequence of events (*ʿalā tartīb al-zamān*)."[167] The message imparted by this structure was one of repentance and return—from Babylonia to Jerusalem, from Exile to Redemption. Bearers of this message to all Israel, the Shoshanim claimed for themselves a unique function. Through their fasts, vigils, prayers, and Bible study they believed that they might hasten the coming of the Messiah. And through this regimented program they self-consciously determined their collective identity as Mourners for Zion.

---

[166] For the twelve themes see above, "Japheth b. Eli and His Commentary on Psalms." For examples of comprehensive Psalms see the comments on 44:1 (Appendix, B.7), Ps.74:1 (Appendix, B.1), and Ps. 90:1 (Appendix, B.8).

[167] See above and Appendix, Text A. A similar tendency is discernible in the Rabbanite order for Passover; cf. the statement in mPes. 10:4, "one should begin with blame and conclude with praise" concerning the recounting of the Exodus.

APPENDIX: TEXTS

A. *Levi b. Japheth, Treatise on Prayer* (al-qawl fīʾl-ṣalāt)

Levi's liturgy is found towards the end of his *Treatise*; see G. Vajda, "La *Lex Orandi* de la communauté karaïte d'après Lévi ben Yefet," *REJ* 134, 1–2 (1975): 41–42 (3–45). The Arabic original is preserved in British Library ms. Or. 2564 (Cat. 308/II), fol. 18ab. For technical reasons the text, which is written in an Arabic *naskhi* hand, has been transcribed into Hebrew characters; Hebrew words are rendered according to masoretic orthography rather than the transcription system of the manuscript.

[18א]

(13) ... ויחסן אן יקד̃ם אלמזאמיר אלתי ללג̇מאעה̈ ובעדהא מזאמיר אלא̆חאד. פאלתי ללג̇מאעה̈ מת̇ל אלהים באזנינו שמענו (תהלים מד) רועה ישראל (תהלים פ) תפלה למשה (תהלים צ). וקבל אלכ̇ל̃ מזאמיר אלקדס מת̇ל למה אלהים זנחת לנצח (תהלים עד) אלהים באו גוים (תהלים עט). ומזאמיר אלא̆חאד מת̇ל אליך ה׳ נפשי אשא (תהלים כה) אליך ה׳ אקרא (תהלים כח) תפלה לדוד (תהלים פו) ומא ג̇אנס ד̇לך. [18ב] וכד̇לך יחסן אן יקד̃ם מזאמיר אלגלות עלי מזאמיר אלישועות עלי תרתיב אלזמאן. וליס פי אלמזאמיר מא יג̇מע אמור אלג̇מאעה̈ ואלאׄזמנה̈ מת̇ל תפלה למשה. פאן ערץ̇ שגל ואא̆ת̇ר אלאכ̇תצאר וצל̃א פואסיק אלתוחיד והודו לה׳ כי טוב אלכביר (תהלים קלו) ופצל אלקרבאן ואתבעה בתהלה לדוד (תהלים קמה) ופואסיק אלקינות ואלהים באו גוים (תהלים עט) ותפלה למשה (תהלים צ) ותפלה לדוד (תהלים פו) ויברך דוד (דה״י א כט, י וגו׳) וקד אתי עלי אכת̇ר אלמראד.

B. *Japheth b. Eli, Commentary on Psalms*

Manuscripts:

A = א
New York, Jewish Theological Seminary of America:
Ms. Mic. 3349 [ENA 95]: text, translation, commentary to Pss. 73–89.
Ms. Mic. 3350 [ENA 96]: text, translation, commentary to Pss. 42–72; 90–106.
Ms. Mic. 3350 [ENA 97]: text, translation, commentary to Pss. 107–150.

B = ב
London, British Library, ms. Or. 2551 (Cat. 290):
Fragments of Japheth's translation and commentary on Pss. (Arabic characters).

P = פ
Paris, Bibliothèque Nationale:
Ms. héb. 286: text, translation, and commentary to Pss. 1–41.
Ms. héb. 287: text, translation, and commentary to Pss. 42–72.
Ms. héb. 288: text, translation, and commentary to Pss. 73–106
Ms. héb. 289: text, translation, and commentary to Pss. 107–150.

Unless otherwise noted, comments on Pss. 42–150 are given according to the JTS, Adler manuscripts; the folio numbers in these manuscripts are indicated in square brackets. Variants from the London and Paris manuscripts are given in the apparatus except in the case of haplographies due to homoeoteleuton; these are supplied within parentheses in the main text.

B.1. *Japheth b. Eli, Commentary on Psalm 74:1*

[**א**16ב]

(א) משכיל לאסף למה אלהים זנחת לנצח יעשן אפך בצאן מרעיתך: רשד לאסף למא ד̇א יא רב כ̇ד̇לת ללג̇איה̈ יתדכ̇ן ג̇צ̇בך פי ג̇נם רעיתך:

אעלם אנה שכי פי אלמזמור אלמתקדם מא יג̇רי עליהם מן אלדולה̈ אלראבעה̈ כמא קלנא פי כי קנאתי בהוללים (תה׳ עג,ג) ופי הד̇א אלמזמור ג̇מע כ̇ל מא ג̇ארי[1] עליהם מן מלכות כסדים[2] ומא יג̇רי עליהם איצ̇א מן מלכות רביעאה. [**א**17א] פמן הרימה פעמיך (תה׳ עד,ג) אלי עד מתי אלהים יחרף צר (תה׳ עד,י) הו שכוי מא ג̇רי עליהם מן כסדים[3] ומן עד מתי אלי אכ̇ר אלמזמור ישכון פיה מא יכון יג̇רי עליהם מן מלכו רביעאה. ופיה מענאיין: אחדהמא הו אנ̇ה כאן גרצ̇ה פי מעני אלקדס אד̇ כאנו קד נג̇סוה כשדים ואחרקוה וכד̇לך ישמעאל ינג̇סוה דאימא והם מקימין יחרפו אלהים ויאנצו שמו[4] כקו׳ ינאץ אויב שמך לנצח (פסוק י). ואלת̇אני אנה ד̇כר אלמלכין אלטרפאניין חתי ידכ̇ל אלמלכאן אלמתוסטאן בינהמא.

קאל פי ענואנה משכיל אד̇ פיה רשד ותעלים לשארית ישראל כיף ירפעון שכואהם אלי אללה תע׳[5] ויסלונה תג̇ייר חאלהם וחאל קדסהם וקולה למה אלהים יג̇רי מג̇רי אלמסלה ואלדעא מת̇ל קול סיי׳ משה ע׳ אלס׳ למה יוי יחרה אפך (שמות לב,יא) למה יאמרו מצרים (שמות לב,יב). וקולה זנחת לנצח יג̇מע [**א**17ב] פיה מא ג̇רי עליהם מן מלך כשדים אלי חית̇ אנתהאינא. ומעני זנחת הו תרך אלמעונה̈ חתי וצלת אלאעדא אלי מראדהם פיהם וקולה יעשן אפך ישיר בה אלי אוקאת אלשדאיד אלצעבה̈. פאו̇להא וקת כ̇ראב מקדש יוי ביד מלך בבל אלד̇י כאן ד̇לך מן חרון אף יוי כקולה כלה יוי את חמתו וג׳ (איכה ד,יא) פג̇מע פי הד̇א[6] אלפסוק כ̇ל מא יג̇רי עליהם פי אלג̇אליה̈ פכ̇ל שי הו מקים פהו פי קולה זנחת לנצח מת̇ל ארור אתה בעיר (דב׳ כח,טז) וסאיר אלקללות וכל שי יג̇רי עליהם פי בעץ̇ אלאוקאת מת̇ל כ̇ראב אלביתין ואוקאת יטאלבון בתרך אלדין ווקת אלמצאדרה̈ כ̇ל הד̇ה פי קולה יעשן אפך בצאן מרעיתך[7] וקולה בצאן מרעיתך לירק̇ק באלקול יודו[8] אן הד̇ה אלאמ̇ה̈ הם צאן מרעיתך מנד̇ כאנו פליס [**א**18א] להם מדב̇ר סואך מת̇ל אלג̇נם אלד̇י ליס תדב̇רהא נפסהא ואנ̇מא אלראעי אלמשפק ידב̇רהא ויצונהא.

---

[1]ג̇רי, **פ**. [2]כשדים, **פ**. [3]כשדים, **פ**. [4]השווה פסוק יח. [5]ליתא, **פ**. [6]הד̇ה, **פ**. [7]בצאן מרעיתך: ליתא, **פ**.
[8]צ״ל יורי; יודי, **פ**.

B.2. *Japheth b. Eli, Commentary on Psalm 74:10*

(י) עד מתי אלהים יחרף צר ינאץ אויב שמך לנצח:
אלי מתי יא אללה יעיّר אלמצאדם ירפ̇ץ אלעדו אסמך אלי אלגאיה̈:

הד̇א שכוי חאלהם מן מלכו רביעאה פקאלו עד מתי ענד תטאול אלגלות ובעד אלקץ וקד צ̇גרו אד̇ קד אחרף עליהם אלעדו פי הד̇ין אלשיין אלמד̇כורין פי אלפסוק והמא [**א**24א] יחרף ינאץ. פאמّא יחרף פהו מא יעיّרון ישראל במא נזל בהם מן אלד̇ל ואלבלא ויקולון להם מע ד̇לך איה אלהיכם כמא שרחנא ד̇לך פי תפסיר ברצח בעצמותי (מזמור מב, יא). ואמّא ינאץ אויב פהו פי מעני אלדין אלד̇י ירפצ̇ו תורת יוי ויתכלّמו פיהא בכ̇ל קביח כמא יקולון דאימאً לישראל קד גייّרתם אלתוראה̈ וחרّפתמוהא וקד יקול אלואחד מנהם ען נפסה אנّה כאפר במן אמר בהד̇ה אלתוראה̈ ויצחّח אלקלון אלממלו נאצות ושקרות ותפלות פלד̇לך קאל ינאץ אויב.[1]

[1] השווה דבריו על פסוק כב.

B.3. *Japheth b. Eli, Commentary on Psalm 74:23*

(כג) אל תשכח קול [**א**30א] צורריך שאון קמיך עלה תמיד:
לא תטרח צות מצאדמיך ולא תטרח ג̇לבת מקאומיך אלד̇י הו
צאעד דאימאً:

קאל פי מא תקדّם חית ענייך אל תשכח לנצח (פסוק יט) עלי אלמעני אלד̇י שרחתה, וקאל פי כ̇אתמה̈ אלמזמור לא תטרח איצ̇א מא פעלוה פי קדסך. וג̇מע פי הד̇א אלפסוק פעל כסדים ופעל ישמעאל ג̇מיעא פקולה קול צורריך ישיר בה אלי קולה שאגו צרריך בקרב (מועדך) (פסוק ד) והו ג̇אמע לסאי̇ר מא ד̇כרתה פי כל הרע אויב בקדש (פסוק ד). וקולה שאון קמיך ישיר בה אלי קולה יחרף צר ינאץ (אויב) (פסוק ד). פד̇כר אעט̇ם חרוף וניאוץ והו אג̇תמאעהם פי אלקדס ולהם ג̇לבה̈ עט̇ימה כ̇אצّה פי וקת צלואתהם אלד̇י ירגיזו[1] בכל יום חמשה פעמים ולד̇לך קאל עלה תמיד. ואראד בקולה אל תשכח יעני אפניהם מן [**א**30ב] קד̇אמך ומן[2] קדסך כקו' מקרב חיקך כלה (פסוק יא). וקולה פי פעל כשדים אל תשכח פאנّה אראד בה אסרע במא תואעדתהם בה ושלמתי לבבל ולכל יושבי כשדים את כל רעתם אשר עשו בציון וג' (ירמיה נא, כד).

[1] **פ**. + יגדיזו, **א**. [2] קדאמך ומן: ליתא, **פ**.

B.4. *Japheth b. Eli, Commentary on Psalm 79:8*

(ח) אל תזכר לנו עונת ראשנים מהר יקדמונו רחמיך כי דלונו מאד:
לא תד̇כר לנא ד̇נוב אלאולין[1] סריעאً יסתקבלנא רחמאתך פאנّא
צ̇עפנא[2] גדאً:

בעד אן קאלו עד מה יוי תאנף לנצח (פסוק ה) רג̇עו יסאٔלו[3] אללה פי אן יתג̇אוז עמّא ג̇רי להם מן אלד̇נוב אלכבّאר[4] וקולה עונות ראשנים יריד בה [**א**82ב] ד̇נוב אקתרפוהא אלאٓבא ונחן תבענאהם ואכ̇ד̇נא את̇ארהם פיהא ואלאٓן פקד יבאן[5] לנא אנّהא עלי גיר צואב פקד רג̇ענא ענהא פנסלך אן לא תד̇כרהא לנא ויג̇ב אן תעלם אן ד̇נוב אהל אלגלות תנקסם פמנהם[6] ד̇נוב כאנת לאהל אלדולה̈ מת̇ל גלוי עריות[7] אסורות וחלול שבת וקסמים ונחש וכשוף ומא ישבה ד̇לך וגזל ועשק וגנבה ומא ישבה ד̇לך ומנהא ד̇נוב כ̇אצّה̈ לאהל אלג̇אליה̈ מת̇ל אלעבור אלד̇י גייّר[8] אלאעיאד ען אוקאתהא ותרכו טמאה וטהרה ומאכלות גוים[9] ורבّיו עליהא פי אלגלות ואלّפוהא[10] פקאלו שבי פשע ביעקב יא רב נסלך אן לא תד̇כר לנא ד̇נוב אלקדמא אלד̇י כנّא נעמלהא ואלאٓן קד רג̇ענא ענהא [**א**83א] וקולה מהר יקדמונו רחמיך יענון אסרע באלפרג̇ אלד̇י קד אבטאٔ ענّא וקולה כי דלונו מאד ידלّ עלי אן הٔולאי אלמצ̇ליין הם קום בלגו אלי אנקץ̇ אלאٓחואל אלד̇י קד סבק אלועד להם פי ידין יוי עמו וגו' (דב' לב,לו) פקולה כי דלונו מאד הו כי אזלת יד (שם) וקד ערّף פי מוצ̇ע אכ̇ר אן פי ד̇לך אלזמאן יתובון בני ישראל פירחמהם רב אלעאלמין כקולה בצר לך ומצאוך וגו' (דב' ד,ל) פערّף אן ישראל יתובון פי עת צרה ת̇ם ערّף אן אללה ירחמהם ענד תובתהם בקולה כי אל רחום יוי אלהיך (דב' ד,לא) פקאלו הٔולאי אלד̇ין יתובון פי עת צרה יא רב הוד̇א דלונו מאד ואנת ועדת אלתאיבין אנך תרחמהם פארחמנא כמא ועדתנא. פאן אזלת יד ואפס עצור ועזוב (דב' לב,לו):

[1]אלאולי, **פ**. [2]צועפנא, **פ**. [3]יסלו, **פ**. [4]אלכבאיר, **פ**. [5]באן, **פ**. [6]פמנא, **פ**. [7]ערוות, **פ**. [8]גיירו, **פ**.
[9]ליתא, **פ**. [10]ואלפנהא, **א**.

B.5. *Japheth b. Eli, Commentary on Psalm 79:13*

(יג) ואנחנו עמך וצאן מרעיתך נודה לך לעולם לדור ודר נספר תהלתך:
ונחן שעבך וגֿנם רעיתך[1] נשכרך ללדהר לגֿיל וגֿיל נקץׄ מדיחתך:

אעלם אן הדֿא אלמזמור יתצֿמֿן כֿמסהֿ צֿרוב אחדהא הו פעל אלגוים בישראל פי תֿלתֿ אבואב פי מעני דכֿולהם פי [א86ב] נחלתהם ונגֿסו קדסהם וכֿרבוה ופי מא קתלו פיהם ופימא עיֿרוהם במא נזל בהם מן אלבלא. ואלתֿאני מסלתהם פי אן יגפר להם אלדֿנוב אלתי הי סבֿבת עליהם כל בלא ואלתֿאלתֿ הו מסלתהם אלרחמהֿ ואלפרג ואלראבע אכֿדֿ חקֿהם מן אעדאיֿהם ואלכֿאמס הו צֿמאנהם עלי אֿנפסהם אלשכר ואלמדיחהֿ ללה. פקאלו נחן אלקום אלדֿי נחן שעבך מנסובין אליך וגנם רעיתך תדבֿרנא כמא תרי[2] ותכֿלֿצנא מן אלרעים[3] ומן יד מלכי גוים ותרעאנא כמא קלת אני ארעה צאני ואני ארביצם וג׳ (יחזקאל לד,טו) ונחן נשכרך דאימאً ולא נפתר ען מדחתך בל פי כלֿ גֿיל וגֿיל נקץׄ מדחתך כקולה ואני [א87א] תמיד איחל וג׳ (תהלים עא,יד).

---

[1]רעיותך, **פ**. [2]במא תרי גרי, **א**. [3]מן יד אלרועים, **פ**.

B.6. *Japheth b. Eli, Commentary on Psalm 80:1*

קד כֿנֿא דֿכרנא פי אלמגֿלהֿ אלמתקדֿמהֿ אלי מן ישיר בהוֿלאי אלשושנים וכדֿלך ביֿנֿא איש מעני עדות וקלנא אן האוֿלי[1] אלשושנים הם אלקום אלדֿין ינבתֿון פי מא בין אלשוך והם אלדֿין וצפהם פי אשרי תמימי דרך (תהלים קיט) ופי תפלה לעני (תהלים קב) וקלנא אן מעני עדות הי אלנסבהֿ כמא שרחנא פי למנצח על שושן עדות (תהלים ס) פדֿאך פי אלמשיח והדֿא מקול פי אלשושנים אלדֿין הם מן תולעת יעקב (ישעיה מא, יד) פדֿכרהם פי צדר אלתֿלתֿ מזאמיר רחש לבי (תהלים מה) והושיעני אלהים (תהלים סט) והדֿא אלמזמור ליערֿף אן הדֿא אלמזמור הו צלאתהם:

---

[1]האוֿלאי, **פ**.

B.7. *Japheth b. Eli, Commentary on Psalm 44:1*

קאל פי ענואנה משכיל לאן פיה רשד ותעלים לישראל כיף ירפעון קצ̇תהם בין ידי אללה. ואעלם אן הד̇א[1] אלמזמור הו אעראב[2] ען אמ̇ה̈[3] ישראל וכ̇רג̇ה בלשון רבים. וליס פי אלתהלות מז׳ ישאכלה פי ג̇ואמע[4] מעאניה לאנ̇ה יבתד̇[5] מן מצרים וינתהי אלי אכ̇ר אלגלות. ופי הד̇א אלמז׳ ג׳ פסוקים[5] תכ̇רג̇ בלשון יחיד והו אתה הוא מלכי אלהים (פסוק ה) כי לא בקשתי אבטח (פסוק ז) כל היום כלמתי (פסוק טז) כל̇ ואחד מנהא למעני נד̇כרה פיה.

[1]הד̇ה, **פ**. [2]אערב, בשוליים של **א**. [3]+ בני, **פ**. [4]גאמע, בשוליים של **א**. [5]ת̇לת̇ פואסיק, **פ**.

B.8. *Japheth b. Eli, Commentary on Psalm 90:1*

[**א**189ב] ... והד̇ה אלתפלה תג̇מע סתה̈ מעאני אחדהא ד̇כר אלכ̇אלק ג̇ל ד̇כ(רה) ואנה אלקדים אלדא̇ים ואלת̇אני ד̇כר אלכ̇לא̇יק ואנ̇ה עז̇ וג̇ל̇ מג̇דהא[1] ואלת̇אלת̇ ד̇כר אעמאר בני אדם עלי אכ̇תלאפהא ואנ̇הם קצירי אלאעמאר ואלראבע ד̇כר מא נזל [**פ**137א] בישראל מן אף יוי וחמתו וסא̇יר מא ילחקהם פי אלגלות[2] ואן ג̇מיע ד̇לך סבב אלעונות ואלכ̇אמס מסא̇לה̈ אללה תע׳ פי תעריפ(ה)ם אלקץ חתי יתחק̇קוה[3] ואלסאדס אנג̇אז̇[4] אלמואעיד אלמנתט̇רה̈ פהי ג̇אמעה̈ לכל̇ מא יחתאג̇ אלי ד̇כרה פי מעני אלגלותיין.

[1]ואולי צ״ל מוג̇דהא, ״יוצרם.״ [2]+ באכ̇תצאר, **פ**. [3]חתי יתחקקוה: ליתחקקוה, **פ**. [4]אתמאם, **פ**.

B.9. *Japheth b. Eli, Commentary on Psalm 44:16–17*

(טז) כל היום כלמתי נגדי ובשת פני כסתני:
כל̇ אלזמאן כ̇גלתי חד̇איי וכ̇זיה̈[1] וג̇הי גטתני:

(יז) מקול מחרף ומגדף מפני אויב ומתנקם:
מן צות אלמעי̈ר ואלקאד̇ף מן קבל אלעדו [א12ב] ואלמנתקם:

קו׳ כל היום יחתמל וג̇הין אחדהמא[2] טול אלנהאר מבקר לערב ואלת̇אני[3] טול זמאן אלגלות. וקאל כלמתי נגדי ובי̈ן פי אלפסוק אלד̇י בעדה מקול מחרף ערף אנ̇ה יכ̇גל[4] דאימאً ממ̇א יסמע קול מחרף ומגדף ויריד בה אלד̇י יעי̈ר דיני ויקד̇ף שריעתי ומעבודי מת̇ל קו׳ אשר גדפו נערי מלך אשור אתי (מלכים ב׳ יט, ו; ישעיה לז, ו). ת̇ם קאל מפני אויב ויריד בה ובושת פני כסתני מפני אויב ומתנקם. וקאל ובושת פני כסתני למעני והו אנה ערף אן אלחיא[5] אלד̇י תכון[6] עלי אלאנסאן פי וג̇הה הי אלתי אשמלת בדנה[7] והד̇א ידל̇ עלי עט̇ם אלבושה. והד̇א הו אלד̇י קאל אויב ומתנקם אן אלתורה נסכ̇ת בגירהא וליס לכם רגעה̈ ואיש כ̇ברכם אליום אלף וכ̇מס מאיה̈ סנה̈ תחת אלד̇ל. פאלי הד̇ה ונט̇ראהא ישיר בקו׳ כלמתי נגדי מקול מחרף ומגדף. ואמ̇א ובושת פני פהו מא יעי̈רון ישראל במעאציהם מן ג̇נס מא יקולון יא עבדת אלעגל וקתלת[8] אלאנביא פהד̇ה[9] ונט̇ראהא פי קו׳ ובשת פני כסתני. וקו׳ אויב ומתנקם ישיר בה אלי ישמעאל ואדום ואיצ̇אً גירהם ממן יעי̈ר ישראל[10]:

---

[1]ובזייה, **א**. [2]אחד, **א**. [3]ואלבי׳, **א**. [4]כ̇גל, **א**. [5]אלחיא, **א**, **פ**. אלחיאיה, בשוליים של **א**. [6]יתביין, **פ**. [7]בדלה, **א**. [8]יא עבדת ... וקתלת: יא מן עבדתו ... וקתלתו, **א**. [9]פהד̇א, **א**. [10]ואיצ̇א ... ישראל: ליתא, **פ**.

B.10. *Japheth b. Eli, Commentary on Psalm 44:18–19*

(יח) כל זאת באתנו ולא שכחנוך ולא [**א**13א] שקרנו בבריתך:
כל̈ הד̇ה[1] ג̇אתנא[2] ולם[3] ננסא̇ך ומא כד̇בנא בעהדך:

(יט) לא נסוג אחור לבנו ותט אשרינו מני ארחך:
לא יזג אלי קהקרי קלבנא ולא מאלת אקדאמנא מן סבילך:

ד̇כרו אלא̇שיא אלתי ג̇מלת[4] אלאמ̈ה̈ עליהא והי ד׳ אשיא: או̈להא ולא שכחנוך ומענאה יחוד השם אלד̇ין כל יום פי אלדניא יקולון שמע ישראל יוי אלהינו יוי אחד (דברים ו,ד): ואלב׳ ולא שקרנו בבריתיך ומענאה ומא אבטלנא שריעתך בל נקול דא̇ימא̇ תורת משה אמת ואיצ̇א̇ יקרו̇ן באן אלל̈ה עאהדהם תחת הר סיני ואן תלך אלברית תלזם אג̇יאל ישראל עד סוף כל הדורות כקו׳ ולא אתכם לבדכם וג׳ כי את אשר ישנו פה (דברים כט,יג-יד). ת̇ם קאל ולא נסוג אחור לבנו וארא̇דו בה ולם ינחרף קלבנא אלא דין סוא דינך פד̇כרו פי אלפסוק אלאו̈ל ט̇אהר קולהם ת̇ם ד̇כרו באטנהם. פקאל לא נסוג אחור לבנו וקולהם ותט אשורינו מני ארחך ישירון בה אלי פרא̇יץ̇ הי א̇צול יפעלהא צאלחהם וטאלחהם מת̇ל אסתקבאל אלקבלה̈ ואלכ̇תאנה̈ ואכל אלפטיר ומא שאכל ד̇לך:

---

[1]הד̇א, **א**. [2]ג̇תנא, **פ**. [3]ולא, **א**. [4]ג̇מלה̈, **פ**.

PART THREE

RELIGIOUS PHILOSOPHY, MYSTICISM, AND SPIRITUALITY IN ISLAM AND JUDAISM

YŪSUF AL-BAṢĪR: THEOLOGICAL ASPECTS OF HIS HALAKHIC WORKS

David E. Sklare

The writings of Yūsuf al-Baṣīr were part of the "Golden Age" of Karaite literature; an extraordinary flowering of intellectual creativity and industry which occurred during the tenth century and the first part of the eleventh. This literary activity took place for the most part in Jerusalem, which had become the sect's spiritual and intellectual center. Karaites from throughout the diaspora were attracted by the call to renounce the material benefits of the Exile and to come to Jerusalem to live an ascetic life of mourning for Zion.[1] The scholars who assembled there formed a school of Karaite learning which produced works of biblical exegesis, grammar and lexicography, law and theology; works which served as the foundations of Karaite culture for generations.[2] The Crusader conquest of Jerusalem brought this school to a sudden end.

This age of cultural efflorescence can actually be divided into two stages. The first, which lasted until approximately the turn of the tenth century, was typified by strident anti-Rabbanite polemics and a strong aversion towards non-Jewish learning. Daniel al-Qūmisī at the beginning of the century and Salmon ben Jeroham and Japheth ben Eli at its end denounced the study of "foreign books" and philosophy.[3] Salmon also criticized spending time and money on the study of the Arabic language, even though the

---

[1] The major figures of this community were surveyed in the fifteenth-century chronicle by Ibn al-Hītī; see G. Margoliouth, "Ibn al-Hītī's Arabic Chronicle of Karaite Doctors," *JQR* o.s. 9 (1897): 429–43. For secondary literature on this community and its central figures, see S. Poznanski, "Reshit hityashevut ha-qara'im bi-yerushalayim," in *Jerusalem*, ed. A.M. Luncz, vol. 10 (1913), 83–116; idem, "The Karaite Literary Opponents of Saadiah Gaon," reprinted in *Karaite Studies*, ed. P. Birnbaum (New York, 1971), 142–83 in particular; Jacob Mann, *Texts and Studies in Jewish History and Literature* (Philadelphia, 1935), 2:3–155; Moshe Gil, *A History of Palestine, 634–1099* (Cambridge, 1992), 784–820; H. Ben-Shammai, "The Karaites," in *The History of Jerusalem: The Early Islamic Period (638–1099)*, ed. J. Prawer (Hebrew) (Jerusalem, 1987), 163–78. Concerning the "Mourners for Zion" (*avelei ṣion*), see now H. Ben-Shammai, "Poetic Works and Lamentations of Qaraite 'Mourners of Zion'—Structure and Contents," in *Knesset Ezra: Literature and Life in the Synagogue, Studies Presented to Ezra Fleischer* (Hebrew), ed. S. Elizur et al. (Jerusalem, 1994), 191–234.

[2] Some of these works were also known to Andalusian Rabbanite scholars. Abraham Ibn Ezra, for example, refers in a number of places in his commentary on the Torah to the exegesis of Japheth ben Eli and Yeshuʿah ben Judah.

[3] Foreign books are referred to as *kalām al-barānī* or *kutub al-barānī*. For al-Qūmisī, see

major part of the literary production of this school (including that of Salmon himself) was written in Arabic.[4] Opposition to the study of foreign books and of Arabic did not mean, however, that elements of Arabic culture were not absorbed by these individuals. Quite the opposite was true. For example, the works of these authors demonstrate an awareness and absorption of the terminology and theological values of the Kalam.[5] The Jerusalem Karaite community in this period had the characteristics of a young movement consolidating its ideology, looking inward in order to define its strengths and sources of vitality and reacting against outside challenges.

In the second stage, the Jerusalem Karaite community demonstrated a more mature sense of identity. Argumentation against Rabbanite positions continued, but in a more respectful tone, without the *ad hominem* vituperation. Rabbinic sources were carefully studied and used extensively in the writings of this period, either to be refuted or as sources of authentic traditions. The maturity of the community can also be seen in its openness to the contributions which Arabic culture could make to its intellectual life, particularly in the areas of theology, linguistics and exegesis. Karaite scholarship in this period was institutionalized in the "House of Learning" maintained by Yūsuf ibn Nūḥ in which, it is reported, seventy scholars gathered.[6] Yūsuf al-Baṣīr was one of the leading figures in this group.

Al-Baṣīr apparently immigrated from Iraq to Jerusalem where he became a student of Yūsuf ibn Nūḥ and where, during the second quarter of

---

J. Mann, "A Tract by an Early Karaite Settler in Jerusalem," *JQR* n.s. 12 (1921–22), 273 (trans. L. Nemoy, "The Pseudo-Qumisian Sermon to the Karaites," *PAAJR* 43 (1976): 55) and al-Qūmisī's commentary on the Minor Prophets, *Pitron Shneim Asar*, ed. I. Markon (Jerusalem, 1958), p. 8, n. 21 and p. 4, n. 23 for other similar occurrences. For Salmon ben Jeroham, see his commentary on Psalms quoted in S. Pinsker, *Lickute Kadmoniot*, pt. 2 (Wien, 1860), appendix, 133–4 and his commentary on Ecclesiastes, translated by G. Vajda, *Deux commentaires karaïtes sur l'Ecclesiaste* (Leiden, 1971), 62. For Japheth ben Eli, see H. Ben-Shammai, "The Doctrines of Religious Thought of Abu Yūsuf Yaʿqūb al-Qirqisānī and Yefet ben ʿEli," (Ph.D. diss., Hebrew University, 1977), 1:105–108.

[4] Salmon ben Jeroham's commentary to Lamentations, ed. S. Feuerstein, (Cracow, 1898), 31. A similar complaint is found in an interesting Genizah fragment, T-S Ar. 27.9, which is probably either from a biblical commentary by Salmon or from his circle. The relevant passage from this fragment was published by David Sklare, "The Religious and Legal Thought of Samuel ben Ḥofni Gaon: Texts and Studies in Cultural History," (Ph.D. diss., Harvard University, 1992), p. 191, n. 92 (referred to below as Sklare, "Samuel ben Ḥofni").

[5] Concerning al-Qūmisī, e.g., see M. Zucker, *Rav Saadya Gaon's Translation of the Torah* (Hebrew) (New York, 1959), 168–219, 481–485 and Mann, "Tract." See also Ben-Shammai, "Doctrines."

[6] See Ibn al-Hītī's chronicle, 433, 439. The number seventy is not to be taken as exact, but was probably given in imitation of the Gaonic Yeshivah of the Rabbanites.

the eleventh century, he seems to have composed most of his theological and halakhic writings.[7] Al-Baṣīr achieved a position of religious and intellectual leadership in the Karaite community. His eminent status and authority are demonstrated by the fact that he is one of the few Karaites of the period who wrote responsa, on both theological and legal topics. His intellectual leadership was particularly noteworthy when one takes into account that he was apparently blind. Because of his blindness, he was known by the euphemistic cognomen, "the Seer" (*al-baṣīr*).[8] He counted among his own pupils Abu'l-Faraj Furqān ibn Asad (Yeshuʿah ben Judah), who succeeded al-Baṣīr as religious leader of the Jerusalem community, and Tobias ben Moses from Constantinople, who translated a number of al-Baṣīr's works from Arabic into Hebrew.[9] The date of his death was apparently around 1040 C.E.[10]

Yūsuf al-Baṣīr the theologian has been fairly well known to scholars for a number of years. His two main works of Kalam theology, *Kitāb al-tamyīz* and *Kitāb al-muḥtawī*, were translated by Tobias ben Moses and have been available in manuscript in western libraries. These works, particularly *al-Muḥtawī*, were closely studied by Georges Vajda.[11] In his studies, Vajda thoroughly demonstrated the impact of the Basran school

---

[7] Ibn al-Hītī refers to al-Baṣīr in one place as "Abū Yaʿqūb al-Baṣrī," i.e. from the town of Basra in Iraq. Margoliouth corrects this to read "al-Baṣīr"; see "Ibn al-Hītī," p. 433, n. 7. This correction, although reasonable, is unnecessary. Ibn al-Hītī at this point refers to al-Baṣīr together with Abū Hārūn al-Maqdasī (i.e. Abū ʾl-Faraj Hārūn who was from Jerusalem); apparently, his specific concern here is to indicate the scholars' respective places of origin. Japheth ben Eli also came from Basra.

[8] It has been suggested that his name does not indicate blindness, but was taken from the title of his halakhic magnum opus, *Kitāb al-istibṣār*. The fact that al-Baṣīr dictated his writings has also been taken as an indication of his blindness. This, however, was a common scholarly practice: the Muslim judge and theologian ʿAbd al-Jabbār, for example, also dictated his voluminous works. For another example of this practice by a Jewish author, see Sklare, "Samuel ben Ḥofni," p. 388, n. 28.

[9] Concerning Yeshuʿah ben Judah, see H. Ben-Shammai, "Yeshuah Ben Yehudah—A Characterization of a Karaite Scholar of Jerusalem in the Eleventh Century" (Hebrew), *Peʿamim* 32 (1987): 3–20. Yeshuʿah also wrote responsa; see Poznanski, "Karaite Literary Opponents," 183. For Tobias ben Moses, see Z. Ankori, "The Correspondence of Tobias ben Moses the Karaite of Constantinople," in *Essays on Jewish Life and Thought Presented in Honor of Salo Wittmayer Baron* (New York, 1959), 1–38; idem, *Karaites in Byzantium* (New York, 1959), index; M. Gil, *History of Palestine*, 814–818.

[10] Ankori dates his death to 1040 on the basis of a letter of Tobias ben Moses. See Z. Ankori, "Ibn al-Hītī and the Chronology of Joseph al-Baṣīr," *JJS* 8 (1957): 71–81. Gil, however, dates this letter to 1048; see *History of Palestine*, p. 815, n. 22.

[11] Vajda published a series of studies and annotated translations of *Kitāb al-muḥtawī* which appeared posthumously in collected form along with an edition of the Arabic text edited by David Blumenthal, *Al-Kitāb al-Muḥtawī de Yūsuf al-Baṣīr* (Leiden, 1985). See the reviews by H. Ben-Shammai in *KS* 62 (1988): 407–26 (referred to below as Ben-Shammai, "Review") and B. Chiesa, "Due note di letterature caraita: 1. Il "Kitāb al- Muḥtawī" di Yūsuf al-Baṣīr," *Henoch* 10 (1988):

of the Mu'tazilite Kalam on al-Baṣīr's theological world-view. The influence of this school—particularly of one of its later representatives, Qâḍî Abû 'l-Ḥasan 'Abd al-Jabbâr—on al-Baṣîr was so great that the Karaite can almost be considered as one of its representatives.[12] Al-Baṣīr was well acquainted and up-to-date with the writings of this school and in his *Muḥtawī* refers to the works of Ibn Khallād (the teacher of 'Abd al-Jabbār's teacher) and the works of his older contemporary, 'Abd al-Jabbār. He even wrote a commentary on a work by a student of 'Abd al-Jabbār.

Yūsuf al-Baṣīr the halakhist, however, has been much less known. Most of the large manuscripts of his major halakhic work, *Kitāb al-istibṣār fī'l-farā'iḍ* (Book of the Examination of the Commandments), have been preserved in the Firkovitch collections of the Russian National Library in St. Petersburg and were not available for the most part to scholars until recently. I do not intend, however, to discuss his legal teachings as a whole, but rather to focus on the interaction between these two parts of his intellectual world, Kalam and law.

In his *Muḥtawī*, he explains the relationship between his works of theology and law as follows:

> Even though this book is entitled *al-Muḥtawī* because it encompasses the fundamentals of religion—and (this would certainly include) the sources of religious law (*uṣūl al-fiqh*) and the detailed exposition of the commandments—I have limited myself to instruction relating to the (fundamentals of religion) as a whole out of fear of being verbose and straying far afield. I have already dictated (some books) concerning the *miṣvot* which I hope will complete and complement (what I have written here). (Those works provide) a detailed treatment of what I mention here (only) in a general fashion. In this book, however, I will not depart from the method of books (which deal with) fundamental principles.[13]

Al-Baṣīr may have divided his literary activity by genre, but he viewed his various books as parts of a whole. This literary unity reflects the conceptual continuity which he understood as existing between theology and law.

355–76. Vajda's last study of al-Baṣīr, edited by Paul Fenton, is entitled "Definitions of the Terminology of the Mutakallimun in the Writings of Yusuf al-Baṣīr" (Hebrew) *Da'at* 26 (1991): 5–34.

[12] It is possible that al-Baṣīr's knowledge of Mu'tazilite Kalam was acquired in Iraq, as he is the first of the Jerusalem Karaites to demonstrate such a deep and up-to-date familiarity with the subject. It is also likely that in Iraq he encountered the writings of his older contemporary, Samuel ben Ḥofni Gaon, who was head of the Yeshivah of Sura in Baghdad. Samuel ben Ḥofni was perhaps the first author to introduce Mu'tazilite Kalam of the Basran school into Jewish thought. Al-Baṣīr polemicizes against the calendrical views of Samuel ben Ḥofni Gaon in a number of places in his *Kitāb al-istibṣār* as well as in a special book (see below).

[13] *Kitāb al-Muḥtawī*, p. 756.

In the sections below, I wish to explore the nature and content of this continuity and interaction. First, I will briefly sketch the Muʿtazilite theory of law and theology to which al-Baṣīr subscribed. Because al-Baṣīr's oeuvre is so little known, this section will be followed by a survey of his writings with an emphasis on the halakhic works in which al-Baṣīr dealt with these issues. Finally, I shall focus on some specific questions examined by al-Baṣīr which illustrate the interaction of theology and halakhah in his thought.

* * *

The approach which saw a unifying dynamic between theology and law was not unique to al-Baṣīr. Indeed, the slogan "knowledge leads to action" could have been inscribed on the banner of the Muʿtazilite Kalam, the dominant school of Islamic systematic theology during the tenth century. It was the axiom of this Islamic school of thought that a fully developed and utilized rational faculty will directly intuit or demonstrate to itself the outlines of ethical behavior, producing rational obligations or commandments—what we would call in a general way natural law. Similarly, a properly grounded knowledge of God's unity and His justice will lead to knowledge of the necessity for His revealed legislation and of the veracity of His prophets, as well as acceptance of the obligations of revealed laws. Both reason and revealed law are therefore seen as imposing obligation (Ar. *taklīf*) upon man. Opposed to this position was the view of the Ashʿariyya which held that good and evil are not objective values, but are determined only by Divine will (known to man by way of revelation and tradition). Thus, according to the Ashʿariyya, obligation is created only by Divine law. This is the view which eventually became dominant in Islam.

The teachings and argumentation of the Muʿtazila (specifically of the dominant Basran branch of this school) are known to us best through the extensive writings of Abu ʾl-Ḥasan ʿAbd al-Jabbār.[14] ʿAbd al-Jabbār was

[14] ʿAbd al-Jabbār's surviving writings are almost the only primary source available to us for Muʿtazilism's middle period when the school reached a comprehensive synthesis. Until the 1950's, when manuscripts of most of his theological summa, *Al-mughnī fī abwāb al-tawḥīd wa'l-ʿadl*, were discovered in a the library of a Yemenite mosque, most of our knowledge of Muʿtazilite Kalam came from citations and discussions in its opponents' works. A survey of his theology can be found in J.R.T.M. Peters, *God's Created Speech: A Study in the Speculative Theology of the Muʿtazilī Qāḍī ʾl-Quḍāt Abū ʾl-Ḥasan ʿAbd al-Jabbār ibn Aḥmad al- Hamadānī* (Leiden, 1976). For a study of his ethics see George Hourani, *Islamic Rationalism: The Ethics of ʿAbd al-Jabbār* (Oxford, 1971). The central ideas of this school were described by R.M. Frank, "Several Funda-

born about 935 C.E. in western Iran. He first associated himself with the Ash'arite theological school, but after traveling to Basra and later to Baghdad in order to further his theological studies, he switched to Mu'tazilism. In 977, he was appointed to the position of chief judge (*qāḍī 'l-quḍāt*) of Rayy, one of the Buyid capitals, where he remained until his death in the year 1024. 'Abd al-Jabbār was renowned as a theologian during his life and later scholars saw him as the head of the Mu'tazilite school in his generation.

The norm- or law-directedness of Mu'tazilite theology is emphasized by 'Abd al-Jabbār in the beginning of his book, *Al-muhīṭ bi'l-taklīf*.[15] In a chapter on the order or arrangement of knowledge he sets forth a theory of divine commandment which can be paraphrased as follows: Knowledge of God's unity includes knowing that God exists, that He is unique, that He is the creator of the world and that certain characteristics, such as knowledge, will, and self-sufficiency can be attributed to Him. When combined with an analysis of such categories of action as good, bad, and obligatory, knowledge of divine unity will lead to knowledge of God's justice. The main consequence of our knowing that God is just is our certainty that God cannot do evil and necessarily acts for good. Since God is necessarily benevolent and since He knows the limitations of the human beings He created, He is obliged to help them overcome their inherent weaknesses and shortcomings. This divine assistance (*lutf*) includes the sending of prophets who communicate divinely revealed commandments which benefit man in ways which could not be known through human reason alone. One aspect of God's justice, therefore, is His *taklīf* or imposition of obligation upon humanity for its own benefit. The benefit (*luṭf, maṣlaḥa*) derived from performing the revealed commandments lies, however, in the support and encouragement people receive to perform the rational obligations. The religious conception resulting from this approach then, is that an individual who has internalized true theological knowledge through rational analysis will properly discharge both his rational and revealed obligations and will lead a life of moral and religious nobility.

---

mental Assumptions of the Basra School of the Mu'tazila," *SI* 33 (1971): 5–18; idem, "The Autonomy of the Human Agent in the Teaching of 'Abd al-Gabbār," *Le Museon* 95 (1982): 323–55.

[15] 'Abd al-Jabbār, *Kitāb al-majmū' fi'l-muḥīṭ bi'l-taklīf*, ed. J.J. Houben (Beyrouth, 1965), 1:11–14. This text is actually an abridged version by 'Abd al-Jabbār's student Ḥasan ibn Mattawayh. The original has apparently been lost for the most part. Some fragments of the original work have been preserved in Judeo-Arabic manuscripts. See H. Ben-Shammai, "A Note on Some Karaite Copies of Mu'tazilite Writings," *BSOAS* 37 (1974): 295–304.

In this period, many Muʿtazilites were also active as jurisprudents, perhaps reflecting the sect's interest in both law and theology.[16] ʿAbd al-Jabbār himself is a good example of this tendency. These two interests met in the investigation of the theory of law and the analysis of its sources, the science of *uṣūl al-fiqh*, which was pursued by some of the leading figures of the Basran Muʿtazilite school. ʿAbd al-Jabbār, for example, wrote a work on legal theory, *Kitāb al-ʿumad*, as did his student, al-Ḥusayn al-Baṣrī, who wrote the influential *Kitāb al-muʿtamad*.[17] Even though some Muʿtazilites were jurists, however, no Islamic Muʿtazilite works of law or *fiqh* have been preserved. Yūsuf al-Baṣīr's *Kitāb al-istibṣār* offers us, therefore, an unusual opportunity to gain some sense of what a Muʿtazilite discussion of *fiqh* would look like: how the theological abstractions and highly developed epistemology interacted with the nitty-gritty of positive law.

* * *

Yūsuf al-Baṣīr's literary corpus was quite extensive and can be divided roughly into works of pure theology, polemics, and halakhah.[18] Among the latter are books dealing with legal theory. The dividing line between these categories is often not clear (which in a sense is the point of this article) and they are suggested only to help organize the relatively large number of titles.

As mentioned above, his major theological work, *Kitāb al-muḥtawī* (The Comprehensive Book), was written as an expansion of his *Kitāb al-tamyīz* (Book of Discernment) which he deemed to have been too terse for the

---

[16] For a number of examples, see Joel L. Kraemer, *Humanism in the Renaissance of Islam: The Cultural Revival during the Buyid Age* (Leiden, 1986), 74–76.

[17] Parenthetically, I might point out that the whole question of the relationship between the development of the *uṣūl al-fiqh* genre and Kalam is a highly interesting one which has not yet been investigated properly. Montgomery Watt has expressed the opinion that much more attention needs to be given to the study of the *uṣūl al-fiqh* literature, as it is there that one can get a broader sense of how Muslims understood the law which governs their lives. See M. Watt, "The Closing of the Door of Iğtihād," in *Orientalia Hispanica*, ed. J.M. Barral (Leiden, 1974), 1:675–78.

[18] The following description of al-Baṣīr's works is strictly provisional. It is based on only limited access to the Firkovitch manuscript collections which only now are becoming available at the Institute of Microfilmed Hebrew Manuscripts, Jerusalem. Full exploration of the collections will undoubtedly expand our knowledge of his writings.

Abbreviations: II Firk. = manuscripts in the second Firkovitch collection, Hebrew-Arabic section, first series; II Firk. NS = the second Firkovitch collection, Hebrew-Arabic section, new series; JTS = manuscripts in the library of the Jewish Theological Seminary in New York; ENA = the Elkan Adler collection of the JTS library; T-S = the Taylor-Schechter collection of Genizah manuscripts in the Cambridge University Library; B.L. = the British Library; Bod. = the Bodleian Library of Oxford University.

average reader.[19] In his *Muḥtawī*, which was one of his later books, al-Baṣīr refers to a number of his smaller theological works, most of which do not seem to have been preserved.[20] They are as follows:

1. *Sharḥ uṣūl al-labbād*, a commentary on the *Kitāb al-uṣūl* of Abū Muḥammad ʿAbdallāh ibn Saʿīd al-Labbād, a student of ʿAbd al-Jabbār. Al-Labbād's book probably dealt with theological principles.[21]
2. *Aḥwāl al-fāʿil*, a work on different states or conditions of the agent.
3. *Aḥkām al-muʾaththirāt*, on the conditions or qualities of influencing factors.
4. *Kitāb al-istidlāl biʾl-shāhid ʿalā ʾl-ghāʾib*, a work about using phenomena of the present world to prove something about invisible or transcendent reality.[22]
5. *Masāʾil al-istiqtāl*, evidently answers to questions concerning the justification for the death penalty and specifically the question of the value of the repentance performed by someone sentenced to death.[23]

Al-Baṣīr wrote at least five, possibly six polemical works directed against Rabbanites, Samaritans and Islam. They may be described as follows:

---

[19] I will not describe these books here, as it would take us too far afield. The interested reader can consult Vajda's edition of *al-Muḥtawī* and the reviews by Ben-Shammai and Chiesa. The known manuscripts of *al-Muḥtawī* are listed in Ben-Shammai, "Review," p. 411 and n. 9. Manuscripts of *al-Tamyīz* are listed in Vajda, 781 and Ben-Shammai, ibid., 410–411.

Al-Tamyīz was also commonly known as *al-Manṣūrī*. Ben-Shammai, "Review," 412–13, suggests that this name perhaps derived from one Manṣūr ben Hillel who in the year 1030 either ordered or received a copy of the book. As Ben-Shammai points out, however, al-Baṣīr already used the title *al-Manṣūrī* in his *al-Muḥtawī* which was written sometime before 1021. I would like to suggest that the book was named after a different individual, Abū Manṣūr Judah ben Daniel. A manuscript of *al-Istibṣār* (II Firk. 1793, f. 26a–b) mentions: "Answers to the questions of Abū Manṣūr Judah ben Hillel, may God support him." This person evidently put a number of questions to al-Baṣīr and it is quite possible that *Kitāb al-tamyīz* originated as an answer to one of his theological questions (or perhaps from a query or request of his son or father). A number of his books were produced in this fashion; see below.

[20] Ben-Shammai, "Review," 410 and p. 412, n. 14.

[21] According to Ibn al-Murtaḍā, al-Labbād wrote many books; see *Tabaqāt al-muʿtazila*, ed. S. Diwald-Wilzer (Beirut, 1961), 116. Ibn al-Murtaḍā does not, however, mention his *Kitāb al-uṣūl*. In a booklist found in the Cairo Genizah, the title "al-Labbād" figures several times. This could be a reference either to al-Labbād's work or to al-Baṣīr's commentary on it (a number of al-Baṣīr's works appear in this list). See Moshe Sokolow, "Four Booklists from the Cairo Geniza" (Hebrew), *Sefunot* 21 (1993): 257–312. The references to al-Labbād appear on pages 272, 276 and 278.

[22] This work is also mentioned in his critique of Samuel ben Ḥofni, II Firk. 3025, f. 40b.

[23] On this work, see Ben-Shammai, "Review," 425. Ben-Shammai suggests the book be identified with a responsum on this topic, most of which has been preserved in a collection of al-Baṣīr's responsa (JTS Mic. 3443 and 3448). It was written as an answer to questions asked by

1. *Naqḍ shemuel rās al-mathība* (Response to Samuel Head of the Yeshivah). This is a critique of the arguments advanced by Samuel ben Ḥofni, Gaon of Sura, in his book *ʿAshar masāʾil* (Ten Essays). A central issue in both works is the calendar: while the Rabbanites calculate the date, the Karaites insist that the calendar be fixed by the observation of the new moon.[24] Al-Baṣīr actually met Samuel ben Ḥofni in Baghdad and reports that he was not impressed by Samuel's ability as a theologian.[25]

2. *Kitāb [al-radd] ʿalā ʾl-qāʾilīn biʾl-iʿtidāl* (Response to those who hold the position of using the equinox in calculating the calendar). Another anti-Rabbanite polemic relating to the calendar.[26]

3. *Al-kalām ʿalā al-samāra* (Debate with the Samaritans). This was possibly a response to claims made by the Samaritans concerning Mount Gerizim and the Samaritan position that prayers should be directed towards it rather than towards Jerusalem.[27]

4. *Kitāb al-istiʿāna* (Book Seeking [Divine] Help). This work was also called *Al-naqḍ ʿalā abī jaʿfar al-Ṭabarī* (Answer to Abū Jaʿfar al-Ṭabarī).[28] It is likely that the al-Ṭabarī referred to here was the renowned

---

Mubarak ben [. . .] ben Josiah, the physician. The work is mentioned in II Firk. 1811, f. 1b, 55b.

[24] This work of al-Baṣīr is mentioned in the responsum on prophecy, II Firk. 1805, f. 34a and in *al-Istibṣār*, II Firk. 1793, f. 53b (and elsewhere in this manuscript), II Firk. 1811, f. 60b and II Firk. 1794, f. 31b (where he describes some of its contents). It is also mentioned in T-S 8 Ka. 8, f. 13a which seems to be a defense of Samuel ben Ḥofni Gaon. The booklist mentioned above also contains a number of references to this work, sometimes as "Response to Samuel ben Ḥofni's Book" and sometimes as "Response to Samuel ben Ḥofni's Debate (*kalām*)"; see Sokolow, "Four Booklists," 266, 272 and 278. It is most likely to be identified with the work preserved in manuscripts II Firk. 3016, 3025–27.

A question which remains to be investigated is the relationship between this work and al-Baṣīr's *intizāʿāt* (debates) against Samuel ben Ḥofni and other Rabbanites. For example, ENA 4016.7–8, 10 is a Genizah fragment containing an *intizāʿa* of al-Baṣīr against Samuel ben Ḥofni Gaon on the matter of the new barley (*aviv*). This may be related to the *muntazaʿāt* (debates), preserved in the Jewish National and University Library in Jerusalem, Yahuda ms. Ar. 985 (Naskhi script), which deal in part with the calendrical differences between Karaites and Rabbanites. A large part of Samuel ben Ḥofni's *Ten Essays* was edited in Sklare, "Samuel ben Ḥofni," 2:61–113.

[25] See II Firk. 3025, f. 52b.

[26] Mentioned in II Firk. 1793, f. 104a.

[27] This work is mentioned in II Firk. 3025, f. 27a. It also appears twice in the above-mentioned booklist, once as *al-qibla radd ʿalā al-samāra* ([Book concerning] the direction of prayer, response to the Samaritans). See Sokolow, "Four Booklists," 272, 278. This work may possibly be identified with B.L. ms. Or. 2528 (Cat. # 1098). It should be noted that a student or follower of al-Baṣīr also wrote a book against the Samaritans, found in II Firk. 1681. In both of these last two manuscripts, the authors respond to the claims made by "the author of the book." It is possible that the author in question is Abū ʾl-Ḥasan al-Sūrī in his work *Kitāb al-tubāh* (Book of Insight). This possibility is made somewhat difficult due to the fact that *Kitāb al-tubāh* is usually dated to 1030–40. This would make al-Baṣīr's response to it one of his last works. On Abū ʾl-Ḥasan al-Ṣūrī, see Alan Crown, *The Samaritans* (Tübingen, 1989), 468–80, 627–28.

[28] On *Kitāb al-istiʿāna*, see the comments of Ben-Shammai, "Review," p. 412, n. 14. *Al-naqḍ*

ninth-century Muslim historian and exegete. Among other things, al-Baṣīr evidently reacted to al-Ṭabari's criticism of the biblical traditions relating to the miracles performed for Moses, and discussed the epistemological quality of information known from traditions.

5. A polemic against Islam. Al-Baṣīr was moved to write this work after the difficulties he experienced when participating in a theological disputation (*majlis*), evidently in Baghdad. In this work, he attacks the concept of the inimitability of the Qur'an (*iʿjāz al-qurʾān*). This idea was one of the Muslims' central arguments for the Qurʾān's authenticity as a divine revelation.[29]

6. *Masʾala ʿalā man iddaʿā naskh sharīʿatinā*. Al-Baṣīr planned to write a work concerned with the abrogation of a revelation by another revelation, but it is not known if he actually did so. This was a hot polemical topic between Jews and Muslims as well as an internal issue of legal theory.[30]

Our main concern, however, is with al-Baṣīr's halakhic writings, albeit in connection with their theological aspects. Al-Baṣīr's halakhic works can be divided into three categories: responsa, short treatises, and his halakhic code, *Kitāb al-istibṣār fīʾl-farāʾiḍ*.

Concerning his responsa, it should be emphasized that he answered questions on both halakhic and theological matters. Sometimes copyists collected his theological responsa separately, but more frequently collections of his responsa contain a mixture of both types.[31] These responsa were often referred to by the names of their questioners. Names of such

ʿalā abī jaʿfar al-ṭabarī is mentioned in II Firk. 1805, f. 35a. The two names of this work are mentioned together in II Firk. 1681, f. 30b (*Naqḍ shemuel rās al-mathība*) where some of its content is also indicated. In II Firk. 3016, f. 14b (also *Naqḍ shemuel rās al-mathība*), *Kitāb al-istiʿāna* is described as an "Answer to one of the non-Jews (*baʿḍ al-goyim*)."

[29] This work is preserved in a number of Firkovitch and Cairo Genizah manuscripts (II Firk. 2133, 2980, 3022; Br. Lib. Or. 5554B, ff. 34–35; T-S 8 Ka. 8, ff. 5–6) and will be the subject of a forthcoming article. The identification of the work—which cannot be made from the manuscripts themselves—can be established from citations by the author of the anti-Samaritan work (n. 27 above) who sometimes even quotes al-Baṣīr in Hebrew translation. I would like to thank my colleague, Sarah Stroumsa, who brought some of these Firkovitch manuscripts to my attention as well as the manuscript mentioned in n. 78 below.

[30] Mentioned in II Firk. 1793, f. 1a. II Firk. 1811, f. 81b has: "Perhaps I will explain this in an epistle (*risāla*) which will include the issue of the possibility of abrogation (*naskh*)."

[31] Ms. JTS Mic. 3450 (in Arabic script) contains the beginning of a collection of theological responsa, called *masāʾil ʿaqlīya*. The table of contents lists twenty-three responsa, one of which may be referred to in *al-Muḥtawī*; see Ben-Shammai, "Review," p. 410, n. 7. Other collections are: (1) JTS Mic. 3443, in Arabic script, partly copied in 1047/48 C.E. (f. 53b); (2) JTS Mic.

questioners which have been preserved include Manṣūr Judah ben Daniel, Mubārak ben [. . .] ben Josiah, the physician, Abū Bishr Sulaymān ibn Bishr,[32] and Azariah ben Ṣalaḥ.[33] Responsa were sometimes also named after the country from which they were sent, such as the "Egyptian Responsa."[34] The questions from these questioners often stimulated al-Baṣīr to write lengthy expositions which were subsequently published (and perhaps re-edited) as independent works. For example, various sections of *al-Istibṣār* still preserve elements of the style of a responsum with phrases such as "You inquired" or "Your question has three parts."[35]

A responsum dealing with certain forbidden sexual relationships provides us with a good example of the interaction of law and theory in this genre. In order to clarify his analysis of this issue, al-Baṣīr felt it necessary to include a lengthy exposition comparing the epistemological status of various types of legal analogies (*qiyās*) with that of transmitted traditions.[36]

A second genre is the short treatise devoted to a single topic and which deals, for the most part, with legal theory. As mentioned above, it is not always possible to distinguish between those treatises which originated as responsa and those which arose out of al-Baṣīr's desire to discuss a certain topic. Known treatises include:

1. *Maqālāt al-qiyās*, concerning the use of analogical reasoning in legal matters. According to his description, this work was structured as a comment on Deuteronomy 17:8–12 ("If a case is too baffling for you to decide, be it a controversy over homicide, civil law, or assault . . .") which is one of the classic foci for discussions of Jewish legal theory.[37]

3448, in Arabic script, these two manuscripts were evidently originally together as one manuscript; (3) II Firk. 1805, in Hebrew characters. Bod. 2789.1 is a Hebrew responsum on forbidden sexual relationships by Yeshuʿah b. Judah and Joseph ha-Roʾeh (al-Baṣīr) and signed by Solomon b. David ha-Nasi. This would seem to be a translation from an Arabic responsum. B.L. Or. 2570 (cat. # 596, in Arabic script) has two responsa, one on the *ʿomer* and one dealing with the nature of God. British Library Ms. Or. 2571 (cat. # 597) is a collection of unattributed responsa in Arabic script. The style, however, is that of al-Baṣīr, although they may have been written by his student Yeshuʿah ben Judah. The questioner was Abū ʿAlī Samuel ben Sināʾī (or Sinānī).

[32] The beginning of the responsum to his questions concerning oaths is found in T-S Ar. 48.224.

[33] See B.L. Or. 2570.

[34] *Al-masāʾil al-miṣriyya* are mentioned in II Firk. 3025, f. 16b.

[35] This phenomenon would explain why different parts of *al-Istibṣār* appear to have been written over a fairly long period of time. See n. 45 below.

[36] II Firk. 1805, ff. 17–18, 27–36. This responsum may be the same as that mentioned a number of times in *al-Istibṣār*. See II Firk. 1794, ff. 52a, 64a, 70b, 73b, 85b.

[37] It is also referred to as *al-kalām fī ʾl-qiyās*. This work is mentioned in a responsum, II Firk. 1805, ff. 17a, 27a, 29a; in *al-Istibṣār*, II Firk. 1811, f. 88a and II Firk. 1794, f. 53b (where he

2. *Kitāb al-hidāya* (Book of Guidance). This book dealt with transmitted traditions, particularly those of rabbinic origin.[38]

3. *Kitāb al-shukūk* (Book Concerning Uncertainty).[39] This work deals with one of the central issues of *uṣūl al-fiqh*: whether a legal decision must be based upon certain knowledge (*ʿilm*) or whether probable opinion (*ẓann*) is sufficient.[40]

4. *Masʾalat al-tawriya* (Essay on Concealment or Ambiguity). The nature of this book is not entirely clear, although it may be similar to a work with the same title by his student, Yeshuʿah ben Judah.[41]

5. *Masaʾla fīʾl-nubūwa* (Essay Concerning Prophecy).[42] This responsum is really a short treatise. Al-Baṣīr was asked whether or not it is necessary to travel in order to verify the miracles of a claimant to prophecy; he used the occasion to deal at length with the issues of prophecy, *taklīf*, tradition, and *qiyās*.

---

explicitly mentions that the topic belongs to *uṣūl al-fiqh*), f. 102a–b; and also in his critique of Samuel ben Ḥofni, II Firk. 3025, ff. 31a, 32b.

[38] It is mentioned in *al-Istibṣār*, II Firk. 1793, f. 53b; II Firk. 1681, f. 30b and is described briefly in II Firk. 1794, f. 31b: "Know that I have already discussed the transmission of the Rabbanites' traditions and their claims as to its soundness in a separate book concerning traditions in which I clarified the veracity of our transmission of the Torah from Moses. I called this book the *Book of Guidance*. In it, I explained the difference between the transmission of Moses' miracles by the entire people and other matters known necessarily by dint of their being transmitted concurrently by large groups of people (*tawātur akhbārihim*) and what the Rabbanites claim concerning the transmission of the Mishnah."

[39] The first ten pages of this book have been preserved in B.L. ms. Or. 2572, ff. 109–118. The relationship between this text and the responsum in JTS Mic. 3443, f. 53b ff. which is entitled *ʿibrat al-shukūk* (lesson concerning uncertainties) needs to be clarified. This book is mentioned in II Firk. 1805, f. 30b; II Firk. 1811, f. 58a; T-S Ar. 51.30; and B.L. cat. # 591, f. 25a.

[40] In this book al-Baṣīr takes the position that probable opinion is indeed adequate. His discussion of certain knowledge and opinion here connects with his treatment of traditions in his *Kitāb al-hidāya*. A major topic in the *uṣūl al-fiqh* literature is the epistemological status of a tradition based on a single line of transmission of individuals as opposed to a tradition known universally through concurrent transmission. The latter was considered to provide certain knowledge, while the singly-transmitted tradition was generally regarded as only probable opinion. Al-Baṣīr's acceptance of probable opinion could help to explain why he and his students were so much more open to using Rabbinic traditions in their discussions of law than were earlier Karaites. Even though al-Baṣīr of course did not consider Rabbinic traditions to be authoritative, he does show a surprisingly respectful attitude towards them. This illustrates how the Karaites' absorption of the framework of Islamic legal theory enabled them at least to consider the relevance of Rabbinic traditions instead of rejecting them out-of-hand.

[41] Al-Baṣīr's work is mentioned in a responsum in II Firk. 1805. f. 30b. The work by Yeshuʿah ben Judah appears to be preserved in II Firk. 4816 and is discussed in H. Ben-Shammai, "Yeshuah Ben Yehudah," 14–16.

[42] Preserved in II Firk. 1805, ff. 23a–36b (incomplete).

Finally, there is *Kitāb al-istibṣār* itself, which he sometimes refers to as a *Book of Commandments* (*sefer miṣvot*).[43] It is composed of a series of essays (*maqālāt*) in which various legal topics are treated in depth. From the manuscripts known at present, the first five *maqālāt* of *al-Istibṣār* deal respectively with circumcision, the Sabbath, the new moon, the *aviv*,[44] and the holidays. The ninth *maqāla* is concerned with forbidden sexual relationships (*ʿarayot*). Other essays, whose numbered positions within the larger work are not known, deal with impurity, inheritance, forbidden foods and ritual slaughter.[45] The influence and authority exerted by *Kitāb al-istibṣār* within the Jerusalem Karaite community is shown by the fact that an abridgement was made of it and that parts of it were translated into Hebrew by Tobias ben Moses.[46] It was also analyzed and criticized at length by ʿAlī ben Sulaymān, who was active in Jerusalem and then in Egypt at the end of the eleventh century.[47]

Al-Istibṣār cannot really be considered a legal code which seeks to define normative practice in concise and clear form. It is, rather, a series of legal monographs in which various topics are examined and the relevant sources are carefully analyzed. In this sense it is similar to the legal monographs written by the Geonim of the tenth and early eleventh century, Saadya ben Joseph, Samuel ben Ḥofni, and Hai ben Sherira. It would be of interest to compare *al-Istibṣār* to other Karaite halakhic works of this period (such as those of Levi ben Japheth, Sahl ben Maṣliaḥ and al-Qirqisānī) and to examine its style and methodology in the context of contemporary Gaonic and Islamic legal works. The research in all of these

[43] Such a reference is to be found in II Firk. 3025, f. 13a.

[44] *Aviv* refers to the new barley which appears in the spring. The appearance of the *aviv* helped to determine the intercalation of the year. The Palestinian Karaites would therefore watch for the first appearance of the new barley. The Rabbanites, who used a calculated calendar, opposed this practice.

[45] Known manuscripts of *al-Istibṣār* include: British Library Or. 2576.1–3 (cat. # 591, the first fragment has the date 1019 and the third 1017/8); T-S Ar. 51.30; T-S Ar. 51.35; ENA 2642.17–8; ENA 2779.22; II Firk. 680, 794, 1694, 1793, 1794, 1795, 1811, 3303, 4528; II Firk. NS 318, 1230. Ibn al-Hītī gives 1036/7 as the year in which it was written (Margoliouth, pp. 434, 440). Given the fact that the colophons of several manuscripts indicate earlier dates, it seems likely that Ibn al-Hītī's date is the date of completion of the last section. In *al-Muḥtawī*, al-Baṣīr refers to these *maqālāt* as separate works. This may be due to the fact that they were indeed written as separate books or responsa and then later joined together or, at least, that they were written over a long period of time. Indeed, in *al-Muḥtawī* (which was written before 1021), he says that he hopes to complete *al-Istibṣār* (Vajda, p. 756).

[46] The abridgement is mentioned and briefly quoted by A. Harkavy, *Zikhron ha-gaon rav shemuel ben ḥofni u-sefarav* (St. Petersburg, 1880), p. 44, n. 120. Part of the translation is found in Bod. 2789.3–4. Other manuscripts of the translation may be found in the Firkovitch collection.

[47] The critique is found in II Firk. 1804 and 1812.

literatures, however, is still in its infancy and it is too early to draw significant conclusions.

* * *

Al-Baṣīr's interest in the intersection of theology and law is demonstrated by the short treatises which he wrote on legal theory. It is true that polemical concerns were at least partially the stimulus for the composition of some of them, such as those dealing with legal analogy, abrogation and tradition. Nevertheless, these works also demonstrate how the polemical need can push an inquiring mind such as al-Baṣīr's to explore an issue for its own sake. Al-Baṣīr, however, sought to integrate his theological concerns with the law itself. For examples of this, we turn to his *al-Istibṣār*.

The first *maqāla* of this book provides us with many illustrations of the impact of Muʿtazilite terminology and concerns. Indeed, al-Baṣīr seems to have taken the laws of circumcision, the act by which a Jewish male enters into the covenant, as an opportunity to present the basic issues of religious obligation or *taklīf* as they would be practically applied.

The *maqāla* is roughly divided into two sections. In the first, al-Baṣīr discusses the basic issues of the laws of circumcision: who is obligated to be circumcised, who may perform it, what instrument is to be used, and when the circumcision is to take place. The discussion proceeds through an analysis of the relevant verses intermingled with definitions of such central concepts as obligation (*taklīf*) and divine command. For example, the fact that infants are circumcised at the age of eight days prompts him to point out that *taklīf* can only apply to individuals with fully developed reasoning capabilities (*kamāl al-ʿaql*). This Muʿtazilite position holds that obligation of divine commandments can only apply to individuals who can know that they are being obligated in order that they may receive reward and benefit. Furthermore, they must have the capability of understanding and demonstrating to themselves the basis of the obligation, i.e., that there is a God who sends His prophets to inform mankind of commanded actions.[48] Moreover, the obligation of the revealed commandments is intimately connected to rational obligations. If one cannot understand what is good and what is evil, then the revealed commandments cannot assist him in performing the imperative of his reason. Different individu-

[48] This position is expressed by ʿAbd al-Jabbār in a number of places. See for example *Al-majmūʿ fīʾl-muḥīṭ biʾl-taklīf*, ed. J.J. Houben (Beyrouth, 1962), 1:5–10; ed. J.J. Houben and D. Gimaret (Beirut, 1981), 2:259–62.

als will therefore be obligated by divine command at different ages, according to their own mental development. Al-Baṣīr contrasts this to the Rabbanite position which makes obligation dependent on attaining a certain age.[49]

The new-born infant is obviously not under any obligation to circumcise itself. Since the benefit of a divine commandment only accrues to someone who is obligated by it, he raises the question of how the poor infant benefits from the pain of circumcision. Muʿtazilite thought sees ethical values as being objective and God would not command something which only brought with it pain and was hence evil. The mere fact that God commands the act does not make it essentially good. By way of reply to this question, he has recourse to the Muʿtazilite idea of the compensation (*ʿiwaḍ*) which God gives to those who suffer undeserved pain in this world. While the infant does not receive the benefit of performing an obligatory action, he will receive compensation for the pain.[50]

The second part of the *maqāla* consists of a series of ten short questions or essays, most of which are concerned with the relationship between knowledge (of God, of the nature of the commandments), intention and the performance of the commandments. Here, al-Baṣīr explicitly states that many of the issues upon which he expands relate not only to the commandment of circumcision, but also to most of the other revealed commandments.[51] In order to get a sense of his concerns and how he includes theological issues in his halakhic discussion, it will be sufficient to describe the contents of some of these essays.

The second essay, for example, addresses the following question: Is it necessary for a slave undergoing circumcision to believe in the veracity of God's prophet and in the fact that he is being circumcised for his own spiritual good, or should we circumcise him despite his doubts on these matters? The fourth essay is concerned with the person who fits most of the criteria for someone obligated by the Torah (*mukallaf*), but who has doubts about the issues mentioned in the second question. This is because he has not engaged in the rational investigation of the topics which would lead to a certain understanding and knowledge of the theological basis for

---

[49] Note that Samuel ben Ḥofni Gaon also treats this issue in the beginning of his *Kitāb al-bulūgh wa'l-idrāk* (On Attainment of the Age of Legal Majority, found in II Firk. 1467, f. 2) where he seeks to combine the Muʿtazilite and Rabbinic definitions of the age of legal obligation.

[50] See Vajda, *al-Muḥtawī*, 333–69 for an annotated translation of the section dealing with *ʿiwaḍ* and references to the relevant passages in ʿAbd al-Jabbār.

[51] II Firk. 1793, f. 15a.

the obligation to perform the commandments. Is such a person still obligated to perform the commandments? The sixth essay asks whether the basis for the obligation to perform a commandment is its goodness or simply its obligatory nature. The seventh essay then asks whether one would merit reward if he performed a commandment for a reason other than its goodness or because it is obligatory.[52]

The ninth essay asks further: When performing a revealed commandment, must one keep in mind the basis of its obligation, that basis being that the commandment is a benefit for him? This essay presents the Muʿtazilite view that it is intention which defines certain actions as good or bad. Al-Baṣīr points out that many of the actions made obligatory by revelation, such as circumcision, would normally be considered evil if it were not for the divine law. Therefore, if we were to perform them without knowing why they are obligatory and without being aware of this at the time of the action, we would then be doing something evil and not fulfilling the divine command. Knowledge and intention determine the nature or quality of the action.[53] Furthermore, he says that this applies to knowing the specific goodness of a commandment. For example, if one circumcises a child or slaughters an animal without keeping in mind the fact that they will receive divine compensation for their suffering, then the acts are evil and the commandments have not been fulfilled.[54] Parenthetically, I might point out that Samuel ben Ḥofni Gaon, who was also highly influenced by Muʿtazilite Kalam and was probably the first writer to introduce Muʿtazilite thought into Jewish literature in a major and full fashion, expressed a similar position in his *Kitāb fīʾl-sharāʾiʿ* (Treatise on the Commandments).[55]

The final example of the interaction between theology and halakhah to be discussed here is an issue which crops up in a number of places in *Kitāb al-istibṣār*. This is the question of the boundaries of *taklīf*. Who is actually included within God's imposition of obligation and who receives the benefit from it? Are all peoples of the world obligated to follow the Law of the Torah or only the Jews? While this question appears in relation to circumcision, the Sabbath, forbidden sexual relationships and in-

[52] This question is also taken up by Samuel ben Ḥofni Gaon in part 1, chapter 19 of his *Kitāb fīʾl-sharāʾiʿ* (Treatise on the Commandments), translated and published in Sklare, "Samuel ben Ḥofni," 1:310–315, 2:12–13.

[53] II Firk. 1793, f. 39b.

[54] II Firk. 1793, f. 44a–b.

[55] See Sklare, "Samuel ben Ḥofni," 1:307–310, 313–314. On Samuel ben Ḥofni Gaon and Muʿtazilism, see ibid., 74–75, 85–96.

heritance, al-Baṣīr usually refers the reader to his lengthy discussion of it in the *maqāla* dealing with impurity. Here the question is raised as to whether or not non-Jews can become ritually impure. Al-Baṣīr's treatment of this issue is an excellent example of how he combined analysis and interpretation of his sources, that is, the relevant biblical verses, with his theological framework.[56]

Al-Baṣīr discusses the question of the universality of obligation in two chapters of his *maqāla* on impurity.[57] In the first chapter, he argues against the view that impurity is a quality which inheres in objects. According to this approach (taken by Japheth ben Eli in his commentary on Leviticus), non-Jews can become impure just as inanimate objects become impure.[58] Al-Baṣīr, however, makes the distinction between inanimate objects and beings with will. The presence of volition makes the framework of command and prohibition relevant. As he sees it, impurity results from a divine command to the effect that one becomes impure from a discharge.

The problem of the non-Jew's status vis-à-vis impurity is thus a question of whether or not he is included within the *taklīf* of the Torah. The discussion proceeds on two levels which intertwine and yet are also in tension with one another. First, there is the question of Moses' mission: to whom was he sent as God's messenger? and to whom was the Torah addressed, to the Israelites alone or to all of humanity? In this legalistic discussion, various verses which seem to be general in nature are examined, such as "When any man has a discharge . . ." (Lev. 15:2) or "When a person (*adam*) dies in a tent . . ." (Num. 19:14) which could be taken to indicate that the Torah imposes universal obligation. While these verses can be interpreted in such a fashion, al-Baṣīr insists on the more straightforward reading, derived basically from the sense of the Bible as a whole, which takes all of these verses as addressing the Israelites only and therefore indicating a particularized *taklīf*.

---

[56] This topic and al-Baṣīr's treatment of it has also been discussed by Haggai Ben-Shammai in his recent article, "Some Genizah Fragments on the Duty of the Nations to Keep the Mosaic Law," in *Genizah Research After Ninety Years: The Case of Judaeo-Arabic*, ed. J. Blau and S.C. Reif (Cambridge, 1992), 22–30.

[57] B.L. Ms. Or. 2576 (Cat. # 591), ff. 39b–56b (in Arabic script).

[58] Japheth ben Eli's comments can be found in British Library ms. Or. 2472 (Cat. # 266), ff. 141b–144b (end of his commentary on the pericope *Meṣoraʿ*). Al-Baṣīr reports that this was the view of his teacher, Yūsuf ibn Nūḥ (f. 40a). According to this approach, Lev. 15:1–2 ("The Lord spoke to Moses and Aaron, saying: Speak to the Israelite people and say to them: When any man has a discharge issuing from his flesh, he is unclean") constitutes a report. In other words, Moses is told to inform the people that such a discharge happens to result in impurity, but is not itself the result of a divine command.

The second level of the discussion brings to bear the Muʿtazilite conception of *taklīf*, which, being based on universal reason, provides a ground for universal obligation. If the purpose of the revealed commandments is to stimulate and help man in the fulfillment of the obligations imposed by reason which are universal by nature, then it would seem that the revealed obligation should also apply to all mankind. Al-Baṣīr, however, stresses the particularity of Israel: since the imposition of obligation is a benefit given by God to man and has no other purpose in and of itself, and if the Torah is indeed a particular *taklīf* as indicated by the biblical sources, then it may benefit the Israelites alone. Muʿtazilite theology does admit that God can know that certain obligations will benefit only a specific people and that He might then direct such *taklīf* to them separately.[59] Therefore, if a non-Jew were to perform a commandment of the Torah which was not intended to benefit him, it would be considered an empty, vain (*ʿabath*) and hence, bad action for him. This approach assumes a theoretical universal obligation which may nevertheless vary according to the needs or capabilities of individuals or groups.

A difficulty, however, arises when considering the phenomenon of converts (*gerim*). How can a non-Jew ever enter into the *taklīf* of the Torah if the situation is as al-Baṣīr takes it to be? Samuel ben Ḥofni Gaon solved the problem by suggesting a parallel between the acceptance of the obligation of divine commandments by non-Jews and the acceptance of supererogatory obligations such as vows by a Jew.[60] In his view, the commandments would then benefit the convert when he decided to enter the Jewish religion.

Al-Baṣīr rejects this suggestion by arguing that one cannot choose to take on the obligation of actions which would normally have been considered bad (such as painful circumcision) or useless and are only known to be good through the approval of revelation. Al-Baṣīr suggests, instead, a sort of political approach, deriving perhaps from the Holy Land ideology and biblicism of the Jerusalem Karaite community. He says that the extension of the benefits of the Torah to the convert comes from his living

---

[59] See ʿAbd al-Jabbār, *Kitāb al-mughnī* (Cairo, 1962–), XI:394; XIII:418; XIV:149; XVI:49ff., 84ff., 361. In his *Kitāb fī ʾl-sharāʾiʿ* Samuel ben Ḥofni takes a similar approach to the distinctions found within the commandments of the Torah itself. For example, there are commandments which only apply to priests and not to the ordinary Israelite, or to men and not to women, or which are obligatory only during the day and not at night. These differences, according to him, stem from the different needs of people and the different effects of the different commandments. See Sklare, "Samuel ben Ḥofni," 1:276–81, 294–97.

[60] His discussion of this issue is found in his work *ʿAshar masāʾil* (Ten Essays), published and translated in Sklare, "Samuel ben Ḥofni." For his treatment of this particular issue see 1:388–423. Some of the manuscripts are discussed in Ben-Shammai, "Duty of the Nations."

among the Jewish people as a *ger toshav*. Al-Baṣīr is apparently using the Islamic model of a protected minority, an impression that is reinforced by his use of the terms *dhimma*, *kharaj* and *jizya* in context. He seems to be uncomfortable with the conception of conversion as a purely internal or religious act.[61]

From the ninth through the twelfth centuries, both Karaites and Rabbanites discussed this fundamental question of the Torah's *taklīf* and its boundaries. Karaite discussions, usually connected with the issue of gentile impurity, are already found in the writings of Daniel al-Qūmisī[62] and can be traced through al-Qirqisānī,[63] Japheth ben Eli, Levi ben Japheth,[64] and al-Baṣīr. On the Rabbanite side, we find Samuel ben Ḥofni Gaon (who quotes Saadya Gaon, probably indicating that Saadya also dealt with this topic in his commentary on Leviticus),[65] Abū ʿAlī Samuel ben Joseph al-Baṣrī,[66] Hai Gaon,[67] Nissim ben Jacob,[68] and a certain Nethanel who wrote a work defending Samuel ben Ḥofni against the criticisms of Nissim ben Jacob on a number of topics.[69] All of these individuals, Rabbanites and Karaites alike, were influenced to a significant degree by the Kalam.

I would like to suggest that the discussion of the universality of the Torah is an instance in which Kalam not only provided a larger conceptual structure for discussing a legal issue, but also evidently played a part in stimulating the discussion of the issue amongst Jews in the first place. This is not to say that there were not other factors which prompted this

---

[61] Others at this time treated conversion as an internal act and sought to understand how it comes about. See, for example, the anonymous fragment ENA 2855.3–4 (published in Sklare, "Samuel ben Ḥofni," 2:110–113) which is evidently connected to this larger discussion.

[62] He expresses this position in the text published by Mann, "Tract," 290.

[63] *Kitāb al-anwār waʾl-marāqib*, ed. L. Nemoy (New York, 1939–43), 2:291 (III:14); see also his discussion of the impurity of non-Jews in *Kitāb al-anwār*, 4:1023–29 (X:29). Al-Qirqisānī reports that there was a group of Karaites from Tustar who took the position that the Torah does not include non-Jews at all within its framework of obligation and hence they cannot convert to Judaism. Abū Isā al-Isfahānī also held this view; see *Kitāb al-anwār*, 2:287–88 (III:14).

[64] The relevant sections from Levi ben Japheth's *Sefer ha-miṣvot* were published by H.H. Ben-Sasson, "Tenth and Eleventh Century Karaite Attitudes to Gentiles," in *Salo Wittmayer Baron Jubilee Volume* (Hebrew section) (New York, 1975), 71–90. Japheth ben Eli's discussion of this topic is found in his commentary on Leviticus mentioned above.

[65] See Sklare, "Samuel ben Ḥofni," 1:422.

[66] See Sklare, ibid., 1:388–89.

[67] Hai Gaon was asked about this issue by Elḥanan ben Shemariah to whom he responded. The beginning of his responsum is found in ms. Mosseri IV:5 and published in Sklare, ibid., 1:229, n. 52.

[68] He touches on this issue briefly in the introduction to his *Sefer ha-mafteaḥ*, ed. J. Goldenthal (1847).

[69] Found in II Firk. 311, published in Sklare, ibid., 2:204–26. The topic was also discussed in some sources which at this stage remain anonymous. See the text published by J. Mann, "An Early Theological-Polemical Work," *HUCA* 12–13 (1937–38): 414, 427, 434, 449, 450. Note also II Firk. 2229 and T-S Ar. 47.10.

discussion. It is clear that the question of the universality or authentic particularity of the Torah was part of a web of issues. It was connected to the polemical debate concerning the abrogation of the Torah by subsequent revelations (*naskh*) and to the related idea of the "eternity of the commandments" (*qidam al- farāʾiḍ*).[70]

ʿAbd al-Jabbār, for example, analyzes the theoretical need of various peoples for particular revelations and the universal revelation of Islam within a conceptual framework similar to that found among Muʿtazilite-oriented Jewish writers.[71] He also uses it to explain why earlier revelations were abrogated and to support Islam's claim to universality. He makes this connection in his *Kitāb al-mughnī*:

> Changeability and variety are only admissible in relation to the revealed laws (*samʿīyāt*) for they are built on the benefits (they bring to man) which are not known rationally. For these (benefits), reason is dependent on the guidance which originates from Him who knows all hidden things. According to what we have said above, it is therefore possible that the state of those obligated (by revelation) may vary or (even) the individual's state may differ at two different times. This is the necessary general principle which supports the possibility of abrogation.[72]

Elsewhere, he explains why the Islamic revelation is universal.

> We will now speak about the revealed laws. Prophecy has been sealed by Muḥammad, may God bless him and his people. The Eternal One knows that the benefits required by (His) servants will not vary in relationship to this revealed law such that their obligation (by it) would cease. Insofar as these revealed laws do not change, they have the same status as the laws of reason (which are universal).[73]

Interestingly enough, ʿAbd al-Jabbār took a position similar to al-Baṣīr's on the question of a non-believer's obligation by Islam. Obligation comes

---

[70] On the issue of *qidam al-farḍ*, see the sources mentioned by H. Ben-Shammai, "Duty of the Nations," 27–28. See also the discussion by Yoram Erder, "Early Karaite Conceptions About Commandments Given Before the Revelation of the Torah," *PAAJR* 60 (1994): 101–40. The issue of the universality of the law and related topics need to be analyzed at length, a project which I hope to undertake in the near future.

[71] See n. 59 above. In most of these places, he does not introduce the polemical aspect of the issue.

[72] ʿAbd al-Jabbār, *al-Mughnī*, 16:88. These ideas are developed fully on pp. 76–91. On p. 95, he says explicitly that he has presented this topic as the basis for a polemic against the Jews. He then proceeds in the following chapters (97–142) to discuss specifically the abrogation of Moses' revelation. This same argument was made by Ibn Khallād, a Muʿtazilite who was active two generations before. See B.L. ms. Or. 8613, ff. 73–74.

[73] ʿAbd al-Jabbār, *al-Muḥīṭ*, 1:16; see also 2:311. Also relevant to this issue are the theoretical discussions as to whether or not the unbeliever is obligated by the Islamic revelation. See for example, ibid., 2:223ff.; Abū ʾl-Ḥusayn Muḥammad ibn ʿAlī, *Kitāb al-muʿtamad fī uṣūl al-fiqh* (Damascus, 1964), 1:273ff. (chapter on *dukhūl al-kāfir fī ʾl-khiṭāb fī ʾl-sharʿiyāt*) and the parallel chapter in *al-Mughnī*, Vol. 11.

about when the non-believer understands and accepts the revealed law which thus becomes divine assistance (*luṭf*) for him. This happens when he lives among Muslims and mingles with them (*khāliṭ mukhāliṭunā*).[74]

Discussion of this issue amongst Jews was thus perhaps stimulated by the universal claims of Islam (and by the discussion of such claims by Muslim Muʿtazilites), or perhaps even by the phenomenon of the wide-spread conversion to Islam witnessed by the Jews during the previous few centuries.[75] One might imagine that this brought the question of conversion—of whether it is truly possible to change religions and what it means spiritually—to the center of theological discussion. Polemical considerations aside, the exposure to Muʿtazilite Kalam, which stressed the universality of reason, prompted Jews to consider the implications of universality for their own religious system.

* * *

The question has been asked, first by Maimonides and later by modern historians of Jewish thought, why the Karaites and the later Geonim adopted the Muʿtazilite Kalam as their theological framework, as opposed to some other system, such as the Ashʿarite Kalam or the Aristotelian philosophy of al-Fārābī. The question is sharpened by our knowledge of a number of Jews who were studying and even writing *falsafa*-type works at this time.[76] Maimonides' answer was simply that Muʿtazilism was the first school of speculative thought encountered by the Geonim and the Karaites, who took its opinions to be proven and accepted.[77] To be sure, the element of historical circumstance that Maimonides points to was undoubtedly a significant factor in the choice of Muʿtazilism, even though

[74] *Al-Mughnī*, 16:429–30.

[75] Polemics with Christianity may have also been a factor here. For example, the Christian *mutakallim*, ʿAmmār al-Baṣrī, rejected Judaism because God "made it a particular religion, in which He did not include His whole creation." See S. Griffith, "ʿAmmār al-Baṣrī's *Kitāb al-Burhān*: Christian Kalam in the First Abbasid Century," *Le Museon* 96 (1983): 163.

[76] Even Hai Gaon was familiar with the works of al-Fārābī, or at least with his *Iḥṣā al-ʿulūm*; see A. Harkavy, *Ḥadashim gam yeshanim* (Jerusalem, 1970), 113. What we know about the speculative activity of Jews in the East during the tenth and eleventh centuries has been reviewed most recently in Sklare, "Samuel Ben Ḥofni," 1:145–10. A more accessible survey is to be found in J. Kraemer, *Humanism in the Renaissance of Islam*, 81–84. Concerning Jewish interest in the Aristotelian tradition, see also S. Pines, "A Tenth-Century Philosophical Correspondence," *PAAJR* 24 (1955): 103–36 and H. Ben-Shammai, "A Philosophical Study Group in Tenth Century Mosul" (Hebrew), *Peʿamim* 41 (1989): 21–31.

[77] Maimonides, *The Guide of the Perplexed*, 1:71. Analysis of this passage is to be found in H.A. Wolfson, *The Philosophy of the Kalam* (Cambridge, Mass., 1976), 82–86.

his approach may be a bit simplistic. The Basran Muʿtazilite school may indeed have been the theological system with which Jews in the East had the most contact. We may even speculate that this occurred through theological disputations (*majālis*) and polemical encounters. The Muʿtazilites were known to be particularly disputatious and they undoubtedly played an important role in inter-religious debates.[78] The need to respond to them in a theologically sophisticated manner may have led to absorption of their basic theological positions by Jews. An effective response would be one which addressed the opponent's own conceptual framework. The common ground thus created might then be internalized. Nonetheless, historical dynamics such as those suggested here could only be part of the story.

Maimonides, however, was only relating to "the argument regarding the notion of the unity of God and regarding what depends on this notion," that part of Muʿtazilite doctrine known as *tawḥīd*. Al-Baṣīr and his contemporaries certainly discussed this doctrine extensively. In Muʿtazilism, however, knowledge of God's unity leads to knowledge of God's justice (*ʿadl*), the second part of Muʿtazilite doctrine, as explained by ʿAbd al-Jabbār. It was within the framework of their discussion of God's justice that the Muʿtazilites developed their understanding of prophecy, the interactions between reason and revelation, and the nature of obligation and human intention. In al-Baṣīr's halakhic works, it was this aspect of Muʿtazilite teaching which was emphasized. I would like to suggest that the attraction Muʿtazilite Kalam held for a Yūsuf al-Baṣīr and a Samuel ben Ḥofni Gaon derived, at least in part, from its close affinity for norm coupled with its deep respect for the capabilities of human volition and rational reflection. It fit well with traditional Jewish views on free will and theodicy.[79] It provided the theological underpinnings for what we might call a "talmudist" type of ethic or spirituality, a characterization appropriate even for a Karaite such as Yūsuf al-Baṣīr. The halakhic writings of the Jewish Muʿtazilites reflect their theological concerns which in certain instances molded the legal decision-making process. These legal works were enriched and enlivened by their meta-halakhic dimension.

---

[78] Participation in such a debate was the stimulus behind the composition of al-Baṣīr's polemic against Islam. In this work, he is clearly responding to Muʿtazilite argumentation. Samuel ben Ḥofni countered Muʿtazilite arguments for the abrogation of the Torah in his *Kitāb naskh al-sharʿ* (Treatise on the Abrogation of the Law). In the ninth chapter of this work, he explicitly refutes the arguments of the Muʿtazilites Ibn Khallād and Ibn ʿAbdallāh al-Baṣrī. It is possible that he disputed with the latter in person. The relevant manuscript of this work is found in II Firk. 3024.

[79] See H.A. Wolfson, *Repercussions of the Kalam in Jewish Philosophy* (Cambridge, Mass., 1979), 199–233.

ISMĀʿĪLĪ THEOLOGY AND MAIMONIDES' PHILOSOPHY

Alfred L. Ivry

Of the many approaches which have been offered to interpreting the work of Moses Maimonides (1138–1204), little attention has been paid hitherto to the influence upon his thought of the Egyptian environment in which he lived from 1165 until his death.[1] That period saw the final collapse of the Fāṭimid empire, regnant in Egypt from 969, and its replacement by the Ayyūbid dynasty, led by the forceful Saladin. More importantly, for our purposes, as of 1171 the Shīʿism of the Fāṭimids was replaced by the Sunnī persuasion of their successors as the official state religion. This was more than a change of clerics and courts of law, it betokened endorsement of a different conceptualization of Islam, politically and theologically.

These changes are usually thought to have had little effect upon the Jewish community in Egypt at the time.[2] After an initial brief period of discrimination against minorities, Jews and Christians alike, Saladin reverted to the more tolerant ways of his Fāṭimid predecessors.[3] Maimonides, though

[1] Cf. now J. Drory, "The Early Decades of Ayyūbid Rule," and A. Ehrenkreutz, "Saladin's Egypt and Maimonides," in *Perspectives on Maimonides*, ed. J.L. Kraemer (Oxford, 1991), 295–302, 303–307 respectively.

[2] Cf. Drory and Ehrenkreutz, *Perspectives on Maimonides*, 301 and 307 respectively. It appears that Saladin's seizure of power did not directly affect most Egyptians either. The Fāṭimid rulers had increasingly become estranged from the people, and Ismāʿīlī dominance in religious life, apart from public ceremonial functions in Cairo, the capital city, had ceased by the middle of the twelfth century. Cf. Y. Lev, *State and Society in Fāṭimid Egypt* (Leiden, 1991), 133ff. L. Al-Imad, *The Fāṭimid Vizierate, 969–1172* (Berlin, 1990), 50ff. contends that the Fāṭimid state was run by a vizierate essentially separate from the imāms and theologians of the Ismāʿīlī religious establishment, known as the *daʿwa*.

[3] Following the Mameluke historian Al-Maqrīzī (1364–1442) and other late medieval sources, and the evidence of the Cairo Genizah, scholars have been unanimous in viewing the experience of the Jews under the Fāṭimids positively, with the exception of the reign of the caliph al-Ḥākim (996–1021). The assessment of J. Mann in the early part of this century still commands agreement; cf. his study, *The Jews in Egypt and in Palestine under the Fāṭimid Caliphs* (Oxford, 1920), 2:220. This positive experience continued under Ayyūbid rule, scholars agree, except for an initial period of repression under Saladin, for which cf. al-Maqrīzī's *Sulūk*, translated by R. Broadhurst as *A History of the Ayyūbid Sultans of Egypt* (Boston, 1980), 40. Saladin's behavior may be explained as part of his reaction to the *ancien régime* of the Fāṭimids, and to suspicions that those formerly associated with it were still loyal to it.

The various evaluations of Saladin's character, from that of idealist to pragmatist, have been evaluated now by R. Humphrey, *From Saladin to the Mongols* (Albany, 1977), 20ff. As Humphrey points out (p. 66), Saladin's restoration of Sunnī Islam went hand in hand with his restoration of political unity and his struggle against the Crusaders.

fully occupied as a physician to the court, and with his own busy private practice, was soon appointed *ra'īs al-yahūd,* "Head of the Jews," later called *nagid*, and served in that capacity for some two years initially, and for eight or nine more years, until his death, in a later tenure of office.[4]

We have a considerable body of responsa which Maimonides wrote in his capacity as the rabbinical and nominally political leader of Egyptian Jewry, whose authority was recognized beyond the confines of Egypt as well, and this material does not reveal any significant conflict between the *dhimmī* Jewish community in Egypt and its Muslim rulers. The relatively tolerant ambience which drew Maimonides to Egypt as a young man sustained him there throughout his life, as it was to sustain his descendants there after him.

Maimonides' good fortune in Egypt[5] has led most scholars to minimize the philosophical significance for him of the changes in political and religious orientation which Egypt underwent in his lifetime. Yet these changes were considerable, and may well have had an effect upon his writing and thought, as they surely did upon his life. In order to assess this possibility properly, it will help to sketch here the main lines of Shiʿī thought, and particularly that of the Ismāʿīlī branch of Shīʿism,[6] which prevailed in the Fāṭimid state for close to two hundred years.

Shīʿism as a political movement traces its origins to ʿAlī, the son-in-law of The Prophet; claiming for him and his descendants and followers sole legitimacy as Muḥammad's successors, and thus the right to lead the faithful. The Shīʿīs (or Shīʿa, to adopt the Arabic collective noun) viewed that succession dynastically, though based on divine will. Revelation, in the form of divine inspiration, was thought to continue after Muḥammad, up to a point. The Shīʿa split into different groups on this point, some—the Imāmiyya or "Twelvers"—believed that there were twelve divinely

---

[4] Cf. the comprehensive summary of Maimonides' life in Egypt, and of Egyptian Jewish history of that period, in M. Cohen, "Maimonides' Egypt," in *Moses Maimonides and His Time*, ed. E. Ormsby (Washington, D.C., 1989), 21–33, and see Cohen's bibliographical note on 33f.

[5] This good fortune did not come without a considerable degree of political astuteness on Maimonides' part. His assumption of leadership within the Jewish community, like the continued leadership of his descendants, has to be seen within the larger context of the Islamic politics of the time. Cf. M. Ben-Sasson, "Maimonides in Egypt: The First Stage," in *Maimonidean Studies*, ed. A. Hyman, 2 (1991): 3–30.

[6] Cf. the succinct summary of Shīʿī thought found now in W. Madelung, "Aspects of Ismāʿīlī Theology: The Prophetic Chain and the God Beyond Being," in *Ismāʿīlī Contributions to Islamic Culture*, ed. S.H. Nasr (Tehran, 1977), 53–65; reprinted in W. Madelung, *Religious Schools and Sects in Medieval Islam* (London, 1985). See too the more comprehensive studies of H. Halm, *Die Schia* (Darmstadt, 1988) and F. Daftary, *The Ismāʿīlīs: Their History and Doctrines*, (Cambridge, 1990).

inspired leaders or imāms after Muḥammad, while the Ismāʿīlīs believed in only seven such holy men.

An apocalyptic motif is pronounced in the doctrines of both groups, the faithful waiting for their last great imām to return as a mahdī (or *qāʾim*) to inaugurate a messianic age. Until that eagerly anticipated time, the Shīʿa were—and are—to be guided by the teachings of Muḥammad, ʿAlī and the imāms who followed him; the teachings interpreted, of course, by the religious leaders of succeeding generations, the ayatollahs and other clerics. Though they developed hermeneutic and legal institutions parallel to those of Sunnī Islam,[7] the Shīʿī emphasis upon the inerrant sanctity of their imāms and the salvific role of the mahdī encouraged the development of charismatic leaders[8] and of millenarian, revolutionary movements within the Islamic world, as witnessed recently.

There are, of course, social, political and economic reasons which can be adduced to account for the rise and growth of Shīʿī Islam. We need not be concerned with these factors here, except to mention that among those Shīʿism attracted were people prepared, for one reason or another, to embrace a vision of Islam that was broader[9] than that offered by the Sunnīs, with their textually restricted orientation. For the Sunnīs, the Qurʾān and *ḥadīth* were the last word in God's message to mankind, and all subsequent religious pronouncements had to refer back to them, in one way or another. Muḥammad's successors, both caliphs and *ʿulamāʾ*, were assigned a rank inferior to his, and were considered nominally only as custodians and interpreters of his—that is, really God's—message.

The Shīʿa, while highly respectful of both Muḥammad and the Qurʾān, placed them within what may be seen as a larger theological perspective. While they too considered the Prophet of Islam to be the last of the prophets, and the Qurʾān the last of revealed Scriptures, they believed that God had not ceased communicating with certain individuals, granting them unilateral authority over the believers. Consequently, these persons and their followers did not have to defer to the legal tradition or consensus of the (Sunnī) community, as embodied by the *ʿulamāʾ*, and could adopt their own law. Even this law would be abrogated with the coming of the mahdī,

---

[7] For the Ismāʿīlīs, the *Daʿāʾim al-islām* of Qāḍī al-Nuʿmān b. Muḥammad b. Ḥayyūn (d. 974) is the main legal authority. Cf. the analysis of W. Madelung, "The Sources of Ismāʿīlī Law," *JNES* 35 (1976): 29–40, esp. 32; reprinted in W. Madelung, *Religious Schools*.

[8] The charismatic dimension of Shīʿī authority has now been studied by H. Dabashi, *Authority in Islam* (New Brunswick and London, 1989), 95–120.

[9] Or that presented itself as broader. Cf. S.M. Stern, "Fāṭimid Propaganda Among Jews," in *Studies in Early Ismāʿīlism* (Leiden, 1983), 95.

the *sharīʿa* deemed no longer neccesary in the messianic age. Until then, a Shīʿī law was in fact to be obeyed, though religious inspiration was to come particularly from familiarity with the lives and deaths, teachings and sayings of their revered leaders.

The emphasis upon person and personality in Shīʿism, and its rejection of the Sunnī schools of law, led many to suspect the movement of antinomianism, an accusation the Ismāʿīlī theologians rejected.[10] Liberal attitudes towards other religions, bordering on what has been considered as interconfessionalism, are evident, however, in the writings of the Ikhwān al-Ṣafāʾ, a Basra-based group of tenth-century savants often identified with Ismāʿīlī thought.[11] Their detractors saw these writings as a cover for Ismāʿīlī antinomianism.

The sincerity of the Ismāʿīlī attachment to law was rendered suspect, furthermore, by the theologians' emphasis upon the esoteric dimension of revelation. The revealed law of the community given by The Prophet was thought to have a double level of meaning, the more interesting level not concerned with practical observance.

Ismāʿīlī authors of the tenth century—the most notable of whom were Abū ʾl-Ḥasan al-Nasafī (d. 943), Abū Ḥātim al-Rāzī (d. 933/34), Abū Yaʿqūb al-Sijistānī (d. c. 975) and Ḥāmid al-Dīn al-Kirmānī (d. c. 1021)—were distinguished by the incorporation of Neoplatonic teachings into their theosophical speculations.[12] For these theologians, the first being of the world, the Universal Intellect, is created from nothing by the will of God, and it is followed by the emanation of the two other universal hypostases,

---

[10] In 931 an antinomian manifesto was actually issued by a radical Shīʿī group, upon the appearance of a presumed mahdī, but the Fāṭimid authorities opposed this, considering the *sharīʿa* obligatory until the true messianic advent, the future *qiyāma*. Cf. H. Halm, *Die Schia*, 207, 210. The tenth-century Ismāʿīlī theologians supported this official view; cf., e.g., Abū Yaʿqūb al-Sijistānī's endorsement of Islam's religious *nomoi (al-afʿāl al-nāmūsiyya)*, together with the principle of future emendation of the law, in *Kitāb ithbāt al-nubūʾāt*, ed. A. Tamer (Beirut, 1966), 117–18. Here I wish to acknowledge the assistance of Paul Walker, who both critiqued an earlier draft of this paper and generously shared with me typescripts of the following two studies prior to their publication: "Early Philosophical Shīʿism: The Ismāʿīlī Neoplatonism of Abū Yaʿqūb al-Sijistānī," in *Cambridge Studies in Islamic Civilization* (Cambridge, 1993) and *The Wellsprings of Wisdom: A Study of Abū Yaʿqūb al-Sijistānī's "Kitāb Al-Yanābīʿ"* (Salt Lake City, 1994).

[11] Cf. Stern, "Fāṭimid Propaganda," 85f. While most scholars assume an Ismāʿīlī connection to the Ikhwān, I.R. Netton has cautioned against over-identification of the two groups, given the Ikhwān's lack of emphasis upon the institution of the imāmate. Cf. Netton, "Brotherhood versus Imāmate: Ikhwān al-Ṣafāʾ and the Ismāʿīlīs," *JSAI* 2 (1980): 253–62. See too Stern's view, n. 19 below.

[12] Al-Nasafī is credited with initiating this process, integrating the earlier mythical and theosophic Ismāʿīlī cosmogonies with the more abstract but more coherent Neoplatonic hypostases. Cf. Stern, "Ismāʿīlīs and Qarmatians," in *Studies in Early Ismāʿīlism*, 297 and Halm, *Die Schia*, 215f. See too al-Kirmānī, *Kitāb rāḥat al-ʿaql*, ed. M. Ghālib (Beirut, 1967), 205f., 295, 302.

World Soul and Nature, as first delineated by Plotinus.[13] The souls of individuals here on earth strive to unite with the Universal Soul from which they derive, and beyond it with the Universal Mind, the first created substance. In this attempt they are aided by the secret knowledge conveyed by the prophets and imāms who have successfully bridged the spiritual and physical worlds, and whose assistance is therefore sought.

Now, the medieval "Aristotelians" also had a Neoplatonically inspired emanationist theory, and they also believed in a Platonic-type return of the soul, or intellect, to its heavenly source. They saw this source as the universal Agent Intellect, the last of the separate intelligences of the heavens. Though sometimes the philosophers gave this universal hypostasis a traditional name, such as the Holy Spirit (*ruḥ al-quds*),[14] it was largely conceived of in strictly universal terms, divorced from particular associations with Islam or any other religious tradition.[15] The philosophers' theories of prophecy were similarly universal, with little accommodation to the Islamic experience. Their prophets were naturalized philosophers, possessed of extraordinary imaginative and intuitive powers.[16]

Falāsifa like al-Fārābī, Ibn Bājja, Ibn Rushd and even Ibn Sīnā are remarkably universal in their concerns, studiously avoiding for the most part the particularities of Islamic theology and dogma. The Sunnī theologians and lawyers, on the other hand, explicitly rejected the philosophers' methodology and constructs. It fell to the Ismāʿīlī theologians among the Shīʿa

---

[13] Cf., e.g., al-Sijistānī, *Kashf al-maḥjūb*, trans. H. Corbin, *Le Dévoilement des choses cachées* (Paris, 1988), 47–88, and see A. Ivry, "Islamic and Greek Influences in Maimonides' Philosophy," in *Maimonides and Philosophy*, ed. S. Pines and Y. Yovel (Dordrecht, 1986), 144.

[14] Cf., e.g., al-Fārābī, *Kitāb al-siyāsa al-madaniyya*, ed. F. Najjar (Beirut, 1964), 32. This term is used by the Ismāʿīlī theologians as well, who employ the emanative scheme with a more traditionally religious voluntarism. Cf. al-Sijistānī, *Kitāb ithbāt al-nubūʾāt*, 119. See too Judah Halevi's usage in the *Kuzari*, 1:87 and cf. I. Efros, "Some Aspects of Yehudah Halevi's Mysticism," in *Studies in Medieval Jewish Philosophy* (New York and London, 1974), 142. The philosophers may have borrowed the term from the Ismāʿīlī theologians.

[15] The philosophers' occasional attempts to interpret Islamic symbols and statements philosophically are suspiciously apologetic. Cf., for example, Avicenna's "On the Proof of Prophecies," trans. M. Marmura, in *Medieval Political Philosophy*, ed. R. Lerner and M. Mahdi (New York, 1963), 112–121.

[16] Cf. now H. Davidson, *Alfarabi, Avicenna, and Averroes, on Intellect* (Oxford, 1992), 58–62, 116–123. Rather than seeing the philosophers' prophets as "naturalized philosophers," D. Blumenthal has argued for viewing the philosophers' concept of prophecy, and much of their epistemology, within the context of an "intellectualist mysticism." Cf. Blumenthal, "Maimonides' Intellectualist Mysticism and the Superiority of the Prophecy of Moses," *SMC* 10 (1977): 51–68; reprinted in *Approaches to Judaism in Medieval Times*, ed. D. Blumenthal (Chico, CA, 1984), 27–51. As its Neoplatonic heritage renders much of medieval metaphysics susceptible to the designation of "intellectualist mysticism," the utility of this term becomes questionable; Blumenthal's point, however, is well taken.

to bring the philosophical and religious traditions together in Islamic culture, using their own theosophically inclined synthesis. Al-Kirmānī, the last of the great Ismāʿīlī theologians, even adopted the emanationist structure of the Aristotelian *falāsifa*, with its heavenly bodies and intelligences, conceived as following upon the emanation of the Neoplatonic triad of Intellect, Soul and Nature.[17] He stayed within the tradition of his Ismāʿīlī predecessors, however, in believing in a voluntaristic *creatio ex nihilo*, instead of the philosophers' eternal and necessary universe. He did, though, agree with the philosophers' view of a sempiternal universe, one eternal *a parte post*.[18]

Ismāʿīlī theology conceived of Islam within broad terms. There was a certain appreciation for all faiths, each of which was thought to have had a prophet who gave a law suitable for his community; with all the laws, i.e., all the religions, seen as valid expressions of the one universal truth.[19] The Ismāʿīlī religious philosophy had ecumenical colorations not only in its teachings on prophecy, but also in its reception of the mythical and theosophical suppositions of other religions. As regards Judaism, Ismāʿīlī authors (like their Sunnī counterparts) and particularly al-Kirmānī, were familiar with biblical and extra-biblical mystical themes. The visions of Ezekiel, the travails of ascending to *pardes*/paradise and the throne of God, the existence of angels and divinized men, the figure of the perfect man

---

[17] Cf. *Rāḥat al-ʿaql*, 212–48, and see S. Pines, "Nathanaël Ben al-Fayyūmī et la théologie ismaëlienne," *Revue d'Histoire Juive en Egypte* 1 (1947): 15.

[18] *Rāḥat al-ʿaql*, pp. 171–185, and see Ivry, "Islamic and Greek Influences," p. 145.

[19] Cf. Al-Sijistānī, *Kashf al-maḥjūb*, trans. H. Corbin, *Le Dévoilement des choses cachées*, 107, 111; *Ithbāt al-nubūʾāt*, 160–162 and Al-Kirmānī, *Rāḥat al-ʿaql*, 501. Compare, too, the contemporaneous dispassionate remarks on religion of al-Fārābī, in which he apparently utilizes Shīʿī terminology, in *Kitāb taḥsīl al-saʿādah*, ed. J. al-Yasin (Beirut, 1981), 90–94; trans. M. Mahdi, "The Attainment of Happiness," in *Alfarabi's Philosophy of Plato and Aristotle* (New York, 1962), 44–47; reprinted in *Medieval Political Philosophy*, 77–79. This may indicate al-Fārābī's Ismāʿīlī affinities, though one cannot press this point overly for lack of sufficient evidence. Moreover, unlike the Ismāʿīlī writers, al-Fārābī does not posit a progressive revelation culminating in the advent of the *qāʾim*; cf. al-Sijistānī, *Ithbāt al-nubūʾāt*, 166.

An attitude of religious toleration is unambiguously asserted in the writings of the Ikhwān al-Ṣafāʾ, excerpts of which are to be found in Stern, "Fāṭimid Propaganda," 85f. While B. Lewis, *The Origins of Ismāʿīlism* (Cambridge, 1940), 93–96, thought the Ismāʿīlīs in general sincerely shared this attitude, Stern cautioned against identifying the Ikhwān with the official Ismāʿīlī establishment. The *daʿwa* should not, in Stern's view, be seen as subscribing to the "humanistic and enlightened philosophy" of the Ikhwān. For Stern, the latter were Ismāʿīlīs but not representative of official Ismāʿīlī policy (p. 86).

While noting this distinction, it still seems quite plausible to assume that Ismāʿīlī society, like all others, had both liberal and conservative members, and that within the educated class proponents of a more universalistic understanding of religion such as advocated by the Ikhwān (and, to a lesser degree, by Ismāʿīlī theologians) would have been found. These are the types of individuals and ideas which could have attracted impressionable intellectuals of other faiths.

(known in Arabic as *al-insān al-kāmil*), all have echoes in Ismāʿīlī literature.[20] Al-Kirmānī apparently knew some Hebrew, and quoted biblical and rabbinic statements in that tongue.[21]

The familiarity of Ismāʿīlī authors with Judaism, and the sympathy of Shīʿī rulers for their Jewish subjects, gave rise to accusations of Jewish origins for Shīʿism.[22] This sympathy may well have had an ulterior purpose, however, for the Ismāʿīlīs are known to have made strenuous efforts in the tenth century to convert Jews.[23] Indeed, the Ismāʿīlīs were ardent evangelizers, sending their "missions" far and wide initially in pursuit of converts, of all kinds. The missionary, or *dāʿī*, had to be familiar with the teachings of other faiths to succeed in his mission, or *daʿwa*. Incorporating

---

[20] Much of this literature, and its echoes in Islamic literature of all sorts, is discussed now by D. Halperin, *The Faces of the Chariot: Early Jewish Responses to Ezekiel's Vision* (Tübingen, 1988), 467–90 and passim. Cf. too Halperin's forthcoming article, "Hekhalot and Miʿraj: Observations on the Heavenly Journey in Judaism and Islam," which the author kindly showed me.

Cf. Al-Sijistānī's use of the term "perfect person," *al-shakhs al-kāmil*, for the "perfect man," in *Kitāb al-yanābīʿ*, ed. H. Corbin, in *Trilogie ismaélienne* (Teheran and Paris, 1961), 50. The Sunnīs and Ṣūfīs also made frequent use of the *insān al-kāmil* designation for Muḥammad; for the Ṣūfīs, identification with him entailed annihilation of the self; cf. A. Schimmel, *Mystical Dimensions of Islam* (Chapel Hill, 1975), 216, 237.

[21] Cf. the citations brought by P. Kraus, "Hebräische und syrische Zitate in ismaʿilitischen Schriften," *Der Islam* 19 (1931): 243–63; and see S.M. Stern, "Fāṭimid Propaganda," 93f. Cf., too, S. Pines' discussion, "Shīʿite Terms and Conceptions in Judah Halevi's Kuzari," *JSAI* 2 (1980): 243f.

[22] Cf. B. Lewis, *Origins*, 67. See, too, H. Busse, *Chalif und Grosskönig* (Beirut, 1969), 493, following I. Friedländer, "Abdullah b. Sabā', der Begründer der Šiʿa und sein jüdischer Ursprung," *ZA* 23 (1909): 297–27; 24 (1910): 1–46. This "sympathy" of Shīʿīs for Jews (as well as for Christians) was already evident under the Buyid regime in tenth-century Baghdad; cf. J.L. Kraemer, *Humanism in the Renaissance of Islam* (Leiden, 1986), 79.

[23] Cf. Stern, "Fāṭimid Propaganda," 87–94. While this effort had some success, as Stern believes, others are of the opinion that there was no numerically significant conversion to Islam throughout the two hundred and twenty years of Fāṭimid reign; cf. Y. Lev, *State and Society*, 181, 194. In any event, the evangelical activity of the Ismāʿīlī missions seems to have been spent by the twelfth century, well before Maimonides' arrival in Egypt. This does not mean, however, that the ideology of the *daʿwa* changed, however much its actual practice did.

An interesting parallel case of disparity between the call for missionary activity and actual effort to implement the call may be found in Maimonides' own call to proselytization. This may be found in his interpretation of the third positive commandment in his *Sefer ha-miṣvot* (Book of Commandments), Arabic and Hebrew edition of J. Qafiḥ (Jerusalem, 1971), 59, trans. Ch. Chavel, *The Commandments* (London and New York, 1967), 4. Maimonides there says that the commandment to love God, which he sees as following necessarily from knowledge of Him, "reportedly" (*wa-qad qālū*) includes the obligation to "call all mankind" (*nadʿū al-nās ajmaʿu*) to worship and believe in Him. Maimonides does not give his sources for this interpretation of the commandment, which theoretically obliges Jews to proselytize. Whoever his Jewish antecedents may be, Maimonides has adopted here not only a tenet of Shīʿī (as well as Sunnī) ideology, but also of Ismāʿīlī practice, or rather non-practice. Maimonides' statement is thus of a piece with the rhetorical calls for conversion to the true faith which had become standard Ismāʿīlī practice. As we shall see, this is not the only example of Ismāʿīlī influence upon Maimonides' thought.

elements of the convert's traditions within the Ismāʿīlī creed was surely one way of encouraging acceptance of it; while treating Islam as but one (though the finest and last) expression of a universal truth, had to be another.

Whatever the degree of actual conversion to the Ismāʿīlī creed, some people would have been attracted to the theosophic coloration of the faith, with its dramatis personae and struggles, while others would have been drawn to its philosophical presentation. The latter type of person would have become familiar with the Ismāʿīlī theologians' penchant for allegorization and esoteric interpretation—the cultivation of a hermeneutic presentation which understood sacred texts and tales on both a literal and non-literal level. Each story, each law, the very words themselves, were understood as having a split level reality, or rather a double existence, to be treated both exoterically and esoterically.[24]

For Ismāʿīlī theologians, then, the exoteric level of pronouncements was not to be dismissed; the literal and apparent meaning of the laws and traditions were to be accepted and observed, even while their inner and secret meanings were to be sought after avidly.[25] If the Shīʿa in general were known as *ahl al-ẓāhir waʾl-bāṭin*, literally "the people of the apparent and the hidden" (or "outer and inner"), the Ismāʿīlīs gave their esotericism a particularly intellectualist and philosophical twist. Their secret teachings stemmed from both mystical and "scientific" sources—ultimately a combination of gnostic and monotheistic religious themes—together with a heavy dose of Neoplatonism. Their doctrines required instruction and training, with recognition of the different levels of achievement for those seeking the truth.

The ideal was to produce a philosopher and initiate in the mysteries of the faith, a person who could join spiritually and intellectually with the prophets, the imāms and the Perfect Man they represented, approaching God Himself. This person was, however, not to lose himself entirely in seclusion and meditation; he was not to abandon his political and social obligations completely, even if this meant functioning within a society antagonistic to Shīʿī goals.

To assist the believer to accommodate himself to an imperfect and often hostile world, the Shīʿa legitimized the practice of *taqiyya* (dissimulation).[26] To their critics, the Shīʿī hermeneutic was itself a form of *taqiyya*,

---

[24] Cf. W. Ivanow, *A Creed of the Fāṭimids* (Bombay, 1936), 3f., and see Ivry, "Islamic and Greek Influences," 143.

[25] Cf. Pines, "Shīʿite Terms," 242.

[26] Cf. Ivry, "Islamic and Greek Influences," p. 142, n. 13.

paying lip service only to what they considered the exoteric dimensions of their faith. Consequently, Shīʿī allegiance to the law and caliphate of Sunnī Islam was always suspect.

Saladin was himself antagonistic to the Shīʿa. Reportedly hating philosophers, heretics and "materialists" in general,[27] he was undoubtedly hostile to Ismāʿīlī theology in its philosophical and theosophical, as well as political, dimensions. One of his first military expeditions after consolidating his power in Egypt was to crush an Ismāʿīlī-inspired mahdī and his followers in the Yemen (though he would not stamp out Ismāʿīlism there entirely). Egypt saw no such popular Ismāʿīlī uprising after Saladin's victory,[28] and the appearance there of Ismāʿīlī lectures, books and pamphlets seems to have ceased.[29] Yet the effect of two hundred years of Ismāʿīlī teachings in Egypt cannot have been erased overnight. Presumably the people of Maimonides' generation, Jews and Christians as well as Muslims, would still have been familiar with Ismāʿīlī teachings, its literature was still available to them, and its practitioners and advocates were still known to them.

Such familiarity has already been demonstrated in the twelfth century *Bustān al-ʿuqūl* ("The Garden of the Knowing Ones") of the rather unknown Nethanel al-Fayyūmī, as well as in the *Kuzari* of the well-known and popular Judah Halevi.[30] As Shlomo Pines has said, Halevi's extensive acquaintance in Spain with Ismāʿīlī concepts indicates the wide reach of their ideas.[31] It is therefore reasonable to look for Ismāʿīlī influence, of

---

[27] Cf. M. Winter, "Saladin's Religious Personality, Policy, and Image," in *Perspectives on Maimonides*, 312.

[28] A few attempts at organizing resistance were quickly dispatched. Cf. al-Maqrīzī's *Sulūk*, trans. Broadhurst, 47, 50, 89; Ehrenkreutz, "Saladin's Egypt," 305.

[29] For a few years after Maimonides' arrival in Egypt until Saladin's accession to power, the public dissemination of Ismāʿīlī views, particularly in Cairo, would have continued. Cf. S.M. Stern, "Cairo as the Centre of the Ismāʿīlī Movement," in *Studies in Early Ismāʿīlism*, 236–42. After that, the ideas would have circulated orally in more clandestine fashion.

[30] Cf. S. Pines, "Nathanaël Ben Al-Fayyūmī et la théologie ismaëlienne," 5–22 and idem, "Shīʿite Terms," 165–219.

[31] "Shīʿite Terms," p. 218, n. 289. As Pines says there, "the impact of this theology must be considered as an important factor which must be taken into consideration in any account of the evolution of Jewish religious speculation within the Arabic civilization." The "wide reach" of Ismāʿīlī philosophical and theological concepts may be seen as extending vertically as well as horizontally. We may assume Ismāʿīlī teachings were known to Jewish thinkers in the Maghreb and Egypt from the beginnings of the Fāṭimid dynasty there in the tenth century. The Neoplatonic orientation of Jewish philosophers there as well as in Spain may well have come to them from Ismāʿīlī sources, or from the same sources which the Ismāʿīlīs used and with which they were identified, particularly the writings of the Ikhwān al-Ṣafāʾ. Pines noted already some time ago the possibility of Ismāʿīlī influence on Ibn Gabirol's doctrine of the will and word of God, in "La longue recension de la Théologie d'Aristote dans ses rapports avec la doctrine ismaélienne,"

both a negative and positive kind, in Maimonides' own work, written in the heart of the former Fāṭimid empire. In fact, traces of Ismāʿīlī thought have already been detected in the *Guide*,[32] and I now propose to widen the scope of this inquiry.[33]

In speaking of "negative" influences on Maimonides, I mean those teachings of Ismāʿīlism which he would have viewed negatively, and which I believe he attempted to counter in a variety of ways. Whether reacting positively or negatively, Maimonides makes practically no mention of Ismāʿīlī thought in the *Guide*, nor does he single out Ismāʿīlī authors for derision elsewhere; he responds to them, I shall attempt to show, more obliquely.[34] His style in this is not limited to Ismāʿīlī authors, there are a number of other writers with whom Maimonides is also engaged in a silent dialogue, as recent research has indicated.[35]

REI 22 (1954): 20; H. Ben-Shammai has now written about Ismāʿīlī distinctions in regard to prophecy which presumably entered into Saadya Gaon's treatment of the topic; see "On a Polemical Element in Saadya's Theory of Prophecy" (Hebrew), in *Shlomo Pines Jubilee Volume* (= *Jerusalem Studies in Jewish Thought*, vol. 7), ed. M. Idel et al., Pt. 1 (Jerusalem, 1988): 134ff., 142.

Working at the other end of the chronological spectrum of medieval Jewish philosophy, G. Vajda and D. Blumenthal have documented the continuation of Ismāʿīlī influence on the writings of Moroccan and Yemenite Jews in the late Middle Ages, and cf. now the summary of Y. Tzvi Langermann, "Cultural Contacts of the Jews of Yemen," in *Contacts Between Cultures*, ed. A. Harrak (Lewiston, Queenston, Lampeter, 1992), 282f.

32 Cf. S. Pines, "Shīʿite Terms," appendix vi, pp. 240–43. In the Introduction to his translation of the *Guide*, "The Philosophic Sources of The Guide of the Perplexed," (Chicago, 1963), xcv, ci, Pines already alludes to additional Neoplatonic sources besides those he mentions, and it seems clear he is referring to the Ismāʿīlī authors discussed in this article. Yet Pines apparently did not believe the influence of these sources on Maimonides' thought was particularly significant, nor that they seriously compromised his staunch "Spanish Aristotelianism" (p. cii.)—a depiction of Maimonides' philosophical orientation which is still dominant in the field.

33 This builds upon my earlier study of "Islamic and Greek Influences on Maimonides' Philosophy," 142–46; cf., too, my comments in "Neoplatonic Currents in Maimonides' Thought," in *Perspectives on Maimonides*, 138f.

34 Cf. *Guide* 2:25 (Pines, 328) for the one indirect mention of the Ismāʿīlīs Maimonides permits himself in that work; castigating them, however, for the kind of hermeneutic he is not in principle opposed to; cf. Pines, "Shīʿite Terms," p. 240.

Maimonides is dismissive of the Ikhwān al-Ṣafāʾ also, mentioning them disdainfully in passing in the famous letter to Samuel Ibn Tibbon in which he evaluates various philosophers. Cf. A. Marx, "Texts By and About Maimonides," *JQR*, n.s. 25 (1934–35): 379, found now in I. Shailat, *Letters and Essays of Moses Maimonides* (Hebrew), (Maʿaleh Adumim, 5748 [1987–88]), 2:552. The textual ambiguity surrounding Maimonides' evaluation of Joseph Ibn Ṣaddiq, whom Maimonides sees as influenced by the Ikhwān, has now been clarified; cf. S. Stroumsa, "Note on Maimonides' Attitude to Joseph Ibn Ṣaddiq" (Hebrew), in *Shlomo Pines Jubilee Volume* (Jerusalem, 1990), 2:33–38, esp. 37. Of course Maimonides' expressed negative attitude towards the Ikhwān does not preclude the possibility that he was more affected by their writings than he cared to acknowledge. Certainly their Neoplatonic teachings would have struck a sympathetic chord in him. Cf. Ivry, "Islamic and Greek Influences," 145f.

35 Cf. H. Kreisel's summary of the evidence for the influence on Maimonides of a number of

Yet Maimonides has a special reason to ignore the Ismāʿīlīs, though after their political downfall it would have been possible to be critical of them publicly, and he had good philosophical reasons to do so. The fact that he does not indulge this opportunity may indicate that he would rather not draw attention to Ismāʿīlī thought, and to his indebtedness to it, despite his disagreement with other aspects of their doctrine. For it appears that with all their differences, Maimonides and the Ismāʿīlī theologians had much in common. They and he were appealing to the same type of intellectual: a person steeped in the traditions and lore of his faith and searching for a religious philosophy with which it would be compatible, which would ultimately rationalize religious observance. Unlike the Sunnīs and the *falāsifa* proper, the Ismāʿīlīs had created a synthesis of the sort Maimonides was seeking,[36] a philosophical midrash that respected the original formulations of the faith while essentially transforming them.

It is al-Kirmānī, with his Aristotelian leanings, who is closest to Maimonides' own thought. The similarities noted between them are not insignificant.[37] They approach allegorization in the same terms, and wish to preserve the literal dimension of the text too; they both defend the religious law of their community, while treating it essentially in instrumentalist terms; they are both deeply concerned with the themes of creation and revelation, and advocate, at least exoterically (for Maimonides), belief in creation from nothing. They both subscribe to emanationist ideas, and view the ultimate goal of life in terms of an ascent to and a joining with the world of intelligible and eternal being.[38]

Maimonides' affinities with Ismāʿīlī notions are, however, limited. He does not endorse the structures of Neoplatonism, its hypostatic configurations, to which all the Ismāʿīlī theologians are loyal; nor does he dwell on the nature of the ascent of the soul and its participation in the supernal realm, favorite Ismāʿīlī topics. He is uncomfortable with Neoplatonic

---

Jewish authors, particularly Judah Halevi, in his study "Judah Halevi's Influence on Maimonides: A Preliminary Appraisal," *Maimonidean Studies* 2 (1991): 95–121. See, too, D.J. Lasker, "The Karaite Influence on Maimonides" (Hebrew), *Sefunot* 20 (1991): 145–61. While these scholars point to antecedent Jewish influences upon Maimonides' thought, S. Harvey has detected the influence in the *Guide* of the eleventh-century Muslim ethicist Miskawayh; see Harvey, "A New Islamic Source of the *Guide of the Perplexed*," *Maimonidean Studies* 2 (1991): 33–47.

[36] As W. Madelung says "Ismāʿīlī teaching from its beginnings offered a comprehensive and coherent view of God, the universe and the meaning of history . . . Ismāʿīlī doctrine did not borrow indiscriminately but rather selected what it found congenial to its basic convictions and amalgamated it into a coherent synthesis of its own"; see "Aspects of Ismāʿīlī Theology," 54.

[37] Cf. Pines, "Shīʿite Terms," 240–43 and Ivry, "Islamic and Greek Influences," 144.

[38] Maimonides shares many of these themes, particularly his view of Mosaic prophecy, with the other Ismāʿīlī theologians as well, particularly al-Sijistānī.

metaphysical assumptions, and with the mythical and theosophical representations of these assumptions such as are found in Ismāʿīlī authors.[39] As one who sees himself as an Aristotelian, Maimonides prefers sticking with the observed and observable phenomena of our universe. His quarrel in the *Guide* with the *mutakallimūn*, the Sunnī theologians of Islam, centers on the limits of acceptable speculation.[40] Maimonides makes it clear that he realizes his own bias is towards empirical science; past experience forming for him the basis for logical coherence and acceptable rational discourse.

Given Maimonides' bias, it should not surprise us to find him in *de facto* opposition—however undeclared—to many of the tenets of Ismāʿīlī speculation, both its philosophical and particularly its theosophical assumptions. That he was well aware of their teachings, I have no doubt. I have written elsewhere of the considerable presence of Neoplatonic themes in Maimonides' philosophy,[41] and much of the same literature which brought him that information would have contained peculiarly Ismāʿīlī teachings. As he was drawn to Neoplatonism despite himself, so he may well have been affected by certain aspects of Ismāʿīlī thought beyond those already adumbrated. A good deal of the *Guide of the Perplexed* should thus be seen as a response to, and implicit rebuttal of, various Ismāʿīlī themes and assertions, as well as a qualified, tacit endorsement of others.

The very introduction to the first part of the *Guide* emphasizes the multileveled nature of language, and alerts the reader to Maimonides' approval of an esotericism that does not disparage literalism.[42] This dual appreciation of language is the "other manner of explanation" to which Maimonides alludes regarding everything connected to prophecy; by contrast, he has no compunction deriding the literal meaning of midrashim. As Maimonides states, the person who is a *kāmil fāḍil* will not be hurt by this approach,[43] while an "ignorant rabbanite"[44] will not be upset either.

---

[39] Cf. S.M. Stern, "The Earliest Cosmological Doctrines of Ismāʿilism," in *Studies in Early Ismāʿīlism*, 3–29; H. Halm, *Kosmologie und Heilslehre der frühen Ismāʿīlīya* (Weisbaden, 1978), 28–66; I. Howard, "Shīʿī Theological Literature," in *Religion, Learning and Science in the ʿAbbasid Period*, ed. M.J.L. Young et al. (Cambridge, 1990), 16–32. See, too, al-Kirmānī's relating of the traditional Neoplatonic hypostases to Muḥammad and other Ismāʿīlī symbols and his adaptation of throne imagery to the motions of the spheres, in *Rāḥat al-ʿaql*, 205f., 295, 302.

[40] Cf. *Guide* 1:73, tenth premise, 206–12, and see Ivry, "Maimonides on Possibility," in *Mystics, Philosophers, and Politicians*, ed. J. Reinharz et al. (Durham, 1982), 67–84.

[41] Cf. "Neoplatonic Currents," 127–39.

[42] Cf. Pines, *Guide*, 10.

[43] Cf. *Dalālat al-ḥāʾirīn*, ed. S. Munk, revised I. Joel (Jerusalem, 1929), p. 6, line 1.

[44] *Dalālat al-ḥāʾirīn*, p. 5, line 27: *jāhil min jumhūr al-rabbānīyīn*, literally, with Pines, 10, "an ignoramus among the multitude of Rabbanites."

Now, *kāmil fāḍil*, translated by Pines as "perfect man of virtue," is literally a "perfect, excellent" person, i.e., one accomplished in all the virtues, pointedly broader in scope than only those normally endorsed by the rabbinic tradition. Significantly too, the *kāmil fāḍil* is a term closely akin to *al-insān al-kāmil*, the term used throughout Shīʿī and Ṣūfī literature to express the ideal person.[45] The many excellences of this person extend beyond the purely legalistic, as well as beyond the purely, or conventionally Aristotelian, rational virtues. This person combines philosophical and extra-philosophical virtues, and is closer theoretically to an Ismāʿīlī model than a Ṣūfī one.[46] Moreover, like the term, so the hermeneutical technique being endorsed is that for which the Ismāʿīlīs, and all Shīʿīs, were known.

It is not surprising that Samuel Ibn Tibbon, the Hebrew translator of the *Guide*, did not render this term completely successfully. He translated *kāmil fāḍil* as *shalem ḥashuv*, a "perfect, important" (or possibly "distinguished") person.[47] Samuel, after all, was neither familiar with Ismāʿīlī literature nor advised by Maimonides to familiarize himself with it.

Maimonides concludes his introduction to the first part of the *Guide* with an explanation of no less than seven reasons for a written work to contain contradictory or contrary statements.[48] While all these reasons may well refer to his own composition, Maimonides explicitly acknowledges employing two types of what today we may call "misstatements" in the *Guide*: one (the fifth cause) for reasons of pedagogy, where the reader is not ready yet to receive the exact truth; and the other (the seventh cause) for prudential reasons, which require the use of contradictory premises. The latter is necessary, Maimonides says, in "very obscure matters" (*umūr ghāmida jiddan*),[49] where the masses, *al-jumhūr*, must in no way be aware of the contradiction.

Now, the "very obscure" and most guarded secrets of the Jewish tradition, according to Maimonides, which he yet feels compelled to discuss in the *Guide*, are its teachings concerning creation and revelation, *maʿasei bereshit* and *maʿasei merkavah*. If Genesis 1 is the *locus classicus* for the

---

45 Cf. above, n. 20.

46 In Jewish terms, this person would be a pietistically inclined philosopher, a type which did not as yet exist within Judaism, and one which Maimonides was in the process of developing and personifying.

47 *Sefer moreh ha-nevukhim*, ed. Y. Even Shmuel (Jerusalem, 1981), 9. Judah al-Ḥarizi's translation is more sucessful. He rendered *kāmil fāḍil* as *ish shalem ve-ḥasid*, "a perfect and pious man"; see Scheyer's edition of al-Ḥarizi's translation (Warsaw, 1904), 15.

48 Pines, 17; *Dalālat al-hāʾirīn*, p. 11, line 7.

49 *Dalālat al-hāʾirīn*, p. 12, line 7, ambiguously translated by Ibn Tibbon as *ʿinyanim ʿamuqim*; see *Moreh ha-nevukhim*, ed. Even Shmuel, 16.

former theme, Exodus 19 and Ezekiel 1 are the prime sources for the latter. Hence we must be extra alert, Maimonides is telling us in his introduction, to his treatment of these issues and sources in the *Guide*, and to expect him to be employing stratagems of one sort or another to dissemble his true teaching, lest he see himself traduced by the ignorant. Accordingly, we find Maimonides here giving a full rationale for endorsing the strategy of *taqiyya*, dissimulation, that technique with which the Ismāʿīlīs, as all the Shīʿa, were identified. The introduction of the *Guide* can thus be seen as approving of Ismāʿīlī methodology, never before so explicitly presented in Jewish thought.

Yet, as stated before, Maimonides is not sympathetic to every Ismāʿīlī theme and certainly not to many of their particular teachings and essential religious beliefs. Moreover, many of their philosophical approaches and doctrines are found as well in other philosophers. Correspondences between Maimonides' writing and that of Ismāʿīlī authors do not, therefore, necessarily signify a meaningful relationship between the two.

Thus, for example, the basic technique of allegorization and the problem of divine attributes have a long philosophical history beginning with Philo. They need not be identified particularly with Ismāʿīlī methodology, nor need Maimonides have learned the lesson of philosophical prudence and circumspect writing from the Ismāʿīlīs; it was a lesson communicated already by Socrates and Plato at the beginning of the philosophical tradition and reinforced all too frequently in the medieval Muslim and Jewish (as later Christian) experience. Besides, Maimonides' earlier life in Spain and Morocco would have taught him the virtue of discretion.

Granting all the above-mentioned facts, there yet remain too many resemblances between Maimonides' writing and those of the Ismāʿīlī theologians who preceded him to dismiss the possibility of identifying this group as one whose ideas and approaches particularly helped shape Maimonides' thought. He may be seen as engaged in a dialectical relationship with Ismāʿīlī thought, influenced by it even when he rejects it.

An example of this relationship may be discerned in Maimonides' treatment of Adam, the first man of creation. This comes in the second chapter of Part One of the *Guide*, which at first appears to be out of place. The first chapter and those which follow the second are devoted, as is known, to a sustained critique of biblical terms and passages which depict God in corporeal terms. Maimonides is determined to root out anthropomorphic beliefs—beliefs which obviously had Jewish adherents.[50]

---

[50] It is worth noting that belief in a personal God, a being possessed of discrete actions and

Those who read the Bible literally would have been strengthened in their approach by a body of mystical literature known from early rabbinic times. The *heikhalot* and *merkavah* texts in this widely dispersed tradition not only elevate select human beings to angelic status, having them mingle in the heavens, they even present images of God in human form, as a divine *anthropos*.[51] Accordingly, Maimonides may be seen, in much of the first part of the *Guide*, and elsewhere, as engaged in a prolonged struggle not merely or even essentially with a primitive Jewish fundamentalism, but rather with a highly imaginative theosophy. This theosophical approach, while nourished by earlier Jewish sources, could well have been encouraged by certain parallel religious formulations in Shīʿī literature, particularly those which depict heavenly beings in both abstract and personal fashion, all considered as intermediaries between God and man.[52]

It may well be that Maimonides is inveighing against a traditional but growing religious fashion in his day, one current among Jews and Muslims alike; a fashion that was temporarily stalled with the political defeat of the Fāṭimids and with the success of Maimonides' own efforts, but which, in the form of Kabbalah and later Persian theosophy, was not to be denied much longer in either faith.

Maimonides' discussion of Adam in the Garden of Eden in *Guide* 1:2 is not, therefore, as anomolous as first it seems, it being part of his war against anthropomorphic and theosophical depictions of God and the celestial realm. In his first chapter, Maimonides had asserted the existence of an intellectual conjunction between man and God, both having intellect as their essence. Adam, as the first man, is then described in Chapter Two

---

emotions, is not logically distinct from belief in a corporeal God, assuming that the divine matter of such a being would be, of necessity, incorruptible. Whether as a material or immaterial being, such a deity would be a complex being with distinct attributes, and hence for Maimonides an inappropriate model of God's oneness. Maimonides is fearless in attacking the anthropomorphists, but much more guarded in transmitting his critique of a personal deity. The latter view is part of the very essence of traditional Judaism and Maimonides cannot openly criticize it, or even dispense with it, particularly in his rabbinic writings.

[51] Cf. G. Scholem, *Jewish Gnosticism, Merkabah Mysticism, and Talmudic Tradition* (New York, 1960), 36, 43 and passim; J. Charlesworth, "The Portrayal of the Righteous as an Angel," in *Ideal Figures in Ancient Judaism*, ed. J. Collins and G. Nicklesburg (Chico, CA, 1980), 135–37; and the works of D. Halperin, above, n. 20. For the influence of these traditions on Judah Halevi see E. Wolfson, "Merkavah Traditions in Philosophical Garb: Judah Halevi Reconsidered," *PAAJR* 57 (1990–91): 199–241.

[52] The earliest articulations of Shīʿī theology in the eighth century conceived of God in corporeal terms, but later expositions—possibly under Muʿtazilite influence—rejected this approach. However, the mythical personifications of God's will, *kūnī* and *qadar*, and other representations of the divine presence, retained their place. See, e.g., al-Sijistānī, *Kitāb al-yanābīʿ*, ed. Corbin, 17–19; French translation, 37–39. Cf., too, H. Halm, *Kosmologie*, 53–66; I. Howard, "Shiʿī Theological Literature," 20ff.; and Daftary, *The Ismāʿīlīs*, 141f.

as having been created with a perfect intellect, being created, as we are told in Genesis, "in the image of God."

Maimonides changes gears at this point rather dramatically, to address a philosophical conundrum: how a perfectly intelligent person such as Adam, the very model of intelligent perfection, could have made the mistake of disobeying his creator's wishes. Maimonides, as is known, resolves this problem with a bold, ultimately Aristotelian distinction between Adam's theoretical and practical intellects: the former perfect, the other neglected, presumably unnecessary for Adam in the original scheme of creation.

As scholars have pointed out,[53] Maimonides may well be indicating to us in this interpretation of the Garden of Eden story his own ranking and evaluation of the theoretical and practical virtues, and of the contemplative versus political life. I would like to suggest that Maimonides is making an additional point as well, brought home in the unusual style, structure and substance of his remarks. Maimonides, it should be noticed, treats this story realistically, as a historic occurrence, however odd that appears. He discusses Adam in strictly human terms, though he obviously intends to make a universal statement about the human condition after the fall. It is Adam as a prototypical human being, however, with which Maimonides is exclusively concerned.

Now, the Adam legend has a long history in Jewish, Christian and Muslim tradition, and it was conflated with extra-biblical, often gnostic themes already in late antiquity.[54] These traditions identify Adam as a being of angelic and even cosmic significance. This Adam, Adam I, is viewed as a creative force in the heavens, being the first and prime expression of God's creation. Similar depictions of Adam—though displaced occasionally by Muḥammad—are also found in Ismāʿīlī literature, which tends to use biblical characters freely in this theosophical manner.[55] Bridging the eternal and created spheres of being, Adam is placed in Shīʿī thought at

---

[53] Cf. L. Berman, "Maimonides on the Fall of Man," *AJSR* 5 (1980): 1–15; S. Klein-Braslavy, *Maimonides' Interpretation of the Stories on Adam in Genesis* (Hebrew) (Jerusalem, 1986), passim. Additional studies of Maimonides' treatment of this theme are cited by S. Harvey, "A New Islamic Source of the *Guide of the Perplexed*," 44.

[54] Cf. *EJ* 1:238–40.

[55] Compare the composite portrait of a universal Adam (*adam al-awwal al-kullī*) also known as "Spiritual Adam," (*adam rūḥānī*) in H. Corbin, *Cyclical Time and Ismāʿīlī Gnosis* (London, 1983), 39, 43–47, 78–80. The biblical Adam discussed here is considered to be a "partial Adam" (*adam juzʾī*), i.e. an instantiation of a figure which recurs in each historical cycle. For other depictions of Adam, cf. W. Ivanow, *Studies in Early Persian Ismāʿīlism* (Bombay, 1955), 146, and see the compendium of Ikhwān thought known as *Al-risāla al-jāmiʿa*, ed. M. Ghālib (Beirut, 1974), 65–70. The tale of Adam conveys (p. 65) a knowledge *ghāmidh daqīq*, "obscure and subtle." See

the head of a chain of select and immortal *nuṭaqāʾ* (sing. *nāṭiq*), "enunciators" through whom the word of God was brought to mankind at different times.[56] Judah Halevi, Pines has shown, freely borrowed Ismāʿīlī formulations of this idea and applied them to the Jewish tradition.[57]

In view of all this it seems highly plausible that Maimonides chose to depict Adam in the way he did in order to dethrone him and dismiss him from theosophical speculation. In so doing, Maimonides gave discreet notice to his *kāmil fāḍil* reader that for all his approval of Ismāʿīlī techniques, and even of some of their teachings, he parted ways with them theologically. He could not accept the Ismāʿīlī elevation of human beings to angelic status. His Adam exists to explain the human condition, and has no other part in a cosmic or supernatural drama.

Maimonides' refusal either to allegorize biblical figures or turn them into angelic beings is seen also in his treatment of the patriarchs; this has been shown by Alexander Altmann in his study of the ladder of ascension theme, with its motif of heavenly ascent and journeys, in Islamic and Jewish sources.[58] This is a theme found frequently as well in Ismāʿīlī literature, both in the legends surrounding Muḥammad's night journey, the occultation of the mahdī, and the upward journey of the seeker of truth.[59] This fits with the general Shīʿī view of the prophets and imāms as having saintly, angelic status.

Maimonides' opposition to this belief can be seen in his treatment of

---

too Pines, "Shīʿite Terms," 174, quoting *Al-risāla al-jāmiʿa's* likening of Adam to the Universal Intellect.

In the material assembled by Corbin, Adam is introduced into the cosmic scene at the level of the third emanated hypostasis, but "falls" to that of the tenth—reflecting in this manner medieval versions of both Neoplatonic and Aristotelian cosmogonies; see *Cyclical Time*, 39–40.

[56] Cf. Halm, *Kosmologie*, 103; *Die Schia*, 202f. In Ṣūfī and Shīʿī thought a primordial Muḥammad is often given precedence over the celestial Adam, this Muḥammad being the first created being and recipient of the divine light (Qur'ān 24:35). This light, clearly a version of the logos theme, is then passed on to Adam and those who come after him, down to the Imām, "the light of heaven and earth." Cf. D.M. Donaldson, *The Shīʿite Religion* (London, 1933), 137–40, 340; Schimmel, *Mystical Dimensions*, 214–37; and U. Rubin, "Pre-Existence and Light: Aspects of the Concept of Nūr Muḥammad," *IOS* 5 (1975): 62–117.

[57] Cf. "Shīʿite Terms," 170, and see *Kuzari* 1:47, 1:95. The similarity between Halevi's treatment of Adam and that of Ismāʿīlī thinkers was already noted by D. Kaufmann, *Geschichte der Attributenlehre* (Gotha, 1877; reprinted Amsterdam, 1967), p. 177, n. 136.

[58] Cf. Altmann, "The Ladder of Ascension," in *Studies in Mysticism and Religion Presented to Gershom G. Scholem* (Jerusalem, 1967), 1–32, and esp. p. 17; reprinted in Altmann, *Studies in Religious Philosophy and Mysticism* (Ithaca and London, 1969), 41–72, esp. p. 58.

[59] Belief in the supernatural, quasi-angelic status of Muḥammad is rooted in such Qur'ānic passages as Sura 17 (the Night Journey) and 24:35 (the light verse). As such, this belief is not limited to Ismāʿīlī or Shīʿī circles. Together with the Ṣūfīs, however, the Shīʿa expanded upon this theme and elevated the very personal souls of other humans as well into the celestial plane.

prophecy along natural lines, a subject to which he devotes much attention in the *Guide* and elsewhere. If like Shīʿī authors he distinguishes between classes of prophets and levels of perfection,[60] he differs with them in giving a "scientific" reason for each type of prophecy. The science employed is that of medieval psychology, with the imaginative and rational faculties, abetted by a powerful intuition, invoked to explain the peculiar gifts of the prophet.[61]

Maimonides' discussion of this experience, being naturalistic, is implicitly universal in scope. He follows al-Fārābī and Ibn Sīnā in discussing a phenomenon which he knows is not limited, theoretically at least, to the Jewish people. He does not, as a philosopher, wish to claim for the Hebrew prophets in general any unique or innate special faculties, as did Judah Halevi, and for that matter Ismāʿīlī writers as well. The latter group, as remarked, had an ecumenical view of prophecy, one which embraced the prophets of Judaism and of other religions alongside the Prophet of Islam; according all a special status which allowed them to receive a unique form of revelation.[62]

Now, while Maimonides as a philosopher could not bring himself to accept the metaphysical assumptions of Halevi, neither could he, as a Jew, accept the relativization and consequent attenuation of Judaism which Ismāʿīlī teachings proferred. He thus draws a clear line between the prophecy of all other prophets, certainly the non-biblical but also the biblical prophets—that is, a line between prophecy in general, prophecy as a universal and explicable phenomenon—and the prophecy of Moses. He asserts that Moses had a unique experience, that he was a unique person, and that consequently claims for the superiority and eternal validity of the Torah, Mosaic legislation, are justified.[63]

Maimonides had made this point earlier in his career, in his *Commen-*

---

[60] As noted by Blumenthal, "Maimonides' Intellectualist Mysticism," 38.

[61] Cf. *Guide* 2:32–48, particularly chapters 38 and 45. See now J. Macy, "Prophecy in Al-Fārābī and Maimonides: The Imaginative and Rational Faculties," in *Maimonides and Philosophy*, 195f.

[62] Al-Sijistānī, for example, speaks of a fourth kind of soul which all prophets have, a "sacred soul" (*al-nafs al-qudsiyya*); see *Ithbāt al-nubūʾāt*, 15–23. This does not, however, preclude belief, for Ismāʿīlī writers, in the special cosmic and historic significance of the Prophet of Islam and the anticipated *mahdī* or *qāʾim*.

[63] Cf. *Guide* 2:35, 39. Maimonides' substantive distinction between the prophecy of Moses and that of other prophets is somewhat analogous to the distinction between *ilhām* and *waḥy* drawn by Judah Halevi and before him by Saadya Gaon, under Ismāʿīlī influences. Whereas *ilhām* is considered a more general form of divine inspiration, *waḥy* is reserved for the inspiration which only prophets receive; see H. Ben-Shammai, "On a Polemical Element in Saadya's Theory of Prophecy," 128–35 and I. Efros, "Some Aspects of Yehuda Halevi's Mysticism," 149f.

tary on Mishnah Sanhedrin, chapter 10 (*Pereq Ḥeleq*, Seventh Principle), where he enunciated thirteen principles of the Jewish faith. He repeated the point in the first book of his Code of Jewish law, the *Mishneh Torah*, where he speaks of the principles of the Torah.[64] His statement in the *Commentary on the Mishnah* is the more radical, for there he claims explicitly that Moses is more dear to God than any other mortal that ever lived or that ever would live and that Moses actually attained the ranks of the angels, tearing down all physical barriers, dispensing with all but his intellectual faculty, having become pure intellect.[65]

Interestingly, Maimonides stops himself at this point in his *Commentary on the Mishnah*, writing that he had intended to say much more on this topic, but that he would have had to enter into an extended discussion of difficult biblical passages and of difficult issues, including the existence and ranks of angels, depictions of angels and of the Creator Himself, and even of *shiʿur qomah*, the mystics' mythically proportioned embodiment of divine glory.[66] Maimonides struck the sentence referring to *shiʿur qomah* from later recensions of the *Commentary on the Mishnah*, and it does not appear in the printed editions of the text.[67] As we know from his correspondence,[68] his attitude towards this mythical figure became decidely negative.

It appears that the entire discussion of spiritual forms, of heavenly and cosmic beings, the entire topic of angelology, posed a problem for Maimonides. In a (presumably) later section of the *Commentary on the Mishnah*, in the seventh chapter of his introduction to the Treatise *Avot*,[69] he already qualifies his earlier identification of Moses as pure intellect. There he says that Moses' intellect was inseparable from his body as long as he lived, and that this prevented him from having the full cognition of the divine which he sought.

---

[64] Cf. *Sefer ha-maddaʿ, hilkhot yesodei ha-torah* ("Book of Knowledge, Principles of the Torah"), 7:6.

[65] See Arabic text and Hebrew translation in *Mishnah ʿim peirush rabbeinu mosheh ben maimon: seder nezikin*, ed. J. Qafiḥ (Jerusalem, 1964), 212–14.

[66] Cf. A. Altmann, "Moses Narboni's Epistle on Shiʿur Qomah," in *Jewish Medieval and Renaissance Studies*, ed. A. Altmann (Cambridge, MA, 1967), 227–32. For the description and discussion of *shiʿur qomah*, see the literature cited above, n. 51, and particularly Wolfson, "Merkavah Traditions," 201, 212.

[67] Cf. S. Lieberman's discussion of Maimonides' remarks concerning *shiʿur qomah*, in the *Commentary on the Mishnah* and elsewhere, and his textual analysis of the *Commentary* sources in his Hebrew appendix to G. Scholem, *Jewish Gnosticism*, p. 124.

[68] See now J. Blau ed., *Maimonides' Responsa* (Hebrew) (Jerusalem, 1989), 1:200f. And see Altmann, "Moses Narboni's Epistle," 231.

[69] Cf. *Mishnah ʿim peirush rabbeinu mosheh ben maimon: seder nezikin*, ed. Qafiḥ, 395.

After interrupting his initial *Sanhedrin* commentary on Moses' nature, Maimonides promises to treat the subject more fully in a future book on midrash or one on prophecy. He never wrote either book, and the *Guide* is apparently intended to supply the lack.[70] In *Guide* 2:35, however, Maimonides merely refers to his earlier treatments of the theme, and then only to the phenomenological differences between Moses' prophetic experience and that of the other Hebrew prophets. Moses' prophecy is supposedly distinctive in its requiring him to enter a special dream or visionary state, by being unmediated, received directly from God in clear terms, in its being received with equanimity, and in its being continually operative.

Moreover, Maimonides claims now[71] that he had "proved" (*istadalla*) his assertions concerning this prophecy in the earlier works, which is not at all the case. The claims of a theosophic sort for Moses' uniqueness which are given only in his *Commentary* on *Sanhedrin* are not discussed again in the *Guide*, though as we shall see Maimonides returns to them covertly. He has apparently chosen to obscure his teachings on Moses' nature in the *Guide*, offering them dogmatically on the one hand, and cryptically, if not disingenuously, on the other. In sum, Maimonides adopts the hermeneutic he announced in the opening of the *Guide* for this most sensitive and politically explosive tenet of Judaism.

Why has Maimonides chosen to be reticent regarding an issue on which he had previously spoken so boldly? Has he realized that merely dogmatic utterances will not do in a work ostensibly devoted to philosophical explanation, to reasoned argument and to natural, verifiable phenomena? Can he make the claims concerning Moses' prophecy in the *Guide* which he made in the *Commentary on the Mishnah* without yielding to the *mutakallimūn*, the Sunnī theologians of Islam, on logical grounds, or to the Ismā'īlīs on substantive grounds? For what difference is there between his claims for the supernatural, angelic intellect of a Moses, and Ismā'īlī claims of a similar sort, for Moses too, but also for Muḥammad and all other historical founders and leaders of religions?

Of course, it is true that Moses had long since been idealized, sanctified and even quasi-divinized, i.e., angelicized, in various Jewish circles,[72] and

---

[70] In his *Mishneh Torah*, written between the *Commentary on the Mishnah* and the *Guide*, Maimonides again expresses himself somewhat ambiguously regarding the existence of angels and spiritual beings of all kinds. His very first statement on the issue, in *Sefer ha-madda', hilkhot yesodei ha-torah* 2:4, emphasizes that the visions of angels which the prophets experienced are not to be taken literally, being parables; but then at 2:8, he apparently affirms the literal existence of such spiritual forms.

[71] Pines, 367; *Dalālat al-ḥā'irīn*, p. 259, line 4.

[72] Ex. 7:1 and Deut. 33:1 were seen in antiquity as sanctioning the view of Moses as a divine,

that Muslims other than the Ismāʿīlīs had followed suit, putting Moses alongside Muḥammad in a saintly and cosmic pantheon of sorts. Yet it is the particular distinction of Ismāʿīlī literature to have combined this theosophic view of Moses and prophecy with a philosophical scheme, giving it a certain rational appearance and presumable philosophical legitimacy.[73]

That Maimonides is aware of parallel Ismāʿīlī claims for other prophets may be inferred from the fact that in *Guide* 2:39 Maimonides refers to Moses' vocation as a *daʿwa*, using the standard Shīʿī and Ismāʿīlī term, normally translated as "mission," for all such callings.[74] Though Maimonides again asserts that Moses' *daʿwa* is *sui generis*, the term still places Moses within the conceptual framework of an Ismāʿīlī *dāʿī*. Maimonides may also be seen as implicitly rejecting Ismāʿīlī and Muslim claims to the superiority of their prophet and faith in his statement that no one prior to Moses, from Adam onwards, had such a *daʿwa* as his, nor did "any one of our prophets" subsequently—this being a principle of the Torah, that Moses' Torah or revelation is unique.

While this statement, like the entire *Guide*, is addressed to a Jewish reader, the point here is anti-Muslim, and particularly anti-Ismāʿīlī. For the Ismāʿīlīs, as stated, had placed Moses within a continuum of great prophets, his mission regarded as but one in a series of successive revelations,

---

or at least super-human figure. Hellenistic concepts of royalty as well as Plato's vision of the philosopher-king influenced the image of Moses in early post-biblical times, as can be seen in Philo's *Life of Moses*. Cf. W. Meeks, "Moses as God and King," in *Religions in Antiquity*, ed. J. Neusner (Leiden, 1970), 354–71. Some of the sources Meeks describes (p. 366) have Moses returning, like Enoch, at the end of time, presumably in occultation in the interim. Cf. too, D. Halperin, *The Faces of the Chariot*, 292, for Moses' ascent to heaven and his struggles there to receive the Torah. In an appendix (467–490) Halperin discusses the reflections of this *merkavah* tradition in Islamic literature. Maimonides would thus have been acutely aware of the popular consensus of belief in the super-human, even angelic stature of Moses in both the Jewish and Muslim traditions, and as we have seen, he hesitates over this issue in his earlier compositions. At the end of his description of Moses' prophecy in the *Mishneh Torah, Hilkhot yesodei ha-torah* 7:6, he says that Moses' permanent state of conjunction with the divine rendered him "sanctified as the angels" (*venitqadesh ka-malʾakhim*).

[73] Cf., for example, al-Sijistānī's remarks on the prophets' interaction with angels, their being inspired by the Universal Intellect, understood as the "holy spirit," *Kitāb ithbāt al-nubūʾāt,* 119, 144; see, too, al-Kirmānī, *Rāḥat al-ʿaql*, 489, for the depiction of the imām as the place of the "divine light," *nūr allah.*

[74] Though *daʿwa* is a standard Arabic term utilized by Sunnīs and Shīʿīs alike to designate the calling of a prophet, it had assumed a specific Ismāʿīlī denotation in Egypt by Maimonides' time. *Daʿwa* now frequently referred to the political and institutional role of the *dāʿī*, as well as to his spiritual calling. Pines, following Samuel Ibn Tibbon's use of *qeriʾah* perhaps, translates *daʿwa* (p. 378) as "call," thereby obscuring the Shīʿī/Ismāʿīlī connotation of the term. In this, Pines follows S. Munk's earlier French choice of *appel*; see *Le guide des égarés* (Paris, 1858), 2:301. Judah al-Ḥarizi, for his part, translated *daʿwa* here (which he has as *Guide* 2:40) as *haskamah* (ed. Scheyer, 199), thoroughly misunderstanding it.

each one supposedly revealing more of God's will to mankind than the previous ones.[75] This is the view which Maimonides forcefully denies. As he says in *Guide* 2:35, Moses' "apprehension" (*idrāk*/*hasagah*), his prophetic experience, is not only different from that of the prophets of "other religious communities,"[76] it is completely different as well from the experience of all other biblical personages; i.e., from all others of the House of Israel, or Jews. In the context of Maimonides' circumstances, his mention of "other religious communities" is clearly an allusion to Islam, even as his remark in *Guide* 2:39 on Moses' unique *daʿwa* is pointedly, if discreetly, anti-Ismāʿīlī. It would have been impolitic for Maimonides to be more explicit in his criticism of Islam, even in its Ismāʿīlī version, and hence the examples he brings of laws indicative of inferior religions do not particularly point to Islam.[77]

As Maimonides reiterates, the uniqueness of Moses' *daʿwa* entails the uniqueness of Mosaic law, and he devotes much effort later in the *Guide* to establish the latter assertion. Indeed, it is the perfection of the law which supplies whatever "proof" Maimonides can muster for the superiority of Moses' prophecy, rather than the other way around. Yet these proofs are not philosophically compelling, dealing as they do with relative matters of conventional and non-demonstrable premises, and the addressee of the *Guide* would not have been persuaded by them on philosophical grounds alone. He might, however, have been persuaded by Maimonides' assertions that the counter-claims of the Ismāʿīlīs (as well as of all other Muslim groups) are not true, and that the laws of Judaism are not only not inferior to those of Islam, and not merely equal to those of the *sharīʿa*, but indeed superior to them. This addressee, it should be recognized, would not have been attracted to an Islam presented dogmatically, but he might well have been tempted by the philosophically supported quasi-universalistic presentation of Islam which the Ismāʿīlī theologians had proposed.

A further Ismāʿīlī-induced note may be heard resounding in Maimonides'

---

[75] See Halm, *Kosmologie*, pp. 18–37, and cf. the scheme described by al-Sijistānī, with the seven celestial letters of "*kwny qdr*" tied to the seven great prophets, or "Enunciators" (*nuṭaqāʾ*), in *Kitāb al-iftikhār*, ed. M. Ghālib (Beirut, 1980), 47–56. See too al-Sijistānī, *Kitāb ithbāt al-nubūʾāt*, 184–91, for his description of Moses and the other *nuṭaqāʾ*.

[76] *Sāʾir al-milal*; see *Dalālat al-hāʾirīn*, p. 259, line 19 (rendered by Samuel Ibn Tibbon as *sheʾar ha-umot* in *Moreh ha-nevukhim*, ed. Even Shmuel, 324). Pines, p. 388, n. 8, offers both "religious communities" and "nations" as acceptable alternatives for *milal*; the Islamic nation being a religious community, whatever its internal differences.

[77] See: *Dalālat al-hāʾirīn*, p. 269, p. 13; *Moreh ha-nevukhim*, ed. Even Shmuel, 336; Pines, 380. At the end of the chapter Maimonides names only the Greeks and Sabians—innocuous targets for him—as groups whose laws are not prophetically inspired. The earlier example of monasticism (though not pilgrimage) points to Christianity, rather than to Islam.

description of the theophany at Sinai, in *Guide* 2:33.[78] In that chapter, Maimonides expands upon the rabbinic interpretation of the event as recorded in Exodus 19 and Deuteronomy 5. Like midrashic sources, Maimonides emphasizes the mystery of God's voice, "seen" by all the people but understood only by Moses. The people experience only a sound, Moses hears words. Maimonides then suggests that the people heard the divine voice but once, and that brief sound was sufficient for them to apprehend immediately the first two of the ten commandments, those which, as Maimonides says, the human intellect can affirm even without revelation. Maimonides regards the articulation of that voice, i.e., the transformation of sound into language, as Moses' own doing, however inspired; Moses is responsible for the articulation of the ten commandments, and by extension for the "giving," or rendering intelligible, of the entire Torah.

As Maimonides continues, it becomes clear that the divine voice poses a problem for him.[79] He explains that it is really a "created voice" (or "sound"), *ṣawt makhlūq*, not the actual voice of the Lord. It would of course be impossible for Maimonides to say that God has a voice, having denied it previously in *Guide* 1:46.[80] There we were told that God has no voice, as He has no eyes, ears, or other limbs; indeed that God has no physical attributes at all. As Maimonides explains in detail in the first part of the *Guide*, there are in fact no attributes which may be predicated directly of God, without destroying His (as it were) pure unicity.

Thus, in *Guide* 1:46 Maimonides had said that bodily organs are ascribed to God only figuratively, as a metaphor, to indicate such perfections in the divine being as life, apprehension and activity. God is figuratively described as speaking and possessing the organ of speech to indicate that "notions (or ideas) reach the prophets from Him" (*taṣilu maʿānī minhu taʿālā li'l-anbiyā'*);[81] and again, to indicate "the emanation of the intellects (sic) on the prophets" (*fayḍ al-ʿuqūl ʿalā 'l-anbiyā'*).[82] The "speech" of God is thus a way of describing the process of emanation, beginning with the One (*fayḍ mā fā'iḍ ʿanhū*),[83] and continuing through the intelligences of the spheres, culminating in the last separate intelligence, the Agent Intellect, from where the emanation passes to the intellect of the

78 Cf. my earlier treatment of this issue in "Neoplatonic Currents," 135–37.

79 Cf. Pines, 365, and see H. Kreisel's examination of this concept in medieval Jewish philosophy, and his interpretation of Maimonides' adaptation of it, in "The Voice of God in Medieval Philosophical Exegesis" (Hebrew), *Daʿat* 16 (1986): 29–38, and esp. 34–36.

80 Pines, 99.

81 Cf. *Dalālat al-ḥā'irīn*, p. 66, line 28.

82 Ibid., p. 67, line 22, and compare Pines' less pointed translation, 99–100.

83 *Dalālat al-ḥā'irīn*, p. 67, line 18.

prophet. The special quality of the prophet is his ability to convert the abstract universal truths which his intellect apprehends into specific and compelling laws. This is a function of the prophetic imaginative faculty, the key to successful prophecy in general.

The scheme just outlined is the philosophers' view of prophecy, which Maimonides apparently endorses in this first part of the *Guide*. Yet in the second part, as we have seen, Moses' prophecy is presumably exempted from this process, the revelation received at Sinai described in a very different manner. In *Guide* 2:45[84] Maimonides reiterates what he said in his other compositions concerning Moses' prophecy (though he refers only to the *Mishneh Torah*, i.e., his non-theosophical, description). He now distinguishes Moses' prophecy from ten other degrees of prophecy. He again says, as in his *Commentary on the Mishnah*, that Moses alone had direct access to God, speaking with him "mouth to mouth" (quoting Numbers 12:8); dispensing, that is, with the imaginative faculty and its representation of angels and visions.

It is clear here that for Maimonides, Moses' apprehension of God and of the divine will was purely intellectual, and of the highest order of abstract understanding, an apprehension of the essential nature of the Deity, of His existence, unity and providential relation to the world.[85] In dispensing with the imaginative faculty, Maimonides in effect believes Moses was able to apprehend truth without any human representation, including that supreme iconic achievement of mankind, language.[86]

This being so, what are we to make of Maimonides' discussion of the voice at Sinai in *Guide* 2:33, and thus of his view of Moses? As we have seen, Maimonides himself qualifies it as a "created voice," but that would still place an intermediary between Moses and God, and Maimonides had claimed that all intermediaries in prophecy are functions of the prophetic imagination.[87] The "created voice" is thus as much an embarrassment for Maimonides as the voice of God itself; like his view of the latter he must really regard it too only as a figurative expression.[88] It is, however, a con-

---

[84] Pines, 403.

[85] This apprehension, it should be emphasized, is of God's essential nature, not of His accidental attributes. It is thus, in Maimonides' own terms, beyond that possible for a human intellect to experience. Consequently, it is necessary for Maimonides to posit a superhuman or angelic status for Moses.

[86] Necessarily, the human language Moses uses to communicate his apprehension of God is that of non-essential predication, so that all *we* can know are the accidental attributes. It should be noted, however, that even for us, God's "back" is intelligible as such only once His "face" has been apprehended, however imperfectly.

[87] *Guide* 1:46 (Pines, 103).

[88] In the popular traditions of Maimonides' time, as before and since, many substances were

venient if not necessary metaphor, given the biblical text, and it is amply found in Jewish and Islamic literature; Halevi, for example, makes use of it, both on its own terms and as part of his comprehensive treatment of the "divine command," *al-amr al-ilāhī*; a term and concept which has been traced to Ismāʿīlī sources.[89] Maimonides' apparent acceptance of this voice as a disembodied being would thus not strike his readers as odd, particularly those who were not philosophically attuned to his style and true teachings, and not ready yet to absorb them.

We are led to the conclusion that as God has no voice and speaks in no language, so for Maimonides the entire depiction of the theophany at Sinai is to be viewed as the product of Moses' imagination, a divinely inspired imagination to be sure, but a human creation nevertheless.[90] To follow and paraphrase Maimonides' depiction of the theophany, we may say that Moses put into words the intellectual apprehension of an event which transcends normal understanding and which he alone understood in its entirety and profundity. The voice is Moses' own, as is its interpretation.

This is not to deny that Maimonides believed that Moses had a unique understanding of God's being, one that allowed him to give a Torah to his people. That understanding, however, purely intellectual as it is, cannot be the Torah as we have it, for it is a religious document similar to all

---

believed to exist miraculously, some with recognizable corporeal shapes, others as disembodied forms. Notable in the latter category are the *Shekhinah* or Divine Presence, equated by Maimonides with *or nivra*, the Created Light (*Guide* 1:21, 25, 28). As A. Altmann has written, the concepts of Created Glory and Light are already utilized by Saadya Gaon, prompted as he was by both Jewish and Muslim antecedents; see Altmann, "Saadya's Theory of Revelation: Its Origins and Background," in *Studies in Religious Philosophy and Mysticism*, 152–60. Recently, M. Fishbane has shown the antiquity of the belief among Jews in the hypostatic nature of *ṣurot nivraʾot*, "created forms," and beyond that, in the corporeal nature even of God; see Fishbane, "Some Forms of Divine Appearance in Ancient Jewish Thought," in *From Ancient Israel to Modern Judaism*, ed. J. Neusner et al. (Atlanta, 1989), 2:261–70.

Maimonides' familiarity with these concepts, and his utilization of them, does not, of course, indicate his agreement with the popular view of them; on the contrary, his entire approach is to deny not only the hypostatic nature of all these forms, but even their objective reality (Cf. *Guide* 1:46). Similarly, Maimonides relentlessly disembodies God and likens Him to pure intelligence only. Adam's likeness to God is, necessarily, purely intellectual.

[89] Cf. *Kuzari*, 1:27, 42; 2:36, and see Ivry, "Philosophical and Religious Arguments in the Thought of Judah Halevi" (Hebrew), *Hagut u-maʿaseh*, ed. A. Greenbaum and A. Ivry (Haifa, 1983), 23, 29. I. Goldziher, "*Mélanges Judeo-Arabe*," *REJ* 50 (1905): 34, already pointed out Shīʿī precedents for the notion of a Divine light which accompanies the faithful. See, too, S. Pines' citation of Ikhwān sources for the notion of the *amr* in both cosmic and historical contexts, and his discussion of Halevi's usage, in "Shīʿite Terms," 174–78. Cf. also al-Kirmānī, *Rāḥat al-ʿaql*, 511. H. Kreisel, "Judah Halevi's Influence," 119 discusses Maimonides' rejection of this concept as anything other than a natural force.

[90] See A. Reines, "Maimonides' Concept of Mosaic Prophecy," *HUCA* 40–41 (1969–70): 351–55 and K. Bland, "Moses and the Law According to Maimonides," in *Mystics, Philosophers, and Politicians*, 57, 63.

others, using the language and conventions of the imagination and of political discourse. The uniqueness of Mosaic prophecy for Maimonides must be located in the intellectual apprehension of the divine which Moses supposedly experienced before transmitting it to his people, the transmission itself being in unavoidable imaginative and figurative terms. Maimonides' Moses thus emerges in a dual light, the one a non-human or semi-divine angelic type (the Moses of the *Commentary on the Mishnah*), the other a recognizable mortal prophet. In the former capacity, Moses is thought to have received the full revelation of God's will in a manner beyond human understanding and description, in the latter capacity he is seen as presenting this revelation in human terms, revealing only as much of its universal truth as the chosen few can grasp.

This dual image of the prophet, the combination in one person of an esoteric and exoteric dimension, is pronounced in Ismāʿīlī thought. There have been six great prophets or "Enunciators," (the seventh yet to appear as such), each privy to the world of eternal being and truth understood in its essential unity, beyond discrete words and ideas.[91] Each *nāṭiq* has also had the gift of great speech, communicating his revelation effectively to his community, in terms of their language, circumstances, and traditions. The universal message is thereby particularized and represented symbolically, in words and deeds, for the benefit of the prophet's entire society. The *nāṭiq* thus has a public mission which he accomplishes brilliantly, if at the price of fragmentation and distortion, even concealment of the essentially apolitical and ahistorical truth which he has apprehended.

To rectify this paradoxical situation, and doubtless as a result of their historical circumstances, the Shīʿī thinkers developed the notion of the prophet's executor or trustee, his associate and conduit to those able to grasp the initial mystical truth, if only in part. This person is known as the *waṣī*, sometimes translated as "legatee." He is the expositor of the secret, esoteric teachings which the *nāṭiq* has had but which he has not expressed explicitly.[92]

---

[91] For al-Sijistānī, the *nāṭiq* is in direct communication with the celestial hypostases of Universal Intellect and Soul. From the former he receives a unitary apprehension of the truth, from the latter he receives the ability to express this in discrete ideas and words. At the time of the *qāʾim* or long-awaited messiah all the people will comprehend essential truths in their universal nature, without particular linguistic or legalistic construction. Cf. al-Sijistānī, *Kitāb ithbāt al-nubūʾāt*, 149, *Kitāb al-yanābīʿ*, ed. Corbin, 83–84 (French translation, 107); and see too al-Kirmānī, *Rāḥat al-ʿaql*, 485–95, particularly 489. The non-discursive knowledge of Universal Intellect is a tenet of classical Neoplatonism; see Ivry, "Neoplatonic Currents," 123.

[92] Cf. al-Sijistānī, *Kitāb al-iftikhār*, 65–69, and see Halm, *Kosmologie*, 22.

This paired scheme is maintained for most of the seven *nuṭaqāʾ* of Ismāʿīlī conception; thus Moses has Aaron, Jesus has Simon Peter, and Muḥammad has ʿAlī. The Ismāʿīlī imāms and their adjutants follow next, with the anticipated arrival of the mahdī completing the cosmic cycle.[93] This elaborate scheme may be seen as a graphic expression of the Ismāʿīlī insistence on the esoteric component of every revelation, as well as on the cyclical nature of human history.

This notion of a paired and historically progressive, on-going revelation is completely foreign to Maimonides' thought, though not necessarily unknown to him. For Maimonides, Moses would have been a classic *nāṭiq*, he who had a total vision of the divine realm and who then translated it into the Torah of his people; he whose revelation was both entirely unique and yet recognizable. Moses as *nāṭiq* has both angelic and human aspects, he is able to dispense with all his physical needs on Sinai

---

[93] The seven *nuṭaqāʾ* are Adam, Noah, Abraham, Moses, Jesus, Muḥammad and the occulted imām, Muḥammad b. Ismāʿīl. Cf. Halm, *Kosmologie*, 19, and see his *Die Schia*, 202f. and Daftary, *The Ismāʿīlis*, 234. The cyclical view of history which this theory represents emphasizes the number seven, there being seven *nuṭaqāʾ* and seven imāms which ideally follow each *nāṭiq* and *waṣī*. Indeed, the number seven recurs in each phase of the discussion of prophecy, from its planetary and angelic origins to its earthly manifestations. Cf. al-Sijistānī, *Kitāb al-Iftikhār*, pp. 47–73.

As is known, L. Strauss detected a striking division of the *Guide* into seven sections, with each section but one having seven subsections, the one section which is an exception having seven chapters instead. Cf. Strauss' introduction to the Pines translation of the *Guide*, "How to Begin to Study the Guide of the Perplexed," xi–xiii. Even if one differs with some of Strauss' divisions, it seems that Maimonides is indeed attached to a heptadic principle of organization in this work, and that this may be one of the secrets of the *Guide*. What, though, is the significance of the secret?

In discussing Strauss' view recently in "Maimonides in the Sultan's Palace," *Perspectives on Maimonides*, 60–66, S. Harvey has noted additional instances of the "pre-eminence of seven" in the *Guide*, and he links this to the seven heavens and seven heavenly palaces of the *heikhalot* literature with which Maimonides would have been familiar. Harvey thus sees Maimonides as responding to *merkavah* terminology and symbolism, using them in a non-mystical fashion and co-opting them for philosophical purposes (see his n. 64). The secret essentially, for Harvey, is that philosophy and not mysticism is the path which leads one towards God.

Harvey's thesis is well argued on textual grounds, but it has Maimonides reaching out to possess and reinterpret a mystical tradition with which he is otherwise not concerned, working to keep secret what is perfectly obvious elsewhere in the book. On this interpretation, Maimonides becomes, for strategic and essentially political reasons, a prisoner of his own literary conceit. If, nevertheless, Maimonides is responding to mystical Jewish themes, as Harvey suggests, it could well be due to the presence in the environment of Ismāʿīlī theosophical schemes which stimulated similar Jewish responses. It may well be that Maimonides is accomplishing both purposes, responding to external stimuli by utilizing the sources within his own tradition.

There is, though, a further argument for stressing the relevance of the Ismāʿīlī model for Maimonides' attraction to heptadic structures. He may be expressing thereby a stylistic analogue and response to Ismāʿīlī historiography. As the mahdī is expected to usher in a final era of universal redemption and salvation, so Maimonides believes he is offering the reader of the *Guide* direction towards personal salvation, redemption from sin and suffering, and life eternal.

and is even brought up to heaven eventually in a special way, not dying as mortals do.[94]

Yet Moses does die, and is not occulted, nor will he return, and the messiah whom one should believe will return will not abrogate the law at that time, Maimonides insists. Hence, despite the precedents found in the Jewish tradition, let alone in the Ismāʿīlī, for believing in Moses' angelic status, and despite the temptation to utilize this idea which he cannot entirely resist, Maimonides does not fully subscribe to the model of the prophet which these sources offered him. He may well feel that the permanent elevation of Moses to a cosmic plane is too threatening to his religious and philosophical convictions, as well as too close to the conceptualization of prophecy and sainthood in which the Ismāʿīlīs and mystics of both Judaism and Islam concurred.

Yet, notwithstanding his reservations, Maimonides has adopted for Moses the Ismāʿīlī *nāṭiq* model of prophecy to a considerable degree. It is this model which alone establishes with any rational coherency the claims of an epistemological and political sort which Maimonides wishes to assert.[95] If, then, Moses may be regarded as a *nāṭiq*, whom did Maimonides believe, possibly only unconsciously, to be his *waṣī*? Here I venture to suggest that Maimonides saw himself in this role, or its unnamed equivalent. For the *Guide* is nothing but a discreet explication for the initiated few of the meaning of the deceptively exoteric text of the Bible, of Moses' Scripture. Maimonides saw himself, in *waṣī* fashion, as explaining the inner meaning of the Torah, a meaning which had been forgotten and neglected by the leaders of his people. Of course, Maimonides is not to be bound to a literal formulation of his role as *waṣī*. Given the chronological distance between Moses and himself, he is, in Ismāʿīlī terms, more of a latter-day imām (or even *walī*) than a *waṣī*, or rather he is both. For while the *waṣī* clarifies the esoteric meaning of the revelation transmitted by the *nāṭiq*, the imām and those adjutant or deputy leaders who follow him are obliged also to direct the community in its daily affairs, to be the decisors, the authorities in law as well as tradition.

Maimonides' efforts in his *Mishneh Torah* and other rabbinic writings accomplished this task brilliantly. He gave his generation, and those after it, a definitive formulation of Mosaic *cum* rabbinic law, and he consid-

---

[94] Cf. *Guide* 3:51 (Pines, 628).

[95] Maimonides' resort to utilizing an image of Moses in theosophic terms is in many ways an act of desperation for one supposedly committed to philosophical models of understanding. The alternatives, he may have thought, were either deep skepticism and even agnosticism, or simply unreasoning dogmatism.

ered himself its supreme arbiter. In his hands, the scope of halakhah was to be consolidated, and religious authority unified. In these practical and public pursuits, as in his theoretical and philosophical endeavors, Maimonides may be regarded as influenced in good part by Ismāʿīlī models and ideas, receptive to the surrounding culture even while zealously defending his own.

A MYSTICAL TREATISE ON PERFECTION, PROVIDENCE AND PROPHECY FROM THE JEWISH ṢŪFĪ CIRCLE

PAUL B. FENTON

As in the case of certain other religious revivalist movements, the Ṣūfī-type, Jewish Pietist circle, which flourished in Egypt in the century following Moses Maimonides, gave rise to a rich and variegated literary output.[1] Though a significant proportion of this oeuvre consists of adaptations of Muslim Ṣūfī texts, it also comprises a number of original Jewish compositions in which the Ṣūfī element predominates. Embodying one of the most profound influences of Islam upon the religion of Israel, this literature is one of signal interest for the history of Jewish spirituality.[2] However, with the exception of the works of Rabbi Abraham, son of Moses Maimonides (ob. 1235) which have come down to us in a more or less substantial, albeit incomplete, form,[3] the scholar is confronted, in the domain of Pietist writings, with the frustrating prospect of having to deal with remains of a very fragmentary nature. Indeed, the principal source for these writings are Genizah manuscripts, which by definition—as is well known to all students of Judeo-Arabic—are incomplete and fragmentary. As a result, our knowledge of the doctrines and practices of the Pietists remains very partial. However, the relatively new research in this area may be enriched at any point by the surprise discoveries which the Genizah treasure-trove no doubt holds in store.

In the course of research sponsored by the British Academy and carried out in 1984 at the then Leningrad Public State Library, we had the good fortune of discovering amongst the very rich collection of Judeo-Arabic Genizah manuscripts preserved in the Second Firkovich collection a relatively large Pietist treatise, which substantially enriches our knowledge of Pietist literature.[4]

The impressive spiritual document class-marked Second Firkovich

---

[1] On this movement see our books: *Obadyah Maimonides: Treatise of the Pool* (London, 1981) and *Deux traités de mystique juive* (Lagrasse, 1987).

[2] On the scope of this literature, see *Deux traités*, 28–36.

[3] See our "En marge du *Kitāb kifāyat al-ʿābidīn* de Rabbi Abraham ben Moïse Maïmonide," *REJ* 150 (1991): 385–405.

[4] For a description of this collection see our *Handlist of Judeo-Arabic Manuscripts in Leningrad* (Jerusalem, 1991).

Judeo-Arabic NS 1223, is one of the most extensive Pietist compositions so far located, both from the point of view of volume and doctrinal content. Although it was brought to light nearly a decade ago, the availability of a microfilm of this precious work has only just been made possible in the wake of recent political transformations that have taken place in Russia. Written on paper, the manuscript comprises ninety folios, each carrying twenty-two lines of oriental script. Unfortunately acephalous, the manuscript is lacking at the end with a lacuna also in the middle, and was, therefore, originally more extensive in scope.[5]

A survey of Genizah material brought to light further smaller fragments of this work both in Saint Petersburg and other Genizah collections, which testify to the existence of at least nine different manuscripts, indicating the work's relative popularity.[6] However, none of these provides details of either the author or the title of the work. Occasionally, the author himself refers to his composition as "these booklets" (*karārīs*),[7] alluding perhaps to the fact that the text was progressively composed in sections. At one point, however, he refers to his work as "this book" (*sefer*, in Hebrew).[8]

Although composed in the classical idiom, the work exhibits sporadic features of vulgar Arabic.[9] The preserved text also contains two Persian technical terms.[10] These elements, as well as internal evidence and paleographical considerations, prompt us to date the treatise to the Mameluke period, i.e. the late thirteenth century.

The author's lyrical style is typical of other Pietist compositions. He writes in a spontaneous, often repetitious, rambling prose, steeped in metaphorical expressions, making copious use of Ṣūfī technical terms and concepts set in the philosophical framework of Avicennian Neoplatonism. From the point of view of Ṣūfī literature, the work can be said to belong to the ecstatic school insofar as the author has no qualms about discoursing at length upon the mystical experience, a subject about which Jewish

[5] See the preliminary description in our *Handlist*, 62–63 and *Deux traités*, 30–33, 71, 77, 79, 214. See also Addendum below, p. 334.

[6] St. Petersburg, II Firkovich Heb.-Ar. I.2193 (4 fols.), 2230 (11 fols.), 4809 (14 fols.), NS 812.16, NS 835.12–15, NS 1006.24, NS 1082.28–29; Cambridge University Library, T-S Arabic 43.62 (same scribe), 44.186 and perhaps AS 154.36 (same scribe).

[7] E.g. II Firk. Heb.-Ar. NS 1223, fols. 26a, 29a, 40b.

[8] See fol. 8b.

[9] For instance the sporadic use of the imperfect auxiliary particle "b" typical of Eastern dialects, e.g. fol. 6a: *bi-yushīr*; fol. 6b: *bi-yaqūl*; fol. 44b: *bi-yakshif*; fol. 61a: *bi-yudrik*; fol. 72b: *bi-yūfī*, *bi-yaqūl*.

[10] fol. 65b *buwādhang* = Steingass, *A Comprehensive Persian-English Dictionary* (London, 1892), s.v. *badkhāneh*: "a lattice window, ventilator"; fol. 66a : *shashnakīr* = Steingass, s.v. *chashnigīr*: "a taster to a prince, a cupbearer."

writings, for their part, are usually quite discreet. Indeed, the work conveys the impression that it was composed under the sway of mystic inspiration. In a way, outside of kabbalistic literature—to which the present text is, of course, unrelated—this work is one of the most mystical of all Jewish compositions. The author is conscious that he is writing an esoteric work, for he sometimes alludes to certain secrets which he abstains from disclosing, claiming that they are reserved for the initiated who fulfill certain requirements.

Of particular interest, in this connection, is the author's allegorizing method which gives the impression of being based on a highly elaborate exegetical system, echoes of which are to be found in other Pietist writings. Since the present work is apparently a relatively early Pietist composition, it is a matter of speculation whether its writer had a part in the forging of the school's exegetical approach. Indeed, several key terms and expressions especially remind us of certain writings associated with the circle of Rabbi Abraham he-Ḥasid (ob. 1232).[11] To be sure, specific passages even employ the selfsame phraseology as found in other texts possibly composed by this important Pietist figure.[12] Furthermore, the numerous marginal corrections in the same handwriting as the text itself indicate that the manuscript is an autograph. Now, we know of a certain number of other Pietist texts executed by the same hand which possibly emanated from Rabbi Abraham's pen.[13]

Apart from biblical references, and, to a much lesser degree, rabbinic sources, no work or author is nominally quoted in the preserved chapters, although it is quite clear that the writer had knowledge of and was influenced by the philosophical doctrines of Maimonides.[14] He also exhibits extensive familiarity with Ṣūfī thought, from which he borrowed, in particular, his conceptual framework.

---

[11] On this personality, see our articles "Some Judaeo-Arabic Fragments by Rabbi Abraham he-Ḥasid, the Jewish Sufi," *JSS* 26 (1981): 47–72 and "A Pietist Letter from the Genizah," *HAR* 10 (1986): 157–68.

[12] Our author also composed the text we published as "A Mystical Treatise on Prayer and the Spiritual Quest from the Pietist Circle," *JSAI* 16 (1993): 137–175. This is evident both from the works' doctrinal content as well as their use of identical expressions, such as *huzūz wa-irādāt* (NS 1223, fols. 33b, 60b; "Mystical Treatise," 24, 27, 34, 40) and *yastirenu be-seter kenafav ha-raḥamim* (NS 1223, fol. 23b; "Mystical Treatise," 30).

[13] II Firk I.3116 (autograph), ENA NSI 10 (autograph letter), Budapest, Kaufmann 205e and T-S Arabic 51.52, fragments in Hebrew characters from *Lawāmiʿ anwār al-qulūb*, a Ṣūfī manual on mystical love by Abū ʾl-Maʿālī al-Shaydhala, T-S Arabic 43.3 and 47.58, draft of above-mentioned Treatise on Prayer.

[14] This is particularly evident in certain traits of his prophetology. In "Mystical Treatise" he borrows from both the *Guide* and the *Mishneh Torah*.

The incompleteness of the treatise and the fact that the order of the gatherings as they appear on the microfilm has been disheveled are unhelpful in conveying a clear idea as to the original form and content of the work. However, the impression is gained that behind the author's florid style, lies an elaborate theosophical doctrine which radiates forth from an earnest and powerful spiritual experience. We should like to attempt to present a brief account of the speculative content of the work, as far as it is possible to reconstruct, in order to intimate something of its astounding depth and originality.

The author is very fond of systematizing the phenomena with which he deals and nearly every theme in the work is divided into degrees, categories and subcategories. Notwithstanding this observation, the book as a whole does not seem to follow a systematic structure, though its fragmentary character may be misleading in this respect. Nonetheless, even in the absence of clearly marked chapters, the work does present a conceptual unity. One would have to wait until—if ever—a more complete version of the work came to light before a definitive judgment could be pronounced.

Purpose

Though we do not possess the beginning of the work in which its aim was probably set out by the author, the latter provides a convenient summary of the purpose of his composition in the chapter on prophecy, which seems to have been the ultimate pivot of the book. We have discussed elsewhere the centrality of the preoccupation of the Pietists with prophecy, the renewal of which they apparently believed was imminent.[15] Indeed, our author first insists that his goal was not simply to be informative (*khabar*); he had intended his book to instigate practical action on the part of his readers:

> The purpose of the discourse contained in these chapters is the practical effort of the soul to attain these noble ends so that individuals may obtain and realize them. The first aim of this discourse is to awaken the hearts from the slumber of apathy and arouse them from the darkness of ignorance so that man may recognize the greatness of his Creator and His omnipotence in the bringing into being of all creatures. (Secondly, that he may recognize) more especially God's having created man and elevated him above all other creatures (Ps. 8:7, Ps. 115:16), on the one hand, through the human intellect, enabling him to gain knowledge, and, on

[15] Cf. *Deux traités*, 70–80.

the other, through the rational soul, enabling him to attain spiritual refinement (*tajawhur*) and perception, making him the regent of the lower world, so that he may sustain it through reason (*ʿaql*; margin reads: *ʿadl*, "justice"). [. . .] Thereafter man will realize the nobleness of his own soul and its source and discover how he may return thereunto and exert himself in its salvation. Some mention will also be made of the soul's happiness in this and the next world through drawing near to God [. . .] in order to awaken the souls and incite them to long for this great happiness laid in store for human souls [. . .].

Now all these themes are mentioned in the Torah, especially God's creation of the soul and His love and compassion for it. It speaks of how He has bestowed special favor upon Israel by the gift of the Torah and the promise of special Providence if they observe it [. . .]. It also mentions the nobleness of the soul and the reason for its descent into this world as well as its beatitude in the next world through perpetual nearness to God. The [Torah] also describes that which impedes it from obtaining this felicity and how the soul may avoid going astray in order to ascend the degrees of proximity in the climb towards its supernal world from which it was hewn [. . .]. We have disclosed a small part of these questions, having included them in this book with the intention of facilitating their explanation for the individual who is unaware of the function of the Torah and its lofty aims [. . .]. In order to awaken the soul from its deep slumber [. . .] and to inform it of the deeds by which it may obtain these sublime things so that by enacting them it may be encompassed by the Providence vouchsafed for those that accomplish these deeds [. . .]. Thereupon the soul will find within itself undescribable sweetness of obedience and pleasure of proximity.

Content

The Firkovich manuscript is made up of seven disarrayed segments which in fact form two complete fragments, (A) and (B). Internal references suggest that the shortest consecutive fragment (A) precedes the second one. A thorough reading of the manuscript has led us to establish as follows the original order of folios:

1 2 3 4 5 6 7
(A) 82a – 90b + 79ab lacuna (B) 80ab + 71a – 78b + 81ab + 51a – 70b + 1a – 50b

Since very few of the work's internal divisions bear headings, in order to facilitate the survey of the work's contents we have seen fit to allot our own chapter titles to the different themes which are treated. The contents of the book can thus be summarized in the following table.

Fragment (A)

I. The Soul's Vices:
- (a) health and illness (?) (fragment) (fol. 82)
- (b) strength and weakness (fols. 82–85)
- (c) weakness and its consequences (fols. 85–86)
- (d) proximity and distance (fols. 87–89)
- (e) life and death (fol. 79)

Fragment (B)

I. The Division of Action:
- (a) personal duties of man (fragment) (fol. 80)
- (b) social duties of man (fol. 80)
- (c) divine duties of man (fol. 71)

II. The Faculties of the Soul:
- (a) natural (fol. 81b)
- (b) vital (fol. 51a)
- (c) pneumatic (fol. 51b)
- (d) external (fol. 52a)
- (e) internal (fol. 53b)

III. The Purpose of the Soul: Its Illuminative Faculties, gnosis and *kavod.*

IV. Gnosis and Love (fol. 59)

V. The Two Hearts (fol. 60)

VI. Gratitude (fol. 63)

VII. Obstacles to Salvation:
concupiscence (*ḥirṣ*) and apathy (*ghafla*) (fol. 1)

VIII. The Purpose of Man:
- (a) his universal purpose (fol. 2b)
- (b) his particular purpose (fol. 3)
- (c) his divine purpose (fol. 4)

IX. The Specificity of Man: Reason (fol. 4b)

X. The Threefold Division of Creation:
supernal, lower and intermediate (fol. 8b).

XI. The Ten Categories of Providence (fol. 17a)

XII. The Universal Hierarchy (fol. 18a)

XIII. The Righteous (fol. 19a)

XIV. The Saints (fol. 20b)

XV. The Humble (fol. 21b)

XVI. The Four Moral Qualities (fol. 27a)

XVII. The Path of Holiness (fol. 28b)

XVIII. Three Causes of Providence (fol. 30a)
XIX. The Providential Role of Reason (fol. 37b)
XX. The Degrees of Prophecy (fol. 39a)
XXI. The Four Categories of Prophecy (fol. 43a)
XXII. The Eyes of the Heart (fol. 44b)
XXIII. The Three Qualities Required for Prophecy (fol. 46a)
XXIV. The Theophanies of Majesty and Beauty (fol. 49a)

Analysis of Content

From a passing remark preserved in the latter part of the book (fol. 8b) it would seem that the work may have begun with an exegetical disquisition based on the verse "To understand a proverb, and a figure; the words of the wise, and their obscure sayings" (Prov. 1:6), explaining the primacy of the metaphorical and esoteric interpretation of Scripture. Further passages refer to the book's having dealt at its outset with the vices of the soul, called by the generic name of *ghishsh*. Now the first preserved chapter discusses precisely that very subject and supposedly belonged to the initial part of the work.

The Soul's Vices

Fragment (A) begins with the concluding portion of a chapter dealing with the ailments of the soul which alienate it from God. The first preserved chapter discusses the soul's strength and weakness in its moral struggle. Strength consists in its capacity to dispel vice, whereas weakness stems from forgetfulness. Its avoidance of iniquity is inversely proportional to its reconciliation with God:

> The greater the soul's liberation from its hindrances (i.e. vices), the nearer it draws to God; and the nearer it draws to God, the deeper its preoccupation with Him; and the deeper its preoccupation with Him, the stronger its power; and the stronger its power, the greater the influence it exerts on all below it. This influence is assisted by all that is above it such as angels, the spirits of the prophets, saints and the pious. (84a)

The immediate objective of the author's ethical doctrine is to obtain a spiritual affinity (*munāsaba*)[16] with God through the attainment first of

[16] Based on the concept of the fundamental symmetry of man and God (in whose image man

purity (*ṭehorah*) and then of holiness (*qedushshah*). The former is realized by avoiding vice through the observance of the negative commandments stipulated in the Torah, whereas holiness is acquired through the practice of virtue, equated with the performance of the positive commandments. Having first secured this spiritual affinity, the soul henceforth gains the Divine attention and Providence: "The more the soul increases in holiness, the closer its affinity (*munāsaba*) (to God); the closer its affinity, the nearer it draws; the nearer it draws, the more Providence (*ʿināya*) it enjoys; the more providence it enjoys, the stronger it becomes; and the stronger it becomes, the greater its action and the weaker its passion (*infiʿāl*)" (fol. 86b). This spiritual affinity is conducive to gnosis.

Proximity and Distance

The second preserved chapter from this part of the book goes on to explain how proximity (*qurb*) and distance (*buʿd*) from God[17] affect gnosis: "The instruments of knowledge once acquired by the soul grant it access to the sources of gnosis (*ʿuyūn al-maʿrifa*). These instruments are the qualities with which the soul adorns itself, bestowing upon it affinity with the Creator."

In essence, the author distinguishes a hierarchy in the performance of the precepts comprising three progressive levels:

(1) The observance of the negative commandments which eliminate the vices veiling the soul from its Creator. Moreover, vice and virtue are interdependent insofar as whenever a virtue such as generosity is secured by the soul, its opposite, meanness, is expelled, and vice versa (fol. 87).[18]

(2) The practice of the positive commandments which foster virtue and disclose to man the secrets of his Creator. The final purpose of this

was created), this Ṣūfī doctrine was propagated by al-Ghazzālī (cf. *Iḥyāʾ ʿulūm al-dīn*, 4:4) and Ibn al-ʿArabī, *al-Futūḥāt al-makkiyya*, Chap. 178 (Cairo, 1329 AH), 365. Both Obadiah and David Maimonides made use of it as well; see *Deux traités*, 140, 146, and 284–87. The author devotes an important chapter to this notion in his "Mystical Treatise," 11–15 where this affinity, inherently concealed in the human composition, is—as with Ibn al-ʿArabī—the foundation of love for God. In its dynamic form, it is the result of assimilation of the Divine attributes, which lead to *qurb*, "proximity."

[17] On these Ṣūfī notions, see *Deux traités*, 154 and 188.

[18] Cf. ibid, 138 and 152.

stage is to carry out the precepts to their utmost perfection, thereby realizing their three underlying cardinal virtues. These inner principles, kindness, justice and charity,[19] known as the "pivot" (*quṭb*) or the "spirits of the commandments" (*arwāḥ al-miṣvot*), are ascribed to God Himself (Jer. 9:23). This moral ascent (*taraqqī*) towards the culminating purpose of the precepts, called the "degrees of the saints" (*manāzil al-ḥasidim*), ultimately leads to the third level:

(3) The paths of gnosis (*masālik al-maʿrifa*) (fol. 87) lead to the mysteries of the Torah called "sources of gnosis." Through these the Divine power (*qudra*) is revealed to the soul by virtue of which it perceives the grandeur of its Creator (fol. 88). Thereupon the soul is vouchsafed physical protection, preserving its corporeal body as well as translucence (*shufūf*), which endows it with gnosis.

Three levels of translucence can be distinguished amongst those that observe the commandments: (1) the "gleaming souls" or "righteous" (*ṣaddiqim*) who shun vice and pursue virtue; (2) the "shining souls" or "saints" (*ḥasidim*) who sublimely meditate upon the words of Scripture; and (3) the "brilliant souls" known as the "humble" (*ʿanavim*), who constantly exalt God.[20] Thus the observance of the commandments and the gradual elimination of vice progressively lead to the soul's illumination, which the author compares to the illumination of the moon's surface by the sun's rays when the earth is no longer interposed between them. This stage is known as *haskalah*, alluded to in the aforequoted verse from Jeremiah 9.

The performance of every precept increases this light and the resulting illumination procures intense love of God and a "cleaving to Him," which bestows life upon the soul, as it is written "but ye that cleave unto the Lord your God are alive every one of you this day" (Deut. 4:4). The theme of life, as cleaving to God through gnosis and affinity, and its opposite, the theme of death, form the subject of the following chapter of which only the opening paragraph has been preserved. Thereafter there is a lacuna in the manuscript which resumes in the second larger segment (fol. 79b).

---

[19] Nowhere in the preserved portions does the author clearly define his understanding of these virtues which perhaps correspond to his threefold classification of the spiritual wayfarers: righteous, pious, and humble. Maimonides too attaches a special importance to these virtues, to which he devotes the final chapters of *Guide* 3:53–54 on the perfection of man. In "Mystical Treatise," 14–15, the author discusses "the ultimate performance of the precepts" (*ghāyat al-miṣvot*), which belong to the "station of the saints" and lead to gnosis.

[20] Abraham Maimonides, *The High Ways to Perfection (Kifāyat al-ʿĀbidīn)*, ed. S. Rosenblatt (New York, 1927), 1:133–35, has a similar terminology.

FRAGMENT B

I. *Man's Duties*

The second fragment opens with the concluding paragraph of an incomplete chapter which apparently dealt with man's personal duties towards himself. The first preserved chapter of the second fragment deals with a second category of deeds, i.e. man's social duties. Here as elsewhere in the treatise the key concepts underpinning the author's system are the three cardinal virtues: righteousness, kindness and justice (cf. Jer. 9:23). In dealings with one's fellows, the author distinguishes two levels: on the one hand, the obligatory (*farḍ*) or common duties, characteristic of the righteous (*ṣaddiq*), and on the other, the superlative approach characteristic of the saint (*ḥasid*), which consists in supererogatory devotion (*nāfila*).[21] Practically, this means, for instance, extending kindness to all mankind regardless of their being sinners and lowly people, in order to imitate God Himself who is bounteous to all (Ps. 145:9) (fols. 80–71).

The third category of deeds concerns man's duties towards God. These include first his recognition of God's absolute oneness, sovereignty, omnipotence and omniscience (Gen. 18:14–25, Jer 23:24). The object of this recognition is to adopt an attitude of both humility and gratitude for the Divine bounty, which not only created man in the first place, but secondly provides him with the means of perfection.

II. *The Faculties of the Soul*

With elements culled from vulgarized philosophy, the author then goes on to describe in great detail the faculties of the soul (fols. 72b–81b), classifying them under five headings with numerous subdivisions: (1) the natural faculties, situated in the liver; (2) the vital faculties, situated in the heart; (3) the psychological faculties, situated in the brain; (4) the external faculties, i.e. the five senses, situated on the surface of the body; and (5) the internal faculties, situated in the brain, which mediate between the soul and the heart (fols. 51–53b). Using the *locus classicus* (Eccl. 10:16–17), he personifies these faculties as a ruling king and compares their func-

[21] On the definition of *ḥasidut* as "going beyond duty," see: Maimonides, *Guide* 3:53 and *Commentary on Avot*, 5:6; Abraham Maimonides, *High Ways*, 1:134.

tions to the government of the city, going on to explain how the soul derives benefit from each of these functions in order to maintain the body (fols. 55–56).[22]

III. *The Purpose of the Soul*

According to our author, in addition to the external physical organs of perception, the soul possesses a set of internal spiritual organs, known as "the eyes of the heart"[23] whose function it is to apprehend the spiritual dimension of creation:

> Since the purpose of the soul in this world is to attain perfection (and thus bring about) its conversion to Him who willed its existence, He prepared for it mysteries and notions whose mastery confer knowledge of the power of its Creator and Maker. Indeed, from these mysteries the soul will ascend to Divine gnosis. Moreover, He bestowed upon it illuminative faculties called the "eyes of the heart" which serve the soul as eyes do man [. . .]. Whereas through the five senses, the soul perceives the outward aspect of creation, that is creatures' bodies, it perceives by means of these illuminative faculties the creatures' spirits (*arwāḥ al-makhlūqāt*), their mysteries and concepts. Now these illuminative faculties also possess organs by which these dimensions become manifest. These are the virtues (righteousness, kindness and charity) which, through inurement, refine these faculties, allowing the soul to apprehend the divine secrets concealed within creation. This form of apprehension is called the "gnostic vision," whereby the soul ascends to knowledge of its Creator, as alluded to in the verse: "Know this day, and lay it to thy heart, that the Lord, He is God in heaven above and upon the earth beneath; there is none else" (Deut. 4:39). I.e. through meditation on the supernal and lower creatures, the individual gains proficiency in these illuminative faculties, applying them to the other creatures and through them acquiring knowledge of their Creator. This latter knowledge is the goal of the first, as it is written "(Let him that glorieth glory in this), that he understandeth and—as a result—knoweth Me" (Jer. 9:23) (fol. 56a–b).

If, however, the soul contravenes these three virtues, explains the author, then:

> The faculties are blinded and the sources of gnosis are sealed, Truth is veiled from the soul which is sure to die before death [. . .]. This is the death referred to

[22] Cf. H. Malter, "Personifications of Soul and Body: A Study in Judaeo-Arabic Literature," *JQR* n.s. 2 (1912): 453–79.

[23] The "eye of the heart," a Ṣūfī motif already used by al-Hallāj, signifies "a subtle spiritual perception," for according to the Ṣūfīs the heart is the organ of mystical knowledge; cf. *Dīwān al-ḥallāj*, ed. L. Massignon (Paris, 1955), 46, 163. The term is also used by the author in his "Mystical Treatise," 39; cf. *Deux traités*, 279.

> (in Scripture) as "slumber" (*tenumah*), signifying, by contrast with "natural sleep" (*shenah*), total submersion in the world of the senses. This is the state of those ignorant of this purpose who grasp solely the sensibilia, as it is written "Awake and sing, ye that dwell in the dust—for thy dew is as the dew of light" (Is. 26:19) (fol. 57a).

The homonymy of the two Arabic terms "eye" and "source" enables the author to describe the unveiling of the heart's eyes through the diligent cultivation of the three above-mentioned cardinal virtues, in terms of the gushing forth of water:

> Thereupon, the fountains of gnosis will well up within the source (eyes) of the soul's heart, which are known as the "wells of salvation" (*ʿuyūn al-ghayth*) and "portals of mercy," as it is written "Therefore with joy shall ye draw water out of the wells of salvation" (Is. 12:3). Then they will inundate the (hearts) with the illuminative bounties the Creator holds in store for man's soul (. . .) until thy soul is engulfed by these lights, just as a dwelling encompasses thy body (. . .), as it is written: "As the mountains surround Jerusalem, so the Lord surrounds His people" (Ps. 125:2) (fol. 57a–b).

Our author hastens to add "and such verses cannot be discussed overtly, only allusively intimated." He goes on to observe, by way of comparison, that this is also the esoteric meaning of the word "dwelling" mentioned in the verse "And it came to pass, because the midwives feared God, that He made them dwellings" (Exod. 1:21), "as has been explained by him to whom the Creator has revealed this great mystery. He employed, however, a subtle expression in order to conceal (it)."[24]

The result of this unveiling of the internal vision and the unleashing of the "springs of salvation" is a spiritual insight into the Divine power which pervades all creation:

> Once the eyes of its heart have been opened, the soul, upon beholding one of God's creatures, will perceive by means of this luminous sight not only the Divine mystery inherent therein but also the Divine power (*al-qudra*) which brought that creature into existence from non-existence, nay the very subsistence of its being through the existential power (*al-qudra al-kaynūniyya*) and the Creator's energy pervading that creature. (fol. 57b)[25]

---

[24] This is possibly a reference to Saadya's translation which adds "to protect them"—understood by the author as divine Providence. Cf. also Obadiah Maimonides' exegesis of the word "dwelling" in Gen. 30:30, *Deux traités*, 164.

[25] The author also addresses this Sūfī concept in a private letter; see "A Pietist Letter," 161. A similar formulation to the wording found there is to be read in another Pietist treatise, possibly authored by our writer: "These are the spiritual stations of the initiates (*maqāmāt al-qawm*), i.e. 'the seekers of God,' of which the highest is the station of extinction (*fanāʾ*) [. . .] wherein they behold in each creature its Creator, blessed be His Name, and in each being, its Maker, Supporter, Sustainer and Mover. Through that [being] they attain Him and through Him they attain all that exists through Him" (Ms. Strasbourg, BNU 4110, 61b–62a). The Sūfī term *fanāʾ*, a key

This insight is conducive to an intuition of God's grandeur and thence to gnosis. The profundity of the latter depends upon the individual's spiritual capacity, just as physical perception depends on the strength of eyesight. The following page goes on to equate gnosis with the term "Glory" (*kavod*):

> Divine gnosis is a part of His Glory as has been stated in connection with the verse "They shall see the Glory of the Lord" (Is. 35:2). Now this "Glory" possesses an initial stage and a final stage. The former follows from the obligation incumbent upon mankind, i.e. the covenant between God and each individual who plies the Divine path, as is clear from the verse "And as for Me, this is My covenant with them, saith the Lord; My spirit that is upon thee" (Is. 59:21). As for the final stage of "Glory," it reaches the very face of God. Now, the expedients which lead to gnosis (*kavod*) are the immaterial notions called Divine attributes, such as "justice," "truth," and "peace." Now the expedients bearing such names are those which are close to man, whereas those approaching the final stage are nameless. This succession of intermediaries leading to gnosis can be compared to a number of entities, placed one behind the other. When the sun shines upon the first in line, it penetrates all [. . .] but the further the light is from the principle, the weaker and dimmer it becomes until it reaches the entity adjoining man,[26] that is true man, traveling the Way of God. For this entity hails the soul on behalf of its Creator in order to guide it along the Path of God (. . .) and the closer the soul draws to God, the more the light waxes strong and increases until the soul arrives unto God and He allots it an everlasting place in His Presence (Prov. 4:18) (fols. 58–59).

IV. *Gnosis and Love*

The following chapter begins with a description of the soul's beatitude accruing from gnosis. Since the purpose of gnosis is love of God, the Creator provided the soul with an organ capable of communing with the immaterial beings, thereby enabling it to taste of their spiritual delights (*madhāqāt ruḥāniyya*).[27] After having experienced the savor of the spiritual world, the soul will frown upon all else and turn wholeheartedly towards the source of this sweetness, enamored with its love, cleaving unto it, abiding with it, delighting in its intimacy and ever relishing its contemplation (Ps. 30:13) (fol. 59).

---

notion in Ibn al-ʿArabī's doctrine of existential unity (*waḥdat al-wujūd*), signifies "the total annihilation of man's subjective conscience [. . .] being completely absorbed by the underlying unity of existence"; see T. Izutsu, *Unicité de l'existence et création pérpetuelle en mystique musulmane* (Paris, 1980), 60.

[26] The reference is to the Active Intellect which communicates with the human intellect.

[27] I.e. grasped through *dhawq*, or spiritual intuition. On this technical term, see our article "Some Judaeo-Arabic Fragments," 64–65. The author also uses this expression on fol. 60b and in his "Pietist Letter," p. 162, line 12.

V. *The Two Hearts*

Man is composed of both a physical and a spiritual substance, declares our author, each of which possesses a heart, as it is said, "My heart and my flesh sing for joy unto the living God" (Ps. 84:3). In turn, each heart possesses an organ containing a kernel:

> The kernel of the physical substance is an igneous light, whereas the kernel of the spiritual substance is divine luminosity.[28] Now each kernel has a specific purpose. Just as the function of the physical heart is to preserve the body from destruction, so that of the spiritual heart is to preserve the soul from transient pursuits and to ensure that it cleaves to that which is permanent (fol. 59b). This heart is endowed both with a tongue and with sight, as it is said: "O taste and see that the Lord is good" (Ps. 34:9). With the former man savors the hidden mysteries (*maʿānī ghaybiyya*) with spiritual relish (*madhāqāt ruḥāniyya*), whereas the latter apprehends wisdom, as it is said: "My heart has seen much wisdom and knowledge" (Eccl. 1:16). If man preserves this heart from all evil then the "wells of life" (*yanābiʿ al-ḥayāt*) will spring forth therefrom (Prov. 4:23) (fol. 60).

This instrument, which the author also calls a "hand," is bestowed upon the "righteous" (*ṣaddiqim*) in order to sustain the bond (*wuṣla*)[29] between the soul and its Creator. Providing the soul shuns that which distracts it from God's gnosis and love, this bond will go from strength to strength, and thus help the soul assimilate the intelligible forms known as God's "gates and courtyards" which assist it in its ascent (fols. 61–62).

VI. *Gratitude*

Access to these higher states is gained through the gratitude felt for all the blessings with which God has favored man, as it is said, "Enter into His gates with thanksgiving, and into His courts with praise" (Ps. 100:4).[30] Here the author enters into a long demonstration of the wonders of the divine gifts through the example of the bodily functions, again harking back to the comparison of the body to the political organization of a city.[31]

[28] *Sirr*, lit. "secret," is the innermost recess of the soul and one of the hierarchical locii of Divine manifestation. Cf. Jurjānī, *Definitiones*, ed. G. Flügel (Leipzig, 1845), 118.

[29] Cf. the mystical interpretation of the term "hand" in Exodus 24:11 given by Abraham he-Ḥasid and quoted by Abraham Maimonides, *Commentary on Genesis and Exodus*, ed. E. Wiesenberg (London, 1956), 379. See also our "Some Judaeo-Arabic Fragments," p. 58, n. 39. On the term *wuṣla*, see *Deux traités*, 140.

[30] *Shukr*, "gratitude," also occupies an important place in the "Mystical Treatise," 35–38.

[31] Cf. supra, n. 22.

Interestingly, his exposition includes a host of popular information, often of a physiological and medical nature (fols. 63a–67a). He concludes: "And these great gifts should be an incitement for the soul's perfection and its knowledge and love of God, the return of the soul to Him and its continuous sojourn in His Presence, eternally delighting in His proximity and rejoicing in the vision of His Beauty. 'Seek you me, and live'"(Amos 5:4).

As a supreme example of one such seeker, the author cites King David, whom he depicts as a mystic lover, in terms similar to those used in Ṣūfī love literature:

> One who unceasingly pursued this great and noble goal, enraptured with desire, was David the lover, intimate with the object of his love, constant in his faithfulness, diligent in his state of purity, steadfast in the station of servitude, intoxicated with the wine of love and passion, enraptured (*wahlan*) with the thought of the Beloved, repeating the praise of his Master and monarch, uttering with the tongue of desire, imploring with the entreaty of an intimate, "Thou makest me to know the path of life, (in Thy presence is fulness of joy, in Thy right hand bliss for evermore)" (Ps. 16:11) (fol. 67b).[32]

A description of the torment lying in store for insensitive individuals occupies the remainder of the chapter, which concludes:

> Woe betide the heedless, shame upon the losers, and misfortune upon the slumberers, sorrow upon the dead who have fallen prey to the swords of their passions and desires [. . .], fallen in the pit of their souls: "For she hath cast down many wounded" (Pr. 7:26) and they shall never have repose since they have not wrought any [good] deeds enabling them to return to their origin which is the permanent dwelling-place [. . .]. That soul will certainly remain in everlasting torment, [. . .] abandoned by the body, now returned to its earthly element, that led it astray to the sensual world, suspended between the supernal and lower worlds until the Day of Judgment, wandering remorseful, far from its Creator and consumed in the flame of separation (Jer. 2:13) (I Sam. 25:29)[33] (fol. 70).

VII. *Obstacles to Salvation*

As an appendix to these eschatological considerations, the author discusses the obstacles to the soul's salvation which he claims are of two kinds: concupiscence and apathy. Individuals who are subject to these two vices,

---

[32] David is considered by the Pietists the archetype of the Divine lover. See our author's "Mystical Treatise," p. 12, n. 30 and *Deux traités*, 172, 267, 291.

[33] This is reminiscent of the Neoplatonic doctrine of the eschatological errance of the unmeritorious soul. Cf. *Theologia Aristotelis*, ed. A. Badawi (Kuwait, 1977), 23.

called metaphorically in Scripture "ox" and "ass" (Is. 32:20), are known as "people of the earth" (fols. 1a–2a).

VIII. *The Purpose of Man*

A new chapter opens with the statement:

> Every creature in this world, from the ant to the elephant, consists of matter endowed with a form containing a spiritual attribute (*maʿna*). The latter is comprised of a kernel (*sirr*)[34] emanated from the Divine generosity, in which God has deposited this form for a particular purpose [. . .]. Now, the prophets, having perceived the kernels of some of these creatures, understood their purposes but not those of others. Since man's matter is the most harmonious and his form the most noble, the Creator entrusted him with two exalted features, the one spiritual and noble, capable of refinement (*tajawhur*, marg. *tahdhīb*) and perception (*idrāk*), i.e. the rational soul, and the other divine and lofty, prone to instruction (*taʿlīm*, marg. *takhrīj*) and gnosis, i.e. the human intellect. By virtue of these two noble features, man possesses manifold purposes which can be subsumed under three headings: (1) a universal purpose; (2) a particular purpose; and (3) a divine purpose.
>
> The universal purpose of man in relation to the world is to become therein a representative of God by acting with equity and emulating the Divine attributes (Ps.115:16).[35]
>
> Man's second purpose, that concerning his personal perfection, is the pursuit of knowledge whose objective is in turn twofold: (a) the soul's felicity (*tawfīq*) through obedience to God (Deut. 11:13); and (b) love of God (Deut. 6:5), leading to "attachment" to Him (*deviqah*) (Deut. 13:5).[36] This attachment involves two goals: first, the soul's edification through the continuous [benefits bestowed by] the Divine effluence (*fayḍ*) throughout life in this world (Deut. 4:4), and second, the soul's enjoyment of God's intimacy (*qurb*) after leaving the body, and its eternal delight in His Presence (I Sam. 25:29).
>
> The third purpose of man, that pertaining to his Creator, is the unveiling of the heart's vision and the perception of the existential power (*al-qudra al-kaynūniyya*) which sustains and pervades all creation in its various forms. Were it not for man, the Creator's power would have remained unappreciated, like a beautiful garden with no one to stroll therein (2b–4b).

[34] See supra, n. 28.

[35] This notion of Qur'ānic origin (Sura 2:28) is particularly accentuated in Islamic esotericism. Through his realization of the Divine attributes, man—who is created in God's image—also becomes His vicegerent. Cf. R. Nicholson, *Studies in Islamic Mysticism* (London, 1978), 113.

[36] Here is an early occurrence of an important technical term which later designated mystical union. Cf. G. Scholem, "*Devekuth*, or Communion with God," *Review of Religion* 14 (1950): 115–139.

IX. *The Specificity of Man*

It is well known, according to the present treatise, that the specific name which designates each species of creatures is derived from its particular attribute or characteristic.[37] Now, man owes his name not to a specific physical feature but to the concomitants of the human state (*lawāzim al-insāniyya*) belonging to his intellectual faculty: discernment (*tamyīz*), imagination (*taṣwīr*), analysis (*tafṣīl*), ponderation (*tarjīḥ*), intelligence (*fiṭna*) and comprehension (*fahm*).[38] The function of these concomitants is to acquire virtue, which though ultimately deriving from the three cardinal virtues, can be classified under seven basic headings: (1) the consumption of a suitable diet; (2) truthful speech; (3) harmonious demeanor; (4) impeccable conduct; (5) judicious acts; (6) pure thoughts; and (7) scrupulous mind. As we have seen, the author equates these virtues (*faḍā'il khalqiyya*) with the "positive commandments" of the rabbinic tradition.[39] Their practice is to be accompanied by the precautions referred to in the verse "Guard thy foot when thou goest to the house of God" (Ecc. 4:17).[40] Now this verse can be understood as referring to external cleanliness, such as the ablutions required for outward worship. However the real significance of this verse is contained in its inner meaning (*bāṭin*), according to which "feet" signifies "the resources of the human condition" (*asbāb insāniyyatihi*). The house in question, whose glory is infinite, is therefore not one made of stone, as it is written: "Where is the house that ye may build unto me? And where is the place that may be my resting-place?" (Is. 66:1). "House," in fact, alludes to "first gnosis" (*maʿrifa ūlā*), i.e. recognition of the existential Divine omnipotence and proximity, which is realized through the practice of ethical virtues.[41] In other words, the prophet is saying: "O man, seeking proximity to God and waiting upon His Presence, if your aim be to strive towards His Presence, then safeguard the means (*asbāb*) by which you attain knowledge of Him and reach His presence [. . .]. Shelter your good deeds from the snares of evil to avoid being diverted from this great and noble aim (cf. also I Sam. 2:9)" (fols. 5–6).

In reply to his own observation that the verse just commented upon employs the expression "house of the Lord" (*beit elohim*) and not the "house

---

[37] According to the Kabbalah, the names of objects designate their spiritual essence.

[38] Although all the terms of this enumeration of the intellectual faculties are known in Arabic philosophy, as far as can be gathered, they cannot be identified with a particular system.

[39] Cf. supra, n. 19.

[40] Cf. the interpretation given by Obadiah Maimonides, *Deux traités*, 144.

[41] Cf. supra, n. 25.

of the Eternal" (*beit ḥavayah*), the author states that "this belongs to the secrets (*sodot*) which cannot be disclosed in a book, but can only be revealed to an individual fulfilling the conditions laid down by the [Rabbis], to wit 'that he be wise and understandeth of himself, and then only the headings of the chapters are entrusted to him'" (bḤag. 13a).[42] The author, however, feeling somewhat obliged after having slightly raised the veil of secrecy, resolves to disclose a hint which "nonetheless is without risk of endangering the soul by revealing a doctrine it is incapable of understanding." Whereas virtuous deeds are the means of reaching the "house of the Lord" and dwelling therein (Ps. 84:5), i.e. perceiving the Divine power pervading all existence, access to the "elevated paths" (*al-masālik al-rafʿīa*)[43] comes about through an uplifting by means of the metaphysical entities (*al-taraqiyyāt biʾl-maʿānī ʾl-mujarrada*). This constitutes the Way reaching (*wuṣūl*)[44] the "house of the Eternal" (fols. 5a–8b). With the conclusion of this chapter, the author's ethical considerations draw to an end and the following chapters develop his anthropological doctrine.

X. *The Threefold Division of Creation*

The whole of creation can be divided into the three categories of superior, inferior and intermediate beings, each in turn being divisible into numerous subsections. Some of these categories enjoy a status both in existence and in God's Knowledge; others occupy a position in the degrees of existence but do not have status in the Divine Knowledge. To the former category belong the superior beings—angels, heavenly bodies and the spheres—and the intermediate beings—the human elite called "the people of God," who dwell in His house. The third category which does not figure in God's Knowledge is divided into minerals, vegetables and animals. However, base human beings whose deeds are defective are assimilated to this category.[45] The real intermediate beings are the pilgrims who ply the "Way of God." They constitute the elite of humanity and enjoy a position

[42] Cf. *Deux traités*, 145–46, no doubt based on Maimonides, *Guide*, Introduction.

[43] The expression "high ways" is also employed by Abraham Maimonides, *High Ways*, 1:144, 148–152; 2:418–20.

[44] *Wuṣūl* is also used by Abraham Maimonides; see *High Ways*, 1:95–101; 2:422. On the term see *Deux traités*, 273–74.

[45] This concept no doubt derives from Maimonides' theory of Providence according to which "only individual beings hav[ing] real existence [. . .] are endowed with Divine Intellect [. . .] and therefore Divine Providence acts upon them"; see *Guide* 3:19.

(*manzila*) in God's Knowledge in addition to their status in the world, to which they belong by virtue of their material bodies (fols. 8b–10a).

What is the nature of the status conferred by Divine Knowledge? The author compares the latter's action to that of the sun. Just as the physical sun generates and matures the material entities, so the sun of Divine Knowledge, called the spiritual sun or the sun of hearts, illumines the wayfarer's soul. On the other hand, if the soul does not behold this sun during its passage in this world, it will not have fulfilled its aim, and it would have been better to have been stillborn (Eccl. 6:4–5).[46] For a light extends from this sun to man's vital soul (Prov. 20:27), with which it must maintain a bond, otherwise it is doomed to be extinguished in darkness (Job 21:17).

> Not so the lamp of the righteous which derives from this sun, i.e. the sun of hearts, as it is said, "The path of the righteous is as the light of dawn that shineth more and more unto the perfect day" (Prov. 4:18). In other words, the light of the righteous increases continuously until the time of separation from the physical world [. . .]. Just as the moon arrives at its fullness the fourteenth night [of its cycle] in harmony with the sun of the physical world, so the plenitude of the soul is related to the sun of hearts. Indeed, the soul's bond with its principle while in this world, and its return thereunto after separation from the body are brought about solely through the apprehension (of intelligibles) mediated through Knowledge which is the sun of hearts.

Every soul belonging to each of the three degrees of humankind receives a portion of sunlight in accordance with the refinement (*tajawhur*) of its conduct. If it perseveres in its refinement, then it will necessarily be vouchsafed "permanence" in the afterlife. Indeed, the soul will obtain Divine gnosis from the sun of knowledge to the extent of its assimilation of the Divine attributes, with the result of its being favored with intimacy and Providence (fols. 11a–12a).

An intermediate paragraph discusses the actions of the various categories of existence, from the angels down to the lowest forms of humanity. Man alone is capable of perpetrating the worst evils, precisely by means of the faculties of discernment and imagination, which, intended for his perfection, are utilized instead by the wicked to wreak destruction (Hos. 14:10). These evildoers, ranking in wretchedness in accordance with the gravity of their sins, are the lowliest of all beings and are inferior even to minerals (fols. 15a–16a).

---

[46] Cf. similar exegesis *apud* Obadiah Maimonides, *Deux traités*, 142.

The author then resumes his discussion of the intermediate category who enjoy Divine recognition and an existential status. Because of the middle position they hold between the superior and lower beings, they constitute the "elite of humanity" and the "heart of the world." Individuals in this category either belong to the class of (1) prophets or (2) wayfarers (*sālikun*), the latter being themselves divided into three groups called "degrees of humankind" (*marātib al-insāniyya*): righteous, saints, humble ones (fols. 16a–18b).

XI. *The Ten Categories of Providence*

At this point, the author begins to set forth what seems to have been the central part of his doctrine related to the theme of Divine Providence. Since creatures occupy various degrees in the Knowledge of God, there must be a hierarchy in Divine Providence in accordance with the extent of God's concern with them. These degrees, ten in number, are designated by the following names: (1) universal; (2) particular; (3) dependent; (4) independent; (5) retributive; (6) complete; (7) perfect. The three remaining degrees of Providence are peculiar to the angelic beings, celestial bodies and spheres. Universal Providence concerns all existents, whereas the following six degrees are vouchsafed to man according to the quantity of Divine attributes assimilated by him. For instance, the sixth form of Providence is extended to the individual who has acquired all Divine qualities and who is practically devoid of their opposite traits (fols. 17a–18b).

Providence is thus proportional to spiritual degree. Our author distinguishes five levels, in ascending order: the righteous (*ṣaddiqim*), who possess two or three Divine attributes and deserve the second and third degrees of Providence; the saints (*ḥasidim*), who deserve the fourth degree of Providence; the humble (*ʿanavim*), who deserve the fifth; and prophets, who deserve the sixth degree. As for the seventh degree, it was attained solely by Moses, the prophet-legislator (*rasūl*).[47]

XII. *The Universal Hierarchy*

As stated, the universe is divided into three levels: (1) higher, comprising angels, constellations and spheres; (2) lower, comprising minerals, veg-

---

[47] The author adopts the Islamic distinction between the prophet-preacher (*nabī*) and the prophet-cum-politician (*rasūl*).

etables, animals and inferior men; and (3) intermediate, inhabited by (a) prophets and (b) spiritual pilgrims, who can enter into the prophetic degrees. The prophets in turn are divided into three classes which cannot be discussed, whereas the pilgrims are divided into (a) "righteous ones," (b) "saints" and (c) "humble ones." "These spiritual wayfarers travel the noble path, i.e. the sole *sharīʿa* of Moses, for just as God is One, so is His Path, that is His Law is One" (fol. 18).

XIII. *The Righteous*

Next there follow three chapters, each devoted to an exposition of one of these three categories.

The righteous are those who, through the exoteric practice of the Law, that is the only Law, that given to Moses, have acquired the quality of uprightness (*ʿadāla*), with which God is described (Ps. 145:7). In fact this category entails three virtues, within each of which eight grades can be distinguished, which means that this category entails, in all, twenty-four grades. Their components enjoy the first three types of providence depending on the spiritual levels they have attained. Their spiritual states (*ḥāl*)[48] in relation to God are those of patience (*ṣabr*), gratitude (*shukr*), refuge (*iltijāʾ*), reliance (*ittikāl*) and contentment (*riḍāʾ*) and they in turn are beneficiaries of His protection (Ps. 34:16).

XIV. *The Saints*

The saints are those who have gone beyond their duty in the practice of virtue, showing kindness even to those who do not act kindly towards them.[49] Their spiritual states (*ḥāl*) towards God are those of fear (*khawf*), love (*maḥabba*), desire (*shawq*), proximity (*qurb*) and continual remembrance (*dhikr*). In return, God reveals to them the exoteric as well as the esoteric aspects of the Law and continuously maintains within their hearts the bond with His overflowing generosity, never forsaking them (Ps. 37:28). In addition to possessing the three aforementioned virtues, they also practice "saintliness" (*ḥesed*) and like the foregoing group are divided into twenty-four grades (fols. 20b–21b).

---

[48] *Aḥwāl* are the mutable spiritual states of the classical Sūfi path, as opposed to *maqāmāt*—permanent spiritual stations.

[49] Cf. supra, n. 21.

XV. *The Humble*

As for the third category, they are called "humble" for they are people of humility (*tawaḍḍuʿ*), modesty (*dhill*) and contrition (*inkisār*)[50] [. . .] their preoccupation is God, their spiritual state (*ḥāl*) is with Him, their objective (*qaṣd*) is God and their speech proceeds from Him. They are absorbed (*ghāʾibīn*) by His gnosis, enraptured by the contemplation of His grandeur, and are in a simultaneous state of distraction and guidance on account of Him. Upon seeing a creature, these adepts (*qawm*) perceive its Creator within it, upon inhaling a perfume, they apprehend the existential force pervading and perpetuating it. Upon tasting a savor, they likewise perceive the pervading force and quality within it [. . .]. In a word, at every instant they cognize God in all things.[51] This category, referred to in the verse "Happy are they that dwell in Thy house" (Ps. 84:5), possess the fifth virtue, that of truth (*emet*) which consists in giving every thing its due and assigning every object to its appropriate place.[52] In return God continuously bestows His gifts upon them, and, furthermore, all of creation, from the highest to the lowest entity pledge obedience to them, as it is written "But unto the humble He giveth grace" (Prov. 3:34) (fol. 22b).

They enjoy the fullest form of Providence, known as retributive Providence, insofar as they master most of the attributes of spiritual affinity (*ṣifāt al-munāsaba*), without, however, possessing them to perfection (*biʾl-tammām*), in which case they would have become prophets. The author explains that perfect possession of the attributes involves a sort of *coincidentia oppositorum*, consisting in mastering both an attribute and its opposite trait. Thus, for example, he who feels compassion (*raḥma*) for a penitent could also display severity to those disobedient to God. The simultaneous possession of an attribute and its opposite is a characteristic of the prophets, "for through the divine faculty and supernal gnosis (*al-maʿrifa al-rabbāniyya*) they employ each attribute in its appropriate place."[53]

While these three degrees, with all their numerous grades, constitute the "Path to God," the degree of the "humble" is the highest. Those that attain it are described as inhabiting (*ḥulūl*) the rank nearest to God, that of correlation (*manzilat al-muqābala*), insofar as they possess lowliness

---

[50] These three notions are also referred to in the author's "Mystical Treatise," 19, 21–23, as being the most sublime virtues.

[51] Cf. supra, n. 26.

[52] According to Ibn al-ʿArabī "Truth confers on each being in the universal hierarchy a degree or right, and guidance or truth." See D. Gril, "*Adab* and Revelation," in *Muḥyiddīn Ibn ʿArabī*, ed. S. Hirtenstein and M. Tiernan (Shaftesbury, 1993), p. 230, n. 52.

[53] Cf. Ibn al-ʿArabī's definition of the *adīb* or sage who: "comports himself with each spiritual station according to the station (. . .) uniting in himself noble virtues while he knows the ignoble ones but does not adopt them" (quoted by Gril, ibid., 229).

in the extreme which is in inverse correspondence to God's loftiness. In its initial stages, the degree of humility manifests itself externally in their countenance, limbs, movements and actions. In its final stage, it impregnates their spirit and the heart of their soul, that is the heart of their spiritual substance (*al-jawāhīr al-ruḥāniyya*). The latter is the element in man, which, when perfected, returns to its source and abides in perpetuity (Is. 57:15) (fols. 24a–b).

These individuals, by virtue of their humility and restraint, enjoy God's protection (Ex. 14:14). They are those named the elite of the elite, who are unknown in their reality except to God, who shields them "in His innermost chambers as an owner cherishes a jewel."[54] The adepts of this third category are those who have been capable of preserving from defilement the divine kernel (*al-sirr al-ilāhī*) entrusted to those who walk the Way of the Torah. Had this kernel been defiled, then they would have remained powerless to attain this noble degree of humility. For lowliness and contrition can only reside in a heart totally free from uncleanliness (fol. 26 a–b).

XVI. *The Four Moral Qualities*

Now this divine kernel possesses four qualities (*ʿalāʾim*) which enable it to pursue its lofty objectives, i.e. knowledge of the Creator and of the mysteries embodied in His creatures, the soul's assimilation of the divine attributes, and the soul's cleaving to Him and abiding in His eternity. Their function is to "lift" (*rafʿ*) the gates of the heart, unveil its sight [. . .] so that it may behold the pure effluence emanating from its source, as it is said "Lift up your heads, O ye gates [. . .] that the King of glory may enter" (Ps. 24:9). These qualities are four in number: (1) etiquette (*adab*);[55] (2) kindness; (3) meekness; and (4) awe. The first is divided into (a) outward etiquette, which concerns restraint of the external senses and speech, and (b) inward etiquette, involving the discipline of thought and the heart. The second quality comprises softness of speech and a conciliatory nature, whereas the third quality implies silence and refraining from dispute. The last quality consists in a constant awe of the consequences of one's actions (fols. 26b–28b).

[54] This is perhaps a reference to the hidden character of the saints. See our article, "La Hiérarchie des saints dans la mystique juive et dans la mystique islamique," in *Studies in the Literature of Jewish Thought presented to A. Safran* (Ramat Gan, 1990), 54–56.

[55] On the Ṣūfī notion of *adab*, see Abū ʾl-Ḥafṣ al-Suhrawardī, *ʿAwārif al-maʿārif* (Beirut, n.d.), Chap. 32 and Gril, "Adab and Revelation." Our author also insists on the discipline of restraint (*ḥifẓ al-adab*) in his "Mystical Treatise," 24–27.

XVII. *The Path of Holiness*

These qualities are known as the "path of holiness," whereas the obstacles in this path are known as impurities. The latter are either physical defilements such as death or leprosy, or spiritual impurities through misuse of the ear, eye, tongue, limbs or heart. In addition to the foregoing, the vices of greed, apathy, indolence and ignorance also constitute a hindrance to spirituality (fols. 29–30).

XVIII. *The Three Causes of Providence*

At the outset of the soul's path, Providence is induced by three motives. First, there is the refinement of the soul through the practice of ethical virtues which strengthen it in much the same way as material food fortifies the physical body. Second, in accordance with the extent of his endeavor, man's quest and virtuous conduct arouse the attention of Reason. Third, Providence stems from the generosity and compassion of God who created the world so that man, whose purpose is self-perfection and drawing near to God, would clothe himself in the Divine attributes such as compassion, forgiveness and kindness. For if mankind were devoid of these attributes, then God's generosity and compassion would be prevented from being realized through them. Indeed, in response to man's endeavor, God will send man His angels to protect and succor him so that none shall stand in his way (Ps. 91:11) (I Chr. 28:9). The practice of the positive precepts, i.e. the ethical virtues, leads to the soul's ascent to the elevated paths (*al-masālik al-rafīʿa*) in the same way as an antechamber gives access to the inner chamber. Thus, the purging of the soul from iniquity is the outer chamber (*al-dahālīz al-burrāniyya*), while acquisition of virtue is the inner chamber (*al-dahālīz al-juwāniyya*). The "elevated paths" are situated in the centre of the chamber, whereas the [attainment of] the knowledge of mysteries is the unsealing of the chamber's treasure chests. Attending the Divine Presence is to be placed in the forefront of the chamber, while [the gift of] prophetic vision is to be informed of the Creator's command ere it is issued to His subjects (fols. 30–33a).

Providence will assist him in the overcoming of his evil inclinations for God desires the repentance of the wicked and not his death, i.e. his being cut off from the Divine source (*al-inqiṭāʿ*) (Ez. 33:11) (fol. 34a).

XIX. *The Providential Role of Reason*

The author momentarily interrupts his line of thought in order to paint a majestic fresco of the wonders of nature:

> And God established the creatures in their positions, such that the universe is likened unto a garden containing every wonderful fruit and marvelous form. Now God vested each particular form with a kernel (*sirr*),[56] resembling an open eye between it and God so that the beings constantly contemplate Him, His bounty never being veiled from them so that the flow of His generosity continuously penetrates the heart of every being (35b). [. . .] Then, having assigned a unique kernel to each being, He placed within man the kernels of all those beings having preceded him in creation. Hence, He endowed man with the totality of kernels, so that the man was entirely made up of "eyes." Then, He assigned to man a wonderful kernel, divine and luminous, in order to guide him in the right path, and direct him through its light. This kernel is Reason (36b). In addition to this source of guidance, God also gave man "a noble science to direct the soul from the moment it enters this world until the moment it forsakes it—the holy Torah (*sharīʿa*), perfecting virtue and concepts." (37b).

XX. *The Degrees of Prophecy*

Having outlined the causes of Providence, the author propounds his theory of prophecy, which seems to have been the culminating theme of the work. The chapter on this subject, which contains one of the most remarkable descriptions of the prophetic experience in Jewish literature, begins with the following declaration, from which it is clear that the author is writing not from a theoretical standpoint but from a practical one:

> A discourse on the prophetic process, its categories and degrees would serve no use, since the purpose of the discussion of prophecy and prophets is not simply to be informative about these noble and great things but to instigate the soul to arrive at these sublime notions and realize them through action. Indeed the ultimate purpose of this discussion is to arouse the souls from the slumber of apathy and to extract them from the darkness of ignorance [. . .] in order that they obtain the ultimate felicity." (fols. 39–40)
>
> [. . .] What can and must be said concerning prophecy is that which is conducive to the opening of the eyes of the soul's heart, the heightening of its longing for these noble ends and its craving to attain them. Thus this exposition [is intended]

---

[56] Compare this with the following doctrine of Ibn al-ʿArabī: "God created Man as an epitome of all the subtle rays of the universe. From man a subtle ray proceeds towards every thing in the universe. This ray transmits to man that which God deposited in that thing for man. Through the intermediary of this ray, the gnostic moves that thing towards its purpose"; see *Futuḥāt*, 1:157.

to bring about awareness of the noble treasures lying within man, which if unpursued, will never be obtained. Indeed, if he were apprised that in his very abode a real treasure lies hidden, would his resolve not be to seek it unceasingly until God revealed it to him and brought him to it? In truth, within the self of the human soul lies a spiritual and luminous light derived from the Divine radiance, as it is written: "the soul of man is the light of God" (Pr. 20:27). However, at the outset of its existence in the sensual world, this light, which is the soul, though pure, is not yet luminous. Likewise, a mirror, when it first emerges from the hand of the craftsman, has to be polished and refined before it can reflect the sun's rays. The state of the human soul upon entering the world is similar to that of the mirror,[57] pending the cultivation of the heart through hearkening to different kinds of wisdom, referred to in the verse "incline thine ear" (Ps. 45:11). This verse alludes to the soul's hearkening by means of the heart. This signifies that a voice passes from the faculty of hearing to the heart of the soul and thence radiates in the midst of that heart. In this manner, the purport of the message permeates the domain of the heart, moving it to action, if this be its implication. If, on the other hand, the message implies knowledge, then the soul will preserve it in its midst and act in accordance with that knowledge as it sees fit (fol. 41b).

The author goes on to enumerate the levels of knowledge imparted by the salutary messages (*aqwāl nafiʿa*) which eventually lead to prophecy: knowledge of God's creative power, of His universal omnipotence, Providence, compassion and goodness towards all beings, of His special compassion for man, of the gift of Reason to the human soul to guide it and conduct it in the ways of the Torah, of God's love for the soul and the latter's desire to draw near to Him, of the special precepts given to Israel to direct them to these great things.

If the eyes of the soul's heart are then opened through this knowledge of which it receives communication and the soul acts thereupon until it shines forth, then the veils will fall away from its face. Therefore the soul will begin to turn towards its source, that is its Master, Creator of the Universe and will constantly engage in remembrance, praise and exaltation of Him. The soul will become luminous and the reverence of His magnitude which will radiate in its heart will clothe it in modesty and humility. Through constant contemplation of the aforementioned knowledge, the soul will become pure until the dawn of the heart's sun breaks forth into its heart, that is the Divine kernel, and it will comprehend the reality of that knowledge. Thereupon, the kernel, which is the heart of the soul, will be permeated by the light of knowledge so that the soul will become totally oblivious to the phenomenal world of the senses. Now in its rapture (*ghaybatihā*), the soul will perceive a grandeur which will dazzle it to a point where its existence will be effaced (*yamtaḥiq*). Thereupon the soul will find itself bathing in the presence of an overwhelming light, called the "majestic light" (*al-*

[57] On the comparison of the soul to a mirror, a frequent metaphor in Ṣūfī literature, see "Mystical Treatise," 16–17, 29 and *Deux traités*, p. 154, n. 65 and p. 249.

> *nūr al-rabbānī*).[58] Henceforth the soul will perceive the mysteries (*ghayb*) which appear within this light before they become manifest to the senses. To the soul they will take the shape of combined letters or exhibit the form of sensible phenomena, these forms acting for the soul as images and parables so that the soul may distinguish the allegory from the allegorized object and inform its fellows of it, as it is said: "And by the ministry of the prophets have I used similitudes" (Hos. 12:11). And this is prophecy.

The profundity of the perception depends on the strength of the vision. Some will perceive visions of the present while others will envision events which are to transpire in years, even centuries to come. These individuals, by reason of their dearness to God are never absent from the world for they constitute the "pillars of the universe"[59] (*qawāʾid al-ʿālam*). Unto them He reveals His will (Am. 3:7), unless there is overwhelming darkness, or mankind has no need of them, or they are just prophets unto themselves.[60] Prophecy is either concerned with future or past events, both communicated through the "majestic light," as it is said: "Through Thy light do we perceive light" (Ps. 36:10) (fols. 42–43).

XXI. *The Four Categories of Prophecy*

The author distinguishes four categories of prophecy:[61]

(1) unveiling of the senses (*al-kashf al-ḥissī*), which is a sort of clairvoyance solely concerning individuals known to the person prophesying, as, for example in the case of Elisha and the Shunamite woman (II Kgs. 27:3);

(2) imaginative revelation (*al-tajallī al-khayālī*), which is communicated by angels appearing in human form or as birds, or takes place as a vision of the "spirits of the prophets." In all these cases, a vision is perceived unaccompanied by speech, unless it is combined with a form of the third category. This category is reserved for prophets but can be vouchsafed to "saints" and even more so to "humble ones."

---

[58] The vision of light in Jewish mystical experience has been discussed by M. Idel, *The Mystical Experience in Abraham Abulafia* (Albany, 1987), Chap. 3:2.

[59] Term designating the high-ranking saints. Cf. "La Hiérarchie," 49 and 59.

[60] The expression was coined by Maimonides; see *Guide* 2:37. Abulafia uses it to designate the kabbalists; cf. Idel, *Mystical Experience*, Chap. III:2, n. 26.

[61] Maimonides (*Guide* 2:45) enumerates eleven degrees which can be reduced to three: internal inspiration, angelic vision and hearing of speech.

(3) intelligible perception (*al-fahm al-fikrī*) concerns, more particularly, knowledge of the mysteries of beings and of the mysteries of the meanings of prophetic texts, as well as the Divine government if it approaches the phenomenal world. This form of prophecy is accompanied by the appearance of a form of speech known as "intelligible speech" (*al-khiṭāb al-fahmī*).

(4) true unveiling (*al-idrāk al-ḥaqīqī* or *al-kashf al-ḥaqīqī*) consists in the soul's perception of future events in accordance with its degree of refinement. This category embraces the perception of the divine statutes (*aḥkām*), and divine government and the spiritual effluence which pervades and sustains all beings.[62]

All these categories are effectuated by the eyes of the soul's heart (fols. 43–44).

XXII. *The Eyes of the Soul's Heart*

At this point the author introduces an extremely strange doctrine which is an extension of the notion of the soul's heart and which as far as the present writer is aware is unique in the whole of Jewish ethical literature. The author claims that the soul possesses twelve such "eyes," this number corresponding to the pair of eyes possessed by the faculty of speech and each of the five senses—sight, hearing, smell, taste and touch—six to the right of the heart and six to its left.[63] Just as the soul apprehends the sensibilia through the intermediary of the senses, so the heart perceives through its eyes the intelligibilia, simple and compound notions. The author then reviews these "eyes" explaining their respective positive and negative functions. For example, in the case of the pair of eyes assigned to hearing, the purpose of the right-hand one is to perceive the sounds and melodies (*aṣwāt wa-naghamāt*) made by the separate entities,[64] whereas the left-hand eye

---

[62] Cf. supra, n. 25.

[63] Cf. al-Ghazzālī, who contrasts the defects of the physical eyes with the virtue of the inner eye of intelligence, which "breaks through into the inwardness of things and into their secrets; apprehends the reality of things and their essential spirits (. . .) what rank of Being they occupy, what their relation is to all other created things"; see *Mishkāt al-anwār*, Chap. 1, trans. W. Gairdner (Lahore, 1952), 81–91, esp. 86. Cf. also Suhrawardī, *ʿAwārif*, Chap. 3:5, trans. H. Wilberforce Clarke (Delhi, 1984), 135–36: "God gave the (soul) two glances of divine blessing: one for beholding the majesty of *qudrat*, the other for beholding the beauty of *ḥikmat*."

[64] A reference to the "Music of the spheres." See the important note in G. Vajda, *Juda ben Nissim Ibn Malka* (Paris, 1954), pp. 101–102, n. 3. Our author's expression is close to that of the *Rasāʾil ikhwān al-ṣafāʾ*, Pt. III, Ch. 31.

is to perceive the speech of the composite entities, that is the entities attached to matter:

> Now this resonance is not an audible sound like that which is heard by the human ear but it is an utterance emanating from the kernel of that composite or simple entity into the kernel of the hearkening prophet. It communes with him by means of an interior voice. The prophet then articulates from this form which expresses its state and the mysteries and concepts with which the Creator has endowed it (fols. 44b–45a).

> There are prophets who possess only a single eye of vision and others who possess both, or just those of hearing or those of both vision and hearing [. . .] in short, they differ greatly in respect to this perception and constitute a limitless hierarchy. The acquisition of all these eyes within the person of a single prophet is a rare occurrence but words would fail even partially to exhaust the reasons for this situation. Now all of these eyes were to be found in our master, the prophet-legislator [Moses], may peace be upon him, as God Himself testified: "If there be a prophet among you, I the Lord do make Myself known unto him in a vision, I do speak with him in a dream. My servant Moses is not so; he is steadfast in all My house" (Num. 12:7), that is, he possessed all of the [eyes] in their reality with no exception, either in the realm of total or partial perception (fol. 45a–b).

XXIII. *The Three Qualities Required for Prophecy*

These prophetic categories are subject to three qualities whose intensity determines the degree of prophetic perception. These are: wisdom, strength and fortune, as the Sages have said, "Prophetic inspiration is only vouchsafed to an individual who is wise, strong and rich" (bShab. 92a).[65] First, the wise man is he who possesses three qualities, the first of which comprises the seven virtues, mentioned earlier.[66] Second, the would-be prophet must possess a behavior characterized by goodness, kindness, sincerity, truthfulness, and compassion. Third, he must be endowed with foresight. The second condition of prophecy is strength which implies, not physical prowess, but the capacity to dominate the soul and its faculties so that they do not deviate from the Truth. The third condition, fortune, entails not material but psychological well-being—the state of contentedness with the least portion of all that exists in the world (fol. 46a–b).

Of course the predisposition to prophecy is not to be found in equal proportion in every soul. The reasons for this discrepancy are numerous

[65] This is the formulation used by Maimonides; see *Guide* 2:32, *Eight Chapters*, Chap. 7, and *Mishneh Torah*, "Yesodei ha-Torah," 7:1.

[66] Supra, n. 39.

but follow from three principles. The first is genetic (*tarkīb*) and concerns the intellectual and ethical constitution of the prophets' forebears. If the latter were righteous at the time of the child's emergence into the world of creation,[67] then with Divine assistance the child could be counted among the saints. Similarly if the parents were "humble" (*ʿanavim*), the child could become a great prophet. The second principle involves a positive education (*tarbiyya*) which the parents are also instrumental in transmitting. The third element is environment (*ʿishra*), for a child will be influenced by the surrounding society and absorb the virtues and vices practised by his contemporaries (fol. 47b).

From this point of view humanity can be divided into five groups: (1) the souls of totally unperceptive brutes, who are compared to black and tarnished stones; (2) the souls of righteous individuals (*ṣaddiqim*), compared to a shiny mirror as yet unaffected by light; (3) the souls of saints—comparable to a transparent vessel penetrated by light but which does not illuminate others; (4) the souls of the humble, comparable to crystal which reflects light on others; (5) the souls of prophets, comparable to the stars which shine forth, each according to its reception of light to provide others "with illumination, knowledge, physical and spiritual excellence, salvation from mortal disease and innumerable and varied influences." Amongst these, Moses' soul occupied the rank of the sun, whereas Samuel occupied that of the moon. The planets are the apostles and the fixed stars are the prophets who were not apostles (fol. 48 a–b).[68]

The Prophetic Hierarchy

The last section of the preserved chapters deals further with prophetic aptitude and its development. The author claims that [the limitations] of physical dispositions account for variety in the respective degrees of prophecy. Some of these are unmodifiable, while others can be improved by moral training consisting in the coaching of the vital faculty. This process is known as mortification and is referred to in the verse "Precious in the eyes of the Lord is the death of his saints" (Ps. 116:15).[69] In accordance

[67] The determining influence of the parents' spiritual status at the time of procreation is also of importance in kabbalistic doctrine. Cf. Ch. Mopsik, *Lettre sur la sainteté* (Lagrasse, 1986), 45–163.

[68] See supra, n. 47.

[69] The author uses this verse in his "Mystical Treatise," 163 to designate the soul's "initiatory death" before its "resurrection" through gnosis.

with the degree of mortification of the vital faculty, the veils will disappear and God will appear to the subject.

XXIV. *The Theophanies of Majesty and Beauty*

As an enlargement of this, the author provides an interesting exegesis of the introductory verse to the vision of Isaiah: "In the year that king Uzziah died I saw the Lord sitting upon a high and exalted throne (Is. 6:1)." He insists that the fact that the Divine name mentioned in this context is not the Tetragrammaton, is based on a great mystery, which, however, cannot be divulged. The unveiling (*kashf*) experienced by Isaiah is known as a theophany (*tajallī*), which can be of two sorts: a theophany of majesty (*tajallī jalāl*) or of beauty (*tajallī jamāl*).[70] The human condition is unable to bear the first but is annihilated by reason of its grandeur and nobility (Ex. 33:20).[71] Indeed, this is the unveiling of the face of greatness in whose presence even the angels, i.e. the separate intellects[72] are consumed (Job 4:18). On the other hand the human condition can endure the theophany of beauty, which is the revelation of the "eye of clemency" imbued with compassion for the creatures (Ex. 33:19), sparkling with a light known as the light of guidance. The intensity and limpidity of this light will vary according to the degree of mortification or of the prophetic qualities of the individual:

> However, amongst humankind there is no human form that does not possess a share of this unveiling and prophetic disposition, providing the individual prepares himself for its reception. But if he again defiles himself, then it will be withheld from him [. . .] and most souls can never regain their previous refinement (*jawharuhā*) if they suffer defilement, especially if the latter is due to a natural effect which cannot then be erased [. . .]. And these obstacles to prophecy and revelation (*kashūfāt*) are the cause of the death of the rational soul, its severance from its Creator and its loss of eternal life, either by the treason of the vital faculty's rebelliousness, or its having itself acted as the instrument of vice.

---

70 These are the Divine attributes of severity and grace as propounded in Ṣūfī doctrine. Our author also evokes these two attributes in his "Mystical Treatise," 21.

71 Cf. Ibn al-ʿArabī, *On Majesty and Beauty: The Kitāb al-Jalāl wa-l-Jamāl*, trans. R.T. Harris, *Journal of the Muḥyiddin Ibn ʿArabi Society* 8 (1989): 5–32. Interestingly, Ibn al-ʿArabī discusses (p. 15) the Quranic account of Moses' request to behold God (Sura 7:143), whereupon he was nearly annihilated by the Divine Majesty.

72 The identification of the separate intellects with the angels was borrowed from Ibn Sīnā, notably by Maimonides, *Guide*, 1:49.

Conclusion

Having reached the limit of the synopsis of this interesting treatise as far as it has been preserved, it will not be unwarranted by way of conclusion to rehearse some of the salient points of our author's doctrine. Broadly, the author divides the spiritual path into two phases, the "degrees of the saints" and the "paths of gnosis," or the "elevated paths." The former is subdivided in turn into the path of "purity," obtained by the avoidance of vice through the practice of the negative precepts, and the path of "holiness," obtained by the acquisition of virtue through the practice of the positive commandments.[73]

On the other hand, the spiritual way is plyed by three types of wayfarers (*sālikūn*): (a) the righteous ones; (b) the pious ones or saints; and (c) the humble ones. These three categories probably correspond to the common Ṣūfī distinction between the legal path (*sharīʿa*), the path of spiritual discipline (*ṭarīqa*) and the path of Truth (*ḥaqīqa*). Indeed, the "righteous" fulfill the exoteric law to its utmost, whereas the "pious" integrate the esoteric teachings, or "spirit of the precepts." Through the assimilation of the Divine attributes they create a spiritual affinity with the supernal world and attract its illuminative effluence (*fayḍ*) through the intermediary of the Active Intellect, whom the author calls the "Sun of Hearts." Having thus induced Divine Providence, the soul of the pious individual gains access to the higher phase of the "paths of gnosis" through the illumination (*haskalah*) of his [rational] soul by the Active Intellect, eventually winning the intimacy of the Divine Presence, and, in consequence, life everlasting, which is man's goal. In this upward process, certain privileged souls, predisposed by their parental and social context, as well as by their personal ethical and intellectual capacity, are vouchsafed prophethood. The author of the present treatise expatiates on the theme of prophecy with great frankness, insisting that his intention is to instigate his readers to undertake practical steps to obtain this end, which, as other Jewish Pietists held at the time, was about to become an actuality.

---

[73] In his "Mystical Treatise," the author expounds a similar doctrine: "Providence is subject to spiritual affinity, itself a condition of purity resulting from the observance of the negative precepts, and holiness resulting from the performance of the positive precepts"; "by the ordinary practice of religious duties man disciplines his soul and takes on human attributes, while the supererogatory performance of the precepts, 'the station of the saints,' through assimilation of Divine attributes; procures spiritual affinity which engenders 'proximity' and 'love.' Thereupon the veils are dissipated—his mortal attributes are effaced—between the soul and its Creator and it accedes to gnosis."

APPENDIX

A. *The Ten Categories of Providence*

World	Content	Attributes	Type of Providence
Lower	Minerals, vegetables animals, non-spiritual man	_______	Universal
Intermediate	(1) Wayfarers (*sālikūn fī derekh ha-shem*)		
	(a) saints (*ṣaddiqim*)	righteousness (*ṣedeq*)	Particular Dependent 24 degrees
	(b) pious (*ḥasidim*)	piety (*ḥesed*)	Independent 24 degrees
	(c) humble (*ʿanavim*)	humility	Retributive 24 degrees
	(2) Prophets		
	(a) Non-Mosaic	all	Complete
	(b) Moses	all + opposites	Perfect
Higher	Angels Stars Spheres		

B. *Categories of Prophecy*

1. Unveiling of the senses —clairvoyance
2. Imaginative revelation —angel
3. Intellective perception —secrets of creation and Scripture
4. True unveiling —full prophecy

Unveiling of the twelve eyes of the heart corresponding to the two pairs (left/righthand) of eyes of the five senses and speech, e.g. sight—right eye perceives descending influence, left eye perceives ascending influence.

ADDENDUM

During a visit to St. Petersburg in the spring of 1994, the author discovered further fragments of this work:

II Firk. Heb.-Ar. I.3040 (4 fols.)
II Firk. Heb.-Ar. N.S. 136 (4 fols.)
II Firk. Heb.-Ar. N.S. 812, fols. 11–14 (4 fols.)
II Firk. Heb.-Ar. N.S. 1102, fols. 28–29 (2 fols.)

YEMENITE PHILOSOPHICAL MIDRASH AS A SOURCE FOR THE INTELLECTUAL HISTORY OF THE JEWS OF YEMEN

Y. Tzvi Langermann

During the period ranging from the mid-thirteenth to the mid-sixteenth century, the Jews of Yemen produced some eight philosophical midrashim on the Torah. These works are, in the main, compilations of citations from the Talmud, earlier midrash, and the writings of Maimonides, appended to the verses of each weekly portion. The authors added to these citations their own disquisitions in Judeo-Arabic, contributions which are decidedly philosophical in both tone and content.[1] Besides their philosophical midrashim on the Torah, the Yemenites composed a few similar works on other parts of the Bible, e.g. the Prophets and the Song of Songs.[2]

Midrashim on the Torah served as an important—perhaps the most important—vehicle for intellectual expression in the Yemen over the course of at least three centuries. The Yemenites continued to compile midrashim after the period in question; but these later works, the most famous of which is Shalom Shabbazi's *Ḥemdat yamim*, exhibit the influence of the Kabbalah, which ultimately displaced philosophy as the main preoccupation of Yemenite thinkers. In this paper I shall touch upon a number of issues in

---

[1] The authors of these midrashim and their works are: David al-ʿAdanī, *Midrash ha-gadol*; Nethanel b. Isaiah, *Nūr al-ẓalām* (or *Nūr al-ẓulm*); Zechariah ha-Rofé, *Midrash ha-ḥefeṣ*; Ḥoṭer b. Solomon, *Sirāj al-ʿuqūl*; Alu'el (David) b. Yeshaʿ, *Al-wajīz al-mughnī*; Saadya b. David, *Midrash ha-be'ur*; an anonymous, short midrash, written in 1525; and Shalom al-Rābiʿah, *Derash ha-mazhir*. All but the last two are well-attested in the scholarly literature. For a fuller discussion of the genre and full bibliography see my anthology, *Yemenite Midrash: Philosophical Commentaries Upon the Torah* (forthcoming). Most of the passages referred to in this paper will appear in full translation in that volume. I recently identified the midrash of 1525 and *Derash ha-mazhir* in unique manuscripts in the British Library; see Y. Tzvi Langermann, "Two Unknown Philosophical Midrashim from the Yemen" (Hebrew), *KS* 63 (1990/1): 1334–7. David Blumenthal made good use of much of this material in his two books on Ḥoṭer b. Solomon: *The Commentary of R. Ḥoṭer ben Shelomo to the Thirteen Principles of Maimonides* (Leiden, 1974); and *The Philosophic Questions and Answers of Ḥoṭer ben Shelomo* (Leiden, 1981).

[2] On Abraham b. Solomon, the author of *Midrash al-ṣayyānī* on Prophets, see Blumenthal, *Philosophic Questions*, pp. 33, 35, 38, 95, and references. Zechariah ha-Rofé's commentary on the Song of Songs has been published twice: J. Qafiḥ published an edition based on three manuscripts in private collections, along with a Hebrew translation, in his *Ḥamesh megillot* (Jerusalem, 1962). Y.L. Naḥum printed a facsimile of another manuscript in *Ḥasifat genuzim mi-teiman* (Holon, 1971), 203–37; Naḥum's manuscript contains significant additions to Qafiḥ's edition, and these are noted at the bottom of each page.

Yemenite intellectual history as they relate to our midrashim. In particular, I shall argue on the basis of these sources that only in the Yemen did Maimonidean religious philosophy—which I define here as Maimonides' call for critical thinking, moderate allegorization, and strict observance of the Law—succeed in establishing itself as the dominant trend of religious thought in a Jewish community for any significant period of time.

Our first subject is the reception and absorption of the Maimonidean oeuvre. Maimonides was certainly venerated in the Yemen to an extent unparalleled elsewhere. Yemenite scholars, including many of our authors, prepared commentaries on Maimonides' *Commentary to the Mishnah*, *Book of Commandments*, *Mishneh Torah*, and *Guide of the Perplexed*; as we have already noted, moreover, the Yemenite midrashim contain extensive quotations from Maimonides' works.[3] It seems, indeed, that Maimonides' writings achieved canonical status in the Yemen and were universally regarded as authoritative. To the best of my knowledge, no Yemenite thinker openly opposed Maimonides.[4]

Nevertheless, on a number of specific matters the Yemenites deviate from what seems to be Maimonides' position. That qualification is necessary, incidentally, so long as there is disagreement with regard to Maimonides' own true positions. As we become more sensitive to some of the non-Aristotelian (in particular, Neoplatonic) currents in Maimonides' thought, we may come to regard the Yemenite understanding of Maimonides to be more in line with his intentions than we had previously thought.[5] While there is no point in belaboring the Yemenites' admiration for their acknowledged master, it may be instructive to look more closely at several issues in which their views appear to have differed from his.

We will begin with cosmology. The cosmologies which we encounter

[3] Almost none of these commentaries have been published or even surveyed; many have been listed in Y. Ratzaby, "The Literature of the Jews of Yemen" (Hebrew), *KS* 28 (1953): 274–78, section 6. Blumenthal utilized some of these compositions, particularly in his second book. The commentary of Aluʾel (David) b. Yeshaʿ to Maimonides' *Laws Concerning the Sanctification of the New Moon*, which I published (with Hebrew translation and notes) in my *The Jews of Yemen and the Exact Sciences* (Jerusalem, 1987), is just one part of a comprehensive commentary on the *Mishneh Torah*. Y. Ratzaby has seen and made use of what may be a complete copy of this commentary—and if it is, then it is the only one known to exist—but, unfortunately, the Institute of Microfilmed Hebrew Manuscripts [IMHM] has not yet been able to make a film of it; see Y. Ratzaby ed., *R. Jehoshua Hannagid, Responsa* (Hebrew) (Jerusalem, 1989), 12f.

[4] Occasionally, we do encounter a veiled criticism. See, e.g., the dissension from Maimonides' attack (or so it seems) on the cosmogony of *Pirqei de-Rabbi Eliezer* which I noted in "The Yemeni Treatise known as *Ḥafiṣah*" (Hebrew), *KS* 61 (1986/7): 363–67, esp. 366.

[5] See, in particular, A. Ivry, "Neoplatonic Currents in Maimonides' Thought," in *Perspectives on Maimonides*, ed. J.L. Kraemer (Oxford, 1990), 115–140, and his "Ismāʿīlī Theology and Maimonides' Philosophy" in this volume.

in Yemenite-Jewish writings include a number of structures that are entirely absent from Maimonides' writings; the most common of these, perhaps, is the "universal soul" (*al-nafs al-kulliyya*). We encounter the universal soul in lists of the cosmological/cosmogonic sequence, as well as in discussions of psychology and epistemology.[6] Three of our midrashic authors display complete cosmological schemes in the form of circular diagrams. It has already been noticed that such figures are quite common in Ismāʿīlī works, e.g., *Kanz al-walad*.[7] These illustrations serve not only to schematize the principal ingredients of the universe. Their ordering conveys the cosmogonic sequence, and their circular form contains some philosophical lessons.

Aluʾel b. Yeshaʿ displays the cosmological circle in his midrash on Genesis.[8] The figure and accompanying text are quoted from one "Abū Naṣr."[9] In this scheme the ten items are: the one (*al-waḥda*); the intellect (*al-ʿaql*); the soul (*al-nafs*); primal matter (*al-hayūlā*); nature (*al-ṭabīʿa*); body (*al-jism*); the orbs (*al-aflāk*); the elements (*al-arkān*); generated things (*al-mawlūdāt*); and man (*al-insān*). In the accompanying and rather recondite text, the figure is invested with additional layers of meaning. The total of ten items possesses numerological significance and the "limit" of the "one" is "ten." The "one" is identified with the "word" (*al-kalima*), and the circular progression is related to man's perfection and the attainment of prophecy.[10] Ḥoṭer b. Solomon also includes a circular diagram in his *Sirāj*, though he does not refer to Abū Naṣr. Ḥoṭer draws an important lesson from the

---

[6] For an example of the invocation of the universal soul in cosmology and cosmogony, see the passage from "Abū Naṣr" discussed below, and also *Midrash ha-beʾur* on *parashat Wa-yishlaḥ* (see the manuscript belonging to an anonymous collector that I consulted on film at the IMHM, fol. 51a); on the other functions see, e.g., *Midrash ha-ḥefeṣ*, Cambridge ms. Or. 551, fol. 43b. Both quotations from Yemenite midrashim are included in my *Yemenite Midrash*. The second passage is available in the Hebrew translation of M. Havazelet, *Midrash ha-ḥefeṣ (Bereishit-Shemot)* (Jerusalem, 1990), 145–46. See also the figurative interpretation of Jerusalem in the midrash of 1525 which I quoted in "Two Unknown Philosophical Midrashim," 1336–37. Cf. Blumenthal, *Philosophic Questions*, Index of Subjects, *s.v.* "soul, universal."

[7] Blumenthal, ibid., p. 179, n. 5.

[8] Oxford ms. Opp. Add. 59, fol. 8a.

[9] Franz Rosenthal has identified al-Ghazzālī's *Al-maʿārif al-ʿaqliyya* (ed. A. ʿUthmān [Damascus, 1963], 29f.) as the source of this quotation; see "From the 'Unorthodox' Judaism of Medieval Yemen," in *Hommages à Georges Vajda*, ed. G. Nahon and C. Touati (Louvain, 1980), 279–90, esp. the discussion and notes on p. 283. This same passage is cited in the name of "Abū Naṣr" both in one of the Jewish texts described by Rosenthal and in one of the three Yemenite texts published by Qafiḥ, "Three Treatises by a Yemenite Author" (Hebrew), *Sefunot* 16 (1980): 83–189 (reprinted in his *Ketavim*, ed. Y. Tobi [Jerusalem, 1989], 1:260).

[10] I believe that the circle should be interpreted as follows: there is a cycle of creation progressing from the intellect to the soul through to the material creations that culminate in man. So much for ordinary man; but another circuit through the circle yields a higher man, a prophet. The

circular form, wherein the end closes in on the beginning, viz., that man, the last item, is closest to his Creator.[11] Several manuscripts of *Nūr al-ẓalām*—although not, unfortunately, the one used by Qafiḥ in his publication—also reproduce this figure.[12] Needless to say, these conceptions are quite alien to Maimonides' thought.

Maimonides is famous for his repudiation of astrology; in his letter to Montpellier, for example, he asserts that all true philosophers reject astrology.[13] Now it is true that Maimonides does acknowledge the stars to have some physical effect on terrestrial processes.[14] Nevertheless, it seems that the Yemenites assimilated astrological doctrines that Maimonides would not have allowed. In his *Midrash ha-ḥefeṣ*, Zechariah ha-Rofé lists the associations of the seven planets with the four qualities, and their effect upon emotions, career, etc.—all of this, he says, is "according to the view of the philosophers."[15] Nethanel b. Isaiah, Ḥoṭer b. Solomon, and Zechariah all relate the traditional life span of one hundred and twenty years to the motions of the heavenly bodies.[16]

Maimonides was also forceful in his rejection of magic, in no small measure because of its connection to astrology.[17] Yet Nethanel b. Isaiah admits that Pharaoh's advisers successfully employed astral magic—"a precise and delicate art," in his words—in order to mimic the divine omens brought by Moses.[18] Ḥoṭer b. Solomon declares that magic "is a lie and a delusion; there is no truth at all to it."[19] Yet in his discussion of Balaam's

---

chief conclusion to be drawn from this observation is that the prophet differs completely from ordinary man, in his spiritual makeup, stellar correlates, and bodily matter. I hope to refine, expand, and substantiate this idea on some other occasion. Rosenthal's references to al-Baṭalyawsī (see "Unorthodox Judaism," p. 263, n. 7) do not seem to be relevant in this context.

[11] New York, HUC-JIR ms. k:148, fol. 68a. Cf. Blumenthal, *Philosophic Questions*, 178–9.

[12] *Nūr al-ẓalām* to Gen. 3:22–24. The figure can be found in Sassoon ms. 1009, p. 7, and in several other copies, e.g. Sassoon ms. 1176, Oxford ms. Neubauer Cat. no. 2346, Berlin ms. Steinschneider Cat. no. 90, and Moscow-Günzburg ms. 1025. Cf. the edition and translation of J. Qafiḥ, *Me'or ha-afelah* (Jerusalem, 1982), 49; the manuscripts cited also contain a goodly amount of text that is missing from the printed version. It should be noted that "Abū Naṣr" is not mentioned in these texts.

[13] See I. Twersky, *A Maimonides Reader* (New York, 1972), 466: "Never did one of those genuinely wise men of the nations busy himself with this matter or write on it. . . ."

[14] Y. Tzvi Langermann, "Maimonides' Repudiation of Astrology," *Maimonidean Studies* 2 (1991): 123–58, esp. 140–43.

[15] Cambridge ms. Or. 551, fol. 11b; Havazelet, *Midrash ha-ḥefeṣ*, 47–8.

[16] *Nūr al-ẓalām*, ed. Qafiḥ, 56; *Midrash ha-ḥefeṣ*, Cambridge ms. Or. 551, fol. 319b; *Sirāj al-ʿuqūl*, New York, JTSA ms. Mic. 5254, fols. 7b–8a. Nothing of the sort is found in Maimonides; see, e.g., G. Weil, *Maimonides über die Lebensdauer* (Basel and New York, 1953).

[17] Langermann, "Maimonides' Repudiation," 147.

[18] *Nūr al-ẓalām*, ed. Qafiḥ, 201–202.

[19] *Sirāj al-ʿuqūl*, New York, JTSA ms. Mic. 5254, fol. 92a.

attempt to curse the Jewish people—specifically his effort to determine the precise moment of divine anger—Ḥoṭer seems rather comfortable with astral magic.[20]

We could cite additional examples from the fields of prophecy and miracles. But let us turn straight-away to the central question: how did the Yemenite scholars manage to reconcile themselves to these sundry non-Maimonidean views? David Blumenthal has presented detailed evidence for the coexistence in the Yemen of non-Maimonidean—in particular, Neoplatonic—materials with what he calls the "Maimonidean-neoaristotelian" tradition.[21] Blumenthal summarizes his analysis as follows:

> There can be no doubt, then: (1) that there did exist a neoplatonic tradition in Yemen, beginning with the *Bustan al-ʿUqul* and continuing until (at least) the generation after Hoter; (2) that, there existed a Maimonidean-neoaristotelian tradition alongside the earlier tradition; and (3) that there existed, beginning with the *Nur al-Zalam*, a conscious effort to integrate these traditions, (at least) until the time of Daʾud al-Lawānī who sought to separate them again.[22]

Statements (1) and (2) are certainly correct. I cannot accept, however, Blumenthal's third conclusion. First, it is my impression that the Yemenites did not consciously differentiate between philosophical traditions. The Yemenites either quote specific authorities (other than Maimonides) by name or, more commonly, they refer to the "scholars" or "sages" (*al-ḥukamāʾ*), a collective name for all who engaged in legitimate speculation. Other "traditions," for example, the *kalām*, are named in order to indicate that they stand outside the boundaries of legitimate philosophy.[23] On rare occasions, the Yemenites note that different views on a particular subject are registered in the philosophical literature.[24] But even then, such disparities reflect differences of opinion between individuals or schools, all of which find their place within legitimate philosophy. By "legitimate philosophy" I mean—speaking on behalf of the Yemenites as I understand them—speculation concerning *al-wujūd*, "reality" or "existence," a concept

---

[20] *Sirāj al-ʿuqūl*, New York, HUC-JIR ms. k:148, fols. 57a–b.

[21] *Philosophic Questions*, 34–41. Blumenthal was responding, at least in part, to certain criticisms of his earlier book on Ḥoṭer.

[22] *Ibid.*, 41. Daʾud al-Lawānī is another name of Aluʾel b. Yeshaʿ, the author of *Al-wajīz al-mughnī*. On the name "Aluʾel," derived numerologically from "David," see my *The Jews of Yemen and the Exact Sciences*, 20.

[23] See Y.T. Langermann, "The Debate between the Philosopher and the *Mutakallim*," *PAAJR* 60 (1994): 189–240.

[24] Aluʾel does this in the essay (*faṣl*) on the soul which he placed at the beginning of *Al-wajīz al-mughnī*; see Oxford ms. Opp. Add. 59, fols. 2a–b; and cf. Blumenthal, *Philosophic Questions*, p. 36, n. 140.

which includes not only the sensible universe, but also (and especially) metaphysical structures culminating in the deity, which are, from this point of view, even more real.[25] They enjoy the highest ontological rankings, and man's final purpose is their apprehension. Illegitimate speculation, by contrast, relies upon the imagination rather than the intellect and, therefore, its discourse concerns pure fantasy, things which, in philosophical parlance, appertain to non-being (*ʿadam*) and impossibility (*mumtaniʿ al-wujūd*). How one concludes that a certain notion or school of thought is legitimate or not—how one decides that their discourse concerns phantasms rather than reality—is not of concern to us at the moment. What is important is the observation that, within the framework of legitimate philosophy, there is no need to harmonize approaches whose apparent disparities may in any event often be reduced to different terminologies.[26]

Now some matters *do* call for harmonization, and calling attention to them will, I trust, sharpen the point I wish to make. The Yemenites often felt the need to harmonize traditional rabbinic dicta with other information that was available to them. Two features of this tendency must be noted: (1) The harmonization is conscious and deliberate, i.e. it is explicitly stated that the two views presented are either identical or, at least, not contradictory—which is to say that the intelligent reader could be forgiven for suspecting that a contradiction exists. (2) The harmonization more often than not reconciles rabbinic texts with non-Maimonidean doctrines. Both of these points are illustrated by the passage from *Al-wajīz al-mughnī* which I shall quote presently, in which a classical midrash is harmonized with a Hermetic notion.[27]

The problem may be posed in the following way: did the Yemenites consciously take it upon themselves to integrate two different philosophical traditions (Blumenthal)? or did they view the Maimonidean, the Neoplatonic, and the other sources at their disposal as all belonging to a single body of wisdom that needs no harmonization (Langermann)? I readily concede that when dealing with this sort of question there is considerable room for interpretation. On another point, however, I feel that Blumenthal is simply wrong. Daʾūd al-Lawānī (Aluʾel b. Yeshaʿ) did not undertake to

[25] I employ the term "metaphysical" somewhat loosely. Strictly speaking, I do not know whether the "universal soul" may be called a "metaphysical" structure but my intention, I trust, is patently clear.

[26] See for example the two figurative interpretations of "Jerusalem," the one "Aristotelian" and the other "Neoplatonic," from the midrash of 1525 which I cite in "Two Unknown Philosophical Midrashim," 1336–37.

[27] In the anonymous Yemenite commentary to *Yeṣirat ha-welad* that I have recently discovered, the author goes to considerable trouble on several occasions to harmonize his text with contemporaneous science and medicine; see Y.T. Langermann, "Ms. Moscow-Günzburg 1020: An Important New Yemeni Codex of Jewish Philosophy," *JAOS* 115 (1995).

separate two traditions. His *Al-wajīz al-mughnī*, as we have seen, is no less informed by non-Maimonidean materials than the other midrashim. Blumenthal's remark that, "over and over again, he gave evidence of knowing well the alternate tradition," simply begs the question. Nowhere does Aluʾel explicitly or even implicitly reject the "alternate tradition." He uses non-Maimonidean materials no differently than do his predecessors and, in fact, he incorporates a range of alternative traditions virtually unknown to his predecessors, including Indian, Hermetic, and other sources. We shall offer here only a few brief examples. Aluʾel refers to Hermes three times in connection with the creation story. In his commentary on Genesis 1:1, he equates the opinion of the Jewish sages with that of Hermes: "The Sages said that God took together fire and water, mixed them up, and produced from them the firmament (*raqiʿa*). This is just as Hermes explained in the book *Ṭabāʾiʿ al-khalq*."[28] Abraham's offer to Lot, "If you turn to the left, then I shall turn to the right" (Gen. 13:9) serves as a springboard for review of the symbolism of "right" and "left." The "right" is more perfect than the "left"; as the verse says, "The wise man's heart is on his right, but the fool's heart is on his left" (Ecc. 10:2). Aluʾel continues, "This is something natural, and the author of *Mirʾāt al-maʿānī* mentioned it."[29] *Mirʾāt al-maʿānī* is al-ʿAmīdī's translation (perhaps also a reworking) of *Amṛtakuṇḍa*, an Indian work on Yoga.[30] On the other hand, he strongly dissents from *Midrash ha-gadol*—which, according to Blumenthal, represents the very line of thought to which Aluʾel wishes to return—on a number of issues. Other non-Maimonidean notions are displayed without citing any source, or indeed, without any clue that the assertion runs counter to the express position of Maimonides. In his comment on Exodus 31:13, Aluʾel states offhandedly, as if the matter were universally accepted, "For it (i.e. the Sabbath) is a proof for the creation of the world, and the creation of the world is a proof for His existence (may He be exalted)."[31] Now Maimonides dissents rather strongly from that view, which had been professed by earlier thinkers, most notably Saadya Gaon; but Aluʾel gives no indication of this.[32]

---

[28] Oxford ms. Opp. Add. 59, fol. 1b. The identification of *Ṭabāʾiʿ al-khalq* remains a mystery; no such title is listed by M. Ullmann, *Die Natur- und Geheimnisswissenschaften im Islam* (Leiden-Köln, 1972).

[29] Oxford ms. Opp. Add. 59, fol. 15b. Again, a full citation of this and other passages will be included in my forthcoming *Yemenite Midrash*.

[30] See S.M. Stern, "al-ʿAmīdī," *EI*, 2d ed., 1:434–35.

[31] Oxford ms. Opp. Add. 59, fol. 76a.

[32] See Moses Maimonides, *Guide of the Perplexed*, 1:71, trans. S. Pines (Chicago and London, 1963), 1:180–81.

Blumenthal relies for his interpretation on the introduction to *Al-wajīz*, certainly one of the more important documents for Yemenite-Jewish intellectual history.[33] Alu'el's criticisms of the shortcomings and/or excesses of his predecessors seem to me rather standard justifications for the compilation of a new work. In light of the evidence that we have assembled, it can no longer be maintained, as Blumenthal does, that his target is "the conflations of ideas, themes, and images that the harmonistic tradition had developed." If and when Alu'el is polemicizing, his target is none other than the school of antinomian interpretation that, as we shall see, had developed in the Yemen. This is borne out by a close reading of that text translated by Blumenthal—most especially, of a passage which he omitted. I cite from Blumenthal's translation:

> In addition there is disagreement among them on the aforementioned matters of definition and truth. Scarcely do two of them agree on one matter in the verse whose esoteric meaning is being expounded. They excuse themselves, however, by saying 'The Torah can be interpreted in many ways.' Yet it is not so. . . .[34]

Here is the omitted passage which is indicated by elision points in Blumenthal's translation:

> For the truth (*al-ḥaqq*) is one relative to the expression of that truth. The intrinsic truth (*al-ḥaqīqa*) is the intrinsic truth of the thing which does not require determination (*taʿrīf*; literally, "making it known"), for it is the most known (*aʿraf*) of [all] things. It is that which knows,[35] and it is that by means of which things are known. It is that which knows, it is that which is known, and it is the knowledge itself (*nafs al-maʿrifa*). Our master of blessed memory said that the final aim of the truth (*al-ḥaqq*) is that we know that He is true, that the religious laws are true, and that their purpose is to be obeyed. It has already been clarified for you that obedience to the Law is one of the paths to science and knowledge. The intrinsic truth of the Torah cannot be apprehended as it is. However, the final purpose is that it be obeyed, as our master of blessed memory noted. You now know (*fa-qad ʿalamta*) our final intention in this composition.

The first part of this passage presents some subtle arguments which make use of different forms of the Arabic roots *ḥ.q.q.*, whose basic meaning is "truth," and *ʿ.r.f.*, whose basic meaning is "to know." It is nearly impos-

---

[33] Partially translated by Blumenthal, *Philosophic Questions*, 41. For a full Hebrew translation see Y. Tobi, "Rabbi David ben Yeshaʿ ha-Levi (Yemen, fifteenth century)" (Hebrew), *Alei Sefer* 16 (1989/90): 87–90. I shall provide a full English translation in the introduction to my *Yemenite Midrash*.

[34] *Philosophic Questions*, p. 41.

[35] Tobi apparently read *tuʿarrif*, even though the *shadda* is not indicated, and accordingly translated "makes things known"; but there is no need for emendation, since it is stated explicitly that *al-ḥaqīqa* is *ʿārifa*, i.e. it knows.

sible to find exact English equivalents for all the forms which appear in our text. Most important is the distinction which Alu'el draws between *al-ḥaqq* and *al-ḥaqīqa*.[36] I have translated *al-ḥaqq* as "truth" and *al-ḥaqīqa* as "intrinsic truth." Both of these terms are semantically loaded. *Al-ḥaqq* is used of God Himself. But Alu'el also says that *al-ḥaqīqa* "is that which knows, it is that which is known, and it is the knowledge itself"—a phrase which immediately calls to mind a similar statement made about the deity, i.e. that He is the One who employs intellect, He is the object of intellection, and He is intellect itself. Alu'el's assertion that *al-ḥaqīqa* (plural: *al-ḥaqā'iq*) is not the final aim of the Torah is undoubtedly a thrust against the radical allegorists who were associated with *Kitāb al-ḥaqā'iq*.[37]

The radical allegorists excused themselves for finding different intrinsic truths in the Torah by citing the dictum, "The Torah can be interpreted in many ways." But they misunderstood the meaning of that saying. The sages wished to indicate that there is more than one way to express the same truth, not that there are many truths. This is what I understand Alu'el to be saying. Despite the difficulties of this passage, the basic point is clear: *al-ḥaqīqa*—the intrinsic truth of the Torah and the focus of the radical allegorists—is recondite, if not inscrutable. But *al-ḥaqq*, the essential message of the Torah, is clear: the laws must be obeyed. Alu'el's primary worry is not non-Maimonidean philosophy, but allegorization which implies or teaches that the Law need not be obeyed.

Alu'el, we may add, took a serious interest even in some rather arcane halakhic matters, and developed a pointed criticism of *Nūr al-ẓalām* on questions of ritual purity, sacrifice, and the like. Despite Blumenthal's contention that Alu'el criticizes his predecessor for harmonizing philosophical notions, his numerous disagreements with *Nūr al-ẓalām* appertain with few exceptions to the field of halakhah, not philosophy.[38] Moreover, in those relatively few instances where Alu'el argues with Nethanel over the proper understanding of Maimonides, his complaint centers upon an

---

[36] This distinction is introduced in the phrase which Blumenthal translates "matters of definition and truth." I accept Tobi's correction of *al-ḥadd* to *al-ḥaqq*, so that the sentence reads "matters of *al-ḥaqq* and *al-ḥaqīqa*"; see Tobi, "Rabbi David ben Yesha' ha-Levi," p. 83, n. 2.

[37] See J. Qafiḥ, "A Yemenite Defense of the Allegorical Method of Scriptural Interpretation" (Hebrew), *Ketavim*, 1:341f.; F. Rosenthal, "From Arabic Books and Manuscripts V: A One-Volume Library of Arabic Philosophical and Scientific Texts in Istanbul," *JAOS* 75 (1955), p. 22, n. 1; and Langermann, "Ḥafiṣah," 365.

[38] Alu'el even employs a special shorthand expression, indicating his criticism of Nethanel; see Oxford ms. Opp. Add. 59, fol. 62b: "Know that whenever we state to you the word *khilāf* ('the opposite of what has been stated') we mean the contradiction that we found between the *derash* of Ibn Yesha'yah and the words of our master [Maimonides]. We have pointed this out, and we do not need to repeat it. Understand it!"

imprecision on the part of his predecessor, rather than a conflation of Maimonides with Neoplatonic teachings.[39] Aluʾel does attack Nethanel for including fantastic stories in his midrash: "[He] said about this something which is hardly possible. The *darshanim* record many similar impossibilities."[40] But he levels the same accusation against David al-ʿAdanī: "Al-ʿAdanī recorded in his *Midrash ha-gadol* sea creatures which are well-nigh impossible . . . and he mentioned elsewhere many things that are impossible. . . ."[41] Aluʾel also disagrees with al-ʿAdanī concerning the interpretation of a passage in Maimonides' *Guide*, though in Blumenthal's reading, he ought to be in close agreement with *Midrash ha-gadol*.[42] In short, there is nothing in Aluʾel's criticisms of his predecessors—both the general criticism raised in the introduction and the specific criticisms found in the text—which justifies Blumenthal's analysis.

A number of alternative explanations for the coexistence of Maimonidean and non-Maimonidean materials may be offered. As we have already suggested, the Yemenites may sincerely have felt that they were not actually straying from the Maimonidean path. Since Maimonides' esotericism consists in skillfully leaving things unsaid, his words are open to interpretation. His Yemenite readers, like his interpreters elsewhere, assumed the task of discovering his hidden meaning.[43]

Then again we must take into account the Yemenites' renowned eclecticism. We have seen that Aluʾel b. Yeshaʿ names his source for the cosmic circle, and in the preceding discussion we have noted a number of other sources utilized by that writer. Indeed, a long and diverse list of sources are quoted in the Yemenite midrashim, and further research is likely to uncover other sources that are not cited by name. In this connection it is noteworthy that the *Sirāj al-ʿuqūl* cites a variant of the Mishnah's well-known dictum; according to Ḥoṭer, the sages said: "Who is the wise man?

[39] See, e.g., ibid., fol. 44b, concerning the psychological explanation for Moses' rescue of Jethro's daughters and its connection to Maimonides' theory of prophetic (or proto-prophetic) inspiration.

[40] Ibid., fol. 139b.

[41] Ibid., fol. 4b.

[42] I discuss the disagreement concerning the passage in Maimonides' *Guide* in my "'The Making of the Firmament': R. Hayyim Israeli, R. Isaac Israeli, and Maimonides" (Hebrew), in *Shlomo Pines Jubilee Volume, Part I* [Jerusalem Studies in Jewish Thought, 7] (Jerusalem, 1988), pp. 473–74, n. 52 (461–76). This may reflect a legitimate disagreement between two strict Maimonideans; but then so would Aluʾel's dispute with Nethanel mentioned above.

[43] I strongly dissent from the trend, now quite popular, to view Maimonides' esotericism as deliberate disinformation. Maimonides may have placed some false scents, but he did not prevaricate. The big lie and the official lie are features of our civilization, not of medieval religious thought.

He who collects from everywhere (*eizehu he-ḥakham ha-me'assef mi-kol maqom*)."[44] Nevertheless, the Yemenites were not indiscriminate: Ḥoṭer himself urges his readers to select correct teachings, rather than rely upon correct authorities.[45] As we shall see presently, some teachings were forcefully rejected.

The explanation that I favor is, perhaps, a combination of both of the preceding suggestions. In my view, the Yemenites were eclectic in matters of philosophy because, as they understood it, the Maimonidean imperative was not necessarily to accept a given body of philosophical doctrine—for example, that which is offered in the *Guide of the Perplexed*—but rather, to engage in philosophical inquiry and submit to the judgment of reason. Entertaining alternative cosmological schemes or theories of prophecy, even stretching a bit the allowable influences of the stars—all of these, again, to the extent that the Yemenites were cognizant of their divergence from Maimonides' opinions—were perceived to do no violence to the essence of the Maimonidean legacy.

The second question that I should like to consider concerns controversies within the Yemenite community. The philosophical midrashim (and some other sources as well) testify to the fact that both an extreme "right" and an extreme "left" were found in the Yemen. That is to say, there were literalists, who repudiated speculative thought, and there were also radical allegorists. Two midrashim present fictitious debates which, we may assume, mirror actual encounters. Nethanel b. Isaiah depicts an exchange between a "philosopher," who denies that Moses could have endured forty days and nights without food or water, and an adherent of Scripture (*mutasharri*ʿ),[46] who defends the literal truth of the biblical account, on scientific grounds, as well as those of traditional belief.[47] Nethanel's solution, which he claims represents the middle ground, is actually a figurative interpretation: "bread and water" is a metaphor for practical religious matters (*umūr shar*ʿ*iyya*). During his forty days on Mount Sinai, Moses

[44] New York, HUC-JIR ms. k:148, fol. 86b. Avot 4:1 states, "Who is the wise man? He who learns from everyone."

[45] New York, HUC-JIR ms. k:148, fols. 26a–b.

[46] That is, a member of one of the religions which finds its basis in a revealed Scripture. There is no direct connection between Nethanel's fictional encounter and Judah Halevi's exposition of the differences between the *mutasharri*ʿ and the *mutafalsif* in *The Book of the Khazar* 4:13. Since the intellectual atmosphere of eleventh- and twelfth-century Spain was permeated with Neoplatonism, it is likely that many parallels exist between Jewish writings from Andalusia and the Yemen. But I know of no direct quotations or any other solid proof that the Yemenites read that literature.

[47] *Nūr al-ẓalām*, 493–96. A full translation of this text will be included in my *Yemenite Midrash*.

occupied himself with metaphysics alone and he communicated this to the masses by telling them that he was without bread or water. This "middle ground" may give the appearance of a somewhat radical stance, especially if we recall that the interpretation which Maimonides offers towards the end of his *Guide* is not very different from—though, of course, not identical with—the stance taken by Nethanel's adherent of Scripture.[48] Nethanel, however, is quite vociferous in his criticism of the "left." He blasts those esotericists (*ahl al-bāṭin*) who read the Flood story as an allegory, wherein the ark stands for reality, the flood for ignorance, and Noah for intellect; this same school, he continues, maintains that the Torah contains a "kernel" and a "shell." They allegorize the Flood story, Nethanel contends, in order to get across the message that sinners need not fear severe punishment.[49]

Ḥoṭer b. Solomon offers a fictitious debate between a *mutakallim*—in fact a *muqallid*, i.e. one who upholds the uncritical acceptance of tradition—and a philosopher who argues for critical and rational inquiry.[50] Needless to say, it is the philosopher who emerges victorious. Indeed, on some half-dozen occasions in his *Sirāj*, Ḥoṭer denounces the "mutakallimūn" of his time. He accuses them of "hating" philosophy and, interestingly, he identifies them with Karaites and other heretics.[51]

We learn from quite a few sources, notably Maimonides' treatise, that the single most controversial issue in medieval Yemen was the doctrine of the resurrection of the dead (*teḥiyyat ha-metim*); not surprisingly, some of our midrashim address the question.[52] The most thorough discussion is found in *Al-wajīz al-mughnī*, and perhaps the most interesting information to emerge from that text is the fact that there were those in the Yemen who impugned the authenticity of Maimonides' treatise.[53] Now in his treatise, Maimonides defends the belief in actual bodily resurrection. As we have already noted, no one in the Yemen seems to have been willing to

---

[48] See Moses Maimonides, *Guide of the Perplexed*, 3:51, trans. S. Pines, 2:620. Note also that Maimonides identified himself as a *mutasharri*ʿ, e.g. in his attack on Galen in the last section of *Fuṣūl mūsā*. There is as yet no edition of the Judeo-Arabic text, but the section in question was published with Hebrew translation by J. Qafiḥ, *Iggerot ha-rambam*, 2d printing (Jerusalem, 1987), 155.

[49] *Nūr al-ẓalām*, 71.

[50] See Langermann, "Debate," 193–94.

[51] For the identification of the *mutakallimūn* with Karaites, see *Sirāj*, Jerusalem ms. JNUL 8° 2059, *parashat Bo* (the pages are unnumbered). For a fuller discussion, see my "Debate," 193.

[52] On this controversy see, e.g., F. Rosenthal, "From the 'Unorthodox' Judaism of Medieval Yemen," 285f.; D. Blumenthal, *Commentary*, 181–200; and Y.T. Langermann, "A Fragment of Abū al-Barakāt al-Baghdādī's *al-Muʿtabar*" (Hebrew), *KS* 61 (1986/7): 361–62.

[53] Oxford ms. Opp. Add. 59, fols. 219b–220a.

attack Maimonides outright. Therefore, the only path open to those who denied the literal meaning of the doctrine was to deny Maimonides' defense as well.

At the beginning of this paper I submitted that philosophy—the Maimonidean philosophy, as earlier defined—was the dominant trend in the Yemen, and that the philosophical midrashim were the chief instruments for its propagation. Proof for both statements comes from the survival of manuscript sources. In addition to the ten midrashim and the commentaries to Maimonides mentioned earlier, we have many Yemenite philosophical treatises and fragments.[54] Yet none of the writings of either the extreme allegorists or the traditionalists has survived.[55] This indicates that it was philosophy—middle-of-the-road Maimonidean philosophy—which triumphed.[56]

---

[54] Three codices may be mentioned here, one of which I have described in detail; see "The Yemeni Treatise known as *Ḥafiṣah*." The mss. are: (1) Sassoon ms. 864; see D. Sassoon, *Ohel Dawid* (Oxford, 1932), 2:1052–53; (2) Chicago, Spertus College ms. C11; see N. Golb, *Spertus College of Judaica Yemenite Manuscripts: An Illustrated Catalogue* (Chicago, 1972), 15–16 and cf. Y.T. Langermann, "Three Singular Treatises from Yemeni Manuscripts," *BSOAS* 65 (1991): 568–71; and (3) Moscow Günzburg 1020; see Langermann, "Ms. Moscow-Guenzburg 1020." Dozens of fragments of philosophical works are found in the collection of Y.L. Naḥum (Holon, Israel); and even if most of these cannot be identified, they collectively testify to the great interest displayed by the Yemenites in philosophy.

[55] A few quotations from *Kitāb al-ḥaqā'iq*, written out in Arabic characters, are found in the marginalia to Carullah 1279. See Rosenthal, "From Arabic Books and Manuscripts."

[56] Again it is to the manuscript sources that we must turn to substantiate our second claim. While most of the philosophical treatises (and some of the midrashim) survive only as *unica*, most of the midrashim are extant in several copies, and some—*Midrash ha-gadol*, *Nūr al-ẓalām*, and *Midrash ha-ḥefeṣ*—survive in over a dozen copies. I rely here upon the inventories of the IMHM.

INDEX OF MEDIEVAL AUTHORS

Jewish Authors

Muslim Authors

Christian Authors

INDEX OF MODERN AUTHORS

ÉTUDES SUR LE JUDAÏSME MÉDIÉVAL

ISSN 0169-815X

1. SIRAT, C. *Les théories des visions surnaturelles dans la pensée juive du moyen-âge.* 1969. ISBN 90 04 02990 7
2. METZGER, M. *La Haggada enluminée, 1.* Étude iconographique et stylistique des manuscrits enluminés et décorés de la Haggada du XIIIe au XVIe siècle. Préface par R. Crozet. 1973. ISBN 90 04 03714 4
3. SCHLANGER, J. *La philosophie de Salomon ibn Gabirol.* Étude d'un neoplatonisme. 1968. ISBN 90 04 00566 8
4. VAJDA, G. *Deux commentaires karaïtes sur l'Ecclésiaste.* 1971. ISBN 90 04 02658 4
5. *Azriel de Gérone.* Commentaire sur la liturgie quotidienne. Introduction, traduction annotée et glossaire des termes techniques par G. Sed-Rajna. 1974. ISBN 90 04 03822 1
6. *The Commentary of R. Ḥōṭer b. Shelōmō to the* Thirteen Principles *of Maimonides.* Edited, translated and annotated by D.R. Blumenthal. With a foreword by S.D. Goitein. 1974. ISBN 90 04 03909 0
7. SHAMIR, Y. *Rabbi Moses ha-Kohen of Tordesillas and his Book* 'Ezer ha-Emunah. A Chapter in the History of the Judeo-Christian Controversy. 1975. ISBN 90 04 04254 7
8. MESCH, B. *Studies in Joseph ibn Caspi, Fourteenth-century Philosopher and Exegete.* 1975. ISBN 90 04 04221 0
9. GELLES, B.J. *Peshat and Derash in the Exegesis of Rashi.* 1981. ISBN 90 04 06259 9
10. MARCUS, I.G. *Piety and Society.* The Jewish Pietists of Medieval Germany. 1981. ISBN 90 04 06345 5
11. *The Philosophic Questions and Answers of Ḥōṭer b. Shelōmō.* Edited, translated, and annotated by D.R. Blumenthal. With a supplementary essay by Y. Tobi. 1981. ISBN 90 04 06541 5
12. VAJDA, G. *Al-Kitāb al-Muḥtawī de Yūsuf al-Basīr.*Texte, traduction et commentaire. Edité par D.R. Blumenthal. 1985. ISBN 90 04 07302 7
13. *Dāwūd ibn Marwān al Muqammiṣ's Twenty Chapters ('Ishrun Maqāla).* Edited, translated and annotated by S. Stroumsa. 1989. ISBN 90 04 09216 1
14. HARY, B.H. *Multiglossia in Judeo-Arabic.* With an edition, translation and grammatical study of the Cairene Purim Scroll. 1992. ISBN 90 04 09694 9
15. YEROUSHALMI, D. *The Judeo-Persian Poet 'Emrānī and his* Book of Treasure. 'Emrānī's *Ganǰ-nāme,* a versified Commentary on the Mishnaic Tractate *Abot.* Edited, translated and annotated together with a critical study. 1995. ISBN 90 04 10301 5
16. FRANK, D. (ed.). *The Jews of Medieval Islam.* Community, Society, and Identity. 1995. ISBN 90 04 10404 6